Methods of Interpretation

Methods of Interpretation: How the Supreme Court Reads the Constitution

LACKLAND H. BLOOM, JR.

OXFORD

UNIVERSITY PRESS

OXFORD
UNIVERSITY PRESS

Oxford University Press, Inc., publishes works that further Oxford University's objective of excellence in research, scholarship, and education.

Oxford   New York
Auckland   Cape Town   Dar es Salaam   Hong Kong   Karachi   Kuala Lumpur   Madrid
Melbourne   Mexico City   Nairobi   New Delhi   Shanghai   Taipei   Toronto

With offices in
Argentina   Austria   Brazil   Chile   Czech Republic   France   Greece   Guatemala   Hungary
Italy   Japan   Poland   Portugal   Singapore   South Korea   Switzerland   Thailand   Turkey
Ukraine   Vietnam

Library of Congress Cataloging-in-Publication Data
Bloom, Lackland H., Jr.
  Methods of interpretation : how the Supreme Court reads the constitution /
  Lackland H. Bloom, Jr.
    p. cm.
  Includes bibliographical references and index.
  ISBN 978-0-19-537711-8 ((hardback) : alk. paper)
1. United States. Supreme Court–History. 2. Judicial process–United States. 3. Law–
    United States–Interpretation and construction. 4. Judicial review–United States. I. Title.
  KF8742.B56 2009
  347.73'26–dc22   2008037195

1 2 3 4 5 6 7 8 9

Printed in the United States of America on acid-free paper

Note to Readers
This publication is designed to provide accurate and authoritative information in regard to the subject matter covered. It is based upon sources believed to be accurate and reliable and is intended to be current as of the time it was written. It is sold with the understanding that the publisher is not engaged in rendering legal, accounting, or other professional services. If legal advice or other expert assistance is required, the services of a competent professional person should be sought. Also, to confirm that the information has not been affected or changed by recent developments, traditional legal research techniques should be used, including checking primary sources where appropriate.

*(Based on the Declaration of Principles jointly adopted by a Committee of the
American Bar Association and a Committee of Publishers and Associations.)*

You may order this or any other Oxford University Press publication by
visiting the Oxford University Press website at www.oup.com

This book is dedicated to my wife, Janice, whose continuous support, encouragement, and editorial assistance helped to make this project a reality, and to Sylvia, Jason, Lackland III, Barbara, and Mom and Dad.

Contents

Introduction

The Supreme Court's Methods of Interpreting the Constitution

THE POINT OF THIS BOOK is to look inside of the Supreme Court's toolbox; that is, to identify and examine in some detail the various methods that the Court as well as individual justices have employed throughout history when interpreting the Constitution. Obviously, this is not the first book ever written about constitutional interpretation by the Supreme Court. I believe, however, that this book takes a somewhat different approach from those that have come before. Rather than attempting to set forth an overall theory of constitutional interpretation or plunge into the never-ending scholarly debate over interpretative theory, I focus exclusively on what the Court and individual justices have done and said about constitutional interpretation in the course of deciding constitutional cases. Moreover, I attempt to do so at a level of great specificity and detail. I make no attempt to comprehensively examine all instances of constitutional interpretation by the Court throughout its history. Considering that the Court has been interpreting the Constitution for over 200 years and has filled over 500 volumes of the United States Reports with cases, many of which raise constitutional issues, it would take a multivolume treatise to survey the entire landscape. Instead, I attempt to identify many of the best and a few of the worst examples of particular interpretative methods as well as the best examples of the Court and justices' explicit discussion of constitutional interpretation.

In this book, I draw heavily on cases decided throughout the Court's history. Some methods of constitutional interpretation have changed over this 200-year period but most have not. Indeed, several of the most prevalent methods of constitutional interpretation and adjudication are simply variations of techniques often employed in statutory interpretation and common law adjudication. As such, many of these methods were employed by lawyers and judges well before and since the Constitution was drafted and ratified. Indeed, many of the finest examples of constitutional interpretation, especially with respect to textual analysis, can be found in the Marshall Court's classic foundational opinions. Sitting shortly after the ratification of the Constitution, the Court wrote on a relatively blank slate that permitted it to apply various interpretive methods for the very first time to the Constitution and its specific provisions. The value of these examples is enhanced by the fact that Justices Marshall and Story were extraordinarily skilled jurists and often wielded interpretive tools in a manner which have rarely been equaled since.

In order to select the best examples of interpretive methods available, I often cite and quote from concurring and dissenting opinions and, in a few instances, from majority opinions that have subsequently been overruled or at least ignored. All of these are part of the Court's larger interpretive canon. Often, techniques that are best illustrated in a dissenting or concurring opinion are also employed by a majority of the Court as well on other occasions. Likewise, the interpretive techniques employed in an overruled opinion may remain quite valid even when the specific result has been rejected. But even in those instances in which the approach of a concurring or dissenting justice has not been adopted by the Court as a whole, it may still provide valuable insight into the thinking of one or more justices as to how constitutional interpretation should be approached. However, when I do cite or quote from opinions that did not command a majority, I have always clearly so indicated.

Even though most of the examples that I have employed are derived from relatively important and well-known cases, I have also relied on some examples from more obscure cases when they have proven particularly illustrative of a given point. I rely on cases that span the entire range of constitutional interpretation rather than those that fall within the boundaries of the traditional law-school course in Constitutional Law. This book is definitely not intended to be a treatise on constitutional law or doctrine as opposed to interpretative methodology. When I discuss a case, I include a very brief summary of the issue and holding to place it in context, especially for readers unfamiliar with constitutional doctrine. However, given that the cases that I employ have been selected as illustrative of interpretive methods rather than doctrinal development, they will inevitably provide a very incomplete picture of constitutional law as a whole. I do not believe that a working familiarity with constitutional law is absolutely essential to an appreciation of this book, but it would certainly help.

In order to focus on specific interpretive techniques such as textualism or original understanding, for instance, it is necessary to take a very segmented and perhaps somewhat distorted look at the Court's opinions. More often than not, the Court relies on a variety of interpretive techniques in reaching its decision. It may argue based on text, original understanding, structure, precedent, and doctrine in order to reach a particular result. As such, the holding is essentially a result of the sum of these parts. None of these techniques could be said to have dictated the decision independently. However, in order to examine how the Court employs particular methods such as textual analysis in a disciplined manner, it is necessary to extract these examples from the cases and consider them in isolation. Thus as a word of caution, when I discuss a particular instance as providing an excellent example of textual or precedential analysis, for instance, that does not mean that it was entirely responsible for the result that the Court reached. Frequently some interpretive arguments are employed by the Court not so much to directly justify its conclusion but rather to respond to counterarguments by the dissent or by counsel.

Nor do I assert that these interpretive techniques either singularly or in the aggregate are responsible for the results that the Court has reached in a particular case. Sometimes they probably are. That is, in some cases, it is likely that the Court examines the issue raised, applies methods of interpretation, and reaches the result that those methods suggest is correct. In other words, the methodologies, at least as applied by the Court, do in fact dictate the outcome. Often, that is probably not the case, however. Rather, it is likely that the justices make an intuitive decision as to how the case should be decided and then utilize accepted methods of constitutional interpretation to explain and justify the decision. Even if that were the case, this use of constitutional interpretation is not insignificant. It is well accepted that the Court's ultimate power, or moral capital as it is sometimes called, is derived from its credibility. And that credibility in turn is largely derived from its ability to convince its informed audience that its decisions are legally sound, even if not inevitably dictated by the interpretive principles. As such, the interpretive arguments employed by the Court play a crucial role in preserving its position as the ultimate interpreter of the Constitution, even when they do not inevitably dictate or require the result reached by the Court in a given case. Whether these approaches constitute interpretation or merely explanation, they still matter a great deal.

I would not suggest that the interpretive methods employed by the Court necessarily lead to a particular result in most cases that the Court decides. Sometimes they do. Sometimes the arguments are quite one-sided. But that is not generally the case. Almost by definition, the Court tends to decide hard cases. Most of the cases on its constitutional docket throughout its history have either been cases of first impression or cases in which the lower courts have already reached conflicting results. As such, employing accepted methods of interpretation, reasoned arguments can generally be made for opposing results. Sometimes, one line of argument will appear to be more persuasive than an alternative. Often, however, preference for one argument over another is heavily influenced by an attachment to a particular approach such as originalism that in a given case may lend more support to one side than another. Perhaps even more often, a justice's preference for one argument over another in a particular case will be influenced by his or her views on the substantive merits of the case. If a justice believes strongly that a certain result should be reached, either in one case or in an entire area of the law, it is only human nature to consider the arguments that support that result to be more persuasive than those that do not.

I do not stake out a position in favor of any particular interpretive method. The point of the book is to illustrate how the Court does in fact interpret the Constitution as opposed to how it should. I believe that it is particularly useful to focus on the Court's approaches to constitutional interpretation because it is the Court that, as a practical matter, sets the standards. Commentators may have the final word on what constitutional interpretation should be; however, the Court essentially has the final word on what it is. Although I take the approach that all of the methods employed by the Court with some consistency are legitimate tools of interpretation or justification, I do maintain from time to time in the book that some arguments, at least as set forth in particular contexts, are more or less persuasive than their alternatives. I attempt this relatively light critique not from the standpoint of any particular overarching, normative point of view, but instead from a more pragmatic standpoint of whether a given argument, however valid in general, is well executed and sensible as applied. Obviously this involves a large degree of personal judgment, and not everyone will agree with my conclusions. Indeed, if I conclude that an argument endorsed by the Court seems unpersuasive, I do so with the knowledge that a majority of the justices, or at last some justices at a given time, certainly thought otherwise.

I divide the book into several chapters, highlighting well-recognized methods of constitutional interpretation. Several of these were prominently identified in Phillip Bobbit's excellent book *Constitutional Fate*, although they have been around throughout our constitutional history. In Chapters One and Two, I discuss Textual Analysis. The Constitution is a legal text in the most literal sense of the word. As such, close reading has always played a significant role in constitutional interpretation. Textual analysis played a most prominent role during the era of the Marshall Court as many textual provisions received their first judicial interpretations in that period; however, it has remained a significant mode of constitutional analysis throughout constitutional history. In Chapter One, I consider how the Court has used various established canons of textual analysis in specific contexts. Included among these are expansive construction of the text, reliance on the plain meaning, understanding terms of art, resolving linguistic ambiguities, avoiding surplus and redundancy, implying an affirmative from a negative, defining a category by its exceptions, and construing the text as written. Then in Chapter Two, I consider the approach known as intratextualism,[1] that is, the Court's use of the constitutional text itself as a guide for construing the text. In this section, I consider how the Court has employed the text as a guide to proper usage of terms, has utilized context within the text to discern meaning, has relied upon congruent readings of textual provisions, and has made use of constitutional architecture as well. I then discuss the Court's use of the purpose of a provision as a guide to its proper construction of the text. Finally, I examine the limitations of textual analysis, not the least of which is an absence of relevant text.

Chapters Three and Four address the use of Original Understanding to interpret the Constitution. At the outset, I attempt to explain what is meant by original understanding, contrasting it with the concept of original intent. In Chapter Three, I review in some detail the wide variety of sources for determining the original understanding. These include preconstitutional sources such as English history, English common law, colonial developments, Blackstone's Commentaries, the Declaration of Independence, and the Articles of Confederation and the experience thereunder. I then review various aspects of the drafting and ratification process, including statements and debates during those processes, changes made to the text during drafting, the significance of rejected provisions, the absence of debate and the influence of the *Federalist Papers*. In Chapter Four, I consider how the Court has used a variety of contemporaneous sources to derive constitutional meaning, including dictionaries, state constitutions, and congressional, executive, judicial, and state legislative practice. I then discuss the Court's reliance on specific influential actors and commentators—such as Madison, Hamilton, Jefferson, Story, and Cooley—as evidence of the original understanding. I consider a variety of issues that the Court has confronted in the context of original understanding, including employing original understanding to illuminate purpose, resolving conflicting accounts of original understanding, revising the original understanding, using of original understanding as a method of exclusion, dealing with inconclusive original understanding, determining whether a broad or narrow conception of original understanding is appropriate, and reconciling original understanding with societal change.

Chapter Five addresses the use of evidence of Tradition and Practice in constitutional interpretation. At the outset, I consider the significance of long and continuous federal practice, including practices extending back to the framing era. In this chapter, I examine the reliance upon practice and tradition in three specific areas in which it has played a significant role–Separation of Powers, the Establishment Clause, and Due Process of Law. I also discuss the Court's attempts to define the appropriate level of generality at which a tradition should be assessed as well as its consideration of evolving tradition. Finally, I consider the Court's treatment of issues that arise with respect to the decline or absence of a tradition.

In Chapter Six, I consider the Court's use of structural argument in con- stitutional interpretation, that is, drawing conclusions about constitutional meaning from the structure of the institutions it has created as well as the implicit assumptions underlying the creation of these institutions. After explaining the nature of structural argument, I review some of the classic structural arguments set forth by the Marshall Court. I then address what I characterize as the Court's use of "big picture" structural argument. Next, I consider various sources from which the Court has derived structural argument and whether such an argument needs be derived from any source other than the structure of the Constitution itself and the government that it creates. I then discuss various contexts in which structural argument has played a role, including judicial review, rights, and separation of powers. I conclude the chapter with a review of the Court's approach to competing structural arguments.

In Chapter Seven, I discuss the use of precedent by the Court in constitutional interpretation. I draw a distinction between precedent and doctrine. By precedent, I refer to the way in which the Court relies on the facts and specific holdings of prior cases in a classical common law manner. By doctrine, which I discuss in two subsequent chapters, I mean the rules that the Court derives from its precedents which then seem to assume a life of their own with no real attachment to the cases or contexts in which they initially appeared. I begin with a case study of the development of a line of constitutional precedent by focusing on the adoption and limitation of the exclusionary rule under the Fourth Amendment. I then discuss in some detail the ways in which the Court interprets and shapes precedent, both in terms of expanding and narrowing it, as well as the weight that is accorded to precedent, and the usage of prior judicial dicta. I then consider the ways in which the Court distinguishes constitutional precedent either factually or legally. Finally, I address the circumstance under which the Court overrules constitutional precedent.

In Chapters Eight and Nine, I consider the development and use of constitutional doctrine. Two chapters are necessary because doctrine plays such an enormous role in constitutional adjudication, especially since the middle of the twentieth century. In Chapter Eight, I concentrate on the derivation of doctrine. First I focus on the derivation of general principle, and then the process of converting general principle into more concrete doctrine, using the Establishment Clause as an example. I follow that with several other leading examples of the creation of constitutional doctrine. I then consider the various sources from which the Court derives its doctrine. In Chapter Nine, I address how the Court shapes, clarifies, and changes its constitutional doctrine. I then discuss different types of doctrinal approaches employed by the Court, including bright line rules, balancing, and ad hoc assessment. Finally, I examine how the Court clarifies doctrine and cleans up doctrinal messes from time to time.

In Chapter Ten, I consider how and when the Court relies on consequential arguments in constitutional adjudication. Specifically I discuss the circumstances under which the Court or individual justices take account of the possibility of adverse consequences in determining whether to interpret the constitution in a particular manner; I discuss, for example, the likelihood of occurrence as well as the Court's ability to prevent the occurrence of such consequences.

In Chapter Eleven, using the Eighth Amendment death-penalty decisions as the primary example but also considering length-of-sentence decisions, I examine the degree to which the Court relies on ethical argument in constitutional law. In addition, I consider how ethical argument may have played a role in the substantive due process punitive damage and right to privacy cases as well as in the one person, one vote case.

In Chapter Twelve, I discuss the role that rhetoric plays in constitutional interpretation. Employing the Court's reliance on Jefferson's "wall of separation" between church and state as an example, I examine the use of rhetoric to bolster constitutional principle and discuss the role of metaphor as a rhetorical device.

Finally in Chapter Thirteen, I attempt to bring these divergent methods together by working through five important cases from different historical periods, in which the Court and the justices relied upon several different interpretive methods in order to reach or at least explain its decision. I attempt to show how the justices wove several different interpretive methods together in order to create coherent and persuasive opinions as well as how different justices relied on alternative approaches to decide the cases in issue.

I make no attempt to cite or quote justices equally or randomly. On issues of interpretation, some courts and justices have provided far more useful material than others. On questions of textual as well as structural analysis, the opinions of John Marshall in particular have never been equaled. The decisions themselves in Marshall's great landmark opinions stand strong nearly 200 years later. The reasoning is as solid today as when it was first written. Likewise, cases addressing issues of separation of powers, for the most part decided in the latter half of the twentieth century, have relied heavily on structural argument as well as tradition and practice. Cases addressing the religion clauses, especially the Establishment Clause—again, decided almost exclusively in the second half of the twentieth century— have relied very heavily on both original understanding and tradition and practice. With respect to these methods, I quote Justices Scalia and Thomas with some frequency because they subscribe heavily to these approaches. Reliance on tradition and practice has played a very large role in the area of substantive due process as the Court has long taken the position that, to a very large extent, the concept of protected liberty, central to such analysis, is defined to a very significant degree by our traditions and practices. Reliance on precedent as well as the limitation of precedent extends throughout the Court's history and throughout all areas of constitutional law. The same is true with respect to the development of constitutional doctrine, although several prominent examples will be emphasized, including the development of standards for evaluating seditious speech by Holmes and Brandeis early in the twentieth century; the creation of the "wall of separation" and the *Lemon* test under the Establishment Clause; the creation of standards of review under the Equal Protection Clause; and the development of complex rules for evaluating obscenity and defamatory speech pursuant to the First Amendment, just to mention a few. Some of the approaches of certain justices who have played a particularly prominent role in doctrinal formulation will be reviewed, including Holmes, Stone, the second Harlan, Brennan, and Powell. As for the use of rhetoric in constitutional interpretation, several of the Court's greatest stylists are highlighted, including Marshall, Holmes, Brandeis, Stone, Frankfurter, and Jackson.

A book of this length can scarcely encompass all of the Court's jurisprudence of constitutional interpretation but it does aspire to capture the best and most prominent examples. An earlier version of the chapter on Consequential Reasoning was first published as *Bad Consequences*, 55 SMU L. Rev 69 (2002). And discussions of interpretative issues raised by the Eleventh Amendment decisions in *Seminole Tribe of Florida v. Florida* and *Alden v. Maine* first appeared in Some Interpretive Issues in Seminole and Alden 55 SMU L. Rev. 377 (2002).

Textualism and Its Canons

M. I. Defining Textualism

Perhaps the most obvious method of interpreting the Constitution is to simply read its text and attempt to determine what it means. Indeed, to the lay person this may primarily, if not exclusively, be how the Constitution is interpreted. In fact, however, textual analysis is only one method of divining constitutional meaning, and it is often not a very useful one. Still, textual analysis plays a significant role in constitutional interpretation. The Supreme Court has relied on textual analysis throughout its 200-plus-year history. This chapter will discuss why textualism has been and remains an important source of constitutional understanding, identifying and critiquing different canons or rules of textual analysis that the Court has employed.

By textualism or textual analysis, I mean the attempt to discern the meaning of constitutional provisions through a close reading of the specific language of the document. Textualism is one of many accepted methods of constitutional interpretation. Other methods include original understanding, structure, precedent, doctrine, tradition, and practice, as well as standard techniques of legal reasoning. Each of these methods can be helpful and persuasive, and more often than not the Court relies on a mixture of them to justify its decisions. Sometimes the text does not speak to the particular issue before the Court. Or it may address the issue at a level of generality that is not particularly helpful. Or even if the issue was once addressed through textual analysis, it is now dominated by a thick overlay of precedent and doctrine. Occasionally, the Court will choose to interpret a constitutional provision in a manner that seems to fly in the face of the text. Still, textual analysis continues to play an important role in constitutional interpretation.

I will attempt to isolate and focus on textual analysis with the understanding that in most cases in which it is employed, it is one of several interpretive techniques utilized by the Court. Moreover, it is not always easy or even possible to disentangle textualism from other methodologies, especially originalism. Obviously, one method of attempting to understand what the language in a document means is to try to determine what it was intended to mean by the draftsmen or ratifiers, or what it was understood to mean by informed contemporary readers. These approaches may be referred to as original intent or original understanding. In this chapter on textualism, I will provide a taste of textual analysis based on original understanding, and I will discuss that methodology in far greater depth in subsequent chapters. Likewise, to the extent that the Court relies on tradition and practice or structure as a method of defining textual meaning, I will discuss those modes of analysis in the chapters on those subjects. These distinctions are inevitably somewhat arbitrary. However, in order to focus on analytical techniques in a discrete manner, which is to a large extent the very purpose of this book, it is necessary to separate concepts that are not always readily separable. Hopefully, a sufficiently complete picture will emerge from a holistic reading of the book.

II. The Allure of Textualism

Textualism is unquestionably a leading methodology of constitutional interpretation. There are a number of explanations for its resonance. Perhaps most significantly, it is intuitively sensible. Most people believe that when they write a document, it will be capable of conveying a relatively determinate meaning to a reader, be it a letter, an article, a will, a grocery list, or a constitution. However difficult this may be for erudite scholars to grasp, it is quite obvious to the average person. In a nutshell "words have meaning." This is especially true in the field of law where it is standard procedure for lawyers and judges to closely interpret legal texts, including statutes, regulations, contracts, wills, and prior judicial opinions. The same holds true for a constitution. In the early case of *Brown v. Maryland*, Chief Justice Marshall noted that

> [i]n performing the delicate and important duty of construing clauses in the constitution . . . it is proper to take a view of the literal meaning of words to be expounded, of their connexion with other words, and of the general objects to be accomplished by the prohibitory clause, or by the grant of power.[1]

Indeed the preeminence of textualism as an interpretive method may be gleaned from perhaps the most foundational of all constitutional cases—*Marbury v. Madison*.[2] There, in the course of justifying the legitimacy of judicial review of congressional legislation, Chief Justice Marshall emphasized the written nature of the Constitution. He explained that

> [t]he powers of the legislature are defined and limited; and that those limits may not be mistaken or forgotten, the constitution is written. To what purpose are powers limited, and to what purpose is that limitation committed to writing; if these limits may, at any time, be passed by those intended to be restrained?[3]

Marshall was building the argument that "all those who have framed written constitutions contemplate them as forming the fundamental and paramount law of the nation."[4] Moreover he considered the Constitution to be quite capable of judicial application, considering that "[i]t is emphatically the province and duty of the judicial department to say what the law is."[5] Thus for Marshall the underlying rationale for judicial review itself was dependent on an understandable and legally applicable text.

The fact that the Constitution is meant to be a binding law capable of interpretation and application by judges does not necessarily mean that in interpreting it, judges must rely on textual analysis. Indeed, the very argument that Marshall made in *Marbury* is a prime example of structural as opposed to textual analysis.[6] Thus *Marbury* can hardly be read as suggesting that textual analysis is the only appropriate methodology. It does make two important points, however. First, the Constitution was intended to have a sufficiently determinate and understandable meaning in order to serve its purpose of effectively limiting the branches of government. Second, the Constitution is a law and as such is subject to interpretation by the techniques used by lawyers and judges to determine legal meaning.

Both points bolster the significance of textual analysis. Marshall's insistence that the constitutional text is capable of yielding a determinate enough meaning to serve the purpose of maintaining constitutional boundaries makes the obvious, though crucial, point that the framers of the Constitution were capable of employing language that could be sufficiently understood by the judicial reader to accomplish that purpose. Marshall was asserting that the words in the text have meaning, and it is the duty of the judges to discover that meaning. The determinacy of language is a necessary condition of the textual enterprise. If words mean whatever the reader wants them to mean, then textual analysis, at least as understood as an enterprise devoted to determining what the words were meant to signify, would seem to be a waste of time. Moreover, if a constitutional text is a legal text to be interpreted by the legally trained, then it stands to reason that the standard methods of legal interpretation, including textual analysis, should be employed. Chief Justice Marshall hardly invented textual analysis in *Marbury*. It had been around for centuries and indeed had been employed by the Supreme Court in constitutional interpretation from the very outset.[7] However, the prominence of *Marbury* in our constitutional heritage underscores the privileged status of textualism.

Justice Scalia is perhaps the strongest contemporary advocate of textualism on the Court. In his dissent in *Planned Parenthood v. Casey*, he wrote that

> [a]s long as this Court thought (and the people thought) that we justices were doing essentially lawyers' work up here—reading text and discerning our society's traditional understanding of that text—the public pretty much left us alone. Texts and traditions are facts to study, not convictions to demonstrate about. But if in reality our process of constitutional adjudication consists primarily of making value judgments . . .[,] then a free and intelligent people's attitude toward us can be expected to be (ought to be) quite different. The people know that their value judgments are quite as good as those taught in any law school—maybe better. . . . Value judgments, after all, should be voted on, not dictated. . . .[8]

Justice Scalia's point is that textual analysis, at least carried out in a lawyer like and unbiased manner, bears the promise of bolstering the Court's credibility against charges that it is simply imposing its own values on the country through the guise of constitutional analysis. Perhaps this is true to some extent. However, in hard cases, which are often at the heart of the Court's docket, the text is capable of yielding multiple meanings, and the choice among plausible alternatives may well be driven by ideology or at least judicial philosophy.

In this and the next chapter, I will examine several facets of textual analysis employed by the Court throughout its history. In this chapter I will consider several of the well-recognized canons of constitutional interpretation employed by the Court, including giving the text its "plain meaning," construing the Constitution flexibly, and construing the text to avoid surplus and redundancy, just to name a few. In the next chapter I will consider several issues involving what Professor Akhil Amar has referred to as intratextualism, that is reading the constitutional text with reference to other parts of the document or with respect to the document as a whole. Next I will consider the important technique of reading constitutional text in light of its purpose. Finally I will look at the question of when, if at all, the Court concludes that it is justified in deviating from what would appear to be the relatively plain meaning of the text. The derivation of textual meaning from other sources, including the original understanding, tradition, practice, and constitutional structure will be considered in subsequent chapters.

A disproportionate number of the best cases illustrating textual analysis comes from the Marshall Court. This is probably attributable to a variety of factors. First, the Court had not yet accumulated a large body of precedent, doctrine, and practice to rely upon. Second, the Court did not yet have access to much of the materials setting forth the original understanding that are now available, and the methodology of original understanding as it has developed was not yet in fashion. Third, the early Court was heavily influenced by the common law method in which all of its justices would have been trained, and close textual analysis played a large role in that methodology. Finally, either Chief Justice Marshal or Justice Joseph Story wrote the vast majority of the Court's foundational constitutional decisions during the first three-and-half decades of the nineteenth century, and both of them were excellent textual expositors. Although now over 200 years into its role as constitutional interpreter, the Court rarely has occasion to address a constitutional provision that it has never before considered, the forms of textual analysis developed during the Marshall Court remain vital and are quoted, cited, and utilized where relevant.

III. Some Basic Canons of Textualism

Over its history, the Court has developed several often utilized canons of textual interpretation. Some of these are well-established rules of thumb that apply to the interpretation of any written legal document, and others make sense only with respect to legislative enactments. Still others are concerned only with the explication of a constitution. These canons are often too general to be outcome-determinative where applicable. Moreover there are sometimes countercanons that lead in the opposite direction. Still on occasion they can prove to be useful analytical devices. They remain well-established legal tools that will almost certainly be employed where applicable.

A. The Constitutional Text should not be given a Strict Construction

At times throughout our constitutional history, it has been argued that the Constitution should be strictly construed, arguably to avoid unnecessary errors, to defer to the more representative institutions of government and to provide a check against the injection of judicial value judgments. Chief Justice Marshall confronted this argument at the very outset of his opinion in *Gibbons v. Ogden*,[9] the Court's foundational exposition of the federal commerce power. In the course of invalidating a state-created monopoly over the ferry boat trade on the Hudson River, Marshall noted that "strict construction" was not controversial if it simply meant that the text should not be given a broader meaning than the language warranted.[10] But there was no basis for:

[a] narrow construction which, in support [of] some theory not to be found in the constitution, would deny to the government those powers which the words of the grant, as usually understood, import, and which are consistent with the general views and objects of the instrument. . . .[11]

This is arguably an example of the principle relied on throughout *Gibbons* that constitutional language must be read in light of its purpose, and the purpose of the grants of power to Congress was to permit it to accomplish great deeds, and as such the text must be read broadly enough to permit that to occur.[12] However, Marshall clearly rejected strict construction as a rule of interpretation designed to promote judicial restraint.

Marshall returned to this theme and made the same argument even more famously in *McCulloch v. Maryland* where he counseled that "we must never forget that it is a constitution we are expounding."[13] He made this remark in the course of a general discussion of the nature of the Constitution and of constitutional interpretation. However, in *McCulloch* as in *Gibbons*, Marshall ultimately addressed an issue of the interpretation of congressional power and concluded that textual grants of power, in that case the Necessary and Proper Clause, must be read with sufficient liberality to allow Congress flexibility in the accomplishment of legitimate ends.[14] So as with *Gibbons*, this may be taken as another example of Marshall reading constitutional text in light of its purpose as opposed to an endorsement of broadly reading constitutional text in all circumstances. In the context of Marshall's discussion of the very nature of the Constitution in *McCulloch*, this declaration can also be taken to mean that the Constitution should be read with sufficient flexibility to permit it "to endure for the ages to come, and consequently, to be adapted to the various crises of human affairs."[15] Moreover, Marshall also set forth the argument in *McCulloch* that the Constitution was a "great outline" as opposed to "the prolixity of a legal code," and as such, it must be read with sufficient liberality to fill in the gaps, at least in order to render it effective.[16] Taken as a whole then Marshall's classic opinion in *McCulloch*, arguably the greatest of all constitutional opinions by the Court, is readily understood as a charter for an expansive reading of the document.

Chief Justice Marshall set the tone for much subsequent constitutional interpretation with his opinion in *McCulloch*. Indeed, in his concurrence in *Youngstown Sheet and Tube v. Sawyer*, the Korean War steel seizure case, Justice Frankfurter referred to Marshall's "constitution we are expounding" remark as the "[t]he pole-star for constitutional adjudications."[17] For Frankfurter that required "a spacious view in applying [the] instruments" with "as narrow a delimitation of the constitutional issues as the circumstances permit."[18]

Likewise, in his influential concurring opinion in *Poe v. Ullman*,[19] an important precursor to the Court's substantive due process privacy precedent, Justice Harlan also cited *McCulloch v. Maryland* as the authority for a flexible reading of the Constitution. He contended that

> [t]he basis of judgment as to the Constitutionality of state action must be a rational one, approaching the text which is the only commission for our power not in a literalistic way, as if we had a tax statute before us, but as the basic charter of our society, setting out in spare but meaningful terms the principles of government.[20]

Justice Harlan understood that the obvious concern about this approach would be that it created too much discretion for judges to impose their own values under the guise of constitutional interpretation. He attempted to deflect that critique by arguing that courts must be guided by history and tradition in construing the due process concept of liberty.[21] The utility of that approach will be discussed in detail in the chapter on Tradition and Practice.[22]

The question of how flexibly constitutional language should be read was addressed in two of the Court's foundational Fourth Amendment cases. In *Boyd v. United States*, one of the earliest Fourth and Fifth Amendment cases, the Court maintained that "[a] close and literal construction deprives [constitutional protections] of half their efficacy, and leads to the gradual depreciation of the right, as if it consisted more in sound than in substance."[23] This lead the Court to conclude that it was impermissible for the government to seize private papers of a testimonial nature, a result which was subsequently abandoned by the Court.[24] Although the specific result in *Boyd* has been rejected, its interpretive approach remains influential though not always followed. In *Olmstead v. United States*,[25] the Court's overly literal interpretation of the Fourth Amendment well illustrated what the Court in *Boyd* intended to reject. In *Olmstead*, the Court held that tapping of a telephone by federal authorities did not constitute a search and seizure because intangibles such as conversations are not a "person, house, papers or effect" within the coverage of the Fourth Amendment.[26]

This literal approach was vigorously criticized by Justice Brandeis in dissent.[27] He quoted Marshall's "Constitution we are expounding" language as well as the language from *Boyd* in maintaining that the Constitution should be read more flexibly. Forty years later in *Katz v. United States*, the Court overruled *Olmstead* and took a more expansive privacy-oriented approach to the purpose and coverage of the Fourth Amendment.[28] The Court's opinions in the Fourth Amendment cases from *Boyd* through *Katz* provide a famous and classic example of the Court ultimately adopting a spacious approach to constitutional language, with direct reliance on Marshall's opinion in *McCulloch*. This is not to say, however, that there have been no instances since Katz in which the Court has construed the concepts of search or seizure more narrowly.[29]

One final example of this approach may be seen in one of the Court's rare constitutional explications of the Copyright Clause. In *Burrows & Giles v. Sarony*, relying in part on a broad construction of constitutional language by the First Congress, the Court concluded that the terms *writing* and *author* in the Copyright Clause should not be restricted to books and their creators, given that "both these words are susceptible to a more enlarged definition."[30] Consequently the Court concluded that by "author," the Constitution should be understood to mean "he to whom anything owes its origin."[31] As such, a photograph could be a "writing" and a photographer an "author" within the meaning of the Copyright Clause.[32] A literal construction of the language would almost certainly have led to the opposite conclusion.

The Court is especially inclined to read constitutional text broadly and flexibly when that text itself tends to be written in general or even vague language. Interpreting such provisions can present a serious challenge in that the very lack of specificity can easily lead to the improper imposition of the justices' own value preferences. Justice Jackson addressed this problem in his concurrence in *Edwards v. California* where he argued that the Court should not shrink from attempting to give meaning to the Privileges or Immunities Clause of the Fourteenth Amendment.[33] He explained that

> the difficulty of the task does not excuse us from giving these general and abstract words whatever of specific content and concreteness they will bear as we mark out their application, case by case. That is the method of the common law, and it has been the method of this Court with other no less general statements in our fundamental law. This Court has not been timorous about giving concrete meaning to such obscure and vagrant phrases as "due process," "general welfare," "equal protection" or even "commerce among the several States." But it has always hesitated to give any real meaning to the privileges and immunities clause lest it improvidently give too much.[34]

For Justice Jackson the harm from reading a provision too narrowly justified the risk of reading it too expansively. In this specific instance, however, the Court has largely stuck with the restrictive interpretation of the clause placed on it shortly after its passage by the Supreme Court in the *Slaughter-House Cases*[35] over strong dissents calling for a broader reading.[36] The *Slaughter-House Cases* are indeed a leading example of an unduly narrow construction of a significant constitutional provision and will be discussed in some detail later in this and subsequent chapters.[37] As a result of the narrow construction of the Privileges or Immunities Clause in the *Slaughter-House Cases*, the Due Process and Equal Protection Clauses of the Fourteenth Amendment have arguably been construed more broadly than was initially warranted in order to provide protection that should have been recognized under the former clause.[38]

The canon that the Constitution should be interpreted broadly to accomplish its purposes is not always honored. There are many instances in which that has not been done. But the canon still expresses a general if imperfect truth about the Court's approach to constitutional interpretation throughout its history. There is certainly not a frequently quoted countercanon that the Constitution should be interpreted tightly or narrowly.

B. The Constitutional Text should be given its Plain Meaning

In many of its foundational decisions, the Marshall Court often started with the assumption that the framers were capable draftsman and as such, as Chief Justice Marshall put it in *Gibbons v. Ogden*, they "must be understood to have employed words in their natural sense, and to have intended what they have said."[39] That is, as a general rule, the framers were writing in plain language rather than using legal terms of art. Marshall then relied on this "plain meaning" approach in *Gibbons* to explicate the meaning of the word *commerce* in the Commerce Clause.[40] He observed that "commerce undoubtedly, is traffic, but it is something more: it is intercourse. It describes the commercial intercourse between nations, and parts of nations. . . ."[41] To define this crucial constitutional concept, Marshall appeared to rely largely on the common understanding of the word in everyday parlance. He took the same approach later in the opinion announcing that "[t]he word 'among' means intermingled with."[42] He also opined that "the power to regulate . . . is [the power] to prescribe the rule by which commerce is to be governed."[43]

The meaning that Marshall attributed to these terms was fairly straightforward, so no further source was necessary. Often, language in the text is of such obvious meaning that no authority beyond an appeal to common usage is necessary to illuminate it. For instance in *Marbury v. Madison*, Chief Justice Marshall could unquestionably proclaim with no further authority that "[i]t is the essential criterion of appellate jurisdiction, that it revises and corrects the proceedings in a cause already instituted, and does not create that case."[44] Nothing more needed to be said to establish that a case brought in the first instance in the United States Supreme Court was not brought in the exercise of its appellate jurisdiction.[45]

Chief Justice Marshall relied on the plain-meaning approach as well in *Sturges v. Crowninshield*[46] in holding that a New York insolvency law that discharged a debtor from liability violated the clause prohibiting the passage of state laws impairing the obligations of contracts. Marshall rejected an attempt to show that the framers had more limited objectives in mind, pointing out that "[i]t would be dangerous in the extreme, to infer from extrinsic circumstances that a case for which words of an instrument expressly provide, shall be exempted from its operation."[47] In other words, where the text is clear and applicable, there is no room for further "interpretation."

Likewise, in the course of expounding on the nature of constitutional interpretation in the landmark case of *Martin v. Hunter's Lessee*,[48] Justice Story, perhaps early America's greatest constitutional scholar, remarked that "[t]he words [of the Constitution] are to be taken in their natural and obvious sense, and not in a sense unreasonably restricted or enlarged." Story relied on this canon to refute Virginia's argument that the Supreme Court could not constitutionally exercise appellate jurisdiction over a decision of the Supreme Court of a state, pointing out that under Article III that "[i]t is the case, then, and not the court, that gives the jurisdiction . . . [and] [i]f the judicial power extends to the case, it will be in vain to search in the letter of the constitution for any qualification as to the tribunal where it depends."[49] Here Story used the plain-meaning rule quite effectively to cut the legs out from under Virginia's primary argument. Later in the opinion, Story was again able to use plain meaning to undermine Virginia's claim of immunity from federal appellate review. In response to the argument that the Constitution did not permit Congress to regulate the states in their sovereign capacity,[50] Justice Story noted that the Constitution "is crowded with provisions which restrain or annul the sovereignty of the states in some of the highest branches of their prerogatives," citing Article I, section 10.[51] So much for untrammeled state sovereignty.

Justice Story returned to the plain meaning of the text once more in *Martin* where in response to Virginia's argument that appellate review by the Supreme Court seemed to assume that state judges might be biased, he pointed out that though he and the Court had the greatest respect for the competence and integrity of state judges, the Constitution itself seemed to exhibit concern over potential state court prejudice by providing for federal jurisdiction in cases between different states, citizens of different states, or a citizen and a state.[52] Thus whether an assumption of possible state bias is warranted or not, "[t]he constitution has presumed" that it is a potential problem worth avoiding according to Story.[53] Consequently, the constitutional language itself disposed of the Virginia court's concern.

In *Okanogan v. United States*,[54] known as the *Pocket Veto* case, the Court quoted the plain-meaning language of Justice Story from *Martin*, noted above, in the course of rejecting the argument that the word *days* in the

Presentment Clause referred to legislative days rather than calendar days. The Court explained that

> [t]he word "days," when not qualified, means in ordinary and common usage calendar days. This is obviously the meaning in which it is used in the constitutional provision, and is emphasized by the fact that "Sundays" are excepted. There is nothing whatever to justify changing this meaning by inserting the word "legislative" as a qualifying adjective."[55]

The Court also concluded that the word *adjournment* in the clause was not limited to final adjournments.[56] Consequently, as the president was not presented with the bill in issue ten days prior to the adjournment of the first legislative session, it did not become law when he failed to sign it.[57] This is an excellent example of the Court construing common language in the text in a straightforward, nontechnical manner.

Similarly in *Hawke v. Smith*, the Court concluded that the term *legislature*, "was not a term of uncertain meaning when incorporated into the Constitution. What it meant when adopted it still means for the purpose of interpretation. A Legislature was then the representative body which made the laws of the people."[58]Consequently, it concluded that where the Constitution called for a constitutional amendment to be approved by state legislatures, it was impermissible to attempt ratification by a popular referendum. As with *Okanogan*, the Court made a persuasive case that even in a structural setting, words in the Constitution should be read in an ordinary as opposed to a specialized manner.

The Court continues to rely on the plain-meaning canon where appropriate. For example, recently, in *City of Boerne v. Flores*,[59] it employed a plain reading of the text to conclude that the power to "enforce" the substantive provisions of the Fourteenth Amendment (and the Bill of Rights) simply cannot be read as permitting Congress to alter the meaning of those provisions. Therefore, Congress could not use its enforcement power to change an interpretation of the Free Exercise Clause, previously adopted by the Court. Likewise in *Plyler v. Doe*, the Court gave the phrase in the Fourteenth Amendment—"persons within its jurisdiction"—the rather obvious meaning of being geographically present as opposed to the strained meaning put forth by the state of being legally within the country.[60] As a result, the Court concluded that the children of illegal immigrants were not excluded from the coverage of the Amendment, considering that they were physically present in Texas even if they had entered the country illegally.

And in *Employment Division v. Smith*, Justice O'Connor, concurring, objected to the majority's conclusion that the Free Exercise Clause of the First Amendment provided complete protection for religious belief but not religiously based conduct, noting that the text of the clause recognized no such distinction and the Court should not read such a distinction into the text.[61]

A predictable problem with the plain-meaning approach, however, is that constitutional meaning will often be far less plain to some justices than to others. For instance, in the *Slaughter-House Cases*,[62] where the Court found that a state-created monopoly in the butchering trade did not violate the recently enacted Fourteenth Amendment, Justice Swayne, dissenting, disagreed with the Court's understanding of the meaning of text. He explained that

> [n]o searching analysis is necessary to eliminate [sic] its meaning. Its language is intelligible and direct. Nothing can be more transparent. Every word employed has an established signification. There is no room for construction. There is nothing to construe. Elaboration may obscure, but cannot make clearer, the intent and purpose sought to be carried out.[63]

Contrary to Justice Swayne's understanding, the plain meaning of the text of the Fourteenth Amendment has been one of the most hotly contested issues in constitutional law ever since.[64]

It is not uncommon for justices to agree upon a plain-meaning approach but disagree as to what the plain meaning is. For instance, in the *Civil Rights Cases*, the majority invalidated a congressional statute passed pursuant to the Fourteenth Amendment that prohibited racial discrimination in certain private businesses, pointing out that the three central protective provisions of the second sentence of Section One of the Amendment—Privileges or Immunities, Due Process, and Equal Protection—were all directed at "state action."[65] Thus for the majority, the text plainly limited congressional enforcement to addressing action by the state. Justice Harlan looked at the text of the Fourteenth Amendment through a somewhat larger lens, however, and concluded that the plain meaning was quite the opposite from that deduced by the Court in that Section Five of the Amendment authorized the Congress to enforce "the provisions of this article" and not simply the prohibitions of sentence two cited by the majority.[66] Because sentence one of Section One of the Amendment defines federal and state citizenship and does not contain a state action limitation, Congress could reach private discrimination simply by fleshing out that concept.[67] This is a very nice example of a justice deriving plain meaning through a more comprehensive reading of the text.

Adamson v. California and the debate over whether the Fourteenth Amendment should be understood as applying the provisions of the Bill of Rights against the states presented another classic disagreement over plain meaning. Rejecting the argument that the Due Process Clause of the Fourteenth Amendment was intended to apply all of the provisions of the Bill of Rights against the states, Justice Frankfurter, concurring, observed that "[i]t would be extraordinarily strange for a constitution to convey such specific commands in such a roundabout and inexplicit way."[68] Justice Black, however, responded that the "the first section of the Fourteenth Amendment, taken as a whole[,]" was thought by the framers and ratifiers as "sufficiently explicit" to require the incorporation of the Bill of Rights against the states.[69] From a plain-meaning perspective, Justice Frankfurter clearly had the better argument. Even if Justice Black was correct in believing that the Privileges or Immunities Clause was intended to apply all provisions of the Bill of Rights to the states, something beyond the plain meaning of the text would be necessary to make the case because, on its own, the language says no such thing.

C. Understanding Legal Terms of Art

Despite the plain-meaning rule, some words and phrases in the Constitution are clearly terms of art, that is, they are not merely elements of common understanding but rather have a technical or historical meaning.[70] As Justice Chase noted in *Calder v. Bull*, "[t]he prohibition, 'that no state shall pass any ex post facto law' necessarily requires some explanation; for, naked and without explanation, it is unintelligible, and means nothing."[71] He then turned briefly to English history to find such an explanation.[72] Later in the opinion, he noted that "[t]he expressions 'ex post facto laws,' are technical, they had been in use long before the Revolution, and had acquired an appropriate meaning by Legislators, Lawyers, and Authors."[73] The Court has continued to view the Ex Poste Facto Clause as a historical term of art, relying heavily on Justice Chase's initial interpretation of it to this day.[74] Once it is recognized that terms such as these have a somewhat specific historical meaning, defining that meaning requires an inquiry into the historical background of the language as well as the original understanding at the time of the framing. For the most part, this inquiry will be discussed in greater depth in the chapters on Original Understanding.

It might seem that the term "Bill of Attainder" that appears in the same clause as Ex Poste Facto should also be interpreted as a legal term of art; however, though the Court has consulted history in the course of defining it, it has been less inclined to consider it limited to its precise historical meaning. In *Cummings v. Missouri*[75] and *Ex parte Garland*,[76] the first two cases to construe the clause, the Court applied it to invalidate federal and state post-Civil War test oaths that precluded individuals unable to swear that they had not, among other things, evaded military service or sympathized with those in rebellion from entering a variety of occupations, including the practice of law and the clergy. Justice Miller, dissenting, in *Cummings* and *Garland* maintained that the term "bill of attainder" was derived from the terms *attincta* and *attinctura*, meaning "the stain or corruption of the blood" resulting in the loss of inheritance rights for those attainted.[77] Citing Story's Commentaries on the Constitution he explained that the concept carried a fairly precise historical meaning that simply did not apply to the provisions at issue in these cases.[78] The majority in Cummings conceded that the test oaths were not Bills of Attainder in the most pristine historical sense, but concluded nevertheless that they carried the same impact and as such must be invalidated because "what cannot be done directly cannot be done indirectly."[79]

Over 100 years later in *United States v. Lovett*, citing *Cummings*, the Court again construed the Bill of Attainder Clause broadly in terms of its purpose in order to invalidate an act of Congress that effectively dismissed several federal employees on the ground that they were subversives.[80] Justice Frankfurter concurred on statutory grounds but rejected the majority's approach to the Bill of Attainder Clause. Like Justice Miller, dissenting in *Cummings*, Frankfurter argued that some constitutional provisions such as the prohibition on bills of attainder have "their source in definite grievances."[81] As such, "[t]heir meaning was so settled by history that definition was superfluous."[82] Because Justice Frankfurter did not believe that the act in question was intended to punish the employees in question, it simply could not qualify as a bill of attainder, at least as that concept had been understood historically. As such, the broader purpose of the provision, if there was one, was simply irrelevant.[83]

Several years later in *United States v. Brown*, where the Court invalidated an Act of Congress that prohibited a member of the communist party from serving as an officer of a labor union, it continued its broad interpretation of the Bill of Attainder Clause,[84] concluding that "while history thus provides some guidelines . . . [the writings of the framers indicate that] the . . . Clause was intended not as a narrow, technical (and therefore soon to be outmoded) prohibition, but rather as an implementation of the separation of powers, a general safeguard against legislative exercise of the judicial function."[85] The dissent in *Brown* no longer bothered to limit the clause to its narrow historical context as had the dissents in the earlier Bill of Attainder cases but merely argued that the decision was inconsistent with precedent.[86] The Court finally placed some limitation on its expansive reading of the Bill of Attainder Clause in *Nixon v. GSA* where it concluded that a Bill of Attainder does not exist whenever Congress fails to legislate at the most general level possible, and, furthermore, in the context of preservation of presidential records, Richard Nixon was "a legitimate class of one."[87] The Court concluded that the Congressional Act depriving former President Nixon of the immediate custody of his presidential papers was not punitive within either an historical or functional understanding of the Bill of Attainder Clause.[88] The contrast between the Court's approach to the Ex Post facto and Bill of Attainder Clauses, each of which involves somewhat unfamiliar terminology derived from distant historical events, illustrates that the Court exercises considerable discretion in determining in the first instance whether constitutional language carries a plain meaning or is a term of art. That decision will in turn be quite influential in the subsequent scope of coverage of the provision.

In *Cohens v. Virginia*, Chief Justice Marshall addressed the meaning of the Eleventh Amendment.[89] He pointed out that the term *suit* was a term of art; "[i]n law language, it is the prosecution of some demand in a Court of justice."[90] He then turned to respected legal scholars such as Blackstone and Bracton for further elucidation.[91] The main point was that this was a technical term that was in need of some professional explanation as opposed to a phrase with a meaning immediately evident to the lay person. Marshall then reasoned that a writ of error to a lower court from a verdict in a suit brought against that person by the state was hardly a suit prosecuted by that individual against the state within the correct meaning of the Eleventh Amendment.[92] This is an example of the Court finding a term of arguably common understanding to constitute a term of art.

In one of its earliest opinions addressing the Due Process Clause, the Court in *Murray v. Hoboken Land Co.* proclaimed that "[t]he words 'due process of law,' were undoubtedly intended to convey the same meaning as the words, 'by law of the land,' in the Magna Charta," quoting Lord Coke to that effect and noting that several early state constitutions used the latter instead of the former phrase.[93] The Court followed this approach in *Twining v. New Jersey* where it noted that

> "[w]hat is due process of law may be ascertained by an examination of those settled usages and modes of proceedings existing in the common and statute law of England before the emigration of our ancestors, and shown not to have been unsuited to their civil and political condition by having been acted on by them after the settlement of this country."[94]

This placed a distinct historical focus on the interpretation of the concept of due process of law. The Court went on to recognize, however, that in spite of this historical focus, due process also protected against the "arbitrary exercises of the powers of government."[95] After an extensive examination of several famous English and American legal proceedings, the Court concluded that the Privilege Against Self Incrimination was not "a part of the law of the land of Magna Charta or the due process of law."[96] The Court would later reverse that conclusion[97] as well as this method of analysis, substituting a more evolutionary approach to ascertain the meaning of due process of law with little or no regard to the meaning of the concept in prerevolutionary England.[98] This illustrates that a concept that may have started out as a term of art can evolve into a term of common understanding.

Even terms of art will not necessarily be given a clear and static interpretation by the Court. In *Rochin v. California*, Justice Frankfurter writing for the majority opined in dicta that

> [t]he requirements of the Sixth and Seventh Amendments for trial by jury in the federal courts have a rigid meaning. No changes or chances can alter the content of the verbal symbol of 'jury'—a body of twelve men who must reach a unanimous conclusion if the verdict is to go against the defendant.[99]

Justice Frankfurter conceded that under the fundamental fairness approach that permitted different standards of protection for the federal and state systems, many states permitted civil juries to be composed of fewer than twelve persons and render nonunanimous verdicts.[100] However, when faced directly with the question of whether twelve-person unanimous juries were constitutionally required, the Court affirmed Justice Frankfurter's assertion that they were so required by the Sixth Amendment in federal courts, but although it conceded that the right to jury trial is fundamental, it concluded that Fourteenth Amendment Due Process did not impose these rules on the states.[101] Instead of adhering strictly to the historical approach stated by Frankfurter in *Rochin*, the Court in *Williams v. Florida*[102] and *Apodaca v. Oregon*[103] took account of the functional role that the jury plays and concluded that neither twelve members nor unanimity was essential for the jury to serve its purposes. Thus over time a purely definitional approach gave way to an approach that focused on the underlying purpose of the provision.

D. Ambiguous Language and Multiple Meanings

The plain-meaning approach will work only if there is a plain meaning. Words often have more than one meaning, however. Chief Justice Marshall expressed the point well in *McCulloch v. Maryland* where he observed the following:

> Such is the character of human language, that no word conveys to the mind, in all situations, one single definite idea; and nothing is more common than to use a word in a figurative sense. Almost all compositions contain words, which, taken in their rigorous sense, would convey a meaning different from that which is obviously intended.[104]

Marshall's explication of the meaning of the words "*necessary* and *proper* in *McCulloch*—discussed in the next chapter—provides an excellent example of the Court confronting and then resolving questions of multiple meanings.[105]

Justice Johnson, concurring in *Martin v. Hunter's Lessee*, also expressed strong reservations as to the ability of the Court to resolve the meaning of constitutional language through a close reading. In rejecting one of Justice Story's textual arguments, Justice Johnson proclaimed the following:

> I have seldom found much good result from hypercritical severity, in examining the distinct force of words. Language is essentially defective in precision; more so than those are aware of who are not in the habit of subjecting it to philological analysis.[106]

So much for textualism. It should be noted, however, that Justice Johnson was focusing on two of Justice Story's weaker textual arguments in the majority opinion. Justice Story engaged in an arguably strained reading of the text when he attempted to find significance in the fact that Article III refers to "all cases" but only to "controversies."[107] Starting with the plausible assumption that Congress deliberately omitted the word *all* before controversies, he speculated that Congress may well have believed that the specified cases were of greater importance to "national sovereignty" than the specified controversies, and consequently some of the latter but all of the former needed to be included within the federal judicial power.[108] Story also argued that the phrase "shall extend" in Article III was used in the imperative sense and therefore made all federal jurisdiction mandatory. Story seemed to recognize, however, that he was only guessing as to the meaning of these terms and ultimately set the whole argument aside and moved on. In his concurring opinion, Justice Johnson noted that he found this argument implausible. His disdain for close textual analysis is at best only partially correct. As will be seen, there are many instances in which a more expansive mode of interpretation is correct. However, the Constitution is a legal document and as such, in many instances, close attention to the precise language employed will often be a helpful approach.

Sometimes the Court admits that there may be multiple meanings to a word, and indeed that words may carry multiple meanings within the Constitution itself. In *Texas v. White*,[109] where the Court was faced with determining whether a state that had seceded during the Civil War remained a "state" for federal jurisdictional purposes as well as with respect to the legality of its actions, the Court explained that "[i]n the Constitution the term state most frequently expresses the combined idea . . . of people, territory, and government."[110] It noted that in some clauses the Constitution seems to focus primarily on the state as a political community (as opposed to a government), while in others it is used primarily in a "geographical sense."[111] It concluded that for purposes of the clause in which the Constitution agrees to guarantee the states a republican form of government, the term *state* was used to signify a political community as opposed to a government, as the clause quite explicitly distinguishes between the state and its government.[112] This is an excellent example of a clause that appears to reveal which of several alternative interpretations is intended by its very own terms. Ultimately the Court concluded that Texas was acting as a state for purposes of conducting legitimate governmental business, but it was not a state when engaging in activity in support of the Civil War against the United States.[113]

When language is ambiguous and there is no clear guidance as to its meaning, the Court must simply do the best that it can to explicate the terms in question using a variety of analytical tools. In *Nixon v. United States*,[114] the Court argued that the clause giving the Senate the "sole" power to try impeachments creates a strong inference against judicial review because if the Court were to have a say on impeachment matters, then the Senate would not have the "sole" authority. Justice Stevens read the word *sole* rather differently from the Court, however.[115] Considering that the word also appears in the parallel clause stating that the House "shall have the sole Power of Impeachment," Justice Stevens reasoned that the framers used *sole* to differentiate the role of the Senate from that of the House rather than from that of the Court.[116] Given the use of *sole* in these two complementary provisions, Justice Stevens's reading seems more persuasive than that of the majority; however, either reading is at least plausible. It is perhaps even more plausible that both were correct; that is, that *sole* was meant to exclude both the House of Representatives and the courts.

In *Morrison v. Olsen*, where the Court upheld the constitutionality of the Independent Counsel statute, it struggled to determine whether an independent prosecutor was an "inferior" as opposed to a "principal" officer within the Appointments Clause.[117] If she was a principal officer, nomination by the president and confirmation by the Senate would be required. If inferior, then appointment by a court, as was called for by the statute would be constitutional. Conceding that "[t]he line between 'inferior' and 'principal' officers is one that is far from clear, and the Framers provided little guidance . . .[,]" the Court found the independent counsel to be an "inferior" officer on the grounds that she could be removed by an executive official; she was authorized to perform only limited duties and she was given only a limited jurisdiction.[118] Justice Scalia disagreed vigorously with the Court's analysis of these factors, but more important, he argued that they were irrelevant to the question before it.[119] Instead, relying on a definition of inferior as "subordinate" from Samuel Johnson's eighteenth-century dictionary, as well as constitutional structure and some originalist material, he argued that the independent counsel was not an inferior officer in view of her protection against removal for anything but cause, and that she was not subordinate to the Attorney General.[120] Justice Scalia's interpretation of this admittedly vague term seems far more persuasive and far better supported by traditional interpretive methodology than the majority's approach. Still the word is easily capable of different meanings, and as the competing approaches show, those meanings can be derived through different forms of analysis.

These cases indicate that when words or phrases in the constitutional text carry multiple meanings, the Court will need to engage in further explication in order to arrive at the "correct" meaning. Sometimes the Court will be able to justify a particular reading of a constitutional term primarily if not exclusively with the tools of textual analysis. Perhaps more often, the Court will rely on other methodologies of interpretation such as original understanding or structure to resolve the ambiguity. Even though the Court must make a choice, in many cases it is faced with a word or phrase that can plausibly carry more than one meaning, and as such more than one reading is easily defensible.

E. The Text should be Read to Avoid Surplus and Redundancy

A common canon of legal interpretation is that a text should be read to avoid rendering another portion meaningless or redundant.[121] Justice Field made that argument in his dissent in the *Slaughter-House Cases* where he noted that under the Court's interpretation of the Privileges or Immunities Clause of the Fourteenth Amendment, the clause has no meaning or significance given that all of the privileges and immunities identified by the majority were independently protected by the Constitution prior to passage of the Amendment.[122] The point was well taken and indeed, as a result of the Court's decision, the clause, which had been intended to be a crucial substantive provision of the Fourteenth Amendment has had almost no impact at all.

In *Hurtado v. California*,[123] the Court concluded that the Fourteenth Amendment Due Process Clause did not require that a defendant in a state criminal trial be indicted by a grand jury because the Fifth Amendment also contained a Due Process Clause and in addition required that a federal criminal defendant must be indicted by a grand jury. The Court reasoned that if due process required indictment by a grand jury then the specific provision of the Fifth Amendment so requiring would be mere surplus.[124] In his concurring opinion in *Adamson v. California*, Justice Frankfurter argued that "[i]t ought not to require argument to reject the notion that due process of law meant one thing in the Fifth Amendment and another in the Fourteenth."[125] However, in *Powell v. Alabama*, the Court cut back on this approach, explaining that "[t]he rule is an aid to construction, and in some instances may be conclusive; but it must yield to more compelling considerations. . . ."[126] Ensuring that indigent defendants in a capital case obtained adequate representation was obviously such a compelling consideration. Consequently the Court concluded that the right to counsel, at least in limited circumstances, was extended into state criminal proceedings as a matter of Fourteenth Amendment Due Process despite the fact that the Fifth Amendment provided for due process of law while the Sixth Amendment explicitly protected the right to counsel. This could be explained by recognizing that Fourteenth Amendment Due Process is a more expansive concept than Fifth Amendment Due Process in that part of its function, at least as understood by the Court, is to apply all tenets of fundamental fairness in adjudication to the states, including some which were set out in detail in the Bill of Rights with respect to the federal government. Thus despite the identity of language, the clauses serve different purposes and as such carry somewhat different meanings.

It is quite plausible that the framers of the Fourteenth Amendment did in fact intend Fifth and Fourteenth Amendment Due Process to have the same scope and meaning and intended for the Bill of Rights to be applied against the states through the Privileges or Immunities Clause. Once the Court gutted that clause in the *Slaughter-House Cases*, however, that was no longer possible, so the Court turned to and arguably distorted the Due Process Clause to achieve this important goal.

In response to the argument that the Ninth Amendment was rarely relied upon by the Supreme Court, Justice Goldberg, concurring in *Griswold v. Connecticut*, cited the maxim proclaimed by Chief Justice Marshall in *Marbury* that all constitutional provisions should be presumed to mean something.[127] Consequently, disagreement as to its meaning was no reason to ignore it completely.[128] The Ninth Amendment provides that "[t]he Enumeration in the Constitution of certain rights shall not be construed to deny or disparage others retained by the people."[129] The question was not whether the Ninth Amendment was redundant but rather whether the Court could confidently discern its scope and meaning, period. Despite Justice Goldberg's plea in his *Griswold* concurrence, the Court has continued to ignore it perhaps to a very large degree because it does not really know what to make of it.

Justice Thomas raised the redundancy argument in his concurrence in *United States v. Lopez* to challenge the Court's well-established doctrine that Congress has the power to regulate activities that "substantially affect" interstate commerce.[130] He maintained that the "substantially affect commerce" theory renders most of the other Article I powers redundant because Congress could pass bankruptcy laws, copyright and patent laws, and maintain a postal system under the broad Commerce Clause theory.[131]

Perhaps so, but as Justice Thomas must certainly realize, it is far too late in the day to uproot doctrine as deeply entrenched as the substantial affects test. Assuming that his reading is correct, there are times when precedent and doctrine overpower text, and this would be such a case.

In his concurring opinion in *First National Bank of Boston v. Bellotti*, Chief Justice Burger argued that the Freedom of Press Clause of the First Amendment was not intended to confer special institutional protection on the press.[132] In reply to the argument that a failure to read the Press Clause as providing special protection would render it redundant, given the Speech Clause, he suggested several alternative interpretations, including that the Speech Clause protects speaking while the Press Clause protects dissemination; the Press Clause focuses specifically on disapproved historical practices such as prior restraint, and that the Press Clause focuses on the written while the Speech Clause focuses on the oral.[133] A majority of the Court has never adopted any of these alternatives and has treated the Speech and Press Clauses as interchangeable. Regardless of whether his alternatives are persuasive interpretations, Chief Justice Burger's recognition of the very need to respond to the redundancy argument is proof of its power.

The canon against surplus and redundancy does not always prevail, however. In *Trop v. Dulles*, Chief Justice Warren writing for a plurality addressing the Eighth Amendment's "Cruel and Unusual Punishment" Clause questioned "[w]hether the word 'unusual' has any qualitative meaning different from 'cruel.'"[134] He noted that in the past, the Court had applied the provision "without regard to any subtleties of meaning that might be latent in the word 'unusual.'"[135] Thus the Court wholly ignored the potential redundancy argument with respect to this clause. However, it did explain that "[i]f the word 'unusual' is to have any meaning apart from the word 'cruel[,]' . . . the meaning should be the ordinary one, signifying something different from that which is generally done."[136]

F. A Negative Inference can be drawn from Affirmative Text

Sometimes it is appropriate to draw a negative inference from an affirmative textual statement. Chief Justice Marshall made this point in *Marbury v. Madison*.[137] Responding to the argument that the grant of original jurisdiction to the Supreme Court should be read as a nonexclusive grant, that is, as a grant that Congress could supplement, Marshall proclaimed the following:

> Affirmative words are often, in their operation, negative of other objects than those affirmed; and in this case, a negative or exclusive sense must be given to them or they have no operation at all.[138]

Marshall correctly recognized that it is certainly not always appropriate to draw a negative inference from an affirmative statement. Rather, he explained that it is at least appropriate in those instances in which the failure to do so would render the text meaningless or ineffective. This would seem to be a logical conclusion. The problem in *Marbury*, however, was that it would not appear to be such a case. In view of the "Exceptions and Regulations" Clause that Marshall conveniently failed to mention, the line between original and appellate jurisdiction would not be "form without substance" as Marshall contended[139] but instead simply an initial distribution pending further rearrangement by Congress through its constitutionally prescribed power. Thus Marshall's interpretive principle was unassailable; however, his application is subject to serious questions.

Marshall engaged in similar reasoning in construing the Commerce Clause in *Gibbons v. Ogden*.[140] In defining the reach of the commerce power, he stated that "[t]he enumeration presupposes something not enumerated; and that something, if we regard the language or the subject of the sentence, must be the exclusively internal commerce of a state."[141] In other words, had the framers meant to say that Congress has the power to regulate all commerce, they would have said so plainly and would not have limited its reach to only "interstate" commerce. The word *interstate* has boundaries, and wholly intrastate is obviously beyond the pale. This is a sensible reading that prevails to this day.[142]

On the other hand, sometimes it is not appropriate to infer a negative from an affirmative. In *Cohens v. Virginia*, Marshall recognized that a negative should sometimes be implied from affirmative language; however, he went on to observe that "where it would destroy some of the most important objects for which the power was created; then, we think, affirmative words ought not to be construed negatively."[143] Applying this principle, Marshall concluded, quite correctly, that the affirmative grant of original jurisdiction to the Supreme Court in cases in which the state is a party should not be read as precluding appellate jurisdiction in cases in which the state is a party where a federal question is raised.[144] In reaching that conclusion, he emphasized that many federal question cases could not originate in the Supreme Court for no other reason than that the federal question may not be apparent at the outset.[145] Moreover, it would preclude the Court from exercising appellate jurisdiction in cases brought in state courts involving the interpretation of treaties that would clearly be inconsistent with the intent of the jurisdictional provisions.[146] In the process, he backed off from some of the "dicta" in *Marbury*, suggesting that Article III by its terms definitively apportioned all of the Court's jurisdiction.[147] This is a good example of the recognition of the obvious limits of an otherwise helpful canon of construction.

Likewise in the *Legal Tender Cases*, the Court reasoned that the clause granting Congress power to "coin money" and "regulate the value thereof" should not be read to imply that Congress could only make precious metals legal tender.[148] In reaching this conclusion, the Court relied on the fact that given the purpose of the Article I powers of Congress, such as the power to coin money, "if any implications are to be deduced from them, they are of an enlarging rather than a restraining character."[149] This is similar to the argument made by Marshall in *McCulloch v. Maryland* with respect to the Necessary and Proper Clause, a case on which the majority in the *Legal Tender Cases* placed heavy reliance. Justice Field, dissenting in the *Legal Tender Cases*, disagreed, however, arguing that "[t]he Constitution has specifically designated the means by which funds can be raised ... taxation, borrowing, coining and the sale of its public property."[150] He concluded that "[t]he designation of the means is a negation of all others, for the designation would be unnecessary and absurd if the use of any and all means were permissible without it."[151] This is often a persuasive argument; however, in this context, the majority's inference seems stronger.

In *Griswold v. Connecticut*, Justice Goldberg argued that the very purpose of the Ninth Amendment was to refute the inference that the explicit enumeration of rights in the first eight amendments of the Bill of Rights should be read to mean that there were no other constitutional rights.[152] In fact, he quoted Madison and Story for this very proposition. It is strong evidence as to how powerful and persuasive the inference that an affirmative grant implies a negative exclusion is if the framers of the Bill of Rights felt compelled to place an explicit disclaimer in the Constitution where they did not wish that inference to be drawn. If this is the correct reading of the Ninth Amendment, then the canon of drawing a negative from an affirmative is all that much stronger in other places within the Constitution where the framers did not explicitly provide for the contrary.

Quirin v. Cox[153] provides another example of the Court's conclusion that the affirmative does not necessarily imply the negative. The question there was whether Nazi saboteurs captured in the United States could be tried before military tribunals. The Court rejected the argument that because "cases arising in the land or naval forces" are excluded from the coverage of the Fifth Amendment, then all other cases including the cases involving spies and saboteurs are included within the Fifth and, by implication, the Sixth Amendment as well, entitling the defendants to a jury trial.[154] The Court reasoned that the exception in the Fifth Amendment was intended to exclude cases that would otherwise be within the scope of Article III of the Constitution, and as the trial of saboteurs for violating the laws of war would not have been covered by Article III to begin with, the failure to exclude it under the Fifth Amendment should not be read as an intention to include it, thereby granting the defendants a right to a jury trial.[155] The Court's reasoning on this point is sensible in that the exclusion must be evaluated against the category to which the exclusion is attached and should not be interpreted to extend any farther.

The Court relied on the affirmative implies a negative argument in *INS v. Chadha* when it concluded that a one house legislative veto was not constitutionally authorized, considering that the Constitution explicitly set forth four instances in which one house of Congress could act on its own—impeachment by the House, conviction on impeachment charges by the Senate, confirmation of presidential appointments by the Senate, and ratification of treaties by the Senate.[156] The "explicit, unambiguous" specification of these four single house proceedings convinced the Court that this was intended to be an exclusive list.[157] The Court reached a similar conclusion in *Nixon v. United States*. Because the Constitution gives the Senate the "sole" power to "try" impeachments and then provides that witnesses shall be under oath, conviction shall be by a 2/3 vote and the Chief Justice shall preside, a strong inference exists that no other limitations should be implied.[158] In both of these instances, the inference of and implied negative is highly plausible though not wholly beyond question.

G. Exceptions Define the Extent of Power

One method of determining what may be included in a grant of power is to consider what has been expressly excluded. Chief Justice Marshall relied on this technique in *Gibbons v. Ogden*.[159] In the course of attempting to determine whether the word *commerce* included navigation, Marshall observed that "[i]t is a rule of construction, acknowledged by all, that the exceptions from a power mark its extent."[160] Marshall then cited Article I, section 9 that provides that "no preference shall be given, by any regulation of commerce or revenue, to the ports of one State over those of another"[161] as evidence that commerce must obviously include navigation if there is to be no discrimination among ports. This is a persuasive use of the comparison between two constitutional clauses evaluated by a time-honored canon of legal construction. Later in *Gibbons*, Marshall used the exceptions argument again, pointing out that the clause of the Constitution that precluded Congress from prohibiting the slave trade prior to 1808 necessarily recognized the power of Congress under the Commerce Clause to regulate vessels employed in transporting persons in commerce.[162]

A few years later, Marshall relied on the same principle again in *Brown v. Maryland*.[163] In the course of determining whether a tax on an imported article was covered by Article I's prohibition on "duties on imports or exports," he focused on the exception that allowed such duties when "[a]bsolutely necessary for executing its inspection laws."[164] He noted that

> [i]f it be a rule of interpretation to which all assent, that the exception of a particular thing from general words, proves that, in the opinion of the lawgiver, the thing excepted would be within the general clause had the exception not been made, we know no reason why this general rule should not be as applicable to the constitution as to other instruments.[165]

Applying the rule, Marshall concluded that it indicated that the framers assumed that taxes similar to those imposed for purposes of inspection fell within the prohibition.[166]

H. The Court should Focus on the Precise Words of the Text and not some Paraphrased Alternative

Strict textualists on the Court insist that the Court focus on the words of the text itself as opposed to abstract concepts embodied in the text. Justice Black made this argument in his dissent in *Griswold v. Connecticut* where he noted that

> One of the most effective ways of diluting or expanding a constitutionally guaranteed right is to substitute for the crucial word or words of a

constitutional guarantee another word or words, more or less flexible and more or less restricted in meaning. This fact is well illustrated by the use of the term 'right of privacy' as a comprehensive substitute for the Fourth Amendment's guarantee against 'unreasonable searches and seizures." 'Privacy' is a broad, abstract and ambiguous concept which can easily be shrunken in meaning but which can also, on the other hand, easily be interpreted as a constitutional ban against many things other than searches and seizures.[167]

Objecting to Justice Douglas's attempt to find a right to privacy in the penumbras of several Bill of Rights guarantees, Justice Black continued, "I like my privacy as well as the next one, but I am nevertheless compelled to admit that government has a right to invade it unless prohibited by some specific constitutional provision."[168]

Justice Black continued this argument in his dissent in *Katz v. United States*[169] in the context of the Fourth Amendment. In the course of concluding that the protection against unreasonable searches and seizures applied to conversations placed from a public telephone, the Court had emphasized that the Amendment was intended to protect privacy and not simply certain "protected areas" such as houses.[170] As in *Griswold*, Justice Black replied that the Court had no authority to "arbitrarily substitut[e] [its] language, designed to protect privacy, for the Constitution's language, designed to protect against unreasonable searches and seizures."[171] According to Justice Black, a focus on the actual language of the Fourth Amendment would have lead to the conclusion that a telephone conversation, especially one that had not yet occurred could not reasonably qualify as "persons, houses, papers [or] effects" within the text of the Amendment.[172] In response to Justice Black, the majority insisted that it was not transforming the Fourth Amendment into "a general constitutional 'right to privacy.'"[173] But as Justice Black pointed out, the concept of privacy, not mentioned in the Amendment itself loomed large in the Court's analysis.

It may be appropriate for the Court to abstract a general principle such as privacy out of the Fourth Amendment in order to better comprehend its purpose. However, if the Court then substitutes the abstract principle for the textual language, as Justice Black charged, it may very well distort the original constitutional meaning. There can be little question that the Court's emphasis on privacy as analytical concept under the Fourth Amendment tends to expand its coverage beyond the categories stated in the text. Whether this is simply an example of the type of generous reading favored by the Court since *McCulloch* or an inappropriate expansion of constitutional meaning is open to debate.

Likewise in his concurring opinion in *Terry v. Adams*, Justice Frankfurter contended that by translating the phrase "any state" in the Fifteenth Amendment into "state action," the Court has given "rise to a false direction [by implying the need to find] some impressive machinery or deliberative conduct normally associated with what orators call a sovereign state[,] when in fact all that is necessary is that "somewhere, somehow, to some extent" "state responsibility" is shown.[174] For Justice Frankfurter, the addition of the word *action* changed and narrowed the constitutional meaning. This would indeed seem to be the case. On the other hand, the majority could have responded that Justice Frankfurter's concept of state "responsibility" would arguably broaden the constitutional text just as much as state "action' would narrow it.

In *Kelo v. City of New London*, Justice O'Connor, dissenting, argued that in two prior cases, the Court had perhaps inadvertently diluted the meaning of "public uses" in the Fifth Amendment Takings Clause by equating it with the police power, which is a very different and broader concept.[175] In the same case, Justice Thomas, dissenting, made a similar point, arguing that the Court had changed the clear meaning of the "Public Use" Clause by substituting the terms "public purpose" or "public necessity," which is not at all the same thing as the public does not have to use the property for there to be a public purpose or necessity.[176] The Court's almost certain deliberate transformation of "public use" to "public purpose" significantly changed the meaning of constitutional analysis in this area in a way which seems quite inconsistent with the clear textual language. The dissent points were well taken.

In his dissenting opinion in *Gonzales v. Raich*, Justice Thomas argued that the Court was expanding the coverage of the Commerce Clause well beyond the original understanding by substituting terms such as *commercial*, *economic*, *production*, *distribution*, and *consumption* for the term *commerce*, which, according to Justice Thomas, had a more defined and limited meaning.[177] This led him to conclude that "[t]he majority is not interpreting the Commerce Clause but rewriting it."[178] Even if Justice Thomas is correct on this point, which he may well be, the line of precedent to which he objects is far too entrenched to dislodge at this point.

In *United States v. Gonzalez-Lopez*, in the course of holding that denial of a criminal defendant's choice of counsel is a per se violation of the Sixth Amendment regardless of any proof of prejudice, Justice Scalia cautioned that the right protected by the Sixth Amendment is "the right to counsel of choice, not the right to a fair trial."[179] However, Justice Alito, dissenting, argued quite persuasively that it was Justice Scalia who was in fact distorting the text, because what the Sixth Amendment literally protects is "'the assistance,' that the defendant's counsel of choice is able to provide."[180] As such, there can be no violation if that assistance proves to be adequate.

It is inevitable that the Court will use alternative phrasing during the course of its opinions perhaps to better explain its analytical process. There is often a danger, however, as these dissents and concurrences of Justices Black, Frankfurter, O'Connor, Thomas, and Alito maintained that by substituting terminology for the language in the text, the Court will deliberately or unconsciously change constitutional meaning. The charge that the text is being altered seems to be an argument raised almost exclusively by dissenters dissatisfied with the Court's approach. How serious of a threat this technique poses will depend to a large extent on the degree of importance placed on adherence to the text as written as well as the degree to which the substituted phrasing alters the meaning of the text. As these cases indicate, once precedent accepts and builds upon an arguably misleading paraphrase of the actual text, it will be difficult if not impossible to shift the Court's focus back to the text itself.

TWO

Intratextualism and Textual Purpose

𝍌 I. Intratextualism—Using the Text to Read the Text

A. Usage within the Constitution

One obvious method of determining the meaning of a word in a legal document is to consider how it is used in other places within the document. This is a technique which Professor Akhil Amar in a brilliant article calls intratextualism.[1] Chief Justice Marshall made excellent use of this technique in *McCulloch v. Maryland* as he explicated the meaning of the word *necessary* in the Necessary and Proper Clause.[2] A well-accepted canon of legal, including constitutional, interpretation holds that a word will generally be used to convey the same meaning throughout the document unless there is some good reason to conclude otherwise.[3] Marshall pointed out that in addition to the Necessary and Proper Clause, the word *necessary* is also used in Article I, section 10, "which prohibits a state from laying 'imposts or duties on imports or exports, except what may be absolutely necessary for the executing of its inspection laws.'"[4] Marshall argued persuasively that if *necessary* was read as meaning "essential," as the state of Maryland contended, then there would be no need to qualify *necessary* with "absolutely" in the Import/Export Clause because it would already bear that strict meaning.[5] Because a word in the Constitution is ordinarily given the same meaning throughout and because the Constitution is construed to avoid surplusage, then *necessary* must mean 'convenient' rather than 'essential'.[6] Here, Marshall made a lawyer-like textual argument executed with devastating effectiveness.

In dicta in *Martin v. Hunter's Lessee*,[7] Justice Story relied on the fact that the Constitution uses the phrase "shall be vested" in Articles I, II, and III with respect to the legislative, executive, and judicial powers in support of his argument (never to be accepted by a majority of the Court) that all of the judicial power catalogued in Article III must be vested either automatically or by act of Congress in the federal courts. Story read the imperative "shall" to mean that it all must be vested. The more obvious, and now well-accepted, reading of the Vesting Clauses is that they explain where the particular powers are to be placed within the government—that is, judicial power in the judicial branch. At least with respect to the judicial power, the Clause says little, if anything, about whether "all" of it must be vested. In this case, the intratextual argument was strong. Justice Story simply missed its point.

In attempting to determine whether the word *person* in the Due Process Clause of the Fourteenth Amendment should be understood to include a fetus, Justice Blackmun in *Roe v. Wade* pointed out that *person* is used in several other places in the Constitution, including clauses setting forth qualifications for office as well as apportionment.[8] He noted that in none of these other instances is it likely that the unborn were contemplated as constitutional persons.[9] Relying then on the canon that words within the Constitution should be given the same meaning from one clause to the next, Justice Blackmun reasoned that it was unlikely that the framers of the Fourteenth Amendment intended to include a fetus within the concept of person.[10] This is a respectable argument; however, the canon provides that a word used at different places within the document should be given the same meaning unless there is good reason based on context to give it a different meaning. Arguably, there could be good reason to construe the concept of person differently—for instance, for purposes of legislative apportionment or qualifications for office rather than for protection of basic civil rights. Thus, although the argument carries some weight, it is hardly dispositive.

In *United States v. Verdugo-Urquidez*, the Court reasoned that the term *the people* was used consistently in the Constitution to "[refer] to a class of persons who are part of a national community or who have otherwise developed sufficient connection with this country to be considered part of that community."[11] The Court cited usage of the term in the Preamble, the Second Amendment, the Ninth and Tenth Amendments, Article I, section 2, clause 1, the First Amendment, and the Fourth Amendment in support of this determination.[12] This led it to conclude that the Fourth Amendment text—which provides that "the right of the people to be secure . . . against unreasonable searches and seizures. . . ."—did not extend protection to a citizen of Mexico whose home in Mexico was searched by United States drug enforcement officers, because such a person was not part of the community described by the concept of "the people."[13] This reading proved to be controversial, however. The Court itself conceded that "this textual exegesis is by no means conclusive."[14] Justice Kennedy concurred in the opinion but expressly did not rely on the Court's textual argument with respect to the meaning of "the people."[15] Justice Brennan, dissenting, rejected the Court's reading, arguing instead that the framers had not used the term "the people" in the Fourth Amendment to connote a political community but rather to simplify the language, as it would have been awkward to say "the right of persons to be secure in their persons."[16]

In *District of Columbia v. Heller*, the Court focused on the phrase "right of the people" and concluded that as used in the Second, First, and Fourth Amendments, it referred to individual rather than collective rights.[17] This consistent use of the phrase to connote an individual right suggested that the prefatory clause of the Second Amendment should not be read to limit its protection more narrowly to gun possession as an aspect of service in the state militia.[18] Dissenting, Justice Stevens disagreed, arguing that the prefatory clause limited the "people" protected to those employing weapons in militia service.[19]

Although he concluded that "right of the people" carried the same meaning in different contexts in *Heller*, Justice Scalia concluded that the term *state* carried different meanings within the Constitution.[20] Usually, when the word was used to connote one of the states of the Union, it was preceded by a modifier, yielding phrases such as "each state," "several states," "any state," "that state," "particular states," "one state," "no state."[21] Reference to a "foreign state" in Articles I and II indicated that *state* did not always denote a state of the Union.[22] Consequently, Justice Scalia reasoned that "the word 'state' did not have a single meaning in the Constitution" and the term in the phrase "security of a free state" in the Second Amendment referred to a free country and not to a state of the Union.[23] Thus, the majority opinion in *Heller* provides examples of the canon that a word or phrase should be understood to carry the same meaning as well as the qualification unless there is reason to believe otherwise.

Just as a word used in more than one place in the Constitution should be read to mean the same thing in both contexts unless there is good reason to construe it otherwise, a word used in one place in the Constitution to apply in two different places should also carry the same meaning in both. Such is the case with the religion clauses of the First Amendment, which reads "Congress shall make no law respecting an establishment of religion, or prohibiting the free exercise thereof." In his dissenting opinion in *Everson v. Board of Education*, Justice Rutledge argued that

> '[r]eligion' appears only once in the Amendment. But the word governs two prohibitions and governs them alike. It does not have two meanings, one narrow to forbid 'an establishment' and another, much broader, for securing 'the free exercise thereof.' 'Thereof' brings down 'religion' with its entire and exact content, no more and no less, from the first into the second guaranty, so that Congress and now the states are as broadly restricted concerning the one as they are regarding the other.[24]

This is a powerful example of a classic textual argument even though made in dissent. There should probably be a presumption that religion carries the same meaning in both clauses. The presumption should not be absolute, however, given that the clauses do serve quite different functions, and a decent argument can be made that religion for purposes of creating an establishment could be different from religion as protected for free exercise. Indeed, the precedent suggests that the Court has in fact construed the concept of religion differently in these contexts.

B. Usage in Context

One way of defining the meaning of a word is to focus on the context in which it is used. Chief Justice Marshall did this in *McCulloch v. Maryland* by arguing that a strict reading of *necessary* in the Necessary and Proper Clause would be in conflict with the more permissive word *proper*.[25] This would be a persuasive argument if *proper* inevitably carried the flexible meaning of "appropriate," as Marshall seemed to suggest. However, it could well mean "legal," in which case there would not seem to be a conflict between the two words.

Contrasting language in the text can elaborate meaning. In his separate opinion in *Chisholm v. Georgia*, Justice Jay pointed out that the failure of the text of Article III to distinguish between suits in which a state is a plaintiff and suits in which it is a defendant was significant in that in the very same article, the text does distinguish between suits in which an Ambassador is a plaintiff and those in which he or she is a defendant.[26] That provided strong textual support for his argument that the text should not be read to imply a principle of state sovereign immunity. As a matter of textual analysis, this is a persuasive argument, although the ultimate conclusion does not inevitably follow.

In construing constitutional text, it is important to read it in full. The Court often speaks of the "right to counsel"; however, that is simply an abbreviation of the Sixth Amendment guarantee. For instance, in *Faretta v. California*, where the Court held that the Sixth Amendment guarantees a criminal defendant a right of self-representation if he so chooses, the Court focused on the fact that the language provides for the "assistance" of counsel.[27] The Court explained that

> an assistant, however expert, is still an assistant. The language and spirit of the Sixth Amendment contemplate that counsel, like the other defense tools guaranteed by the Amendment, shall be an aid to a willing defendant—not an organ of the State interposed between an unwilling defendant and his right to defend himself personally.[28]

This is a clever textual argument and is worthy of consideration. However, Chief Justice Burger responded in dissent that even though the attorney is an assistant, given the complexity of legal proceedings and the need for orderly procedure, the state may insist that the accused be represented by a legally trained assistant.[29] As such, the majority's argument was not by itself powerful enough to carry the day. However, it was only one of many reasons why the Court concluded that a criminal defendant does have an implied constitutional right of self-representation.

Context does not always resolve ambiguity. In construing the Second Amendment in *District of Columbia v. Heller*, the majority and dissents argued over the relationship of the prefatory clause, which reads "[a] well regulated Militia, being necessary to the security of a free State" with the operative clause "the right of the people to keep and bear Arms, shall not be infringed." Justice Scalia, writing for the majority, concluded that— in view of the fear both in England and the colonies that the government would disarm the people—the prefatory clause should be read as explaining the purpose for which the Amendment was placed in the Constitution, that is, to ensure that Congress was not understood as having the power to disarm the militia.[30] The right to keep and bear arms for any lawful purpose, including self-defense, was a preexisting right, however, and as such the Second Amendment was not intended to narrow its scope by limiting it to service in the state militia.[31] Justice Stevens disagreed completely. Relying on the text as well as state constitutional analogs, he maintained that "[t]he preamble . . . both sets forth the object of the Amendment and informs the meaning of the remainder of the text."[32] That purpose, as stated by the preamble, was the preservation of the militia.[33] Thus, for Justice Stevens the right to bear arms protected by the Amendment was for the purpose of and limited to militia service. There was no constitutional protection beyond that objective. Justice Breyer, dissenting, conceded that the Amendment seemed to create an individual right to keep and bear arms that could be used for self-defense, among other things. However, the prefatory clause indicated that the primary purpose of the right was to provide for the arming of the militia, and that all other interests served were subsidiary and, as such, they could readily be overridden by important countervailing interests.[34] The relationship between the two clauses of the Second Amendment is indeed ambiguous. The attempt to untangle it in *Heller* led to three different interpretations. Justice Scalia, writing for the Court, concluded that the prefatory clause did not limit the operative clause at all. Justice Stevens, dissenting, maintained that the prefatory clause limited and controlled the operative clause completely. Justice Breyer argued that the first clause subordinated the second to a significant degree. All three found it necessary to supplement the text with historical understanding in order to draw a conclusion. Context alone could not provide a clear answer.

C. Congruence with Other Clauses

It is a well-recognized canon of constitutional interpretation that constitutional clauses must be read in light of other clauses to produce a harmonious rather than a discordant meaning.[35] However, it is not always easy to make the constitutional pieces fit neatly together. In *Martin v. Hunter's Lessee*,[36] Justice Story argued in dicta that Congress is under a duty to create lower federal courts; otherwise some of the appellate jurisdiction of the Supreme Court may be unusable if there is no lower court from which an appeal might be taken. Although this arguably provides a more sensible meaning to the clause establishing the Supreme Court's appellate jurisdiction, it does so at the expense of the clause that seems to vest Congress with broad discretion as to whether to establish lower federal courts at all. The tension between these two clauses actually suggests that Story was incorrect in assuming that all of the judicial power necessarily "shall" be vested somewhere, a position that in fact has never prevailed.

Later in the opinion in *Martin*, however, Story read several clauses of the Constitution together to build a very persuasive argument for the Supreme Court's right to review a decision interpreting federal law by the highest court of a state. Story pointed out that the Supreme Court's appellate jurisdiction extends to all cases, and because the Constitution seemed to grant Congress discretion as to whether or not to create lower federal courts at all, the framers must have contemplated that some of those cases (indeed possibly all of them in the absence of the creation of lower federal courts) must come from the state court system.[37] In addition, the Supremacy Clause of Article VI explicitly contemplates that federal issues will be litigated in state courts in that it proclaims that federal law shall be "the supreme Law of the Land, and the Judges in every State shall be bound thereby, any Thing in the Constitution or Laws of any State to the Contrary notwithstanding."[38] Story then provided a few examples of how federal issues would readily arise in state courts.[39] By reading three separate but related constitutional clauses together, Justice Story built a powerful rebuttal to Virginia's claim that the Constitution should not be read to allow the United States Supreme Court to take an appeal from one of its decisions.[40]

Likewise, in the landmark case of *Cohens v. Virginia*,[41] Chief Justice Marshall relied on an argument from congruence among clauses at several different points in his opinion. In *Cohens*, the petitioner had been convicted in Virginia of selling lottery tickets authorized for sale by Congress in the District of Columbia. Writing for the Court, Chief Justice Marshall observed that if two clauses of the constitution are arguably in conflict, it "becomes the duty of the Court . . . to construe the constitution as to give effect to both provisions, as far as it is possible to reconcile them, and not to permit their seeming repugnancy to destroy each other."[42] In applying this principle, Marshall then concluded that the clauses granting the Supreme Court original jurisdiction over a case in which a state was a party, and appellate jurisdiction when a federal question was involved, were not in conflict but should be read as granting original jurisdiction only in those cases in which jurisdiction is based on the very fact that the state is a party, and appellate in those cases in which a state may be a party, but jurisdiction is derived from the fact that there is a federal question.[43]

In the same case, Marshall responded to Virginia's structural argument that the Supreme Court should not hear an appeal from the highest court of a sovereign state with the textual argument that Article III grants jurisdiction to federal courts over cases in which states are parties, so it would be incongruous if the Supreme Court lacked jurisdiction over state tribunals.[44]

Marshall used the text to suggest that Virginia's pure conception of state sovereignty was not consistent with explicit textual inroads. This does not end the argument, however, because it is conceptually possible that the framers could extend jurisdiction over state governmental actors without extending appellate review over state judicial tribunals.

Additionally in *Cohens*, the state of Virginia argued that Congress could only legislate locally for the District of Columbia and could not extend the impact of such legislation beyond the confines of the District itself. In responding to this argument, Marshall cited another provision of Article I, which gave Congress the power to legislate with respect to "forts, arsenals [and] dockyards."[45] He then pointed out that legislation passed implementing this provision clearly allowed federal officers to exercise jurisdiction beyond the immediate confines of these facilities, where, for instance, someone committed a crime within one of these federal enclaves but then escaped to the surrounding state.[46] By analogy, Marshall argued that the principle must be the same with respect to legislation passed for the District of Columbia.[47] The analogy is apt and persuasive if the legislation with respect to forts is assumed to be constitutional. However, Marshall made no attempt to establish that in fact it was. *Cohens* is one of the best examples in all of constitutional law of perhaps our greatest justice successfully employing several arguments in which the congruence between various constitutional provisions is used to great effect.

Chief Justice Marshall also relied on the fit with other clauses in the Constitution in *Barron v. City of Baltimore*.[48] The question before the Court was whether the Bill of Rights applied to the states. In the course of concluding that it did not, Marshall pointed out that Article I, section 10 explicitly set forth various prohibitions against actions by states.[49] Consequently, had the framers of the Bill of Rights meant to cover the states, it is safe to assume that they would be equally explicit. Marshall's conclusion is clearly correct but perhaps more easily justified by the undisputed purpose of the Bill of Rights as he later argued.[50]

Marshall provided yet another excellent example of relying on the congruence among clauses to interpret the text in *Cherokee Nation v. Georgia*.[51] In concluding that within Article III an Indian tribe was not properly considered a foreign state capable of suing in federal court, he relied on the fact that the Commerce Clause speaks both of Indian tribes and foreign nations.[52] He reasoned that "[w]e cannot assume that the distinction was lost in framing a subsequent article, unless there be something in its language to authorize the assumption."[53] Rather, as Marshall noted, had the framers believed that Indian tribes constituted foreign nations, they would presumably have drafted the Commerce Clause to allow Congress "to regulate commerce with foreign nations, including the Indian tribes. . . ."[54] Marshall admitted that "the same words have not necessarily the same meaning attached to them when found in different parts of the same instrument: their meaning is controlled by the context."[55] But he concluded that there was nothing in the contexts here to suggest that they should have different meanings.[56] Justice Baldwin, concurring, pointed to the clause in Article I "excluding Indians not taxed" from being counted in legislative apportionment and reasoned that the very necessity for including this clause was testimony to the fact that the framers did not regard Indians as members of foreign states.[57]

Changes in wording in closely related clauses may provide fairly compelling evidence that a change in meaning was intended. For instance, in the *Slaughter-House Cases*, the majority pointed out that it would be incongruous to conclude that the Privileges or Immunities Clause of the Fourteenth Amendment was intended to protect privileges or immunities of state citizenship, considering that the clause spoke only of privileges or immunities of "citizens of the United States," whereas the preceding sentence referenced both state and national citizenship.[58] As the Court noted, "the change in phraseology was adopted understandingly and with a purpose."[59] The Court was certainly correct in concluding that the clause only protected the privileges or immunities of United States citizenship, although it then went on to define them in an unduly narrow manner.

Justice Scalia made a similar argument in *Harmelin v. Michigan*, where he argued that the fact that the Eighth Amendment prohibited excessive fines, but only cruel and unusual punishments should be understood as not imposing a proportionality requirement with respect to criminal punishments because where the Constitution uses "different language to address the same or similar subject matter, a difference in meaning is assumed."[60] Still, it is possible to argue that to some extent the terms *cruel* or *unusual* can be understood as encompassing some inquiry into proportionality.

Sometimes the interest in textual congruence is simply overridden by other considerations. The Court's landmark desegregation cases *Brown v. Board of Education*, invalidating racial segregation in a state school system, and *Bolling v. Sharpe*,[61] reaching a similar result with respect to segregated schools in the District of Columbia, presented the Court with a challenging issue of textual interpretation. In *Brown*, the Court invalidated racially segregated schooling in state systems under the Equal Protection Clause of the Fourteenth Amendment. There was, however, no Equal Protection Clause applicable to the federal government, although there was a Due Process Clause in the Fifth Amendment. Finding an equality principle capable of invalidating segregated schooling in Fifth Amendment Due Process presented some obvious interpretive problems, however. The Fifth Amendment Due Process Clause had been part of the Constitution since 1791. During its first seventy years, slavery was apparently constitutional in at least a portion of the nation. When the Reconstruction Congress sought to address the problem of racial discrimination through the Fourteenth Amendment, it adopted both a Due Process Clause and an Equal Protection Clause.

There is every reason to assume that because the wording of Fifth and Fourteenth Amendment Due Process is identical, they were intended to carry the same meaning. If so and if due process contains an equality principle capable of invalidating racial segregation in public schools (as *Bolling* would hold), then the question arises as to whether equal protection is redundant and unnecessary. The Court must have been aware of these difficulties, but it did not specifically address them. Rather, it attempted to blend the purposes of equal protection and due process by arguing that at a higher level of generality, both are about fairness.[62] Because racial segregation violates basic conceptions of fairness and is otherwise unjustifiable, it violates Fifth Amendment Due Process.[63] This was essentially a sleight of hand intended to deflect attention from the clear textual incongruity.

The decision in *Bolling* was ultimately dictated by necessity. The Court simply could not credibly condemn segregated schooling in the state systems while permitting it in its own backyard. The Court obliquely admitted as much when it observed that "it would be unthinkable that the same Constitution would impose a lesser duty on the Federal Government."[64] The problem, however, is that it is not at all so unthinkable. The Congress that drafted the initial Bill of Rights did not intend to impose an equality principle on either the federal or the state government. The Reconstruction Congress was focusing exclusively on abuses by the states and thus intended to impose an equality principle only on the states. To put it another way, the Reconstruction Congress trusted itself (the federal government) but not the states. As such, there is a reasonable explanation as to why the Constitution imposes an equality obligation on one level of government but not the other. *Bolling* is simply an example of a case in which real-world political necessity had to trump ordinary principles of textual explication. This is not so much a criticism of the decision as it is a recognition of the larger context in which the Court operates.

Cases involving constitutional challenges to the death penalty also provide an example of reliance on textual congruence. In the course of rejecting the argument that the death penalty necessarily constituted cruel and unusual punishment under the Eighth Amendment of the Constitution, Justice Stewart, writing for the plurality in *Gregg v. Georgia*,[65] emphasized that the text of the Fifth Amendment added to the Constitution at the same time as the Eighth Amendment's Cruel and Unusual Punishment Clause presumes that the death penalty may constitutionally be imposed in three separate provisions. First the Fifth Amendment provides that "no person shall be held to answer for a capital, or otherwise infamous crime, unless on presentment or indictment of a Grand Jury." Next, it provides that "nor shall any person be subject for the same offense to be twice put in jeopardy of life or limb." And finally it states that "nor [shall any person] be deprived of life, liberty, or property, without due process of law." Moreover, the third provision was included in the Fourteenth Amendment enacted seventy-five years later. Although this does not establish that capital punishment however imposed could never constitute cruel and unusual punishment, the *Gregg* plurality was certainly correct in recognizing that the framers and ratifiers of the Bill of Rights as well as the Fourteenth Amendment saw no inherent conflict between the concept of cruel and unusual punishment and capital punishment. As such, textual congruence provided a solid presumption in favor of the constitutionality of the death penalty at least in the abstract.

Wesberry v. Sanders,[66] the Court's congressional reapportionment case, provides another example of the Court favoring other considerations over strong arguments of textual congruence. In a lengthy dissent, Justice Harlan relied on the interaction of several different constitutional provisions to make the argument that the sentence in Article I, section 2—providing that Representatives are to be chosen "by the people of the several states"—does not mean that they must be selected on a one person, one vote basis. He started out by noting that the very sentence in which that phrase appears also states that Electors in each State shall have the Qualifications requisite for Electors of the most numerous Branch of the State Legislature."[67] He then pointed out that under this provision the state could presumably structure its electorate in a way that by definition would be inconsistent with popular equality—for instance, by adopting a property qualification.[68] He discussed several other constitutional provisions, which also seemed inconsistent with a deep commitment to one person, one vote, including the composition of the Senate, 3/5 representation for slaves (who certainly could not vote), and provision of one representative for every state, including those with very sparse population.[69] Finally, he noted that Article I, section 4 gave Congress, not the courts, the power to police congressional representation.[70] Taking these provisions as a whole, Justice Harlan provided a compelling textual refutation of the majority's conclusion that a popular equality theory of representation was central to the framers' thinking.[71] Ultimately, however, the Court's decision was prompted by contemporary notions of fairness and equality rather than, or more accurately, in spite of, the text and original understanding.

In response to the government's argument in *Youngstown Sheet and Tube v. Sawyer* that the Commander-in-Chief Clause gave the president the power to seize steel mills during the Korean War in order to avoid a work stoppage, Justice Jackson, concurring, pointed to several other clauses that undercut this argument.[72] Most pertinently, he pointed out that although the Constitution made the president Commander in Chief of the armed forces, it also explicitly vested in Congress the power to "'raise and support Armies' and 'to provide and maintain a Navy.'"[73] More generally, he explained that the president does not have an unrestrained hand in the area of war because Congress has clearly been given a significant role through the power to declare war and "make rules for the Government and Regulation of land and naval forces."[74] These limitations led Justice Jackson to conclude that although the president was Commander-in-Chief of the Army and Navy, he was not intended to be "Commander-in-Chief of the country, its industries and its inhabitants."[75] This is an example of a powerful argument derived from a reading of the Constitution as a whole, as opposed to focusing on one specific phrase or clause in isolation.

Also in *Youngstown*, Justice Douglas relied on congruence between constitutional clauses. He argued that the seizure of private property (such as a steel mill) was a taking under the Fifth Amendment, if only a temporary one.[76] A taking of property by the government required "just compensation," and because only Congress could raise and appropriate the funds to pay for the taking, as a matter of symmetry, only Congress should be allowed to authorize the taking.[77] This was a clever argument, although no other Justice in *Youngstown* endorsed it. Its obvious flaw is that there will be occasions in which the president will in fact be constitutionally warranted to engage in a compensable taking of property without specific congressional authorization—such as in a valid exercise of his Commander-in-Chief power.

Constitutional symmetry may be important, but it is not the only consideration.

Arguments in favor of textual congruence, like any other constitutional argument, can reach too far. In *Boyd v. United States*, the Court argued that there was "an intimate relation" between the Fourth and Fifth Amendments and that

> "[t]hey throw great light on each other. For the 'unreasonable searches and seizures' condemned in the fourth amendment are almost always made for the purpose of compelling a man to give evidence against himself, which in criminal cases is condemned in the fifth amendment; and compelling a man 'in a criminal case to be a witness against himself,' which is condemned in the fifth amendment, throws light on the question as to what is an 'unreasonable search and seizure' within the meaning of the fourth amendment."[78]

This was a case in which the Court pushed too hard to find congruence between two constitutional clauses. The Court's statement that most searches are conducted to obtain documentary evidence against an accused is simply not true (although it would have been more true prior to the demise of the "mere evidence" rule); and the discovery or production of documentary evidence incriminating a person does not generally result in compulsion within the meaning of the Privilege Against Self-Incrimination. Consequently, the congruent reading of the Fourth and Fifth Amendments expounded in *Boyd* has since been quite properly rejected by the Court.[79] This is yet another case illustrating that although textual congruence is important, it is far from determinative.

D. Congruence over Time

One problem raised by attempts to fit the textual provisions together in a congruent manner is that the Constitution, as amended, was drafted at different times throughout our history. As such, there was not one common set of drafters. On the one hand, it is safe to assume that the drafters of subsequent amendments were aware of the existing text and did consider it carefully when adding amendments. On the other hand, societal changes could well influence subsequent drafters to use language or concepts different from that of earlier drafters.

One such problem of congruence over time has arisen with respect to the propriety of incorporating the Establishment Clause against the states through the Fourteenth Amendment. Although the Court has applied the Establishment Clause to the states,[80] Justice Stewart argued in his dissenting opinion in *Abington Township v. Schempp* that unlike other provisions of the Bill of Rights, the Establishment Clause was specifically intended to protect certain state activity, that is, state religious establishments against federal intrusion.[81] As such, incorporating the Establishment Clause against the states would not simply distort it, but it would in fact give it the opposite meaning than that understood by the framing generation.[82]

Justice Brennan acknowledged but rejected this argument in his concurring opinion in *Abington Township v. Schempp*.[83] He argued that even assuming that the framers of the Establishment Clause had intended to protect state establishments against federal interference, the fact that the last state establishment had expired thirty-five years prior to the drafting of the Fourteenth Amendment, in 1868, indicates that "the problem of protecting official state churches from federal encroachments could hardly have been of any concern of those who framed the post–Civil War Amendments.[84] Thus, under Justice Brennan's approach, societal change had caused the very purpose of the Clause to shift significantly over time.

E. Constitutional Architecture

One clue in divining the meaning of constitutional text is constitutional architecture—that is, the placement of a word or phrase in a particular location in the Constitution. Chief Justice Marshall made this type of argument effectively in several of his landmark opinions, including *McCulloch*, *Marbury*, and *Cohens*. He made such an architectural argument in favor of his broad, empowering reading of the Necessary and Proper Clause in *McCulloch v. Maryland*.[85] He pointed out that the Clause was placed in Article I, section 8, which set forth the affirmative powers of Congress rather than Article I, section 9, which lists the specific restrictions imposed on Congress.[86] Although this does not end all debate over the proper reading, it is indeed a powerful argument for Marshall's position that the Clause was meant to expand rather than limit congressional power.

Marshall also relied on an argument of constitutional architecture in *Marbury v. Madison*.[87] In developing the argument that delivering Marbury's commission was not an integral part of the appointment process, Marshall emphasized that the appointing and commissioning powers are "given in two separate and distinct parts of the constitution."[88] Consequently, the fact that Marbury's commission was never delivered did not preclude him from asserting a legal right to the judicial office.

And in *Cohens v. Virginia*,[89] Chief Justice Marshall stated that it "may be considered as a political axiom . . . that the judicial power of every well constituted government must be co-extensive with the legislative, and must be capable of deciding every judicial question which grows out of the constitution and laws."[90] Marshall was quick to emphasize that his argument was not based on symmetry or architecture alone, noting that "[w]e do not mean to say, that the jurisdiction of the Courts of the Union should be construed to be co-extensive with the legislative, merely because it is fit that it should be so; but we mean to say, that this fitness furnishes an argument in construing the constitution which ought never to be overlooked. . . ."[91] Thus architecture does not necessarily dictate a particular interpretation, but it certainly may bolster it.

II. Reading the Text in Light of Its Purpose

If constitutional meaning is obvious, it should be so understood, but more often than not, there will be room for disagreement as to the "plain meaning." Where the meaning of the text is not obvious, the Court will need to look beyond the text itself to discern its meaning. Two very important sources for discovering constitutional meaning are the original understanding of the text and consistent postenactment practice. Each of these will be discussed in great detail in subsequent chapters. Yet another method of interpreting constitutional text is to look to its purpose. That method will be discussed in detail here, although it will also be considered to some extent in the chapter on the Derivation of Doctrine.

Chief Justice Marshall, recognizing the possibility of textual ambiguity in *Gibbons v. Ogden*, observed that "[i]f from the imperfection of human language, there should be serious doubts respecting the extent of any given power, it is a well settled rule, that the objects for which it was given, especially when those objects are expressed in the instrument itself, should have great influence in the construction."[92] Thus, Marshall propounded the canon that constitutional language should be construed in light of its purpose.[93] He then applied this principle to his construction of "commerce," concluding that the term *commerce* must include navigation because "[t]he power over commerce, including navigation, was one of the primary objects for which the people of America adopted their government."[94] By injecting purpose into the interpretive equation, Marshall necessarily raised the question of how that purpose is to be discovered. On occasion, as he noted, perhaps the purpose can be found within the Constitution itself. Often, that will not be the case. At that point, presumably the Court must turn to some other source to discover the purpose of the provision, such as the original understanding. Marshall purported to do just that in *Gibbons*, but in his characteristic fashion he cited no source whatsoever as evidence of that understanding but rather simply asserted that covering navigation was clearly what everyone had in mind.[95] As a member of the framing generation and an active participant in the Virginia ratifying convention, perhaps we can grant Marshall the right to rely on such bald assertion. However, a justice more temporally removed from the framing era would certainly need to produce some evidence of constitutional purpose, which would take the textual analysis into the domain of original understanding, a place that Marshall himself had warned us is off-limits when the text is sufficiently clear.[96]

Sometimes purpose may indeed be derived from the text itself. *McCulloch v. Maryland*[97] is another of Chief Justice Marshall's great cases in which he turned to constitutional purpose in order to illuminate text. Granting that the word *necessary* in the Necessary and Proper Clause admits of more than one meaning,[98] Marshall reasoned that the purpose of the Clause, obvious on its face, of facilitating Congress's ability to carry out its enumerated powers would be well served by reading *necessary* to mean convenient and hampered by reading it to mean "essential."[99] This is a relatively easy and yet persuasive example of reading the text in light of purpose, in that the purpose is indeed easily discernable from the text itself.

Kentucky v. Dennison is another example of a case in which the Court relied heavily on its conception of the purpose of a clause in explicating its meaning.[100] The Court rejected the argument that the phrase "treason, felony or other crime" in the Extradition Clause was intended to limit the "Crimes," giving rise to extradition to those crimes which were recognized at common law and by the usage of nations in view of the fact that felonies and treasons were necessarily crimes and hence need not have been listed unless the framers meant to restrict the meaning to only some crimes.[101] The Court rejected what might have otherwise been a logical legal argument in reliance on both the history and purpose of the language.[102] It reasoned that, in fact, the words "treason and felony . . . were introduced for the purpose of guarding against any restriction of the word 'crime.'"[103] It noted that as between nations there was a practice of making an exception in extradition proceedings for political crimes. But according to the Court, as this was not a compact between separate nations, but rather a constitution intended to promote peace and harmony between states of one nation, an exception for crimes of a political nature would not only be inappropriate but also positively harmful.[104] Thus, the Court's understanding of the provision's purpose as deduced from a combination of text, structure, and history dictated the construction of its language.

Sometimes the Court deduces purpose from its own logical or common-sense understanding of what the provision in question was intended to accomplish. That seemed to be the case in *Okanogan v. United States* (the *Pocket Veto Case*).[105] Article I, section 5 provides that if the president declines to sign a Bill submitted to him by Congress, he "shall return it, with his Objections to that House in which it shall have originated, who shall enter the Objections at large on their Journal, and proceed to reconsider it." The Court rejected the argument that the Bill could become law if returned to an agent of the House while the House was in adjournment.[106] It concluded that "it was plainly the object of the constitutional provision that there should be a timely return of the bill, which should not only be a matter of official record definitely shown by the journal of the House itself, giving public, certain and prompt knowledge as to the status of the bill, but should enable Congress to proceed immediately with its reconsideration."[107] As understood by the Court, the purpose of the provision clearly undermined the argument for what the Court referred to as a "fictitious return."[108]

Reading a constitutional provision in order to implement its purpose can readily extend its protection well beyond the limits of the constitutional language itself. This was certainly the case with respect to the Court's interpretation of the congressional speech and debate privilege. In the leading case of *Gravel v. United States*, the Court explained the following:

> It is true that the Clause itself mentions only 'Senators and Represen-tatives,' but prior cases have plainly not taken a literalistic approach in applying the privilege. The Clause also speaks only of "Speech and Debate," but the Court's consistent approach has been that to confine the protection of the Speech or Debate Clause to words spoken in debate would be an unacceptably narrow view. Committee reports, resolutions, and the act of voting are equally covered. ... Rather than giving the clause a cramped construction, the Court has sought to implement its fundamental purpose of freeing the legislator from executive and

judicial oversight that realistically threatens to control his conduct as a legislator.[109]

Consequently, recognizing that "it is literally impossible . . . for Members of Congress to perform their legislative tasks without the help of aides and assistants," the Court extended protection of the privilege to them as well, at least to the extent that they were engaged in activity that would be privileged if performed by the Member.[110] Even so, the Court declined to extend the privilege to cover a Senator's arrangement to have the Pentagon Papers published by a private publisher, concluding that it was not "essential to the deliberations of the Senate."[111]

One of the great arguments for reading constitutional language in light of its purpose in an effort to expand the coverage beyond the limits of the text itself was set forth by Justice Brandeis in his classic dissent in *Olmstead v. United States*.[112] The Court had excluded wiretapping of telephone conversations from the coverage of the Fourth Amendment on the ground that they were not "persons, houses, papers and effects" within the textual language.[113] Justice Brandeis replied that

[t]he protection guaranteed by the amendments is much broader in scope. The makers of our Constitution undertook to secure conditions favorable to the pursuit of happiness. They recognized the significance of man's spiritual nature, of his feelings and of his intellect. They knew that only a part of the pain, pleasures and satisfactions of life are to be found in material things. They sought to protect Americans in their beliefs, their thoughts, their emotions and their sensations. They conferred, as against the government, the right to be let alone—the most comprehensive of rights and the right most valued by civilized men. To protect that right, every unjustifiable intrusion by the government upon the privacy of the individual, whatever the means employed, must be deemed a violation of the Fourth Amendment.[114]

Here Brandeis attempted to defeat the formalistic textual arguments that conversations did not fall within the categories specifically protected by the text of the Fourth Amendment, and in any event were incapable of seizure by appealing to his conception of the abstract purpose of the Amendment. Although he cited little other than the Court's own precedent in support of his conception of the Amendment's larger purpose, the power of his rhetoric alone went a long way toward carrying the day as the *Olmstead* majority's result as well as its analytical approach were eventually discarded by the Court. The Brandeis dissent has lived on as one of the great opinions in Supreme Court history.

Purpose could be derived from the original understanding but that will not necessarily be the case. In *Flast v. Cohen*,[115] the Court relied heavily on its perception of the purpose served by the Article III "case or controversy" requirement in interpreting that phrase. After rejecting an original understanding based on interpretation set forth by Justice Frankfurter in earlier opinions,[116] the Court concluded that the basic function of the "case and controversy" requirement is to ensure that federal courts address "questions presented in an adversary context and in a form historically viewed as capable of resolution through the judicial process" as well as to ensure that "federal courts will not intrude into areas committed to the other branches of government."[117] Thus, in defining these terms, the Court looked to the role that "case and controversy" plays in adjudication and in the separation of powers as opposed to an attempt at close textual explication of the phrase or, for that matter, its original meaning. The Court relied on purpose, but it derived that purpose from function rather than from language or history. This in turn led the Court to conclude that a taxpayer had standing to challenge an appropriation under the congressional spending power on the ground that it violated the Establishment Clause.[118] The Court's conception of purpose seemed to be based on what the Court believed the provision should mean, at least in a contemporary context.

The Court has also tended to interpret the First Amendment's prohibition on the establishment of religion on the basis of its conception of the Clause's purpose, as opposed to a linguistic or historical explication of the term *establishment*. For example, in *Lemon v. Kurtzman*,[119] conceding that it would not always be obvious whether a particular law was one "respecting" the establishment of religion, the Court concluded that the Clause should be interpreted "with reference to the three main evils against which the Establishment Clause was intended to afford protection: sponsorship, financial support, and active involvement of the sovereign in religious activity," quoting the Court's earlier opinion in *Walz v. Tax Commissioner*. Having determined what the purpose of the Amendment was, to some extent based on historical considerations, the Court relied on that purpose to read the text as well as shape the doctrine. The Court continues to rely on purpose in construing the Establishment Clause; however, the justices disagree vigorously as to exactly what the purpose or purposes of the Clause are.[120]

The Court has also relied heavily on its understanding of the Eighth Amendment's purpose in interpreting its scope. In concluding that the Excessive Fines Clause did not apply to awards of punitive damages in *Browning-Ferris Industries v. Kelco Inc.*, the Court reasoned that "the primary focus of the Eighth Amendment was the potential for governmental abuse of its 'prosecutorial power,' not concern with the extent or purposes of civil damages."[121] As such, the latter fell beyond its scope.

Rice v. Cayetano[122] provides a recent example of the Court's interpretation of text driven primarily by its conception of its overriding purpose. There the Court concluded that reason behind the Fifteenth Amendment's ban on the denial of the vote based on "race" was that such exclusion "demeans the dignity and worth of a person to be judged [by such a characteristic] instead of by his or her own merit and essential qualities."[123] Concluding that "ancestry can be a proxy for race," the Court extended the protection of the Amendment to disenfranchisement based on ancestry as well, given that it was equally inconsistent with the underlying purpose of the Amendment.[124] In so doing, the Court did not attempt to come to grips with the meaning of the word *race* either as of the time of the ratification of the Fifteenth Amendment or as of the time of the decision, but instead focused on the rationale for the limitation. The Court's conception of the Amendment's purpose was no doubt driven as much by its own jurisprudence as by the original understanding, given that the text itself did not divulge the purpose of the provision at issue. *Rice* suggests that reliance on a provision's purpose, or more accurately, on the Court's conception of a provision's purpose, allows the Court to steer the text in whatever direction it so desires.

In *Escobedo v. Illinois*,[125] the Court attempted to employ a purpose- or function-oriented approach to define the meaning of the term *accused* within the Sixth Amendment in the context of police interrogation. Previously, the Court had held that a person did not become an "accused," and thus entitled to the right to counsel, until formal charges had been brought.[126] The majority rejected this approach in the context of custodial interrogation, holding that whether the defendant had been formally indicted make[s] no difference since he had requested and been denied an opportunity to speak with his attorney and the purpose of the interrogation was to get him to implicate himself in the crime.[127] As such the "[p]etitioner had become the accused."[128] Given that an attorney could have been of great assistance to the defendant when faced with custodial interrogation as to his participation in a murder, "[i]t would exalt form over substance to make the right to counsel, under these circumstances, depend on whether . . . the authorities had secured a formal indictment."[129] In other words, the Court concluded that the more textually oriented approach that it had followed in the past undermined the very purpose of the provision as understood by the Court. As a result, purpose at a general level trumped a more literal textual analysis.

Although the text should be interpreted in light of its purpose, the "purpose" should not necessarily trump the clear text in the event that they are inconsistent. In the *Slaughter-House Cases*, for instance, the Court concluded that the purpose of the Fourteenth Amendment was to protect the rights of recently freed slaves and their descendants.[130] Consequently, the Court opined that "[w]e doubt very much whether any action of a State not directed by way of discrimination against the negroes as a class, or on account of their race, will ever be held to come within the purview of this provision."[131] The text of the clause in question, however, guarantees equal protection of the laws to "any person," and it says nothing at all about the type of discrimination that is prohibited, as Justices Field[132] and Bradley[133] noted in their dissents. The Court's construction was thus at war with the text and not surprisingly its dicta has not been followed.

III. The Limits of Textualism

A. Absence of Relevant Text

One limitation on reliance on the constitutional text arises where there is no relevant text on which to rely. In such an instance one response is simply to conclude that if the text does not prohibit or address a practice even at an abstract or general level, then in must be constitutional. In *Ray v. Blair*, for instance, the Court was asked to decide whether an Alabama law, which required an elector in the state primary to take a pledge to support the candidate of the national convention, violated the Twelfth Amendment, which provided the procedure for electors to cast their ballots in presidential elections.[134] The Court upheld the requirement, noting that nothing in the text of the Constitution, nor implicit therein, addressed the issue, and the obligation of party loyalty by electors was supported by lengthy tradition.[135] Essentially, the Court concluded that it would simply be too much of a stretch to find that a pledge of loyalty was prohibited, given that the text did not seem to contemplate that question at all.

Just as the absence of text can convince the Court that a practice is permissible, it can also on occasion persuade the Court that it is not constitutionally authorized. For example, in *Youngstown Sheet and Tube v. Sawyer*, Justice Jackson, concurring, rejected the government's claim that the president had inherent emergency powers that would allow him to seize the steel mills during war time—at least in part due to the absence of any constitutional authorization of such procedures.[136] Justice Jackson explained that the framers certainly "knew what emergencies were," but with the exception of the power to suspend the writ of habeas corpus during time of rebellion or insurrection, they "made no express provision for [the] exercise of extraordinary authority because of a crisis."[137] The absence of such a provision, given the crises that the framers had seen, was strong evidence that they meant to omit it.

The absence of explicit text does not necessarily lead to the conclusion that there is no constitutional protection. In *Nixon v. Fitzgerald*, the Court rejected the argument that the absence of an explicit presidential privilege of immunity against suit precluded the recognition of one, even though the Speech and Debate Clause provided explicit protection to Congress.[138] The Court concluded that an explicit textual basis was not essential, however, considering that it had previously recognized judicial and executive immunity in spite of the fact that neither was embodied in the text.[139] Moreover, the Court noted that the framers seemed to assume that the president was immune from liability, and hence they may not have felt the need to embody that principle in the Constitution itself.[140]

Sometimes, the absence of explicit constitutional text can be answered with the argument raised by Marshall in *McCulloch v. Maryland*.[141] In response to the argument by *Maryland* that the Constitution does not provide an explicit power to create a corporation or a bank, Marshall made the classic argument that the constitutional text was to be read as a great outline rather than a detailed legal code.[142] This is a powerful argument in contexts in which it makes sense, such as the enumeration of congressional powers. But in *McCulloch*, Marshall pointed out that there were indeed great powers such as the Commerce Clause and Taxing and Spending Clause, which justified the creation of a national bank.[143] There simply wasn't a detailed specification as to how Congress could implement them. Marshall's approach will not be useful, however, in an instance in which the Constitution does not address the question at all, as opposed to failing to address it in great detail.

B. Disregarding Text—The Case of the Eleventh Amendment

The text would seem to be an obvious place to start when attempting to discern constitutional meaning. Arguably, if the text is relatively clear, it should take precedence over any alternative meaning suggested by other interpretive methods. The Eleventh Amendment cases are one of the most stunning examples, however, of other methodologies trumping the text. By its terms, the Eleventh Amendment prohibits suits in federal courts by out-of-state citizens against a state. In *Hans v. Louisiana*,[144] however, the Court extended the immunity to suits by a state's own citizens against the state. In so doing, it relied upon the original understanding, including the *Federalist Papers*, as well as remarks in the Virginia Ratifying Convention by Madison and Marshall.[145] The Court argued that the ultimate principle behind the rapid passage of the Eleventh Amendment, reversing *Chisholm v. Georgia*,[146] which had permitted a suit against a state by an out-of-state citizen, was one of state sovereignty as against citizen suits altogether, and not simply with respect to suits by out-of-state citizens, as the language of the Amendment seems to say.[147]

The *Hans* Court's reading of the Eleventh Amendment, as extending immunity well beyond its language, has prevailed in important recent Eleventh Amendment decisions such as *Seminole Tribe of Florida v. Florida*,[148] which held that Congress could not abrogate a state's Eleventh Amendment immunity against suit under the Indian Commerce Clause. In the subsequent case of *Alden v. Maine*,[149] holding that Congress could not abrogate a state's Eleventh Amendment immunity and subject the state to suit in state courts without its consent, the Court extended the *Hans* Court's reading of the Eleventh Amendment even further. *Alden's* extension of immunity to suits based on federal causes of action in state courts as well appears to be inconsistent with the text of the Amendment both with respect to the class of plaintiff, in-state citizens, as well as the forums covered, state courts.

In his dissent in *Seminole*, Justice Souter charged that the majority was making no serious attempt to construe the text.[150] He argued that there were two straightforward readings of the text to choose from, but neither supported the Court's result. Justice Souter maintained that arguably the Amendment was designed to deprive federal courts of jurisdiction over suits based on diversity of citizenship.[151] He argued that this reading was bolstered by the fact that the language of the Eleventh Amendment precisely tracks that of Article III.[152] In *Seminole*, Justice Rehnquist conceded that the text seemed to support this reading.[153] Alternatively, Justice Souter noted that the text could be read as prohibiting any suit against a state by an out-of-state citizen in federal court, whether based on diversity or on federal question jurisdiction.[154] Neither of these readings would support the results in *Seminole* or *Alden*.

Given that the *Hans* Court's reading of the Eleventh Amendment had been followed for 100 years, the question presented by *Seminole* and *Alden* was not whether in the first instance the plain meaning of the text may be trumped by other interpretive methods, but rather whether the text should be given such primacy, that a correct reading of the text (assuming for sake of argument that one of Justice Souter's suggested readings was correct) should override a century of precedent to the contrary. This presented a value choice with respect to the respective weight of two different but important methods of interpretation. These cases are particularly notable because it might seem that the justices in the majority, especially Justice Scalia, would generally be most receptive to a strong textualist approach.

These Justices did have a response to Justice Souter's textualist arguments, however. The majority did not ultimately agree that *Hans* misinterpreted the text. Instead, it argued that the text of the Eleventh Amendment, like any constitutional text, must be read and understood in historical context, as it was originally understood.[155] Using this approach, the majority argued that the framing generation understood the states to be sovereign entities protected by sovereign immunity against all citizen suits.[156] The Court in *Chisholm v. Georgia* misunderstood this and was immediately rebuked by passage of the Eleventh Amendment.[157] Because the original understanding was one of near complete sovereign immunity, there was little need to assert this but rather simply repeal the holding of *Chisholm* on its facts.[158]

In *Alden*, Justice Kennedy, writing for the majority, pointed out that the Eleventh Amendment does not purport to erect an immunity against suits as such, but instead states that the judicial power shall not be "construed" to reach suits like the one brought in *Chisholm*.[159] Consequently, the Amendment by its terms addressed misinterpretation of the prior understanding.[160] So the Court's response to Justice Souter's plain meaning approach was to argue that the meaning was not at all so plain when read in proper historical context. Even so, the disparity between the wording of the text and the interpretation placed on it in *Hans* and reaffirmed in cases such as *Seminole* and *Alden* is significant and presents a serious challenge to strict textualism as the predominate mode of constitutional analysis.

〽 IV. Conclusion

Close textual analysis is without question a very significant method of constitutional interpretation. However, once the text has been interpreted and precedent, doctrine, and practice begin to accumulate, textual analysis starts to recede as the primary method of providing meaning to the particular provision. More often than not, the initial reading of the text will continue to provide the foundation for further analysis. Even after an initial interpretation of the text has been rendered, new questions will arise, which often can best be answered by a return to the text, as opposed to simply consulting existing precedent and doctrine. Moreover, prior interpretations of the text are not beyond challenge and can be replaced by better readings in the future.

The recognized canons of constitutional interpretation—many of which are standard canons of legal interpretation period and almost all of which have been utilized since the Marshall Court—provide useful guidance but rarely provide the only reason for interpreting a provision or deciding a case one way rather than another. As with any interpretative aid, these canons are useful tools; however, they can be subject to manipulation and they can on occasion point in opposite directions. The Constitution itself, read as a whole, can provide important interpretive guidance, but this approach alone will not necessarily present a single clear answer either.

When the text itself does not produce one clear meaning, as is often the case, the Court will turn to other sources of understanding, including purpose, original understanding, structure or practice, and tradition. Even when turning to a provision's purpose, the Court will usually need to turn to some other source to determine what the purpose is.

In reaching a conclusive interpretation of a constitutional provision, the Court will almost certainly rely on a combination of interpretive methods, of which textual analysis may often be one. Finally, there will be cases from time to time in which the Court rejects a relatively plain reading of the text because other factors support a contrary reading.

THREE

Original Understanding
Preconstitutional Sources and the Drafting and Ratification Process

※ I. What Is Original Understanding?

One of the most significant methods of constitutional interpretation is original understanding. That is, the Court attempts to interpret the constitution by explicating how the text was understood at the time that it was ratified. Original understanding can be closely linked with a textual approach. Textualism assumes that words are capable of conveying a relatively objective meaning. Originalism provides an important source for discovering that meaning. The basic assumption of originalism is that those who possessed the legitimate authority to make the Constitution the supreme law of the land meant to set forth certain principles, powers, and limitations within the text that was ratified, and it is the obligation of constitutional interpreters to attempt to understand what the ratifying generation understood the text to mean. There has been a revival of the use of original understanding over the past two decades, which has caused much controversy as well.

Originalism raises several vexing questions, including the extent to which it is possible, especially for judges untrained in historical analysis, to discover the original understanding. There is also a question of whether original understanding, even if properly appreciated, is capable of providing sufficient guidance to the Court today, given that the framing generation may have held conflicting views on the meaning of constitutional provisions. Likewise, the framers will often have failed to anticipate the changes in circumstance, which give rise to so many of the difficult constitutional questions that come before the courts today. In addition, the values of the framing generation may be different from, or even in conflict with, our own. Ultimately, the question is not whether original understanding is an appropriate method of constitutional interpretation—given that the Court has relied upon it throughout its history—but rather how much weight it should be given, especially when alternative methodologies might appear to point in a different direction. This chapter will consider the issues raised by originalism from the Court's perspective as it has addressed these questions throughout its history.

In the debate over the propriety of original understanding as a methodology of constitutional interpretation, original understanding should be distinguished from what is sometimes called original intent. Original understanding focuses on how a constitutional provision was in fact understood by the informed public at the time, especially, but not exclusively, those who participated in the ratification process. Under this approach, the intent of the drafters is of more limited relevance. This is so because it was the ratifiers, as opposed to the drafters, who were authorized to make the Constitution the supreme law of the land.

In *Maxwell v. Dow*, for instance, the Court pointed out that statements made in Congress during the drafting of the Fourteenth Amendment were of less significance than statements made during the drafting of legislation because the Amendment still needed to be ratified by three-fourths of the states before it could take effect.[1] However, the intent of the drafters—such as the members of the Philadelphia Convention, or in the case of the Fourteenth Amendment, the Reconstruction Era Congress—may be highly relevant, not because they were responsible for the words of the text themselves, but because such statements could provide powerful evidence of how these provisions were in fact understood at the time. This assumes of course that the understanding of the drafters was either known or at least widely shared by those who ratified the text. As Justice Frankfurter observed in his concurring opinion in *Adamson v. California*, "any evidence of design or purpose not contemporaneously known could hardly have influenced those who ratified the Amendment."[2]

The distinction between original understanding and original intent is sometimes, but by no means always, recognized by the Court. Justice Scalia, writing for the Court in *District of Columbia v. Heller*, did explicitly recognize such a distinction, endorsing original understanding as a methodology, but cautioning that preenactment statements were "considered persuasive by some not because they reflect the general understanding of the disputed terms, but because the legislators who heard or read those statements presumably voted with that understanding."[3] Clearly, he did not approve of the latter usage.

In order to discover the original understanding of the Constitution, it is first necessary to know where to look. Depending on the provision in question, the legitimate sources are numerous. Because many constitutional provisions address issues that had troubled the framing generation and its predecessors, important elements of the original understanding can often be derived from English and colonial history as well as the preratification history of both the states and the nation. Preexisting legal texts—including the Declaration of Independence, the Articles of Confederation, state constitutions, as well as the common law both as it existed in England as it was received in the colonies and states—have proven useful to the Court.

Obviously, the Court has also focused upon events surrounding the drafting and ratification of the Constitution, including early drafts, debates in both the Drafting Convention (or in the case of the reconstruction amendments, the Congress) and the ratifying conventions, as well as commentary such as the *Federalist Papers*. The Court has also relied on events contemporaneous with the ratification, including federal legislation, state legislation, and litigation and societal practices in an effort to discern the original understanding. It has also looked to the views of particularly influential members of the framing generation—including Madison, Hamilton, and Jefferson—with respect to the initial Constitution, or to Senator Bingham, with respect to the Fourteenth Amendment. Likewise, it has considered the works of a few of the great early treatise writes, such as Justice Story and Judge Cooley, for enlightenment on the original understanding.

In this chapter, I will discuss the Court's use of preconstitutional historical sources as a means of discovering the original understanding as well as the Court's use of source material pertaining to the drafting and ratification of the Constitution and its amendments. In the second chapter on originalism, I will discuss the use of postratification sources to distill the original understanding as well as some familiar issues that the Court confronts in its use of original understanding.

II. Preconstitutional History and Sources

A. English History

Because many provisions in the Constitution are derived from English antecedents, detailed accounts of English history sometimes provide evidence of the original understanding.[4] Early on, the Court was more likely to view some constitutional provisions as simply codifying existing practices or principles. For instance, in *Robertson v. Baldwin*, the Court stated that

> the first 10 amendments commonly known as the Bill of Rights were not intended to lay down novel principles of government but simply to embody certain guarantees and immunities which we had inherited from our English ancestors, and which from time immemorial, had been subject to certain well-recognized exceptions, arising from the necessities of the case. In incorporating these principles into the fundamental law, there was no intention of disregarding the exceptions which continued to be recognized as if they had been formally expressed.[5]

Under such an approach, a careful understanding of the historical antecedents would be crucial.

The Court continued with this approach in *Munn v. Illinois*.[6] Having concluded that the concept of due process was derived from the "law of the land as embodied in the Magna Carta," Chief Justice Waite turned to English history to comprehend the nature of state regulation of property that would be consistent with due process of law.[7] The Court then concluded, citing Lord Chief Justice Hale, that "[l]ooking . . . to the common law, from whence came the right which the Constitution protects, we find that when private property is 'affected with the public interest, it ceases to be juris private alone.'"[8] Justice Field, dissenting, questioned the relevance of this English practice to the issue before the Court. *Munn* followed in the footsteps of *Murray v. Hoboken Land*,[9] where the Court had applied the same approach. For the most part, however, the Court has strayed far from this mode of analysis in interpreting the Bill of Rights, relying instead on the contemporary significance of the rights and limitations.[10]

In *Hurtado v. California*, for instance, the Court recognized that the concept of due process of law originated from the phrase "law of the land" in the Magna Carta.[11] But it cautioned against limiting its interpretation to either the Magna Carta or common law. It pointed out that "in England, the words of Magna Charta stood for very different things at the time of the separation of the American colonies from what they represented originally."[12] As such, the Court noted that "it is better not to go too far back into antiquity for the best securities for our 'ancient liberties'"[13] This was especially true with respect to England, given that the Magna Carta itself was adopted exclusively as a check on executive power, whereas the concept of due process of law was intended to provide a check against legislative abuse as well.[14] The Court warned against placing too much weight on English history, given that

> [t]he constitution of the United States was ordained . . . by descendants of Englishmen, who inherited the traditions of the English law and history; but it was made for an undefined and expanding future, and for a people gathered, and to be gathered, from many nations and of many tongues. . . . There is nothing in Magna Charta . . . which ought to exclude the best ideas of all systems and of every age.[15]

Thus, the English background of the Bill of Rights can be both relevant and misleading at the same time.

Nevertheless, since the Magna Carta is viewed as one of the foundation stones of the protection of civil liberties, tracing the origin of a right back to that document carries at the least significant rhetorical impact. Thus, in concluding that the Speedy Trial Guarantee of the Sixth Amendment was fundamental and worthy of incorporation against the states, the Court in *Klopfer v. North Carolina* noted that "[i]ts first articulation in modern jurisprudence appears to have been made in [the] Magna Carta (1215)."[16] It is certainly interesting that the Court thinks of events occurring in the early thirteenth century as a part of "modern jurisprudence."

Recently, in his concurring opinion in *Pacific Mutual Life Insurance Co. v. Haslip*, Justice Scalia argued that

> *Hurtado* . . . clarified the proper role of history in a due process analysis: If the government chooses to *follow* a historically approved procedure, it necessarily *provides* due process, but if it chooses to *depart* from historical practice, it does not necessarily *deny* due process.[17]

Whether or not this is a correct understanding of what the *Hurtado* Court meant, the Supreme Court has not necessarily followed this approach, as Justice Scalia conceded later.[18] Even in the context of punitive damages, which Justice Scalia was addressing in *Pacific Mutual Life*, the Court subsequently held that an award thus imposed by a jury in a manner not inconsistent with that known to the framers of the Fourteenth Amendment could nevertheless violate due process of law.[19]

Sometimes the Court finds that English historical antecedents are relevant to the interpretation of constitutional provisions, but such antecedents must be employed with caution. In *Kilbourn v. Thompson*, for instance, the Court engaged in a lengthy discussion of the origin of the use of contempt power by the Houses of Parliament for the purpose of showing that the development of that power in England—arising as it did from the fact that both the House of Lords and House of Commons wielded significant judicial powers—was quite different from the origin of the Houses of Congress. As such, English practice "rest[s] on principles which have no application to other legislative bodies, and certainly can have none to the House of Representatives . . . a body which is in no sense a court."[20] Later in the same opinion, however, the Court relied on the fact that the Constitution's Speech and Debate Privilege had been modeled after a similar privilege in the English Bill of Rights, and as such, "it may be reasonably inferred that the framers of the Constitution meant the same thing by the use of the language borrowed from that source."[21]

Ninety years later, in *United States v. Brewster*,[22] the Court again emphasized the differences between the English and American contexts, rather than the similarities. It cautioned that:

> We should bear in mind that the English system differs from ours in that their Parliament is the Supreme Authority, not a coordinate branch. Our speech or debate privilege was designed to preserve legislative independence, not supremacy.[23]

The Court did not ignore the English history of the Clause. In fact, it relied on it quite heavily, but with a certain degree of caution as to the differences in context.

Sometimes, the Court cites incidents that occurred in England and were fresh in the minds of the framing generation as shedding light on the meaning of the text.[24] In *Powell v. McCormack*,[25] for instance, it was faced with the question of whether a decision by the House of Representatives to exclude Adam Clayton Powell for misconduct that took place during a previous congress was a nonjusticiable political question, or whether it presented an issue of constitutional interpretation fit for the Court to decide. In order to decide the issue, the Court found it necessary to first determine whether there was a textual commitment of the question to another branch of the government, that is, the House of Representatives.[26] To determine whether Congress had the power to exclude a member for anything other than a failure to meet the three Article I standing qualifications, the Court consulted English precedents in some detail, as the English practice had clearly influenced the framers. It concluded that the historical record indicated that the battle over the exclusion of John Wilkes from Parliament shortly before the Constitutional Convention—resulting in vindication of the principle that an elected member could be excluded only for failure to meet standing qualifications—met with a high degree of approval among the framing generation. This lengthy historical analysis led the Court to conclude that there was no textual commitment to the House and hence no political question. This is a striking example of the Court's use of English history, familiar to the framers, to provide the primary basis for its reading of the text.

Boyd v. United States[27] provides another example of the Court relying heavily on a famous incident in English history, fresh in the minds of the framers, as evidence of the correct interpretation of a constitutional provision. Coincidentally, like *Powell v. McCormack,* this incident also involved the infamous John Wilkes, in this instance, a search of his personal papers. In interpreting the Fourth and Fifth Amendments in Boyd, the Court quoted extensively from the opinion by Lord Camden in the case of *Entick v. Carrington*[28] in 1765, which it referred to as "one of the landmarks of English liberty."[29] It believed that *Entick* provided sound guidance as to the meaning of our Bill of Rights, given that

> [e]very American statesman, during our revolutionary and formative period as a nation, was undoubtedly familiar with this monument of English freedom, and considered it as the true and ultimate expression of constitutional law, it may be confidently asserted that its propositions were in the minds of those who framed the fourth amendment to the constitution, and were considered as sufficiently explanatory of what was meant by unreasonable searches and seizures.[30]

The key to the Court's heavy reliance on *Entick* was its belief that the framers were undoubtedly familiar with the case and that it influenced the drafting of the Bill of Rights. These assumptions may well have been correct; however, the Court did not cite any authority to confirm that belief. Although the stirring rhetoric of *Boyd* has been influential in leading to an expansive interpretation of the Fourth Amendment,[31] the holding that the Fourth and Fifth Amendments read together preclude the search for private papers has since been rejected by the Court.[32]

Talley v. California[33] is yet another case in which the Court relied upon incidents in English history and their impact on the framers as evidence that a provision of the Bill of Rights should be interpreted in an expansive manner. The question there was whether the guarantee of freedom of speech in the

First Amendment protected anonymous speech. In holding that it did, and thus invalidating an ordinance requiring that pamphlets distributed in public identify their source, the Court cited several events from English as well as colonial history that demonstrated the need for such a right. The Court referred to the infamous English press licensing and seditious libel laws and noted that

> John Lilburne was whipped, pilloried and fined for refusing to answer questions designed to get evidence to convict him or someone else for the secret distribution of books in England. Two Puritan Ministers, John Penry and John Udal, were sentenced to death on charges that they were responsible for writing, printing or publishing books.[34]

These incidents led the Court to conclude that "[a]nonymous pamphlets, leaflets, brochures and even books have played an important role in the progress of mankind."[35] It is certainly true, as the dissent pointed out, that the First Amendment does not by its terms protect "freedom of anonymous speech."[36] However, the historical background provided sound reason for the Court's conclusion that anonymity could well be a crucial bulwark of effective critical speech.[37]

Perhaps there is no area in which the Court relies on history and original understanding to a greater extent than the Establishment Clause of the First Amendment. Most of the emphasis is placed on events occurring in America both before and after the ratification of the Bill of Rights. However, on occasion, justices have referred to English history as well. In *Everson v. Board of Education*, the Court's first significant Establishment Clause opinion, Justice Black pointed out that the shape and very existence of the provision was determined to some extent by religious persecution and strife in England, which had in turn led to a significant amount of the colonization of North America.[38] He then maintained that these practices continued in the colonies as well.[39]

Justice Black emphasized English practices again in even more detail in *Engel v. Vitale*,[40] as he saw a direct parallel between the disputes over the legislative adoption of the *Book of Common Prayer* in England in the sixteenth century and the adoption of the Regents Prayer in New York. He explained that the adoption of the *Book of Common Prayer* led to dissension and religious persecution and eventually the emigration of many religious minorities to North America.[41] He pointed out that the same practice of governmental adoption of prayer occurred in the colonies but was repudiated by events leading to the Virginia Bill of Religious Freedom and the religion clauses of the First Amendment.[42] Justice Stewart, dissenting, dismissed Justice Black's invocation of these historical antecedents as largely irrelevant, given that England and several of the colonies did in fact establish churches, which of course was not the case in New York in the early sixties.[43] Rather than looking at "the history of an established church in sixteenth century England or in eighteenth century America," he would look instead to "the religious traditions of our people, reflected in countless practices of the institutions and officials of our government."[44] It is fair to say that Justice Stewart's approach has been more influential in Establishment Clause jurisprudence.

Recognizing the necessity for some reasonable limitation on relevant historical antecedents, Justice Frankfurter, in evaluating the religious influence in the origin of Sunday closing laws in his concurrence in *McGowan v. Maryland*, noted that the Fourth Commandment, an edict of Constantine and "prohibitions by the Carolingian, Merovingian and Saxon rulers and later of the English kings of the thirteenth and fourteenth centuries may be passed over."[45] Rather, he began his study in 1481.[46]

Where a provision in the Constitution is modeled after some piece of English legislation, such as a provision in the English Bill of Rights, the Court may refer to English case law in order to determine how the provision was understood in England. To the extent that the English case law postdates the inclusion of the similar provision in the United States Constitution, however, it can have only the most indirect effect on the original understanding. In *Kilbourne v Thompson*,[47] for example, the Court discussed the English case of *Stockdale v. Hansard*, which had held that republication outside of Parliament of a libelous statement made on the floor of Parliament was not protected by legislative privilege.[48] Despite the fact that *Stockdale* was decided over fifty years after the United States Constitution was ratified, the Court in *Kilbourne* assumed that it provided a reasonable basis for inferring "that the framers of the Constitution meant the same thing by the language borrowed from that source."[49]

Ninety years later, the Court in *Gravel v. United States*[50] quoted this language approvingly and noted that in reaching its decision, *Stockdale* had analyzed and relied on several earlier cases, some of which were contemporaneous with the ratification of the United States Constitution, thereby attempting to solidify the argument for viewing the case as at least somewhat relevant to original understanding of the Speech and Debate Clause. Justice Brennan, dissenting, did express doubt as to the relevance of "authority post-dating the adoption of our Constitution,"[51] but disagreed with the Court's interpretation of English history in any event. He relied instead on the conviction and exile of Sir William Williams for republishing a report about a plot against the Crown which ultimately lead to the creation of the English Speech and Debate Privilege.[52] Thus, Justice Brennan was able to argue that the William Williams incident was not only far more probative of the original understanding of the English provision, but also bore strong similarities to the facts before the Supreme Court.

Events in English history may be particularly relevant when there is reason to believe that the right in question was in fact established in that historical context. For instance, in *District of Columbia v. Heller*, Justice Scalia, writing for the Court, maintained that "it has always been widely understood that the Second Amendment, like the First and Fourth Amendments codified a *pre-existing right*."[53] Consequently, the events that gave birth to the right in late seventeenth-century England define the nature of the right. Justice Scalia explained that in response to the disarming of Protestants by King James II, the people obtained a guarantee from William and Mary as part of the English Bill of Rights that the King could not disarm Protestants.[54] He then noted that "[t]his right has long been understood to be the predecessor to our Second Amendment [and] [i]t was clearly an individual right having nothing whatsoever to do with service in the militia."[55] Citing a variety of sources, including Blackstone, Justice Scalia concluded that "by the time of the founding [the right was] understood to be an individual right protecting against both public and private violence."[56] Justice Stevens, dissenting, dismissed the English history relied on by the Court as largely irrelevant, as it arose in a "different historical and political context."[57] To a significant extent, that could be said with respect to virtually all pre-Constitutional English historical events.

As with the Second Amendment, historical events leading to the passage of the English Bill of Rights definitely have a bearing on the meaning of the Eighth Amendment's Cruel and Unusual Punishment Clause, as the language of the latter was based on the former. However, there has been vigorous argument on the Court as to exactly what lessons are to be learned from these events. In *Harmelin v. Michigan*, Justice Scalia, in an opinion joined by Justice Rehnquist announcing the judgment of the Court, reviewed the historical incidents (including the Bloody Assize) in great detail and concluded, based on the work of some historians, that the evil that the provision in the English Bill of Rights was intended to rectify was not disproportionate punishment, but rather legally unauthorized punishment.[58]

B. The Common Law of England

Sometimes the Court cites the common law as providing the background for a practice that the framers arguably intended to incorporate in the Constitution. This has been particularly true with respect to the law of arrest. In *Gerstein v. Pugh*, the Court relied on common-law practice in concluding that the Fourth Amendment requires that a person arrested must be brought before a magistrate for a determination of whether probable cause to arrest and detain exists.[59] It pointed out that "[a]t common law it was customary, if not obligatory, for an arrested person to be brought before a justice of the peace shortly after arrest."[60] The Court then concluded that "[t]his practice furnished the model for criminal procedure in America immediately following the adoption of the Fourth Amendment."[61] As such, the requirement of a probable cause hearing before a magistrate had a solid historical pedigree, even if it was not absolutely required. Essentially, the Court argued that the common-law practice was at the very least familiar to the framing generation and almost certainly met with its approval.[62]

The Court continued this approach in *United States v. Watson*,[63] holding that a postal inspector could constitutionally arrest a suspect in a public place without a warrant, relying largely on the common law of arrest as it existed at the time of the ratification of the Fourth Amendment. This historical review convinced the Court that the common-law rule permitting a warrantless arrest for a felony in a public place when the officer had probable cause was known to Congress at the time of the drafting of the Fourth Amendment and was embodied in federal law at that time, suggesting that this was clearly consistent with the original understanding of the Fourth Amendment.[64] Justice Marshall dissented, arguing that the reliance on the common-law rule was misleading and inappropriate, given that far fewer crimes were recognized as felonies at common law, and hence the breadth of the exception to a warrant requirement would be far greater today than then.[65] Justice Marshall's dissent does serve as a caution that it is easy to misunderstand the significance of historical incidents if the context is not examined closely.

Payton v. New York is yet another case involving the Fourth Amendment in which the Court relied heavily on the common law as evidence "of what the Framers of the Amendment might have thought to be reasonable" with respect to an arrest.[66] At the outset, the Court cautioned that "the common-law rules of arrest developed in legal contexts that substantially differ from the cases now before us."[67] It conceded that the leading common-law commentators—including Coke, Blackstone, and Hale—"disagreed sharply" on the scope of the power to arrest.[68] It then relied on this "diversity of views" as well as the "prominence of Lord Coke" to support the proposition that "the common-law rule on warrantless home arrests was not as clear as the rule on arrests in public places."[69] This led the Court to conclude that

> [o]ur study of the relevant common law does not provide the same guidance that was present in Watson. Whereas the rule concerning the validity of an arrest in a public place was supported by cases directly in point and by the unanimous views of the commentators, we have found no direct authority supporting forcible entries into a home to make a routine arrest and the weight of the scholarly opinion is somewhat to the contrary.[70]

Consequently, "the issue is not one that can be said to have been definitively settled by the common law at the time the Fourth Amendment was adopted."[71] Thus, in *Payton* the Court focused on the common law largely to distinguish *Watson* and the heavy reliance that the Court had placed on it in that case. Justice White, dissenting, argued that the common-law rule favoring warrantless arrests in the home had much more support than the Court acknowledged.[72] Moreover, in response to the Court's reliance on Lord Coke, Justice White emphasized that Blackstone disagreed, which was "particularly significant in light of his profound impact on the minds of the colonists at the time of the framing of the Constitution and the ratification of the Bill of Rights."[73] Justice White also maintained that the absence of common law precedent upholding warrantless home arrests is most probably explained by the fact that they were so clearly accepted as legal, that no one would have bothered to bring a challenge.[74]

On many occasions the Court has explicitly rejected the common-law rule upon concluding that that was precisely what the framing generation intended to do as well. For instance, in *Grosjean v. American Press Co.*, the Court concluded that the First Amendment was intended to prohibit licensing taxes on the press, which, though controversial in England at the time of the ratification of the Amendment, was not prohibited by the common law.[75] It recognized that "the range of constitutional provisions phrased in terms of the common law sometimes may be fixed by recourse to the applicable rules of that law."[76] However, "it is subject to the qualification that the common law rule invoked shall be one not rejected by our ancestors as unsuited to their civil or political conditions."[77] The Court concluded that licensing taxes on the press had been so rejected.[78]

Likewise, in *Bridges v. California*, the Court concluded that the English common law permitting a lenient use of the contempt power to punish speech critical of the conduct of judges was irrelevant, given that "'one of the objects of the Revolution was to get rid of the English common law on liberty of speech and press.'"[79] As a result, "the First Amendment cannot reasonably be taken as approving prevalent English practices."[80] In dissent, Justice Frankfurter emphasized the deep historical roots of the contempt power.[81] However, the Court's citation of specific historical incidents would seem to effectively counter Justice Frankfurter's more generalized history.

On other occasions, the Court has rejected the common-law rule not because the framers necessarily meant to reject it as such, but rather because it was not appropriate in the American context. In *The Daniel Ball*, for purposes of the Commerce Clause,[82] the Court rejected the English common-law rule that navigable waters are defined by the ebb and flow of the tides. It noted that such a rule was well and good for England, where the tides and navigability all but completely overlap,[83] but that it would make no sense for the United States, where many rivers are quite navigable hundreds of miles beyond the highest ebb and flow of the tides.[84] Consequently, in the United States "rivers must be regarded as public navigable rivers in law which are navigable in fact."[85] Twenty years earlier, in *The Propeller Genesee Chief v. Fitzhugh*,[86] for purposes of determining admiralty jurisdiction under Article Three of the Constitution, the Court had rejected the same common-law ebb and flow of the tide rule for essentially the same reasons.

C. Blackstone's *Commentaries on the Law of England*

On questions of the original understanding, the Court has frequently cited William Blackstone's *Commentaries on the Law of England* as providing insight into the framers' legal understandings, recognizing that Blackstone "provided a definitive summary of the common law but was also a primary legal authority for eighteenth- and nineteenth-century American lawyers."[87] For instance, in *Marbury v. Madison*,[88] Chief Justice Marshall relied on Blackstone for support for the principle that in our legal system, derived as it is from the common law of England, the law must generally afford a remedy where there has been a violation of a legal right. As Justice White put it in his dissenting opinion in *Gertz v. Welch*, quoting John Williard

Hurst, "[t]hey read Blackstone, a classic tradition of the bar in the United States and 'the oracle of the common law in the minds of the American Framers.'"[89] Justice White went on to conclude that from Blackstone, the framers learned that the primary purpose of the First Amendment had been to prevent prior restraints.[90] Even so, from the outset of free speech jurisprudence, the Court has not limited the First Amendment to a prohibition on prior restraints.[91] In *Alden v. Maine*, the Court proclaimed that Blackstone "constituted the preeminent authority on English law for the founding generation."[92] And in the course of incorporating the Fifth Amendment's guarantee against Double Jeopardy against the states, the Court in *Benton v. Maryland* paid heed to Blackstone's influence, noting that "[a]s with many other elements of the common law, it was carried into the jurisprudence of this Country through the medium of Blackstone, who codified the doctrine in his Commentaries."[93]

For instance, the Court has cited Blackstone for the proposition that the standing qualifications for legislators were intended to be exclusive,[94] freedom of the press was especially threatened by prior restraints,[95] at common law, a jury consists of a body of the defendant's peers,[96] judicially derived rules applied retroactively,[97] the pardoning power was extremely broad,[98] Sunday closing laws had acquired a secular meaning in eighteenth-century England,[99] suicide was strictly prohibited at common law,[100] just to name a few examples.

In using Blackstone, or for that matter, any historical secondary source, it is helpful if the Court can show that the framers were familiar with the particular passages on which the Court relies. In his dissenting opinion in *Hamdi v. Rumsfeld*,[101] Justice Scalia quoted from Blackstone's *Commentaries* on the importance of ensuring that a person may be imprisoned by the Executive only pursuant to legal process. He then pointed out that "[t]hese words were well known to the Founders given that Hamilton quoted from this very passage in Federalist No 84."[102] This transformed the principles from Blackstone from general background history to a conception which very well may have influenced the framing generation.

Likewise, in his dissent in *Kelo v. City of New London*, Justice Thomas cited Blackstone as well as Chancellor Kent for the proposition that the common law at the time of the framing would permit suppression of a nuisance on private property but would not allow the condemnation of private property for nonpublic use.[103] Justice Thomas argued that the framers understood this and meant to enshrine this principle in the Takings Clause of the Fifth Amendment.[104]

In his opinion for the Court in *District of Columbia v. Heller*, Justice Scalia emphasized the importance that the framing generation attached to Blackstone and relied on the fact that Blackstone's Commentaries established that the right to bear arms was a fundamental individual right of Englishmen; and furthermore, "the most important early American edition of Blackstone's Commentaries (by the law professor and former Antifederalist St. George Tucker)" also recognized the right as an individual right of "self-preservation."[105] As such, Blackstone was a prominent authority on the common law of England and, at least as revised by St George Tucker, on the law of the colonies as well.

The Court has also placed heavy reliance on Coke's Institutes because it seemed to have influenced the framing generation. In *Klopfer v. North Carolina*, for instance, where the Court cited Coke for the importance of the Speedy Trial Guarantee,[106] it quoted Thomas Jefferson for the proposition that " 'Coke Lyttleton was the universal elementary book of law students,' "[107] and John Rutledge for the statement that " 'the Institutes seemed to be almost the foundation of our law.' "[108]

D. Colonial History

Events that occurred in colonial and postrevolutionary America prior to the drafting and ratification of the Constitution are often cited by the Court as shedding light on the meaning of its provisions.[109] One event that preceded the drafting of the Constitution by almost twenty five years but is nevertheless sometimes cited by the Court as helping to explain the meaning of some of its provisions, especially those guaranteeing civil liberties, is the Letter of the Continental Congress of October 26, 1774, to the Citizens of Quebec.[110] In *Near v. Minnesota*, for instance, the Court quoted from the section of the letter explaining the importance of freedom of the press as evidence of its significance under the First Amendment as well.[111] Likewise, the Court in *Lovell v. Griffin* noted that the role that the pamphlets of Thomas Paine played in the establishment of American liberty is proof that the coverage of the First Amendment was "not confined to newspapers and periodicals," but "necessarily embraces pamphlets and leaflets" as well.[112]

The significance of preconstitutional pamphleteering also played a significant role in *Talley v. California*.[113] There, in the course of finding a right to anonymous speech protected by the First Amendment, the Court explained that "[b]efore the Revolutionary War colonial patriots frequently had to conceal their authorship or distribution of literature that easily could have brought down on them prosecutions by English-controlled courts."[114] The Court also noted that "[a]bout that time the Letters of Junius were written and the identity of their author is unknown to this day."[115] These as well as similar incidents from English history convinced that Court that First Amendment protection of anonymous speech was crucial.[116]

E. Declaration of Independence

Occasionally, the Declaration of Independence is cited as part of the historical background for constitutional provisions, but as Justice Scalia acknowledged in his dissent in *Troxel v. Granville*, it "is not a legal prescription conferring powers upon the courts."[117] It can prove some evidence of what was particularly important to citizens in colonial America. For instance, in *Duncan v. Louisiana*, in the course of incorporating the right to jury trial in criminal cases against the states, the Court quoted a provision of the Declaration limiting the right to jury trial in the colonies.[118] And in rejecting the government's argument in *Youngstown Sheet and Tube v. Sawyer* that the Clause vesting the president with executive power should be read as "of all the executive powers of which the Government is capable," Justice Jackson, concurring, pointed out that the exercise of such extraordinary powers by King George III had led rather directly to the Declaration of Independence.[119]

F. Articles of Confederation and Experience Thereunder

The Constitution was not our first constitution. Previously, there were the Articles of Confederation. The Constitution does not track or amend the Articles of Confederation so, as a general rule, textual comparisons with the Articles are of limited utility. There are instances, however, in which differences between the Articles and the Constitution may shed light on the meaning of the text of the latter. This is especially true as the Constitutional Convention was called specifically to address the shortcomings of the Articles. Consequently, most changes from the Articles of Confederation were made quite deliberately.

Chief Justice Marshall provided an example of such a purposeful change in *McCulloch v. Maryland*, where he pointed out that unlike the similar provision in the Articles, the Tenth Amendment "omits the word 'expressly,' and declares only, that the powers 'not delegated to the United States, nor prohibited to the states, are reserved to the states or to the people.'"[120] Moreover, Marshall argued that given the difficulties encountered under the Articles of Confederation, the word was "probably" omitted consciously.[121] Thus, a comparison between the language of the Articles of Confederation and a parallel provision in the Constitution in this instance arguably shed some light on the correct interpretation of the latter.

Just as differences between the Articles of Confederation and the Constitution can be useful in understanding the latter, so can similarities. For instance, in *Martin v. Hunter's Lessee*, in the course of refuting the state of Virginia's argument that the Supreme Court of the United States could not hear an appeal from a decision by the state supreme court, Justice Story pointed out that under the Articles of Confederation, which were "framed with infinitely more deference to state rights and state jealousies," a federal court was created, which could hear appeals from state court decisions in prize cases.[122] This certainly suggested that the framing generation did not consider a state court decision as beyond revision by federal courts.

In the *Slaughter-House Cases*,[123] Justice Miller, writing for the majority, noted that the term "privileges or immunities," which is used in Article IV of the Constitution, also appeared in the Articles of Confederation and was almost certainly meant to carry the same meaning. Moreover, because the clause in the Articles then provided a few specific examples of what was encompassed by the phrase, such as free egress and ingress to other states and the privileges of trade and commerce, then these examples should provide solid evidence of what was intended by the same language in the Constitution.[124]

Likewise, in his dissenting opinion in *Saenz v. Roe*, Justice Thomas argued that the phrase "privileges in immunities" in the Fourteenth Amendment should be limited to "fundamental" rights because that provision was modeled after the similar Clause in Article IV, which was in turn modeled after the Privileges and Immunities Clause of the Articles of Confederation.[125] Justice Thomas argued that because it was relatively clear that the framers of the Articles would have understood "privileges and immunities" to be limited to "fundamental rights," it is likely that such understanding was carried over into the nearly identical language in the Constitution as well.[126] This was especially true given that *Corfield v. Coryell*, an important case interpreting the phrase after the ratification of Article IV and before the drafting of the Fourteenth Amendment, so understood it.[127]

In *Kentucky v. Denison*,[128] the Court noted that the fact that the Articles had permitted extradition of persons charged with "treason, felony or other high misdemeanor" indicated that when the Constitution changed the phrase to "treason, felony and crimes," the framers meant simply to clarify the language and certainly did not intend to omit "political crimes" from the coverage of the term *crimes*. In addition, the Court concluded that "in adopting the same words" as used in the Articles, they clearly intended to sanction the same method of proceeding under the Clause as had been utilized under the Articles.[129] This is an instance in which the Court concluded from the language and history that continuity rather than rejection was intended.

One source of the original understanding would surely be consideration of the obvious problems encountered under the Articles of Confederation, which the framers of the Constitution sought to avoid. In *Cohens v. Virginia*,[130] without explicitly referring to the Articles of Confederation, Chief Justice Marshall relied heavily on the experiences under that document in construing the reach of governmental powers under the Constitution. He observed that the states as well as the people "have been taught by experience, that this Union cannot exist without a government for the whole; and they have been taught by the same experience that this government would be a mere shadow, that must disappoint all their hopes, unless invested with large portions of that sovereignty which belongs to the independent States."[131] A modern Court would almost certainly provide some specific citations to the Confederation experience. That was not Marshall's style, however, and given that the incidents in question occurred during his adult lifetime and considering that his account coincides with conventional history of the times, his argument is potent.

Marshall returned to the problems under the Articles of Confederation and the common understanding of the defects in the Articles later in the opinion, pointing out that the laws enacted by Congress under the Articles were "habitually disregarded" and "[w]ith the knowledge of this fact, and under its full pressure, a convention was assembled to change the system."[132] Understanding that the evil the Constitution was designed to address was inadequate respect for federal law by the states, Marshall argued that it would make little sense to interpret the Constitution as vesting those very states with the final say over the meaning of the Constitution and federal law. This was quite a persuasive example of the use of the problems that occurred under the Articles to justify a different approach under the Constitution.

G. The Virginia Experience and the Religion Clauses

Perhaps no series of preconstitutional events has had as much influence on constitutional interpretation, however, as the dispute over religious liberty in Virginia in the mid-1780s, combined with Jefferson's letter to the Danbury Baptist Association some fifteen years later. In its very first freedom of religion case, *Reynolds v. United States*,[133] the Court set the stage for heavy reliance on original understanding as a means of interpreting the religion clauses in the course of rejecting a claim that a federal law that criminally prohibited polygamy violated a Mormon's First Amendment right of free exercise of religion.[134]

In order to determine the meaning of the Free Exercise Clause, Justice Waite focused on a series of events around the time of the drafting of the First Amendment. First he noted that in colonial America, the free exercise of religion was often infringed by colonial legislatures, including by the adoption of taxes to support favored churches as well as by punishment for failure to attend church.[135] The Court then called attention to the debate on religious liberty that erupted in Virginia in the mid-1780s.[136] It explained that when the Virginia legislature considered reauthorizing a tax to support the state church, James Madison and Thomas Jefferson led the opposition and not only defeated the reinstatement of the tax but also succeeded in getting the legislature to enact a Bill of Religious Liberty.[137] Justice Waite quoted from James Madison's famous "Memorial and Remonstrance" as well as from the Preamble of the Act Protecting Religious Liberties in each instance as evidence that Madison and Jefferson assumed that freedom of religion protected the exercise of religious belief but not the exercise of religiously motivated conduct.[138]

Of course the Court was attempting to interpret and apply the Free Exercise Clause of the First Amendment and not the Virginia Bill of Religious Liberty. To show the relevance of the events in Virginia to the First Amendment, it noted that the enactment of the Virginia Bill predated the Constitutional Convention by only a year.[139] Moreover, there was a movement supported by Jefferson and several states to amend the Constitution to provide protection for civil liberties, including freedom of religion.[140] The Court noted that Madison, then along with others, proposed the First Amendment.[141] It quoted from Jefferson's now famous letter to the Danbury Baptist Association, written a decade after the ratification of the First Amendment, in which Jefferson declared that the religion clauses of the First Amendment have the effect of "building a wall of separation between church and State."[142] That statement would eventually take on a life of its own in First Amendment doctrine; however, the *Reynolds* Court's interest in the Danbury Baptist letter was not on account of the wall of separation metaphor, but rather on the next sentence, in which Jefferson reaffirmed that the religion clauses protect beliefs but not actions, the principle that the Court would use to decide the Mormon polygamy case.[143] Indeed, the Court found the enactment of the Virginia Bill of Religious Liberty so relevant to the meaning of the Free Exercise Clause that it maintained that the fact that Virginia legislature imposed the death penalty for polygamy a few years after it had enacted the Bill of Religious Liberty illustrated that criminally punishing polygamy could not be considered inconsistent with freedom of religion.[144]

Thus, in its very first significant freedom of religion case, the Court chose to interpret the clause on the basis of events which preceded and followed the actual drafting and ratification of the Amendment. The significance of these events turned on the participation of Madison in the creation of the religion clauses in 1791. Essentially, the Court's thesis seemed to be that Madison wrote "Memorial and Remonstrance" and Jefferson wrote the Virginia Bill of Liberties a few years prior to the drafting and ratification of the First Amendment. Although Jefferson was out of the country, Madison was a prime mover in the drafting of the religion clauses. Jefferson commented on the meaning of the religion clauses a decade after they were enacted in a private letter. Therefore, Madison's "Memorial and Remonstrance," Jefferson's Bill of Religious Liberties and Jefferson's letter to the Danbury Baptist Association provided powerful if not definitive evidence as to the meaning of the religion clauses. It is notable that in *Reynolds*, the Court relied on these events, which are generally considered milestones in the struggle for freedom of religion for the express purpose of giving the Free Exercise Clause a narrow and restrictive, as opposed to an expansive, reading.

In *Everson v. Board of Education*, the Court's first significant Establishment Clause opinion, Justice Black relied on the history of religious persecution "transported" from Europe to the colonies as background information to explain the reason why the Establishment Clause of the First Amendment was adopted.[145] Citing and quoting from *Reynolds*, Justice Black also placed heavy reliance on the dispute over religious liberty in Virginia in 1785–86, starting with Madison's famous "Memorial and Remonstrance" and culminating in the Virginia Bill of Religious Liberty, drafted by Jefferson, as well as Jefferson's subsequent letter to the Danbury Baptist Association. Justice Black explained that in 1785 the Virginia legislature considered whether to continue to use taxpayer funds to pay salaries of ministers and to build churches.[146] Madison wrote "Memorial and Remonstrance" opposing this practice and setting forth several arguments in favor of religious freedom.[147] Justice Black noted that the bill to continue the financial support of the churches was defeated and the Bill of Religious Liberties was enacted.[148] He then concluded that "the provisions of the First Amendment, in the drafting and adoption of which Madison and Jefferson played such leading roles, had the same objective and were intended to provide the same protection against government intrusion on religious liberty as the Virginia statute."[149] So, according to Justice Black this dispute in the Virginia legislature six years prior to the drafting of the First Amendment provided the very foundation and purpose of that Amendment.[150]

Justice Rutledge, dissenting in *Everson*, discussed the battle in Virginia over the Assessment and Bill of Religious Liberty in even more depth than did Justice Black, and if anything gave them more weight in interpreting the Establishment Clause, even attaching a copy of Madison's "Memorial and Remonstrance" as an appendix to the opinion.[151] He argued the following:

[a]ll of the great instruments of the Virginia struggle for religious liberty thus became warp and woof of our constitutional tradition, not simply by the course of history, but by the common unifying force of Madison's life, thought and sponsorship. He epitomized the whole of the tradition in the Amendment's compact, but nonetheless comprehensive, phrasing.[152]

Consequently, Madison's "Memorial and Remonstrance" became Justice Rutledge's lodestar for interpreting the religion clauses. Contrary to the manner in which the *Reynold's* Court employed the Virginia events to read the Free Exercise Clause restrictively, the *Everson* Court used the same events to read the Establishment Clause expansively, even though Justice Black and the majority found the practice in issue in that case to be constitutional.

As was the case with *Reynolds* and the Free Exercise Clause, the pre-First Amendment Virginia history can be employed to uphold practices as consistent with the Establishment Clause as well. In *McGowan v. Maryland*, Justice Warren, writing for the majority of the Court and upholding Sunday closing laws against an Establishment Clause challenge, relied heavily on Madison's actions and the Virginia history.[153] Chief Justice Warren emphasized the significance of the Virginia religious debates and especially Madison's role in those debates on the meaning of the First Amendment.[154] He then pointed out that not only did Virginia maintain its Sunday closing laws before and after the passage of the Virginia Bill of Liberties and the

Establishment Clause but, in addition, that Madison himself presented the Virginia legislature a "bill for Punishing . . . Sabbath Breakers" in the very same year that the Virginia Bill of Religious Freedom was passed.[155] Thus Madison, who Justice Warren called "the First Amendment's architect,"[156] saw no inconsistency between Sunday closing laws and religious freedom. Similarly in his concurrence in *Walz v. Tax Commission*, Justice Brennan argued that given the importance of the Virginia religious controversy to the meaning of the First Amendment, the fact that the Virginia legislature reenacted a property tax exemption for "houses for divine worship" after the enactment of the Virginia Bill of Religious Liberties is strong evidence that it saw no inconsistency between this practice and freedom of religion.[157] In this instance, Justice Brennan was actually relying on events that occurred almost a decade after the First Amendment was drafted and ratified; however, he justified this on the ground that "Virginia remained unusually sensitive to the proper relation between church and state during the years immediately following ratification of the Establishment Clause."[158]

The Court's reliance on the Virginia controversy and Madison's "Memorial and Remonstrance" as the key to understanding the First Amendment's religion clauses has not escaped criticism. In his dissenting opinion in *Flast v. Cohen*, Justice Harlan, citing recent historical publications, noted that "we have recently been reminded that the historical purposes of the religion clauses of the First Amendment are significantly more obscure and complex than this Court has heretofore acknowledged."[159] He continued, "[c]areful students of the history of the Establishment Clause have found that 'it is impossible to give a dogmatic interpretation of the First Amendment, and to state with any accuracy the intention of the men who framed it'" quoting a recent historical work.[160] He explained that "[a]bove all, the evidence seems clear that the First Amendment was not intended simply to enact the terms of Madison's Memorial and Remonstrance against Religious Assessments."[161] Nevertheless, in Establishment Clause cases, the Court and various justices continue to place very heavy reliance on these events.

III. Drafting and Ratification of the Constitution and its Amendments

Not surprisingly, evidence of the drafting and ratification process has often played a central role in the Court's attempt to determine the original understanding of the Constitution. This type of evidence has included the debates during the Constitutional Convention and the state ratifying conventions, changes and omissions during the drafting process, and important contemporaneous commentary such as the *Federalist Papers*.

A. Statements and Debate during the Drafting Process

The Court frequently relies on statements or debate during the process of drafting a constitutional provision as shedding light on what it was understood to mean. For instance in *INS v. Chadha*,[162] where the Court struck down the legislative veto on the ground that it violated the textual requirements of presentment and bicameralism, it cited and quoted speeches from the Constitutional Convention pertaining to the relevant provisions. The Court noted that the Presentment Clause was added to the text after Madison "expressed concern" that the prerequisite of presidential signature could readily be evaded by simply calling a proposed law a "resolution or vote."[163] Likewise the Court quoted a statement by James Wilson during the Convention attesting to the importance of the requirement of bicameral approval to the validity of legislation and noted that it was the Great Compromise creating a bicameral legislature that allowed the Convention to break the deadlock that had threatened its very mission.[164] These examples as well as support from the *Federalist Papers* convinced the Court that "the Framers were acutely conscious that the bicameral requirement and the Presentment Clauses would serve essential constitutional functions," and hence the legislative power must "be exercised in accord with a single, finely wrought and exhaustively considered, procedure."[165]

The debates on the meaning of the language by those who drafted it may offer significant insight into its meaning. In *Reynolds v. Sims*, for instance, Justice Harlan, in his dissenting opinion, relied heavily on the statements in Congress by Representative Bingham and others to show that sections 1 and 2 of the Fourteenth Amendment, when read together, were clearly not intended to give Congress (or, by implication, the federal courts) any authority over state voting rights with one exception.[166] Justice Harlan's argument was well documented and quite powerful but nevertheless rejected by the majority. *Reynolds* is an example of a case in which the majority rejected the result consistent with the original understanding in favor of a result supported by contemporary conceptions of political fairness.

It demonstrates that for the Court original understanding is generally just one of several guides to interpretation and scarcely the final word.

There are limits to the utility of speeches and comments made during the drafting process, however. One of the most extensive uses of drafting history in Supreme Court is the lengthy appendix that Justice Black attached to his dissent in *Adamson v. California* for the purpose of showing that the framers of the Fourteenth Amendment intended to incorporate all of the guarantees of the Bill of Rights against the states.[167] Justice Frankfurter was not swayed by this history. He noted in his concurring opinion in *Adamson* that "[r]emarks of a particular proponent of the Amendment, no matter how influential, are not to be deemed part of the Amendment. What was submitted for ratification was his proposal, not his speech."[168] As such, speeches and comments have the potential at least to be more misleading than informative on questions of original understanding, and therefore must be used with some caution.

Although he argued in favor of placing reliance on statements made in the Convention and the ratification debates in his dissenting opinion in the *Legal Tender Cases*, Justice Field acknowledged that a court must proceed with caution because

> [m]embers . . . who did not participate in the debates may have entertained different views from those expressed. The several state conventions to which the Constitution was submitted may have differed widely from each other and from its framers in their interpretation of its clauses. We all know that opposite opinions on many points were expressed in the Conventions, and conflicting reasons were urged both for the adoption and rejection of that instrument.[169]

Nevertheless, Justice Field concluded, contrary to the majority that in this instance "there was an entire uniformity of opinion," that Congress was prohibited from making paper money legal tender.[170]

The Court made a similar point in the course of rejecting a statement made by a senator during the course of debate on the Fourteenth Amendment in *Maxwell v. Dow*.[171] It observed that

> [i]t is clear that what is said in Congress . . . may or may not express the views of the majority of those who favor the adoption of the measure . . . and the question whether the proposed amendment itself expresses the meaning which those who spoke in its favor may have assumed that

it did, is one to be determined by the language actually used, and not by the speeches made regarding it.[172]

B. Changes in the Text during the Drafting Process

The drafting history of the religion clauses of the First Amendment has proven to be a rich source for coming to grips with original understanding. Chief Justice Warren reviewed that history in *McGowan v. Maryland*,[173] a case in which the Court upheld the constitutionality of Sunday closing laws. He pointed out that Madison added the word *national* before the word *religion* in the initial draft in the House of Representatives in recognition of existing state establishments.[174] The House committee changed the language to "no religion shall be established by law."[175] Chief Justice Warren then quoted Madison as understanding the language to mean "that Congress should not establish a religion, and enforce the legal observation of it by law, nor compel men to worship God in any manner contrary to their conscience."[176] The amendment as passed by the House provided that "Congress shall make no law establishing religion."[177] The provision as passed by the Senate stated that "Congress shall make no law establishing articles of faith, or a mode of worship."[178] The language that finally emerged from the reconciliation of the two provisions stated that Congress shall make no law "respecting an establishment of religion."[179] The Court concluded that the progression through this drafting history showed that Congress intended to produce a principle that would be "[far] more extensive than merely to forbid a national or state church."[180] Likewise, in his concurring opinion in *Lee v. Weisman*,[181] Justice Souter made a similar argument working through the changes in language from draft to draft in an attempt to show that Congress intended to adopt a broader principle than mere nonpreferentialism of one religion over another.

Looking at this history in detail and Madison's role in it, Justice Rehnquist, dissenting in *Wallace v. Jaffree*, read it quite differently than had the Court in *McGowan*.[182] He argued that it showed that Madison was primarily concerned with prohibiting a national religion or discrimination among sects, but that it did not suggest that Madison was attempting to carry over his approach to the religious struggles in the Virginia General Assembly earlier in the decade into the drafting of the First Amendment.[183] Moreover, he concluded that there was no evidence at all that any member of the Congress that drafted the First Amendment contemplated that it "would require . . . the Government [to] be absolutely neutral as between religion and irreligion."[184] The legislative history of the drafting of the Religion Clauses provides an excellent example of an instance in which there is a fairly significant amount of detailed legislative history and yet still room for vigorous debate over exactly what it reveals.

The Court has taken the position that changes made in the Committee on Style during the Convention of 1787 should not be read as changing the substance of the provision because the charge to the Committee was only to alter the style, and not the substance.[185] As such, the Court will "presume that the Committee did its job."[186] Dissenting from the Court's decision in *Payton v. New York* that the Fourth Amendment prohibited a warrantless arrest in the suspect's home, Justice White emphasized the extensive common-law history suggesting that fear of the "general" warrant was the primary, if not exclusive, concern of the framers of the Fourth Amendment.[187] In response to this argument, the Court noted that the initial draft of the Fourth Amendment only addressed warrants; however, the subsequent addition of the clause prohibiting unreasonable searches and seizures made it "perfectly clear that the evil the Amendment was designed to prevent was broader than abuse of the general warrant."[188] Justice White responded, however, that this second clause "was adopted virtually at the last moment by the Committee of Three, which had been appointed only to arrange the Amendments rather than to make substantive changes in them."[189] Quoting Lasson, Justice White noted that "[t]he Amendment passed the House, but the House seems never to have consciously agreed to the Amendment in its present form."[190] Consequently, Justice White concluded that "because the sanctity of the common-law protections was assumed from the start, it is evident that the change made by the Committee of Three was a cautionary measure without substantive content."[191] Here Justice White used general background and legislative history to argue persuasively, though ultimately in a losing cause, that a significant textual change in the drafting process should be understood as having no substantive impact whatsoever.

C. The Significance of Rejected Provisions

Sometimes the focus is on what the framers failed to do rather than what they actually did. One argument against a particular interpretation of the Constitution is to point out that the framers of the Constitution considered and rejected something quite similar. The rejection of the Council of Revision by the Philadelphia Convention has often been cited as an objection to the validity of aggressive judicial review, especially of state legislation.[192] During the Convention, on several occasions James Madison had proposed the adoption of a Council of Revision, composed of members of the federal judiciary, which would have the power to invalidate national and state legislation before it took effect.[193] In his dissenting opinion in *Griswold v. Connecticut*, Justice Black cited the rejection of that provision as proof that the framers did not intend for federal judges to substitute their views for those of legislative bodies.[194] That is certainly one inference that could be drawn from the rejection of the proposal, although the eighteenth-century Council of Revision is readily distinguishable from the institution of judicial review as exercised in the twentieth century. The opposite conclusion from Justice Black's might be drawn from this historical incident as well. That is, the framers rejected the proposal of a Council of Revision as unnecessary because they believed that courts exercising the power of judicial review would impose a sufficient constitutional check on legislatures. The same qualification must be attached to that inference as well, however. That is, the form of judicial review that could have been contemplated by the framers would have been far less aggressive and intrusive than its modern counterpart. Thus, it does not follow that the rejection of the Council of Revision necessarily could justify the full extent of modern judicial review.

In *Bowsher v. Synar*, where the Court invalidated a law that would have permitted congressional removal of an official exercising executive authority for "'inefficiency,' 'neglect of duty' or 'malfeasance,'" the Court pointed out that the Constitutional Convention had rejected language that would have permitted impeachment of officers for "maladministration."[195] The Court concluded that the statute before it was far too close to a standard that the framers had explicitly rejected as one of several reasons why it was unconstitutional. The parallel was sufficiently close in this instance to provide this argument with some weight.

Likewise, in *Carter v. Carter Coal*, the Court pointed out that during the Constitutional Convention, William Randolph had proposed that the Congress be vested with power to "legislate in all cases to which the Separate States are incompetent, or in which the harmony of the United States may be interrupted by the exercise of individual Legislation," but that this provision was rejected in favor of defined and limited powers.[196] The Court relied on this history to reject the argument that Congress should have the authority to address problems that the states cannot adequately manage. *Carter Coal* has since been rejected and congressional power has been construed far more expansively.[197]

In *New York v. United States*, in the course of concluding that Congress does not have the right to commandeer state legislatures to carry out federal programs, the Court pointed out that the Constitutional Convention had considered the Virginia proposal, which required the federal government to act directly on states, and the New Jersey plan, which required it to obtain the consent of states before acting.[198] By rejecting the New Jersey plan, and essentially using the Virginia plan as the model for the new Constitution, the Court concluded that the Convention meant for the federal government to act on individuals directly, and not through the states.

In *City of Boerne v. Florence*,[199] the Court relied heavily on the drafting history of section 5, the enforcement provision of the Fourteenth Amendment, in support of its conclusion that the framers clearly did not intend to give the Congress authority to define the meaning of the Fourteenth Amendment guarantees. The Court noted that the Reconstruction Congress definitively rejected representative Bingham's initial proposal, which would have granted the Congress the power to make all laws "necessary and proper" to secure the amendment's substantive guarantees.[200] The Court noted that many members of Congress vigorously objected to this provision on the ground that it gave Congress too much legislative power at the expense of Constitutional structure.[201] Consequently, it was rejected and replaced with the language that now appears in the Fourteenth Amendment, which simply gave Congress the power to "enforce" the Amendment.[202] The Court concluded that "[u]nder the revised Amendment, Congress power was no longer plenary but remedial."[203] Thus, in this instance, according to the Court, the rejection of an alternative during the drafting process of the amendment provided definitive guidance as to its meaning.

There has also been debate over the significance of the rejected Blaine Amendment, which, following the passage of the Fourteenth Amendment, would have explicitly prohibited states from creating religious establishments or violating the right of free exercise of religion.[204] The very attempt to pass such an amendment has been raised as proof of the position that the Fourteenth Amendment itself did not incorporate the Establishment Clause, given that that clause was arguably intended to protect state establishments against federal interference.[205] Justice Brennan rejected this argument in his concurring opinion in *Abington Township v. Schempp*.[206] He noted that the Blaine Amendment also created a free exercise right against the states as well, but unlike the Establishment Clause, there was no viable argument to the effect that the Free Exercise Clause was not to be extended to the states.[207] As such, the argument that the rejection of the Blaine Amendment indicted a belief that the Establishment Clause would not otherwise apply against the states seemed tenuous at best.

Although the Court will sometimes draw inferences from the rejection of language or specific provisions by the framers, Justice Scalia cautioned in his opinion for the Court in *District of Columbia v. Heller* that "it is always perilous to derive the meaning of an adopted provision from another provision deleted in the drafting process."[208] There, Justice Scalia was responding to Justice Stevens's argument in dissent that Madison's early draft of the Second Amendment, which included an exemption for conscientious objectors, could only mean that the expression "to keep and bear arms" referred exclusively to service in the militia.[209] Justice Scalia disagreed with Justice Stevens's reading of Madison's language, arguing that the most natural reading was that those opposed to the use of weapons for any type of violent confrontation were excused from doing so in a military context.[210] Justice Stevens responded that the Virginia and North Carolina proposals upon which Madison's amendment was based permitted a person of religious scruples to be exempted from bearing arms upon payment "to another to bear arms in his stead."[211] It may be an overstatement to claim, as does Justice Scalia, that it is always perilous to rely on deleted text to ascertain meaning, but it would certainly be fair to say that it often is. It may not be clear why the provisions were rejected. It could be due to substantive disagreement with the principle, but it might also be because it was assumed that the principle was already implicit in the document itself. Consequently, reliance on rejection of a similar provision will generally be at best a supplemental argument but rarely the primary justification for the Court's result.

D. Understanding during the Ratification Process

The understanding of a provision during the ratification process is powerful evidence of its true meaning, given that the ratifying conventions were the bodies that had the authority to make the Constitution operative.[212] In the landmark case of *McCulloch v. Maryland*, Chief Justice Marshall relied on the very existence and nature of the ratification process as conclusive evidence of the origin and structure of the nation itself.[213] *McCulloch* raised the foundational argument over whether, as the state of Maryland urged, the Constitution was a compact between preexisting sovereign states or whether its existence, legitimacy, and authority flowed instead from the people, that is, from the popular sovereignty theory propounded by the federal government.[214] Marshall concluded that the latter was the correct theory of constitutional creation.[215] He based this almost exclusively on the fact that the document drafted in Philadelphia "was a mere proposal," and it became the Constitution only after having been ratified by popularly elected conventions in the states.[216] Although these conventions occurred within the states, "the people were at perfect liberty to accept or reject [the constitution] and their act was final."[217] Consequently, "[t]he government of the Union . . . is, emphatically and truly, a government of the people."[218] Thus, in *McCulloch*, a unanimous Supreme Court adopted the popular sovereignty theory and rejected the compact theory largely based on the structure of the ratification process. However, the latter theory actually gained political momentum in subsequent years and provided the justification for the secession of the southern states in the early 1860s. Despite *McCulloch*, it was only the Civil War that ultimately established the popular sovereignty as the true constitutional foundation.

Justice Story, one of the Constitution's greatest scholars, relied on debate in the ratification process in *Martin v. Hunter's Lessee*, where he stated that "[i]t is an [sic] historical fact, that this exposition of the constitution, extending its appellate power to state courts, was, previous to its adoption, uniformly and publically avowed by its friends, and admitted by its enemies, as the basis of their respective reasonings, both in and out of the state conventions."[219] He took judicial notice of this but did not provide any specific examples. A modern court would obviously provide details. Likewise, in *Barron v. City of Baltimore*, Chief Justice Marshall pointed to the various amendments designed to limit federal power suggested in several state conventions during the process of ratifying the Constitution as evidence that the subsequently enacted Bill of Rights was intended to apply only to the federal government, and not the states.[220]

In *U.S. Term Limits v Thornton*, the Court made good use of the ratification debates to support its conclusion that the states lacked the authority to add conditions such as term limits to congressional office seekers.[221] The Court pointed out that during the debates, critics argued that the Constitution itself should have imposed term limits.[222] Defenders of the Constitution responded that that would have been a bad idea.[223] The Court found "compelling the complete absence in the ratification debates of any assertion that States had the power to add qualifications."[224] It concluded that "[t]he failure of intelligent and experienced advocates to utilize this argument must reflect a general agreement that its premise was unsound."[225] On the other hand, Justice Thomas, in dissent, argued that a lack of discussion during the ratification debates might prove very little because "the surviving records of those debates are fragmentary," given that "[w]e have no records at all of the debates in several of the conventions . . . and only spotty records from most of the others."[226] The more comprehensive nature of the records of the Philadelphia Convention as well as the drafting of the Bill of Rights as compared to those of state ratification conventions may at least partially explain why the former are usually given greater consideration than the latter, even if the latter are arguably of greater significance in describing the original understanding. Because the focus of the ratification conventions was on the Constitution itself and not necessarily the reserved powers of the states, it is certainly possible that the opponents overlooked what the Court believed to be such a compelling argument. As such, there are limits on exactly what type of inferences should be drawn based on the absence of discussion.

The Court in *New York v. United States*[227] quoted several statements made during ratifying conventions by prominent members of the Constitutional Convention—including Oliver Ellsworth, Charles Pinckney, Rufus King, and Alexander Hamilton—emphasizing that the proposed constitution was designed to create a government empowered to act on individuals rather than states. This would seem to provide quite significant evidence of the original understanding, because the persons in question not only participated in the debates and drafting of the document but also publicized their understanding of the nature of the Constitution in the very forums that possessed the authority to give it legal effect. This hardly shows that all ratifiers held these views, but it is certainly evidence that some of the most informed and prominent did.

Because of the proximity of the ratification of the Constitution to the drafting and ratification of the Bill of Rights, debates and proposed amendments in the ratifying conventions for the original Constitution, may shed light on the meaning of provisions later added to the Bill of Rights. In his concurring opinion in *McGowan v. Maryland*,[228] Justice Frankfurter pointed out that five states proposed an amendment to the Constitution during their state ratifying conventions banning an establishment of religion and all five at the time had Sunday closing laws. Moreover, four of them reaffirmed these laws within five years.[229] Given that this occurred in the period immediately preceding the drafting and ratification of the First

Amendment, it is some evidence at least of the view that the framing generation saw no inconsistency between such laws and the Establishment Clause. Justice Douglas, dissenting, responded that state practices at the time were irrelevant, given that it is clear that the Establishment Clause would only apply to the federal government.[230]

E. Absence of Discussion

Sometimes the fact that a particular issue was not discussed during the drafting or ratification process may be relevant.[231] The absence of discussion might suggest that at the time everyone considered the question to be settled one way or the other, or perhaps that it was simply of no interest or concern. The meaning of such an absence of discussion, if discernable at all, will be contingent on the historical context.

In *Duncan v. Louisiana*,[232] Justice Harlan, dissenting, relied heavily on Professor Fairman's examination of the state convention debates over the ratification of the Fourteenth Amendment. Professor Fairman had concluded that the absence of any discussion of the question of whether the Fourteenth Amendment would apply the Bill of Rights to the states was powerful evidence that the state ratification conventions could not have assumed that it did, as such a radical change in the law would have provoked significant debate had it been contemplated.[233] Justice Black found such evidence unpersuasive. In his dissent in *Duncan*, responding to Justice Harlan's reliance on the Fairman article,[234] Justice Black wrote that his own experience as a United States senator convinced him that "it is far wiser to rely on what was said" than on what was not said.[235] Certainly, the absence of discussion is almost inevitably open to divergent explanation. Still, it may have some probative value at least in some circumstances.

Similarly, in *Faretta v. California*, after detailing the importance of the right of self-representation in England and colonial America, the Court stated that

> [i]f anyone had thought that the Sixth Amendment, as drafted, failed to protect the long-respected right of self-representation, there would undoubtedly have been some debate or comment on the issue. But there was none.[236]

In his concurring opinion in *Walz v. Tax Commission*, Justice Brennan argued that the absence of any discussion of the constitutionality of tax exemptions for churches at the time of the drafting of the First Amendment must be understood as an indication that the framers had no doubt as to the constitutionality of the practice, given that it was widespread and well known at the time.[237] This is a logical assumption; however, it is always possible that no one thought of the issue. The absence of discussion must always be used with care, as inevitably there will be more than one possible explanation for that absence, and the actual reason will at best be a matter of speculation.

Sometimes, however, the absence of discussion suggests that the meaning of a provision was well understood by the framers. In *United States v. Johnson*, for instance, the Court observed that "[t]he Speech or Debate Clause of the Constitution was approved at the Constitutional Convention without discussion and without opposition."[238] The Court attributed this to the fact that the language was nearly identical to that of the Articles of Confederation, which was in turn copied from the English Bill of Rights of 1689.[239] One hundred years of historical understanding preceded the incorporation of that phrase into the Constitution. As such, it was the events that gave rise to the creation of the privilege in England that shed the most light on its meaning.

The Court has taken the same approach with the Eighth Amendment, noting in *Browning-Ferris Industries v. Kelco Disposals Inc.* that "[t]he Eighth Amendment received little debate in the First Congress . . . and the Excessive Fines Clause received even less attention."[240] The Court attributed this to the fact that several states had excessive fines clauses in their own constitutions, and thus, the concept was well understood.[241] The Court then turned to eighteenth-century dictionaries to confirm that the word *fine* meant a payment to the government as opposed to a private party.[242]

F. The *Federalist Papers*

The *Federalist Papers* have long provided an important source for gleaning original understanding of the Constitution.[243] No one has played a greater role in popularizing the significance of the *Federalist Papers* than Chief John Marshall. In *Cohens v. Virginia*, he explained that

> [t]he opinion of the Federalist has always been considered as of great authority. It is a complete commentary on our constitution; and is appealed to by all parties in the questions to which that instrument has

given birth. Its intrinsic merit entitles it to this high rank; and the part two of its authors performed in framing the constitution, put it very much in their power to explain the views with which it was framed. These essays having been published while the constitution was before the nation for adoption or rejection, and having been written in answer to objections founded entirely on the extent of its powers, and on its diminution of State sovereignty, are entitled to the more consideration where they frankly avow that the power objected to is given, and defended it.[244]

Here Marshall gave several reasons why the *Federalist Papers* should be taken seriously as a source of constitutional meaning. First, he pointed out that everyone involved in argument over constitutional meaning does rely on them. By 1821, they had already carried the day in the court of informed public opinion. Next, he supported them on the basis of their "intrinsic merit;" in other words, they are correct and persuasive. Then, Marshall explained that because the authors (at least two of them) were involved in the framing of the Constitution, they should be able to offer firsthand information on the original intent. Finally, given that the papers were published during that ratification process, they provided especially strong evidence of original understanding with respect to the proper construction of governmental powers, as this was a primary front on which the document was challenged and these were the defenses raised, which apparently were persuasive to at least some of the ratifying conventions. Thus, in this single paragraph, Marshall offered a multilayered explanation for why the *Federalist Papers* ought to be highly regarded by constitutional interpreters. He then quoted a passage from Hamilton in *Federalist*, which supported the position he was taking in the case.[245]

In the landmark case of *McCulloch v. Maryland*,[246] Chief Justice Marshall again endorsed the *Federalist Papers* but cautioned that they must be read carefully and critically.

[T]he opinions expressed by the authors of that work [The Federalist] have been justly supposed to be entitled to great respect in expounding the constitution. No tribute can be paid to them which exceeds their merit; but in applying their opinions to the cases which may arise in the progress of our government, a right to judge their correctness must be retained; and to understand the argument, we must examine the proposition it maintains, and the objections against which it is directed.[247]

Marshall made three basic points: (1) that the *Federalist* is entitled to great respect, (2) even so, it is not conclusive, and (3) it is important to read it carefully, understanding the point it is making. Taking up the third point, Marshall then dismissed *Maryland*'s reliance on the *Federalist*, noting that the stated fear of federal taxation choking off state power scarcely supported the ability of a state to tax federal instrumentalities.[248] Indeed, it might more readily support the opposite conclusion.[249] Marshall pointed out that *Maryland* was attempting to rely on an argument that the *Federalist* was setting forth only to demolish.[250] As such, the source provided no support for the argument at all.

The Court often places reliance on the *Federalist Papers* on questions of constitutional structure, as that was perhaps their primary concern. For instance, in *New York v. United States*, in the course of deciding that the federal government could not constitutionally "commandeer" state legislatures to carry out federal programs, the Court quoted Hamilton in *Federalist 15* for the proposition that, unlike the deeply flawed Articles of Confederation, the new Constitution was designed to allow the federal government to act on persons in their individual capacity, "the only proper objects of government," rather than on the states in their corporate capacity.[251] Likewise. in *Mistretta v. United States*, the Court placed heavy reliance on the *Federalist Papers* to bolster its conclusion that, properly understood, the concept of separation of powers was concerned with aggrandizement of power by any one branch of the government as well as encroachment by one branch on the domain of another.[252]

The *Federalist Papers* do not always provide a definitive answer, however. In *Printz v. United States*, for instance, Justice Scalia, writing for the majority, and Justice Souter, dissenting, argued vigorously about the proper lesson to be drawn from the *Federalist Papers* on the question of whether Congress could require state executive officials to carry out obligations under federal policies. Justice Souter relied heavily on a statement by Hamilton in *Federalist 27* to the effect that state officials will be "incorporated into the operations of the national government" and "will be rendered auxiliary to the enforcement of the laws."[253] Justice Scalia, writing for the majority, argued that the statements that Justice Souter relied on were ambiguous, distinguishable from the issue before the Court and inconsistent with established precedent.[254] Moreover, he maintained that since Hamilton, the author of *Federalist 27*, was far and away the most nationalistic of the framers, his views on questions of federal power should not be considered indicative of the original understanding of the framing generation.[255] In other words, on at least some questions, the views of Madison would be more persuasive than those of Hamilton.

Ordinarily, the Court will cite or quote the *Federalist Papers* to illuminate provisions of the original Constitution of 1789, which the *Federalist Papers* themselves were addressing. On occasion, however, the Court will also use the *Federalist Papers* in the course of discussing subsequent developments. For instance, in *Griswold v. Connecticut*,[256] Justice Goldberg quoted from the *Federalist Papers* as evidence of the meaning of the Ninth Amendment, which still would not be drafted for a few years. Specifically, Justice Goldberg quoted Madison in *Federalist 37* and Hamilton in *Federalist 84* for enlightenment as to the nature of the problem that the Ninth Amendment was drafted to address.[257] He quoted Madison for the point that language can give an inaccurate impression, and Hamilton for the proposition that the very existence of a Bill of Rights might suggest that Congress has the affirmative power to pass laws that would abridge rights when, in fact, it does not.[258] Justice Goldberg cited these statements from the *Federalist Papers* as evidence of the problems that Madison and the Congress were attempting to solve a few years later with the drafting of the Ninth Amendment.[259] This would seem to be an appropriate use of the *Federalist Papers*. They were written close enough in time, and Hamilton in particular was addressing a specific issue that arguably did have a bearing on the drafting of the Ninth Amendment. As such, they provide legitimate evidence of the original understanding. Obviously, the greater the temporal lag between the *Papers* and the subsequent occurrence, the less persuasive is the argument that they provide pertinent information.

FOUR

Original Understanding
Contemporaneous Understanding and Interpretive Issues

※ I. Contemporaneous Practice and Understanding

As Justice Clifford observed in his dissent in the *Legal Tender Cases*, "[c]ontemporaneous acts are certainly evidence of intention."[1] Perhaps it would have been even more accurate to have said that they are evidence of original understanding, although that terminology was not well established at the time. In light of this observation, the Court has relied on several different types of contemporaneous acts to provide evidence of the original understanding.

A. Contemporaneous Dictionaries and Other Writings

In attempting to discern the meaning of words or phrases at the time that they were incorporated into the Constitution, the Court and various justices frequently turn to contemporary dictionaries.[2] In *Eldred v. Ashcroft*, for instance, the petitioners argued that the term "limited times" within the Copyright Clause meant that once the copyright term was set, it could not be altered.[3] Justice Ginsburg writing for the majority rejected this reading, however, pointing out that both at the time of the framing, quoting from definitions in Johnson's dictionary of 1785 and Sheridan's dictionary of 1796, and today quoting from Webster's 1976 dictionary, the word *limited* was defined as meaning "confined within certain bounds" or "limits."[4] The Court ultimately concluded that a law extending the term of existing copyrights did not violate the clause.

Similarly, Justice Scalia writing for the Court in *District of Columbia v. Heller* explained that "[t]he 18th-century meaning [of 'arms' in the Second Amendment] is no different from the meaning today[,]" citing the dictionaries of Samuel Johnson, Timothy Cunningham, and Noah Webster.[5] He argued that the term was applied to weapons of nonmilitary use.[6]

Further explicating the clause, Justice Scalia explained that to "keep" meant "to have in custody" according to Johnson, and "to hold; retain in one's power or possession" according to Webster.[7] He then cited Johnson, Webster, and Sheridan's respective dictionaries for the proposition that "to 'bear' meant to 'carry.'"[8] This convinced Justice Scalia that the phrase to "keep and bear arms" did not carry an exclusively military meaning. Justice Stevens, dissenting, cited contemporaneous dictionaries, including Samuel Johnson's, to show that the phrase "bear arms" often if not usually carried a military meaning.[9] Both justices conceded that the phrase "to bear arms" could carry a military as well as a nonmilitary meaning. For Justice Scalia, it was enough that it did not carry an exclusively military meaning. For Justice Stevens the important point was that the military meaning was most common and familiar.

Original meaning can also be established by reference to other sources as well. For example, in his concurring opinion in *United States v. Lopez*,[10] Justice Thomas quoted from three contemporaneous dictionaries to establish that the word *commerce* was understood to mean "trade" or "exchange." He then tied this meaning into the original understanding of the phrase as used in the constitutional text by citing several instances from the contemporaneous constitutional debate, including three from the *Federalist Papers* and one from the *Federal Farmer*, in which commerce was used to mean trade or exchange.[11] He bolstered this argument that commerce had a relatively restricted meaning by quoting several originalist sources, including the *Federalist Papers*, as drawing clear distinctions between trade on the one hand and agriculture and manufacturing on the other.[12] Thus by relying on contemporary usage by those engaged in the debate over the meaning of the Constitution, Justice Thomas was able to move beyond dictionary definitions into the world of constitutional discourse. This strengthened his argument, although as a practical matter, the precedent to the contrary is simply too entrenched to overcome even if the originalist argument is correct.

Just as in our own time, words and phrases at the time of the framing of the Constitution often carried multiple meanings. As such, simply consulting a dictionary will not necessarily resolve the issue. Justice Thomas recognized this in his dissent in *Kelo v. City of New London*, conceding that contemporaneous dictionaries offered alternative meanings for the word *use*.[13] Citing Dr. Johnson's dictionary, Justice Thomas argued that the most natural reading of *use* was "to employ," and thus a public use of property would connote government ownership or at least a public right of access to the property.[14] He noted, however, that Johnson's dictionary also defined *use* as "to help" or to "make a thing proper for any purpose."[15] He maintained that within the context of the Constitution, the narrower reading made more sense.[16]

B. Pre- and Post-Ratification State Constitutions

One source of original understanding, at least as to some matters, is pre- and post-ratification state constitutions.[17] For instance, in the early case of *Calder v. Bull*, in attempting to establish the meaning of the term of art "ex poste facto law," Justices Chase and Patterson in seriatim opinions quoted from or cited the Constitutions of Massachusetts, Maryland, North Carolina, and Delaware for the proposition that the term applied to retrospective criminal laws.[18] Likewise, in the course of rejecting the English common law rule that denied counsel in felony cases, the Court in *Powell v. Alabama* engaged in a thorough review of the pre-ratification state constitutions and concluded that twelve of the thirteen states had rejected the English rule.[19] The Court quite properly considered this to be compelling evidence that a complete denial of counsel in a capital case did not comport with due process of law.[20]

As with other sources of the original understanding, the inferences to be drawn from these documents are indeed subject to debate. Justice Scalia cited provisions in nine contemporaneous state constitutions in *District of Columbia v. Heller*, which used the phrase "to bear arms in defense of themselves and the state" as significant evidence that to the framing generation, the phrase "to bear arms" was not limited to an exclusive militia-oriented meaning.[21] He pointed out that if "to bear arms" carried an exclusive military meaning, a purposive qualifier, such as one which permitted a person to bear arms "for the purpose of killing game," for instance, would contradict the phrase that it modifies, leading to a nonsensical construction.[22] Dissenting in *Heller*, Justice Stevens was able to turn the reliance on contemporaneous state constitutions around on the Court, however, by pointing out that the fact that at least two of them explicitly stated that a person had the right to bear arms in self defense undermined the argument that the Second Amendment should be so read, given that it does not contain such language.[23]

The language of contemporaneous state constitutions can be employed to qualify the meaning of the federal constitution. Given that there is little direct source material with respect to the Freedom of Speech Clause of the First Amendment, justices have frequently cited contemporaneous state constitutional provisions to attempt to clarify its scope. In *Dennis v. United States*, Justice Frankfurter, arguing that the First Amendment was not absolute, cited the fact that there were political libel trials in Massachusetts despite a freedom of speech provision in the Massachusetts constitution, as well as the fact that the Pennsylvania and Delaware constitutions adopted at about the same time as the First Amendment had express provisions imposing liability for the abuse of free speech.[24] It is hard to see how these examples shed much light on the meaning of the First Amendment, especially as prior to the passage of the Fourteenth Amendment, the Bill of Rights had no application to the states; but in this instance, it hardly matters because the point Frankfurter was making was rather obvious.

Other justices have also relied on existing state constitutional provisions as proof that the First Amendment was not understood as being as absolute as its language might suggest. In his dissenting opinion in *Gertz v. Welch*, Justice White pointed out that although ten of the fourteen states that had ratified the Constitution by 1792 had provisions in their own constitutions protecting freedom of expression, thirteen of the fourteen provided for the prosecution of libel.[25] From this, Justice White concluded that "scant, if any, evidence exists that the First Amendment was intended to abolish the common law of libel."[26]

Likewise in *Roth v. United States*, Justice Brennan cited historical evidence showing that despite protection of freedom of speech by thirteen of fourteen state constitutions at the time the First Amendment was drafted, virtually all of these states had laws on the books banning obscenity, blasphemy, and profanity.[27] From this evidence, he concluded that "the unconditional phrasing of the First Amendment was not intended to protect every utterance."[28] This is a striking example of where very clear text— "Congress shall make no law. . . ."—is read as being qualified by historical understanding.

Recently, in *Locke v. Davey*,[29] the Court cited provisions in several state constitutions contemporaneous with the ratification of the United States Constitution that restricted the use of tax funds to support churches. The Court cited these provisions to bolster its conclusion that the Free Exercise Clause permitted states to exempt programs in devotional theology from state-funded scholarship grants.[30] In dissent, Justice Scalia responded that the provisions cited by the Court were off point because they prohibited targeted grants to religious institutions while the program in question involved an exemption to an otherwise broad-based and general scholarship program.[31] Regardless of who had the better argument on the relevance of these state constitutional provisions to the program before the Court, there seemed to be general agreement that if the analogy was sound, then these provisions would be of significant evidentiary value.

The presence of a provision in a contemporaneous state constitution might give rise to an inference to be drawn from its absence in the federal constitution. In *Harmelin v. Michigan*,[32] for instance, Justice Scalia joined by Chief Justice Rehnquist argued that the fact that the New Hampshire, Pennsylvania, and South Carolina constitutions contained provisions explicitly requiring that criminal sentences be proportional to the offense suggested that the framers of the Cruel and Unusual Punishment Clause did not mean to require proportionality without saying so.

C. Contemporaneous State Practice

In interpreting the meaning of the Fourteenth Amendment, contemporaneous state legislation or practice can provide some guidance as to the understanding of the framing generation.[33] For instance, in *Roe v. Wade*, Justice Rehnquist argued unsuccessfully in dissent that the concept of liberty in the Due Process Clause of the Fourteenth Amendment could not have been understood to include a right to abortion, given that in 1868, at the time the Amendment was ratified, thirty-six states prohibited abortion.[34] This would seem to be a fairly compelling evidence of the general understanding at the time if in fact the decision were to be driven by original understanding, which ultimately it was not.

In *U.S. Term Limits v. Thornton*,[35] the Court relied in part on contemporaneous state practice in concluding that the Constitution does not permit states to impose additional qualifications on congressional candidates. The Court pointed out that several states imposed term limits on state legislative candidates at the time of the ratification of the Constitution but made no attempt to do so with respect to congressional candidates.[36] This suggested to the Court that the states understood that they lacked the power to impose additional qualifications on federal candidates.[37] It also pointed out that those states with property qualifications for congressional candidates soon abolished them.[38] Justice Thomas, dissenting, responded that, as of the first election, five states did in fact impose property qualifications on congressional candidates, certainly indicating that they believed that they had the power to do so.[39] Thus the subsequent abolition was best regarded as a matter of policy as opposed to one of constitutionality. This was an instance in which competing plausible inferences could readily be drawn.

Interpretation of the Due Process Clause presents a particularly intriguing case for the use of contemporaneous source materials as the Constitution contains two Due Process Clauses added to the Constitution roughly eighty years apart. In *Munn v. Illinois*, in the course of defining the word *deprive* in the Due Process Clause of the Fourteenth Amendment, Chief Justice Waite pointed out that both in England "from time immemorial" and in the United States, the government had consistently regulated certain businesses affected with the public interest, including common carriers, inn keepers, and wharfingers.[40] This practice convinced the Court that such regulation pursuant to the police power did not constitute a "deprivation" of property without due process of law.[41] In a sense this was an instance of the Court relying on both pre- and post-enactment legislative practice to define the meaning of constitutional text as the Due Process Clause of the Fifth Amendment was enacted in 1791 while the Due Process Clause of the Fourteenth Amendment that the Court was construing was enacted in 1868. The English practice was pre-Fifth and Fourteenth Amendment. The American practice was post-Fifth Amendment but pre-Fourteenth Amendment. Because the Court presumed that the Due Process Clause of both amendments should be construed similarly, the post-Fifth Amendment practice was especially pertinent as it seemed to provide examples of regulation that apparently was not considered as having amounted to a deprivation under the very same language as would later appear in the Fourteenth Amendment.

Sometimes, because of relevant differences, contemporaneous state practice does not say much about the original understanding. As the Court pointed out in *McDaniel v. Paty*, although six of the original thirteen states disqualified clergy from holding at least some public offices, the relevance of this is severely undermined by the fact that the religion clauses of the First Amendment clearly did not apply to the states, and indeed several states at the time had established state churches.[42] As such, the plurality concluded that this evidence of early state practice was hardly conclusive,[43] and Justice Blackmun's concurrence found it to be wholly irrelevant.[44]

Likewise in his concurring opinion in *City of Boerne v. Flores*,[45] Justice Scalia argued that the fact that state legislatures prior to the enactment of the Free Exercise Clause may have provided significant protection for religious liberty might simply be evidence of what the framing generation considered good legislative policy as opposed to what it considered constitutionally required. It simply does not follow that the Free Exercise Clause was intended to enshrine these practices, especially as it would not even apply to the states.

D. Contemporaneous Congressional Practice

The Court has frequently drawn evidence of original understanding from legislation passed by the Congress of 1787 that was in session at the same time that the Constitution was being drafted, especially as some of the membership of Congress and the Constitutional Convention overlapped.[46] The Northwest Ordinance of 1787 has often been cited as providing insight into the meaning of various constitutional provisions. For instance, in his concurring opinion in *Charles River Bridge v. Warren Bridge*, Justice Baldwin contrasted the language protecting contracts in the Northwest Ordinance with that in the Contract Clause of the Constitution.[47] The provision in the Ordinance prohibited any law which "'shall in any manner interfere with, or affect, private contracts, or any agreements, bona fide and without fraud, previously formed.'"[48] Justice Baldwin noted that the substitution of the word *impair* in the Constitutional Clause may provide somewhat weaker protection than the Ordinance; however, the omission of *private* extends the protection further.[49] He concluded, however, that the changes in language were almost certainly conscious and as such shed light on constitutional meaning.

The Northwest Ordinance should be employed with some caution, however. Although there was overlap between the Constitutional Convention and the Congress that passed the Ordinance, the Ordinance was passed before the Constitution was ratified. As such, it cannot be considered a definitive guide to original understanding. However, it is significant that the Northwest Ordinance was reenacted by the First Congress and thus provides some guidance as to what the very first federal legislative actors following ratification believed that the Constitution required.[50]

In *Reynolds v. Simms*, for instance, in the course of arguing that the fact that the Constitution allocates two senators to each state does not mean that the framers approved of malapportionment of legislatures, the Court cited the fact that the Congress of 1787 provided for representation based on population in the Northwest Territory under the Northwest Ordinance.[51] This does support the Court's argument that the framers did not assume that the "federal analogy" would automatically apply at the territorial or state level. But it certainly does not establish that they believed that malapportionment was unconstitutional as opposed to unwise.

Just as the presence of Congressional practice in the framing era can give rise to an inference that the practice was constitutional, the absence of such a practice, at least to the extent that it is the type of practice that might have been expected could give rise to an inference that it was not constitutionally acceptable. In his opinion for the Court in *Printz v. United States*, Justice Scalia maintained that the fact that there is no evidence that early Congresses ever attempted to require state executive officials to aid in the implementation of federal programs indicates that they did not consider such a course of action to be constitutionally permissible.[52] Justice Scalia found this to be especially true, given that the Congress did impose certain obligations on state courts.[53] Obviously, the absence of a practice cannot possibly provide as strong a proof of the framing generation's belief of its unconstitutionality as its presence could of its constitutionality. As Justice Stevens pointed out in his dissenting opinion, Congress may have chosen not to utilize state executive employees either because it was not necessary or because it simply decided that it did not constitute sound policy even if it believed that there was no constitutional problem.[54]

The fact that the Congress authorized the appointment of legislative chaplains three days prior to its agreement on the final language of the Bill of Rights was taken by the Court in *Marsh v. Chambers* as strong evidence that opening a legislative session with prayer should not be considered to be inconsistent with the Establishment Clause.[55] In this instance, the evidence would indeed seem to be exceedingly strong because it is hard to imagine that Congress would sanction a practice that it almost immediately intended to render unconstitutional. Justice Brennan, dissenting, criticized the Court for placing too much weight on congressional practice at the time of the drafting of the Bill of Rights because these provisions did not become part of the Constitution until ratified by the states.[56] This is certainly correct. However, Justice Brennan was then forced to acknowledge that "[a]s a practical matter, 'we know practically nothing about what went on in the state legislatures' during the process of ratifying the Bill of Rights."[57] Still something is better than nothing, and as such the congressional history that is available should obviously carry far more weight than the nonexistent state ratification materials.

The proper interpretation of a constitutional provision might well be deduced from implementing legislation passed by the same Congress that drafted the provision. Justice Field made just such an argument in his dissenting opinion in *The Slaughter-House Cases*.[58] In support of the argument that the Thirteenth Amendment was intended to guarantee basic rights to all persons and not simply to prohibit racial discrimination or slavery, Justice Field quoted the Civil Rights Act of 1865 passed pursuant to the Thirteenth Amendment by the same Congress that drafted that Amendment. That act guaranteed the protection of a variety of rights against racial discrimination which indicated that the purpose of the Amendment was to provide protection against far more than slavery. This would seem to be a very compelling argument because the connection between the Amendment and the legislation was so close.

E. Early Congressional and Executive Practice

From the earliest days, the actions of the First Congress has been accorded great weight on questions of the original understanding of the Constitution, given that there was significant overlap between the Constitutional Convention and that Congress.[59] For instance, Justice Story invoked early congressional understanding in support of his conclusion that the Supreme Court could hear an appeal from a state supreme court's decision on a matter of federal law in *Martin v. Hunter's Lessee*.[60] He proclaimed that

> [i]t is an [sic] historical fact, that at the time when the judiciary act was submitted to the deliberations of the first congress, composed, as it was, not only of men of great learning and ability, but of men who had acted a principal part in framing, supporting, or opposing that constitution, the same exposition was explicitly declared and admitted by the friends and by the opponents of that system.[61]

Thus Justice Story made the point that the understandings of the First Congress are of great value not simply because of their proximity in time to the adoption of the Constitution but also due to the substantial overlap of participants. Making a similar argument in *Cohens v. Virginia*,[62] Chief Justice Marshall cited the Judiciary Act, noting that several of the members of the Congress that had passed it "were . . . eminent members of the Convention which formed the constitution." In *Lynch v. Donnelly*, the Court noted that "seventeen Members of that First Congress had been Delegates to the Constitutional Convention. . . ."[63] Two years later in *Bowsher v. Synar*, the

Court listed twenty members of the First Congress who had been delegates to the convention.[64]

Chief Justice Marshall began his landmark opinion in *McCulloch v. Maryland*[65] with an invocation of early legislative and executive practice. He noted that the power to create the Bank of the United States, the power challenged in *McCulloch*, "was exercised by the first congress elected under the present constitution."[66] Moreover, he observed that the act "did not steal upon an unsuspecting legislature" but "was completely understood, and was opposed with equal zeal and ability" and was then the subject of debate "in the executive cabinet, with as much persevering talent as any measure has ever experienced, and being supported by arguments which convinced minds as pure and as intelligent as this country can boast, it became a law."[67] Without explicitly naming them, Marshall made reference to the famous debate in President Washington's cabinet between Secretary of the Treasury Alexander Hamilton and Secretary of State Thomas Jefferson over the constitutionality of the First Bank of the United States Act. As Marshall pointed out, governmental action could scarcely carry a more impressive pedigree.

In addition in *McCulloch*, in the course of arguing that the word *necessary* in the Necessary and Proper Clause should be read flexibly to mean convenient rather than strictly to mean essential, Marshall noted that several well-established exercises of congressional power could only be justified under the latter reading, such as inferring a right to carry the mail and to punish theft of the mail from the clause permitting Congress "to establish post-offices and post-roads."[68] Thus Marshall took a practice that was presumably well accepted and reasoned backwards to illustrate that a more controversial exercise of power must also be justified.

In *Powell v. McCormack*, the Court declared that the "relevancy of [congressional practices, in that case exclusion of elected members] is limited largely to the insight they afford in correctly ascertaining the draftsmen's intent. Obviously, therefore, the precedential value of these cases tends to increase in proportion to their proximity to the Convention of 1787."[69] As a result, the Court placed great weight on congressional practice shortly after the Constitutional Convention and de-emphasized counterexamples that occurred seventy years later at the time of the Civil War.[70]

Actions by the early congresses and presidents play an important role in the debate on the Court over governmental acknowledgment or support of religion. In his dissenting opinion in *McCreary County v. ACLU*, Justice Scalia has emphasized that the First Congress instituted the practice of opening its session with legislative prayer.[71] The Congress authorized paid chaplains for the House and Senate the same week that it sent the Establishment Clause to the states for ratification.[72] The Congress asked the president to proclaim a day of thanksgiving and prayer the day after the First Amendment was proposed.[73] Shortly thereafter, President Washington offered the first Thanksgiving Proclamation.[74] The same Congress reenacted the Northwest Ordinance that authorized building of schools in the territory for the teaching of "[r]eligion, morality and knowledge."[75] Presidents Adams and Madison also offered Thanksgiving Proclamation, although Jefferson did not on the grounds that it would be inconsistent with religious freedom.[76] Justice Scalia concluded that "[t]hese actions of our First President and Congress . . . were not idiosyncratic; they reflected the beliefs of the period."[77] He also pointed to prayers or invocations of God in speeches or official correspondence by Presidents Washington, Adams, Jefferson, and Madison.[78] In *Wallace v. Jaffree*, Justice Rehnquist, dissenting, pointed out that Congress appropriated money to be spent on religious schools for Indians from the earliest congresses up until 1897.[79] Together, Justice Scalia and Justice Rehnquist have read these historical incidents as proof that the Court's principle requiring strict governmental neutrality toward religion was inconsistent with the original understanding of the Establishment Clause.[80]

However, Justice Souter, writing for the majority in *McCreary County v. ACLU*, cited contrary statements by Presidents Jefferson and Madison and drew the conclusion that the original understanding was inconclusive.[81] In response, Justice Scalia pointed out that unlike Justices Souter and Stevens,[82] he had relied on official statements that were at least contemporaneous with or subsequent to the drafting of the Establishment Clause.[83] By way of contrast, Justices Souter and Stevens relied on documents written prior to the drafting of the First Amendment, such as Madison's "Memorial and Remonstrance" or private letters written by former presidents.[84] Consequently Justice Scalia maintained that the public actions on which he had relied were better evidence of the original understanding of the Establishment Clause than the private and predrafting items relied on by Justices Souter and Stevens. Thus they had failed to show that the original understanding was inconclusive as they had claimed.[85]

One response to the recitation of historical examples to define the meaning of a constitutional provision is simply to argue that sometimes, even the framers violated the principles they had embodied in the Constitution. For instance, in his concurring opinion in *Lee v. Weisman*, Justice Souter responded to Justice Scalia's reliance on public prayers delivered by early presidents by first noting that some of them admitted they should not have done so but also contending that these practices indicate "at best, that the Framers simply did not share a common understanding of the Establishment Clause, and, at worst, that they, like other politicians, could raise constitutional ideals one day and turn their backs on them the next."[86] As another prominent example of such presidential and congressional "backsliding" in the founding era, he cited the passage of the Alien and Sedition Acts that are well recognized as violative of the freedom of speech and press.[87]

The dispute over the Sedition Act of 1798 enacted within the same decade as the First Amendment does indeed provide important information as to the original understanding of the guarantee of the freedom of speech. Under the law, criminal sanctions could be and were imposed on citizens for making false and defamatory statements about high governmental officials. However, it is not the enactment and enforcement of this law but rather its repeal and repudiation on which the Court has relied as evidence of the original understanding of the First Amendment. Writing in *New York Times v. Sullivan*, Justice Brennan argued that the quick repeal of the law by Congress with the repayment of the fines, the pardoning of those convicted by President Jefferson, and the condemnation of the act as inconsistent with the principles of freedom of speech by Madison, along with the resolution of the Virginia legislature condemning the act provide compelling evidence that the framing generation did not understand the First Amendment as authorizing prosecution for making false statements about government officials.[88]

This is a stunning example of how a reaction against contemporaneous legislation provided a more convincing picture of the original understanding than the initial legislation. Justice Brennan then used this original understanding to bolster his claim that strict civil liability for defamation of public officials was inconsistent with the freedom of speech in spite of the fact that up until the *Sullivan* case in 1963, the First Amendment had never been applied as a limitation on defamation law at all.[89] Justice Brennan's original understanding argument in Sullivan was clever but quite significant in its impact on constitutional law.[90]

F. Contemporaneous Judicial Understanding

The understanding of a constitutional provision by judges who ruled in close temporal proximity to the ratification of that provision may be taken as strong evidence of original understanding by a subsequent court.[91] In the *Slaughter-House Cases*, decided only four years after the ratification of the Fourteenth Amendment, the Court relied on its understanding of "events, almost too recent to be called history, but which are familiar to us all" in concluding that the central purpose of the Amendment was to establish freedom and protection for the recently freed slaves.[92] Nevertheless, with respect to the majority's narrow interpretation of the Privileges or Immunities Clause of the Amendment, the dissent charged that it had clearly misunderstood the recent original understanding of the framers and ratifiers.[93] Some seventy years later, the conclusion of the Court in the *Slaughter-House Cases* that privileges or immunities of United States citizens did not protect basic civil rights was accorded near conclusive weight by the Court in *Adamson v. California*.[94] As the *Adamson* Court put it, this was "the construction placed upon the amendment by justices whose own experience had given them contemporaneous knowledge of the purposes that led to the adoption of the Fourteenth Amendment."[95]

On the other hand, relying on the influential case of *Corfield v. Coryell*[96] in his dissent in *Saenz v. Roe*, Justice Thomas argued that the very same clause should in fact be understood to protect "fundamental rights."[97] He reasoned that in *Corfield*, decided some thirty-five years after the framing of the Article IV Privileges and Immunities Clause, Justice Bushrod Washington had captured the original understanding of that language, and that when the framers of the Fourteenth Amendment used similar language some forty years later, they were familiar with *Corfield*, referred to it, and meant to insert its conception of privileges and immunities as fundamental rights into the Fourteenth Amendment.[98] Thus relatively contemporaneous judicial construction of the Privileges and Immunities Clause of Article IV and of the Privileges or Immunities Clause of the Fourteenth Amendment have played a significant role in the understanding of the latter clause in the Fourteenth Amendment.

Similarly in *Cohens v. Virginia*,[99] in arguing that the Constitution did not prohibit the Supreme Court from granting review in cases from state supreme courts, Chief Justice Marshall cited the fact that state courts had almost unanimously accepted such review from the very outset. This provided significant though not conclusive evidence that the contrary position of Virginia was not supported by a sound construction of the Constitution.

In *Kilbourn v. Thompson*, after noting that many state constitutions contained speech and debate privileges similar to that in the federal constitution, the Court quoted from the 1808 case of *Coffin v. Coffin* an early Massachusetts decision construing that state's speech and debate privilege. It concluded that "[t]his is perhaps, the most authoritative case in this country on the construction of the provisions in regard to freedom of debate in legislative bodies and being so early after the formation of the Constitution of the United States, is of much weight."[100] Thus in its first significant interpretation of the Speech and Debate Clause, the Court placed heavy reliance on a state case interpreting an analogous state provision based on the belief that is was likely to be quite indicative of the original understanding.

The absence of litigation may also be of some relevance on the original understanding. In his concurring opinion in *City of Boerne v. Flores*,[101] Justice Scalia disputed Justice O'Connor's claim that there was a clear understanding that state constitutional and statutory protections of free exercise rights extended protection against burdens imposed by neutral and general laws. He argued that if this were so, it is quite surprising that there was not a single state or federal case enforcing free exercise rights against the application of such a law.[102]

G. Prominent Framers and Sources

The views of prominent framers often carry significant weight in assessing the original understanding of the Constitution. This is especially true of individuals such as Madison who played a major role in the drafting and ratification of the Constitution; Hamilton who authored several of the *Federalist Papers*; and Jefferson, who, though not a framer as such, was certainly one of the leading political thinkers of the time. However, Justice Brennan signaled a word of warning on this consideration in his dissenting opinion in *Marsh v. Chambers* where he noted that "members of the First Congress should be treated, not as sacred figures whose every action must be emulated, but as the authors of a document meant to last for the ages."[103] As such, "a proper respect for the Framers themselves forbids us to give so static and lifeless a meaning to their work."[104]

Likewise, statements made in the framing era, even by those involved in the drafting or ratification of a constitutional provision, may be of little relevance if there is reason to believe that they do not reflect a widely held understanding of the provision in question. For instance, in his concurring opinion in *Cutter v. Wilkinson*, Justice Thomas maintained that a quote from

Madison at the Virginia Convention to ratify the Constitution in 1788 arguing that the federal government may not regulate religion at all sheds no light on the meaning of the Establishment Clause drafted three years later.[105] As Justice Thomas noted, Madison was clearly addressing the question of limits of congressional power and not the as yet unproposed First Amendment.[106]

1. James Madison

As "the father of the Constitution" and as the moving force behind the Bill of Rights, the writings of Madison are almost always taken very seriously as evidence of original understanding.[107] As general background on the significance of the freedom of the press, the Court in *Near v. Minnesota* quoted extensively from Madison's assessment of the significance of the protection of the freedom of the press under state constitutions to the very survival of the young nation.[108] Madison's statements did not directly support the Court's specific conclusions but added flavor and pedigree to its general point that the freedom of the press was quite important.

Madison's famous "Memorial and Remonstrance" against the proposed renewal of the Virginia bill to support a state establishment of religion has played a crucial role in the understanding of the Establishment Clause of the First Amendment,[109] although its meaning has been subject to some debate by various justices. In *Rosenberger v. University of Virginia*, Justice Thomas, concurring,[110] and Justice Souter, dissenting,[111] each relied on the "Memorial and Remonstrance" but read it very differently. Focusing on specific parts of Madison's famous document as well as scholarly interpretations of it and various other actions taken by Madison, Justice Thomas argued that it was best understood as simply objecting to state financial aid that preferred some churches over others.[112] Justice Souter, emphasizing other parts of the "Memorial and Remonstrance" and relying on other scholarly interpretations, argued that the better reading rested on a principle of opposition to all financial aid to the religious mission of religious institutions and not simply nonpreferentialism.[113] A case can be and has been made for each approach, although the text of the "Memorial and Remonstrance" itself squares more readily with Justice Souter's reading. The debate illustrates, however, that the writings of someone like Madison can be as difficult to understand, if not more so, than the Constitution itself and as such may obscure as much as they clarify.

Silence by the likes of Madison or Jefferson may even be probative of original understanding. In his concurring opinion in *Walz v. Tax*

Commissioner, Justice Brennan observed that tax exemptions for churches were passed by Congress while Jefferson was president and by the Virginia General Assembly while Madison was a member, and neither of them commented on these acts.[114] For Justice Brennan this was evidence that they saw no conflict between such exemptions and the Establishment Clause. He argued that "[i]t is unlikely that two men so concerned with the separation of church and state would have remained silent had they thought the exemptions established religion."[115] Justice Brennan's inferences may be correct; however, inferences drawn from silence are always somewhat problematic because there are virtually always alternative explanations.

Several years later Madison did write an essay in which he contended that tax exemptions of churches did violate the Establishment Clause; however, Justice Brennan dismissed this as "an extreme view of church-state relations, which Madison himself may have reached only late in life."[116] In any event, "[h]e certainly expressed no such understanding of the Establishment during the debates on the First Amendment . . . [a]nd even if he privately held these views at that time, there is no evidence that they were shared by others among the Framers and Ratifiers of the Bill of Rights."[117] Justice Brennan is certainly correct in concluding that privately held views, even of Madison, tell little if anything of value about original understanding.

2. *Madison v. Hamilton*

As the two most prominent authors of the *Federalist Papers* and as two of the leading statesmen of the early republic, the views of Madison and Hamilton are taken seriously, but they did not always agree. When they disagreed, an interesting debate is presented in terms of the correct original understanding. *United States v. Butler* is a case in which the Court considered the conflicting views of the two. The question was whether the clause permitting Congress to tax and spend and "provide for the general welfare" limited Congress to taxing and spending to carry out powers otherwise set forth in Article I of the Constitution or whether providing for the general welfare was separate from the aggregation of the other enumerated powers. As the Court pointed out, Madison supported the former reading while Hamilton supported the latter.[118] Noting that Story agreed with Hamilton, the Court adopted his view.[119] The Court observed that Hamilton recognized that the term generally still imposed limits on what Congress could do.[120] Ultimately, the Court provided little more defense for its conclusion than simply concluding that the combination of Hamilton and Story trumps Madison. By ultimately deciding, however, that the Congress could not tax and spend to effectively regulate agriculture within a state as that extended beyond the reach of interstate commerce and invaded the reserved powers of the states,[121] the Court arguably came closer to the Madisonian view in the end. However, this was no longer the case once the Court rejected its narrow interpretation of the Commerce Clause a few years later.

In *Printz v. United States*, in the course of discounting Hamilton's views on the extent of national power, Justice Scalia argued that the *Federalist Papers* read with "'a split personality' on matters of federalism[,]" with Hamilton taking a more nationalistic and Madison taking a more state sovereignty oriented position.[122] This led Justice Scalia to argue that "[t]o choose Hamilton's view, as Justice Souter would, is to turn a blind eye to the fact that it was Madison's—not Hamilton's—that prevailed not only at the Constitutional Convention and in popular sentiment . . . but in the subsequent struggle to fix the meaning of the Constitution by early congressional practice. . . ."[123] This is an important reminder of the very real differences of opinion that existed in the times of the framers, especially between Madison and Hamilton. As such, it is hazardous to rely too heavily on the views of any one person no matter how prominent absent evidence that those views were widely shared.

3. Thomas Jefferson

As one of, if not the most respected members of the framing generation, and as an extremely prolific writer, statements by Jefferson are often cited as evidence of original understanding even though he played no direct role in the drafting or ratification of either the original Constitution or of the Bill of Rights. As such, his statements are often cited for their wisdom, or for the Jefferson pedigree, or as simply evidence of the general understanding at the time.[124]

No single statement made in a private letter has had such a profound impact on constitutional interpretation as Jefferson's statement in his letter to the Danbury Baptist Association that the First Amendment intended to erect "a wall of separation between church and state." The controversial history of this phrase is discussed in detail elsewhere in this book.[125]

In the course of concluding that the president enjoyed absolute immunity against civil liability for acts within the outer perimeter of his office, the

Court in *Nixon v. Fitzgerald* quoted Jefferson's letter to the prosecutor in trial of Aaron Burr where he wrote that

> [t]he leading principle of our Constitution is the independence of the Legislature, executive and judiciary of each other, and none are more jealous of this than the judiciary. But would the executive be independent of the judiciary, if he were subject to the *commands of* the latter, & to imprisonment for disobedience; if the several courts could bandy him from pillar to post, keep him constantly trudging from north to south & east to west, and withdraw him entirely from his constitutional duties?[126]

This colorful statement by Jefferson provided nice support for the majority's approach. Justice White, dissenting, was able to respond, however, that this was one of many issues on which Jefferson took somewhat contradictory positions at different times in his career.[127] However, the dissent relied on statements made by Jefferson with respect to separation of powers under the Virginia Constitution that quite obviously was not as pertinent as the majority's reliance on his position with respect to the U.S. Constitution.[128] In fact, ten years earlier in *Gravel v. United States*, the Court had relied on statements by Jefferson for the proposition that the privilege against arrest of members of Congress should be construed narrowly because "legislators ought not to stand above the law."[129]

However, Justice Brennan, dissenting in *Gravel v. United States*, quoted at great length a protest written by Jefferson in 1797 and forwarded to the Virginia House of Delegates, objecting to the investigation of several congressmen by a grand jury.[130] He characterized Jefferson's letter as the "most cogent analysis" of the privilege and argued that contrary to the Court's holding, it supported the conclusion that Senator Gravel was privileged in arranging for publication of the *Pentagon Papers*.[131]

4. Justice Story's *Commentaries on the Constitution*

Joseph Story was a justice on the Supreme Court and a professor at the Harvard Law School. He also wrote a multivolume treatise on the Constitution entitled *Commentaries on the Constitution* that remained the dominant academic exposition of the Constitution for at least the first half of the nineteenth century. The Court continues to take Story's treatise quite seriously as an important source for original understanding of the Constitution.[132]

For instance, in *Browning-Ferris Industries v. Kelco Disposal*, in the course of holding that the Excessive Fines Clause of the Eighth Amendment did not apply to punitive damages in a civil suit, the Court noted that "Justice Story was of the view that the Eighth Amendment was 'adopted as an admonition to all departments of the national government, to warn them against such violent proceedings as had taken place in England in the arbitrary reigns of some of the Stuarts,'" quoting Storey's Commentaries.[133] Thus at least in this context, the Court considered Story to be an authoritative source as to the original understanding of the framers of the Bill of Rights.

In *Nixon v. Fitzgerald*, in the course of concluding that the president was absolutely privileged against claims of liability when exercising authority within the "outer perimeters" of the presidential office, the Court quoted Justice Story's Commentaries for the proposition that "his person must be deemed, in civil cases at least, to possess an official inviolability."[134] The Court concluded that "Justice Story's analysis remains persuasive."[135]

In his concurring opinion in *Griswold v. Connecticut*, Justice Goldberg quoted from Story for the propositions that the Ninth Amendment was meant to refute the argument that "'the affirmance of certain rights might disparage others.'"[136] He then concluded that statements by Madison and Story showed that the framers did not intend for the first eight amendments to constitute an exclusive catalogue of constitutional rights, seemingly considering the views of Story as equivalent to those of Madison, the draftsman of the Ninth Amendment.[137]

In *New York v. United States*, the Court quoted Story's Commentaries for the proposition that the Tenth Amendment means "that which is not conferred, is withheld, and belongs to state authorities."[138] In this instance, reliance on Story added little to the analysis because the Court conceded that this had been its consistent understanding of the Amendment.[139] In *INS v. Chadha*, in the course of ascertaining the significance of Presentment and Bicameralism to the legislative process, the Court quoted Story for the proposition that absent a check on its will, a legislature will rarely consider a matter long enough to fully understand its implications, noting that Hamilton had made the same point in the *Federalist Papers*.[140]

In *Field v. Clark*,[141] the petitioners argued that the clause in Article I requiring each house to keep a journal of its proceedings that it would publish from time to time meant that a bill could not become law unless its passage was recorded in the respective journals. Relying on Justice Story's Commentaries, the Court rejected this reading on the ground that it was inconsistent with the purpose of the Journal Clause that was to ensure that legislative proceedings were publicized in order to protect against corruption and intrigue.[142]

As highly respected as Story was and is, his views do not always carry the day. In his treatise, he explicitly concluded that the original understanding of the Establishment Clause was to preclude the national government from preferring one Christian sect over another and not to prohibit a preference for Christianity over other religions or over nonbelief.[143] In *Wallace v. Jaffree*, the Court noted Story's position but rejected it as inconsistent with the principle of freedom of conscience that it had derived from the religion clauses.[144] Justice Rehnquist, dissenting, quoted Story as capturing the true understanding of the Establishment Clause.[145]

Likewise, in *Weems v. United States*, the Court rejected Story's conclusion that the Cruel and Unusual Punishment Clause was simply intended to ban those punishments condemned by the English Bill of Rights of 1688.[146] Upon studying Story's analysis of the issue, the Court concluded that "his citations do not sustain him."[147]

Responding to the majority's reliance on Story's Commentaries,[148] Justice Thomas, in his dissenting opinion in *U.S. Term Limits v. Thornton*, cautioned against giving Story's Commentaries undue weight on questions of original understanding.[149] He noted that

> Justice Story was a brilliant and accomplished man, and one cannot casually dismiss his views. On the other hand, he was not a member of the Founding generation, and his Commentaries on the Constitution were written a half century after the framing. Rather than representing the original understanding of the Constitution, they represent only his own understanding. In a range of cases concerning the federal/state relation, moreover, this Court has deemed positions taken in Story's commentaries to be more nationalist than the Constitution warrants.[150]

Thus Justice Thomas would use Story with caution as Justice Scalia had warned about using Hamilton.

5. Thomas Cooley's Constitutional Limitations

One of the most authoritative treatises of constitutional law during the latter half of the nineteenth century was Thomas Cooley's Constitutional Limitations.[151] Justice Rehnquist declared that "Cooley's eminence as a legal authority rivaled that of Story."[152] Indeed, Cooley published an influential update of Storey's Commentaries. The Court continues to rely on Cooley's treatise as an important source on original meaning, especially with respect to the Reconstruction Amendments as it was written much closer in time to those than to the original Constitution or the Bill of Rights.[153] The Court and various justices have relied on Cooley for his insight on the original understanding of the initial Constitution as well.[154] For instance, in District of *Columbia v. Heller*, Justice Scalia, writing for the Court, quoted Cooley at length for the proposition that the Second Amendment right to keep and bear arms was not limited to the protection of the use of arms with respect to militia service.[155]

II. Interpretive Issues Regarding Original Understanding

A. Unsourced Original Understanding

An appeal to original understanding or the framers often bolsters a constitutional argument. Frequently, justices will claim that a particular position reflects the views of the framers without any citation to originalist materials. Such claims about the original understanding may or may not be accurate; however, it is difficult for the reader who does not have an in-depth knowledge of the historical period in question to assess the claim in the absence of citations. It was common in the early days of the Court to claim support from the intent of the framers without citing any specific source. Chief Justice Marshall did this with great frequency. This practice is quite understandable, given that many if not most of the significant sources pertaining at least to the constitutional convention were not yet available, and Marshall and other early justices were not only contemporaries of the framers but in Marshall's case, for instance, participated actively in the ratification debates. Given such firsthand knowledge, they can be forgiven for their lack of specificity even though some of their claims with respect to original understanding may have reflected little more than their own preferences and opinions.

A sterling example of an argument seemingly based on claims of original understanding but with no citation whatsoever of source material is Justice Brandeis' famous concurrence in *Whitney v. California*[156] where he engaged in a brilliant and eloquent discussion of the values furthered by the freedom of expression. For several paragraphs he attributed virtually every claim that he made to the framers' constantly prefacing nearly every statement with "they believed" or "they recognized."[157] Justice Brandeis supported these many claims with nothing more than one footnote quoting Jefferson twice. As such, Brandeis' references to the framers, whether or not wholly accurate, would appear to be more of a rhetorical device than a serious claim about original understanding and presumably should be recognized as such by the readers. The *Whitney* concurrence is without question one of the most influential judicial opinions ever written on free speech theory and values. However, the impact of the opinion depends on the strength of Justice Brandeis' reasoning and rhetoric rather than his attribution of his claims to the founders.

Justice Frankfurter warned against the dangers of unsourced claims of original understanding in his opinion for the Court in *Minersville v. Gobitis*, noting that "[j]udicial nullification of legislation cannot be justified by attributing to the framers of the Bill of Rights views for which there is no historic warrant."[158] That is, if no source is cited for the claim, it is at least possible that the claim itself is false or at least misleading.

B. Original Understanding to Illuminate Purpose

Perhaps the most common use of original understanding is to illuminate the purpose of a constitutional provision.[159] It is frequently stated that constitutional language must be read in light of its purpose, and often that purpose is best gleaned from the original understanding of the provision. In *Maxwell v. Dow* the Court noted that

> [t]he safe way is to read [constitutional] language in connection with the known condition of affairs out of which the occasion for its adoption may have arisen, and then to construe it . . . to forward the known purpose.[160]

Thus in *Baldwin v. Seelig*, the Court recognized that "a chief occasion of the commerce clauses was 'the mutual jealousies and aggressions of the States, taking form in customs barriers and other economic retaliation[,]'" quoting the lower court and citing Farrand's *Records of the Federal Convention*, *The Federalist Papers*, Curtis's *History of the Constitution*, and Justice Story's *Treatise on the Constitution*.[161] This led the Court to reject the state's argument that it was applying its minimum milk price to a purchase from another state not to discriminate against interstate commerce but rather to ensure the economic health of its own milk industry.[162] In response to the state's contention, Justice Cardozo declared that

> [t]he Constitution was framed under the dominion of a political philosophy less parochial in range. It was framed upon the theory that the peoples of the several states must sink or swim together, and that in the long run prosperity and salvation are in union and not division.[163]

Thus with stirring rhetoric, Justice Cardozo transformed the recognized original understanding of the Commerce Clause into constitutional principle, relying on the well-accepted purpose of the Clause.

In the *Slaughter-House Cases*,[164] the Court concluded that "the one pervading purpose" of the post–Civil War amendments was "the freedom of the slave race, the security and firm establishment of that freedom, and the protection of the newly-made freeman and citizen from the oppressions of those who had formerly exercised unlimited dominion over him."[165] It based this on a short history of the events leading up to the passage of the Amendment that, as it noted, was "almost too recent to be called history, but which are familiar to us all."[166] Citing the *Slaughter-House Cases*, the Court again turned to the purposes animating the Fourteenth Amendment a few years later in *Strauder v. West Virginia*, leading it to conclude that the "spirit and meaning" of the Amendment to provide legal protection against racial discrimination to recently freed slaves should cause it "to be construed liberally."[167] Unfortunately, the Court strayed from this principle for the better part of a century thereafter.

In the foundational Establishment Clause case of *Everson v. Board of Education*, Justice Black discussed the history of religious persecution in England and the colonies, as well as the battle over religious liberty in Virginia in the mid-1780s for the purpose of divining the meaning of the Establishment Clause.[168] From this history he derived the principles that neither the federal or state government could:

> [s]et up a church . . . pass laws which aid one religion, aid all religions, or prefer one religion over another. . . . force nor influence a person to go to or to remain away from church against his will or force him to profess a belief or disbelief in any religion. No person can be punished for entertaining or professing religious beliefs or disbeliefs, for church attendance or non attendance. No tax in any amount, large or small, can be levied to support any religious activities or institutions . . . to

teach or practice religion . . . participate in the affairs of any religious organizations or groups or vice versa. . . .[169]

Justice Black closed his summary with the conclusion that "[i]n the words of Jefferson, the clause against establishment of religion by law was intended to erect 'a wall of separation between Church and State[,]'"[170] citing not to Jefferson's Letter to the Danbury Baptist Association from which the metaphor comes but rather to the Court's earlier decision in *Reynolds v. United States*.[171] Thus the concept of a "wall of separation between church and state" was introduced into modern Establishment Clause jurisprudence without any consideration of its historical context or for that matter whether it even did capture the essence of the more specific historical principles that Justice Black had previously set forth. No sooner had Justice Black introduced the "wall of separation" as an Establishment Clause metaprinciple than he concluded that state-funded bus transportation for children attending religious schools did not breach that wall because the state could neither favor nor disfavor religion.[172]

In *McCollum v. Board of Education*, the next Establishment Clause case to come before the Court, Justice Reed, dissenting, pointed to incidents in early American history, including Jefferson and Madison's acceptance of theology schools at the University of Virginia as evidence that the Establishment Clause was not intended to create total separation between church and state.[173] Thus from the outset of Establishment Clause jurisprudence, battle was joined over the proper lessons that history teaches about the original understanding of the purpose of the clause. That battle continues to rage on and off of the Court to this very day.

In *INS v. Chadha*, the Court cited the original understanding of the Presentment Clause as reflected in the Convention Debates, the *Federalist Papers*, and Justice Story's Commentaries on the Constitution to illustrate that "[t]he decision to provide the President with a limited and qualified power to nullify proposed legislation by veto was based on the profound conviction of the Framers that the powers conferred on Congress were the powers to be most carefully circumscribed."[174] In this instance, the meaning of Presentment and Bicameralism were quite clear. The Court employed originalist materials to illuminate the underlying purposes of the provisions in order to explain why a legislative veto would compromise that purpose that in turn would lead to the conclusion that it was unconstitutional.

In *Griswold v. Connecticut*, Justice Goldberg argued that the recognition of a fundamental right to privacy by the majority was supported by reference to the enigmatic Ninth Amendment rarely relied upon by the Court.[175] To make this argument, he needed to explicate the Amendment. Specifically, he needed to explain what type of rights was meant by "others retained by the people." To do this he turned to the purpose of the Amendment as explained by its draftsman James Madison.[176] He quoted Madison for the proposition that the Amendment was designed to meet the argument that rights which were not explicitly enumerated in the Bill of Rights would go unprotected by providing assurance that such an inference should not be drawn.[177] Consequently the "others" to which the Amendment referred were indeed rights of federal constitutional stature and not simply those rights previously recognized as a matter of state law. Despite this Madisonian pedigree, the Court has never taken up Justice Goldberg's challenge to give substance to the Ninth Amendment, perhaps for fear that it would be unable to develop a limiting principle.

C. Dueling Histories

Frequently, the majority and the dissent in an opinion will look at originalist materials and draw opposite conclusions.[178] In *Wesberry v. Sanders*,[179] for instance, the Court was faced with the question of whether the clause stating that representatives shall be elected by "the People of the several states" in Article I, section 2 means, as the majority held, that they must be elected on a basis of population equality ("one person, one vote") or whether it simply means that they are to be chosen by the people of the state in question as opposed to someone else, as Justice Harlan argued in dissent. Both the majority and Justice Harlan cited and quoted statements from the Philadelphia Convention as well as the ratification conventions in favor of their positions.[180] As Justice Harlan pointed out, many different and opposing views were expressed during these conventions and thus it is not difficult to sift through the records and pull out statements that appear to support one thing or another.[181] In this particular case, Justice Harlan's use of drafting and ratification history appeared to be more persuasive in that many of the majority's quotes are out of context and beside the point.[182] But the case does illustrate that resourceful lawyers and judges can often find support for their contentions in the originalist materials whether or not these statements actually capture the "original understanding" to the extent that it exists. It serves as a warning that when history is used to advocate a particular position or to support an argument, it may be deliberately or unconsciously misleading and should be assessed carefully.

In *Flast v. Cohen*,[183] the Court was faced with discerning the meaning of the terms *case* and *controversy* in Article III. At the outset, it noted that "those two words have an iceberg quality, containing beneath their surface simplicity submerged complexities which go to the very heart of our constitutional form of government."[184] The Court rejected Justice Frankfurter's earlier argument that *case* and *controversy* were defined by practices of the English courts of Westminster,[185] because those courts could clearly issue advisory opinions, and from the very outset it has been established by the Supreme Court that an advisory opinion would not qualify as a case and controversy.[186] The Court was not rejecting original understanding as a helpful methodology but rather asserting that Justice Frankfurter had clearly misunderstood the original understanding, given that in one of its earliest official acts the Court had explained to President Washington that it could not constitutionally issue advisory opinions.[187] That particular incident was in fact far more authoritative in establishing the original understanding of the terms than anything Justice Frankfurter had to offer in support of his theory.

In *City of Boerne v. Flores*,[188] Justices Scalia and O'Connor engaged in a lengthy debate over the meaning of the colonial and state Free Exercise provisions that predated the First Amendment. Justice O'Connor argued that the fact that several colonies and states enacted Free Exercise Clauses that protected religious liberty except where it was in conflict with public order indicated that the free exercise of religion was generally protected even when it was in conflict with neutral and general laws.[189] The public order type qualification would be unnecessary if a general law automatically prevailed over a Free Exercise claim,[190] as Justice Scalia, writing for the majority, had held in *Employment Division v. Smith*.[191] Justice Scalia interpreted these early enactments quite differently, however, arguing that they may well show that the framers of the First Amendment simply assumed that the very concept of Free Exercise was necessarily limited by neutral and general laws and as such they did not need to explicitly so state.[192] Consequently, the existence of these state laws does not clearly reveal the principle behind the Free Exercise Clause. Either inference is plausible, and as there is no proof as to why these qualifications were written, the justices essentially battled to a draw on the question of original understanding.

Stogner v. California[193] provides an example of vigorous debate between the majority and dissent over the significance of long, distant historical events.

The question in *Stogner* was whether a state statute reviving criminal charges where the statute of limitations had run constituted an Ex Poste Facto law barred by the Constitution. That led Justice Breyer, writing for the majority, and Justice Kennedy, responding in dissent, to engage in a protracted argument over the rationale for the attempt by the House of Commons to banish the Earl of Clarenden in 1667, as that event in turn was highly influential to the development of the constitutional concept of Ex Poste Facto. The majority argued that Parliament had added a new punishment, banishment to the crime of treason of which Clarendon was charged and convicted.[194] Justice Kennedy's dissent on the other hand maintained that Parliament actually changed the nature of the offense, convicting Clarendon of treason based on conduct that would not have qualified as treason at the time he engaged in it.[195] Each side marshaled historical material in support of its own position, and it is not possible for the nonhistorian to sort it out and determine for certain who had the better argument.

In the context of the case, however, Justice Breyer would seem to be correct in his contention that what mattered most was how Justice Chase understood the incident 150 years later (who in turn was acting on the assumption that the framers of the Constitution were familiar with and had relied on the incident) as opposed to what actually occurred, as it was his interpretation of its significance in *Calder v. Bull* that essentially defined the law of Ex Poste Facto.[196] So the event raises at least three separate historical questions: (1) What in fact happened to Clarendon?; (2) what did the framers of the Ex Post Facto Clause believe happened to Clarendon?; and (3) what did Justice Chase believe that the framers thought had happened to Clarendon? A reading of the point-counterpoint arguments of the majority and dissent on the Clarendon incident emphasizes how precarious and indeterminate reliance on history can sometimes be, especially when buried in the layers of complexity encountered in *Stogner*.

In several of its sovereign immunity decisions, the Court has argued that the original understanding of the Eleventh Amendment must be viewed as including an essential postulate of state sovereign immunity from suit in federal court significantly broader than the text of the Eleventh Amendment itself would suggest. In his dissenting opinions in both *Seminole Tribe of Florida v. Florida* and *Alden v. Maine*, Justice Souter argued that just as the Court misunderstood or ignored the plain text, so it misunderstood the original understanding or context as well. Contrary to the Court's conclusion that the sovereign immunity of the states was overwhelmingly accepted by the framing generation, that it was an "essential postulate," as the Court has put it, in fact sovereign immunity was a controversial concept by no means universally accepted at the time.[197]

In Alden, Justice Kennedy writing for the majority in turn replied that the Court's showing of support for sovereign immunity at the time of the framing of the Constitution was far stronger than Justice Souter's proof to the contrary.[198] Assuming that this was true, as it appears to be, the question then becomes to what extent should proof of conflicting views of the original understanding undermine reliance on such an understanding. It is no doubt a given that history will rarely if ever be clear and undisputed. If the Court demands certainty, it will almost never be able to establish the original understanding with respect to any constitutional provision.

Ordinarily a solid showing should suffice even if there is some evidence to the contrary. But there may be reason for a higher burden of proof here. Arguably the majority was not simply attempting to employ original understanding to define the meaning of the plain text but rather to contradict the plain meaning of the text, or at least to employ historical context to support a meaning that would otherwise be far from obvious. Consequently, Justice Souter argued that the proof of significant dispute as to the status of sovereign immunity destroyed any claim that it was in fact the type of unstated essential postulate on which the majority relied.[199] There is certainly some logic behind this argument. The recognition of "essential postulates" arguably in tension with the text itself should require a fairly compelling showing. Even so, the majority may nevertheless have satisfied that heavy burden although the dissent as well as the historians upon which it relies may disagree.

Nixon v. Fitzgerald[200] presents another excellent example of a debate on the Court over what the original understanding actually was. There the question to be resolved was the scope of presidential immunity from civil damage litigation and awards. Although the majority relied primarily on structural considerations to support absolute immunity with respect to acts within the outer perimeter of the presidential office, it cited originalist sources in support of this argument, though conceding that the materials regarding the framers' intent on this issue were fragmentary.[201] The dissent disputed the majority's reading of the materials it relied on and cited other originalist sources to the contrary, including remarks by Hamilton, Wilson, and Pinckney.[202] The Court responded by noting that

[H]istorical evidence must be weighed as well as cited. When the weight of evidence is considered, we think we must place our reliance on the contemporary understanding of John Adams, Thomas Jefferson, and Oliver Ellsworth.[203]

In other words, the Court concluded that our framers are more important than your framers.

One of the lengthiest and most detailed debates over the original understanding took place in *Pollock v. Farmers Loan and Trust Co.*[204] where the Court invalidated a federal tax on the income of a corporation from its real estate on the grounds that it was a direct tax not apportioned among the various states as required by Article I, section 2. The majority devoted sixteen pages to the original understanding of the meaning of a "direct tax," relying on the *Federalist Papers*; influential authors with whom the framers were familiar, including Turgot and Adam Smith; statements in the Constitutional Convention of Pinckney, Randolph, Patterson, Morris, Ellsworth, Wilson, and Gerry; debates in the ratifying conventions, including statements by Martin, Livingston, Ellsworth, King, Jay, Marshall, Randolph, Nicholas, and Madison; Madison's correspondence with Jefferson; and Gallations Sketches on the Finances of the United States.[205] From these sources, the Court drew several conclusions, the most important of which was that taxes on real estate, personal property, rents, or income were direct taxes requiring apportionment among the states.[206]

Justice White, dissenting, disagreed with the Court's conception of the original understanding of the framers and ratifiers, arguing that "they did not well understand, but were in great doubt as to the meaning of the word 'direct.'"[207] More important, however, he rejected the Court's preratification approach by focusing upon events that occurred shortly thereafter, including early Supreme Court litigation. Justice White argued the passage by Congress in 1794 of a tax on carriages despite Representative James Madison's contention that it was an unconstitutional direct tax constituted a complete rejection of the principle adopted by the Court and provided decisive proof that the framing generation in fact rejected that view as well.[208] Even more important, the constitutionality of the tax was thereafter sustained in *United States v. Hylton*,[209] with two justices who had been members of the constitutional convention voting to uphold it.[210] Justice White concluded that since *Hylton*, the approach contrary to that of the majority had become "a part of the hornbook of American constitutional interpretation, has been taught as elementary in all of the law schools and has never since been anywhere authoritatively questioned."[211] The majority attempted to distinguish *Hylton* as not having set down any general principle.[212] Ultimately, however, *Pollack* represents a classic battle over the original understanding, pitting an emphasis on preratification events versus an emphasis on postratification occurrences.

D. Revising History

Sometimes, the Court or at least one or more justices will determine that earlier conclusions about original understanding were incorrect. The question then becomes whether the Court should revise its understanding of original understanding or whether instead it must simply accept arguably incorrect historical conclusions as a matter of precedent. Justice Rehnquist confronted this issue in his dissenting opinion in *Wallace v. Jaffree*.[213] He examined the drafting history of the religion clauses and pointed out that Madison had inserted the word *national* before *religion* in the suggested language of the Establishment Clause that read "Congress should not establish a religion."[214] From this and other actions by Madison, Justice Rehnquist concluded that the Court in *Everson* was "demonstrably incorrect" in attributing to Madison a strong separationist approach when he served as the "architect" of the First Amendment even if he had held such a view several years earlier in the course of the religious controversies in the Virginia legislature.[215] Justice Rehnquist concluded that "stare decisis may bind courts as to matters of law, but it cannot bind them as to matters of history."[216]

In *Alden v Maine*, the majority and Justice Souter quarreled over whether prior opinions had in fact misunderstood the original understanding of the Eleventh Amendment. The majority in *Alden* provided a fair amount of historical support for its claim that the framing generation considered state sovereign immunity from citizen suits in federal court to be an essential postulate of the system created by the Constitution.[217] However, in response to Justice Souter's argument to the contrary, the Court in both *Alden* and earlier in *Seminole Tribe of Florida v. Florida* also argued that its position had been adopted by the Court over 100 years earlier in *Hans v. Louisiana*, and it was simply too late in the day to reopen the question.[218] Justice Souter responded that the original understanding is a matter of history, and it simply cannot be definitively resolved by prior judicial decisions.[219] If subsequent historians make the case that the Court's earlier historical conclusions are inaccurate, the Court should pay attention and if need be correct its errors. Justice Souter is certainly correct that the Supreme Court does not and cannot have the last word on history. Historians will always continue to discover, revise, synthesize, and correct. However, the Court is not attempting to have the final say on history but rather the final say on constitutional meaning that of course may be heavily be influenced by history. Getting it right is important to the judicial process but so is certainty and stability.[220] Stare decisis assumes that courts will make mistakes but that many of those mistakes are best left uncorrected. This should generally be true of historical interpretation as well as other forms of legal interpretation. Presumably there will be cases in which the need for stability is so great that it is worth perpetuating clear historical error by the Court. As long as the Court can still marshal strong historical evidence in support of its position in the Eleventh Amendment area, the existence of conflicting evidence, even if supported by a significant portion of contemporary historians, should not necessarily cause it to revisit its earlier conclusions. The Court is not a participant in an on going historical seminar. Justice Souter is correct that prior Supreme Court precedent is not a primary source of history, but it often must be the Court's primary source.

E. Original Understanding as a Method of Exclusion

Sometimes, original understanding materials are incapable of clearly defining what a constitutional provision was intended to mean but can be useful in explaining what it clearly did not mean. In other words, it can be useful as a method of exclusion. In *Williams v. Florida*, the Court confronted the question of whether the jury trial provision of the Sixth Amendment was understood by the framers as adopting the common law meaning of jury with the understanding that a jury be composed of twelve persons.[221] The Court worked through the drafting of the Sixth Amendment jury trial guarantee carefully, concluding that changes in language between the version sent by the House to the Senate and then sent back from the Senate to the House ultimately leading to Committee agreement on the final language of the Sixth Amendment indicated that the Senate meant to exclude some elements of the common law concept of jury, including trial in the "vicinage."[222] After reviewing the originalist evidence, the Court explained the following:

> We do not pretend to be able to divine precisely what the word 'jury' imported to the Framers, the First Congress, or the States in 1789. . . . [T]he most likely conclusion to be drawn is simply that little thought

was actually given to the specific question we face today. But there is absolutely no indication in the 'intent of the Framers' of an explicit decision to equate the constitutional and common-law characteristics of the jury.[223]

This is a text book example of the Court carefully using original understanding to eliminate at least one possible alternative meaning. Sometimes, that is the most that originalism can be expected to accomplish.

F. Inconclusive Original Understanding

Evidence of original understanding can often provide great enlightenment in the effort to discern constitutional meaning. But it will not always resolve difficult questions. *Brown v. Board of Education* (*Brown* I)[224] illustrates the limits of original understanding. After extensive briefing and oral argument devoted to the question of the original understanding of the Fourteenth Amendment and school segregation, the Court noted that while "these sources cast some light, it is not enough to resolve the problem with which we are faced."[225] The Court concluded that

> [at]t best, [the sources] are inconclusive. The most avid proponents of the post-War Amendments undoubtedly intended them to remove all legal distinctions among 'all persons born or naturalized in the United States.' Their opponents, just as certainly, were antagonistic to both the letter and the spirit of the Amendments and wished them to have the most limited effect. What others in Congress and the state legislatures had in mind cannot be determined with any degree of certainty.[226]

The Court then noted that it was not surprising that the original understanding was inconclusive on this point, given that public education itself was in its infancy.[227] Looking at the originalist materials surrounding the adoption of the Fourteenth Amendment, the Court recognized at least three things. First, it recognized that often there is a clear conflict in the intention or understanding of a constitutional provision. Thus although it is possible to find originalist material that supports one reading or a very different one, relying heavily on either as the correct reading presents an incomplete and misleading picture. Second, the Court recognized that often, a review of the existing source material falls short of telling us all we might like to know. As the Court pointed out, "what others . . . had in mind cannot be determined with any degree of certainty."[228] Finally, the Court recognized that original understanding materials will often have little if anything to say about an issue that is of great interest to the present generation, such as school segregation in *Brown*, but which was of little concern to those who drafted and ratified the Amendment.[229]

Likewise in the famous concurring opinion in *Youngstown Sheet and Tube v. Sawyer*, Justice Jackson recognized the limits of original understanding in the context of separation of powers, pointing out the following:

> Just what out forefathers did envision, or would have envisioned had they foreseen modern conditions, must be divined from materials almost as enigmatic as the dreams Joseph was called upon to interpret for Pharaoh. A century and a half of partisan debate and scholarly speculation yields no net result but only supplies more or less apt quotations from respected sources on each side of any question. They largely cancel each other.[230]

Justice Jackson recognized that originalist materials are often taken out of context and used to support preexisting positions rather than in an objective attempt to discover what the original understanding actually was. In addition, they simply do not tell us all we would like to know in order to fully comprehend the limits of a constitutional provision in our contemporary context.

In *McCreary County v. ACLU*, in response to Justice Scalia's appeal to original understanding in dissent, the Court, citing divergent opinions by influential members of the founding generation declared that "[t]he fair inference is that there was no common understanding about the limits of the establishment prohibition. . . ."[231] Instead, it concluded that "the evidence does show . . . a group of statesmen . . . who proposed a guarantee with contours not wholly worked out, leaving the Establishment Clause with edges still to be determined."[232] Obviously few constitutional provisions written at any level of generality are capable of resolving every issue at the outset. Some interpretation and honest disagreement will occur. On the other hand, disagreement at the time of the framing should not be taken to mean that nothing was decided and that the Court has complete freedom to interpret a provision however it sees fit. Presumably the provision in question meant something, or it would hardly have been worth including in the Constitution.

In interpreting the Cruel and Unusual Punishment Clause of the Eighth Amendment, the Court has relied on its historical antecedents, including the English Bill of Rights and the Virginia Bill of Rights. In his concurring opinion in *Furman v. Georgia*, effectively invalidating the death penalty procedures then in existence in all states that imposed capital punishment, Justice Brennan, concurring, attempted to minimize an historical approach to the provision on the ground that there is "little evidence of the Framers' intent in including the Cruel and Unusual Punishments Clause . . . in the Bill of Rights."[233] Justice Brennan discussed the two statements made by opponents of the clause during the House debate in some detail but concluded that aside from a prohibition of barbarous or torturous punishments, "we cannot know exactly what the Framers thought cruel and unusual punishments were."[234] This left Justice Brennan free to reject an "historical interpretation" that would have limited the prohibition to those punishments that were considered cruel and unusual at the time of the ratification of the Amendment and instead adopt an evolving-standards approach as the Court had essentially done as of the *Weems* case decided in 1910.[235]

G. Broad Principle v. Specific Conceptions

It is sometimes argued that it is crucial to discern broad principles from the original understanding as opposed to the framing generation's specific conceptions of what the constitutional provisions meant in their own times. The Court made this point in *Weems v. United States* where it wrote that

> Legislation, both statutory and constitutional, is enacted, it is true, from an experience of evils but its general language should not, therefore, be necessarily confined to the form that evil had theretofore taken. Time works changes, brings into existence new conditions and purposes. Therefore a principle, to be vital, must be capable of wider application than the mischief which gave it birth. This is particularly true of constitutions. They are not ephemeral enactments, designed to meet passing occasions . . . In the application of a constitution, therefore, our contemplation cannot be only of what has been, but of what may be. . . . [Otherwise] [i]ts general principles would have little value, and be converted by precedent into impotent and lifeless formulas. Rights declared in words might be lost in reality.[236]

This statement from *Weems* is a classic and elegant recognition of the need of law in general and constitutions in particular to set forth principles at a relatively high level of generality. This follows the lead of Chief Justice Marshall in his classic opinion in *McCulloch v. Maryland*, where he wrote that a constitution by "[i]ts nature requires, that only its great outlines should be marked" and that the details be worked out over time.[237]

In attempting to discern the original understanding of constitutional text, the fact that the framers and ratifiers may not have had a specific case or factual situation in mind certainly does not mean that it cannot be covered by the language in question. Chief Justice Marshall recognized this in *Trustees of Dartmouth College v. Woodward* when he observed that

> It is not enough to say, that this particular case was not in the mind of the convention, when the article was framed, nor of the American people, when it was adopted. It is necessary to go further, and to say that, had this particular case been suggested, the language would have been so varied, as to exclude it, or it would have been made a special exception.[238]

In his classic dissent in *Olmstead v. United States*, Justice Brandeis relied on this principle, arguing that the Fourth Amendment should be construed to protect against means of evading privacy that did not exist in the framers' day such as wiretapping.[239] Forty years later when in *Katz v. United States*, the Court finally accepted Justice Brandeis' position, overruled *Olmstead*, and held that wiretapping did in fact constitute a search, Justice Black responded in dissent that although the framers were unfamiliar with electronic surveillance, they were quite familiar with eavesdropping and yet elected to employ language in the Fourth Amendment that did not readily cover it.[240] This can be viewed as an example of the issue of the levels of abstraction at which historical concepts are viewed. As the level of abstraction increases in generality, so does the likelihood of protection. If the question is whether the framers specifically intended to cover electronic surveillance, the answer must be no because the technology was at that time nonexistent. If the question is whether they meant to cover eavesdropping, Justice Black at least would still argue no as they were aware of it and used language that did not seem to encompass it. If on the other hand the framers intended to cover any means by which privacy might be invaded as the majority concluded, then the electronic surveillance of telephone conversations falls within the ambit of the Fourth Amendment. As such, in cases like *Katz*, the level of abstraction appears to be outcome-determinative.

And yet there does not seem to be an accepted method for determining which level of abstraction is correct.

In his concurring opinion in *Abington Township v. Schempp*, Justice Brennan conceded, based on historical materials, that Madison and quite possibly Jefferson as well did not consider school prayer to be inconsistent with the Establishment Clause[241] He argued, however, that "an awareness of history and an appreciation of the aims of the Founding Fathers do not always resolve concrete problems."[242] Rather he maintained that the question should be whether "the practices here challenged threaten those consequences which the Framers deeply feared."[243] The task of the Court according to Justice Brennan is "to translate the majestic generalities of the Bill of Rights, conceived as part of the pattern of liberal government in the eighteenth century, into concrete restraints on officials dealing with problems of the twentieth century."[244] Thus under this approach to originalism, the Court "must limit itself to broad purposes, not specific practices."[245]

The Court followed up with this approach in *Wallace v. Jaffree*.[246] There, it reversed a district judge's conclusion that the Establishment Clause was intended only to prohibit preferences among religions and was not intended to prohibit a preference by state governments of religion over nonreligion.[247] The Court conceded that this may have been the original understanding of the Establishment Clause, quoting Joseph Story's *Commentaries on the Constitution* for that proposition.[248] Despite the Court's respect for Justice Story's scholarship, however, it concluded that such a view was inconsistent with the broad principle that it had previously recognized under that clause.[249] It argued that a failure to respect the beliefs of the nonreligious as well would be inconsistent with a principle prohibiting coercion of belief central to its understanding of both of the religion clauses.[250] Despite Joseph Story's position, the Court could maintain that its principle was hardly inconsistent with the original understanding because it found some support in Madison's famous "Memorial and Remonstrance."[251] This is a case in which the Court made it clear that it would be quite willing to rely on the abstract principle that it had derived in order to reject a specific application that the framing generation presumably had endorsed.

Finally, in *Rice v. Cayetano*, where the Court held that limiting voting rights based on ancestry rather than race violated the Fifteenth Amendment, it noted that although the Amendment was passed "to guarantee emancipated slaves the right to vote . . . the Amendment is cast in fundamental terms transcending the particular controversy which was the immediate impetus for its enactment."[252] In other words, the principle or concept was significantly broader than the context that gave rise to it. This is an instance where the Court found that the broader purpose of the Amendment transcended not simply its original context (protecting the voting rights of recently freed slaves) but its specific language as well.

H. Taking Account of Change

Given the enormous societal changes that have occurred since the framing of the Constitution as well as many of its significant amendments, historical understanding cannot necessarily be transposed effortlessly into the modern world. Justice Jackson recognized this in his famous opinion in *West Virginia Board of Education v. Barnette* where he explained that

> [t]he task of translating the majestic generalities of the Bill of Rights, conceived as part of the pattern of liberal government in the eighteenth century, into concrete restraints on officials dealing with the problems of the twentieth century, is one to disturb self-confidence. These principles grew in soil which also produced a philosophy that the individual was the center of society, that his liberty was attainable through mere absence of governmental restraints, and that government should be entrusted with few controls and only the mildest supervision over men's affairs. We must transplant these rights to a soil in which the laissez-faire concept or principle of non-interference has withered at least as to economic affairs, and social advancements are increasingly sought through closer integration of society and through expanded and strengthened governmental controls. These changed conditions often deprive precedents of reliability and cast us more than we would choose upon our own judgment. But we act in these matters not by authority of our competence but by force of our commissions.[253]

In this quotation Justice Jackson attempted to capture the difficulty of transporting legal principles through time. He used two different metaphors to describe the task—that of translation and of gardening (i.e., transplanting into different soil). The use of these metaphors as well as his explicit expression of self-doubt help to convey both the ill-defined nature of the process itself as well as the degree to which it is guided by judicial discretion. Although Justice Jackson perceived the task as a judicial duty to be confronted rather than avoided, he did caution that it must be approached with a fair degree of humility.

Because of societal change, practices that were significant to the framers of the Constitution may be less relevant today. For instance, in his dissent in *Duncan v. Louisiana*, Justice Harlan argued that the right to jury trial in criminal cases should not be regarded as essential to the protection of liberty as it was in colonial times given that

> [w]e no longer live in a medieval or colonial society. Judges enforce laws enacted by democratic decision, not by regal fiat. They are elected by the people or appointed by the people's elected officials, and are responsible not to a distant monarch alone but to reviewing courts, including this one.[254]

As such, the principal rationale for the criminal jury protection from "a tyrannous judiciary–has largely disappeared."[255] This is hardly to suggest that the right to jury trial is anachronistic or irrelevant but rather that the nature of the threat that it was designed to guard against may have changed somewhat and that should be taken into account in construing it.

The Court's emphasis on the growth and expanded significance of education in the modern world in *Brown v. Board of Education* is yet another notable example of it taking account of major societal changes, especially with respect to the role of public education in society since the time that a constitutional provision was drafted and ratified.[256] The Court noted that in the South at the time of the framing of the Fourteenth Amendment, public education was almost nonexistent, especially for black children, and in the north it was still quite different than as of the time of *Brown*.[257] It observed that "[a]s a consequence, it is not surprising that there should be so little in the history of the Fourteenth Amendment relating to its intended effect on public education."[258] The Court then concluded that "we cannot turn the clock back to 1868 when the Amendment was adopted" but rather "must consider public education in the light of its full development and its present place in American life throughout the Nation."[259] It then explained in a frequently quoted paragraph how "[t]oday, education is perhaps the most important function of state and local governments."[260] Thus according to the opinion, the extreme changes in the role of public education over the period of about a century was one of the driving forces behind the Court's decision in *Brown*.

I. Unacceptable Outcomes

One argument that is sometimes raised against originalism is that it can lead to results that are simply unacceptable in the modern world. Justice Stevens offered this argument in his dissent in *Van Orden v. Perry*[261] in response to the opinion of Chief Justice Rehnquist for the plurality in that case,[262] and Justice Scalia in dissent in the companion case of *McCreary County v. ACLU*[263] that religious acknowledgment by public officials is not inconsistent with the original understanding of the Establishment Clause. Justice Stevens argued that the framing generation did not believe that religious liberty should be extended to non-Christians, nor did it believe that the principles of the Establishment Clause should apply against the states.[264] He argued that these views are highly inconsistent with contemporary understanding of religious liberty and as such discredit the original understanding of the Establishment Clause as a source of interpretive authority.[265] Justice Stevens also contended that Justice Scalia's argument that the framers endorsed acknowledgment of a monotheistic God should not be accepted as a guiding principle because the historical record indicates that they in fact limited their extension of religious concern to a Christian God; a view that would clearly "eviscerate the heart of the Establishment Clause."[266]

Essentially, Justice Stevens argued that the specific original understanding should be rejected because it is inconsistent with well-established and sound constitutional principle settled by decades of precedent. Justice Scalia responded by citing George Washington's Letter to the Hebrew Congregation of Newport, Rhode Island, stating that "[a]ll possess alike liberty of conscience and immunities of citizenship."[267] The arguments raised by Justice Stevens acknowledges that there will be occasions when the original understanding, at least at a relatively specific level, is so out of place with contemporary values that it simply must be ignored or rejected even where the constitutional provision in issue has not been amended or altered. If this is so, it is likely to be the exception and not the rule. Justice Stevens argued that that is what in fact occurred in *Brown v. Board of Education* despite the fact that the Court there dismissed the original understanding as inconclusive.[268]

ⅢⅢ III. Conclusion

Original understanding is clearly a staple technique of constitutional interpretation. Intuitively, proof that the framing generation understood a constitutional provision to carry a certain meaning or, alternatively, exclude a particular meaning is worthy of serious consideration. Debate exists over how much weight should be given to evidence of original understanding, at least if other methods of interpretation point in a different direction. The Court has considered a wide variety of sources for evidence of original understanding, including English and colonial history, the constitutional drafting and ratification process, contemporaneous state and federal legislation, public debate, the writings of prominent individuals, and state and federal practice following ratification. Each of these presents its own particular interpretive problems that the Court has addressed over time. Moreover the search for original understanding raises a variety of issues, including the problem of incomplete history, historical conflict, societal evolution, and choice of the appropriate level of abstraction. The Court has confronted and discussed each of these issues although they are not necessarily capable of final resolution. As with textual analysis, once the Court has mined the original understanding in the first few cases interpreting a particular provision, precedent, and doctrine may predominate in analyzing it from then on. However, there are certain areas in which the originalist materials are so rich and complex, such as the religion clauses, the Eleventh Amendment, and the separation of powers, that the debate on the Court over the meaning and significance of the original understanding continues decade after decade.

FIVE

Tradition and Practice

※ I. Introduction

In a variety of contexts, the Court has relied upon tradition and practice as one method of providing meaning to certain constitutional provisions. In this context, tradition refers to patterns of behavior that have been accepted and acted upon socially and culturally and are generally embodied in law, be it legislative or judicial. Practice refers to the way in which governmental bodies, whether legislative, executive, or judicial, have responded to a particular constitutional provision; that is, essentially how they have interpreted it through their actions over time. There can be a variety of sources for discovering and evaluating tradition and practice, but for the Court's purposes in interpreting the Constitution, the embodiment of tradition and practice, either in government action or inaction, is by far of the greatest significance. Evidence of tradition and practice is used in several different ways. In certain areas, especially separation of powers, evidence that the Congress or the Congress and the president have over a lengthy period of time acted in a certain manner with respect to a particular constitutional provision may provide solid evidence as to the correct understanding of that provision. If this practice extends back to the framing generation, such practice may be understood as strong evidence of the original understanding. If not, it may still be taken seriously as the proper interpretation developed by those governmental bodies charged with acting pursuant to that provision on a regular basis.

There are certain constitutional provisions for which tradition and practice have played an especially significant role. Perhaps most prominently among these would be the religion clauses where there is extensive evidence of tradition and practice over time, often dating back to the drafting and ratification and beyond. This evidence is often relied upon very heavily by the Court or individual justices to show the original understanding of the provision, the accepted and settled understanding of the provision by the American people and their institutions, or in some instances, it is used to argue that principles and doctrines developed by the Court are incorrect in that they are in conflict with longstanding and widely shared tradition and practice.

Evidence of tradition and practice is used in a somewhat different way in interpreting the concept of due process of law. There, the Court has long taken the position that, to a significant extent, the concept of Due Process, especially the meaning of the term *liberty*, is properly defined by tradition and practice. That is, whether a right under due process is recognized as fundamental may turn on whether it is a right that has a lengthy historical tradition behind it. As such, in this area, evidence of tradition plays a far more dominant role than elsewhere in constitutional interpretation.

The consideration of tradition and practice as a significant methodology of constitutional interpretation gives rise to other important issues. First, at what level of abstraction should tradition and practice be considered? The more general the level at which a tradition is described, the more conduct or practice it is likely to encompass. Consequently determining the proper level of generality is crucial. This is an issue with which the Court has struggled over time. Second, given that tradition and practice changes over time, does that suggest that constitutional meaning should change as well? Does this mean that at least in some areas we have an evolving or living Constitution as is sometimes argued?

This chapter will address several of these issues. First it will consider the role of long and continuous federal legislative and executive practice. Next it will use the Establishment Clause decisions as a case study of the role played by state and federal practice and tradition in interpreting a specific constitutional provision with strong historic roots. Then it will focus on the relatively unique questions raised with respect to due process where the Court has long held that tradition and practice is often determinative of the meaning of the constitutional concept. The chapter will also consider the issue of the level of generality at which tradition should be considered, along with question of whether, like tradition, the constitution should be viewed as a living or evolving document. Along the way various other issues regarding tradition and practice will be discussed.

II. Long and Continuous Federal Executive or Legislative Practice

A. Practices Extending to the Time of the Framing

A practice engaged in by Congress and or the Executive at the time of the framing will be treated by the Court as providing strong evidence of the original understanding. A long-sustained practice that does not date back to the inclusion of the provision in the Constitution will still generally provide significant proof that the practice in issue is settled and should be considered constitutional.

If challenged action has been part of a longstanding practice extending back to the times of the framers, the Court is likely to award it an especially strong presumption of constitutionality.[1] As the Court put it in *United States v. Curtiss-Wright Exporting Co.*, "[a] legislative practice . . . evidenced not only by occasional instances, but marked by the movement of a steady stream for a century and a half of time, goes a long way in the direction of proving the presence of unassailable ground for the constitutionality of the practice."[2] At the very outset of his opinion in *McCulloch v. Maryland,*[3] Chief Justice Marshall observed that the Act incorporating the Bank of the United States "was introduced at a very early period of our history, has been recognised [sic] by many successive legislatures, and has been acted upon by the judicial department, in cases of peculiar delicacy as a law of undoubted obligation."[4] He also noted that after the original act had expired, it was reenacted.[5] The case was decided only three decades after the ratification of the Constitution and the action by the first Congress to which Marshall referred, but he considered that a more than sufficiently entrenched and respected legislative and executive practice.

Likewise in *Gibbons v. Ogden*, Marshall explained that the power over navigation "has been exercised from the commencement of the government, has been exercised with the consent of all, and has been understood by all to be a commercial regulation."[6] Although Marshall made this point quite briefly, he did note that the practice had existed since the very outset and had been without dissent or controversy. It is unclear whether these qualifications were essential conditions to reliance on practice or simply persuasive facts.

In *Stuart v. Laird,*[7] the Court brushed aside a challenge to the practice of Supreme Court justices riding circuit with the observation that

[the] practice and acquiescence under it for a period of several years, commencing with the organization of the judicial system, afford an irresistible answer, and have indeed fixed the construction. It is a contemporary interpretation of the most forcible nature. This practical exposition is too strong and obstinate to be shaken or controlled.[8]

Here the existence of the practice (eliminated not too long thereafter) for a mere fifteen years was deemed to be conclusive of its constitutionality.

A single instance of a practice may also be of some probative value as well. In *Gibbons v. Ogden*,[9] Marshall relied on the fact of a commercial embargo by Congress (obviously Jefferson's infamous embargo of 1807 of Britain) as evidence that it was well accepted that commerce included navigation.[10] If it did not, then what would have been the source of the congressional power to impose the embargo, given that Marshall argued that it was not a war time measure?[11] He pointed out that although it was challenged on other constitutional grounds, no one argued that it was unconstitutional because Congress had no right to regulate navigation pursuant to the commerce power.[12] Essentially, Marshall was saying that the failure to raise a Commerce Clause based challenge to the embargo shows that the argument would have been rejected if it had been raised. Otherwise, he would simply be citing one arguably unconstitutional act in support of another. The argument may well correctly capture the understanding at the time of the dispute over the Embargo Act; however, as presented, it does involve a fair amount of speculation on Marshall's part.

In *Cooley v. Board of Wardens*, the Court noted that the federal laws regulating pilotage, like the one before the Court,

> have existed and been practised [sic] on in the states since the adoption of the federal Constitution [citing such a law passed by the First Congress in 1789] and that this contemporaneous construction of the Constitution since acted on with such uniformity in a matter of much public interest and importance, is entitled to great weight, in determining whether such a law is repugnant to the Constitution. . . .[13]

Thus the Court relied on the fact that (1) the practice had the blessing of the very First Congress, providing fairly strong evidence of original understanding; (2) there has been a lengthy and consistent legislative adherence to the tradition involving both state and federal legislation; and (3) it had involved a matter of some importance and thus presumably had been well considered. Near the end of its opinion, the Court argued that this lengthy legislative practice also gave rise to the concern that dire consequences would flow from a rejection of this tradition in that sixty years of now illegally collected pilotage fees might well have to be repaid.[14] The Court acknowledged that if the constitutional violation was sufficiently clear, then this was a cost that would simply have to be borne.[15] However, the imposition of such cost and inconvenience would be worthy of consideration in a close case.[16]

And in *Carroll v. United States*, in the course of upholding the search of a car for contraband where probable cause was present but there was no search warrant, the Court explained that

> contemporaneously with the adoption of the Fourth Amendment we find in the First Congress, and in the following Second and Fourth Congresses, a difference made as to the necessity for a search warrant between goods subject to forfeiture, when concealed in a dwelling house or similar place, and like goods in course of transportation and concealed in a movable vessel where they readily could be put out of reach of a search warrant.[17]

The Court then noted that Congress had passed similar legislation in 1815, 1822, and 1899, noting that Congress had recognized the distinction in question from the outset up through the present and that this was entitled to substantial weight in construing the meaning of the Fourth Amendment. Not only was this a long-standing practice, but the fact of consistent reenactment gave it particular weight in that the Court could assume that it had not simply been passed early on and then forgotten.

Recently, in the course of upholding a twenty-year extension of copyright terms to those who were currently protected by copyright, the Court in *Eldred v. Ashcroft*[18] relied on "an unbroken congressional practice of granting to authors of works with existing copyrights the benefit of term extensions." Moreover, the Court pointed out that this practice was followed by the very First Congress when it passed the Copyright Act of 1790.[19] Ultimately, the Court concluded that the unbroken congressional practice from the founding generation on refuted the petitioner's argument that the Copyright Term Extension Act's recent extension of existing copyright fails as a matter of law to promote the purpose behind the Copyright Clause.[20]

These cases confirm that longstanding congressional or executive practice can carry significant weight in establishing the constitutionality of a challenged practice.

B. Separation of Powers and Congressional Practice

The Court has long been especially deferential to continuous legislative and or executive practice as evidence of the constitutionality of such practices in the area of separation of powers. This may be because the text itself is often somewhat vague on these matters, and as the other branches are also under a constitutionally imposed oath to carry out their duties pursuant to the Constitution, long-engaged practices within their own domain should be seen as reflecting careful consideration. In *Youngstown Sheet and Tube .v Sawyer*,[21] perhaps the Court's leading separation-of-powers decision, Justice Frankfurter, concurring, made the case for the significance of accepted practice to constitutional understanding in the area of separation of powers. He wrote the following:

> [D]eeply embedded traditional ways of conducting government cannot supplant the Constitution or legislation, but they give meaning to the words of a text or supply them. It is an inadmissibly narrow conception of American constitutional law to confine it to the words of the Constitution and to disregard the gloss which life has written upon them. In short, a systematic, unbroken, executive practice, long pursued to the knowledge of the Congress and never before questioned, engaged in by presidents who have also sworn to uphold the Constitution, making as it were such exercise of power part of the structure of our government, may be treated as a gloss on "Executive Power" vested in the President by section 1 of Art. II.[22]

Justice Frankfurter argued that historical practice can place a "gloss" on the text of the Constitution; however, the criteria he imposed were high. The practice must be (1) long standing, (2) unbroken, (3) pursued with knowledge of the Congress, and (4) never before questioned. If these conditions are taken seriously, such a historical gloss will be the exception and not the rule. Justice Frankfurter attached a lengthy appendix to his opinion analyzing every purported instance of the presidential use of emergency power in American history and concluded that these examples failed to meet the criteria he had set forth.[23] He did not require that the practice extend back to the days of the founding, however.

Chief Justice Vinson, dissenting in *Youngstown*, also believed that long-standing tradition could provide constitutional justification for presidential action. He detailed many instances of the exercise of emergency power without prior congressional approval by several presidents, including Washington, Adams, Jefferson, Jackson, Lincoln, Wilson, and Franklin D. Roosevelt.[24] Unlike Justice Frankfurter, however, Chief Justice Vinson did in fact believe that these examples were sufficiently analogous to President Truman's seizure of the steel mills to provide constitutional support for that action.[25] Chief Justice Vinson obviously did not hold historical practice to the same demanding standards as Justice Frankfurter.

In *Okanogan v. United States*, the *Pocket Veto Case*,[26] the Court held that a bill returned by the president when Congress was in adjournment did not become law. In so holding, the Court relied on the fact that of the 119 bills returned by presidents during adjournments from the Madison administration to the present case, none had become law.[27] That provided powerful evidence that a return during adjournment did not comply with the Constitution, a result which the Court reached on other grounds as well. In an area involving consistent congressional practice over a lengthy period of time, such evidence should indeed have been all but conclusive.

Likewise, in concluding that it did not violate separation of powers for Congress to place federal judges on the Federal Sentencing Commission, the Court in *Mistretta v. United States* detailed and relied on the history of judicial appointments to nonjudicial commissions and tasks dating back to the earliest days of the republic.[28] This "200 year tradition of extrajudicial service," though these practices were not without controversy, provided strong evidence that it did not violate separation of powers.[29] This is yet another example of the weight that the Court will often give to long-standing congressional practice in the area of the separation of powers.

C. Serious Legislative or Executive Consideration

The Court shows greater respect for a legislative or executive practice if these branches have seriously considered the constitutional issues raised by it. For instance, in *McCulloch v. Maryland*, Chief Justice Marshall pointed out that "[t]he Bill incorporating the Bank of the United States did not steal upon an unsuspecting legislature, and pass unobserved."[30] Rather "its principle was completely understood"[31] and was vigorously debated in both Congress and in the cabinet prior to its passage. Although the Court always reserves the right to pass final judgment on constitutionality, it has accorded greater deference to legislation that has received serious constitutional scrutiny by the other branches of government.

Similarly, in *Rostker .v Goldberg*,[32] in the course of upholding a congressional decision not to require women to register for the draft, the Court took account of the fact that Congress had considered the issue very carefully, although it is not clear from the Court's discussion that Congress had thought about the constitutional implications.

※ III. Long-standing Practice and the Establishment Clause

Long-standing executive and legislative practice, both at the federal and state levels, has played a very significant role in the interpretation of the Establishment Clause. One reason for this is simply because there is a great amount of seemingly relevant material with respect to tradition and practice for the Court to draw upon. In part this is because the Establishment Clause was enacted against a rich historical context with respect to the freedom of religion. Many incidents pertaining to religious practice and government predated and immediately followed the ratification of the First Amendment, rendering them relevant to questions of the original understanding. Moreover, as the Court's Establishment Clause jurisprudence essentially begins with *Everson v. School Board* in 1946, practice and tradition was able to develop for a century and one half absent judicial influence. Finally, at least some of the doctrines that the Court did develop from *Everson* on appear to be inconsistent with well-established tradition and thus give rise to the use of such tradition as counterargument by dissenters. Consequently evidence of tradition and practice has played a major role in interpretation of and argument over the meaning of the Establishment Clause.

In his dissenting opinion in *Engel v. Vitale*, one of the Court's earliest decisions in the area, Justice Stewart argued that Establishment Clause jurisprudence should be guided not by "the history of an established church in sixteenth century England or in eighteenth century America, but the history of the religious traditions of our people, reflected in countless practices of the institutions and officials of our government."[33] He then provided a lengthy recital of religious acknowledgment in American history. He noted that the Court had begun its session with "God Save the United States and this Honorable Court" dating back to the days of Chief Justice Marshall.[34] The daily sessions of both houses of Congress begin with prayer.[35] Every president from Washington through Kennedy had "upon assuming his Office asked the protection and help of God."[36] "The Star Spangled Banner" was made the national anthem by an Act of Congress and contains a stanza invoking God.[37] The Congress added the phrase "under God" to the Pledge of Allegiance in 1954.[38] In 1952, Congress passed legislation asking the president to proclaim a national day of prayer each year.[39] "In God We Trust" has appeared on coins since 1865.[40] Justice Stewart then argued that theses practices as well as the Regents prayer at issue in *Engel* did not establish a state religion in violation of the First

Amendment but rather "recognize and . . . follow the deeply entrenched and highly cherished spiritual traditions of our Nation. . . ."[41]

Writing for the majority in *Lynch v. Donnelly*, Chief Justice Burger also emphasized this lengthy history, including the proclamation of thanksgiving, the appointment of chaplains, and the opening of congressional sessions with prayer, creating national holidays for Thanksgiving and Christmas, placing "In God We Trust" on coins and "under God" in the Pledge of Allegiance, the placing of religious art in public art galleries and representations of the Ten Commandments in the Supreme Court's chamber, and proclamations of National Days of Prayer.[42] Thus as of *Lynch*, reliance upon this lengthy catalogue of public acknowledgments of God in one context or another was endorsed by the Court in the course of upholding a practice against challenge and not simply by dissenters objecting to the majority's approach.

Objecting to the Court's use of various public acknowledgments of religion in his dissenting opinion in *Lynch v. Donnelly*, Justice Brennan argued that the Court should only take account of the history and traditions surrounding the particular practice in issue as opposed to analogous practices.[43] He went on to argue that there was no long-standing acceptance of public celebration of Christmas as a religious holiday and that in fact "the development of Christmas as a public holiday is a comparatively recent phenomenon;" he provided a detailed discussion of that history.[44] He pointed out that Christmas was not made a public holiday until the middle of the nineteenth century, and nativity scenes did not become common until the later part of the nineteenth century.[45] Consequently, he concluded that "there is no evidence whatsoever that the Framers would have expressly approved a Federal celebration of the Christmas holiday including public displays of a nativity scene."[46] Nor has there been a showing that support for such public displays "extends throughout our history."[47] Consequently, the tradition was simply not long enough, according to Justice Brennan, to be of value in understanding constitutional meaning.

More recently, in the course of upholding the constitutionality of a Ten Commandments monument placed on the grounds of the Texas State Capitol in *Van Orden v. Perry*, Justice Rehnquist, writing for a plurality of the Court, cited a congressional resolution in 1789 asking President George Washington to issue a Proclamation of Thanksgiving as well as the subsequent Proclamation itself.[48] Justice Rehnquist also cited several examples of depictions of the Ten Commandments on government buildings in Washington, D.C., including within the Supreme Court's own courtroom.[49]

He explained that "[t]hese displays and recognitions of the Ten Commandments bespeak the rich American tradition of religious acknowledgments."[50] This history illustrated that a display of the Ten Commandments can have historical as well as religious significance and as such can coexist with the Establishment Clause.[51] Justice Rehnquist did not apply any recognized doctrinal test in upholding the Ten Commandments monument, and the significance of tradition and history to the outcome remained murky.

Justice Souter, in dissent, argued that all of the other Ten Commandments monuments or depictions in Washington, D.C., cited by Justice Rehnquist were readily distinguishable in that the text was not legible at all, only the nonreligious commandments were presented, or Moses, or the commandments were surrounded by secular laws or law givers.[52] Justice Stevens, dissenting in *Van Orden*, challenged the reliance on historical antecedents on the ground that there were a number of significant historical events pointing in the opposite direction, including the refusal of President Jefferson to issue a Thanksgiving Proclamation on the ground that doing so would violate the Establishment Clause.[53] He also responded that the instances cited by Chief Justice Rehnquist only served to illustrate that those "who drafted and voted for a text are eminently capable of violating their own rules."[54] The Souter and Stevens dissents in *Van Orden*, like the Brennan dissent in *Lynch*, maintained that evidence of tradition, though not irrelevant, must be employed with some precision to ensure that it truly supports the practices at issue before the Court.

The fact that a particular law is widespread throughout the states may provide some evidence that it has been and is considered consistent with the Constitution.[55] In his concurring opinion in *McGowan v. Maryland*, Justice Frankfurter pointed out that forty-nine states have at least some form of Sunday closing law, and thirty-four have fairly broad Sunday closing laws.[56] In addition, the fact that many of these had been repeatedly reenacted provided at least an inference that they were not simply remnants of a time when the purpose of such laws was predominantly religious in nature. Justice Frankfurter also noted that Sunday closing laws had been challenged as violating religion clause of state as well as the federal constitution for over 150 years, and with the exception of one state court case subsequently overruled, the challenges had all been rejected.[57] He explained that even though the Court must make its own independent judgment on constitutionality, "this does not mean that we are indifferent to the unanimous opinion of generations of judges who, in the conscientious discharge of obligations as solemn as our own, have sustained the Sunday laws as not inspired by a religious purpose."[58] This was a powerful tradition-based argument in favor of the constitutionality of a practice that the Court did in fact sustain.

In deciding that property tax exemptions for churches (and other public service oriented institutions) did not violate the Establishment Clause, the majority in *Walz v. Tax Commission* emphasized the long and continuous congressional practice of enacting such exemptions starting in 1802.[59] Justice Burger conceded that "no one acquires a vested or protected right in violation of the Constitution by long use, even when the span of time covers our entire national existence and indeed predates it."[60] Nevertheless, he recognized that "an unbroken practice of according the exemption to churches, openly and by affirmative state action, not covertly or by state inaction, is not something to be lightly cast aside."[61] The Court pointed out that tax exemptions were provided in all fifty states often as part of the state constitutions.[62] If anything, Justice Brennan, often a critic of reliance on tradition and practice, concurring, put even more emphasis on the lengthy history and tradition of tax exemptions for churches.[63] He also recognized that tradition, no matter how rooted, was not conclusive.[64] He contended, however, that

[t]he more longstanding and widely accepted a practice, the greater its impact upon constitutional interpretation. History is particularly compelling in the present case because of the undeviating acceptance given religious tax exemptions from our earliest days as a Nation. Rarely if ever has this Court considered the constitutionality of a practice for which the historical support is so overwhelming.[65]

Justice Brennan then provided an even more detailed review of the history of legislative approval of property tax exemptions for churches than had Chief Justice Burger.[66] His argument, like that of Justice Frankfurter in *McGowan*, gained strength from the pervasiveness and near unanimity of the practice. The following year in *Lemon v. Kurtzman*, the Court cited the fact that there was no similar lengthy history of state-supported salary supplements for teachers in parochial schools in the course of invalidating such programs under the Establishment Clause.[67] Thus just as the presence of a lengthy tradition in the Establishment Clause area may bolster its constitutionality, so can the absence of tradition undermine it.

The Court relied almost exclusively on history and consistent practice in *Marsh v. Chambers*[68] in sustaining the constitutionality of a legislative prayer by the chaplain of the Nebraska legislature. The Court pointed out that prayers opening legislative sessions began with the Continental Congress and have been employed by Congress since the very First Congress.[69] This led the Court to conclude that "[i]n light of the unambiguous and unbroken history of more than 200 years, there can be no doubt that the practice of opening legislative sessions with prayer has become part of the fabric of our society" and as such was constitutional.[70] Thus *Marsh* is an example of a case in which the history of the practice played a dominant if not decisive role.

Although widespread societal acceptance of a practice arguably provides some evidence of its constitutionality, it does not always carry the day. In his dissenting opinion in *McCreary County v. ACLU*, the companion case to *Van Orden v. Perry*, Justice Scalia argued that historical and traditional acknowledgment in American society of a single God coupled with the fact that "Christianity, Judaism, and Islam—which combined account for 97.7% of all believers [in the United States] are monotheistic" and that all three religions honor the Ten Commandments indicate that acknowledgment of these practices by the government "cannot be reasonably understood as a government endorsement of a particular religious viewpoint."[71] The majority in *McCreary* rejected this view,[72] as did Justice O'Connor, concurring, who wrote that "we do not count heads before enforcing the First Amendment" and "[t]here is no list of approved and disapproved beliefs appended to the First Amendment—and the Amendment's broad terms ('free exercise,' 'establishment,' 'religion') do not admit of such a cramped reading."[73] Consequently, the question of whether proof of tradition or practice is strong enough to vouch for its constitutionality is always a matter to be decided in the context of the specific case, and there will be instances in the Establishment Clause where evidence of tradition and practice will be overridden by other considerations such as accepted principle and doctrine. Moreover, there continues to be a dispute on the Court over how precisely analogous the practice in question must be in order for it to be relevant. In addition, there will be instances in which the Court determines that a lengthy historical practice is simply too inconsistent with contemporary values.

IV. Tradition and the "Public Forum" Doctrine

The Court's First Amendment public forum doctrine is yet another area in which it has relied quite heavily on tradition in order to construct and apply constitutional doctrine. This doctrine is central to the determination of the extent to which speakers may utilize government property as a means or venue for propagating their messages In his plurality opinion in *Hague v. CIO*, Justice Butler provided the foundation for what has since become known as the First Amendment "public forum" doctrine with his conclusion that

> [w]herever the title of streets and parks may rest, they have from time immemorially been held in trust for the use of the public and, time out of mind, have been used for purposes of assembly, communicating thoughts between citizens, and discussing public questions. Such use of the streets and public places, has from ancient times, been a part of the privileges, immunities, right and liberties of citizens.[74]

The entire explanation provided for the right of the people to freely use the streets and sidewalks for expressive activity was grounded in history and tradition. Following *Hague*, over the next several decades, the Court consistently ruled that speakers and protestors had a right to use traditional public forums such as streets, sidewalks, and parks for expressive activity; however, the state had the power to impose reasonable time, place, and manner regulation on such use.[75]

After having decided several "public forum cases," the Court set forth a doctrinal framework for deciding these cases in 1983 in *Perry Educ. Assn. v. Perry Local Educ. Assn.*[76] It divided instances in which speakers attempted to use government property for speech-related activity into three possible categories—traditional public forums, dedicated public forums, and nonpublic forums, with a strong First Amendment right of access in the first two but not in the third.[77] The determination of whether government property would be characterized as a traditional public forum would turn on whether it had continuously been used for expressive activities as first recognized in *Hague*.[78] The Court concluded that teacher mail boxes had not been so used traditionally nor had the school dedicated them to wide-open use for expressive purposes; therefore, they did not qualify as a public forum under either category.[79]

Despite criticism, the Court has continued to rely on tradition in order to determine whether governmental property qualifies as a traditional public forum. Writing for a plurality in *International Society for Krishna Consciousness v. Lee*,[80] Chief Justice Rehnquist concluded that an airport terminal did not qualify as a traditional public forum. He reasoned that "given the lateness with which the modern air terminal has made its appearance, it hardly qualifies for the description of having 'immemorially . . . time out of mind' been held in the public trust and used for purposes of expressive activity."[81] He also concluded that this would follow even if the focus were on "the rather short history of air transport."[82] In addition, Chief Justice Rehnquist rejected the argument that in examining tradition the Court should focus on "transportation nodes" including bus and train stations as opposed to airport terminals alone.[83] He noted that comparison to other transportation facilities would be misleading because many were privately owned, and more importantly they each bore unique characteristics affecting the degree of regulation that was appropriate, such as the greater need for security at airports.[84] Consequently, the plurality applied and defended a narrowly focused historical approach.

Justice Kennedy, concurring in part in the judgment, challenged the Court's reliance on history to define traditional public forums, noting that even the "quintessential" public forums such as streets, sidewalks, and parks have primary uses other than speech and thus would not qualify for protection if the analysis was applied literally.[85]

Justice Kennedy argued that by limiting traditional public forums to types of government property long utilized for expressive purposes, the Court would unduly constrict the types of venues available for public speech in an increasingly mobile and insular society.[86] Thus Justice Kennedy would extend "public forum status to other forms of property, regardless of their ancient or contemporary origins and whether or not they fit within a narrow historic tradition" if the use for public speech was compatible with their ordinary functions.[87] This led Justice Kennedy to conclude that airport terminals were public forums.[88] Justice Souter, dissenting, expressly agreed with Justice Kennedy's critique of traditional public forum analysis.[89] The public forum cases are illustrative of an area in which tradition has and continues to play a dominant role in analysis and yet has come under fierce attack in dissent. The dispute highlights the obvious weakness of a heavily tradition-based approach, that is, that it can be unresponsive to significant societal change and in the process undermine the very constitutional provision that is employed to interpret it.

✄ V. Tradition and Practice and Due Process

The Due Process Clause presents a somewhat singular example of the role of tradition in constitutional interpretation in that the Court has long taken the position that tradition as well as social evolution must play a significant role in defining what due process and the concept of protected liberty mean. In other words, tradition is not simply evidence that may occasionally prove helpful in understanding constitutional meaning. Rather with respect to due process, it is a primary source of defining that meaning.[90] As Justice Holmes put it early in the twentieth century in *Jackman v. Rosenbaum*:

> The Fourteenth Amendment, itself a historical product, did not destroy history for the States and substitute mechanical compartments of law all exactly alike. If a thing has been practiced for two hundred years by common consent, it will need a strong case for the Fourteenth Amendment to affect it. . . .[91]

The Court has relied heavily on tradition in two separate but related areas under the Due Process Clause. Throughout the first half of the twentieth century, the Court frequently consulted tradition and practice as embodied in state law as a significant means of determining what Process was Due under the Fourteenth Amendment in state criminal proceedings. The question was often posed whether a particular procedural guarantee in the Bill of Rights was sufficiently fundamental to be incorporated against the states under the Fourteenth Amendment. In the second half of the twentieth century, the Court relied on tradition and history again largely to the extent that it was embodied in positive law to determine whether particular aspects of liberty were fundamental and thus accorded a high level of protection as a matter of substantive due process. Although the two questions were different, the methods analysis, especially with respect to the consideration of tradition, were quite similar.

A. Tradition and Incorporation

Throughout most of the first half of the twentieth century, at least into the 1960s, a majority or at least a solid plurality on the Court followed the fundamental fairness approach in determining whether a Bill of Rights provision was applicable to the states under the Fourteenth Amendment. Under this approach, recognition of the significance of the right historically by various organs of government played a prominent role in the determination.

In *Twining v. New Jersey*,[92] one of the earliest incorporation decisions, the Court cited a wide array of historical sources as evidence of constitutional significance, including the Magna Carta (1215), the Petition of Right (1629), the English Bill of Rights (1689), colonial charters, the Stamp Act Congress (1765), the Declaration of Rights of the Continental Congress (1774), and the Ordinance for Governance of the Northwest Territory. In addition, the Court might look to the amendments suggested by state ratifying conventions or state constitutions.[93] To some extent these sources would provide evidence of the original understanding, but they also spoke to long-standing tradition and practice that the Court took quite seriously in fleshing out the concept of Due Process.

During the period prior to the incorporation of most of the provisions of the Bill of Rights against the states in which the Court applied a fundamental fairness approach to determine whether a particular state practice violated due process of law under the Fourteenth Amendment, the Court paid close attention to whether most states mandated the practice in question. In *Betts v. Brady*,[94] for instance, the Court held that appointment of counsel was not required in a noncapital felony case after an exhaustive survey of state law concluded that the great majority of the states permitted but did not require the appointment of counsel in such cases.[95]

Justice Frankfurter, writing again for the Court, made a similar showing in *Wolf v. Colorado*[96] in concluding that the exclusionary rule was not a constitutionally required remedy for an unreasonable search and seizure in a state criminal proceeding. Justice Murphy, dissenting, argued that the Court should not "decide due process questions by simply taking a poll of the rules in various jurisdictions."[97] Several years later in *Mapp v. Ohio*,[98] when the Court overruled *Wolf* and applied the exclusionary rule to the states, Justice Clark, writing for the majority, maintained that the weight of state authority was not crucial to the resolution of the issue but did point out that half of the states that had rejected the rule as of *Wolf* had now adopted it.

Near the end of the incorporation debate, a solid plurality of the Court adopted the selective-incorporation approach under which all of the specifics of a particular guarantee would apply against a state if the guarantee was deemed to be fundamental. This approach was set forth most comprehensively in *Duncan v. Louisiana*.[99] In determining that the right to jury trial was fundamental and hence must be incorporated against the states, the Court relied on its historical pedigree, citing the Magna Carta, the English Declaration of Rights, Blackstone, the First Continental Congress, the Declaration of Independence, various provisions of the Constitution, original state constitutions as well as current state constitutions.[100] But the Court did not rest on tradition and history alone. If anything, it placed even greater weight on the functional role that the jury places in the American system of criminal justice by providing a buffer of protection between the accused and the potential for abuse by the state in a criminal case.[101] Thus by the end of the incorporation debate, the purpose served by the provision had eclipsed historical tradition as the most significant factor in determining whether it was fundamental. In his dissent in *Duncan*,[102]

Justice Harlan, generally a proponent of tradition-based analysis in the due process area, was critical of what he believed to be the Court's overreliance on history and tradition in determining that the right to jury trial in a criminal case applied to the states, arguing that the fact that a practice was "old" was insufficient reason to impose it on the states. By the early seventies, the Court had in fact incorporated almost all the provisions of the Bill of Rights against the states, and this important debate came to an end.

B. Tradition and Substantive Due Process Liberty

Tradition analysis has played a central role in modern substantive due process analysis since its origin in the early sixties to the present. Perhaps the most significant and influential argument in favor of the use of tradition-based analysis as a method of interpreting the meaning of liberty within the Due Process Clause appeared in Justice Harlan's dissent in *Poe v. Ullman* where the Court refused to hear a case challenging a Connecticut law subsequently invalidated in *Griswold v. Connecticut*[103] criminalizing the use of contraceptives. In the course of arguing that the Court should decide that case on the merits, Justice Harlan maintained that history and tradition provided an objective means of determining the extent to which various aspects of "liberty" are protected by the Due Process Clause of the Fourteenth Amendment.[104] He reasoned thus:

> Due process has not been reduced to any formula; its content cannot be determined by reference to any code. The best that can be said is that through the course of this Court's decisions it has represented the balance which our Nation, built upon postulates of respect for the liberty of the individual, has struck between that liberty and the demands of organized society. If the supplying of content to this Constitutional concept has of necessity been a rational process, it certainly has not been one where judges have felt free to roam where unguided speculation might take them. The balance of which I speak is the balance struck by this country,

having regard to what history teaches are the traditions from which it developed as well as the traditions from which it broke. That tradition is a living thing. A decision of this Court which radically departs from it could not long survive, while a decision which builds on what has survived is likely to be sound. No formula could serve as a substitute, in this area, for judgment and restraint.[105]

In the following paragraph, in the course of rejecting the notion that due process liberty was limited to the application of the Bill of Rights provisions to the states, Justice Harlan explained that

[t]he character of [Constitutional provisions] must be discerned from [their] larger context. And inasmuch as this context is one not of words, but of history and purposes the full scope of [that] liberty . . . cannot be found in or limited by the precise terms of the specific guarantees elsewhere provided in the Constitution. This "Liberty" is not a series of isolated pin points pricked out in terms of [various constitutional provisions]. It is a rational continuum which broadly speaking, includes a freedom from all substantial arbitrary impositions and purposeless restraints.[106]

A few years later, Justice Harlan incorporated the reasoning of his *Poe* dissent by referencing it into his concurring opinion in *Griswold v. Connecticut.*[107] In *Poe* and *Griswold*, he argued that it was not inappropriate for judges to exercise discretion in defining due process liberty. In other words, judging requires the exercise of judgment. But it is channeled judgment. In response to critics such as Justice Black who argued that substantive Due Process analysis inevitably leads to judges imposing their own value preferences through the balancing process,[108] Justice Harlan relied upon tradition and history to provide a sufficiently objective benchmark. Still he made it quite clear that tradition is not static but rather evolving, and only those aspects of tradition that survive the continual winnowing process of history are worthy of consideration by the Court.

Applying this tradition-based analysis to the Connecticut law that made it a crime for anyone including a married couple to use contraceptives, Justice Harlan concluded that such a law cut too deeply into the "private realm of family life."[109] Because "the intimacy of husband and wife is necessarily an essential and accepted feature of the institution of marriage, an institution which the State not only must allow, but which always and in every age it has fostered and protected,"[110] the state may not intrusively regulate that intimacy. Over time, Justice Harlan's emphasis on tradition and history became the central focus of substantive due process analysis.[111]

Eight years after *Poe* in *Roe v. Wade*, Justice Blackmun set forth a lengthy history of abortion regulation from ancient times to the present. It was not entirely clear what the point of this history was, but presumably he was arguing that the prohibition on abortion was not as strict in the past as it had become from the nineteenth century on, and that throughout most of human history, the reason for prohibition was protection of the health of the mother rather than protection of the life of the fetus.[112] If so, Justice Blackmun's use of history and tradition was at most only partially successful. He certainly was not able to establish that there had been a long tradition of permissive abortion but rather at best that the prohibitions were not as strict in the past as in the present.[113] This scarcely amounted to the type of deep-seated societal protection that Justice Harlan spoke of in his *Poe* dissent. And the state certainly has the right to shift its reason for abortion regulation from one ground to another.

The Court continued to refine its tradition-based analysis of substantive due process liberty in *Washington v. Glucksberg*, where it held that there was no constitutionally protected right of assisted suicide.[114] There, the Court cited the fact that "[i]n almost every State—indeed, in almost every western democracy—it is a crime to assist suicide"[115] in the course of rejecting a constitutional challenge to the prohibition. The Court characterized these laws as "longstanding expressions of the States' commitment to the protection and preservation of all human life," pointing out that the common law had taken this position "for over 700 years."[116] This a classic instance of widespread state authority as testament to the significance of the state interest. In determining whether a right is fundamental and therefore highly protected, the majority in *Glucksberg* emphasized that first such a right must be "found to be deeply rooted in our legal tradition" and second it must be carefully described.[117] Thus *Glucksberg* appeared to establish tradition as a crucial element in the definition of fundamental rights under due process.

Justice Souter, concurring, argued that the Court should follow Justice Harlan's *Poe* analysis that he believed authorized the Court to explicitly balance the importance of individual liberty against state interest.[118] The majority replied that it had never endorsed the Harlan *Poe* approach as the proper mode of analysis.[119] The Court scarcely needed to distance itself from Justice Harlan's analysis in *Poe*, however, because, if anything, an emphasis on history and tradition was as consistent if not more so with that approach than Justice Souter's balancing approach. The balancing of interests that Justice Harlan spoke of in *Poe* was to occur within the very context of tradition and history rather than apart from it, as Justice Souter seemed to suggest. To read Justice Harlan's opinion as endorsing an interest-balancing approach divorced from history and tradition seems in direct conflict with his attempt to answer Justice Black's charge that the substantive Due Process analysis was not unduly subjective through its reliance on tradition and history. Thus properly understood, *Glucksberg* was the logical exposition of Harlan's tradition-oriented approach.

The justices disagreed over the significance of tradition in two cases addressing the constitutionality of state laws criminalizing homosexual sodomy. In 1986 in *Bowers v. Hardwick*, the Court declined to find that a right of homosexual sodomy was "'deeply rooted in this Nation's history and traditions' and thus a highly protected aspect of Due Process liberty."[120] The Court cited the fact that sodomy was a criminal offense in all thirteen states at the time the Bill of Rights was ratified, in thirty-two of thirty-seven states when the Fourteenth Amendment was ratified, and in all fifty states as recently as 1961.[121] In his concurrence, Justice Burger made the same point, citing Roman law, Western Christian tradition, and Blackstone.[122]

The dissenting justices in *Bowers* objected to what they considered to be the Court's unduly narrow characterization of the right in question as a right to engage in homosexual sodomy. Justice Blackmun would have characterized it as a right to privacy or "intimate associations"[123] and Justice Stevens would have analyzed it as a right to engage in "intimate relations."[124] This debate over the appropriate level of generality at which a right is defined will be discussed in the next section of this chapter. Both dissents objected to the amount of weight that the majority placed upon tradition. Justice Blackmun explained that "I cannot agree that either the length of time a majority has held its convictions or the passion with which it defends them can withdraw legislation from the Court's scrutiny."[125] Likewise, Justice Stevens argued that the cases established that "the fact that the governing majority in a State has traditionally viewed a particular practice as immoral is not a sufficient reason for upholding a law prohibiting the practice. . . ."[126]

Eighteen years later in *Lawrence v. Texas*, a case which overruled *Bowers*, the majority cited historical material that contended that the traditions that the Court had relied on in *Bowers* pertained to sodomy in general and not homosexual sodomy as the Court had seemed to suggest and were enforced only against public as opposed to private acts.[127] It also maintained that the laws targeting same-sex acts are of relatively recent origin.[128] Ultimately the *Lawrence* Court did not completely reject the conclusions about tradition and history relied on in *Bowers* but concluded that the history was "more complex," "not without doubt and, at the very least ... overstated" in *Bowers*.[129] Justice Scalia, dissenting, responded by citing legislation and case law that had criminalized and upheld the criminalization of sodomy or homosexual sodomy.[130]

The majority and Justice Scalia employed tradition and history for quite different purposes. *Bowers* used history and tradition to establish that there was not a fundamental right to engage in homosexual sodomy.[131] The majority in *Lawrence* argued that the traditions and history that *Bowers* had relied on were not as clear or as currently respected as the *Bowers* Court had assumed.[132] However, it did not make the further argument that there was an affirmative tradition of treating homosexual sodomy as if it was a fundamental right, such as Justice Harlan had argued with respect to the right to enjoy sex within marriage in *Poe* and *Griswold*. To some extent, the Court's showing with respect to the erosion of the tradition of criminalizing homosexual sodomy in *Lawrence* served to undercut the state's interest in upholding such laws. Relying on the Court's prior privacy cases, including *Griswold*, Justice Scalia argued that the central question was whether evidence of tradition established that homosexual sodomy has been treated as a fundamental right such as marital intimacy, and he concluded that the lengthy and continuing history of criminalizations clearly showed that it had not been so.[133]

This illustrates that a particular tradition may point in different legal directions if it is utilized for different purposes. A showing that there has not been a tradition of condemnation of a particular practice does not automatically translate into a showing that the practice has been highly revered and protected. Unlike *Glucksberg*, decided six years earlier, the Court in *Lawrence* did not base its decision on tradition or the lack thereof. However, the context in which the issue arose in the two cases was quite different. In *Glucksberg*, the plaintiff needed to show that there was a tradition of assisted suicide in order to strike down the law prohibiting it. In upholding the law, the Court found that the tradition was quite to the contrary. In *Lawrence* on the other hand, it was the state that was relying on the tradition in order to defend the law in reliance on *Bowers*. In finding insufficient support for such a tradition, the Court merely held that the basis of its earlier decision in *Bowers* was flawed. It did not purport to find a fundamental right to engage in intimate relations, and as such *Lawrence* should not be read as undermining *Glucksberg*'s holding that a grounding in tradition is in fact the basis for identifying fundamental interests as a matter of substantive Due Process.

VI. Reliance on International Practice

Occasionally, the Court will place some reliance on the practice of other nations in determining whether a specific practice is consistent with one of the more explicitly value-oriented provisions of the Constitution such as due process of law or cruel and unusual punishment.

In *Trop v. Dulles*, for instance, in the course of holding that revoking a person's citizenship for desertion of duty in the military violated the Eighth Amendment's ban on cruel and unusual punishment, a four-justice plurality noted that "[t]he civilized nations of the world are in virtual unanimity that statelessness is not to be imposed as punishment for crime."[134] More specifically, the Court pointed out that the United Nations had found that only two of eighty-four nations surveyed employed denationalization as a penalty for desertion.[135] In this context, a comparative approach made some sense because only a nation is capable of imposing the penalty in question.

Within the past decade, the Court or at least some justices have cited international laws and practices in some substantive due process and cruel and unusual punishment cases as evidence of consensus. This in turn has provoked a sharp rebuke from other members of the Court, especially Justice Scalia.

In the course of holding that the Due Process Clause of the Fourteenth Amendment did not protect a right of assisted suicide, Justice Rehnquist, writing for the majority in *Washington v. Glucksberg*, relied heavily on tradition and practice within the United States but also dropped a footnote pointing out that Canada, England, and New Zealand declined to adopt such a right, and Australia rejected such a right after the Northern Territory had adopted it.[136] The Court also cited the recent Dutch experience as evidence that the creation of such a right tends inevitably to lead to serious abuse.[137] Justice Souter, concurring, also cited the Dutch experience and noted that there was enough controversy over whether it did tend to lead to abuse; he thus cautioned against recognition of such a right.[138] The majority and concurrence relied on the Dutch experience not as a source of tradition to define the scope of Due Process liberty, but rather as proof that in the context before the Court, the slippery-slope problem could be quite real.

There would not appear to be anything particularly controversial about this use of international practice.

In his concurring opinion in *Bowers v. Hardwick* in 1987 where the Court held that there was no Due Process right to engage in homosexual sodomy, Chief Justice Burger declared that the conduct in question had been "subject to state intervention throughout the history of Western civilization."[139] In 2003 in *Lawrence v. Texas* when the Court overruled *Bowers*, it took issue with this contention.[140] It noted that prior to *Bowers*, Britain had in fact decriminalized consensual homosexual conduct, and the European Court of Human Rights had struck down a statute of Northern Ireland criminalizing it.[141] The Court cited these incidents explicitly to undermine Chief Justice Burger's claim in *Bowers*.[142] Near the end of its opinion, the Court cited several other similar decisions of the European Court of Human Rights and stated that "other nations, too have taken action consistent with an affirmation of the protected right . . . ."[143]

The Court concluded that the right in question "has been accepted as an integral part of human freedom in many other countries. . . ." and "[t]here has been no showing that in this country the governmental interest in circumscribing personal choice is somehow more legitimate or urgent."[144] At this point, the Court seemed to argue that foreign practice was relevant either to the existence of the Due Process right or at least the weight of the competing governmental interest. Justice Scalia dissenting was quite critical of the majority's citation of foreign practice. He rejected the contention that the *Bowers* Court had relied on internationally based values and dismissed the Court's citation of foreign practice as "meaningless" though "dangerous dicta" because "this Court should not impose foreign moods, fads or fashions on Americans . . ."[145]

ⅶ VII. Level of Generality

A crucial question raised by the use of tradition as a method of determining what aspects of liberty are fundamental under the Due Process Clause is the level of generality at which the tradition is defined. This issue was debated in detail but was not definitively resolved in the case of *Michael H v. Gerald D*.[146] The strange factual background of the case involved a claim of visitation rights by a man, who had apparently fathered a child with a woman who was and remained married to another man, against the wishes of the mother and her husband.[147] The constitutional issue was whether the biological father had a liberty interest protected by Due Process permitting such visitation. Justice Scalia wrote the opinion for the Court, holding that he had no such interest. In a controversial footnote joined only by Chief Justice Rehnquist, Justice Scalia argued that the Court should define the liberty interest at stake narrowly as dictated by the facts of the case at hand.[148] Thus according to Justice Scalia, the interest was properly defined as "whether the States in fact award substantive parental rights to the natural father of a child conceived within, and born into, an extant marital union that wishes to embrace the child."[149] Consequently, Justice Scalia considered whether the states had awarded parental rights to such "adulterous natural fathers" and concluded that they had not.[150]

Justice Brennan, dissenting, in contrast would have focused on a more general liberty interest in "parenthood."[151] Justice Scalia defended his analytical framework, arguing that the facts of the case provided an objective basis for defining the interest narrowly; however, there was no such basis for choosing a broader or more general approach.[152] Consequently, defining the interest more broadly than the facts of the case warrant allows the judges to choose whatever level of generality leads to the result that they would like to reach.[153] He noted that there would be no basis for choosing "parenthood" rather than "family relationships," "personal relationships," or "emotional attachments."[154] Justice Scalia would turn to a broader statement of tradition only if there was no history with respect to a narrower tradition.[155] Justice Brennan argued that tradition will often be difficult to discern.[156] However, Justice Scalia responded that this is all the more reason to choose that tradition that is dictated by the facts of the case as it will generally be the most readily discernable.[157] Justices Brennan and Scalia quarreled over whether prior cases could adequately be explained pursuant to Justice Scalia's analytical framework.[158] Justice Brennan also argued that a focus on tradition narrowly defined would not take sufficient account of societal evolution.[159]

The constraint on the judiciary that Justice Brennan viewed as a weakness was the very characteristic that Justice Scalia viewed as a strength.[160] In *Gerald D*, Justices Scalia and Brennan essentially battled to a draw. Justices O'Connor and Kennedy otherwise joined the opinion but did not concur in footnote 6.[161] Justice Scalia lost the battle four years later, however, when in *Planned Parenthood v. Casey*, a majority of the Court explicitly rejected his approach to defining Due Process liberty at the fact-specific level, citing a variety of cases in which the Court had defined liberty at a more general level.[162] Citing Justice Scalia's footnote in *Gerald D*, the Court concluded that it would be inconsistent with precedent to define liberty interests at the most specific level.[163] The Court cited *Loving v. Virginia*[164] where it had held that a ban on interracial marriage violated the Due Process Clause of the Fourteenth Amendment as proof that liberty is not necessarily defined at the narrowest level because the case would presumably have come out the other way were that so, given that the practice had been widely prohibited by the states.[165] Rejecting an approach that would define liberty at the most specific level, the Court instead quoted Justice Harlan's language in *Poe v. Ullman* dissent where he maintained that liberty is "a rational continuum which broadly speaking includes a freedom from all substantial arbitrary impositions and purposeless restraints. . . ."[166]

Five years later in his concurring opinion in *Washington v Glucksberg*, where the Court rejected the claim that due process liberty protected a right to assisted suicide, Justice Souter acknowledged the problem of determining the appropriate level of generality but concluded that "[s]electing among competing characterizations demands reasoned judgment about which broader principle, as exemplified in the concrete privileges and prohibitions embodied in our legal tradition, best fits the particular claim asserted in a particular case."[167] In other words, determining the level of generality to assess claims of due process liberty is similar to any other difficult interpretive issue where judicial discretion must be employed and where reasonable minds can differ.

The case of *Bowers v. Hardwick*,[168] later overruled in *Lawrence v. Texas*,[169] provides a stunning example of the debate over the appropriate level of generality. There, the question was whether a Georgia law criminalizing sodomy was unconstitutional.[170] The majority defined the issue as "whether the Federal Constitution confers a fundamental right upon homosexuals to engage in sodomy."[171] As so narrowly defined, the question virtually answered itself in the negative. Justice Blackmun, dissenting, was unwilling to accept that definition of the issue, however, arguing instead that the case was about "the right to be let alone" or the "constitutional right to privacy" or "freedom of intimate associations."[172] Criticizing the Court's reliance on tradition to uphold the Georgia sodomy law against constitutional challenge, Justice Blackmun quoted Justice Holmes famous dictum that

"[i]t is revolting to have no better reason for a rule of law than that so it was laid down in the time of Henry IV. It is still more revolting if the grounds upon which it was laid down have vanished long since, and the rule simply persists from blind imitation of the past."[173]

Holmes hardly rejected tradition as a source of legal understanding, however, but rather simply tradition lacking any other ground of support. Justice Blackmun reasoned that

> [t]his case is no more about "a fundamental right to engage in homosexual sodomy" . . . than *Stanley v. Georgia* . . . was about a fundamental right to watch obscene movies, or *Katz v. United States* . . . was about a fundamental right to place interstate bets from a telephone booth.[174]

This was a nice illustration of the fact that the Court had not always reasoned in terms of the most specific level of generality, although it should be noted that neither of the cases cited involved the definition of substantive Due Process liberty, the issue before the Court in *Bowers*. Justice Stevens, dissenting, would have characterized the liberty interest in question as a right to "voluntarily conduct intimate relations" or a "right to engage in nonreproductive, sexual conduct that others, may consider offensive or immoral."[175]

In the course of overruling *Bowers* several years later in *Lawrence v. Texas*, the Court criticized the *Bowers* Court's "failure to appreciate the extent of the liberty at stake."[176] It explained that the liberty in question was not "simply the right to engage in certain sexual conduct" but rather involved the "most private human conduct . . . in the most private of places, the home."[177] *Bowers* and *Lawrence* were cases in which the characterization of the conduct in question for purposes of determining whether it fell within a protected aspect of Due Process liberty was essentially outcome-determinative. By the time of *Lawrence*, the Court had rejected the narrow fact specific conception of liberty relied upon in *Bowers* and favored by Justice Scalia and had instead adopted a broader approach. It has explained that such an approach provides greater protection to liberty, especially aspects of liberty that may fall outside of the traditional mainstream. As such, the Court believes this to be more consistent with the broad purposes of the Due Process Clause as well as the Court's precedents interpreting it.[178] Such an approach does come at the cost of amplifying the role of arguably unbounded judicial discretion, however.

VIII. Evolving Standards—The "Living" Constitution

The Court does not always interpret constitutional provisions in terms of tradition and past practice. In certain instances, it has taken a more evolutionary approach. At a general level, perhaps the classic statement of the significance of an evolutionary approach was made by Justice Holmes in *Missouri v. Holland* where he noted that the words of the Constitution

> have called into life a being the development of which could not have been foreseen completely by the most gifted of its begetters. It was enough for them to realize or to hope that they had created an organism; it has taken a century and has cost their successors much sweat and blood to prove that they created a nation. The case before us must be considered in the light of ou[r] whole experience and not merely in that of what was said a hundred years ago.[179]

This is ringing rhetoric to be sure. The case for a "living constitution" has never been stated more eloquently. Holmes basically created an atmosphere without providing any guidance as to how the task of understanding what the Constitution has become is to be divined.

Justice Frankfurter echoed this same theme on several occasions. In his concurring opinion in *Joseph Burstyn v. Wilson*, he explained that "[t]he Constitution . . . is an organism, not merely a literary composition."[180] And in his concurrence in *Dennis v. United States*, he rejected an absolutist reading of the First Amendment that

> [t]reats the words of the Constitution as though they were found on a piece of outworn parchment instead of being words that have called into being a nation with a past to be preserved for the future.[181]

He also relied on this evolutionary approach in his concurring opinion in *Martin v. Struthers* where he explained that

> [f]rom generation to generation fresh vindication is given to the prophetic wisdom of the framers of the Constitution in casting it in terms so broad that it has adaptable vitality for the drastic changes in our society which they knew to be inevitable, even though they could not foresee them.[182]

This led him to conclude in that case that the conflict between the rights of those who wished to distribute literature door to door and cities that wished to ban such practices could not be resolved by reliance on the rural conditions that existed at the time of the framing but rather must take account of the degree to which people were now "crowded together in large human beehives."[183]

Similarly in *Home Building and Loan v. Blaisdell*, where the Court drastically altered its traditional interpretation of the Contract Clause, it proclaimed that if "the great clauses of the Constitution must be confined to the interpretation which the framers, with the conditions and outlook of their time, would have placed upon them, the statement carries its own refutation."[184] The Court quoted the above dictum from *Missouri v. Holland* as well as Marshall's famous dictum from *McCulloch* that it is a Constitution we are expounding. Justice Sutherland, dissenting, viewed the Court's interpretation of the Contract Clause, which permitted state courts to extend the redemption period on a mortgage, not as a logical evolution of principle but instead as a radical change. He declared that "[a] provision of the Constitution . . . does not admit of two distinctly opposite interpretations." As a matter of text, original understanding, and precedent, Justice Sutherland had the better argument. As a practical matter, the Court's construction of the Contract Clause in *Blaisdell* "evolved" it from a relatively significant constitutional protection to near irrelevance.

In *Hurtado v. California* the Court wrote that due process was not restricted to rules fixed in the past, for that "would be to deny every quality of the law but its age, and render it incapable of progress or improvement."[185] This should be especially true with respect to a phrase that is as abstract as Due Process, especially given that understandings of procedural fairness will almost certainly change over time. In his concurring opinion in *Griffin v. Illinois*, where the Court invalidated an Illinois law that required indigents to pay for a transcript in order to obtain an appeal of a criminal conviction, Justice Frankfurter observed that "'due process' is, perhaps, the least frozen concept of our law—the least confined to history and the most absorptive of powerful social standards of a progressive society."[186] But even so, it does not "disregard procedural ways that reflect a national historic policy."[187] That is, Due Process evolves, but history and tradition guide and check that evolution.

In *Harper v. Virginia State Board of Elections*,[188] the Court struck down poll taxes although they were once quite common. In the process, it noted that

> the Equal Protection Clause is not shackled to the political theory of a particular era. In determining what lines are unconstitutionally discriminatory, we have never been confined to historic notions of

equality. . . . Notions of what constitutes equal treatment for purposes of the Equal Protection Clause do change.[189]

In a sharp dissent, Justice Black responded that this approach was "an attack . . . on the concept of a written constitution which is to survive through the years as originally written unless changed through the amendment process . . ."[190] The debate here between Justices Black and Douglas highlights the issue surrounding the concept of a living or evolving constitution. On the one hand, the very idea of a constitution assumes that certain enduring principles can be embodied in the text and are capable of being understood and applied into the indefinite future. Were this not so, there would be little point to the creation of the Constitution in the first instance. On the other hand, if those principles are to remain entirely static, they may over time become obsolete or at least not wholly effective. There is presumably some need for growth and change, but the question is how much and how should it be determined?

There is no constitutional provision to which the Court has applied a more evolutionary approach than the Eighth Amendment's prohibition of cruel and unusual punishment. As Chief Justice Warren, writing for the plurality in *Trop v. Dulles* in the course of striking down the penalty of loss of citizenship for military desertion, put it, "[t]he Amendment must draw its meaning from the evolving standards of decency that mark the progress of a maturing society."[191] The manner in which the Court has applied an evolving-constitution approach under the Eighth Amendment to various punishments, especially the death penalty, is considered in great detail in the chapter on ethical reasoning.

⅔ IX. Change, Decline, and Absence of Tradition and Practice

A. Insufficient Length to a Practice

Before a practice or tradition is worthy of judicial respect, it must have been in existence for a sufficient length of time. In *Republican Party of Minnesota v. White*, for instance, the Court held that state prohibitions on the speech of judicial candidates were "neither long nor universal."[192] The Court pointed out that during the first century in which judges were selected in many states by popular elections, there seemed to be no restrictions at all on the speech of judicial candidates.[193] The Court noted that by the end of World War II, only eleven states had adopted Canons of Judicial Ethics.[194] Moreover, of thirty-one states selecting judges by election, only four had adopted rules similar to the one at issue in *White*.[195] As a result, the Court concluded that the practice in issue "relatively new to judicial elections and still not universally adopted, does not compare well with the traditions deemed worthy of our attention in prior cases."[196]

B. Deliberate Change to Legislative Practice

Perhaps even more telling than a long-standing legislative practice is one that was reconsidered and deliberately changed. Justice Harlan provided an example of this in his dissent in *Wesberry v. Sanders*.[197] In the course of arguing that Article I, section 2 of the Constitution did not impose a "one person, one vote" requirement on congressional districts, he noted that under its Article I power to regulate congressional elections, Congress had initially required that congressional districts have roughly equal populations, but later dropped this requirement in 1929 following debate over its continued inclusion.[198] He argued that this change along with the thirty-five year period subsequent to the change in which there was no congressionally imposed population equality requirement tended to indicate that Congress certainly did not believe that such a requirement was constitutionally mandated.[199] Given that Justice Harlan interpreted Article I, section IV as granting Congress plenary power to regulate congressional elections, this practice was not merely evidence of constitutional meaning from which the Court could draw guidance in its own interpretive efforts but rather a near definitive conclusion as to what the Constitution required.[200]

C. Declining Legislative or Judicial Practice

Just as a continuous legislative practice can provide evidence that the practice in question is consistent with constitutional provisions, a declining legislative practice could send the opposite signal. For instance, in *McDaniel v. Paty*,[201] the Court pointed out that although at the time of the adoption of the Constitution, seven of the original thirteen states disqualified clergy from holding at least some public offices, as did six new states, by the time the Court was faced with the issue of a law prohibiting clergy from holding legislative office in 1978, Tennessee was the only state that still had such a ban in place.[202] As such, it could hardly be said that there was a long-standing and continuous practice by the states but rather only by one isolated state. Likewise, in *Bowers v. Hardwick* the Court had relied on the long tradition of prohibiting homosexual sodomy in upholding a statute that criminalized it.[203] In overruling *Bowers* several years later, the Court relied in part on the fact that even as of the time of Bowers and certainly in its wake, the tide had turned against the criminalization of homosexual sodomy in the state as well as in Europe.[204]

In *Payton v. New York*,[205] the Court was faced with a state court tradition and practice that was inconsistent with the rule that it intended to adopt. The Court acknowledged that at the time of its decision, twenty-four states permitted warrantless arrests in the home whereas only fifteen states clearly prohibited the practice.[206] It argued, however, that these figures "reflect a significant decline during the last decade in the number of States permitting warrantless entries to arrest."[207] The Court noted that "[a] longstanding widespread practice is not immune from constitutional scrutiny."[208] However, "neither is it lightly to be brushed aside," especially when attempting to define "a standard as amorphous as the word 'reasonable.'"[209] Still, the statistics in question, especially when coupled with the fact of a declining trend, did not present the type of "virtual unanimity" that was present in *Watson*.[210]

In *Atkins v. Virginia*, the Court relied on the fact that several state legislatures that had previously permitted the execution of mentally retarded persons had recently rejected this practice as proof that a consensus against the practice was emerging.[211] The Court reasoned that "[i]t is not so much the number of these States that is significant, but the consistency of the direction of change."[212] In addition, the Court emphasized the fact that those states that changed their laws tended to do so by overwhelming margins.[213] Finally the Court pointed out that mentally retarded persons are almost never executed, even in those states that permit the practice.[214] Putting all of this together, the Court concluded that "it is fair to say that a national consensus has developed against [the practice]."[215]

Justice Scalia, dissenting, had a very different take on the evidence relied on by the majority. He argued that the trend that the Court purported to have identified was both misleading and irrelevant. He pointed out that only eighteen of the thirty-eight states authorizing the death penalty had turned against the execution of the mentally retarded, and of those, eleven had applied this ban only prospectively.[216] This caused Justice Scalia to ask, "[h]ow is it possible that agreement among 47% of the death penalty jurisdictions amounts to consensus?"[217] As for the trend relied on by the Court, Justice Scalia noted that given that almost all death-penalty states formerly permitted execution of the mentally retarded, in the short term at least, change could only move in one direction.[218] Justice Scalia's analysis cast serious doubt on the weight and persuasiveness of the proof set forth by the majority. It also illustrated that evidence of tradition or a decline in tradition must be subjected to careful analysis if it is to be useful. It suggested that the majority's use of this data was arguably a makeweight that did not play a determinative role in its ultimate decision.

D. The Absence of Practice

The very absence of a particular practice or procedure might well provide some evidence as to its unconstitutionality. For instance, in *Near v. Minnesota* the Court reasoned that

> [t]he fact that for approximately one hundred and fifty years there has been almost an entire absence of attempts to impose previous restraints upon publications relating to the malfeasance of public officers is significant of the deep-seated conviction that such restraints would violate constitutional right.[219]

There may be other reasons for this absence, but given the familiar historical condemnation of prior restraints recounted by Blackstone, it is safe to assume that there was at least some truth in the Court's assumption.

Likewise in *Tumey v. Ohio*, the Court "conclude[d] that a system by which an inferior judge is paid for his service only when he convicts the defendant has not become so embedded in general practice, either at common law or in this country, that it could be regarded as due process of law."[220] *Tumey* was decided at a time when common law and state practice played a larger role in determining the scope of due process than it does today. The complete absence of such a practice in the common law in England, combined with a relatively minor recognition of it by the states, seemed to be the conclusive factors in the Court's decision.

In *Printz v. United States*,[221] Justice Scalia argued that the absence of instances in the decades after the ratification of the Constitution of congressional imposition of duties to enforce federal law upon state executive officers despite the imposition of such duties on state courts suggests that Congress did not believe that it had the constitutional authority to impose such duties on state executive officers.

Dissenting in *Baker v. Carr*, Justice Frankfurter set forth a lengthy review of English and American history to demonstrate that the system of population-based representation—"one person, one vote" had never been the dominant operative political theory, and as such was not embodied in the Constitution.[222] He concluded that pure population-based representation

> [h]as never been generally practiced, today or in the past. It was not the English system, it was not the colonial system, it was not the system chosen for the national government by the Constitution, it was not the system exclusively or even predominantly practiced by the States at the time of adoption of the Fourteenth Amendment, it is not predominantly practiced by the States today.[223]

Consequently, the Court had no business imposing it on the country through the Equal Protection Clause.[224] Nevertheless, relying perhaps on basic notions of political equality and fairness, the Court adopted the "one person, one vote" principle in *Reynolds v. Simms*,[225] illustrating that historical tradition is at best only one consideration, and even a solid tradition can be rejected in favor of other considerations.

X. Evaluating Tradition

In *Burson v. Freeman*, in the course of upholding a 100-feet "campaign-free" zone around polling places, the plurality set forth a lengthy history of the abuses that had marred early American elections and then explained that virtually all states had attempted to curb these abuses through the adoption of the secret ballot as well as by banning electioneering near polling places.[226] The Court then concluded that "this widespread and time tested consensus demonstrates that some restricted zone is necessary in order to serve the State's compelling interests in preventing voter intimidation and election fraud."[227] Justice Stevens, dissenting, was highly critical of the plurality's heavy reliance on tradition.[228] He charged that the plurality "confuses history with necessity, and mistakes the traditional for the indispensable."[229] He pointed out that even in the area of voting rights, many long-standing traditions had been rejected as unconstitutional by the Court, including poll taxes, "stringent petition requirements," property-ownership requirements, lengthy residency requirements, and malapportionment of districts.[230] He noted that the Court must take account of political and cultural changes that have undermined the need for some of these traditions, including the one before the Court.[231] The plurality made a very persuasive case for the significance of the tradition on which it relied in *Burson*. At a more general level, however, Justice Stevens identified some of the problems inherent in judicial reliance on tradition in constitutional adjudication. Tradition and practice can be quite nebulous and difficult to define. It is a type of evidence that can be useful and at times compelling, but it is also readily susceptible to misunderstanding and misuse.

If societal agreement is relevant, the question arises as to how the Court can discern such a consensus. In *Atkins v. Virginia*, where it held that execution of mentally retarded persons violated the Eighth Amendment ban on cruel and unusual punishment, it cited position papers by interest groups as well as polling data in support of the conclusion that a societal consensus against such practice had formed.[232] Justices Rehnquist and Scalia, dissenting, were both highly critical of even the Court's passing reference to this material.[233] Chief Justice Rehnquist questioned the Court's "uncritical acceptance of the opinion poll data . . . [since] we lack sufficient information to conclude that the surveys were conducted in accordance with generally accepted scientific principles or are capable of supporting valid empirical inferences. . . ."[234] He also argued that the opinions of interest groups were of far less significance than the enactments of state legislatures.[235] Justice Scalia also criticized the relevance of this information.[236]

⚿ XI. Conclusion

Evidence of tradition and history has played a significant role in constitutional interpretation. Traditions and practices that can be traced back to the founding era carry great weight with the Court as evidence of the original understanding. Long-standing traditions that do not extend back quite that far are still taken seriously in showing that a particular practice is well settled and accepted. This does not mean that it is beyond constitutional challenge, but it does certainly provide it with a presumption of constitutionality. Tradition and practice has played a particularly significant role in the areas of the Separation of Powers, Establishment Clause, Due Process, and the First

Amendment Public Forum Doctrine. When tradition and practice evidence is cited, arguments will often arise over what it establishes as well as how much weight it should be given. Reliance on tradition and practice also presents the question of the level of generality at which the tradition or practice should be defined. After some disagreement, the Court has moved toward defining it in a relatively expansive manner. Reliance on tradition also raises the question of whether the Constitution is static or dynamic in nature. Throughout its history the Court has endorsed the idea that the Constitution, at least in certain areas, is capable of growth or evolution. There must be limits to this evolutionary process, however, if the Constitution is to continue to preserve foundational and enduring principles.

SIX

Structural Reasoning

%% I. Nature of Structural Reasoning

One of the oldest and most widely accepted methods of constitutional interpretation is structural reasoning. Structural reasoning was popularized by Charles Black in his classic volume *Structure and Relationship in Constitutional Law*.[1] As Professor Black illustrates, however, it has been an important method of constitutional interpretation since the very earliest days.[2] Indeed, structural reasoning was crucial to the opinions in what are perhaps three of our most foundational constitutional cases—*Marbury v. Madison*,[3] *Martin v. Hunter's Lessee*,[4] and *McCulloch v. Maryland*.[5]

In a nut shell, structural reasoning is the method by which constitutional meaning is derived from the structure of the Constitution itself and the government it establishes along with the obvious purposes of that Constitution and government.[6] As such, structural reasoning often seems grander in scope and paints with a broader brush than other interpretive methodologies such as textual analysis, original understanding, or precedent. Structural reasoning should be distinguished from cases involving structural issues such as separation of powers or federalism. Structural reasoning plays a larger role in cases explicitly addressing issues of governmental structure than in any other area of constitutional law; however, governmental structure is often discerned through other interpretive methodologies as well, and structural reasoning can prove useful in cases that do address issues pertaining to the structure of government.

This chapter will consider several of the early foundational cases in which the Marshall Court relied heavily on structural reasoning. It will then discuss cases confronting a variety of issues raised involving structural reasoning, including "big picture" structural reasoning, the source of structural argument, structural reasoning and original understanding, purpose, judicial review, and rights. It will also examine a series of cases in which the Court has had to choose between competing structural arguments.

II. Classic Structural Arguments

One reason why structural reasoning is such a well-respected method of constitutional interpretation is because it played such a crucial role in several foundational constitutional opinions.

A. *Marbury v. Madison*

Perhaps no constitutional opinion is as widely recognized and hallowed as Chief Justice Marshall's opinion in *Marbury v. Madison* in that it is largely responsible for establishing the institution of judicial review of congressional action. Although Marshall raised some textual arguments, he seemed to concede that they were essentially makeweights.[7] To justify his conclusion that a court must invalidate a congressional law that is in conflict with the Constitution, Chief Justice Marshall advanced the following thesis. The people established a government in which "[t]he powers of the legislature are defined and limited; and that those limits may not be mistaken or forgotten, the constitution is written."[8] Courts must decide cases based on all of the applicable law or in Marshall's memorable phrase "[i]t is emphatically the province and duty of the judicial department to say what the law is."[9] Because "the constitution is superior to any ordinary act of the legislature; the constitution, and not such ordinary act, must govern the case to which they both apply."[10] Otherwise the legislature could do "what is expressly forbidden" and it would reduce "to nothing what we have deemed the greatest improvement on political institutions—a written constitution. . . ."[11]

This is the very heart and soul of *Marbury v. Madison*. In deciding the issue, Chief Justice Marshall looked for guidance to the nature of the Constitution itself, a written document intended to impose real limits; as well as the traditional role of courts, the adjudication of disputes based on all of the applicable law. He constructed the edifice of judicial review, the Court's very destiny as a significant governmental institution, not on text, original understanding, precedent, or doctrine, but rather on structural reasoning. And he did it for the good and simple reason that constitutional structure was the best argument he had. Thus structural reasoning won a favored place in the Court's interpretive tool box from the very dawning of constitutional judicial review.

B. *Martin v. Hunter's Lessee*

The place of structural reasoning was further cemented a decade later in *Martin v. Hunter's Lessee*[12] in an opinion by Justice Story, yet another of the Supreme Court's greatest justices. Martin also raised the issue of judicial review, this time whether the United States Supreme Court could reverse a state supreme court's interpretation of federal law. The issue presented to the Court in *Martin* was easier than the one in *Marbury*. Unlike Marshall in *Marbury*, Story in *Martin* had strong arguments from text,[13] original understanding,[14] and precedent[15] in his favor, and he used them well. But perhaps the most persuasive of Justice Story's arguments were structural in nature. Granting that state courts are as learned and capable as the United States Supreme Court, he pointed out that the courts of different states would inevitably disagree on difficult questions of federal law (and indeed the construction of the federal treaty at issue in *Martin* was exceedingly difficult); and "if there were no revising authority to control these jarring and discordant judgments, and harmonize them into uniformity, the laws, the treaties, and the constitution of the United States would be different in different states, and might, perhaps, never have precisely the same construction, obligation, or efficacy, in any two states."[16]

This argument is all but unanswerable. It is derived from the structure of the Constitution and the nation. Even though states and state courts retain significant autonomy and are obligated to decide questions of federal law, the obvious interest in developing and maintaining a coherent and uniform body of federal law demands an umpire, "a revising authority" as Story put it, and what institution other than the United States Supreme Court could possibly fill that role? If the Constitution creates a nation rather than a weak confederation as the structure and purpose of the Constitution would seem to indicate on its face, then Story's conclusion must be correct.

C. *McCulloch v. Maryland*

The case most clearly identified as the fountainhead of structural reasoning is *McCulloch v. Maryland*.[17] There were two major constitutional issues in *McCulloch*, whether the Constitution should be read broadly to permit Congress to choose among permissible means to effectuate its legitimate ends and whether a state could impose a targeted tax on a federal instrumentality. Chief Justice Marshall relied in part on structural reasoning to answer both questions. He did make a very solid and convincing textual argument construing the Necessary and Proper Clause flexibly to provide Congress with a broad choice of means to achieve its goals under its enumerated powers. Before turning to the text, however, Marshall built an elegant and compelling structural argument reaching the same result based on, as he put it, "general reasoning."[18]

The specific issue was whether Congress had the power to charter the Bank of the United States, given that the Constitution did not explicitly provide a power to create a corporation or a bank. Chief Justice Marshall grounded his argument on the very nature of the Constitution itself, pointing out that in order for it to be comprehensible and enduring, "only its great outlines should be marked, its important objects designated, and the minor ingredients which compose those objects,[must] be deduced from the nature of the objects themselves."[19] Thus if Congress was to be able to effectively legislate pursuant to the great powers, it must be allowed flexibility in choosing the means of effectuating them.[20] Otherwise it would be hamstrung. Creating a bank was simply one reasonable mean of exercising various enumerated powers, including the power to regulate commerce, to raise and maintain armies and navies, and to tax, borrow, and spend.[21] Marshall was able to justify this flexible reading of congressional power independently under the Necessary and Proper Clause, but had there been no such clause, his structural argument was fully capable of carrying the day.

Marshall also built a structural argument on the second issue of the case, whether the state of Maryland could impose a specific tax on the Bank of the United States. Indeed, Marshall described the source of his argument as follows:

> There is no express provision for the case, but the claim has been sustained on a principle which so entirely pervades the constitution, is so intermixed with the materials which compose it, so interwoven with its web, so blended with its texture, as to be incapable of being separated from it, without rending it into shreds.[22]

The great principle he referred to is "that the constitution and the laws made in pursuance thereof are supreme; that they control the constitution and laws of the respective states, and cannot be controlled by them."[23] From this, Marshall deduced the following axiom and corollaries:

> 1st. That a power to create implies a power to preserve: 2d. That a power to destroy, if wielded by a different hand, is hostile to, and incompatible with these powers to create and to preserve: 3d. That where this repugnancy exists, that authority which is supreme must control. . . .[24]

This lead Marshall to the conclusion that, for fear of destroying it, the part could not tax the whole.[25] On the other hand, there was no such danger if the whole taxed the part[26] or for that matter if the part taxed the whole through a neutral and generally applicable as opposed to a specifically targeted tax.[27] This was because as Marshall noted, "security against the abuse of this power, is found in the structure of the government itself";[28] that is, voters will presumably prevent their elected officials from imposing abusive or destructive taxes on them. This is the judicial genesis of the important constitutional structural argument that has come to be known as "the political safeguards of federalism."[29] The political process provides an ineffective check when the state imposes a targeted tax on a federal instrumentality because the citizens of the nation are not fully represented in the state legislature; hence there is an incentive to export tax liability to a different governmental entity.[30] Thus *McCulloch v. Maryland*, widely considered one of if not the greatest of all constitutional opinions, firmly entrenched structural reasoning as a significant methodology of constitutional interpretation. It did so by building structural arguments that were both elegant and persuasive.

III. Big Picture Structure

One form of structural argument is to paint the constitutional landscape with a very broad brush. Chief Justice Marshall did this in *Cohens v. Virginia*.[31] In rejecting Virginia's argument that state sovereignty precluded Supreme Court review of a state criminal case raising federal issues, Marshall emphasized that in war, peace, and commerce, "we are one people."[32] As such, the national government must have control of those matters that fall within its competence, and there can be no reason why it should have any less authority over the products of a state court than of a state legislature.[33] The argument is powerfully stated and properly applied in the case before the Court, but taken to its logical conclusion, it could all but obliterate the concept of federalism that likewise has strong support in constitutional structure. *Cohens* was not a case in which Marshall needed to define the limits of the structural concept, however.

In fact, structural argument has often been raised by the Court to protect federalism and state autonomy. In *Coyle v. Smith*,[34] the Court relied on structural reasoning to conclude that as the Constitution contemplated a union of equal states, Congress did not possess the authority to condition Oklahoma's admission as a state on the location of its capital in a specified city. The Court's conclusion was clearly dictated by the Court's understanding of the structure of the Union that it believed the Constitution created. A union of states with at least some degree of governmental autonomy demanded that the federal government could not dictate the location of the state capital.

Perhaps there has been no bigger-picture structural issue than that addressed by the Court in *Texas v. White*,[35] that is whether the Union was indivisible. The case raised the question of whether the sale of U.S. government bonds by Texas to raise money to support the Confederacy during the Civil War constituted the legitimate action of a state. This in turn caused the Court to reflect on whether the act of secession was constitutionally permissible. Relying primarily on its conception of the very nature of the Constitution and the nation, with little else in the way of authority, the Court concluded that "[t]he Constitution, in all its provisions, looks to an indestructible Union, composed of indestructible states."[36] As such, as the Court put it, Texas's decision to join the Union was "final," "complete," "perpetual," "indissoluble," and "[t]here was no place for reconsideration, or revocation. . . ."[37] Writing only a few years after the end of the Civil War, the Court could hardly be expected to proceed on any other set of foundational beliefs.

As a matter of constitutional theory, the nature of the Union may have been debatable prior to the Civil War, although Chief Justice Marshall had definitively rejected the "compact theory" in *McCulloch v. Maryland*.[38] Following the Civil War, however, the debate was over and *Texas v. White* simply provided a judicial obituary for the theory of a divisible union.

The Court has on occasion relied on the same broad-based structural approach to congressional control over aliens and immigration. In *Fong Yue Ting v. United States*, in the course of upholding Chinese Deportation Act of 1892 that permitted the deportation of Chinese aliens with nothing approaching any form of due process protection, the Court recognized

> [t]he right to exclude or to repel all aliens, or any class of aliens, absolutely or upon certain conditions, in war or in peace, being an inherent and inalienable right of every sovereign and independent nation, essential to its safety, its independence, and its welfare. . . .[39]

Thus the right to control immigration was derived not from the structure of the Constitution as such but rather from the even larger structural principles pertaining to the nature of nationhood. Justice Brewer, dissenting, rejected such an open-ended approach, focusing on the Constitution itself and arguing that "its framers . . . gave to this government no general power to banish."[40] Likewise, Justice Field, dissenting, set forth the more orthodox view of constitutional power, explaining that

> [t]he government of the United States is one of limited and delegated powers. It takes nothing from the usages or the former action of European governments, nor does it take any power by any supposed inherent sovereignty.[41]

Thus from the perspective of the dissenters, the Court's approach was essentially at war with the true structure of the Constitution and the government it had created. Despite the admitted breadth of congressional and executive authority over immigration, the dissenting vision seems more consistent with well-accepted conceptions of constitutional structure and authority.

In the separation of powers area especially, the Court will rely on the structure of the text itself to support conclusions regarding the limitations on the branches of government. In *Kilbourne v. Thompson* in the course of holding that Congress does not have an unbridled power to hold witnesses in contempt and then imprison them, the Court observed that the Constitution has

> [b]locked out with singular precision, and in bold lines, in its three primary articles, the allotment of power to the executive, the legislative and the judicial departments of the government. It also remains true, as a general rule, that the powers confided by the Constitution to one of these departments cannot be exercised by another.[42]

Consequently, the House could not engage in activity that "was in its nature clearly judicial."[43] This was an instance in which the Court inferred the structure of governmental power from the very structure of the Constitution itself.

Sometimes the Court must make certain general assumptions about background or context in order to interpret the Constitution. For instance, in *Cox v. New Hampshire* where the Court considered the constitutionality of an ordinance prohibiting parading without a permit, it observed that "[c]ivil liberties, as guaranteed by the Constitution, imply the existence of an organized society maintaining public order without which liberty itself would be lost in the excesses of unrestrained abuses."[44] The Court noted that this type of regulation certainly required a city to be able to control its streets. It did not cite text, history, or precedent for these propositions but rather simply deduced it as a matter of common sense. This in turn caused the Court to conclude the following:

> If a municipality has authority to control the use of its public streets for parades or processions, as it undoubtedly has, it cannot be denied authority to give consideration, without unfair discrimination, to time, place and manner in relation to the other proper uses of the streets.[45]

The Court reached this conclusion as a matter of common sense; however, the phrase "time, place and manner" thereafter became a doctrinal standard applied in these types of cases. Thus significant constitutional doctrine was readily deduced from background structural conclusions as to what types of basic conditions are necessary in order to achieve the type of ordered democracy envisioned by the Constitution.

The Court has made similar background assumptions about the relationship of the state and the individual in its efforts to give meaning to the concept of liberty under the Due Process Clause of the Fourteenth Amendment. In *Pierce v. Society of Sisters*, where the Court invalidated a state law prohibiting private schooling of children as a violation of the Fourteenth Amendment Due Process interest in "liberty," it explained that

> [t]he fundamental theory of liberty upon which all governments in this Union repose excludes any general power of the state to standardize its children by forcing them to accept instruction from public teachers only. The child is not the mere creature of the state; those who nurture him and direct his destiny have the right, coupled with the high duty, to recognize and prepare him for additional obligations.[46]

On the other hand, in the course of upholding a Massachusetts law that required that persons be vaccinated against small pox, the Court in *Jacobsen v. Massachusetts*[47] rejected the argument that the word *liberty* in the Fourteenth Amendment means that a person has an absolute right of control over his or her own body. The Court reasoned that

> the liberty secured by the Constitution . . . does not import an absolute right in each person to be, at all times and in all circumstances, wholly freed from restraint. There are manifold restraints to which every person is necessarily subject for the common good. On any other basis organized society could not exist with safety to its members. Society based on the rule that each one is a law unto himself would soon be confronted with disorder and anarchy. . . .[48]

This is an obvious recognition that the Constitution is not written in a vacuum but rather is intended to exist in the context of, as the Court put it, an "organized society." Thus Due Process liberty assumes that the individual is entitled to significant autonomy with respect to certain fundamental decisions; however, that autonomy cannot be without limits. As Justice Harlan later recognized in his important dissent in *Poe v. Ullman*, defining those aspects of liberty that are fundamental entails a process of balancing the "respect for the liberty of the individual" with "the demands of organized society."[49]

IV. Deriving Structural Arguments

A. Structure and Original Understanding

Some structural arguments are derived from or at least supported by the Court's conception of the original understanding. In *United States v. Curtiss-Wright*,[50] the Court relied on a structural argument derived in part from its conception of original understanding to bolster a vigorous conception of presidential authority in the area of foreign affairs. The question was whether the president had the constitutional authority acting pursuant to a joint resolution of Congress to ban arms sales in the Chaco.[51] Both from an originalist and structural perspective, the Court argued that foreign-affairs powers and internal powers "are different."[52] Whether as a matter of historical occurrence or as simply a big-picture structure, the Court argued that sovereignty, including the power to conduct foreign relations, had passed from Great Britain to the colonies as a whole and then to the government under the Articles of Confederation and finally to the United States (as presently structured).[53] As such, the foreign-affairs power was never held by the people but passed directly from government to government.[54] Consequently, the Court concluded that the president would be vested with the foreign-affairs power even if it "had never been mentioned in the Constitution."[55]

This theory of the foreign-affairs power seems quite out of step with the deliberate emphasis on enumerated and limited federal power that permeates the Constitution and which was so crucial to the founding generation. Justice Sutherland's account has been challenged by historians.[56] Although Justice Sutherland purported to describe the theory as an account of what did in fact occur historically, he also seemed to say that as a matter of big-picture structure, it was the way that things must be. "Sovereignty is never held in suspense."[57] That is, the foreign-affairs power would inevitably come to rest in the federal government as a matter of sovereignty whether or not that is what the framing generation intended or understood. It is simply an aspect of the sovereignty of a nation. This is essentially a structural argument writ very large, focusing on the structure of nations. A structurally based counterargument emphasizing the careful delegation and limitation of federal power throughout the Constitution might have been raised in opposition to the Court's rationale and arguably would have been even more persuasive.

As for the location of the foreign-affairs power within the federal government, Justice Sutherland relied on a basic structural argument to justify its near exclusive placement with the president. The Court emphasized that the president was in the best position, as head of state, to represent the nation to other nations and to negotiate with them. The president would have greater access to information, including confidential information, and would be better able to maintain the secrecy of such information.[58] Thus the Court relied on the structure of the presidency as compared to the Congress to draw the conclusion that the president was constitutionally warranted in playing the primary role in the area of foreign affairs, a topic, by the way, which was not even really at issue in the case.

Justice Thomas, dissenting in *Hamdi v. Rumsfeld*,[59] made an originalist-based structural argument somewhat similar to that made by the Court in *Curtiss-Wright*. He argued that the structure of the Constitution indicated that decisions pertaining to the detention of captured enemy combatants are vested in the president, with the possibility of procedural modification by Congress.[60] He argued that the president was in the best position to act decisively and make the most informed decision as to how enemy combatants should be treated, drawing heavily on the framers' decision to create a "unitary" executive.[61] In explaining why constitutional structure favored vesting this authority over war and foreign relations in the president, Justice Thomas quoted Hamilton's *Federalist 70* for the proposition that "'decision, activity, secrecy, and dispatch will generally characterize one man, in a much more eminent degree, than the proceedings of a greater number.'"[62] Although the argument was structural, it drew support from the fact that it was endorsed by at least one prominent member of the founding generation. Justice Thomas supported the argument with statements from precedent as well.[63] Consequently, he concluded that the judiciary was incompetent to review decisions made by the executive branch with respect to the legitimacy of the detention of enemy combatants.[64] The plurality rejected the argument, however, relying on precedent limiting the discretion of the executive in this area.[65]

B. Structure on its Own—The Eleventh Amendment Cases

Occasionally, disputes will arise as to the legitimate source of a structural argument—that is, must a structural argument be derived from or at least bolstered by some other source such as the text or original understanding, or is it sufficient that it is derived from constitutional or governmental structure by itself? Over the years, the Court has relied heavily on structural arguments in its Eleventh Amendment decisions. Two of the Court's more recent major Eleventh Amendment decisions, *Seminole Tribe of Florida v. Florida*[66] and *Alden v. Maine*[67] provide excellent examples of how the Court derives and then applies structural arguments. In 1996 in *Seminole Tribe of Florida v. Florida*, in a five-to-four decision, the Court in an opinion by Chief Justice Rehnquist held that Congress did not have the power under the Indian Commerce Clause to abrogate state immunity from suit in federal court.[68] In a lengthy opinion, the Court concluded that the Eleventh Amendment recognized the "basic postulate" that sovereign immunity shields states from suits by citizens in federal court, and as this protection is of a constitutional stature, Congress may not abrogate it legislatively under any Article I power.[69]

Justice Stevens dissented, arguing that the precedent has recognized that the Eleventh Amendment only creates a presumption of sovereign immunity that Congress has the power to abrogate.[70] In a lengthy and detailed dissent, joined by Justices Ginsburg and Breyer, Justice Souter argued that the Eleventh Amendment provided immunity only against suits based on diversity of citizenship and that any sovereign immunity held by the states in federal suits was attributable to common law rather than the Constitution, and as such, it could readily be abrogated by Congress.[71]

Three years later in *Alden v. Maine*, again in a five -to-four decision with the same split among the justices, the Court held that the Congress could not, pursuant to its Article I powers, abrogate the immunity of states from suit by citizens in state court pursuant to a federal cause of action.[72] Writing for the majority and relying on original understanding, precedent, and, most significantly, constitutional structure, Justice Kennedy concluded that state sovereign immunity, whether in federal or state court, was and has been a crucial aspect of the sovereignty retained by the states from the very outset.[73] In the process, he shifted the justification away from the Eleventh Amendment that he viewed as merely recognizing the existence of the "essential postulates" of state sovereignty in a very specific context to the Tenth Amendment that protects them in a more comprehensive manner.[74] As in *Seminole*, Justice Souter wrote a lengthy dissent, taking issue with the Court on virtually every point and especially maintaining that sovereign immunity was not as well accepted at the framing as the majority believed, that the very concept is largely inconsistent with the nature of popular government, especially with regard to federally based causes of action against state governments.[75] Ultimately Justice Souter and the three justices who joined his opinion expressed a very different conception of constitutional structure than did Justice Kennedy for the majority.

The Court's primary argument in both *Seminole Tribe of Florida v. Florida* and *Alden v. Maine* is structural in nature, although it is not always identified as such. The Court was able to shift from the Eleventh to the Tenth Amendment fairly easily from *Seminole* to *Alden* because in both cases the basic argument was more structural than textual. When the Court relied on "essential postulates" behind the Constitution, it was basically falling back on constitutional structure. It was saying that there are large themes apparent in the constitutional structure—in this instance, a high degree of state sovereignty with respect to citizen suits, which must be taken seriously even if not specifically embodied in the text. The question then became how does the Court or any other constitutional interpreter know that this is so? In its purest form, a structural argument or understanding might be derived simply from reading the full text and contemplating its purpose. The argument might be derived in the abstract. Generally, however, the Court will look to other sources as well to discern or at least validate arguments of constitutional structure. That seems to have been the case in *Seminole* and *Alden*. In *Seminole*, Justice Rehnquist relied on precedent, specifically *Principality of Monaco v. Mississippi*, for the proposition that there are "essential postulates" behind the Constitution, including the primacy of state sovereignty.[76] That does not mean that his ultimate argument was one of precedent rather than structure, but rather that an earlier Court had made the structural argument first.

Justice Kennedy relied on structural argument more explicitly and in much greater detail in *Alden* than Chief Justice Rehnquist did in *Seminole*. Writing for the Court, Justice Kennedy made it clear time and again that constitutional structure was central to his thesis that the states continue to enjoy constitutionally based sovereign immunity against suits by citizens in federal and in some circumstances state courts as well. At the very outset of his opinion he noted the following:

> As the Constitution's structure, its history, and the authoritative interpretations by this Court make clear, the States' immunity from suit is a fundamental aspect of the sovereignty which the States enjoyed before the ratification of the Constitution, and which they retain today (either literally or by virtue of their admission into the Union upon an equal footing with the other States) except as altered by the plan of the Convention or certain constitutional Amendments.[77]

Later in the opinion, he explained that the precedent confirms that "sovereign immunity derives not from the Eleventh Amendment but from the structure of the original Constitution itself"[78] and "the scope of the States' immunity from suit is demarcated not by the text of the Amendment alone but by fundamental postulates implicit in the constitutional design."[79] In a lengthy opinion, Justice Kennedy relied on text, original understanding, practice, and precedent to support his structural argument, but he ultimately set forth a free-standing structural argument emphasizing the myriad ways in which the removal of sovereign immunity would undermine state sovereignty.[80]

Much of Justice Souter's lengthy dissent seemed to be based on the proposition that there must be some independent source for the Court's structural argument other than structure itself. Near the outset of his opinion, he contended that the Court was apparently basing its reasoning on natural rather than common law.[81] Justice Kennedy in turn took sharp issue with that charge, suggesting that Justice Souter's argument was the result of "analytical confusion or rhetorical device."[82] Nevertheless Justice Souter devoted much of his opinion to a thorough and interesting attempt to demonstrate that neither the original understanding nor the precedent supported a natural law justification for state sovereign immunity incapable of abrogation. That seems to be largely beside the point. A structural argument such as the one that Justice Kennedy made need not be derived from some source independent of constitutional structure such as original understanding, precedent, or natural law as Justice Souter seemed to assume. Rather it is a valid constitutional argument capable of standing on its own. It may be a more persuasive argument if confirmed or supported by other interpretive methodologies as Justice Kennedy tried to do, or it may be a weaker argument if undermined by these sources; however, it is not ultimately dependent on them for its validity. But it would be fair to say that stripped to its essentials, Justice Kennedy's argument in *Alden* was structural and easily capable of sustaining the decision reached by the Court.

C. Structure and Purpose

Sometimes the Court justifies structural arguments by explaining the purpose of structural provisions. For instance, in *New York v. United States*,[83] the Court held that given the federal structure of the Constitution, Congress may not "commandeer" state legislatures and force them to enact federally mandated programs. The Court then explained that this limitation was crucial to the preservation of governmental accountability.[84] If unpopular programs, in that particular case locating low level radiation disposal sites, were implemented by state governments but mandated by the federal government, both levels of government might attempt to take cover and avoid true political accountability.[85] This, according to the Court, would be contrary to the democratic federal structure that the Constitution was designed to implement.

Justice O'Connor writing for the majority in *New York v. United States* made yet another important pronouncement about the purpose of the federal constitutional structure. In the course of rejecting the argument that the state of New York could not object to federal commandeering of the state legislature because the state had consented to the program in question, Justice O'Connor observed that

> [t]he answer follows from an understanding of the fundamental purpose served by our Government's federal structure. The Constitution does not protect the sovereignty of States for the benefit of the States or state governments as abstract political entities, or even for the benefit of the public officials governing the States. To the contrary, the Constitution divides authority between federal and state governments for the protection of individuals. State sovereignty is not just an end in itself.[86]

Consequently, the state had no power to waive a type of structural protection that was ultimately intended to protect the liberty of the individual and not simply the sovereignty of the state. The purpose of the structural protection of ultimately safeguarding individual liberty as well as state autonomy attested to its inviolability.

Justice White, dissenting, responded by arguing that the Court's reliance on constitutional structure was overstated under the circumstances. He observed the following:

> I suppose, the entire structure of our federal constitutional government can be traced to an interest in establishing checks and balances to prevent the exercise of tyranny against individuals. But these fears seem extremely far distant to me in a situation such as this.[87]

Although Justice O'Connor's structural argument in the case was solid, Justice White was certainly correct in pointing out that structural arguments are easy enough to raise and can be carried beyond their justification.

D. Structure by Contrast

Structural arguments may be derived by contrasting the provisions of the Constitution with those of other constitutions or other legal systems For instance, in *Cohens v. Virginia*, Chief Justice Marshall relied on the fact that in many states judges are not granted life tenure but rather "are dependent for office and for salary on the will of the legislature."[88] Noting the "importance which that constitution attaches to the independence of judges," Marshall argued that it is unlikely that the framers of the Constitution would entrust "the means of self-preservation" to such politically dependent institutions.[89] Thus Marshall was able to draw a conclusion about the Constitution by contrasting one aspect of its structure (judicial independence) with a differing structure (judicial dependence) of a competing institution. This in turn supported his conclusion that the ultimate interpretation of federal law should not as a matter of constitutional structure be left to judges whose independence is not protected.

V. Structure and Judicial Review

Structural arguments have played an especially prominent role in cases in which the Court has addressed the propriety of or the appropriate level of judicial review in a particular situation. As discussed earlier in this chapter, Chief Justice Marshall relied almost exclusively on structural reasoning to justify judicial review of congressional action in the landmark case of *Marbury v. Madison*. Likewise, Justice Story in *Martin v. Hunter's Lessee*, and Chief Justice Marshall in *Cohens v. Virginia* relied at least partially on structural arguments in explaining why the Court was constitutionally justified in exercising appellate review over state court judgments in civil and criminal proceedings, respectively.

In addition to employing structural reasoning to justify the very exercise of judicial review, the Court, both in the early days and in the twentieth century, has used structural reasoning to explain why it is appropriate to adjust the standard of review to different situations. This approach was initially recognized by Chief Justice Marshall in *McCulloch v. Maryland* where he held that the state could not impose a targeted tax on a federal instrumentality such as the Bank of the United States because the U.S. government would not be adequately represented in the state legislature and thus would be unable to protect its interests through the political process.[90] By the same token, Marshall indicated that a neutral and general tax such as a property tax that applied to in-state and out-of-state owners alike would probably not be unconstitutional because the political process would be capable of protecting against abuse.[91] This theoretical approach was famously characterized by Professor Wechsler as "the political safeguards of federalism."[92]

Marshall reiterated this process based approach to judicial review a few years later in the landmark Commerce Clause case *Gibbons v. Ogden*.[93]

In explaining why the Court should be especially deferential to congressional exercise of it enumerated powers. Marshall noted the following:

> The wisdom and the discretion of Congress, their identity with the people, and the influence which their constituents possess at elections, are, in this, as in many other instances, as that, for example, of declaring war, the sole restraints on which they have relied, to secure them from its abuse.[94]

Thus at least where the scope and exercise of enumerated powers of Congress were at issue, the apparent existence of a political check provided a rationale for relatively extreme judicial deference.

This process-based approach to judicial review was pursued by Justice Stone in several significant cases decided in the 1930s and 1940s. In *South Carolina State Highway Dept. v. Barnwell Brothers*, the Court applied highly deferential review to state highway regulation intended to serve safety purposes when challenged under the dormant Commerce Clause.[95] However, in a footnote, Justice Stone, writing for the Court, indicated that it would find a violation of the Commerce Clause if a state imposed a burden on or discriminated against businesses outside of the state because state "legislative action is not likely to be subjected to those political restraints which are normally exerted on legislation where it affects adversely some interests within the state."[96] In other words, as there is unlikely to be an effective political check to protect constitutional values, a judicial check was warranted. Under this line of reasoning that is purely structural in nature, the role of the Court is somewhat dependent on its judgment as to whether the political process is functioning properly. The Court suggested a willingness to defer to democratic institutions as long as it has reason to believe that they are likely to provide an adequate opportunity for the protection of interests affected by their actions.[97]

A few years later, writing for the majority in *Southern Pacific v. Arizona*, Justice Stone put this theory into action in a case in which an Arizona limitation on maximum train length was deemed by the Court to burden interstate commerce. The Court relied on the political safeguards of federalism argument in a footnote, pointing out that it "has often recognized that to the extent that the burden of state regulation falls on interests outside the state, it is unlikely to be alleviated by the operation of those political restraints normally exerted when interests within the state are affected."[98] Following *Southern Pacific*, the Court has applied a strict standard of review when state regulation arguably burdened or discriminated against interstate commerce. Structural reasoning was the basis for this significant doctrinal development.

The most famous and without doubt the most influential instance of Justice Stone's reliance on structure occurred in *United States v. Carolene Products*[99] where in dicta in a footnote, he sketched a theory that ultimately has served as the backbone for judicial review of civil rights and liberties claims by the Court. In the course of upholding a federal law regulating the contents of milk against a Fifth Amendment Due Process challenge, Justice Stone dropped the famous footnote four in which he suggested that the Court would likely apply a far less deferential standard of review if the law in question burdened a right protected by the Bill of Rights. This conclusion was justifiable on textual grounds.[100] However, he also indicated that a stricter standard of review would be appropriate where the law in question "restricts those political processes which can ordinarily be expected to bring about repeal of undesirable legislation."[101] He then went on to suggest that stricter review would also be warranted where there was reason to believe that a law was the product of "prejudice against discrete and insular minorities . . . which tends seriously to curtail the operation of those political processes ordinarily to be relied on to protect minorities."[102] Both of these theories focusing upon distortions of the normal political processes as justification for more intense judicial review were structural in nature. The impact of the *Carolene Products* footnote will be discussed in far greater detail in the chapter on creating doctrine.[103] It is a classic example of the power and influence that a structural argument can have on the future and on the direction of constitutional law, given that all that Justice Stone predicted came to pass over the next two or three decades and continues to provide the blueprint for levels of judicial scrutiny in civil rights and liberties case to this very day.

A recent dispute over the continuing viability of the political safeguards theory lead to an about-face by the Supreme Court over a fairly short period of time. In *National League of Cities v. Usery*,[104] Justice Rehnquist, writing for the Court, invalidated a congressional extension of the Fair Labor Standards Act to state employees, at least where such extension was likely to impair the state's ability to structure its employer-employee relations in areas in which the state was performing traditional governmental functions. In reaching this conclusion, Justice Rehnquist relied on two structural arguments. The first is that the structure of the Constitution and the government it creates presupposes the existence of states with a fair amount of decision-making autonomy that may not be invaded by Congress, even pursuant to what would otherwise be a legitimate exercise of the commerce power.[105] Second, Justice Rehnquist concluded that it was appropriate for the Court, through judicial review, to protect state decision-making autonomy against congressional intrusion.[106]

In a lengthy and vigorous dissent, Justice Brennan argued that there was no judicially enforceable structural limitation on the ability of Congress to regulate the states as long as it was acting within the proper scope of the commerce power.[107] Instead, Justice Brennan relied heavily on the political safeguards of federalism argument[108] articulated by Chief Justice Marshall in the second part of *McCulloch v. Maryland*.[109] That is, the states must rely on the national political process to protect themselves against congressional overreaching rather than judicially enforced constitutional limitations.[110]

Nine years later in *Garcia v. San Antonio Metropolitan Transit Authority*,[111] by a one vote margin, the Court changed directions, reversed *National League of Cities*, and adopted the structural vision of Justice Brennan's dissent in that case. Justice Blackmun who had concurred with the majority in *National League* now wrote the opinion reversing it. The Court relied on its purported inability to apply the *National League* principles in a coherent manner as its primary reason for reversal.[112] Like Justice Brennan, Justice Blackmun maintained that "the principal means chosen by the Framers to ensure the role of the states in the Federal system lies in the structure of the Federal Government itself,"[113] and that such structure was reasonably effective.[114] Justice Blackmun cited several statements from the framers as well as examples of state success in Congress for this conclusion.[115]

Justice Powell challenged these conclusions in a lengthy dissent. For Justice Powell, a proper understanding of constitutional structure required judicial enforcement of constitutional norms in the area of federalism rather than leaving the states wholly dependent on the political process.[116] By way of contrast to the majority's approach with respect to Commerce Clause based regulation of the states, Justice Powell noted that "one can hardly imagine the Court saying that because Congress is composed of individuals, individual rights guaranteed by the Bill of Rights are amply protected by the political process. Yet the position adopted today is indistinguishable in principle."[117] In addition to arguing that the Court should enforce constitutional limitations on Congress as a matter of constitutional principle, Justice Powell challenged Justice Blackmun's political-safeguards theory on the ground that members of the national legislature will inevitably be biased in favor of national legislative power.[118] Moreover, he argued that even if the political process provided sufficient protection in Chief Justice

Marshall's day, subsequent changes, most importantly the enactment of the Seventeenth Amendment that replaced state legislative appointment of Senators with direct popular election, have significantly undermined the extent to which the members of the national legislature will identify with and protect the interests of states as states.[119] Justice Powell bolstered his structural argument with references to the well-known fears of the framers that the central government might grow too strong and simply overwhelm the states.[120]

Both the majority and dissent were able to set forth reasonable structural arguments for their respective positions. Justice Blackmun relied on the structural vision set forth by Chief Justice Marshall in *McCulloch v. Maryland* and *Gibbons v. Ogden* construing congressional power expansively with states protected all but exclusively through the political process.[121] Justice Powell relied on the structural vision propounded by Chief Justice Marshall in *Marbury v. Madison* emphasizing the necessity of the judicial enforcement of constitutional limitations against Congress.[122] Both of these structural visions have deep roots. The question is whether the ideal of judicial review applies across the board or whether it yields to process-based protection when Congress regulates the states. Given that both visions may be traced back to the Marshall Court classics, it might be argued that Justice Marshall himself reconciled the arguable inconsistency as Justice Brennan and Blackmun did, though he obviously did not confront the actual issue before the Court in *National League* or *Garcia*.

Both visions have support in precedent. Justice Powell's approach is probably closer to the dominant vision of the Court throughout much of our constitutional history. Justices Brennan and Blackmun have much stronger support in the case law since the New Deal revolution of 1937. One might conclude that precedent had simply turned against the structural vision propounded by Justice Rehnquist in *National League of Cities*; however, there can be little doubt that the point of the Rehnquist opinion in that case was to attempt to cut back on that very line of precedent that five members of the Court in 1976 concluded had strayed too far from the original and correct structural conception of the relationship between the federal government and the states. The issue raised by *National League of Cities* and *Garcia* is a good example of a constitutional issue that can be argued vigorously one way or the other with structural reasoning. There is, however, no definitive structural key that will resolve the controversy, although partisans on each side will doubtlessly believe that they have the better argument.

In his concurring opinion in *United States v. Lopez*,[123] where the Court invalidated an act of Congress that made it a crime to bring a gun into a school zone as exceeding the federal commerce power, Justice Kennedy met a structural argument with a structural response. He acknowledged the structural argument that the states are able to protect themselves against federal overreaching through the political process, and thus disputes over whether Congress has exceeded its authority under the Commerce Clause should be resolved through the political process rather than the courts.[124] Like Justice O'Connor in *New York v. United States*, Justice Kennedy pointed out, however, that the ultimate purpose of federalism is to protect individual liberty.[125] This interest preserved by this balance "is too essential a part of our constitutional structure and plays too vital a role in securing freedom for us to admit inability to intervene when one or the other level of Government has tipped the scales too far."[126] Thus at least in the extreme case, judicial review is warranted in order to protect constitutional boundaries even where broad deference is ordinarily the rule. This is simply a recognition that even politically accountable bodies are capable of violating constitutional limitations.

The Court has relied upon structural reasoning to limit judicial review in contexts in which the political-safeguards argument was not pertinent as well. For instance, in *Nixon v. United States*, the Court reasoned that constitutional structure undermined any inference that the framers intended there to be any judicial review of impeachment convictions by the Senate.[127] After noting that the framers deliberately did not give the judiciary the initial power to try impeachment cases as the impeachment of judges would be a primary check against abuse of power by the courts, the Court argued that the same policy obviously would caution against giving the courts authority to review impeachment decisions.[128] Otherwise the intended check on the judiciary would be undermined and a conflict of interest might be presented.[129] However, Justice Stevens, concurring, maintained that the better structural argument would recognize that the check on the courts imposed by impeachment should in turn be checked by judicial review.[130] The majority seems correct in its response that the latter check could readily "eviscerate" the former.[131]

Structural arguments are readily used to expand as well as contract judicial review. In *City of Boerne v. Flores*,[132] the Court relied in part on a structural argument in rejecting a reading of the enforcement provision of the Fourteenth Amendment that would have given Congress the power to substantively alter the meaning of the Amendment's provisions. The Court reasoned that construing the enforcement clause to only grant Congress remedial or preventive authority is crucial in "maintaining the traditional separation of powers between Congress and the Judiciary."[133] The Court noted that providing Congress with nonremedial power under the Fourteenth Amendment would be inconsistent with Justice Marshall's understanding of judicial review providing a check against legislative overreaching recognized in *Marbury v. Madison*.[134]

﹅ VI. Structure and Rights

Structural arguments occur most frequently in cases involving the structure of government, that is, federalism or separation of powers. This is not always the case, however. Occasionally they are employed in cases involving the assertion and definition of constitutional rights as well. Beginning with *Crandall v. Nevada*,[135] the constitutional right to travel has been supported in part by structural arguments. In *Crandall*, the Court invalidated a one dollar tax on persons leaving the state in commercial vehicles for hire.[136] Writing for the majority, Justice Miller cited *McCulloch v. Maryland* as proof of the legitimacy of structural argument, noting that "[n]o particular provision of the Constitution was pointed to as prohibiting the taxation by the State."[137] Reasoning from the proposition that "[t]he people of these United States constitute one nation," Justice Miller explained that citizens have a right to come to the seat of government without obstruction from even a seemingly minimal tax.[138] *Crandall* provided the foundation for the constitutional right to travel recognized and relied on in recent decades.[139] Though various constitutional provisions have been cited to justify this right, its primary foundation is in constitutional structure.

Over 100 years later in *Saenz v. Roe*, one of the Court's most recent right to travel cases, the Court relied on the unified nature of the union in concluding that while "[c]itizens of the United States, whether rich or poor have the right to choose to be citizens 'of the State wherein they reside[,]' . . . [t]he States, however, do not have any right to select their citizens."[140] As with *Crandall*, structural argument in part dictated the existence of and nature of the right to interstate relocation. If there is to be a constitutional right to travel, constitutional structure provides its soundest justification.

Richmond Newspapers v. Virginia,[141] provides a relatively recent example of structural reasoning in a civil liberties case. There the Court held that the public had a First Amendment–based right to attend criminal trials.

Writing for a three-justice plurality, Justice Burger relied largely on arguments of original understanding as well as the purpose of the free speech guarantee.[142] However, in a concurring opinion joined by Justice Marshall, Justice Brennan set forth an explicitly structural justification for the holding. As he explained, the First Amendment "has a structural role to play in securing and fostering our republican system of self-government.... The structural model links the First Amendment to that process of communication necessary for a democracy to survive."[143] Recognizing that this theory could prove limitless, Justice Brennan argued that it should be invoked with care and guided by historical experience as well as the value of access in the specific circumstance.[144] He concluded that public access to criminal trials met both of these criteria. Specifically, he maintained that public trials help to promote the accuracy of fact-finding, ensuring that justice has been done and, most significantly from a structural standpoint, providing a check on the judicial branch of government itself.[145]

As with Marshall's argument in *Marbury*, Justice Brennan looked to the nature of the government created by the Constitution and drew some logical conclusions; that is, if the Constitution creates a democracy, public access to the proceedings of the judiciary, a branch of government, as well as the potential for a public check on such judicial proceedings seems warranted and public access to criminal trials is well designed to serve these goals. Justice Brennan's structural argument, as is the case with most structural arguments, was supported by other interpretive approaches. But in *Richmond Newspapers*, he illustrated that a well-crafted structural argument can often prove to be the most persuasive alternative in a constitutional rights case.

※ VII. Structure and Separation of Powers

There is probably no area of constitutional law where structural argument has played a larger role than separation of powers. To a significant extent, this is the case because the concept of separation of powers is more of a product of constitutional structure than of explicit text.

The question involving the removal of executive or quasi-executive officers has bedeviled the Court on several occasions. In addressing such questions, the justices have relied on constitutional structure to reach diametrically opposite conclusions. One of the great constitutional cases on the removal issue was *Myers v. United States*, decided in 1925.[146] The question presented was whether a postmaster who had been nominated by the president and confirmed by the Senate pursuant to a statute that permitted removal by the president only with the consent of the Senate could nevertheless be removed by the president without Senate participation. In a massive series of opinions running over 150 pages in length, Chief Justice Taft, writing for the Court, held that the president had the sole power of removal over strong dissents from Justices Holmes and Brandeis. Virtually all accepted methodologies of interpretation were employed by the justices, structure being among them. The crux of the issue was that although the Constitution was explicit as to executive appointment, it failed to address removal other than through impeachment. Although Chief Justice Taft relied heavily on text, original understanding and past practice in sustaining the president's power to remove, he made structural arguments as well. Looking at the structure of the Constitution, he reasoned that the president is charged with nominating all executive officials and that "the power of appointment to executive office carries with it, as a necessary incident, the power of removal."[147] Later in the opinion, he argued that as head of the executive branch charged with seeing that the laws are faithfully executed, the president must necessarily have sole power over removal in order to effectively control executive branch subordinates.[148]

In a lengthy dissent, Justice Brandeis met Chief Justice Taft's structural argument head-on and attempted to refute it with a different conception of the federal structure. Unlike Taft, Brandeis did not believe that the power to remove was inherently executive or an incident of the executive's appointment power.[149] Rather Congress was inevitably involved as well, in that it created the office in the first instance and defined its tenure.[150] Just as Justice Taft could argue that removal is incident to nomination, Justice Brandeis could respond that it is at least partially incident to creation and definition of the office. As for the need for the president to be able to control his subordinates in order to be able to faithfully execute the law, Justice Brandeis argued that the president had adequate ability to protect against insubordination through the implied power of suspension.[151] Although he was willing to concede that power to remove a high political official might be indispensable, the same would not follow with respect to an inferior officer appointed to a term of years.[152] Justice Brandeis found reenforcement for this proposition in the fact that none of the states granted their governors independent removal authority.[153] Thus the lesson that Justice Brandeis drew from constitutional structure was that "[t]he doctrine of the separation of powers was adopted by the convention of 1787 not to promote efficiency but to preclude the exercise of arbitrary power."[154]

Justice Holmes with characteristic brevity made much the same structural response as Justice Brandeis in a two-paragraph dissent, noting that "[w]e have to deal with an office that owes its existence to Congress and that Congress may abolish tomorrow."[155] As such, "[t]he duty of the President to see that the laws be executed is a duty that does not go beyond the laws or require him to achieve more than Congress sees fit to leave within his power."[156]

On this crucial and controversial issue of constitutional law, both sides relied at least in part on constitutional structure. Chief Justice Taft, writing for the majority, emphasized the need for the president to control the executive branch. Justices Brandeis and Holmes in dissent emphasized the very real role of the Congress in the creation and definition of executive offices. Both arguments are respectable and plausible, yet the case demands a choice between the two. In 1926, the majority opted for a strict separation-of-powers approach. A decade and one half later in *Humphreys Executor v. United States*,[157] the Court upheld the congressional creation of an independent regulatory agency whose officers were appointed for a term of years and could only be removed for cause.[158] Although *Myers* was distinguished on its facts as involving "a purely executive office," the Court rejected the "dicta" of *Myers* to the extent that it was inconsistent, thereby rejecting the structural vision of the Taft majority in *Myers* and forcefully committing itself to the alternative conception offered by Holmes and Brandeis.[159] Just as the *Myers* Court had argued that constitutional structure required presidential removal control over subordinates, the *Humphreys* Court reasoned that constitutional structure required congressional control over its legislative creations. As proof that two different and inconsistent structural views of the removal question were respectable, a majority of the Court managed to embrace both within the space of two decades.

Structural reasoning also played a role in *Youngstown Sheet & Tube v. Sawyer*,[160] the Court's preeminent modern separation-of-powers decision. There the Court struck down President Truman's seizure of the steel mills during the Korean War to avert a labor strike that arguably could have interfered with the war effort. In a brief opinion for the Court, Justice Black made a text-based structural argument in which he concluded that because the president's action was legislative in nature, it violated the separation of powers.[161]

Justice Jackson wrote a concurring opinion that overshadowed Justice Black's opinion of the Court. He noted that separation-of-powers cases such as this could not properly be decided by focusing on "isolated clauses or even single Articles torn from context."[162] Rather focusing on constitutional structure writ large, he noted the following:

> While the Constitution diffuses power the better to secure liberty, it also contemplates that practice will integrate the dispersed powers into a workable government. It enjoins upon its branches separateness but interdependence, autonomy but reciprocity.[163]

Thus Justice Jackson indicated that constitutional structure as refined by actual practice provided the key to understanding the separation of powers. This in turn led Justice Jackson to introduce his famous tri-part doctrinal framework for analyzing separation-of-powers questions depending upon whether the president was acting with congressional support, without such support or in the teeth of congressional disapproval.[164] Justice Jackson's approach has almost certainly been so well received because it is a common-sense deduction from the structural relationship between the branches of government. Applying this framework, he carefully considered and rejected the arguments that the government raised in defense of the president's actions.[165]

In recognizing an absolute privilege for presidential actions within the outer perimeter of the presidential office, the Court in *Nixon v. Fitzgerald*[166] relied quite explicitly on constitutional structure. The Court noted that because the presidency did not exist at common law, it could not rely on that as a source of authority as it had done in other cases involving the degree of privilege available to state and federal officials.[167] Instead it recognized that it "must draw its evidence primarily from our constitutional heritage and structure."[168] In so doing, the Court relied on the president's "unique position in the constitutional scheme."[169] The Court noted that as chief executive, the president exercises supervisory authority over the entire executive branch and is charged with "policy responsibilities of utmost discretion and sensitivity."[170] Moreover, the broad scope of the president's duties coupled with his visibility and the controversial nature of the decisions he must make could expose him to litigation that would "distract [him] from his public duties, to the detriment of . . . his office [and] . . . the Nation."[171] While citing some evidence of the original understanding, the Court maintained that in view of its "fragmentary character . . . the most compelling arguments arise from the Constitution's separation of powers and the Judiciary's historic understanding of that doctrine."[172] Chief Justice Burger filed a concurring opinion simply to emphasize that the key to the decision was indeed structural separation-of-powers reasoning.[173] Justice White, dissenting, charged that the Court's separation of powers based structural arguments could not readily be distinguished from mere arguments of public policy.[174] Although the Court does appear to be making legitimate structural arguments, the dissents critique illustrates that the very breadth and generality of structural argument lend itself to the charge that it amounts to little more than subjective views of wise policy.

The Court also relied on constitutional structure to some extent in recognizing a qualified privilege with respect to Presidential Communications in *United States v. Nixon*.[175] There a special prosecutor was seeking to subpoena tapes of conversations between the president and his closest advisors for possible use in the criminal trial of several of the president's aides. The president argued for an absolute privilege. The Court relied on structural principles to conclude that a constitutionally based privilege did indeed exist, but it was only qualified in nature. At the outset, the Court rejected the president's contention that he had the exclusive authority to define the existence and scope of the privilege, noting that such a result "would be contrary to the basic concept of separation of powers and the checks and balances that flow from the scheme of a tripartite government."[176] Thus the claim for executive exclusivity was rejected on the basis of structural principle. The Court then recognized, however, that there was indeed a constitutionally based confidential communications privilege "derive[d] from the supremacy of each branch within its own assigned area of constitutional duties."[177] Structural considerations explained why the privilege must be recognized. But they also explained why the privilege was qualified and not absolute as such privilege would interfere with the judiciary's need for evidence in criminal cases.[178] The Court noted that

> [i]n designing the structure of our Government and dividing and allocating the sovereign power among three co-equal branches, the Framers of the Constitution sought to provide a comprehensive system, but the separate powers were not intended to operate with absolute independence.[179]

Relying on the needs and functions of both the executive and judicial branches, the Court struck a balance and created a qualified privilege, although one that could readily be overridden where there was a demonstrated need for evidence. The Nixon tapes case was almost certainly driven by the peculiar circumstance in which it arose, involving a sitting president suspected, quite accurately as it turned out, of attempting to conceal evidence of his own misdeeds. In explaining the decision, however, the Court did rely heavily on structural reasoning.

〰 VIII. Structure v. Structure

Despite its pedigree, structural reasoning is not without its difficulties. Perhaps the most serious problem with structure as an interpretive methodology is that it can be vague and easily subject to manipulation. Thoughtful and learned judges will frequently perceive the constitutional structure quite differently, or focus on distinct aspects of constitutional structure to address and resolve a particular issue or draw different inferences from the same structural base.

In *Cohens v. Virginia*,[180] Chief Justice Marshall met the state of Virginia's structural argument with a structural argument of his own. Virginia, relying on the theory that the Constitution was essentially a compact between the states, contended that constitutional structure, properly understood, would be violated if a decision of the highest court of a sovereign state was subject to appellate review by the United States Supreme Court in spite of the language in Article III extending federal jurisdiction to all cases and controversies.[181] Marshall countered with his own structural argument, emphasizing that congressional powers created by the Constitution obviously cut deeply into any pure conception of state sovereignty and that the Supremacy Clause along with Article III supported the conclusion that state sovereignty must yield to the judicial power as well.[182] In the process, Marshall noted the following:

> While weighing arguments drawn from the nature of government, and from the general spirit of an instrument, and urged for the purpose of narrowing the construction which the words of that instrument seem to require, it is proper to place in the opposite scale those principles, drawn from the same sources, which go to sustain the words in their full operation and natural import.[183]

In other words, structural arguments must often be met with competing structural arguments, and it is for the Court to determine which better captures the proper vision of constitutional structure.

U.S. Term Limits v. Thornton[184] is a recent case in which the majority and dissent squared off with significantly different conceptions of constitutional structure regarding foundational issues. The specific question in the case was whether a state could impose term limits on members of the state's congressional delegation.[185] In very lengthy opinions, Justice Stevens, writing for the majority, and Justice Thomas, in dissent, relied on most of the standard arguments of constitutional interpretation, including text,[186] original understanding, precedent,[187] and practice. They also engaged in a debate over two important structural issues: (1) whether under the constitutional framework the states had any power to regulate qualifications for election to Congress absent explicit constitutional authorization; and (2) whether the addition of qualifications by the states would be inconsistent with the national character of the congressional office.

As to the first issue, Justice Stevens argued that the congressional office was wholly a creation of the new Constitution and did not in any way owe its existence to the preexisting powers of the states.[188] Consequently, any authority to regulate the congressional office could not be a "reserved" power of the states but instead must be a delegated power of or from the federal government.[189] Because the Constitution does not explicitly delegate power to the states to add qualifications for election to Congress, then no such state power exists.[190]

With respect to the second structural issue, Justice Stevens argued that "[t]he Constitution . . . creates a uniform national body representing the interests of a single people."[191] "Members of Congress [though] chosen by separate constituencies . . . become, when elected, servants of the people of the United States . . . [and] not merely delegates appointed by sovereign states. . . ."[192] He argued that the constitutional provisions that authorized Congress to judge the qualifications of its own members,[193] that authorized that members be paid from the Treasury,[194] and that authorized that states set the times, places, and manners of holding elections for senators and representatives,[195] supported the view that the congressional office was primarily national in character.[196] As such, "the right to choose representatives belongs not to the States, but to the people."[197] This led him to conclude that all citizens should have an equal right to elect representatives without encumbrance from particular states.[198]

Justice Kennedy joined Justice Stevens' majority opinion but also filed a concurring opinion in which he explained the following:

> Federalism was our Nation's own discovery. The Framers split the atom of sovereignty. It was the genius of their idea that our citizens would have

two political capacities, one state and one federal, each protected from incursion by the other.[199]

Relying heavily on Chief Justice Marshall's opinion in *McCulloch v. Maryland* for the proposition that within this structure of dual sovereignty, the federal government is supreme within its sphere of authority,[200] he concluded that states are powerless to define or limit service in Congress because it is properly viewed as an aspect of the national political sphere.[201]

Writing for four members of the Court in dissent, Justice Thomas took sharp issue with Justices Stevens and Kennedy on both structural issues. Justice Thomas first addressed the question of whether the states had any power whatsoever to regulate qualifications for congressional election in the absence of any explicit prohibition in the Constitution. Like Justice Stevens, Justice Thomas argued that the Constitution owes its origin to the consent of the people but to "the people of each individual State, not the consent of the undifferentiated people of the Nation as a whole."[202] "Because the people of the several States are the only true source of power[,] . . . the Federal Government enjoys no authority beyond what the Constitution confers."[203] As the initial and ultimate source of constitutional power "the States can exercise all powers that the Constitution does not withhold from them."[204] Given that the Constitution does not explicitly prohibit states from adding qualifications for congressional election, the correct "default rule" is that the power to do so is reserved to the states.[205]

Justice Thomas then addressed the second structural issue of whether a state's addition of qualifications for members of its congressional delegation is inconsistent with the national character of the congressional office. Justice Thomas conceded that once assembled, the Congress is a national body.[206] However, he emphasized that "selection of representatives in Congress is indisputably an act of the people of each State, not some abstract people of the Nation as a whole."[207] As such, state power to set qualifications for its own delegation does not unduly interfere with the functioning of Congress. Likewise, he argued in detail that there is no inconsistency between the three specific clauses cited by Justice Stevens and the promulgation of additional qualifications by a state.[208] To the extent that the Qualifications Clause has been read to preclude Congress itself from adding new eligibility requirements, that should have no application to the states because the problem of bias that would taint congressional manipulation of its own electoral qualifications would not exist with regard to state-generated eligibility requirements.[209]

Term Limits is a fascinating case from the standpoint of constitutional structure in that the Court divided five to four on two foundational structural issues: (1) whether the correct default rule should be that in the absence of explicit constitutional command, a state should be precluded from or permitted to add eligibility requirements for Congress; and (2) whether such additions would be inconsistent with the nature of the office and the overall structure of the Constitution. The underlying issues raised by the first question have deep constitutional roots. To some extent at least, the debate between Justice Stevens and Justice Thomas sounds like the issue purportedly resolved by Chief Justice Marshall in *McCulloch v. Maryland* as to whether the Constitution owes its origin to an act of the "the people" or to a compact between sovereign states. However, Justice Thomas need not and does not go so far as to endorse the long-discredited "compact theory." Like Justice Stevens, he too can support a popular sovereignty approach, but with a somewhat different twist. Justice Thomas acknowledged that "the people" as opposed to the states as institutions are the true originators of constitutional authority, but it is "the people" in each individual state acting through state ratifying conventions. As such, it need not be assumed that the ratifying people were cut loose from state attachments or identification and thereby indifferent to reserving powers to their respective states. Justice Stevens' conception may have greater precedential support; however, Justice Thomas presents a well-developed, credible structural alternative.

On the second question as well, whether state addition of eligibility requirements is inconsistent with the structure of the Constitution and the nature of the congressional office, Justice Stevens and Justice Thomas arguably fought to a draw, at least from a structural perspective. Justice Stevens made a solid structural argument for federal constitutional exclusivity; however, Justice Thomas had an answer for every point that Justice Stevens raised, along with a well-developed counterconception justifying state additions. Term Limit is an excellent example of a case in which contrasting conceptions of constitutional structure may readily be brought to bear. The issue must then be resolved either by concluding that one of the two structural visions is superior to the other or more likely by treating the structural arguments as a wash and deciding the outcome on the basis of other interpretive methodologies.

In *Alden v. Maine*, discussed above, Justice Kennedy, writing for the majority, and Justice Souter, dissenting, relied on different structural arguments to reach very different results. In a nutshell, Justice Kennedy argued that the text of the Constitution, especially in historical context, shows that states continue to possess significant attributes of sovereignty that are inconsistent with being subjected to suit absent consent.[210] He explained that by subjecting states to suit in their own courts, Congress would violate this residual sovereignty by showing a lack of respect for the states, threatening their financial integrity, commandeering their judicial system, hindering the allocation of state governmental priorities and blurring the lines of political accountability.[211] For Justice Kennedy, constitutional structure contains the "unique insight . . . that freedom is enhanced by the creation of two governments not one."[212]

Justice Souter responded by presenting a very different conception of constitutional structure. For Justice Souter, the Court's conception of state sovereignty is deeply flawed in that it is reminiscent of royal prerogative instead of a republican government.[213] Rather the federal structure assumed that each government is sovereign with respect to its own objects, and matters of national law are the object of and hence within the power of the federal government.[214] Thus it is not constitutionally inappropriate for Congress to require state courts to enforce federal law. Justice Kennedy might well have agreed with the Justice Souter's structural proposition that each government is sovereign over its own objects, but simply disagreed as to what the appropriate objects were in the case. Just as Justice Souter argued that the federal government is sovereign with respect to national matters as expressed through national law, Justice Kennedy would likely respond that the state government is sovereign with respect to the operation of its judicial system and, as such, should not be required to entertain suits to which it has not consented.

Justice Kennedy and Justice Souter each set forth compelling arguments based on constitutional structure. Each conception led to a different result. They were engaged in the oldest, most fundamental, and arguably the most intractable debate in American constitutional law: what is the proper relationship between the federal government and the states? Justice Souter invoked a nationalistic conception of federal structure under which the federal government may trump states rights or immunities whenever it is within its constitutionally authorized domain. This is a conception championed Marshall in *McCulloch v. Maryland*, supported by the passage of the Civil War Amendments and bought into full bloom by the constitutional revolution of 1937 and consequent judicial deference. Justice Kennedy described a constitutional structure in which state sovereignty retains inviolable protection against federal intrusion, at least in certain specific instances. This vision is more consistent with the pre-Civil War and pre-New Deal eras; one which has been influential through much of our constitutional history, lost significant ground in the mid-twentieth century, but has regained at least some momentum with the "New Federalism" of the past three decades.[215]

Both conceptions are correct, at least in the abstract. Both conceptions of federal structure have textual, theoretical, and historical pedigrees and find significant support in practice and precedent. Both make sense. If Justice Souter's conception is given complete free reign, especially in view of the enormous expansion of federal power over the past two centuries, there would be little if anything left of state sovereignty. If Justice Kennedy's conception is taken to the extreme, the states would be able to effectively block significant national objectives. Neither vision is completely acceptable. Both are essential. That means that in a specific situation, as this one, a choice must be made, though it need not and should not be a global rejection of the other alternative.

Structure arguments can be quite nebulous. The appropriate constitutional structure often exists in the eye of the bolder. This is illustrated by a few of the Court's more recent separation-of-powers decisions. In *INS v. Chadha*,[216] for instance, both the majority and Justice Powell, concurring, agreed that a one House legislative veto of the suspension of a deportation order violated constitutional structure, but they disagreed radically on exactly what the structural deficiencies were. The majority believed that the House was violating constitutional structure by legislating without complying with bicameralism and presentment.[217] Justice Powell on the other hand also believed that the provision violated constitutional structure not because it was legislative but rather because it resembled adjudication without due process.[218]

A similar disagreement occurred in *Bowshers v. Synar*, the next significant separation-of-powers case to come before the Court where it invalidated a section of the Gramm-Rudman Deficit Reduction Act that required the comptroller general to assess levels of spending, triggering mandatory across-the-board cuts.[219] The majority invalidated this provision because it was inconsistent with constitutional structure in that it allowed an official removable by Congress to exercise executive authority.[220] Justice Stevens, concurring, would also invalidate it for interfering with constitutional structure, but to his mind the comptroller general was exercising legislative, not executive authority, and as there was no presentment to the president, it violated the structural principle set forth in *Chadha*.[221] These cases illustrate that structural arguments can be quite slippery and that reasonable people can see a very different structural arrangement in the same factual circumstances, even when they agree that the law in question violates constitutional structure. As such, structural arguments are easily subject to manipulation.

〰 IX. Conclusion

Structural argument has played a significant role in constitutional interpretation throughout our constitutional history. It has been relied on heavily in some of our most important constitutional precedents. Its pedigree is beyond question. Structural reasoning can often be quite powerful, as well it should be. It simply makes sense to interpret the Constitution in a manner that follows from and is supported by the very nature of the document itself as well as the government it was creating and the general ends that it was attempting to achieve. Indeed, it would seem shortsighted and overly technical not to take constitutional structure into account where it seems relevant. The problem is that constitutional structure is hardly a self-defining concept. Reasonable people can disagree about the correct understanding of constitutional structure in a particular area, as they can with respect to the application of most interpretive methodologies. In *Myers* and *Humphreys Executor*, for instance, the Supreme Court was sharply divided as to the lessons of constitutional structure on the issue of presidential removal of executive officers. Likewise, constitutional structure can often provide competing principles to choose from, as was the case in *National League of Cities* and *Garcia*. The structural principles propounded by both the majority and the dissent were well accepted. The question was which of these admittedly legitimate structural principles should control the cases before the Court. There is no structural principle for resolving such conflicts but rather only judgment.

In the early years of the Court, structural reasoning may have played a more significant role in resolving constitutional controversies simply because precedent and doctrine were not yet well developed and original understanding had not yet blossomed. At present, structural reasoning remains a major method of interpretation, at least in the set of cases to which it is relevant; however, it is rarely the sole technique upon which the Court relies. Rather it tends to be one of several methods employed, often tightly intertwined with arguments from the text and original understanding. As such, the results in constitutional cases rarely stand or fall on the strength of the structural argument alone, and it is often difficult to determine how much weight the structural argument really carries.

Even in the present era, however, structural argument sometimes assumes primacy in constitutional decision making. In *National League of Cities*, for instance, Justice Rehnquist's case for state regulatory immunity was primarily if not exclusively structural. Although Justice Brennan raised several different types of constitutional arguments, his best response was probably the structural political safeguards of federalism as well. Structural argument looms largest in cases involving government structure itself, especially those involving separation of powers, perhaps because by definition these cases raise issue of constitutional structure and because these issues are often not addressed explicitly by constitutional text. Structural argument is not limited to this area, however.

Structural argument will continue to be a significant interpretive tool employed by the Court in constitutional litigation. Although it can often provide justification for a result, in most instances, arguments from constitutional structure will be hotly contested and will need support from other interpretive sources.

SEVEN

Precedent

🎞 I. Introduction

Precedent plays an extraordinarily important role in constitutional interpretation. The Supreme Court decides cases much like a common law court, incrementally building upon its past decisions. When interpreting an authoritative, written document such as the Constitution, the Court begins with the text but, as precedent accumulates, analysis tends to focus on the most recent cases or the doctrine developed in those cases and becomes farther removed from the text, its original understanding, or its structure. In areas in which a substantial line of case law has developed, constitutional interpretation tends to focus all but exclusively on precedent and doctrine.

To simplify analysis, I have divided this material into chapters dealing with precedent and doctrine. The difference between the two can appear to be somewhat arbitrary; however, there is a distinction worth drawing. *Precedent* refers to traditional common law–type analysis in which the Court takes at least some account of prior cases and their factual contexts in deciding the case at hand. *Doctrine* refers to the rules that are developed from prior cases, which at some point seem to assume a life quite independent of the cases from which these rules arose and which are applied in subsequent cases with no consideration of the factual contexts out of which they initially arose. Under traditional common law reasoning, doctrine is the logical outcome of accumulated precedent. After a certain number of cases have been decided, the reasoning and results of the cases may be seen as formulating a rule capable of governing the outcomes in subsequent cases. Perhaps, initially, the rule will be applied with reference to the case and factual situations that gave it birth, but at some point it will be cut loose to stand on its own. This happens in constitutional law as well. This chapter will focus on the development of constitutional precedent in the traditional common law sense in which cases are decided with reference to the facts before the court, as well as the factual contexts of prior relevant cases. Subsequent chapters will focus on doctrine as defined above.

At the outset, the line of cases recognizing the exclusionary rule under the Fourth Amendment, applying it to the states and then narrowing its scope, will be set forth as an example of precedential development and interpretation. The next section will consider the interpretation of precedent, including its expansion and contraction, as well as the important distinction between the holding of a case and dicta. The following sections will consider how the Court distinguishes and rejects precedent.

II. Developing Precedent—The Exclusionary Rule

To best appreciate the role of precedent in constitutional interpretation, it is useful to trace the development and interpretation of a significant line of constitutional caselaw over time. Dozens of examples could well serve as illustrative. The development of the Fourth Amendment exclusionary rule from its inception in 1914 to its significant modification in the 1980s will provide an excellent example of how precedent develops and is shaped.

At the outset, the line of cases began with *Boyd v. United States,*[1] the Court's first significant Fourth Amendment opinion. *Boyd* was a civil proceeding—seeking forfeiture of some panes of imported glass on which customs duties had not been paid—although the Court considered it effectively criminal in nature.[2] The trial court had ordered the defendant to produce the invoices for the glass, and they were admitted into evidence against him.[3] In a majestic opinion, quoting heavily from the famous English precedent of *Entick v. Carrington,*[4] the Court recognized that the Fourth Amendment's protection against unreasonable searches and seizures and the Fifth Amendment's privilege against self incrimination when read together provided significant protection for privacy, at least with respect to papers and documentary evidence.[5] The Court invalidated the production order and the statute that authorized it and ordered a new trial.[6]

Some thirty years later in *Weeks v. United States,*[7] the Court unanimously ruled that evidence seized in violation of the Fourth Amendment may not be introduced in a federal criminal trial. It relied heavily on *Boyd* for the proposition that the Fourth Amendment was intended to protect privacy.[8] The Court reasoned that absent exclusion of the evidence the Fourth

Amendment's protection against unreasonable search and seizure would be "of no value and . . . might as well be stricken from the Constitution."[9] The Court did not elaborate on the role of the exclusionary rule, but it did indicate a concern with ensuring that the courts do not become implicated in unconstitutional conduct by receiving illegally seized evidence.[10] Unlike *Boyd*, *Weeks* based its holding squarely on the Fourth Amendment, as opposed to a combination of the Fourth and Fifth. A few years later in *Silverthorne v. United States*, the Court reaffirmed *Weeks*, in holding that not only could illegally seized papers not be used against a defendant before a federal grand jury, but neither could information gleaned from those papers be used.[11]

Thirty years later in *Wolf v. Colorado*,[12] the Court declined to apply the exclusionary rule to the admission of illegally seized evidence in state court proceedings. It conceded that the evidence would have been excluded in a federal proceeding.[13] It did hold that the protection against unreasonable searches and seizures embodied in the Fourth Amendment was a fundamental right protected against state infringement by the Due Process Clause of the Fourteenth Amendment.[14] However, turning to the exclusionary rule, the Court noted that *Weeks* derived the rule by "judicial implication" rather than from "the explicit requirements of the Fourth Amendment."[15] Consequently, the Court seemed to view the exclusionary rule as a matter of policy as opposed to a constitutional requirement. Based on an extensive review of practice in the states and foreign jurisdictions, the Court concluded that it would "hesitate to treat this remedy as an essential ingredient of the right."[16] It reasoned that state practice indicated other effective remedies against state officials who engaged in illegal searches and seizures, including private civil damage actions.[17] Justice Murphy, dissenting, argued that the alternative remedies suggested by the majority would almost certainly prove to be ineffective.[18]

Twelve years later in *Mapp v. Ohio*,[19] the Court overruled *Wolf* and held that the exclusionary rule did apply against the states. The Court began its analysis by quoting extensively from *Boyd* as to the significance of the Fourth Amendment and from *Weeks* as to the importance of the exclusionary rule.[20] The Court confirmed that, despite some dicta to the contrary, the exclusionary rule adopted in *Weeks* was indeed constitutionally based.[21] Although the Court indicated that it was not relevant to its ultimate conclusion, it explained that the state practice that *Wolf* had relied so heavily upon had shifted significantly since *Wolf* to favor the exclusionary rule.[22] The Court argued that once *Wolf* recognized that the Fourth Amendment protection against searches and seizures was applicable to the states, the exclusionary rule, as the most effective remedy for violation, must inevitably apply as well.[23] Justice Black concurred and provided the crucial fifth vote but, harkening back to *Boyd*, maintained that the exclusionary rule could only be deduced from a combination of the Fourth and Fifth Amendments because, unlike the former, the latter did explicitly exclude the use of evidence.[24] Justice Harlan dissented, arguing that, even assuming that the exclusionary rule was constitutionally based, it remained a remedy rather than part of the substantive right itself and should not be imposed upon the states under the Due Process Clause of the Fourteenth Amendment.[25]

The development of the exclusionary rule and application to the states from *Boyd* through *Mapp* provides an excellent example of the Court developing and interpreting precedent, including two major shifts of direction. *Boyd* excluded documentary evidence in reliance on a theory emphasizing the combination of the Fourth and Fifth Amendments. *Weeks* relied heavily on *Boyd* but grounded the rule on the Fourth Amendment alone, emphasizing the need to protect judicial integrity. *Silverthorne* bolstered the rule in reliance on both *Boyd* and *Weeks*. *Wolf* read *Weeks* narrowly as imposing a rule of policy, whereas *Mapp*, in overruling *Wolf*, read it broadly as imposing a constitutionally based rule. The evolution of the precedent hardly stopped with the Court's landmark opinion in *Mapp*, however. The exclusionary rule remained controversial with law enforcement, and, just as the Court was faced with challenges to *Wolf* after it was decided, so it was also faced with challenges to *Mapp*. Over time, the Court did through case-by-case analysis build several limitations into the rule, restricting it far more than the *Mapp* Court itself would have.

The efforts to limit the scope of the exclusionary rule commenced shortly after it was initially extended to the states in *Mapp*. Four years later in *Linkletter v. Walker*,[26] the Court held that the exclusionary rule should not be given retroactive effect. It concluded that the primary purpose of the rule was to deter illegal police conduct, and that purpose would not be furthered by retroactive application because the illegal conduct in question had already occurred.[27] The Court also emphasized that, because there was a significant state reliance interest on *Wolf*, retroactive application would impose severe costs on state criminal justice systems and moreover convictions based on illegally seized evidence were not likely to be unreliable.[28] Justice Black, dissenting, challenged the Court's contention that deterrence of police misconduct had been a primary justification for the extension of the rule in *Mapp*.[29]

A few years later in *United States v. Calandra*,[30] the Court held that a witness before a federal grand jury could not refuse to answer questions on the grounds that they were based on material illegally seized under the Fourth Amendment. Relying on *Linkletter*, the Court declared that

> [t]he purpose of the exclusionary rule is not to redress the injury to the privacy of the search victim. . . . Instead the rule's prime purpose is to deter future unlawful police conduct. . . .[31]

Consequently, the rule is "a judicially created remedy designed to safeguard Fourth Amendment rights generally through its deterrent effect, rather than a personal constitutional right of the party aggrieved."[32] Applying a balancing test, the Court concluded that the adverse impact of applying the exclusionary rule to grand jury proceedings exceeded the incremental deterrent effect of the rule, given that the evidence could not be used in the criminal trial proper.[33] The Court distinguished *Silverthorne*, a seemingly pertinent precedent, on several grounds, including that the defendant there had already been indicted; thus, the grand jury was presumably seeking the illegally seized material for use in the subsequent criminal trial.[34]

Dissenting, Justice Brennan noted that "there is no evidence that the possible deterrent effect of the rule was given any attention by the judges chiefly responsible for its formulation."[35] He quoted extensively from *Weeks* to support the proposition that the actual purpose of the rule was to keep the judiciary from being tainted by the lawlessness of illegal searches and to assure potential victims that the government would not profit from its unlawful behavior.[36] He also quoted *Mapp*'s statements that the exclusionary rule was "'part and parcel of the Fourth Amendment's limitation on (governmental) encroachment of individual privacy' and 'an essential part of both the Fourth and Fifth Amendments'" as proof that it was not merely a judicially created remedy as the majority stated.[37] Justice Brennan also argued that *Silverthorne*, which had applied the exclusionary rule to grand jury proceedings only a few years after *Weeks*, was on point and controlling.[38]

Two years later in *Stone v. Powell*, the Court held that the Constitution does not require that a convicted defendant be allowed to bring a federal habeas corpus action challenging the failure to exclude allegedly illegally seized evidence in his criminal trial if he had obtained a full and fair hearing on the claim in state court.[39] The Court reasoned that protection of judicial integrity was at best a minor justification for the exclusionary rule and that deterrence of illegal police conduct was its primary rationale.[40] Relying on *Calandra*, it conducted a cost-benefit analysis to determine whether the rule should be extended to federal habeas proceedings when the issue had been adjudicated in the state system and concluded that such an extension was unjustified.[41]

Finally, in *United States v. Leon*, the Court held that evidence should not be excluded from a criminal trial when it was obtained pursuant to a search conducted under a warrant that was later struck down as invalid if the officer executing the warrant held an objectively reasonable good faith belief that the warrant was legal.[42] Relying on *Calandra* and *Stone v. Powell*, the Court emphasized that the exclusionary rule was not absolutely required by the Fourth Amendment.[43] Rather, its imposition was a matter of judicial policy to be determined by cost benefit analysis.[44] The Court reasoned that exclusion would have slight if any deterrent effect if the officer had relied in good faith on an apparently valid warrant.[45] Justice Blackmun concurred, emphasizing that because the exclusionary rule was not a constitutional prerequisite of the Fourth Amendment, "the scope of the . . . rule is subject to change in light of changing judicial understanding about [its] effects."[46] Justice Brennan, dissenting, emphasized the role of the exclusionary rule in shielding the courts from participation in illegal conduct, quoting from *Weeks* as he had in his dissent in *Calandra*.[47] He argued that the true purpose of the exclusionary rule was initially recognized in *Weeks*, misunderstood in *Wolf*, reinstated in *Mapp*, but then undermined from *Calandra* on.[48] He concluded that "by basing the rule solely on the deterrence rationale, the Court has robbed the rule of legitimacy."[49] He also engaged in an extensive critique of the Court's empirical data.[50]

The Court has continued to construe the scope of the rule narrowly.[51] Recently, in *Hudson v. Michigan*, it held that the purposes of the knock and announce rule, to prevent violence and to protect property and dignity, would not be furthered by application of the exclusionary rule to its violation.[52] Moreover, the Court argued that developments since *Mapp*, including the expansion of civil rights remedies and the professionalization of the police, decreased the need for deterrence of illegal searches and seizure through exclusion of evidence.[53] Justice Breyer dissented, noting that the Court had rejected this very argument when *Mapp* overruled *Wolf*.[54]

The lengthy line of cases creating and interpreting the Fourth Amendment exclusionary rule provides a classic example of the Court building and working with precedent. Over a period of seventy-five years, the rule was created, expanded, limited, expanded, and then narrowed. During the course of this interpretation and reinterpretation, the justices analyzed and reanalyzed the crucial cases, including *Boyd, Weeks, Silverthorne, Wolf,* and *Mapp.* From *Silverthorne* in 1920 through *Leon* in 1984, the justices continued to argue over the meaning of *Weeks* itself, as well as the rationale for the exclusionary rule. The shape of the ultimate doctrine was justified based on the analysis of the prior precedents. The judicial integrity rationale for the rule was at best only dimly sketched in *Weeks,* but from at least *Linkletter* on the Court quite explicitly replaced it with the deterrence rationale, which in turn gave the Court much more leeway to limit the application of the rule. Perhaps because the rule was imposed by the narrowest of margins and was met with hostility from a substantial minority on the Court from the very outset, its reinterpretation and limitation was all but inevitable with changes in the Court's composition. In any event, the exclusionary rule cases provide a textbook example of the significance of precedential development as a factor in constitutional interpretation.

III. Interpreting and Shaping Precedent

A. Understanding Precedent

Often, the principles underlying precedent or its outer boundaries are unclear. Precedent can be read broadly or narrowly. At some point, the Court may have to confront the ambiguity and make a choice. Writing for the majority, Justice Powell did this in *San Antonio Independent School District v. Rodriguez,*[55] in which the Court upheld the constitutionality of the Texas educational funding program against an equal protection challenge. Prior to *Rodriguez,* the Court had decided several cases that had held that the deprivation of some particular good or service in the context of a criminal case on account of the defendant's inability to pay violated equal protection, due process, or some combination of the two.[56] For instance, in *Griffin v. Illinois,*[57] the Court had held that an indigent was entitled to be furnished with a trial transcript on appeal, and in *Douglas v. California*[58] an attorney on appeal, as long as a person with adequate funds was permitted to purchase these services. Justice Powell read these and several similar cases as standing for the proposition that the state might be constitutionally required to provide certain important benefits, at least in the criminal appellate context, if the person was "completely unable to pay for some desired benefit, and as a consequence, they sustained an absolute deprivation of a meaningful opportunity to enjoy that benefit."[59] Applying this principle to the facts of these cases, he noted that the petitioner in *Griffin* was completely deprived of a trial transcript, and the petitioner in *Douglas* was completely deprived of counsel on appeal.[60] The educational financing plan before the Court in *Rodriguez* did not violate this principle, according to Justice Powell, because the petitioners were not completely unable to pay, nor were they absolutely deprived of an education.[61]

This was not the only possible reading of these cases, however. In dissent, Justice Marshall argued that Justice Powell had mischaracterized the nature of the benefit being sought. The petitioners in these cases were not seeking a trial transcript and an attorney as ends in themselves but rather as a means of obtaining a meaningful appellate review.[62] And the petitioners were not completely deprived of appellate review; rather, they simply did not receive as useful of an appeal as defendants who could afford a transcript.[63] Consequently, the criminal appeal cases, like the educational financing cases, were about relative, not absolute, deprivation.[64] This is an excellent example of how a prior line of authority can be read quite differently depending on how key factors in the decisions are characterized. The criminal appellate procedure cases were opaque, and both interpretations were legitimate attempts to discern the governing principles.

B. Expanding Precedent

1. The Generative Power of Precedent

The very nature of judicial precedent is that it provides a building block for further development. Justice Jackson explained this well in his dissent in *Korematsu v. United States*.[65] Objecting to the Court's reliance on its earlier opinion in *Hirabayashi v. United States*,[66] he observed that once the Court decides a case,

> [t]he principle then lies about like a loaded weapon ready for the hand of any authority that can bring forward a plausible claim of an urgent need. Every repetition imbeds that principle more deeply in our law and thinking and expands it to new purposes. All who observe the work of courts are familiar with what Judge Cardozo described as 'the tendency of a principle to expand itself to the limit of its logic.' A military commander

may overstep the bounds of constitutionality, and it is an incident. But if we review and approve, that passing incident becomes the doctrine of the Constitution. There it has a generative power of its own, and all that it creates will be in its own image.[67]

Justice Jackson argued that, despite the fact that the Court in *Hirabayashi* had explicitly limited its holding to the challenge to a curfew before the Court, the majority in *Korematsu* was now pushing that precedent from "support[ing] . . . mild measures to very harsh ones."[68] Consequently, "[t]he Court is now saying that in Hirabayashi, we did decide the very things we there said we were not deciding."[69]

2. The Creative Use of Precedent—*Griswold v. Connecticut*

Sometimes the Court has used precedent in an imaginative manner to create a new principle or doctrine. Perhaps there is no better example of this in constitutional law than Justice Douglas's famous opinion in *Griswold v. Connecticut,*[70] first recognizing a constitutional right to privacy. To avoid resting on the then thoroughly discredited ground of substantive due process,[71] Justice Douglas wove together bits and pieces from several constitutional provisions and precedents to fashion a freestanding right to privacy. He argued that several constitutional provisions give rise to peripheral rights that are not enumerated as such in the Constitution but are protected to strengthen and help effectuate the enumerated rights.[72]

To back up this claim, he cited *Pierce v. Society of the Sisters* as recognizing a person's right to educate one's children as one sees fit[73] and *Meyer v. Nebraska*[74] as prohibiting the state from contracting the spectrum of available knowledge. Justice Douglas characterized these cases as peripheral to the First Amendment.[75] As initially decided, however, they had nothing whatsoever to do with the First Amendment. Rather, both were based on a substantive due process right to contract approach, which had been thoroughly discredited when the *Lochner*-era jurisprudence was rejected in *Nebbia v. New York*[76] and *West Coast Hotel v. Parrish.*[77] Thus by completely re-rationalizing these two *Lochner*-era decisions, Justice Douglas produced two cases that arguably supported his penumbral rights theory and at the same time resurrected and revitalized two precedents that most observers would have assumed had long since disappeared from the scene.

More conventionally, Justice Douglas cited the Court's more recent decision in *NAACP v. Alabama*[78] as recognizing a peripheral right of freedom of association under the First Amendment.[79] *NAACP v. Alabama* had held that this newly recognized right of association prohibited the state from requiring an organization such as the NAACP to publically divulge its membership lists.[80] This case was especially useful to Justice Douglas's thesis in *Griswold*, given that it not only involved the type of peripheral right on which he was relying but one which involved an aspect of privacy as well, the very focus of the *Griswold* case itself. He concluded that "without those peripheral rights the specific rights would be less secure."[81] After further discussion of cases recognizing a constitutional right to association, he observed that "specific guarantees in the Bill of Rights have penumbras, formed by emanations from those guarantees that help give them life and substance."[82]

Having used these cases to build his argument that various enumerated rights were surrounded by penumbras and emanations, he then argued that several of these amendments, including the First, Third, Fourth, Fifth, and Ninth, and their penumbras were concerned in one way or another with the protection of zones of privacy.[83] This led him to conclude that "the right of privacy which presses for recognition here is a legitimate one."[84] In other words, the fact that several constitutional provisions protected certain aspects of privacy caused Justice Douglas to take a giant leap in recognizing an independent constitutional right of privacy, which the Connecticut law prohibiting the distribution of contraceptives to married couples violated.[85]

This exceedingly novel manipulation of precedent was undertaken for perhaps no other reason than to avoid the force of the Court's precedents, such as *West Coast Hotel* and *Nebbia*, rejecting the substantive due process theory of the *Lochner* era. No one was fooled, however. Justice Harlan, concurring, was quite willing to rest the decision on substantive due process.[86] In a vigorous dissent, Justice Black argued that the vice of *Lochner* and substantive due process was the imposition of judicial value preferences not explicitly set forth in the Constitution itself, and that problem was scarcely avoided merely by characterizing the constitutional vehicle as the right to privacy.[87] Justice Douglas launched the right to privacy decisions in *Griswold*. Not long after *Griswold* was decided, Justice Harlan's analysis carried the day and the right to privacy cases were brought under the rubric of substantive due process, with no further talk of emanations and penumbras. Nevertheless, the Douglas opinion in *Griswold* remains one of the most recognized examples of extreme judicial creativity in constitutional precedential analysis. Ultimately, however, it failed to achieve its apparent goal of producing a rationale that was largely invulnerable to the charge that the Court was simply reading its own preferred values into the Constitution. The right to privacy embodied in due process liberty has become well entrenched in the Court's jurisprudence; however, its legitimacy remains almost as controversial today as when initially introduced in *Griswold*.

3. Expanding Beyond the Limits—*Eisenstadt v. Baird*

Sometimes the decision in a constitutional case is tightly tied to the facts before the Court, but in subsequent cases it is cut loose from its original moorings. Such was the case with the extension of *Griswold v. Connecticut* by the subsequent case of *Eisenstadt v. Baird*.[88] All members of the Court who concurred in *Griswold* wrote opinions that were careful to limit their scope to interference with intimacy within the marital relationship.[89] For instance, in his dissenting opinion in *Poe v. Ullman*, incorporated by reference into his concurring opinion in *Griswold*, Justice Harlan observed that

> [t]he laws regarding marriage which provide both when the sexual powers may be used and the legal and societal context in which children are born and brought up, as well as laws forbidding adultery, fornication and homosexual practices which express the negative of the proposition, confining sexuality to lawful marriage, form a pattern so deeply pressed into the substance of our social life that any Constitutional doctrine in this area must build upon that basis.[90]

The Court did not long abide by this limitation, however. Seven years later in *Eisnstadt v. Baird*, it invalidated a Massachusetts law that prohibited the distribution of contraceptives to unmarried persons.[91] Writing for a plurality, Justice Brennan conceded that "in Griswold the right of privacy in question inhered in the marital relationship."[92] He dismissed this limitation, however, with the assertion that

> [t]he marital couple is not an independent entity with a mind and heart of its own, but an association of two individuals each with a separate intellectual and emotional makeup. If the right of privacy means anything, it is the right of the individual, married or single, to be free from unwarranted governmental intrusion into matters so fundamentally affecting a person as the decision whether to bear or beget a child.[93]

However true Justice Brennan's assertions and however consistent with liberal or libertarian ideology, the limitation of *Griswold*'s privacy principle to the marital relationship appeared to be crucial to its attempt to ground the opinion in objective tradition rather than subjective judicial preference. As such, the disposal of the marital limitation would not appear to be a natural progression of the principle recognized in *Griswold* but rather a discordant break with it. Nevertheless, given that the extension to the unmarried was almost certainly consistent with contemporary mores as well as a significant foundation stone for the Court's forthcoming decision in *Roe v. Wade*, it quickly became an accepted part of the jurisprudence. This is a stunning illustration of the fact that once a Court decides a case, it is not necessarily able to limit the scope of its decision by the mere imposition of verbal restrictions.

4. Broad or Narrow?

a. Barnette and Wooley

In *West Virginia State Board of Education v. Barnette*,[94] the Court had held that requiring a mandatory salute of the flag along with the recitation of the Pledge of Allegiance violated the First Amendment by requiring an affirmation of belief by the individual. Three decades later in *Wooley v. Maynard*,[95] the Court was faced with the question of determining whether a state law that required licensed New Hampshire drivers to display the state motto "Live Free or Die" on their license plates violated the principle of *Barnette*. The Court concluded that it did, noting that "[c]ompelling the affirmative act of a flag salute involve[s] a more serious infringement upon personal liberties than the passive act of carrying the state motto on a license plate, but the difference is essentially one of degree."[96] The Court believed that the principle of *Barnette*, as violated in *Wooley*, prevented the state from "forc[ing] an individual, as part of his daily life . . . to be an instrument for fostering public adherence to an ideological point of view he finds unacceptable."[97] This was a broad reading of *Barnette* and a plausible reading, but certainly not the only plausible reading.

In dissent, Justice Rehnquist argued that *Barnette*, properly understood, required a positive affirmation of belief that was simply not present in a context in which it would have been common knowledge that the license plate motto was a state requirement as opposed to a personal choice and that a person could easily make his disagreement clear with a dissenting bumper sticker.[98] Had the Court chosen to limit *Barnette* closely to its factual circumstances, Justice Rehnquist's active/passive distinction would be sensible. However, the grand principle of freedom of thought and conscience identified in *Barnette* was certainly deserving of more spacious application as the Court concluded in *Wooley*. As such, the Court's reading of precedent was probably driven by its conception of the purpose of its underlying principle as opposed to specific factual predicates.

b. Robinson and Powell

The cases of *Robinson v. California*[99] and *Powell v. Texas*[100] provide another example of a subsequent Court faced with the question of whether a prior precedent should be interpreted narrowly or broadly. In a fairly brief but ground-breaking opinion in *Robinson*, the Court held that a state statute that made it a crime to be "addicted to narcotics" violated the prohibition against cruel and unusual punishment. The Court noted that the statute made "the 'status' of narcotic addiction a criminal offense."[101] The Court explained that it was unlikely that a state would "make it a criminal offense for a person to be mentally ill, or a leper, or to be afflicted with a venereal disease."[102] With little more in the way of analysis, the Court declared the law unconstitutional.

Six years later in *Powell v. Texas*, the Court was faced with the question of whether the conviction of a chronic alcoholic for being intoxicated in public also violated the Cruel and Unusual Punishment Clause. Writing for a four-justice plurality, Justice Marshall distinguished *Robinson* on the fact that the statute in *Robinson* "punish[ed] mere status," whereas the Texas law focused on "public behavior."[103] This would appear to be the most straightforward reading of the admittedly sparse opinion in *Robinson*. However, Justice Fortas, dissenting, read *Robinson* as embodying a far broader principle "which, despite its subtlety, [holds that] [c]riminal penalties may not be inflicted upon a person for being in a condition he is powerless to change."[104] As Justice Fortas's reference to subtlety acknowledges, *Robinson* did not speak in these terms; however, at a higher level of principle, this is not necessarily an extravagant reading of the case.

The plurality rejected the dissent's alternative reading, however. It emphasized that *Robinson* had focused on the distinction between status and behavior.[105] Perhaps even more importantly, Justice Marshall emphasized that the principle expounded by the dissent would cut deeply into substantive criminal law, arguably prohibiting the conviction of a murderer with an uncontrollable compulsion to kill.[106] Justice Black, concurring, conceded that the dissent's reading of *Robinson* was at least permissible but agreed that the plurality's reading was closer to the explicit holding of the case and avoided the difficult problems of determining in subsequent cases how if at all it should apply to a variety of other states of mind.[107] The *Powell* Court's interpretation of *Robinson* illustrates the extent to which a somewhat enigmatic precedent such as *Robinson* is reasonably capable of readings of significantly different breadth and how the Court may well look to factors such as the consequences of alternative understandings in order to determine which decision is best.

C. Understanding Precedent Based on its Facts

Ideally, in common law adjudication, a judicial precedent is limited to the facts before the Court. Nevertheless, either in the specific case or in subsequent decisions, the Court will often abstract a general principle from the case. Still presumably, the principle should be bounded to some extent by the facts that gave rise to it. Frequently, however, the underlying facts will fail to restrain the principle as it develops and is applied. As Justice McLean observed in his dissenting opinion in *Cooley v. The Board of Wardens*, "[t]he noted Blackbird Creek case shows what little influence the facts and circumstances of a case can have in restraining the principle it is supposed to embody."[108] Justice McLean failed to explain why the *Cooley* Court had ignored the factual limitations of *Wilson v. The Blackbird Creek Marsh Co.*,[109] and the majority had not mentioned or relied on the case. Presumably, Justice McLean believed that Chief Justice Marshall's brief opinion in *Wilson*, concluding that state-authorized damming of a navigable stream in order to eradicate marshy conditions, should not have been read as a wholesale invitation to state regulation of interstate commerce as it seems to have been. Justice McLean was certainly correct in recognizing that a brief and obscure opinion soon became the fountainhead of a large and expansive doctrine.

In *Dennis v. United States*,[110] the Court was confronted with the argument that a "clear and present danger" capable of overriding a free speech defense must involve a "threat to the safety of the Republic."[111] To refute the argument, the Court cited the facts of several cases in which convictions for expressive activity had been sustained in which the threat seemed fairly insignificant.[112] In his concurring opinion, Justice Frankfurter emphasized that "[s]ince the significance of every expression of thought derives from the circumstances evoking it, results reached rather than language employed give the vital meaning."[113] Justice Frankfurter then proceeded to work over the facts of these cases in even more detail than did the plurality.[114] *Dennis* is a good example of the Court illustrating that language in earlier cases should be limited by the results in those cases and should not necessarily be read as broadly as is literally possible.

There is room for disagreement as to which facts truly matter, however. In *Flagg Brothers v. Brooks*, the Court held that a Georgia statute that permitted a warehouseman to sell the property of a customer for failure to pay the storage fee without any involvement of state officials did not involve state action and hence did not require notice and hearing pursuant to due process.[115] In reaching this result, the Court distinguished three prior cases in which a hearing was required before a debtor's property could be sold on the grounds that all three involved the participation of a state official to some extent, and that this was crucial to the finding of state action.[116] Justice Stevens's dissent rejected this reading of the prior cases and concluded that what mattered was not the minimal participation of state officials but rather the "State's role in defining *and controlling* the debtor-creditor relationship."[117] Although Justice Stevens's reading of the prior cases is more consistent with their stated rationales, the distinction that the majority drew was significant as a matter of state action doctrine. Consequently, either reading of the precedent was permissible, leaving the Court free to decide which facts were most essential to the holding.

D. Unique Precedent

Some cases arise from circumstances that are so unique as to undermine any precedential value. Or, alternatively, the opinion is written in such a fact-specific manner that as a practical matter there will almost certainly never be another case to which it can readily apply. The classic statement of this phenomena was provided by Justice Holmes in his dissent in *Northern Securities Co. v. United States*, in which he explained that

> [g]reat cases like hard cases make bad law. For great cases are called great not by reason of their real importance in shaping the law of the future, but because of some accident of immediate overwhelming interest which appeals to the feelings and distorts the judgement. These immediate interests exercise a kind of hydraulic pressure which makes what previously was clear seem doubtful, and before which even well settled principles of law will bend.[118]

Occasionally, the Court does find itself involved in the type of "great case" to which Holmes referred, often with an expedited briefing and oral argument schedule. Under these circumstances, the Court is generally hard-pressed to produce a well-reasoned and coherent opinion, and as such it does not create a precedent with much future applicability.

New York Times v. United States,[119] better known as the Pentagon Papers Case, was such a decision. There, the *New York Times* and the *Washington Post* had obtained copies of the Pentagon's highly classified internal history of its decision making process leading up to and during the Vietnam War. The United States obtained an injunction against publication of the papers. The Court of Appeals decisions staying publication were entered on June 23, 1971. The case was argued to the Supreme Court on June 26, and the decision was handed down on June 30.[120] A majority of the Court was only able to produce a three-paragraph per curiam opinion stating that the government had been unable to meet the heavy burden of justification for sustaining a prior restraint against publication.[121] The six justices who joined the opinion each wrote separate concurrences. The three dissenting justices also published opinions.

The justices in the majority did not agree on a single approach or standard for judging prior restraints. As such, the opinion provided little doctrinal guidance. Given the national security implications of the publication of the *Pentagon Papers*, however, the case certainly sent out the message that prior restraints against the press would almost never be tolerated. Justice Harlan began his dissent by quoting the "great cases, like hard cases, make bad law" paragraph from Holmes in *Northern Securities* and argued that even with respect to a prior restraint, the Court should not proceed in such a "frenzied" manner.[122] Occasionally, the Court may find it necessary to decide an important case in the extraordinarily hurried manner that it decided the *Pentagon Papers Case*. However, that decision should provide reason to doubt that it will be capable of producing a coherent majority opinion in the process.

The Court's decision three years later in *United States v. Nixon*[123] is yet another example of an extremely rushed process in a case of great national interest, once again resulting in an opinion providing little in the way of future guidance, although in a somewhat different manner. The case was the culmination of the Watergate investigation, which had been proceeding for over a year. The president had moved to quash a subpoena served by the special prosecutor requesting the production of tapes of conversations between the president and his close advisors for possible evidentiary use in the criminal trials of some of those advisors.[124] The district court denied the motion to quash on May 20, the case was argued to the Supreme Court on July 8, and the opinion was handed down on July 24. The case was handled by the Court on an expedited basis, although not quite as hastily as the *Pentagon Papers Case*.

In the *Pentagon Papers Case*, the Court did not have time to agree upon and write a majority opinion at all. In *Nixon*, on the other hand, considering the Court's fear of the possibility that the president might not obey its mandate, it was essential that the Court produce not simply a majority opinion but a unanimous one at that. Still, given the time available, the novelty of the issues, and the difficulty of obtaining unanimous agreement in any hard case, the Court published an opinion that was so opaque and heavily qualified that as a practical matter it was of little precedential value. Ultimately, the opinion written by Chief Justice Burger held that there was a constitutionally based presidential communications privilege; however, it can be overridden by a proven need for prosecutorial evidence in a criminal case.[125] The Court made it clear that it was not considering military, diplomatic, or national security secrets, or a subpoena in a civil suit or a congressional demand, for information.[126] As a practical matter, the case was driven by the fact that the president had been implicated in the cover-up of illegal activity, and the opinion produced in such a unique context was unlikely to have much bearing on any other situation. In the *Pentagon Papers Case*, an expedited process in a case of great national significance and interest resulted in an inability to produce a majority opinion of any substance. In the *Nixon* case, similar circumstances resulted in a unanimous majority opinion, but one of little precedential significance.

Bush v. Gore[127] is yet one more example of extremely unique precedent. It is another case decided in a highly expedited manner in the midst of a national controversy: the deadlocked 2000 presidential election. The Court's decision halting the Florida electoral recount ensured that George W Bush would be declared the winner of the presidential election. In a per curiam opinion, a majority of the Court relied upon a fairly novel equal protection theory, invalidating the Florida recount procedures for failure to employ a uniform standard for evaluating ballots.[128] Chief Justice Rehnquist's concurring opinion set forth a more limited Article II theory but did not attract a majority.[129] The Court's equal protection approach, read broadly, could well have significant implications for future election challenges, but it is likely that, as a practical matter, the case will be limited to its unusual historical context and as such will have little precedential value, absent another extraordinarily close election.

E. Narrowing Precedent

Sometimes precedent is preserved, at least to some extent, by significantly narrowing it. Such was the case with the Court's decision in *Planned Parenthood v. Casey*[130] which saved *Roe v. Wade*[131] by rejecting several of its tenets. The Court concluded that viability as the point at which the state's interest in protecting the fetus exceeded the woman's interest in obtaining an abortion was at the core of *Roe* and was still good law.[132] On the other hand, it decided that its trimester framework, its limitations on counseling women about other alternatives, and the strict standard of review, all imposed either by *Roe* itself or subsequent cases interpreting *Roe*, were not essential to the holding and to some extent were inconsistent with it.[133] The Court rejected the trimester approach, replaced strict scrutiny with an undue burden analysis, and overruled parts of two cases that limited the ability of the states to counsel women against choosing abortion.[134] Thus the joint opinion saved what it considered the essence of *Roe* but only by rejecting some of its doctrine and significantly changing its standard of review. *Roe* lived on, but in a somewhat different form than it did prior to *Casey*. This did not escape the notice of the dissents. Chief Justice Rehnquist wrote that "[t]he joint opinion, following its newly minted variation on stare decisis, retains the outer shell of *Roe v. Wade* . . . but beats a wholesale retreat from the substance of that case."[135] And Justice Scalia, dissenting, referred to the joint opinion's stare decisis reasoning as a "keep-what-you-want-and-throw-away-the-rest version."[136]

The Court's narrowing of *Roe* in *Casey* was not at all inconsistent with common law adjudication, where, from time to time, courts find it necessary to reevaluate the direction that a line of precedent has taken and to put it back on track by pruning away doctrinal developments, some of which may even be traced to the initial decision but now seem out of step with the core of the holding. This type of reevaluation may at times be essential if precedent is to retain its vitality. The embarrassment for the plurality in *Casey* stemmed from the fact that it relied so heavily on stare decisis in a case in which it was also engaged in such a substantial reworking of the initial decision.

F. Precedent and Analogy

The Supreme Court's "public function" state action cases are a prime example of its use of analogical reasoning first to build and then later to narrow and limit precedent. In *Marsh v. Alabama*,[137] the question was whether a "company town" was sufficiently akin to the state to require that it permit the distribution of religious literature on its streets as would be required by the First Amendment if it were an actual municipality. Answering the question required the Court to reason by analogy almost by definition, because the very issue was whether the private property was sufficiently like a town to incur at least some of the constitutional obligations of a municipality. After setting forth a detailed description of the company town, Justice Black stated that

> [i]n short the town and its shopping district are accessible to and freely used by the public in general and there is nothing to distinguish them from any other town and shopping center except the fact that the title to the property belongs to a private corporation.[138]

Because the company town looked like a municipality, performed many of the functions of a municipality, and provided the only practical location where speakers could communicate with an audience, the Court concluded that the analogy was sufficient to support a finding of state action.[139] Essentially, this was the creation of the Court's public function doctrine, under which it would find state action in instances in which a private party was performing a function ordinarily performed by the state.[140] Sensing that this doctrine could prove quite expansive, Justice Reed, dissenting, noted that in the future the Court could restrict the holding "to the precise facts of this case—that is to private property in a company town where the owner for his own advantage has permitted a restricted public use by his licensees and invitees."[141]

Twenty-two years later in *Amalgamated Food Employees Union v. Logan Valley Plaza*, the Court extended the doctrine of *Marsh* to a suburban, non-enclosed shopping mall, arguing that such a mall was the "functional equivalent" of a city business district.[142] Consequently, labor picketers had a First Amendment right to picket a store in the mall on mall property.[143] As in *Marsh*, the Court reasoned by analogy, comparing the suburban shopping mall to the company town in *Marsh*, as well as the typical city business district.[144] The Court pointed out that in the years since *Marsh*, with increased movement to the suburbs, detached suburban malls had significantly increased their share of the retail sales market.[145] The Court conceded that there were dissimilarities between a company town and a suburban shopping mall, in that the owners of the mall do not own the surrounding residential areas nor do they provide municipal services.[146] Nevertheless, the Court concluded that the similarities outweighed the differences, especially because the picketers would have no effective means of communicating with patrons of the store in the mall if they could not use the mall's property.[147] The Court reserved the question of whether its rationale would extend to speech unrelated to the business of an occupant of the mall.[148] Justice Black, the author of the *Marsh* opinion, dissented, arguing that the differences far outstripped the similarities.[149] He explained that *Marsh* turned on the fact that the company-owned town was in fact a town with "streets, alleys, sewers, stores, residences, and everything else that goes to make a town."[150] As this was hardly the case with a suburban mall, he concluded that "it sounds like a very strange 'town' to me."[151] Dissenting, Justice White pointed out that the mall and its businesses had not thrown themselves open to the public for any reason but rather simply for purposes of shopping at the stores.[152]

Four years later in *Lloyd Corporation v. Tanner*,[153] the Court addressed the question reserved in *Logan Valley* and held that there was no right to hand out literature at a large, enclosed shopping mall where the message of the speakers was not related to the business of the mall. The Court construed *Marsh* as turning on the fact that the private property was in virtually all respects a town and not on the fact that it contained businesses open to the public, despite any language in *Logan Valley* to the contrary.[154] The Court interpreted *Logan Valley* as limited to instances in which the First Amendment activity was directly related to the business of the shopping center and where the speakers could not reasonably communicate with customers of the business from public property.[155] Because the Court found neither of these characteristics present in *Lloyd*, it distinguished *Logan Valley*.[156] Justice Marshall, dissenting, argued that from the standpoint of state action, there could be no logical distinction between the shopping centers in *Logan Valley* and *Lloyd*, and thus the Court had effectively undermined the basis of *Logan Valley*.[157]

Three years later in *Hudgens v. NLRB*,[158] a case involving labor picketing of a store in a mall, the Court concluded that there was no basis for a distinction between First Amendment activity related to a business in the mall and such activity that was not so related and therefore overruled *Logan Valley*. The Court noted that *Lloyd* had relied heavily on the dissenting opinion in *Logan Valley*, which had argued that *Marsh* turned on the fact that the property was a company town and that the analogy between a company town and a private shopping center was too flawed to support an extension of state action to the later.[159] The Court also observed that if the operation of a private shopping mall involved state action, then the First Amendment would not condone a distinction between speech related to the mall and speech that was not.[160]

The line of cases from *Marsh* through *Hudgens* illustrate the limits of reasoning by analogy. An analogy is persuasive only to the extent that the similarities between the items being compared are of greater significance than the differences. The initial analogy between an actual town and a company town was quite close from a First Amendment perspective. For a majority of the Court, however, the further analogy between a company town and a shopping center, though initially appealing, proved to be too much. Ultimately, the Court concluded, as Justice Black argued in his *Logan Valley* dissent, that however dominant shopping centers have become in the world of retailing, ultimately they are not towns and as such should not be treated as if they are for First Amendment purposes. The *Marsh* public function doctrine began with close attention to the facts of the case, expanded by reasoning from factual similarities, and ultimately contracted once factual dissimilarities were seen as predominating.

G. The Weight of Precedent

All constitutional precedent does not carry the same weight. As Justice Frankfurter commented in his concurring opinion in *Adamson v. California*[161] with respect to *Twining v. New Jersey*:

> Decisions of this Court do not have equal intrinsic authority. The Twining case shows the judicial process at its best—comprehensive briefs and powerful arguments on both sides, followed by long deliberation, resulting in an opinion by Mr. Justice Moody which at once gained and has ever since retained recognition as one of the outstanding opinions in the history of the Court.[162]

In the same case, turning to the subject of incorporation of the Bill of Rights, Justice Frankfurter noted that only one of forty-three justices who addressed the issue during the preceding seventy-year period took the position that "the Fourteenth Amendment was a shorthand summary of the first eight

Amendments" and that one justice "may respectfully be called an eccentric exception."[163] He then pointed out that of these 43 justices were "among the greatest in the history of the Court," naming several.[164] Despite this impressive authority, Justice Frankfurter more or less lost this argument, as the Court did incorporate most of the Bill of Rights provisions against the states, though it never adopted the total incorporation theory that he was criticizing in *Adamson*. Still, he made a compelling argument that, as a matter of common sense, the weight of Supreme Court precedent must be influenced by the number of justices who have accepted it along with the reputations of those justices.

However, Justice Black, dissenting in *Adamson*, was not nearly as impressed with the reasoning of *Twining* as was Justice Frankfurter.[165] He argued that the Court's earlier opinion in *Twining*[166] could not have definitively settled the question of whether the Due Process Clause of the Fourteenth Amendment incorporated all of the provisions of the Bill of Rights against the states because it and the prior cases that it had relied on had failed to consider the legislative history of the Fourteenth Amendment. Consequently, its analysis was not as comprehensive as Justice Frankfurter argued but was instead incomplete.

In his concurring opinion in *Kovacs v. Cooper*, which distinguished but arguably cut deeply into the rationale of the recently decided case *Saia v. New York* pertaining to the permissibility of state regulation of sound amplification equipment under the First Amendment, Justice Frankfurter observed that "[a] single decision by a closely divided court, unsupported by the confirmation of time, cannot check the living process of striking a wise balance between liberty and order as new cases come here for adjudication."[167] For Justice Frankfurter this was the opposite of *Twining* and proof that, just as a precedent can be unusually strong, it can be relatively weak as well. It should be noted, however, that many of the Court's most significant precedents have been decided by closely divided courts,[168] though it is probably correct, as Frankfurter maintained, that they did not gain momentum until subsequently reaffirmed.

Ordinarily, precedents that have been overruled would carry no weight at all in subsequent cases. Occasionally, however, the Court will cite dicta in overruled cases as still providing an accurate statement of the law. For instance, in *Employment Division v. Smith*,[169] Justice Scalia quoted *Minersville School District v. Gobitis*[170] for a correct statement of the law under the Free Exercise Clause, even though it had been overruled rather quickly under the Freedom of Speech Clause. However accurate the dicta relied on may remain, it certainly carries a taint if it is the product of an over-ruled case.

H. Dicta

It is a foundational principle of common law adjudication that dicta in an opinion is not necessarily controlling in a subsequent case. Chief Justice Marshall explained this well in *Cohens v. Virginia*,[171] in which he found it necessary to distinguish some of his own dicta in *Marbury v. Madison*. Marshall stated that

> [i]t is a maxim not to be disregarded, that general expressions, in every opinion, are to be taken in connection with the case in which those expressions are used. If they go beyond the case, they may be respected, but ought not to control the judgement in a subsequent suit when the very point is presented for decision. The reason of this maxim is obvious. The question actually before the Court is investigated with care, and considered in its full extent. Other principles which may serve to illustrate it, are considered in their relation to the case decided, but their possible bearing on all other cases is seldom completely investigated.[172]

Applying this principle, Marshall reasoned that it was appropriate in *Marbury* to have proclaimed that the affirmative grant of original jurisdiction precluded Congress from adding to that jurisdiction if the division of jurisdiction between original and appellate was to have any meaning.[173] On the other hand, it would not undermine the purpose of the clause to allow Congress to provide appellate jurisdiction over cases that might also be brought in original jurisdiction.[174] To the extent that *Marbury* had suggested otherwise, its reasoning was "much broader than the decision and . . . in some instances contradictory to its principle."[175] Thus Marshall had no problem cutting back on the dicta of the most foundational case in American constitutional law where necessary.

The reading in *Washington v. Davis*[176] of the Court's earlier decision in *Palmer v. Thompson*[177] provides another example of a close distinction between holding and dicta. In *Palmer* the Court rejected an equal protection challenge to the closure of the public swimming pools in Jackson, Mississippi, where the district court found that it had been done as the city asserted to avoid violence and to avoid losing money,[178] although Justice White made a powerful case in dissent that this was nothing more than another way of saying that it was unwilling to operate the pools on a desegregated basis.[179] The Court rejected the argument that this purportedly legitimate purpose could be impeached by showing that the real reason for the closure was simply opposition to integration of the pools.[180] In the course of so doing, however, Justice Black seemed to argue that the motives behind legislation could never be a reason for invalidation under the Equal Protection Clause or any other constitutional provision.[181]

Five years later in *Washington v. Davis*, the Court held that a racially neutral employment test on which black applicants did proportionately worse than whites did not violate equal protection of the laws, absent proof of some discriminatory intent.[182] The Court recognized that this was at the very least in tension with the language in *Palmer*, suggesting that legislative motive was never constitutionally relevant.[183] The *Washington v. Davis* Court was able to quite properly characterize the language in *Palmer* as dicta, given that *Palmer* could be read as holding that a neutral and legitimate purpose may not be impeached by proof of improper motive and not that intent, purpose, or motive can never be constitutionally relevant.[184] The Court then went on to conclude that intent is not merely relevant but crucial in a racial discrimination case brought under the Fourteenth Amendment.[185] Technically, this was a legitimate reading of *Palmer*, though hardly the only permissible one. The Court could not conceal, however, that there was obvious tension between a conclusion that improper legislative motive may not be employed to impeach a legitimate state purpose and the requirement that an improper purpose is the key to a viable claim. If improper purpose was crucial, why was not improper motive an obvious and legitimate way to establish it? It would appear that even if the broader language in *Palmer* was technically dicta, *Washington v. Davis* cuts more deeply into *Palmer* than the Court was prepared to admit.

The line between what is dicta and what is the holding of a case is often far from clear. In *Duncan v. Louisiana*, the Court held that the Due Process Clause of the Fourteenth Amendment incorporated the Sixth Amendment right to jury trial against the states, such that a person charged with an offense carrying a penalty of a year in prison was entitled to trial by jury even though the person was only sentenced to sixty days in prison.[186] The Court dismissed language in the earlier case of *Maxwell v. Dow*,[187] to the effect that the right to a criminal jury trial did not apply to the states on the ground that these statements were dicta in that *Maxwell* had held that no provision of the Bill of Rights applied to the states, "a position long since repudiated."[188]

Justice Harlan took issue with the majority's characterization of the language in *Maxwell* as dicta, maintaining that

> [a]s a technical matter, however, a statement that is critical to the chain of reasoning by which a result is in fact reached does not become dictum simply because a later court can imagine a totally different way of deciding the case."[189]

Justice Harlan seemed to have the better argument. The Court in *Maxwell* had considered at great length whether the right to jury trial was applicable to the states under either the Privileges and Immunities or Due Process Clauses of the Fourteenth Amendments. Although the Court took a far more restrictive view of the scope of the Fourteenth Amendment than ultimately prevailed, it did not simply dismiss the argument as the Court seemed to imply. Although the Court in *Duncan* could, as it did, reject the language in *Maxwell* as inconsistent with the direction that the Court had taken under the Due Process Clause in subsequent decades, Justice Harlan was correct in concluding that it should not be casually dismissed as near irrelevant dicta.

In *Seminole Tribe of Florida v. Florida*, the majority and Justice Souter argued over what was the holding and what was mere dicta in *Hans v. Louisiana* and subsequent Eleventh Amendment cases, specifically on the issue of whether the sovereign immunity recognized by the Eleventh Amendment is of constitutional or merely common law origin and stature. The majority cited language from several cases, most prominently *Principality of Monaco v. Mississippi*,[190] explaining that the sovereign immunity in question is a constitutional limitation on Article III jurisdiction.[191] Justice Souter responded that this language was mere dicta; because the Court was not faced with the question of whether Congress could abrogate the immunity, it did not matter whether it was of constitutional or common law origin.[192]

The majority responded by citing several cases for the proposition that "[w]hen an opinion issues for the Court, it is not only the result but also those portions of the opinion necessary to that result by which we are bound."[193] Justice Souter did not offer a competing principle for distinguishing holding from dicta. He could have argued, however, that, even under the majority's definition, the statements in question were dicta because the cases could have come out the same way even if the sovereign immunity in question was not constitutionally based. The majority might have responded by contending that the stated rationale of a case is to be taken seriously by subsequent courts, even if it is not absolutely essential to the result, because it is presumably the justification that the prior court relied upon in reaching its decision. In other words, even if common law sovereign immunity may have led to the same result, it is not irrelevant that prior courts clearly believed they were relying on a constitutionally based doctrine. It is quite possible that they would not have reached the same result based on non-constitutionally grounded sovereign immunity even if they could have.[194]

Seminole illustrates the difficulty of employing the holding/dicta distinction. The majority had strong language in support of its holding that may not have been essential to earlier holdings but was probably at least well considered and important. Justice Souter had a variety of arguments as to why this language should not be taken at face value. On balance, the majority survived Justice Souter's attack on this point but barely. In any event the case provided a sharp example of the degree to which dicta and holding are flexible conceptions.

Whether prior dicta will be taken seriously in subsequent cases may depend on whether it was "well considered" or simply a casually aside. In *Afroyim v. Rusk*, for instance, in which the Court concluded that Congress did not have the constitutional power to strip a citizen of his citizenship, the Court cited a statement to that effect by Chief Justice Marshall in *Osborn v. Bank of the United States*, which the Court described as "what appears to be a mature and well considered dictum."[195] However, Justice Harlan, dissenting, disagreed strongly with the Court's characterization of Marshall's dicta, noting that he was simply responding to an unpersuasive analogy raised by counsel.[196] Justice Harlan maintained that the Court's reading of the dicta assumed that Chief Justice Marshall "meant to decide an issue that had to that moment scarcely been debated, to which counsel . . . had never referred, and upon which no case ever reached the Court."[197] This convinced Harlan that Marshall's statement should be accorded no precedential weight.

⁊⁊ IV. Distinguishing Precedent

Often, the Court will distinguish precedent that might otherwise seem applicable. It will do so for a variety of reasons. Sometimes precedent is distinguished on disingenuous grounds. That is, the precedent almost certainly should apply; however, the Court does not care to reach the result that the precedent would seem to support, so it attempts to explain why it is not pertinent. On other occasions, the Court has concluded that the precedent should no longer be followed, at least with respect to new cases or circumstances, but determines that it need not be overruled on its own facts so it simply distinguishes it. In many cases, however, the Court concludes that a precedent is in fact valid but simply is not relevant or controlling in the present situation perhaps because of significant factual or legal distinctions.

A. Precedent Undermined by Subsequent Cases

Sometimes the Court will conclude that a precedent, though never overruled, has been significantly undermined by subsequent cases and thus has lost much of its authoritative force. In *Hamdi v. Rumsfeld*,[198] the Court was faced with the question of whether an enemy combatant seized by the U.S. military was entitled to a hearing on the factual basis for his confinement. In dissent, Justice Scalia relied heavily on *Ex parte Milligan*[199] for the proposition that a U.S. citizen arrested for treason for supporting the enemies of the United States must be tried, if at all, in a federal court and may not be detained indefinitely.[200] Justice O'Connor, writing for the plurality, took the position that *Milligan* was readily distinguishable in that the petitioner was not a prisoner of war captured during battle.[201] But, more importantly, the plurality argued that the *Milligan* opinion had been severely limited by the Court's subsequent decision in *Ex parte Quirin* which permitted a U.S. citizen captured as a spy to be tried by a military tribunal.[202] Thus, *Milligan* had not been overruled, nor was it likely to be overruled. The Court found it simply should not be read as broadly as was once the case. Justice Scalia, in turn, disagreed with the plurality's reading of *Quirin* and argued that it was explicitly limited to its own facts and as such had no impact on *Milligan*.[203] The plurality in *Hamdi* made a convincing case, however, that the broad language of *Milligan* could no longer be taken at face value in light of *Quirin*.

In *McGautha v. California*[204] the Court held that due process did not require that a jury imposing the death penalty be constrained by clear guidelines. The following year in *Furman v. Georgia*, the Court invalidated a death penalty statute under the cruel and unusual punishment provision of the Eighth Amendment, at least in part for failing to provide the fact finder with sufficient guidance and constraint.[205] The dissent in *Furman* recognized that the Court's approach effectively overruled *McGautha*.[206] Four years later in *Gregg v. Georgia*, in which the Court upheld state death penalty statutes that did in fact provide clear guidance to the fact finder, the plurality recognized that "[w]hile Furman did not overrule McGautha, it is clearly in substantial tension with a broad reading of McGautha's holding."[207] Thus, the Court concluded that at most *McGautha* could only stand for "the proposition that standardless jury sentencing procedures were not employed in the cases there before the Court so as to violate the Due Process Clause."[208] The plurality then observed that "McGautha's assumption that it is not possible to devise standards to guide and regularize jury sentencing in capital cases has been undermined by subsequent experience."[209] Thus, the move from *McGautha* to *Furman* is a stunning example of the Court radically reversing course over a short period without overruling the initial decision, with *Gregg* eventually conceding that *Furman* had indeed rejected *McGautha*.

B. Factual and Legal Distinctions

Sometimes an earlier precedent is distinguished based on factual or legal differences. It is often difficult to distinguish factual from legal differences because the significance of factual differences often depends on their legal consequences. The distinctions that the Court draws to distinguish earlier cases are often quite sensible.[210] For instance, in *United States v. O'Brien*, the Court reaffirmed the rule that it would not invalidate an act of Congress simply because some members of Congress voted for the act for improper motives.[211] The Court did find it necessary to distinguish a few cases that, because of the nature of the legal claims raised, had found that improper motives were relevant. For instance, propriety of motive was pertinent to bill of attainder claims because the punitive nature of the measure was one element of the claim, and bad motive was often relevant to that question.[212] Likewise, the Court distinguished its opinion in *Grosjean v. American Press*, which struck down a tax imposed on only one newspaper in the state, and *Gomillion v. Lightfoot*, which invalidated a racially gerrymandered electoral district. The Court maintained that in those two cases the conduct in question was invalidated as unconstitutional on its face rather than on account of illicit motive.[213] These would seem to be meaningful rather than disingenuous distinctions of the prior cases on legal grounds.

Likewise, in *Richmond Newspapers v. Virginia*,[214] the Court concluded that its earlier decision in *Gannett v. de Pasquale*,[215] holding that the Sixth Amendment's public trial guarantee did not provide the public or the press with a right to attend a pretrial suppression hearing that the parties had voluntarily agreed to close, did not preclude a conclusion that the First Amendment provides such a right of public access to criminal trials, given that *Gannett* had involved a pretrial hearing and was based on a different legal theory. Both of these would appear to be quite sensible distinctions because the need for secrecy at the pretrial hearing was arguably more significant, and the purpose of the Sixth Amendment public trial guarantee was primarily concerned with the rights and interests of the accused, whereas the First Amendment access principle clearly focused on the public right to know.

In *Stanley v. Georgia*,[216] the Court recognized that persons have a constitutional right to possess obscene material within their homes. The Court based its decision on the First Amendment. It noted that prior cases had recognized "the right to receive information and ideas,"[217] although none of these cases involved information such as obscenity, which was definitionally unprotected by the First Amendment. The Court went on to characterize the right as "the right to read or observe what he pleases—the right to satisfy his intellectual and emotional needs in the privacy of his own home."[218] It reasoned that permitting the state to prosecute a person for possessing obscene material in his home would be akin to thought control.[219] During the course of its opinion, it repeatedly recognized that this case was readily distinguishable from prior cases such as *Roth v. United States*, which had permitted the government to criminalize the distribution of obscene matter, because this case turned on private possession within the home.[220]

Despite the Court's explicit attempts to distinguish public distribution of obscenity from private possession in the home, it was inevitable that petitioners in subsequent cases would argue that, if there was a right to receive information and to enjoy it in the home, then there must also be a right to provide it. This proved to be an instance, however, in which the Court meant what it said and was prepared to stand behind the distinctions that it had initially drawn. Two years after *Stanley* in *United States v. Reidel*,[221] the Court rejected a challenge to a conviction for transmitting obscene materials through the mail based on *Stanley* and emphasized that the right to possess obscene material in the home in no way implied a right to provide it. Likewise, in *Paris Adult Theatre v. Slaton*, the Court made it clear that the right to possess obscene material in the privacy of the home did not extend to the right to view such material in an adult theater, given that the latter could result in cognizable social harm.[222] It might seem that a right to possess implies a right to provide; however, the Court could readily conclude that commercial distribution of unprotected material lacked the solid constitutional roots in privacy and autonomy of possession and was capable of causing greater societal injury than private possession. These cases also indicate that distinctions drawn at the outset by the Court are to be taken seriously and not simply set aside as meaningless in subsequent decisions.

Occasionally, when the Court would like to distinguish but not overrule earlier precedents, it will differentiate them based upon facts that appear to have been irrelevant to the Court in earlier decisions. As such, these distinctions appear to be disingenuous. In *Chamption v. Ames*, the Court held that Congress had plenary power to prohibit the shipment of an item such as lottery tickets in interstate commerce.[223] Several years later in *Hammer v. Dagenhart*,[224] the Court invalidated an act of Congress that had banned interstate shipment of goods produced with child labor. In the course of doing so, it distinguished *Champion* and several similar cases that had seemed to provide Congress with the plenary power to prohibit the shipment of goods in interstate commerce as holding that Congress only had the power to prohibit the shipment of those goods such as contaminated food that were harmful in and of themselves.[225] Although this may have described the earlier cases factually, it had not been a part of their rationale, as Justice Holmes argued in dissent.[226] Consequently, it appeared to be an artificial distinction designed to limit the scope of the earlier cases. Eventually this distinction was rejected, *Hammer* was overruled in *United States v. Darby*,[227] and the line of cases returned to the earlier and broader meaning.

Likewise, in *Employment Division v. Smith*, the Court concluded that in prior cases it had only applied the compelling state interest standard to free exercise of religion challenges involving hybrid claims, that is free exercise claims coupled with some other independent constitutional violation, often a freedom of speech claim.[228] As Justice O'Connor quite correctly pointed out in her concurrence, this factor, even though true, played no role in the prior decisions.[229] Rather, the Court had applied the compelling state interest analysis independently to both the free exercise and freedom of speech claims with no indication that the conjunction of the two was at all relevant to the standard of review.[230] Thus, *Smith* is an example of a re-rationalization of a prior line of authority that had no realistic grounding in the earlier cases.

The Court's line of "taxpayer standing" cases provide a clear example of the Court drawing arguably disingenuous factual and legal distinctions to limit the scope of earlier decisions. In an opaque opinion in *Frothingham v. Mellon*,[231] the Court held that a taxpayer did not have legal standing to challenge a federal spending program on the grounds that it exceeded congressional authority under Article I of the Constitution. Forty-five years later in *Flast v. Cohen*,[232] it was faced with the question of whether *Frothingham* precluded a taxpayer from claiming legal standing to challenge the expenditure of federal funds in aid of religiously affiliated schools. While recognizing the general validity of *Frothingham*, the Court carved out a narrow exception to allow standing in the type of case before the Court, reasoning that a taxpayer would have standing if the challenge was to a federal spending program and if the challenge was based on the Establishment Clause, which the Court deemed to have imposed a specific limitation on the spending power.[233] Thus, the Court distinguished *Frothingham* largely based on legal as opposed to factual differences.

Justice Harlan dissented, presenting a devastating argument that there was no basis for these distinctions and that they were without meaningful substance.[234] First, he explained that, where the revenue for the tax was not earmarked for a special purpose but was simply placed in the general revenues, the taxpayer had no proprietary interest in the funds more than any other citizen, given that a decision in his favor would have no impact at all on his tax liability.[235] Likewise, Justice Harlan pointed out that there was no basis whatsoever for the Court's conclusion that the Establishment Clause "specifically" limits the spending power, as there is nothing in the clause "expressly directed at the expenditure of public funds."[236] As such, there would be no principled way of limiting the concept to Establishment Clause challenges. Consequently, the *Flast* exception to *Frothingham* appeared to be an ad hoc limitation based on thin legalistic distinctions, lacking any legitimate basis.

In subsequent cases, the Court has distinguished away *Flast* based on arguably minor legal differences, just as *Flast* had distinguished away *Frothingham*. In *Valley Forge Christian College v. Americans United*,[237] the Court read *Flast* literally and held that taxpayers did not have standing to challenge a transfer of surplus governmental property to a religiously based college. The Court maintained that *Flast* did not apply, given that the property was transferred by the executive branch rather than Congress, and the action was taken pursuant to legislation passed under the Article IV Property Clause as opposed to the taxing and spending power.[238] Justice Brennan, dissenting, characterized the Court's effort to distinguish *Flast* as relying on "torturous" and "specious" distinctions gleaned by "wrenching snippets of language from our opinions."[239] Despite his rhetorical bombast, Justice Brennan did have a point in arguing that, from the standpoint of either Establishment Clause values or standing doctrine, it made little sense to differentiate executive branch disposition of surplus property from congressional grants of funds.[240] As such, the majority opinion in *Valley Forge* appeared to be attempting to limit the scope of *Flast* to the greatest extent possible.

The torturous distinctions in the area of taxpayer standing continued in *Hein v. Freedom from Rel-igion Foundation*.[241] The Court declined to extend taxpayer standing under *Flast* to permit a challenge to the organization of conferences by the White House Office of Faith-Based Initiatives, which was created by executive order and supported by general appropriations to the executive branch.[242] The Court relied heavily on the fact that the program in question was not created by Congress nor funded by specific congressional appropriations.[243] The plurality distinguished its prior decision in *Bowen v. Kendrick*[244] on the grounds that the program there challenged was created by Congress, and the funds in question were appropriated for that program.[245] The plurality concluded that it neither overruled nor extended *Flast* but rather left it as it found it.[246]

Justice Scalia, concurring, rejected the plurality's distinctions of the prior cases as illogical and argued that *Flast* should be overruled outright because its logic would require application to the challenge before the Court, which would expand the role of judicial oversight of executive action in such a manner as to undermine separation of powers principles.[247] He maintained that the distinctions that the Court had drawn between the instant case and *Flast* were "meaningless and disingenuous . . . forcing lawyers and judges to make arguments which deaden the soul of the law, which is logic and reason."[248] Justice Souter, dissenting, agreed with Justice Scalia that the plurality's distinctions were meaningless but concluded that this simply meant that under *Flast* standing should in fact be found in the case.[249] Whether or not *Flast* should be overruled, it is difficult to disagree with Justice Scalia's conclusion that this line of precedent has become "incomprehensible," "lawless," and "chaotic."

Sometimes in interpreting precedent, the Court will focus on facts in a prior case that seemed to have been of little if any relevance to the holding. For instance, in *In re Griffiths*,[250] in the course of invalidating a Connecticut law that prohibited resident aliens from becoming members of the bar, the Court noted that the person challenging the law had no intention of becoming a citizen. Subsequently, in *Nyquist v. Mauclet*,[251] the Court invalidated a law that precluded resident aliens who did not intend to apply for citizenship from receiving college tuition benefits. The Court cited *Griffiths* for the proposition that it was irrelevant that the exclusion did not apply to all aliens but only to those who did not intend to apply for citizenship.[252] Justice Powell, dissenting, was quite correct in pointing out that the statement in *Mauclet* "was hardly more than a factual 'aside,'" because the challenge in that case was to a law that excluded all aliens and not simply those who did not intend to apply for citizenship.[253] This particular fact had no bearing on the decision in *Griffiths*, and whether it ought to matter in an appropriate case should still have been very much of an issue in *Mauclet* as opposed to one that had already been decided.

⅋ V. Overruling Precedent

A. Reconsideration of Constitutional Precedent

Even in constitutional law, stare decisis is the rule, and the rejection of precedent is the exception. As the Court explained in *Payne v. Tennessee* in the course of overruling two recent decisions:

> [s]tare decisis is the preferred course because it promotes the even-handed, predictable, and consistent development of legal principles, fosters reliance on judicial decisions, and contributes to the actual and perceived integrity of the judicial process.[254]

One argument for sticking with precedent is simply to avoid creating the perception that cases are decided based on the political preferences of judges and as such are subject to being overruled whenever changes on the Court occur. In his dissenting opinion in *United States v. Rabinowitz*, Justice Frankfurter objected to the Court's continual changes of direction concerning the issue of the legitimate scope of a search incident to arrest.[255] He warned that

> [e]specially ought the Court not reenforce needlessly the instabilities of our day by giving fair ground for the belief that Law is the expression of chance—for instance, of unexpected changes in the Court's composition and the contingencies in the choice of successors.[256]

Likewise, in his dissenting opinion in *Pollock v. Farmers Loan and Trust*, Justice White warned that:

> [i]f the permanency of [the Court's] conclusions is to depend upon the personal opinions of those who, from time to time, may make up its membership, it will inevitably become a theater of political strife, and its action will be without coherence or consistency.[257]

To the extent that precedent has been accepted and regularly followed, there would be slight reason to overrule or abandon it. In *Dickerson v. United States*, for instance, the Court declined to seriously consider overruling its once controversial decision in *Miranda v. Arizona*, concluding that it "has become embedded in routine police practice to the point where the warnings have become part of our national culture."[258]

Nevertheless, the Court is more inclined to reconsider constitutional as opposed to statutory precedent. In *Smith v. Allwright*, the Court explained that "[i]n constitutional questions, where correction depends upon amendment and not upon legislative action this Court throughout its history has freely exercised its power to reexamine the basis of its constitutional decisions."[259] Indeed, in a concurring opinion in *St. Joseph Hospital v. United States*, Justice Stone went so far as to say that "[t]he doctrine of stare decisis . . . has only a limited application in the field of constitutional law."[260] This was definitely an overstatement but is still recognition of the fact that the Court is not infallible and, absent a disposition to occasionally reconsider past decisions, many constitutional errors as a practical matter would be irreversible. The Court in *Allwright* also noted that such a possibility of overruling would necessarily be greater where "the decision believed erroneous is the application of a constitutional principle rather than an interpretation of the Constitution to extract the principle itself."[261] Presumably, the former would cause less harm to the interests in the stability of constitutional doctrine than the latter. In dissent, Justice Roberts argued that frequent overruling would indeed undermine the predictability of the law "bring[ing] adjudications of this tribunal into the same class as a restricted railroad ticket, good for this day and train only."[262]

Rarely has the Court addressed the issue of stare decisis and its limitations in as much detail as it did in *Planned Parenthood v. Casey*.[263] For two decades the Court had been pressured to overrule[264] its controversial decision in *Roe v. Wade*.[265] In the plurality joint opinion of Justices O'Connor, Kennedy, and Souter in *Casey*, it began by noting the obvious tension between the need to follow precedent in order to preserve stability and the need to be able to discard precedent, which has proven to be clearly erroneous.[266] Citing prior case law, the joint opinion of three justices then deduced four instances in which it was appropriate for the Court to overrule prior constitutional decisions.[267] It noted that in deciding whether to overrule a prior opinion the Court has considered whether the principle has proved to be unworkable, whether there has been the type of reliance on the decision that would result in hardship if it were discarded, whether its doctrine has been abandoned, and whether it has been undermined by changes in the underlying facts.[268] The plurality then applied these principles to *Roe* and concluded that it did not meet the criteria that would justify its rejection.

The joint opinion did not stop at that point, however. Recognizing the controversy that continued to swirl around the Court's opinion in *Roe* and the movement to have it overruled, it engaged in a rare discussion of the very theory behind judicial review and its relation to precedent. At the outset, the joint opinion noted that the Court's power was derived from its legitimacy, which in turn was a product of its ability to convince the public that its decisions were grounded in constitutional principle and not simply the result of political pressure.[269] This led the Court to conclude that it must be cautious in overruling prior precedent if it is to maintain its legitimacy.

First, if the Court overrules prior cases too frequently, it may appear that its decisions are not based on enduring constitutional principle but rather the policy preferences of current members of the Court.[270] Second, overruling would be inappropriate in rare cases such as *Roe*, where the Court believes that its " interpretation of the Constitution calls the contending sides of a national controversy to end their national division by accepting a common mandate rooted in the Constitution."[271] This is so, according to the joint opinion, because overruling in these circumstances might lead the public to believe that the Court had simply caved in to political pressure.[272] In addition, those who had relied on the Court's initial resolution of the issue would feel betrayed by a reversal.[273] This could undermine the legitimacy of the Court for an extended period of time.[274]

In dissent, Chief Justice Rehnquist argued that a controversial decision such as *Roe* produces mass demonstrations both in its favor and in opposition, and as a result "[a] decision either way ... can therefore be perceived as favoring one group or the other."[275] Justice Scalia noted that, rather than settling the abortion issue by nationalizing it, *Roe* fanned the flames and has since dominated the selection of Supreme Court justices.[276] He pointed out that the Supreme Court that decided the *Dred Scott*[277] case also apparently believed that it was resolving an intensely controversial issue, that of slavery in the territories, and yet by constitutionalizing the issue, the decision only added more fuel to the fire, which shortly thereafter resulted in a civil war.[278] Consequently, at least some of the rationales that the joint opinion set forth for adhering to precedent were as controversial as the decision to adhere itself. As the joint opinion recognized, however, *Roe* and the massive political controversy that followed from it were quite unusual, and some of the reasons for adhering to it or not would be of little consequence to the typical judicial decision.

B. Departure from Established Doctrine

One common rationale for overruling is to explain that the precedent in question departed from prior established principle or doctrine.[279] The overruling of *Hammer v. Dagenhart*[280] by *United States v. Darby* is an example of this.[281] *Hammer* had held that Congress only had the right to prohibit the shipment in interstate commerce of items that were harmful in and of themselves, and that was not true of products manufactured with child labor.[282] Dissenting in *Hammer*, Justice Holmes argued that none of the Court's prior cases recognizing the plenary power of Congress to regulate the shipment of products in interstate commerce had required that the item itself be dangerous or harmful.[283] In *Darby*, the Court upheld congressional legislation banning the shipment in interstate commerce of items made in violation of the federal Fair Labor Standards Act.[284] The Court recognized that *Hammer* stood squarely in the path of its decision and thus, after citing the precedent relied on by Justice Holmes, as well as a few subsequent cases, overruled *Hammer* on the ground that it "was a departure from the principles which have prevailed in the interpretation of the commerce clause before and since the decision."[285] This is a sterling example of the overruling of a case as inconsistent with developed doctrine.

The Court took this approach in *Adarand Constructors, Inc. v. Pena*[286] in overruling *Metro Broadcasting v. F.C.C.* to the extent that it had applied an intermediate standard of review to "benign" racial classifications enacted by the federal government. The *Adarand* Court explained that *Metro*'s rationale for applying the intermediate standard was inconsistent with prior doctrine in that it rejected the distinction between benign and invidious discrimination, as well as the distinction between state and federal employment of racial classifications.[287] The Court explained that

> [r]emaining true to an "intrinsically sounder" doctrine established in prior cases better serves the values of stare decisis than would following a more recently decided case inconsistent with the decisions that came before it; the latter course would simply compound the recent error and would likely make the unjustified break from previously established doctrine complete. In such a situation, "special justification" exists to depart from the recently decided case.[288]

The Court was not troubled by overruling *Metro*, as it had yet to "become integrated into the fabric of the law."[289]

Likewise, in *Payne v. Tennessee*,[290] the Court was willing to overrule two recent decisions—*Booth v. Maryland*[291] and *South Carolina v. Gathers*[292]—on the grounds that the holdings in those cases—precluding the admission of evidence in the sentencing phase of capital cases of a murder victim's unique nature or of the impact of the murder on the family and community—was simply inconsistent with decades of prior precedent. This was especially true according to the Court in *Payne* when the overruled cases were decided by a one-vote margin over spirited dissents and had been questioned by dissents in subsequent cases as well.[293]

C. Abandoned Precedent

The Court will overturn a precedent that has been effectively abandoned by succeeding cases.[294] The joint opinion in *Planned Parenthood v. Casey* recognized that a case might be overruled if its doctrine had been significantly undermined by subsequent decisions.[295] The plurality then argued that this had not been the case with *Roe*.[296] Justice Scalia, dissenting, argued quite effectively, however, that the joint opinion was able to save *Roe* only by rejecting part of its holding as well as overruling several of the post-*Roe* decisions that had relied on it.[297] Consequently, if not abandoned, *Roe* was at least significantly modified by the very case that concluded it had not been undermined.

Likewise, in urging that *Flast v. Cohen* should be overruled in his concurring opinion in *Hein v. Freedom from Religion Foundation*, Justice Scalia argued that "honoring stare decisis requires more than beating Flast to a pulp and then sending it out to the lower courts weakened, denigrated, more incomprehensible than ever, and yet somehow technically alive."[298] Thus, for Justice Scalia, if a precedent has been effectively undermined, it is better to overrule it than simply to distinguish it into oblivion, given the confusion that the latter course would pose for the lower courts.

D. Rejecting the Underlying Predicates

Sometimes a precedent or a line of precedent is overruled when the Court rejects one or more of its essential predicates.[299] This basically happened with the infamous *Lochner* due process liberty of contract doctrine. For the better part of fifty years, the Court had invalidated many state laws regulating economic affairs because they infringed the right of contract, which was an aspect of Fourteenth Amendment due process liberty. The Court did not, however, generally invalidate even extensive regulation of businesses that "affect the public interest."[300] This concept was crucial to the application of the doctrine in that it essentially differentiated, though not on a principled basis, those businesses that could constitutionally be regulated heavily by the state from those that could not.

In *Nebbia v. New York*,[301] the Court upheld a New York law that set a minimum price for the retail sale of milk. The Court conceded that, though the milk business was important and heavily regulated, it was not a monopoly or a public utility.[302] Still, after a lengthy review of the cases, the Court concluded that "[i]t is clear that there is no closed class or category of businesses affected with a public interest."[303] Rather "the phrase 'affected with a public interest' can, in the nature of things, mean no more than that an industry, for adequate reason, is subject to control for the public good."[304] In other words, "affected with the public interest" was not a concept for qualitatively differentiating one type of industry from another but simply a statement of the conclusion that state regulation of the industry was reasonable and hence constitutional. The Court did not purport to overrule any specific prior case nor did it purport to be revising its prior doctrine. However, it was obvious that without this foundational concept, the due process liberty right to contract would collapse, and it did. Justice McReynolds, dissenting, well understood the significance of the Court's opinion, writing that "[t]he argument advanced here would support general prescription of prices for farm products, groceries, shoes, clothing, all the necessities of modern civilization, as well as labor, when some Legislature finds and declares such action advisable and for the public good."[305] The dissent knew that a sea change in the Court's jurisprudence had occurred.

The Court completed the rejection of the due process right to contract doctrine three years later in *West Coast Hotel v. Parrish*.[306] As with *Nebbia*, the Court emphasized the state's important interest in relieving the economic stress imposed by the Depression, but ultimately it concluded that *Adkins v. Children's Hospital*,[307] its earlier case invalidating a minimum wage for women, was simply incorrect as a matter of law.[308] Consequently, the Court overruled *Adkins* and upheld the New York minimum wage statute for women.[309]

In *Agostini v. Felton*,[310] decided in 1997, the Court overruled its 1986 decision in *Aguilar v. Felton*,[311] thereby upholding the constitutionality of the very program that had been invalidated in *Aguilar* on account of changes in Establishment Clause doctrine between the two decisions. The Court concluded that subsequent cases had rejected the key predicates of *Aguilar*, including its determinations that permitting public schoolteachers to offer remedial educational programs would risk religious indoctrination, create a symbolic link between the state and religion, and involve the state in an excessive entanglement with religion through the monitoring of the program.[312] In view of these changes in the Court's legal analysis under the Establishment Clause, it took the unusual step of overruling the earlier decision in subsequent litigation stemming from the very same controversy.[313]

The overruling of *Olmstead v. United States*[314] and *Goldman v. United States*[315] by *Katz v. United States*[316] provides another example of the Court overruling prior decisions when the predicates of those decisions had been rejected. In *Olmstead*, the defendant's telephone was tapped without a physical trespass on his property.[317] In *Goldman*, government agents had overheard conversations within an office through a listening device placed against the partition wall in an adjacent office. *Olmstead* and *Goldman* had both rejected the application of the Fourth Amendment's guarantee against unreasonable searches and seizures to wiretapping or electronic surveillance on the grounds that intangibles such as conversations were not protected by the Fourth Amendment, and an intrusion into a protected place was not protected absent a physical penetration. However, in *Silverman v. United States*,[318] where federal agents listened to conversations in an adjoining office with a spike microphone that may have resulted in a physical trespass, the Court concluded that proof of such a trespass was not necessary to invoke the protection of the Fourth Amendment. The Court did not purport to overrule *Olmstead* or *Goldman* in *Silverman*. However, six years later in *Katz*, when the Court was confronted with the legality of warrantless electronic surveillance of a telephone call from a phone booth without any physical penetration, the Court concluded that "the underpinnings of Olmstead and Goldman have been so eroded by our subsequent decisions that the 'trespass' doctrine there enunciated can no longer be regarded as controlling."[319] As a result, it overruled both *Olmstead* and *Goldman*, replacing the physical trespass approach with a focus on privacy.[320] This is an example of the Court changing directions and overruling precedent through a two-step procedure in which it initially undermines the underlying premise of a prior decision and then later concludes that the decision must be overruled because the premise is no longer valid.

E. Changed Facts or Circumstances

Sometimes a precedent is overruled because the factual context on which the earlier case was based has changed significantly. In the *Propeller Genesee Chief v. Fitzhugh*,[321] decided in 1851, the Court overruled the *Thomas Jefferson*,[322] decided in 1825, which had held that the admiralty jurisdiction of federal courts was restricted to waters with the ebb and flow of the tide, as was the case with the English common law rule. The Court emphasized that at the time the *Thomas Jefferson* was decided "the question as it now presents itself could not be foreseen," given that "commerce on the rivers of the west and on the lakes was in its infancy, and of little importance."[323] The development of internal commerce on rivers such as the Mississippi and Missouri altered the context in a significant manner, causing the Court to rethink its earlier approach.

In *Wolf v. Colorado*, the Court declined to apply the exclusionary rule to the states in cases in which evidence had been illegally seized under the Fourth Amendment, in part because it believed that alternative remedies, including civil damage actions and administrative and criminal actions against the police, were sufficient.[324] In overruling *Wolf* twelve years later in *Mapp v. Ohio*, the Court emphasized that these alternatives had been found to be ineffective in practice, and hence the exclusionary rule was indeed the only meaningful remedy.[325]

The treatment of the separate but equal principle of *Plessy v. Ferguson* in *Brown v. Board of Education*[326] provides a well-known example of the Court effectively overruling a prior decision due to a change in circumstances. In *Plessy*, decided in 1896, the Court had relied in part on the fact that the Congress that drafted the Fourteenth Amendment had also funded segregated public schools of the District of Columbia as evidence that the Fourteenth Amendment did not prohibit all segregated facilities.[327] Thus, the *Plessy* precedent provided the legal justification for the entire segregated social structure of the South. At the very least, the Court in *Brown* needed to distinguish away *Plessy* into oblivion to hold segregated public schools unconstitutional.

The Court attempted to do this in a variety of ways. First, it observed that, initially, the Court had read the Fourteenth Amendment as "proscribing all state-imposed discriminations against the Negro race,"[328] and the separate but equal concept was first adopted later on in *Plessy*. The Court cited the *Slaughter-House Cases* and *Strauder v. West Virginia* for this point.[329] Although these cases did state the equality principle more expansively than *Plessy*, they were both easily distinguishable in that the *Slaughter-House Cases* did not involve a claim of racial discrimination at all; thus, the statement was simply dicta, whereas *Strauder* did involve discrimination with respect to a civil as opposed to a social right, a distinction that *Plessy* believed the framers of the Fourteenth Amendment had taken seriously.[330]

The Court next distinguished all of the post-*Plessy* separate but equal cases primarily involving graduate education on the ground that none required the Court to reconsider *Plessy*'s premise that separate could be equal.[331] However, the primary argument that the *Brown* Court relied on to distinguish *Plessy* was that times had changed, or more specifically that the societal importance of education had changed.[332] Earlier in the opinion, the Court had noted that, at the time of the adoption of the Fourteenth Amendment, public education was still in a relatively primitive state.[333] By way of contrast, the *Brown* Court proclaimed that "[t]oday, education is perhaps the most important function of state and local governments. . . . .[I]t is doubtful that any child may reasonably be expected to succeed in life if he is denied the opportunity of an education."[334] Thus, even assuming that *Plessy* was correct in its time, it was no longer so.

The Court also rejected *Plessy*'s conclusion[335] that there was no reason to believe that racial segregation was intended to or did in fact stigmatize.[336] It stated that "[w]hatever may have been the extent of psychological knowledge at the time of *Plessy v. Ferguson*, this finding [that segregation leads to a feeling of inferiority which in turn interferes with educational development] is amply supported by modern authority."[337] To support this conclusion, the Court cited social science data that proved to be somewhat controversial.[338] For these reasons the Court "conclude[d] that in the field of public education the doctrine of 'separate but equal' has no place,"[339] distinguishing though essentially overruling *Plessy*. Thus, *Brown*'s treatment of *Plessy* illustrates several different methods of handling deeply troublesome precedent. The Court can argue that the initial precedent incorrectly understood the law, incorrectly understood the facts, or that times have changed and hence the facts are now quite different. *Brown* did all three in the course of burying *Plessy*.

F. Reliance Interest

The Court is less likely to overrule a prior precedent that has given rise to a significant reliance interest.[340] This is especially true where economic or property rights have been created as a result of the legal rule in question. In the course of overruling a prior case that had not given rise to any such economic reliance, the Court in the *Propeller Genesee Chief v. Fitzhugh* explained that there would be a near irrebuttable presumption against overruling a decision that had provided the basis for the creation of either contract or property rights.[341] In *Adarand Constructors, Inc. v. Pena*, in the course of overruling *Metro Broadcasting v. F.C.C.*, the Court noted that "reliance on a case that has recently departed from precedent is likely to be minimal, particularly where, as here, the rule set forth in that case is unlikely to affect primary conduct in any event."[342] Presumably, the Court meant that because the rule in question pertained to the correct standard of review, that is, judicial analytical methodology, private parties or government entities were unlikely to take the change into account in planning their activities. It is hardly obvious that that is so, however. Because the determination of the appropriate standard of review often makes the difference between winning or losing a lawsuit, a well-counseled government entity might indeed take it into account in determining whether to employ a "benign" racial preference, and a potential plaintiff would also take the standard into account in determining whether to challenge it.

Justice Kennedy emphasized the value of stability and reliance interests in his concurring opinion in *United States v. Lopez*.[343] There the Court had invalidated an act of Congress as exceeding its power under the Commerce Clause for the first time in 60 years. Justice Kennedy cautioned that this was an unusual case and that the vast bulk of the Court's Commerce Clause precedent remained firmly in place. He proclaimed that

> [t]he Court as an institution and the legal system as a whole have an immense stake in the stability of our Commerce Clause jurisprudence as it has evolved to this point. Stare decisis opearates with great force in counseling us not to call in question the essential principles now in place respecting the congressional power to regulate transactions of a commercial nature. That fundamental restraint on our power forecloses us from reverting to an understanding of commerce that would serve only an 18th century economy.. . .[344]

This was an important reminder of the need for stability in constitutional doctrine which affects economic transactions.

In *Planned Parenthood v. Casey*, the joint opinion acknowledged that a reliance interest would be strongest where people had entered into commercial transactions as a result of the decision in question.[345] The Court recognized that the reliance claim, with respect to abortion, was arguably quite weak but nevertheless maintained that the fact that people had planned their lives around the ability to control conception should not be dismissed as irrelevant.[346] The Court seemed to recognize that this was a rather unusual if not strained reliance interest. Although it did not say so in so many words, it may have recognized that there was a more abstract reliance on the existence of the right created by *Roe*, even by the vast majority of people who would never have occasion to make use of it. That is, once a right is established and gains a constituency, its very existence creates a psychological reliance interest that is hard to displace. A repeal of the right would not return society to the place it was before its creation.[347] Chief Justice Rehnquist's dissent confirmed this understanding. He characterized the joint opinion's reliance argument as "undeveloped and totally conclusory."[348] Consequently, he maintained that the reliance argument was based only on the joint opinion's "generalized assertions about the national psyche, on a belief that the people of this country have grown accustomed to the Roe decision over the last 19 years."[349] Arguably, Chief Justice Rehnquist understood the nature of the Court's reliance argument but underestimated the social dislocation that might accompany the overruling of *Roe*.

Not every claim of reliance on prior precedent will be taken seriously by the Court. In overruling *Bowers v. Hardwick*, which had upheld the constitutionality of a state law criminalizing homosexual sodomy, the Court in *Lawrence v. Texas*[350] concluded that there had been no significant detrimental reliance on the decision, given that it had restricted rather than expanded liberty and given that the clear societal and legal trend was to the contrary. Justice Scalia in dissent disagreed with this, citing cases and legislation that had relied on *Bowers*.[351] The Court's opinion indicates that general governmental reliance expressed through continued enforcement of existing laws is almost certainly not the type of reliance that the Court considers to be significant in determining whether to overrule a prior decision.

Likewise, in *Hein v. Freedom from Rel-igion Foundation*, in calling for the overruling of the Court's prior decision in *Flast v. Cohen*, which allowed taxpayers standing to challenge congressional appropriation that arguably violated the Establishment Clause, Justice Scalia, concurring, maintained that *Flast* had "engendered no reliance interest, not only because one does not arrange his affairs with an eye to standing, but also because there is no relying on the random and irrational."[352]

G. Unworkability

Sometimes, the Court will overrule prior precedent if it concludes that its principles or doctrinal rules have proven to be unworkable.[353] The Court's decision in *Garcia v. San Antonio Metropolitan Transit Authority*,[354] overruling *National League of Cities v. Usery*,[355] is a prime example of this principle. *National League of Cities* had held that congressional action that impaired a state's ability to "structure integral operations in areas of traditional governmental functions"[356] was unconstitutional.[357] The *Garcia* majority argued that the concept of "traditional governmental functions" was unworkable because neither the Supreme Court nor the lower courts had been able to provide guidance as to the contours of this concept in the nine-year period since *National League of Cities* had been decided.[358] The Court cited several lower court decisions that had reached opposite conclusions on relatively similar facts.[359] The Court found it difficult to find "an organizing principle" in these cases.[360] Justice Blackmun recognized that "[m]any constitutional standards involve 'undoubte[d] . . . gray areas.'"[361] Likewise, the Court would normally assume that "case-by-case development would lead to a workable standard."[362] He was unwilling to indulge that assumption in this instance, however, in view of the previous difficulty the

Court had experienced with a similar standard in the area of state sovereign immunity from federal taxation.[363] Based on this experience, he argued that relying on the history of governmental functions "results in line-drawing of the most arbitrary sort" and fails to take account of the ever-changing role of government.[364] Consequently, Justice Blackmun concluded that *National League of Cities* must be overruled, and protection of state sovereignty must reside in the political branches rather than the courts.[365] *Garcia* provides a prime example of overruling because of unworkability of judicial doctrine.

The area of judicial review of partisan political gerrymandering has also given rise to concerns over unworkability. In *Davis v. Bandemer*,[366] the Court had held that, in an extreme case, drawing districting lines in order to gain partisan political advantage could be invalidated under the Equal Protection Clause; however, a majority was unable to agree on a standard for assessing such claims. The plurality in *Bandemer* concluded that a challenger could prevail if he could show that the redistricting plan was intentionally discriminatory against an identifiable political group and had the effect of discriminating against such group.[367] Eighteen years later in *Vieth v. Jubelirer*,[368] a four-justice plurality argued that *Bandemer* should be overruled on the grounds that, since that case was decided, the lower courts had been unable to devise a workable standard for addressing the issue, resulting in almost no litigated cases in which the plaintiff had prevailed.[369] Because Justice Kennedy, concurring, as well as the four dissenters, believed that it was still possible to develop workable standards in the future, *Bandemer* was not overruled.[370] Still, the plurality made an unusually strong argument for unworkability based not simply on the years of judicial experience but on the very intractability of the underlying issue as well.

In *Seminole Tribe of Florida v. Florida*,[371] the Court did overrule its previous decision in *Pennsylvania v. Union Gas Co.*[372] That case had held that Congress could abrogate a state's sovereign immunity against a citizen suit in a federal court under the Interstate Commerce Clause.[373] *Seminole* presented the question of whether Congress could also abrogate state sovereign immunity under the Indian Commerce Clause. Because the Court readily concluded that the Indian Commerce and Interstate Commerce Clauses were indistinguishable for purposes of abrogation, it needed to consider whether *Union Gas* should be followed or abandoned.[374] In concluding that *Union Gas* should be overruled, the Court relied on several factors. It observed that one recognized ground for overruling was a situation in which a precedent had proved to be unworkable.[375] It maintained that this was such a case because only four justices had joined Justice Brennan's plurality opinion in *Union Gas*, with Justice White adding the fifth vote for the holding but explicitly dissenting from the rationale.[376] That, of course, created confusion as to the meaning and application of the case, and the Court pointed out that such confusion has been reflected in subsequent lower court opinions.[377] As such, no workable doctrine had emerged from *Union Gas*, and the law would be clarified rather than confused by its rejection.

H. Comparison to Other Overruled Decisions

In view of the controversy surrounding *Roe v. Wade* and whether it should be overruled, the joint opinion in *Planned Parenthood v. Casey* compared the circumstances of *Roe* with that of two other famous overrulings—that of *Lochner v. New York* and *Plessy v. Ferguson*.[378] Because in each instance doctrine that had been settled and had become part of the legal fabric for half a century or more was ultimately rejected, it was worth asking whether the same might be true of *Roe*, which had been in place for only 20 years. The joint opinion distinguished *Roe* from *Lochner* and *Plessy* on the grounds that each of those cases were overruled as the result of a change in the factual predicate, or at least a perception that the facts had changed.[379] This appears to be a strained if not wholly disingenuous reading of the overruling of these decisions. To be sure, factual change did play a role in the overruling of *Plessy* and *Lochner*; however, it would not appear to be the dominant reason.

Chief Justice Rehnquist argued in dissent that those decisions were overruled simply because they were incorrect as a matter of constitutional interpretation and not because the underlying facts had changed.[380] This would seem to be a better explanation of the rejection of those two cases. Despite the emphasis in the *Brown* opinion on the changed role of education in society, *Brown* clearly stood for the proposition that state-sponsored racial segregation or discrimination was inconsistent with the core meaning of equal protection of the laws. The summary application of *Brown* to prohibit segregation outside of the area of education in the years following the decision made this quite clear.[381] Likewise, the primary reason why the *Lochner* doctrine was ultimately rejected was the reason expressed by Justice Holmes in his classic *Lochner* dissent; that is, there was simply no basis for considering the right of contract to be a highly protected fundamental right capable of precluding state regulation of economic activity as the Court recognized in *West Coast Hotel v. Parrish*.[382]

I. Incorrectly Decided

At some point, a prior decision should be overruled simply because it was flat-out wrong as a matter of law, recognizing, however, that if stare decisis is to have any meaning, every error of law cannot and will not be corrected.[383] In *Planned Parenthood v. Casey*, however, the joint opinion took the position "that a decision to overrule should rest on some special reason over and above the belief that a prior case was wrongly decided."[384] This generally may be true, but there must certainly be instances in which the Court concludes that a case was so clearly incorrect in its reasoning or its interpretation of the Constitution that it should be rejected.[385]

One of the most remarkable reversals in Supreme Court history was the overruling of *Minersville School District v. Gobitis*,[386] decided in 1940, upholding a compulsory flag salute by *West Virginia State Board of Education v. Barnette*,[387] decided three years later in 1943. What is even more remarkable is that *Gobitis* was decided by a vote of 8-1, while *Barnette* reversed it by a vote of 6-3. The Court's explanation for this rather dramatic reversal was simply that *Gobitis* was incorrect as a matter of First Amendment law.[388] Justices Douglas and Black, who had agreed with the majority in *Gobitis* wrote a special concurrence in *Barnette*, confessing error.[389] It is true that *Gobitis* was based on a rejection of a free exercise claim, whereas *Barnette* found that the provision violated freedom of speech. The *Barnette* Court's primary complaint against *Gobitis* was that the Court had granted far too much deference to the state's educational policies in a civil liberties case.[390] At its heart, *Barnette* was based on a very different conception of the role of the Court in a case involving First Amendment freedoms. As Justice Jackson wrote for the majority:

> [t]he very purpose of a Bill of Rights was to withdraw certain subjects from the vicissitudes of political controversy, to place them beyond the reach of majorities and officials and to establish them as legal principles to be applied by the courts.[391]

This approach was quite inconsistent with the degree of deference that *Gobitis* had granted the school board, and as such the case had to be overruled.

Another example of a precedent that was rejected almost immediately for no other reason than that a majority of the Court believed that it was wrongly decided is *Hepburn v. Griswold*.[392] In *Hepburn* by a 5-3 vote, the Court held that Congress lacked the power to authorize the use of paper money as legal tender. At the time that the opinion was released, Justice Grier, who joined the majority, resigned from the Court. Two justices were then appointed to the Court, raising the total to nine. The following year in *Knox v. Lee* and *Parker v. Davis*, known as the *Legal Tender Cases*, the two new justices, along with the three who had dissented in *Hepburn*, voted to overrule *Hepburn*, relying on the reasoning set forth in the *Hepburn* dissent.[393] The remaining four members of the *Hepburn* majority dissented, arguing that *Hepburn* had been correctly decided. This was certainly the swiftest overruling of a major precedent in Supreme Court history.

In *Chimel v. California*, the Court overruled two prior decisions in which the Court had permitted a search incident to an arrest to extend to the defendant's entire room or house on the grounds that those cases were incorrectly decided, given that the purpose of the doctrine was to permit the police to prevent the arrestee from grabbing a weapon to attack the police or to destroy evidence, and neither of these rationales would support a search beyond the defendant's reach.[394] Given the purpose of the rule, the earlier cases were incorrect to begin with and quite properly rejected.

Even a long-settled precedent might be subject to reconsideration if it has contributed to serious doctrinal error, although the likelihood of reversal is quite small. In his dissenting opinion in *Saenz v. Roe*, Justice Thomas suggested that he would be amenable to the reconsideration of the unduly narrow construction of the Fourteenth Amendment Privileges or Immunities Clause, some 130 years earlier in the *Slaughter-House Cases*, given that "[it] has contributed in no small part to the current disarray of our Fourteenth Amendment jurisprudence."[395] He maintained that the *Slaughter-House Cases* were inconsistent with the original understanding of the clause.[396] Revisiting that error is consistent with his emphasis on construing the Constitution based on the original understanding. It is unlikely that a majority of the Court would be inclined to significantly revise a major holding that had prevailed for well over a century, even if incorrect, in order to bring it into line with original understanding, especially because many of the other justices would be unlikely to agree with Justice Thomas's interpretation of the original understanding. Moreover, Justice Thomas argued that, if it is appropriate to correct the unduly narrow construction of the Privileges or Immunities Clause propounded by the *Slaughter-House Cases*, it would also be appropriate to narrow the improperly broad readings of the Equal Protection and Due Process Clauses that the Court developed to fill the gap.[397] Given the amount of doctrinal water that has passed under the bridge, it is inconceivable that a majority of the Court would agree with that suggestion.

J. Ill-Considered Precedent

Arguably, a precedent should be reconsidered and narrowed (if not overruled) if it failed to take account of relevant considerations when initially decided.[398] For instance, in his dissenting opinion in *Kelo v. City of New London*, Justice Thomas, dissenting, argued that the Court's opinion in *Fallbrook Irrigation Dist. v. Bradley*,[399] the first case to equate the "public use" provision of the Takings Clause with "public purpose," though only in dicta, is of questionable precedential value because it failed to discuss the original meaning or the developed understanding of the clause.[400] Subsequent cases that picked up this dicta and relied on it did so without any further analysis.[401] Justice Thomas concluded that "[w]hen faced with a clash of constitutional principle and a line of unreasoned cases wholly divorced from the text, history, and structure of our founding document, we should not hesitate to resolve the tension in favor of the Constitution's original meaning."[402]

Likewise, in his dissent in *Mapp v. Ohio*,[403] Justice Harlan argued that the Court's adoption of the exclusionary rule was quite inappropriate, given that the question had not been the primary issue briefed or argued to the Court.[404] As such, an important precedent such as *Wolf v. Colorado* should not be overruled, nor should the exclusionary rule be imposed upon the states, absent more thorough consideration by the Court. Justice Souter raised this argument in his dissent in *Church of Lukumi Babalu v. City of Hialeah*,[405] arguing that the Court's prior decision in *Employment Division v. Smith*[406] was vulnerable because the Court had changed the standard of review under the Free Exercise Clause without briefing or oral argument on the issue. This argument should hold some weight in the first case after the initial decision in which the matter is raised, which in this instance was *Lukumi*. However, it should dissolve once the decision has been reaffirmed as binding law in subsequent cases.

In *District of Columbia v. Heller*, writing for the Court Justice Scalia argued that the Court's prior decision construing the Second Amendment, *Miller v. United States* was entitled to little weight, given that the defendant did not make an appearance through counsel before the Court, and thus the government was unopposed.[407] Justice Stevens, dissenting, pointed out that the same thing could be said of *Marbury v. Madison*.[408]

K. Precedent Unsupported by Other Sources

Precedent unsupported by any other legitimate source of constitutional interpretation should be worthy of reconsideration. In his dissenting opinion in *McCreary County v. ACLU*, Justice Scalia argued that the Court's principle of strict governmental neutrality toward religion was not supported by text, history, tradition, or contemporary understanding but rather only by the Court's say-so, which was based only on "the unsubstantiated say-so of earlier Courts going back no farther than the mid-20th century."[409] Justice Scalia concluded that this say-so had been "thoroughly discredited" and as such should be rejected.[410] In his dissent in *Church of Lukumi Babalu v. City of Hialeah*,[411] Justice Souter turned the tables on Justice Scalia and argued that his opinion for the Court in *Employment Division v. Smith*, lowering the standard of review in free exercise cases, should be reconsidered given that it did not discuss evidence of the original understanding of the clause, which quite arguably supported a different result.[412]

L. Precedent Undermined by Extrajudicial Sources

Seminole Tribe of Florida v. Florida raised the issue of whether it is appropriate for a prior opinion to be understood and devalued by an extrajudicial explanation. Justice Souter questioned how *Hans v. Louisiana* could have threatened settled constitutional principle by removing the federal forum in which citizens could sue their own states for violation of federally protected rights.[413] He answered that question by reference to extrajudicial historical material, alleging that the Court in *Hans* withdrew federal jurisdiction to avoid the humiliation of the inability of the federal judiciary to enforce its judgments in Southern states following the removal of federal troops at the end of Reconstruction.[414] The majority scolded Justice Souter, complaining that "[i]ts undocumented and highly speculative extralegal explanation of the decision in Hans is a disservice to the Court's traditional method of adjudication."[415] Justice Souter replied that his point was not to undermine a defensible decision but rather to explain an "utterly indefensible" one.[416] He cited *Puerto Rico v. Branstad's*[417] speculation as to the reasons behind the Court's holding in *Kentucky v. Dennison*[418] as a recent example of the same approach that had been joined by Justice Rehnquist, the author of the majority in *Seminole*, along with two other members of the majority.[419] Whether or not the Court has engaged in such analysis before, the majority surely had a good point. It would indeed undermine the legitimacy of constitutional law and precedent if decisions could be impeached by extrajudicial, conspiratorial explanations. Moreover, it would lead the Court into a morass of historical argument, which would be distracting, complicated, and potentially misleading. The majority was certainly correct in suggesting that this is a road worth avoiding. However, the point was tangential to Justice Souter's arguments against *Hans*, which were based largely on traditionally respected methods of legal analysis.

VI. Conclusion

The American judicial system is a common law system in which case-by-case analysis plays a dominant role. This remains true even when the Court is interpreting a written document such as the Constitution. Indeed, it is especially true with respect to the Constitution, given that so many of its key provisions are vague and flexible and thus readily lend themselves to case-by-case analysis. Creation of precedent, interpretation, and shaping of precedent—including the expansion, narrowing, and distinguishing of precedent and in some instances the overruling of precedent—has always and will always play a significant role in constitutional interpretation and adjudication. For the most part, the techniques that the Court employs in utilizing precedent in constitutional interpretation are the same as those employed in common law analysis. The fact that the Court is ultimately interpreting the Constitution, however, almost certainly has an impact on the way in which it interprets precedent. On the one hand, the fact that the Constitution is the foundational document, both with respect to governmental structure and civil liberties, places a high premium on stability. As the Court has recognized, its very legitimacy would be threatened if the public believed that constitutional interpretations were always in a state of flux and that both structure and rights were subject to radical reevaluation as the composition of the Court shifted. On the other hand, the Court has also recognized that there is perhaps a need for greater flexibility in the reconsideration of precedent in the area of constitutional interpretation, given that the correction judicial error through constitutional amendment is quite difficult. In addition, because the Constitution is so important, it is especially crucial to get it right—even at the expense of some instability and dislocation. As a result, when the Court creates and interprets its precedent, the Court remains no doubt profoundly aware that it is a Constitution that it is expounding.

EIGHT

Deriving Doctrine

🎜 I. Introduction

This chapter treats a variety of issues involving the creation, application, and change of legal doctrine. As explained in the previous chapter precedent, in which the Court relies to some extent on the facts and context of earlier cases in deciding the case, is distinguished from doctrine, in which the principles and rules developed in those cases are largely divorced from the circumstances in which they arose and assume a life of their own. The distinction is not always clear, but it is still somewhat useful for analytical purposes. Justice Holmes noted how doctrine may become divorced from the cases themselves in his dissenting opinion in *Adkins v. Children's Hospital*,[1] arguing that this had happened with respect to the substantive due process liberty of contract. He observed that initially this doctrine began with

> an unpretentious assertion of the liberty to follow the ordinary callings. Later that innocuous generality was expanded into the dogma, Liberty of Contract. Contract is not specially mentioned in the text that we have to construe. It is merely an example of doing what you want to do, embodied in the word liberty. But pretty much all law consists in forbidding men to do some things that they want to do, and contract is no more exempt from law than other acts.[2]

In this chapter, a somewhat arbitrary distinction will be drawn between principle and doctrine. Principle, refers to the broader or more general values that the Court identifies as explaining the core or essence of a constitutional provision. For instance, a principle behind the freedom of speech guarantee of the First Amendment might be the search for truth in the marketplace of ideas. Doctrine adopted to achieve this principle would be prohibition on government censorship of viewpoint out of mere disagreement or the application of the strict standard of judicial review to many instances of governmental interference with freedom of speech. Likewise, a principle behind the Fourth Amendment might be the protection of personal privacy against unwarranted governmental intrusion. Doctrine created to effectuate that principle would be the requirement that the police obtain a warrant from a neutral magistrate based on probable cause before searching a private home for criminal evidence or contraband. As with any distinction, the line between principle and doctrine can be fuzzy around the edges but should be quite apparent in many cases.

This chapter will consider how the Court creates, or at least recognizes, both principle and doctrine. It will consider a variety of sources from which doctrine is derived by the Court, including principle, purpose, precedent, necessity, and whole cloth. The following chapter will consider issues related to the shaping and changing of doctrine.

II. Deriving Principle

One of the most important aspects in the development of constitutional doctrine is the derivation of principle. The most significant provisions in the Constitution are often written at a broad, general, and vague level of abstraction. These provisions are capable of a variety of different readings, some of which are surely in tension—if not inconsistent—with others. The task of identifying the correct principles embodied in a constitutional provision is one of the most important and difficult tasks for the constitutional interpreter. Four areas in which the Court has derived basic principles from various constitutional provisions will be examined. Initially, this chapter will focus upon how the Court developed the marketplace of ideas and self-government principles of freedom of speech, as well as its recognition of differential treatment of speech and the emotive aspect of speech. Then it will examine how the Court developed over a series of cases the individualistic, color-blind theory as its basic principle for assessing racial classifications under the Equal Protection Clause of the Fourteenth Amendment. Next, it will consider how the Court adopted the "one person, one vote" principle as the key to issues of political representation. Then it will examine how the Court initially attempted to justify its decision to protect the right to choose abortion and how it later revised its approach into a more coherent principle. Finally, it will consider how the Court responds to conflicts among competing principles.

A. Freedom of Speech Principle

1. *Abrams v. United States*

One of the most famous examples of a justice attempting to derive the principle behind a constitutional provision is Justice Holmes's famous dissent in *Abrams v. United States*, in which the majority affirmed a conviction under the Sedition Act of 1918.[3] After a thorough discussion of the charges and the evidence in the case, Justice Holmes attempted to explain why the First Amendment must be understood to permit speech that seems misguided, unpatriotic, and even threatening to the best interests of the country during wartime. He began by conceding that it would be logical to suppress potentially dangerous falsehoods as long as we are certain of the truth.[4] But given that "time has upset many fighting faiths," we have come to conclude "that the best test of truth is the power of the thought to get itself accepted in the competition of the market."[5] Consequently, we should be hesitant to prohibit even those "opinions that we loathe . . . unless they so imminently threaten immediate interference" with lawful government objectives.[6]

Rarely has the Court or a justice provided such a straightforward discussion of the theory behind a constitutional provision in a Supreme Court opinion leading to the development of a crucial principle—the marketplace of ideas justification for protection of freedom of speech. Justice Holmes introduced the marketplace of ideas as a theory of freedom of speech and briefly but eloquently explained it. He grounded his theory in skepticism. He started by conceding that suppression of apparent falsehood makes sense if one is certain of the truth. He then explained that history teaches us all that we should be skeptical of such certainty, given the many instances in which we have witnessed the rejection of our previously held certitudes, or "fighting faiths." As such, the wise approach is to let truth and falsehood do battle rather than to attempt to suppress the latter. Justice Holmes certainly did not originate the marketplace of ideas/search for truth theory. It had deep historical roots.[7] But he judicialized it. As with most of Holmes's writing, this cryptic paragraph raised more questions than it answered. It is hardly clear whether Holmes believed that truth is discoverable or whether that even matters. With this brief but piercing theoretical discussion, Holmes launched a debate over free speech theory that continues to this day and began at least to explain why freedom of speech should be regarded as a special and highly protected value.

2. *Whitney v. California*

With all due respect to the Holmes dissent in *Abrams*, by far the most comprehensive and eloquent exposition of free speech theory and principle in the United States Reports appeared in Justice Brandeis's justly famous concurrence in *Whitney v. California*.[8] Brandeis began his discussion by explaining that, in order to develop free speech doctrine, some understanding of the purpose of the First Amendment was necessary.[9] Over the next two or three pages, he eloquently discussed several of the primary values served by freedom of expression. He started by emphasizing the importance of freedom of expression to human liberty. He wrote:

> Those who won our independence believed that the final end of the state was to make men free to develop their faculties, and that in its government the deliberative forces should prevail over the arbitrary. They valued liberty both as an end and a means.[10]

Brandeis linked the value of freedom of expression to human growth, sometimes identified as the autonomy or liberty theory of free expression and with the role of speech in democratic deliberation, the self-government theory. He then turned his attention to the role of freedom of speech to self-government, writing that the founders believed that

> freedom to think as you will and to speak as you think are means indispensable to the discovery and spread of political truth; that without free speech and assembly discussion would be futile; that with them, discussion affords ordinarily adequate protection against the dissemination of noxious doctrine; that the greatest menace to freedom is an inert people; that public discussion is a political duty; and that this should be a fundamental principle of the American Government.[11]

Thus, Brandeis discussed the interrelationship of speech as a means of discovering truth, especially political truth, and speech as an essential component of democratic self-government, melding two of the central theories or values identified with freedom of expression. In doing so he emphasized that citizens must not simply be passive recipients of information but are instead under a duty to be active participants in the process. Brandeis then explained how freedom of speech can provide a safety valve against bottled-up dissatisfaction, noting that

> [f]ear breeds repression: repression breeds hate: that hate menaces stable government; that the path of safety lies in the opportunity to discuss supposed grievance and proposed remedies . . .[12]

A theme than runs throughout the opinion is the danger of fear and repression in a free government. He emphasized that

> [t]hey [the founders] recognized the risks to which all human institutions are subject. But they knew that order cannot be secured merely through the fear of punishment for infractions . . . they eschewed silence coerced by the law—the argument of force in the worst form . . . Fear of serious injury cannot alone justify suppression of free speech and assembly. Men feared witches and burnt women. It is the function of speech to free men from the bondage of irrational fears . . . Those who won our independence were not cowards. They did not fear political change. They did not exalt order at the cost of liberty. To courageous self reliant men, with confidence in the power of free and fearless reasoning applied through the processes of popular government, no danger flowing from speech can be deemed clear and present, unless the incidence of the evil apprehended is so imminent that it may befall before there is opportunity for full discussion.[13]

Brandeis repeatedly returned to the theme that in a democracy citizens must not fear the impact of speech. Rather, they must rely on the power of speech to defeat that which they fear. This theme is particularly relevant to at least three points. First, Brandeis was writing in a case in which the state had convicted a person for engaging in associational activity of an arguably seditious nature. This was one of many cases decided by the Court during this period affirming convictions for seditious speech and activity.[14] Brandeis was obviously trying to make the point that society was overreacting to the potential threat. Next, the emphasis on the need for tolerance of seditious speech, as opposed to action, supported the doctrinal changes that Brandeis urged. Finally, the emphasis on civic courage with respect to speech was obviously a central tenet of Brandeis's theory of how freedom of expression should operate.

As is often the case with opinions that delve into constitutional theory, Brandeis was not writing for the majority. Presumably, a concurring or dissenting opinion has greater latitude to reason at a more abstract level. The opinion has been entirely vindicated by history, however, and is without any question one of the cornerstones of the Court's freedom of speech jurisprudence.

3. *Chaplinsky v. New Hampshire*

The Court has long recognized that some types of speech are more constitutionally significant than others are and that some types of speech are more likely to cause serious social harm. In order to develop doctrines that strike the correct balance between speech and legitimate state concerns, the Court needed a framework for drawing distinctions among different categories of speech. The Court took an initial stab at this in *Chaplinsky v. New Hampshire*, in which it essentially defined certain categories of speech out of the First Amendment entirely.[15] Justice Murphy explained the following:

> There are certain well-defined and narrowly limited classes of speech, the prevention and punishment of which has never been thought to raise any Constitutional problem. These include the lewd and obscene, the profane, the libelous, and the insulting or 'fighting' words—those which by their very utterance inflict injury or tend to incite an immediate breach of the peace.[16]

This recognizes a two-tier theory under which some speech is protected while other speech is excluded. The categorization is based on an assessment of the value of the speech, along with its potential for causing harm. Moreover, in determining what was in and what was out, the Court relied on its understanding of what had been excluded from protection historically. The Court stuck with this theoretical framework for a while and has not entirely abandoned it yet, but eventually extended a lower level of First Amendment protection to most of the initially excluded categories of speech.

4. *Cohen v. California*

Cohen v. California[17] is factually insignificant but from a standpoint of freedom of speech principle a very important case. In reversing a conviction of a person who wore a "fuck the draft" jacket in a courthouse, Justice

Harlan explained why the state may not censor a particular word from the public vocabulary on the grounds that it is offensive.[18] First, he noted that apparent "verbal cacophony" should be considered a strength and not a weakness in a system that is committed to freedom of expression.[19] Moreover, it would be exceedingly difficult in a heterogeneous society to agree on a list of words to be censored as offensive.[20] As Justice Harlan put it, "one man's vulgarity is another's lyric."[21] He then provided the important insight that "linguistic expression serves a dual communicative function: it conveys not only ideas capable of relatively precise, detached explication, but otherwise inexpressible emotions as well."[22] Finally, he reasoned that it may sometimes be difficult to censor the words used to express an idea without censoring the idea itself.[23] Justice Harlan used *Cohen v. California*, a case he acknowledged might seem "too inconsequential to find its way into our books,"[24] to emphasize the emotive function of speech, a new judicial insight into free speech theory. Additionally, he provided a multilayered theoretical explanation for the Court's result, turning this "inconsequential" case into a constitutional gem.

B. Equal Protection and Racial Discrimination

Another clear example of the Court's development of general principle can be found in its cases wrestling with racial discrimination and the Equal Protection Clause of the Fourteenth Amendment. The Court recognized from the outset that protection against racial discrimination to some extent and in some contexts was the driving force behind that amendment.[25] Even so, that left a great deal of room for disagreement.

The issue in *Plessy v. Ferguson*[26] was whether a Louisiana law requiring racial segregation of railroad cars violated equal protection of the law. Relying primarily on a collection of United States Supreme Court and state law precedents, the Court concluded that the Fourteenth Amendment protected against racial discrimination involving civil but not social rights.[27] With respect to the latter category, in which riding on a railroad car fell, according to the Court, a relatively weak formal equality policed by a reasonableness requirement sufficed.[28] That is, as long as whites were prohibited from riding with blacks just as blacks were prohibited from riding with whites, no constitutional harm was done. The plaintiff in *Plessy* argued that private racial segregation (in that case in railroad cars) stigmatizes or "stamps the colored race with a badge of inferiority."[29] The Court's reply, presumably based on nothing more than its own opinion, was "[i]f this be so, it is not by reason of anything found in the act, but solely because the colored race chooses to put that construction upon it."[30] The Court reached this conclusion in spite of the fact that a decade earlier in *Strauder v. West Virginia*, it had well understood that a state law excluding blacks from serving on juries was "practically a brand upon them, affixed by the law, an assertion of their inferiority, and a stimulant to . . . [racial] prejudice."[31] Likewise, prior to *Plessy* in *Yick Wo v. Hopkins*,[32] the Court looked at the application of a discretionary permit system that in operation screened out eighty Chinese laundries and no non-Chinese laundries and refused to sustain it on the grounds that it was neutral but rather struck it down, recognizing that it was administered with "an evil eye and an unequal hand" and as such was a "denial of equal justice."[33] Consequently, the Court in *Plessy* could readily have understood the social meaning of the law before it simply by heeding its own precedents.

In dissent, Justice Harlan found a very different principle in the Fourteenth Amendment. Citing no particular authority, he proclaimed that

> [i]n view of the constitution, in the eye of the law, there is in this country no superior, dominant, ruling class of citizens. There is no caste here. Our constitution is color-blind, and neither knows nor tolerates classes among citizens. In respect of civil rights, all citizens are equal before the law.[34]

There is some inherent ambiguity in Justice Harlan's language. His reference to color blindness arguably points in a somewhat different direction than his anti-caste emphasis, although this may be more of a function of the modern usage of this terminology as opposed to Justice Harlan's contemporary meaning. He argued forcefully for a principle different from the majority's on the basis of little more than rhetoric and perhaps his sense of history and justice. He predicted that the Court's decision would "in time, prove to be quite as pernicious as the decision made by this tribunal in the Dred Scott Case."[35] That indeed proved to be the case. The Harlan opinion is still quoted favorably a century later, whereas the majority opinion is considered one of the Court's great tragedies. The Harlan dissent in *Plessy* is part of the very foundation of the Court's equal protection race discrimination jurisprudence, just as the Holmes and Brandeis dissents are in the area of freedom of speech.

As a matter of principle and doctrine, the Court began to take a far more aggressive approach toward racial discrimination in *Korematsu v.*

United States, where citing nothing it proclaimed that "legal restrictions which curtail the civil rights of a single racial group are immediately suspect."[36] Consequently, the Court would subject such classification to "the most rigid scrutiny," requiring "a definite and close relationship" to a "pressing public necessity."[37] Even though the Court in *Korematsu* sustained the order excluding Americans of Japanese origin on the West Coast from their homes during World War II in deference to military authority, the case marks the beginning of the Court's modern approach to racial discrimination. The Court in *Korematsu* did not attempt to set forth a comprehensive theoretical approach for addressing racial discrimination under the Equal Protection Clause. It did, however, indicate that the deferential approach of *Plessy* had been replaced with far more searching review.

Although *Brown v. Board of Education*[38] effectively overruled *Plessy* and led to a lengthy series of decisions invalidating state-sponsored racial discrimination, the Court avoided any discussion of the larger principles behind the prohibition of racial discrimination, at least in a majority opinion. It was not until the Court began to face challenges to the use of race in affirmative action plans that it found it necessary to examine the principles behind its near prohibition of racial discrimination.

In the landmark case of *Regents of the University of California v. Bakke*,[39] Justice Powell wrote an influential concurring opinion that began to sketch out the theory behind equal protection and racial discrimination. In the course of arguing that the strict standard of review should apply to all racial distinctions, whether for invidious or benign purposes, Justice Powell maintained that "the 'rights created by . . . the Fourteenth Amendment . . . are, by its terms, guaranteed to the individual. The rights established are personal rights.'"[40] This led Justice Powell to conclude a violation of equal protection almost certainly existed if an individual was disadvantaged because of his race, whether or not he belonged to a group that had been the object of racial oppression in the past. He explained that even racial classification enacted for purportedly "benign" purposes could very well have severe negative effects by disadvantaging persons innocent of any previous discriminatory acts, stigmatizing beneficiaries, causing general resentment, and entrenching governmental and societal reliance on race.[41] Moreover, the decisions as to who should benefit and who should be burdened could not readily be resolved on a principled basis.[42] Consequently, Justice Powell concluded that, as a matter of principle, all state classifications must be subject to the strict standard of review.[43] As such, Justice Powell espoused what is generally characterized as the color-blind theory of racial equality.

Writing for a four-justice plurality concurring and dissenting, Justice Brennan argued in favor of a group-oriented approach to equal protection and racial discrimination that would lead the Court to apply a somewhat less demanding standard of review to racial classifications adopted for socially benign purposes. This approach is often characterized as an anti-caste or antisubordination theory of discrimination. Justice Brennan argued that it was "myopic" to attempt to take a "color-blind" approach to racial discrimination in view of the nation's long and tragic history.[44] He conceded that existing precedent did not really address the issue of benign discrimination; however, he contended that it did reject a pure color-blind approach.[45] Justice Brennan agreed that the dangers of benign discrimination warranted the application of a more demanding standard than rational basis but less than strict scrutiny.[46] The four other justices did not reach the constitutional issue.[47] Justice Powell relied primarily on text and potential consequences to derive an individualistic, color-blind principle behind equal protection and race discrimination. Justice Brennan relied on history and precedent to derive a competing group-oriented antisubordination principle. In *Bakke*, Justice Powell was writing only for himself, while Justice Brennan was only one vote shy of a majority. Ultimately, it was the Powell view that carried the day with a majority of the Court, however.

A decade after *Bakke* in *City of Richmond v. J.A. Crosan Co.*,[48] Justice O'Connor, writing for a four-justice plurality, adopted the principle set forth by Justice Powell in *Bakke*. Justice O'Connor began by quoting the same language quoted by Justice Powell, emphasizing that the Fourteenth Amendment created "personal" rights.[49] She relied heavily on the Powell opinion in *Bakke* in concluding that strict review must apply to all governmental classifications based on race, regardless of the race benefitted or burdened.[50] Applying strict scrutiny, the Court invalidated the racial preference program that the city had developed for public contracting.[51] Justice Marshall, dissenting, defended the approach taken by Justice Brennan in *Bakke*, again relying heavily on the history and impact of racial discrimination in the United States.[52]

The individualistic, color-blind approach was finally adopted by a majority of the Court a few years later in the next major affirmative action case to come before the Court, *Adarand Constructors, Inc. v. Pena*.[53] Again writing for the majority, Justice O'Connor worked through the precedent in detail and concluded that it established three basic principles: (1) skepticism: that any racial classification must be subjected to strict scrutiny, (2) consistency: that the same standard applies whether a race is burdened or benefitted, and (3) congruence: that the same standard applies to state and federal government.[54] The Court explained that all three of these conclusions were derived from "the basic principle that the Fifth and Fourteenth Amendments to the Constitution protect *persons*, not *groups*."[55] As of *Adarand*, the approach introduced in the lone opinion of Justice Powell in *Bakke* had become the operative principle for a majority of the Court. Justice O'Connor, again writing for the majority, arguably softened the impact of the principle in the context of affirmative action in higher education in *Grutter v. Bollinger*, though she purported to remain true to the theoretical approach that she had expounded in *Croson* and *Adarand*.[56] This is an outstanding example of how the underlying principle held by the Court on a question as fundamental as racial equality can develop slowly and incrementally from the opinion of a single justice before eventually commanding a majority of the Court.

C. One Person, One Vote

In *Reynolds v. Sims*,[57] the Court was faced with the question of whether grossly malapportioned state legislatures violated the Equal Protection Clause of the Fourteenth Amendment. As of that point, the Court had yet to work out a principle of constitutional apportionment at the state level. Previously, in *Wesberry v. Sanders* the Court had construed the phrase that representatives must be chosen "by the People of the several states" in Article I of the Constitution to require that congressional districts must be apportioned on the basis of "one person one vote."[58] In *Reynolds*, the Court recognized that *Wesberry* involved a different constitutional provision and that the question with respect to state legislatures differed from that of congressional districts.[59] Nevertheless, it relied heavily on its reasoning,[60] contending that "Wesberry clearly established that the fundamental principle of representative government in this country is one of equal representation for equal numbers of people."[61] This went quite a long way toward resolving the issue presented in *Reynolds*. Analogizing to *Wesberry*, the Court reasoned that, because it would be constitutionally impermissible to explicitly create a system of weighted voting under which some citizens' votes would be weighted more heavily, it would be equally unconstitutional to achieve the same result through malapportioned districts instead of explicitly weighted votes.[62] The analogy was persuasive, because it would appear that weighted voting and malapportioned districts shared the crucial similarity of being two somewhat different methods of achieving the same goal—magnifying the voting power of some citizens while diluting that of others.[63] The Court also raised the structural argument that representative government assumes political equality of citizens.[64]

Essentially, the basic issue presented by *Reynolds* and its companion cases was whether, even assuming that there is a strong presumption in favor of equal representation, there could nevertheless be good enough reasons to deviate from such ideal equality in order to serve other state interests, such as providing more political power to particular geographic areas of the state to ensure that their interests were adequately protected in the legislature. The Court attempted to deflect this argument with its assertion that "[l]egislatures represent people, not trees or acres" and that "[l]egislators are elected by voters, not farms or cities or economic interests."[65] But as Justice Harlan pointed out in dissent, people do not seek representation in the abstract but rather for purposes of furthering or protecting their specific interests.[66]

Once the Court turned to the application of the Equal Protection Clause to state legislative apportionment, it reasoned that:

> the concept of equal protection has been traditionally viewed as requiring the uniform treatment of persons standing in the same relation to the governmental action questioned or challenged. With respect to the allocation of legislative representation, all voters, as citizens of a State, stand in the same relation regardless of where they live.[67]

This is certainly the crux of the decision. If voters are similarly situated regardless of where they reside, then presumably equal protection requires a one person, one vote standard as the Court concluded. But the true issue presented by *Reynolds* was whether voters are in fact similarly situated as a constitutional matter, regardless of where they live, and on this point the Court seemed to assume its conclusion. As Justice Harlan noted in dissent, the Court's constitutional analysis rested on the "frail tautology that 'equal' means 'equal.'"[68] From a standpoint of legal reasoning, the Court's derivation of principle in *Reynolds* is quite unsatisfying. Nevertheless, the Court's adoption of the "one person, one vote" principle is not only relatively uncontroversial but is almost certainly one of its more highly regarded decisions, as the result was politically attractive, seemed intuitively fair, and was easily implemented. It illustrates that in the end the Court will often be judged by the social impact of its decision as opposed to the strength of its interpretive approach.

D. The Right to an Abortion

In *Roe v. Wade*, the Court held that the Due Process Clause of the Fourteenth Amendment protected a fundamental liberty right of a woman to obtain an abortion.[69] The Court's explanation of why this particular right was fundamental and thus highly protected was quite unsatisfying, however. The Court listed a series of cases recognizing a variety of fundamental rights, including marriage, procreation, contraception, family relationships, child rearing, and education.[70] The Court then explained that "[t]his right of privacy . . . is broad enough to encompass a woman's decision whether or not to terminate her pregnancy."[71] It then described the detriments that an inability to obtain an abortion might cause the woman.[72]

Twenty years later in *Planned Parenthood v. Casey*, the Court modified *Roe* significantly but purported to preserve its core.[73] In the process the joint opinion of Justices Kennedy, O'Connor, and Souter attempted to provide a more principled basis for the right recognized in *Roe*. After surveying the Court's previous due process liberty/right to privacy cases, the joint opinion concluded that the matters considered fundamental

> [i]nvolv[e] the most intimate and personal choices a person may make in a lifetime, choices central to personal dignity and autonomy. . . . At the heart of liberty is the right to define one's own concept of existence, of meaning, of the universe, and of the mystery of human life.[74]

This is a credible explanation of the principle, uniting the somewhat disparate group of cases protecting decisions regarding procreation, marriage, and the raising of children. The cases had been decided with little if any effort to provide a unifying theme. The joint opinion in *Casey* attempted to provide a viable rationale, although, as the Court recognized, it is dictated by "reasoned judgment" rather than the text of the Constitution.[75] Applying this principle to the abortion decision, the joint opinion concluded that a woman's

> [s]uffering is too intimate and personal for the State to insist, without more, upon its own vision of the woman's role, however dominant that

vision has been in the course of our history and culture. The destiny of the woman must be shaped to a large extent on her own conception of her spiritual imperatives and her place in society.[76]

This relatively libertarian conception of procreational autonomy is certainly a principle that could be derived from the precedent as it stood, but, as the Court noted, it runs counter to the dominant history and culture of the nation, which are the very criteria that Justice Harlan emphasized as constraining the Court's judgment when he essentially launched the Court's right to privacy jurisprudence in his influential dissenting opinion in *Poe v. Ullman*,[77] cited and relied on by the *Casey* Court itself.[78] From the standpoint of identifying underlying principle, *Casey* improved upon *Roe* significantly by attempting to provide a coherent explanation for the somewhat disparate group of cases on which the *Roe* Court had relied. This arguably lent some stability to the underlying right by making it appear to be less of an ad hoc conclusion. Still, the autonomy principle explicated in *Casey* was stated at such a high level of abstraction that its boundaries remain quite unclear and as such is open to challenge as a highly manipulative device.

E. Principle v. Principle

Sometimes important constitutional principles come into conflict, and the Court must either reconcile them or choose between them. In *Miami Herald Co. v. Tornillo*,[79] involving a challenge to a Florida statute that required newspapers to print replies to editorials critical of a candidate's character, the Court was faced with two different conceptions of freedom of the press. The state argued that the statute served the purpose of the First Amendment by ensuring that the public would have access to divergent points of view on political issues in view of the increasingly monopolistic nature of the mass media.[80] The Court noted that its landmark opinion in *New York Times v. Sullivan* had indicated that the First Amendment was intended to ensure that "debate on public issues should be uninhibited, robust, and wide-open."[81] That certainly is an important First Amendment principle. Nevertheless, a unanimous Court invalidated the statute, emphasizing the competing First Amendment principle of avoiding governmental intrusion into the editorial process.[82] In reaching this conclusion, it quoted dicta from a variety of earlier cases, indicating that governmental supervision of the content of newspapers would be highly problematic under the First Amendment.[83]

Indeed, it reasoned that the cost involved in requiring a newspaper to print views that it would prefer not to would actually "[dampen] the vigor and [limit] the variety of public debate" that *New York Times v. Sullivan* had indicated was so essential.[84] Thus, in a relatively brief opinion, the Court considered the competing principles and decided that one of the two had a more solid grounding in First Amendment precedent, while the other, though not insignificant, would be likely to undermine freedom of the press, at least in the context of the case before the Court. The Court scarcely rejected the diversity of viewpoints principle but rather subordinated it to an alternative in a specific setting.

III. From Principle to Doctrine—The Establishment Clause

To truly understand the purpose of constitutional provisions and to be able to apply them correctly and consistently, it is crucial that the Court consider the core principles animating these provisions. But these principles in and of themselves are generally too abstract to provide sufficient guidance to resolve the typical cases that come before the courts. Therefore, it is necessary for the Court to refine those principles into more concrete doctrine, which will provide the day-to-day framework for constitutional adjudication. The line of cases in which the Court has attempted to apply the Establishment Clause, especially to religious influence in public schools, provides an excellent example of how the Court does in fact move from principle to doctrine.

A. The Wall of Separation

One of the best-known principles embodied in all of constitutional law is the metaphor that the First Amendment erects a "wall of separation" between church and state. It has been repeated with such frequency that many laypersons almost certainly believe that this conception is embodied in the text of the Constitution, but of course it is not. How did this figure of speech become so dominant in freedom of religion jurisprudence? The phrase may be traced back to a letter that President Jefferson wrote to the Danbury Baptist Association in 1802.[85] It was first introduced into Supreme Court jurisprudence in *Reynolds v. United States* in the unsuccessful free exercise challenge to the law passed by Congress aimed at the Mormons and banning polygamy.[86] Seventy-five years later in *Everson v. Board of Education*, the Court's first significant Establishment Clause case and the fountainhead of modern freedom of religion jurisprudence, Justice Black, citing *Reynolds*, summarized the purpose of the Establishment Clause as revealed by his cursory discussion of its history as intending "to erect 'a wall of separation between Church and State.'"[87] Justice Black provided no discussion of the context in which Jefferson made that statement; indeed, he did not even provide a citation to the letter but rather only to its prior quotation in *Reynolds*.[88] The dissent approved of the principle but disagreed with Justice Black's application of it.[89] One line in a judicial opinion coupled with the Jeffersonian pedigree and the power of the metaphor launched the "wall of separation" as a constitutional principle. Quite obviously, however, the concept of a wall of separation was far too amorphous and blunt to prove very useful in deciding concrete cases.

Two years later in *McCollum v. School Board*, the next Establishment Clause case to come to the Court, Justice Black, writing for the majority, returned to the wall of separation metaphor as the central principle of the Establishment Clause, noting that it had been endorsed by the dissenters as well as the majority in *Everson*.[90] Concurring in *McCollum*, Justice Frankfurter accepted the wall of separation principle but noted that "[a]ccommodation of legislative freedom and Constitutional limitations upon that freedom cannot be achieved by a mere phrase."[91] He then set forth a lengthy review of the history of religious instruction and the public schools, in which he attempted to show that the principle of a wall of separation had become deeply ingrained in American culture, most especially with respect to education.[92] In the same case, however, Justice Jackson warned in his concurrence that "we are likely to make the legal 'wall of separation between church and state' as winding as the famous serpentine wall designed by Mr. Jefferson for the University he founded."[93]

Justice Black's reliance on Jefferson's metaphor has been subject to serious challenge. In his dissenting opinion in *Wallace v. Jaffree*, Justice Rehnquist argued that

> the Establishment Clause has been expressly freighted with Jefferson's misleading metaphor for nearly 40 years. Thomas Jefferson was of course in France at the time the constitutional amendments known as the Bill of Rights were passed by Congress and ratified by the States. His letter to the Danbury Baptist Association was a short note of courtesy, written 14 years after the Amendments were passed by Congress.[94]

In *Zorach v. Clauson*,[95] the next Establishment Clause to come before the Court after *McCollum*, Justice Douglas tempered the separation principle somewhat. In *Zorach*, the Court upheld the constitutionality of a "released time" law, which, unlike *McCollum*, permitted the students to leave the school during the school day for religious instruction.[96] Justice Douglas began his opinion by reaffirming the separation principle, stating that "the separation must be complete and unequivocal."[97] He continued, however, noting that "[t]he First Amendment . . . does not say that in every and all respects there shall be a separation of Church and State. Rather, it studiously defines the manner, the specific ways, in which there shall be no concert or union or dependency one on the other. . . . Otherwise the state and religion would be aliens to each other—hostile, suspicious, and even unfriendly"[98] He explained that separation in all contexts would cut deeply into well-accepted practice. Justice Douglas recognized that "[w]e are a religious people whose institutions presuppose a Supreme Being."[99] He emphasized, as had Justice Black in *Everson*, that "[g]overnment may not finance religious groups nor undertake religious instruction nor blend secular and sectarian education nor use secular institutions to force one or some religion on any person."[100] Justice Douglas, who had joined the majority opinions in *Everson* and *McCollum*, purported to swear allegiance to the concept of separation of church and state while recognizing that, pressed to the extreme, it would improperly cause "government to be hostile to religion and to throw its weight against efforts to widen the effective scope of religious influence."[101] Thus, the Douglas opinion in *Zorach* would appear to be intended to restore some balance to the separation principle.

Justice Black, the author of *Everson* and *McCollum*, dissented in *Zorach*. He argued that "[i]t was precisely because Eighteenth Century Americans were a religious people divided into many fighting sects that we were given the constitutional mandate to keep Church and State completely separate."[102] He criticized the majority for its "legal exaltation of the orthodox and its derogation of unbelievers."[103] Justice Jackson also objected, declaring that "[t]he day that this country ceases to be free for irreligion it will cease to be free for religion—except for the sect that can win political power."[104]

The principle of a wall of separation was derived from a historical incident; however, as historians and justices have argued, Jefferson's metaphor is almost certainly a misleading summarization of the original understanding of the Establishment Clause. Arguably, Justice Black in *Everson* selected the principle he liked, relatively strict separation, and simply relied on Jefferson, previously served up by the Court in *Reynolds*, for support. It was almost immediately recognized, even by a Justice like Douglas, who seemed to be somewhat partial to the separation principle, that it was simply too severe and blunt of an instrument to capture or confront the richness and complexity of the nation's religious heritage. As these cases indicate, the wall of separation metaphor was either too vague or, if taken seriously, too extreme to provide useful guidance in the decision of cases. Thus, the Court found it necessary to develop more specific doctrinal rules. These eventually were brought together to compose the controversial *Lemon* test.

B. The *Lemon* Test

In *Abington Township v. Schempp*,[105] a case involving school prayer, the Court began to translate the general principles recognized in *Everson, McCollum*, and subsequent cases into a more specific doctrinal test. Starting with the proposition that the Court had adopted a principle of neutrality as the touchstone of constitutionality under the Establishment Clause, it explained that the test to be applied is "there must be a secular legislative purpose and a primary effect that neither advances nor inhibits religion," citing *Everson*.[106] This was essentially the creation of the modern Establishment Clause analytical test. Not all of the justices who concurred in the decision were happy with the Court's analytical approach, however. Justice Goldberg concurred but wrote that "there is no simple and clear measure which by precise application can readily and invariably demark the permissible from the impermissible."[107] He warned that "untutored devotion to the concept of neutrality" can lead to "a brooding and pervasive devotion to the secular and a passive, or even active, hostility to the religious."[108]

In *Board of Education v. Allen*, decided five years after *Schempp*, the Court quoted the test developed there and applied it to uphold a New York statute authorizing the loan of textbooks to all students, including those attending private schools.[109] The majority relied on the fact that the *Schempp* Court had cited *Everson* as consistent with its analytical approach.[110] It reasoned that if the state could pay for bus transportation to religious schools it could also pay for textbooks approved by the State Board of Education and limited to secular subjects, given that there was no proof of misuse in the record.[111]

The Court continued to express discomfort with the broad declarations set forth in *Everson*, as well as its previous attempts to derive applicable Establishment Clause jurisprudence in its opinion in *Walz v. Tax Commission*, where it upheld the constitutionality of income tax exemptions for a variety of public service-oriented institutions, including churches.[112] Chief Justice

Burger explained that

> [t]he Establishment and Free Exercise Clauses of the First Amendment are not the most precisely drawn portions of the Constitution. The sweep of the absolute prohibitions in the Religion Clauses may have been calculated; but the purpose was to state an objective not to write a statute. In attempting to articulate the scope of the two Religion Clauses, the Court's opinions reflect the limitations inherent in formulating general principles on a case-by-case basis. The considerable internal inconsistency in the opinions of the Court derives from what, in retrospect, may have been too sweeping utterances on aspects of these clauses that seemed clear in relation to the particular cases but have limited meaning as general principles.[113]

In addressing the constitutionality of the property tax exemptions for churches, Justice Burger considered both the purpose and the effect of the law, as *Schempp* would seem to require, but on the latter point emphasized that "[w]e must also be sure that the end result—the effect—is not an excessive entanglement of religion."[114] Recognizing that either granting or denying the exemption could lead to entanglement, the Court concluded that the former would result in less government involvement.[115] The Burger opinion in *Walz* clearly illustrated the extent to which the Court was obviously struggling to derive workable doctrine under the Establishment Clause.

The following year in *Lemon v. Kurtzman*, Chief Justice Burger, again writing for the majority, decoupled the concept of "excessive entanglement" from the effects inquiry and propounded a three-part standard that ever since has been known as the "*Lemon* test."[116] Citing *Allen*, he explained that "[f]irst, the statute must have a secular legislative purpose; second, its principle or primary effect must be one that neither advances nor inhibits religion," and finally, citing *Walz*, "the statute must not foster 'an excessive government entanglement with religion'"[117] And so, over the course of precedential accretion, a test was born. In applying the new test in the *Lemon* case, the Court focused almost exclusively on excessive entanglement and concluded that it would exist, given the need to monitor the programs to avoid religious indoctrination as well as the possibility of political divisiveness along religious lines.[118]

Over the years the *Lemon* test has been the subject of much criticism on the Court.[119] One problem with the test was that it became extraordinarily fact-specific in application, depriving it of predictability.

In *Tilton v. Richardson*, Chief Justice Burger explained that "there is no single constitutional caliper that can be used to measure the precise degree to which these three factors are present or absent."[120] Rather the Court must apply "the cumulative criteria developed over many years" in these cases.[121] In *Tilton*, the Court engaged in just such a detailed factual analysis, especially under the "excessive entanglement" prong of the test, explaining why there was less likelihood of governmental entanglement with religion with respect to the building construction grant program available to sectarian colleges, at issue in that case, than in grants of aid to elementary and secondary schools.[122] The distinctions that the Court drew were sensible; however, so many factors were taken into account that little guidance was provided for a different factual situation.[123]

In *Roemer v. Board of Public Works*, a case similar to *Tilton*, the Court continued to subdivide the entanglement test into a variety of influential but nondecisive ad hoc factors, rendering its application even more complicated.[124] A few years later in *School District of Grand Rapids v. Ball*, the Court complicated the effects test of *Lemon* even more by factoring in whether the practice in question might lead to unconscious or subtle indoctrination of religious messages or might give the appearance of a symbolic union between church and state.[125]

In her concurring opinion in *Lynch v. Donnelly* in 1984, Justice O'Connor suggested that the *Lemon* test should be modified.[126] First, she suggested that the Court should limit its inquiry on excessive entanglement to institutional as opposed to political entanglement; that is, the problems with monitoring a particular rule as opposed to the possibility that it might cause divisiveness in the political process.[127] She would have further construed the purpose prong of *Lemon* to focus on an inquiry as to whether the message of the government practice is to endorse religion.[128] Likewise, the effects prong of *Lemon* should turn on whether the practice has the effect of communicating endorsement of religion.[129] She concluded that a nativity scene in the midst of an otherwise secular Christmas display on public property had neither the intent or effect of endorsing religion.[130] The majority in *Grand Rapids v. Ball*[131] purported to apply the endorsement approach. In *Allegheny v. ACLU*,[132] the next holiday display case to come before the Court, a three-justice plurality accepted Justice O'Connor's endorsement test as the controlling standard. Justice Kennedy, dissenting, wondered how an approach propounded by a single justice could suddenly become controlling.[133]

In *Zobrest v. Catalina Foothills School District*[134] and *Agostini v. Felton*,[135] the Court continued to soften the impact of the *Lemon* test in the aid to parochial school setting by rejecting the prior holdings to the effect that there was a near irrebuttable presumption against public school teachers providing secular services on the premises of religious-oriented schools. In *Agostini* the Court continued to deemphasize the independent significance of the excessive entanglement aspect of *Lemon* as well.[136] The trend to undermine the *Lemon* test culminated in an attempt by a four-justice plurality in *Mitchell v. Helms* to essentially replace it with an approach that focused on whether the aid in question results in religious indoctrination or defines its recipients with reference to religion using the concept of neutrality in terms of even handedness of distribution as the primary means of answering these questions.[137] Justices O'Connor and Breyer, concurring in the result, were unwilling to approve of this significant doctrinal shift, however.[138] These developments suggest that the dissatisfaction with the *Lemon* test continues to grow, and it would appear likely that at some point in the future it will be replaced entirely.

The creation of the *Lemon* test illustrates how one of the Court's most famous doctrinal tests was constructed over time from bits and pieces of language in accumulated cases. Almost from the outset, the test was criticized vigorously both on and off the Court, and for a lengthy period of time it has appeared that it was in danger of being overruled, and yet that did not happen. Despite the many faults of the *Lemon* test, it must be acknowledged that the tensions that exist in the area of the Establishment Clause make it particularly difficult if not impossible to develop a truly satisfactory doctrinal test for resolving a wide variety of cases. The Court's Establishment Clause decisions, especially those involving public funding of parochial schools, have been so fact-specific as to provide little guidance. What is worse, they are filled with glaring inconsistencies in the treatment of seemingly similar factual situations, which opens the Court to ridicule. One would hope that the Court could have done a better job; however, the difficulty of creating a principled jurisprudence in this area as well as a doctrinal framework to effectuate it cannot be underestimated.

🦟 IV. Deriving Doctrine

A. The Search for Intermediate Principles

As Justice Harlan pointed out in his dissent in *Duncan v. Louisiana*, citing an article by Professor Jaffee, the Court's task in creating constitutional doctrine is to develop "intermediate premises"; that is, principles that help to bridge the gap between the generality of constitutional provisions such as due process of law and the specificity of the factual situations to which they must be applied.[139] The question then becomes, as Justice Harlan asked, "[w]here does the Court properly look to find the specific rules that define and give content to such terms as 'life, liberty, or property' and 'due process of law'?"[140] Where does the Court get the rules and sub-rules of constitutional law that it applies from one case to the next? For Justice Harlan, at least with respect to the meaning of the Due Process Clause, such principles and doctrine are derived by starting "with the words 'liberty' and 'due process of law' and attempt[ing] to define them in a way that accords with American traditions and our system of government."[141] Doctrine is limited by the power and ability of words to draw significant distinctions. This was perhaps most famously recognized by Justice Cardozo in his concurring and dissenting opinion in *Carter v. Carter Coal Co.*, where, in discussing the dangers of placing too much reliance on conclusions as to whether an effect on commerce was direct or indirect, he observed that "a great principle of constitutional law is not susceptible of comprehensive statement in an adjective."[142]

This section will examine the ways in which the Court has derived significant constitutional doctrine in four different contexts. First, it will examine the development of how the doctrine for assessing seditious speech developed, flowing mainly out of important dissenting opinions. Then it will review the development of the strict standard of review under the Equal Protection Clause, which arguably was implemented pursuant to a judicially created blueprint. Third, it will consider the development of the doctrine that the Court instituted to reconcile freedom of speech with the competing societal interest in protecting reputation. Finally, it will review how in the context of its early desegregation efforts the Court created constitutional doctrine virtually by accident.

B. Doctrine from Dissent—Seditious Speech

The development over a lengthy period of the legal standard for assessing the constitutionality of legislative restraints on seditious speech provides one of the most well-known examples of doctrinal development. In *Patterson v. Colorado*,[143] one of the Court's earliest opinions on freedom of speech, Justice Holmes assumed in passing that the First Amendment was primarily concerned with prior restraints, that is, with efforts by the government to prohibit speech in advance. Thereafter, the Court did apply the First Amendment to subsequent punishments as well. In *Schenk v. United States*,[144] Justice Holmes seemed to tighten the doctrine somewhat with the introduction of the famous "clear and present danger" standard, if it can even be called a standard. He introduced this language not in the self-conscious manner in which the modern court launches a new doctrinal approach, but rather he simply used the phrase in the course of an important explanatory paragraph. Justice Holmes wrote the following:

> We admit that in many places and in ordinary times the defendants in saying all that was said in the circular would have been within their constitutional rights. But the character of every act depends upon the circumstances in which it is done. . . . The most stringent protection of free speech would not protect a man in falsely shouting fire in a theatre and causing a panic. . . . The question in every case is whether the words used are used in such circumstances and are of such a nature as to create a clear and present danger that they will bring about the substantive evils that Congress has a right to prevent. It is a question of proximity and degree. When a nation is at war many things that might be said in time of peace are such a hindrance to its efforts that their utterance will not be endured so as long as men fight. . . .[145]

This is the first significant Supreme Court exposition of free speech theory and doctrine. In his concise style, Justice Holmes made many important points. Perhaps the central theme that runs throughout his exposition is that free speech analysis must be contextual, taking account of relevant circumstances. Holmes recognized that speech is capable of causing harm to important governmental interests, and, at some point and in some circumstances, the government has the right to prohibit or punish such speech. He also explained that First Amendment analysis in the area of seditious speech should focus on the impact of the speech on the government interest (the clear and present danger) rather than the intent of the speaker or the precise nature of the language. Justice Holmes's short opinion in *Schenck* is perhaps best understood as an effort to decide the case before him, offer some explanation of the analysis, and move the Court toward a more speech-protective approach without providing deep or detailed theoretical or doctrinal exposition, as of yet. Given that Justice Holmes appeared to be changing the standard for assessing the validity of a First Amendment defense, it is unclear why *Schenck* did not receive a new trial under the proper standard. Presumably, the Court concluded that it would not have made a difference.

Holmes began to express dissatisfaction with the approach he articulated in *Schenck* in his famous dissent in *Abrams v. United States*.[146] Most of his dissent addressed sufficiency of the evidence and requirements of federal criminal law, rather than free speech theory. However, near the end of his dissent, he did note that we should be hesitant to suppress opinions with which we disagree, unless they "imminently threaten immediate interference with the lawful and pressing purposes of the law."[147] It is not over reading this language to suggest that Justice Holmes would, as of *Abrams*, impose a more stringent standard than clear and present danger.

Holmes continued to express dissatisfaction with the Court's approach in his dissent in *Gitlow v. New York*.[148] Among other things, he concluded that the legislature could not conclude that a certain type of activity or speech constituted a clear and present danger as a matter of law, as the majority had permitted.[149]

Justice Brandeis followed up on Justice Holmes's refinements a few years later in his concurrence in *Whitney v. California*.[150] Recognizing that the clear and present danger test was insufficiently protective of freedom of speech, he proposed that it be modified to permit prohibition or punishment of speech only where there was incitement to unlawful action, the likely occurrence of the danger is imminent, and the harm to society would be serious.[151] Moreover, as with Holmes in *Gitlow*, he argued that the question of clear and present danger or imminence is factual and contextual and must be assessed with respect to the defendant's speech and may not be determined in advance by the legislature as had been done in those two cases.[152]

All of Justice Brandeis's suggestions would ultimately be incorporated into First Amendment doctrine, but not for four decades. Some twenty-five years later in *Dennis v. United States*, the plurality noted that, although *Whitney* and *Gitlow* had not been expressly overruled, "there is little doubt that subsequent opinions have inclined toward the Holmes-Brandeis rationale."[153] Having paid lip service to the Holmes-Brandeis approach, however, the Court ultimately reached a result that, in its deference to the legislative judgment, seems far more consistent with the majority opinions in those cases.[154] Indeed, by explicitly adopting the balancing test propounded by Judge Learned Hand in his opinion for the court of appeals,[155] the Court arguably diluted the "clear and present danger test" even more than the *Gitlow* and *Whitney* majorities.[156]

Finally, in *Brandenburg v. Ohio*, the Court overruled *Whitney*, replacing the clear and present danger test with a requirement that the state prove incitement as well as that the likelihood of danger was imminent,[157] as Brandeis had asserted in his *Whitney* concurrence. It is a classic example of the opinion of a dissenting justice eventually discrediting and replacing the opinion of the Court, although over a quite lengthy amount of time. Perhaps it is an example of the better approach eventually winning out in the marketplace of ideas, as Justice Holmes theorized should happen in his famous dissenting opinion in *Abrams*. Arguably, the Holmes and Brandeis approaches were simply ahead of their time when articulated and needed to wait for the culture to catch up.

In his concurrence in *Dennis*, Justice Frankfurter criticized this process by which the "clear and present danger test" lost its connection to the context from which it had arisen.[158] He lamented :

> It does an ill-service to the author of the most quoted judicial phrases regarding freedom of speech, to make him the victim of a tendency which he fought all of his life, whereby phrases are made to do service for critical analysis by being turned into dogma.[159]

Frankfurter then quoted Justice Holmes on this very proposition to the effect that "[i]t is one of the misfortunes of the law that ideas become encrusted in phrases and thereafter for a longtime cease to provoke further analysis."[160] He also quoted Professor Paul Freund for the proposition that "no matter how rapidly we utter the phrase 'clear and present danger' or how closely we hyphenate the words, they are not a substitute for the weighing of values. They tend to convey a delusion of certitude when what is most certain is the complexity of the strands in the web of freedoms which the judge must disentangle."[161] Justice Frankfurter concluded that it would be better to abandon the clear and present danger test entirely than to continue to apply it in an unreflective manner.[162] The same could almost certainly be said of any doctrinal test developed by the Court that is applied reflexively, absent any consideration of nuance and context.

C. Doctrine by Blueprint—Strict Scrutiny

One of the Court's most prominent doctrinal developments of the twentieth century was the introduction of varying standards of review into its jurisprudence, especially but not only in the area of equal protection of the laws. Traditionally, the Court had reviewed legislation against an equal protection challenge under a relatively deferential standard. That is, as long as the classification in question was reasonably related to a legitimate state purpose, it would survive constitutional attack.[163] Shortly after the Court rejected the *Lochner* doctrine of more aggressive judicial review of state economic legislation pursuant to the Due Process Clause of the Fourteenth Amendment, it began to speculate that a more searching level of scrutiny than rational basis review might be appropriate in a variety of cases involving civil liberties claims.[164]

This doctrine, which was later characterized as "strict scrutiny,"[165] first received theoretical recognition in dicta in a footnote in *United States v. Carolene Products*.[166] In the text, the Court acknowledged that the congressional statute banning the shipment of "filled milk" in interstate commerce was reasonably related to a legitimate purpose and was therefore constitutional.[167] Citing a number of prior cases, Justice Stone dropped the now famous footnote four, in which he traced out three areas in which a higher standard of judicial review might well be appropriate.

First, the Court noted that "[t]here may be a narrower scope for operation of the presumption of constitutionality when legislation appears on its face to be within a specific prohibition of the Constitution, such as those deemed equally specific when held to be embraced within the Fourteenth."[168] Next, the Court observed that "[i]t is unnecessary to consider now whether legislation which restricts those political processes which can ordinarily be expected to bring about repeal of undesirable legislation, is to be subjected to more exacting judicial scrutiny. . . ."[169] Finally, Justice Stone noted that "[n]or need we enquire whether similar considerations enter into the review of statutes directed at particular religious . . . or racial minorities . . . whether prejudice against discrete and insular minorities may be a special condition, which tends seriously to curtail the operation of those political processes ordinarily to be relied upon to protect minorities, and which call for a correspondingly more searching judicial inquiry."[170] The Court was able to cite at least some precedent for each of these statements.[171] None of the prior cases, however, came close to setting forth the type of justification that Justice Stone was propounding for stricter judicial review. Essentially, in dicta in a footnote in an otherwise run-of-the-mill case, Justice Stone attempted to redefine the role that the Supreme Court would play in the constitutional future.

During the fifty-year period before the *Carolene Products* footnote, the Court had devoted much of its energy to policing federal and state economic regulation. With the adoption of a more expansive view of the Commerce Clause in *NLRB v. Jones & Laughlin Steel Corp.*[172] and the rejection of vigorous review of state economic legislation under the Due Process Clause in *Nebbia v. New York*[173] and *West Coast Hotel v. Parrish*,[174] the Court abandoned that role. With the *Carolene Products* footnote four, it tentatively indicated that it was preparing to replace its supervision of the economic marketplace with a more vigorous role in protecting civil rights and liberties. Each aspect of emphasis in the footnote—protecting those rights specified in the Bill of Rights, policing the political process, and scrutinizing laws that might be the result of prejudice against discrete and insular minorities— would in later cases become the source of full-blown doctrinal development. There may be no other instance in American constitutional law where the Court set forth a doctrinal blueprint quite so clearly and then followed through with it. Justice Frankfurter objected to this emerging trend in his concurring opinion in *Kovacs v. Cooper*, noting that "[a] footnote hardly seems to be an appropriate way of announcing a new constitutional doctrine."[175]

Four years after *Carolene Products*, in *Skinner v. Oklahoma*,[176] the Court relied on the Equal Protection Clause to invalidate an Oklahoma statute that imposed sterilization of repeat offenders convicted of certain crimes deemed to be of moral turpitude. Without citing anything, including the *Carolene Products* footnote, Justice Douglas declared that " [w]e are dealing here with legislation which involves one of the basic civil rights of man. Marriage and procreation are fundamental to the very existence and survival of the race."[177] These statements introduced the idea that there were fundamental rights that would trigger a higher degree of judicial scrutiny under the Equal Protection Clause. Justice Douglas then declared that a classification that severely affected these rights would be subject to "strict scrutiny," although he did not clearly indicate what that entailed.[178] Thus, Justice Douglas in *Skinner* began to build on the *Carolene Products* suggestions without explicitly acknowledging that he was doing so.

Two years later in *Korematsu v. United States*, without so much as citing the *Carolene Products* footnote, Justice Black, speaking for the Court, declared

> [t]hat all legal restriction which curtail the civil rights of a single racial group are immediately suspect. That is not to say that all such restrictions are unconstitutional. It is to say that courts must subject them to the most rigid scrutiny. Pressing public necessity may sometimes justify the existence of such restrictions; racial antagonism never can.[179]

In deference to the military judgment, the Court upheld the order excluding *Korematsu*, an American citizen of Japanese origin, from his home during the Second World War. Nevertheless, *Korematsu* ensured that the theory of paragraph three of the *Carolene Products* footnote—that laws that might be the result of prejudice against a racial minority must be subjected to strict judicial review—became part of the constitutional fabric. This approach clearly built upon the third paragraph of the *Carolene Products* footnote.

Several years later in *Kramer v. Union Free School District*,[180] the Court built on the *Carolene Products* footnote dicta by determining that strict scrutiny should apply whenever the state passes legislation limiting the franchise. The Court reasoned that

> [t]his careful examination is necessary because statutes distributing the franchise constitute the foundation of our representative society. Any unjustified discrimination in determining who may participate in political affairs or in the selection of public officials undermines the legitimacy of representative government.[181]

Thus, the Court relied on policing the process theory to justify subjecting legislative limitations of the ballot to more searching judicial review. Several years earlier the Court had shown special concern for laws interfering with the franchise in *Reynolds v. Sims*,[182] in which it adopted the "one person, one vote" standard, effectively invalidating the legislative apportionment schemes of most states; however, it did not explicitly apply a strict standard of review in that case. The Court's application of the strict standard of review to laws affecting voting was the logical progression from paragraph two of the *Carolene Products* footnote four.

The Court extended strict scrutiny under the Equal Protection Clause to laws that interfere with the right to travel in *Shapiro v. Thompson*.[183] It held that there was a constitutional right to travel, without identifying its specific source, though it cited cases that had ascribed such a right to four different constitutional provisions.[184] In dissent, Justice Harlan accused the majority of simply "pick[ing] out particular human activities [and] character[izing] them as 'fundamental.'"[185] He also questioned why the Court even needed to rely on equal protection if in fact there actually was a fundamental constitutional right to travel. Rather, why not simply analyze the statute pursuant to that right?[186] *Shapiro* is an example of the creation of new doctrine; that is, when a legislative classification adversely affects the right to travel from one state to another, it will be subjected to strict scrutiny. However, as Justice Harlan amply illustrated in dissent, the reasoning by which the Court reached this conclusion was at best murky.[187]

Thus, by starting with dicta in a footnote in an otherwise obscure case, over a period of thirty years the Court transformed the Equal Protection Clause, which Justice Holmes had once referred to as the "last resort of the constitutional arguments"[188] into its most potent instrument of judicial review in perhaps all of constitutional law. This transformation took place in an incremental case-by-case manner, but, by the end of the process, the Court had constructed a doctrinal framework that, in retrospect, would appear to have come straight from Justice Stone's blueprint in the famous footnote four. The Court's continuing efforts to explain and stabilize this doctrine will be discussed in the following chapter.

D. Doctrine as Reconciliation—Free Speech and Libel

In *New York Times v. Sullivan*,[189] the Court held for the first time that state defamation law, at least where the plaintiff was a public official, was subject to First Amendment limitations. Because the Court did not intend to wholly displace the state protection of reputation even in this limited context, it was necessary for it to produce doctrine that would protect the First Amendment interest and still allow some protection for reputation. Relying on a state law case from Kansas, as well as the public official's own privilege when sued for libel, the Court crafted a standard that it referred to as actual malice, requiring the official to prove that the statement was made with knowledge of falsity or reckless disregard for its truth.[190] Although this standard had some common law pedigree, it was largely created as a compromise between the interests in freedom of speech and reputation with a heavy bias in favor of the former. Justice Goldberg, concurring, reminded the majority that there was no precedent in this area, and therefore "we are writing upon a clean slate."[191] Justices Black and Goldberg (with Douglas concurring) argued for a complete privilege from defamation liability for citizen critics of the government.[192]

In subsequent cases, the Court struggled in its attempts to develop doctrine for analyzing defamation cases involving private individuals.[193] In *Rosenbloom v. Metromedia*,[194] Justice Brennan, writing for a plurality of the Court, extended the *Times* malice test to a defamation action involving a "matter of public concern." A few years later in *Gertz v. Robert Welch*,

Inc.,[195] Justice Powell, writing for the majority, attempted to bring order and predictability to this area by adopting a series of rules designed to reconcile the competing interests. Justice Powell began by recognizing that both the interest in freedom of speech protected by the First Amendment and the interest in reputation protected by state defamation law were worthy of legal protection.[196] Neither should be wholly overridden by the other. Although Justice Powell accepted the actual malice standard as the correct reconciliation of these interests when a public official was involved, he did not accept the *Rosenbloom* plurality's extension of that standard to matters of public concern.[197] Upon concluding that the *Rosenbloom* standard would result in unpredictability and underprotection of the interest in reputation, Justice Powell settled instead on an approach that distinguished between public and private figures, extending the protection of the actual malice standard only to the former.[198] He argued that this distinction made sense because private figures were more deserving of protection of reputation, given that they generally will not have invited media scrutiny and are less capable of protecting themselves through the media because they are usually not of much interest to the press.[199]

To provide sufficient protection to the press, however, Justice Powell required that even private figure plaintiffs must provide some proof of fault (at least negligence) on the part of the press in order to recover, replacing the strict liability imposed at common law. In addition to altering the standard of liability, the Court also addressed the issue of damages, holding that a plaintiff could not recover presumed or punitive damages absent a showing of actual malice.[200] The Court feared that the risk of substantial damages with little proof of harm could easily be used to punish the press for publishing unpopular views.[201] The doctrines set forth by the Court in *Gertz* were clearly intended to bring some predictability to an area in which predictability is important. Indeed, Justice Blackmun indicated that he did not agree with all of the Court's doctrinal conclusions but was willing to join the majority simply because he was convinced that it was essential to give the press and the lower courts the guidance that a majority opinion could provide.[202]

Perhaps it is some credit to the compromise of interests that Justice Powell managed to construct in *Gertz* that it was attacked vigorously from both sides. Justice Brennan, the author of the rejected *Rosenbloom* "matter of public interest" approach, contended that the Court's approach in *Gertz* failed to give the press adequate protection.[203] Justice White, on the other hand, attacked the majority's approach on the grounds that it cut too deeply into the common law protection for reputation.[204] Justice White was particularly troubled that the Court had paid little if any attention to the fact that libel had coexisted with the First Amendment throughout most of American history and that virtually all states had agreed that the law of libel as it had developed at common law was essential to the preservation of reputation.[205]

The First Amendment libel cases show the Court starting from scratch in 1963 in *Sullivan* and building a fairly complex and stable superstructure for analyzing most issues likely to arise as of *Gertz* ten years later. There was a period of instability and confusion in the interim before the Court could build a majority around any single approach. It is likely that the degree of frustration expressed by the lower courts, commentators, and the press during this period caused the Court to make special efforts to adopt controlling doctrinal standards. The Court achieved that in *Gertz* by carefully balancing the competing interests and setting forth relatively detailed rules intended to cover most foreseeable situations. As such, both *New York Times v. Sullivan* and *Gertz* represent cases in which, due to the perceived need for predictability, especially where the right to freedom of the press was at stake, the Court wrote opinions, including extensive, well-considered dicta, designed to set forth a comprehensive doctrinal framework as opposed to a narrow case-by-case incremental approach. Despite extensive criticism of the Court's approach both on and off the Court, the framework set forth in *Gertz* has provided stability for over thirty years, and the Court has not needed to revisit the area.

E. Doctrine by Accident—All Deliberate Speed

Brown v. Board of Education II[206] provides a well-known example of constitutional doctrine arguably getting out of hand. In *Brown v. Board of Education I*,[207] the Court held that segregated public schools violated the Fourteenth Amendment. The following year, the Court addressed the question of the proper remedy for the violation and, near the end of its decision, wrote that the judgments in favor of the school districts were reversed and remanded to the district courts to enter orders "to admit to public schools on a racially nondiscriminatory basis with all deliberate speed the parties to these cases."[208] The phase "with all deliberate speed" had not necessarily been intended to create a governing doctrinal standard. Apparently, the language came from a nineteenth century English poem, had found its way into an opinion by Justice Holmes during the early part of the century,[209] and then ended up in the opinion in *Brown*. It was then seized upon by parties, lower courts, and the Supreme Court and became something of a litmus test for measuring compliance with *Brown*, until the Court decided that it had had enough of it some ten years later in *Griffin v. Prince Edward County*, where, in the face of continued resistance to the integration of one of the schools involved in the original *Brown* decisions, it declared, "the time for mere 'deliberate speed' has run out."[210]

"All deliberate speed" is a stunning example of arguably insignificant language in an opinion assuming a life of its own and dominating legal analysis of a complicated issue to an extent that was neither intended nor useful. The concept was too malleable to provide guidance and easily utilized to justify delay and avoidance. Eventually, in *Green v. County School Board* the Court replaced it with the command that all aspects of segregated (dual) systems must be "eliminated root and branch," and the school district must "come forward with a plan that promises to work, and promises to work realistically now."[211] The Court had learned that any doctrinal flexibility would simply be employed to resist compliance.

It was not finished with the matter, however, returning to the question of appropriate desegregation remedies in *Swann v. Charlotte Mecklenburg Board of Education*.[212] There, recognizing as did *Brown II* that different school districts would present different remedial problems, the Court combined a general and flexible equitable principle—that the scope of the wrong should dictate the scope of the remedy, with a lengthy approval of various remedial devices that would be constitutionally acceptable.[213] The *Swann* Court seemed to recognize that in the area of school desegregation there was at once a need for specificity to avoid resistance and at the same time a need for flexibility to take account of the diverse circumstances of various school districts. Neither specificity nor generality, by themselves, would be sufficient. Achieving a workable school desegregation plan required both rules and judgment.

V. Sources of Doctrine

The Court creates doctrine in virtually all areas of constitutional law, but where does it come from? What is the source of the Court's "intermediate principles"? The previous sections, which traced the creation of doctrine in a variety of areas, provided examples of how the Court builds its analytical frameworks. The following sections will examine at least some of the sources on which the Court has relied to derive constitutional doctrine.

A. Doctrine from Precedent

1. *Baker v. Carr*

Much doctrine is derived from precedent in one way or another. Often the Court develops specific rules in individual cases and then puts them together into a larger doctrinal framework in a later case. Justice Brennan's opinion for the Court in *Baker v. Carr*[214] is one of the classic examples of the Court deriving doctrine from precedent. In the course of holding that a challenge to the apportionment of a state legislature based on the Equal Protection Clause of the Fourteenth Amendment did not present a political question, Justice Brennan engaged in an extensive review of the messy case law involving the political question doctrine. At the outset, he conceded that "the attributes of the doctrine . . . in various settings, diverge, combine, appear, and disappear in seeming disorderliness."[215] Nevertheless, he set out to show that there were discernable principles in the apparent chaos. Working through the precedents, he maintained that not all questions involving foreign relations, the dates of hostilities, or the status of Indian tribes necessarily involved nonjusticiable political questions.[216]

He then analyzed the Court's earlier opinion in *Luther v. Borden*[217] at great length because it had arguably held that Guarantee Clause claims were political questions and *Colegrove v. Green*, an earlier challenge to the malapportionment of the Illinois legislature, which had been dismissed at least in part on the grounds that it raised a political question.[218] Consequently, it was important for Justice Brennan to establish that not all challenges to malapportioned legislative bodies were necessarily nonjusticiable. He reasoned that the Court's decision not to intervene in *Borden*, which involved a dispute over which of two groups was the legitimate government of Rhode Island, was dictated by several factors, including a lack of judicially manageable standards, a textual commitment of the issue to the Congress, and a decisive response by the president.[219] Ultimately, Justice Brennan concluded that the primary relevance of *Borden* was for the principle that the Guarantee Clause did not present judicially manageable standards.[220]

Justice Brennan then worked through several other political question cases in some detail. The ultimate principle that he distilled from the precedent was that "nonjusticiability of a political question is primarily a function of separation of powers."[221] This lengthy examination of the case law led him to conclude that a political question is likely to be found when there is

> a textually demonstrable constitutional commitment of the issue to a coordinate political department; or a lack of judicially discoverable and manageable standards for resolving it; or the impossibility of deciding without an initial policy determination of a kind clearly for nonjudicial discretion; or the impossibility of a court's undertaking independent resolution without expressing lack of the respect due coordinate branches of government; or an unusual need for unquestioning adherence to a political decision already made; or the potentiality of embarrassment from multifarious pronouncements by various departments on one question.[222]

He then determined that none of these criteria would preclude an equal protection challenge to the malapportionment of a state legislature.[223] Because he read *Colegrove* as resting on the lack of judicially manageable standards under the Guarantee Clause, the existence of well-developed standards under the Equal Protection Clause distinguished that case from the one before the Court.[224]

Justice Frankfurter, dissenting, did not accept Justice Brennan's synthesis of the case law, providing his own analysis instead.[225] If anything, he analyzed the precedent in even greater detail than had Justice Brennan. He did identify many of the same criteria as had Justice Brennan for the majority.[226] However, he placed greater weight on the need for judicial deference to legislative choices, especially in the area of structuring governmental institutions.[227] After a lengthy analysis of *Luther v. Borden*, he concluded that Guarantee Clause challenges were nonjusticiable for several reasons, including sensitivity to "the delicacy of judicial intervention in the very structure of government."[228] Unlike Justice Brennan, Justice Frankfurter believed that the question of whether a legal challenge to the apportionment of a state legislature was justiciable turned on the underlying nature of the problem and not upon the particular legal theory employed.[229] Consequently, *Colegrove* precluded a challenge to malapportionment, whether based on the Guarantee Clause or equal protection.[230] Resolving the question of apportionment would require the Court to select one of several legitimate theories of representative government, which was a political, not a legal, question.[231] *Baker v. Carr* is an example of both the majority and dissent engaging in careful and detailed analysis of complicated precedent and coming to very different conclusions on issues of extreme constitutional importance. It is a classic example of doctrine distilled from precedent. It also illustrates the large extent to which there is room for legitimate disagreement over how precedent should be read and how doctrine should be formulated from that precedent. The criteria that Justice Brennan devised for assessing whether a political question is present have been applied by the Court ever since.[232]

2. *Lopez, Morrison,* and the Limits of the Commerce Clause

For the first three decades of the twentieth century, the Court interpreted the Commerce Clause narrowly, invalidating several exercises of congressional power under the clause. From 1937 on, however, the Court changed its approach and became so deferential that there were questions as to whether there were any judicially enforced limitations at all. For a period of almost sixty years, the Court did not invalidate an act of Congress on the grounds that it exceeded the scope of commerce power. However, in 1995 in *United States v. Lopez*, the Court finally drew the line and struck down a law making it a criminal offense to carry a gun into a school zone on the grounds that such activity was not shown to have had a substantial effect on interstate commerce.[233] In order to justify this decision, the Court derived a number of factors from its precedent to take into consideration in determining when the limits of the commerce power have been exceeded.

First, the Court cited *Wickard v. Filburn,*[234] which it described as "perhaps the most far reaching example of Commerce Clause authority over intrastate activity," as involving economic activity, which was not the case with the Gun Free School Zone Act.[235] The Court also cited several cases for the proposition that federal criminal legislation regulating activity traditionally left to the states should be strictly construed.[236] Next, it cited its opinions in *United States v. Bass*[237] for the proposition that the absence of a "jurisdictional element" such as an "in" commerce requirement undercut the validity of the statute in a close case.[238] Then the Court cited *Preseault v. ICC*[239] for the proposition that congressional fact-findings would be useful in sustaining the legislation in close cases.[240] Finally, the Court concluded by citing the landmark Commerce Clause case of *Gibbons v. Ogden* for the proposition that the enumeration of a power such as the right to regulate interstate commerce presupposes something not enumerated, that activity which has no substantial effect on interstate commerce.[241] Consequently, a regulatory theory that would appear to reach intrastate activity without apparent limitation is almost certainly constitutionally suspect.[242] Thus, from existing precedent, the Court was able to glean several considerations that could provide guidance in evaluating extreme extensions of commerce power. Relying on these factors, the Court invalidated the law that made it a federal crime to knowingly bring a gun into a school zone.[243]

Justice Kennedy wrote a concurring opinion emphasizing the importance of established precedent in the Commerce Clause area and arguing that the Court's decision was quite consistent with that precedent.[244] Justice Thomas concurred but argued that the Court's Commerce Clause precedent had strayed far from the original understanding and should be cut back severely.[245] Although the dissents argued that the Court's holding was a radical break with longstanding precedent, which had upheld a fairly extreme extension of the commerce power over in-state activity,[246] the majority was able to build an argument for some outer limits on that power, almost exclusively from the Court's prior decisions. These precedents did not necessarily compel the decision in *Lopez*; however, they did provide a basis for developing a multifactored doctrinal approach that could be used to place at least some constraint on the seemingly infinite expansion of the commerce power.

In striking down the legislation, in *Lopez*, the majority simply listed several factors that played a role in its decision. Perhaps concluding that the multifactored analysis in *Lopez* was too unwieldy, the Court in *United States v. Morrison*[247]—a subsequent case in which the Court relied on *Lopez* to invalidate federal legislation—summarized *Lopez* as turning on four central factors: (1) whether the law regulated economic activity, (2) whether there was a jurisdictional element, (3) whether there were congressional fact-findings supporting the interstate commerce connection, and (4) whether the link between the activity regulated and interstate commerce was too attenuated.[248] Thus, *Morrison* molded *Lopez* into a more typical and rigid doctrinal test. Applying this test to the facts, the Court concluded that, although Congress had made extensive fact-findings, unlike *Lopez*, the other three factors were not satisfied, and as a result the law was unconstitutional.[249]

B. Doctrine from Purpose

1. The Right of Association

Often the Court will look to the purpose of a constitutional provision to develop the doctrine needed to achieve that purpose.[250] The Court's landmark case of *NAACP v. Alabama*[251] is an excellent example of doctrine derived from purpose. There, the Court was faced with an Alabama law that required every organization operating within the state to file a list of its Alabama members with the secretary of state, which would then be available for public inspection.[252] The Alabama chapter of the NAACP challenged this requirement on the grounds that it deterred persons from joining their organization out of fear of retribution in the then racially segregated South.[253] The Court acknowledged that "[e]ffective advocacy of both public and private points of view, particularly controversial ones," which the guarantee of freedom of speech is designed to protect, "is undeniably enhanced by group association."[254] The Court cited previous cases in which it had recognized the importance of group association to effective exercise of freedom of speech.[255] This led to the conclusion that "[i]nviolability of privacy in group association may in many circumstances be indispensable to preservation of freedom of association, particularly where a group espouses dissident beliefs."[256] Thus, by focusing on the purpose of the First Amendment in promoting speech on controversial public issues, the Court reached the conclusion that association for the purposes of engaging in such speech must be protected, and that privacy in such association must also be protected. *NAACP v. Alabama* provides an excellent example of the Court creating principle and doctrine by reasoning from the purpose of a constitutional provision.

The Court continued this process of explication in subsequent right of association cases. For instance, in *Roberts v. United States Jaycees*, it recognized that, as an aspect of substantive due process liberty, it had long protected "certain intimate human relationships . . . against undue intrusion by the State because of the role of such relationships in safeguarding the individual freedom. . . ."[257] The Court explained that such associations were of constitutional significance because they are important in "cultivating and transmitting shared ideals and beliefs," and, in addition, "such relationships [reflect] the realization that individuals draw much of their emotional enrichment from close ties with others."[258] In view of these purposes underlying the right, the Court then explained that, in determining whether a particular form of association was protected by the right, it would consider the "relative smallness, [the] high degree of selectivity . . . and seclusion from others in critical aspects of the relationship,"[259] because these were factors that tend to distinguish those relationships that serve the constitutional purposes from those that do not. Thus, the purpose of the right was the driving consideration in defining its scope.

2. Racial Gerrymandering

In *Shaw v. Reno*,[260] the Court held that an extremely bizarre-shaped voting district, which appeared to be gerrymandered based on race, could give rise to a constitutional violation even if it did not result in vote dilution. This was the first occasion on which the Court had recognized that the strange appearance of a district, if created for racial purposes, could constitute cognizable harm. To justify this conclusion, the Court argued that such extreme racial gerrymandering was inconsistent with the underlying purpose of the Equal Protection Clause, in that it appeared to be based on an improper stereotype that all members of a minority group think alike and share common interests and that elected officials should perceive themselves as representing racial groups instead of individuals.[261] Thus, the purpose of the provision, treating persons as individuals rather than racial group members, dictated the doctrine and the result.

3. Public Access to Criminal Trials

The fact that doctrine might promote a useful purpose may provide a reason to adopt it. For instance, in *Richmond Newspapers v. Virginia*, in the course of concluding that the Constitution required that criminal trials be presumptively open, both Chief Justice Burger's plurality opinion and Justice Brennan's concurrence emphasized the several useful purposes served by open trials, including providing a check against governmental abuse, assuring the public that the trials were fair, educating the public about the justice system, catching the attention of potential witnesses, and providing a catharsis following a particularly alarming crime.[262] These were not the only reasons for the decision; however, they provided solid support.

4. The Market Participant Doctrine

In *Hughes v. Alexandria Scrap*,[263] the Court was faced for the first time with the question of whether a state could provide a subsidy to in-state businesses, scrap metal processors, in order to accomplish a legitimate state purpose, cleaning up abandoned vehicles within the state. After noting that the purpose of the Commerce Clause was to prevent the states from engaging in trade wars by imposing tariffs on each other's goods, the Court concluded that "[n]othing in the purposes animating the Commerce Clause prohibits a State . . . from participating in the market and exercising the right to favor its own citizens over others."[264] With this, the "market participant" exception to the dormant Commerce Clause was created. The Court's conception of the purpose of the constitutional provision defined the outer limits of its coverage in other words. If a practice did not interfere with that purpose, it did not violate the provision. Justice Brennan, dissenting, criticized the Court for creating an ill-defined rule in a fairly off-handed manner.[265]

C. Doctrine from Structure

Youngstown Sheet and Tube v. Sawyer is perhaps the Court's most significant exposition of the doctrine of separation of powers, even though there was extensive disagreement among the justices. In that case, the Court invalidated President Truman's wartime seizure of steel mills. Despite the fact that Justice Black wrote the opinion for the Court, Justice Jackson, concurring, set forth a three-part analytical framework for assessing the constitutionality of exercises of executive authority that the Court has relied on ever since.[266] Obviously impatient with the overly rigid nature of Black's analysis, which simply concluded that the seizure constituted legislation and as such was beyond the power of the president, Justice Jackson attempted to set forth a more nuanced and flexible approach. Relying to a significant extent on constitutional structure as well as historical practice, Jackson noted that the Constitution does not contemplate air-tight separation of the branches but rather "separateness but interdependence, autonomy but reciprocity."[267] Building on this theme, he maintained that exercises of executive power must be assessed in light of congressional action. The executive power is at its strongest when it is supported by congressional action. It is somewhat weaker when Congress has neither approved nor disapproved, and it is "at its lowest ebb" when in direct conflict with congressional action.[268]

In retrospect, this seems like common sense, yet it had not been previously articulated by the Court. In separation of powers cases since *Youngstown*, the Court has consistently relied on Justice Jackson's tri-part analysis and has ignored Justice Black's opinion for the majority.[269] In creating this approach, Justice Jackson warned repeatedly of the dangers of overreliance on legal doctrine, especially in the area of separation of powers, noting that judicial decisions in this area have tended to "accentuate doctrine and legal fiction" over experience.[270] In an obvious reference to Justice Black's approach, Justice Jackson noted that his own approach gave "enumerated powers the scope and elasticity afforded by what seem to be reasonable practical implications instead of the rigidity dictated by doctrinaire textualism."[271] Justice Jackson's analysis illustrates the power of well-crafted doctrine. By providing a simple but sensible analytical framework for addressing separation of powers questions, he basically set the agenda for constitutional analysis in this area for the foreseeable future.

D. Doctrine from Necessity

1. First Amendment Due Process

Sometimes the Court derives doctrine from necessity. The Court confronts a constitutional problem and creates doctrine to help resolve it. *Freedman v. Maryland*[272] provided an excellent example of this. There, the Court was faced with an ordinance that required that films be submitted to an administrative review board for prior approval before they could be exhibited.[273] The Court had previously held that prior administrative review of films was not per se unconstitutional; however, it recognized that such a prior restraint posed significant risks of censorship.[274] The Court reconciled the permissibility of a prior administrative review with the need to avoid censorship by adopting several rules of First Amendment due process. First, it concluded that the state must carry the burden of proving that the film is not protected by the First Amendment.[275] Second, in the event that the review board finds the film to be unprotected, the exhibitor must be able to receive judicial review of that decision promptly.[276] Finally, restraint of the film prior to a final decision can only be maintained for the shortest time necessary to complete judicial review.[277] These rules were not explicitly specified in the Constitution, nor were they required by prior precedent. Rather, the Court expounded them as a means of erecting a strategic safeguard for freedom of speech while at the same time preserving the state's ability to prohibit the exhibition of unprotected films. They were the result of a practical attempt to reconcile competing interests and have stood the test of time.

2. Wartime Executive Authority

An argument urging the creation of doctrine from necessity does not always prevail, however. Such an argument was made by the government in *Youngstown Sheet and Tube v. Sawyer*[278] in an attempt to justify the president's seizure of steel mills during the Korean War to avoid a work stoppage. Such a power was based on necessity; that is, the need to be able to adequately defend the country. In an influential concurrence, Justice Jackson denied the existence of such a power for quite a number of reasons, but among them was the lack of necessity. He reasoned that the president did not need inherent emergency powers because in the modern world Congress could be summoned quickly to provide authority in the event of a true emergency.[279] In addition, in today's world, the president, due to the prestige of his office and his ability to communicate through the media, has the power to effectively rally and obtain public support for his position.[280] Consequently, even in an emergency, there is little need to vest such unchecked authority in the executive. Writing for the majority, Justice Black rejected the president's claim on the grounds that his action amounted to legislation that was beyond the power vested in the executive. So from Justice Black's perspective, it simply did not matter whether there was an emergency if the power claimed violated express constitutional limitations. *Youngstown* shows that, even in the area of wartime emergency, necessity will not automatically compel the creation of constitutional doctrine.

3. Dormant Commerce Clause Doctrine

In *Cooley v. Board of Wardens*,[281] a case that as a practical matter is the origin of dormant Commerce Clause analysis, the Court faced the question of whether a local law requiring ships to take on local pilots before entering the harbor was inconsistent with the dormant or unexercised power of Congress to regulate interstate commerce. The Court found that the law was constitutional, focusing largely on the respective needs of the federal and state systems. Essentially, the Court reasoned that if there was a need for a uniform national rule then the Commerce Clause would preempt state legislation, but where differences in state and local conditions required a diversity of approaches, state regulation of interstate commerce in navigation would be permissible.[282] Although this provided the starting point for dormant Commerce Clause doctrine, it was rather obviously a simplistic and conclusory approach that would need significant amplification and adjustment over time.

Almost 100 years later in *South Carolina Highway Dept. v. Barnwell Brothers, Inc.*, relying on dozens of cases decided in the interim, the

Court concluded that state regulation that discriminated against interstate commerce was unconstitutional; however, if the regulation of a predominately local activity such as state highways only imposed a burden on interstate commerce, then the Court would show substantial deference to the state regulation.[283] This provided somewhat more definition than the *Cooley* approach but still left the Court with great discretion in the individual case.

A few years later in *Southern Pacific v. Arizona*,[284] faced with a far more nationally integrated economy, the Court significantly modified the relatively deferential approach it had been using, derived from *Cooley* through *Barnwell*. In view of the tension between an efficient national economy, especially in the area of transportation, and competing state interests such as safety, the Court adopted a balancing test,[285] which with some adjustment remains the approach followed to date. The Court explained that to judge the constitutionality of state regulation of interstate commerce in the absence of federal regulation, courts must balance the burden imposed on interstate commerce against the extent to which the regulation promotes legitimate state interests.[286] Consistent with *Cooley*, the need for national uniformity could weigh heavily on the federal side of the equation.[287] The Court contended that its analytical framework was consistent with its precedent;[288] however, Justice Black's argument in dissent that the majority's approach represented a significant break with the past was far more persuasive.[289]

As the economy changed and the Court decided more cases, it found it necessary to produce a more refined and detailed doctrinal framework, especially since it was important to provide guidance to the lower courts, which would confront this issue with some frequency.

Eventually, in *Pike v. Bruce Church*,[290] the Court pulled the essence of many of its earlier decisions together into a multifaceted balancing approach. It concluded that

> [w]here the statute regulates even-handedly to effectuate a legitimate local public interest, and its effects on interstate commerce are only incidental, it will be upheld unless the burden imposed on such commerce is clearly excessive in relation to the putative local benefits ... If a legitimate local purpose is found, then the question becomes one of degree. And the extent of the burden that will be tolerated will of course depend on the nature of the local interest involved, and on whether it could be promoted as well with a lesser impact on interstate activities.[291]

This is a classic example of the type of multifaceted doctrinal test that the modern Supreme Court tends to gravitate toward. Although the Court did not explicitly rely on its precedent in setting forth the test, virtually all of the components of the test were readily drawn from prior cases, although the less restrictive alternative element had been employed only in discrimination as opposed to burden cases up to that point. Indeed, the test purported to be no more than a summary of what had come before. The Court was no doubt interested in attempting to bring a certain degree of clarity to Commerce Clause burden analysis. However, long after the test was articulated, the justices continued to argue over the correct analytical approach to dormant Commerce Clause burden cases.[292]

The evolution of the Court's approach to state legislation that may burden interstate commerce shows how it responds to the necessities of the situations before it. *Cooley* attempted to balance the state interest in regulating at least some aspects of interstate commerce against the federal need for uniformity. *Barnwell* attempted to provide somewhat more guidance in an area in which the state interests still largely predominated. *Southern Pacific* revised the approach in view of the fact that, in at least some areas, the federal interest in uniformity would be greater than competing state interests. Finally, *Pike Church* responded to the need for a more detailed and nuanced approach by which the courts could regularly address the question of the constitutionality of state-imposed burdens on interstate commerce.

E. Doctrine from Theory

The constitutional theory that the Court holds generally dictates the doctrine it develops. For instance, in *United States v. E.C. Knight Co.*,[293] the Court concluded that regulation of local activity such as manufacturing was reserved to the states and hence beyond the congressional commerce power. It appeared that the Court's conclusion was driven by its theoretical conception of the relationship between the federal government and the states. The Court believed that the regulatory domains of the federal government and the states were largely mutually exclusive, and, as such, permitting federal regulation of local activity would deprive the states of their traditional power to regulate manufacturing, mining, or agriculture.[294] This conception became known as "dual federalism." Had the Court adopted a theory under which federal and state power were seen as largely overlapping rather than mutually exclusive, as Justice Harlan essentially understood it in dissent,[295] there would have been no need to develop doctrine that assigned a particular activity to one realm or the other.

F. Doctrine as Summary

Initially doctrine, including doctrinal tests, may start as a summary of the principles decided in a specific case. That would seem to be true of one of the earliest and most famous of all constitutional doctrinal tests, Chief Justice Marshall's statement of the approach for determining the constitutionality of a congressional exercise of the Necessary and Proper Clause.[296] After pages of analysis of the meaning of the clause, Marshall proclaimed:

> Let the end be legitimate, let it be within the scope of the constitution, and all means which are appropriate, which are plainly adapted to that end, which are not prohibited, but consist with the letter and spirit of the constitution, are constitutional.[297]

This was essentially a summary of the points that Marshall had previously considered. Yet this sentence launched a doctrinal test that remains viable nearly 200 years later. Having set forth the test, it is somewhat surprising that Marshall made little effort to apply it to the facts of the case in any detail. Had he done so, it would have readily confirmed the result he reached in the case.

Building doctrine from a summary of the analysis in the case was also present in *Terry v. Ohio*,[298] in which the Court decided that a police officer had a limited degree of authority, consistent with the Fourth Amendment, to stop and frisk a suspect for the officer's self-protection, absent probable cause to arrest. During the course of its opinion, the Court considered and balanced the competing interests carefully. Having done so, it concluded the following:

> [W]e merely hold today that where a police officer observes unusual conduct which leads him reasonably to conclude in light of his experience that criminal activity may be afoot and that the persons with whom he is dealing may be armed and presently dangerous, where in the course of investigating this behavior he identifies himself as a policeman and makes reasonable inquiries, and where nothing in the initial stages of the encounter serves to dispel his reasonable fear for his own or others'

safety, he is entitled for the protection of himself and others in the area to conduct a carefully limited search of the outer clothing of such persons in an attempt to discover weapons which might be used to assault him. Such a search is a reasonable search under the Fourth Amendment, and any weapons seized may properly be introduced in evidence against the person from whom they were taken.[299]

This paragraph summarized all of the factors that the Court had taken into consideration in analyzing the issue. Piecing all of these elements together, the Court created a complex doctrinal test for evaluating the constitutionality of stop and frisk incidents that both the Court and lower courts would apply in the future.

G. Borrowing Doctrine

Occasionally, the Court borrows doctrine from one area of the law and inserts it into another. This happened in *Dean Milk v. City of Madison*,[300] where the Court held that a state may not employ a regulation that discriminates against interstate commerce unless there are no less discriminatory alternatives. As Justice Black pointed out in dissent, the Court had never before used the less discriminatory alternatives principle in the dormant Commerce Clause area but had developed it in its First Amendment jurisprudence.[301] The Court did not cite any First Amendment cases or acknowledge that it was borrowing the standard from that area,[302] but clearly it was. Justice Black had no problem with a less discriminatory alternative approach in freedom of speech cases but believed that it limited legitimate state policies too severely in the economic area.[303]

H. Doctrine from Whole Cloth

Sometimes, constitutional doctrine seems to be created out of whole cloth. The Court simply makes an assertion based on no apparent authority, and doctrine appears. For instance, in the early case of *Calder v. Bull*, Justice Chase, in a seriatim opinion, listed four categories of laws that would qualify as ex post facto laws.[304] Apparently, these were derived from his analysis of historical sources. They have been accepted as the very definition of ex post facto laws ever since.[305]

Lochner v. New York[306] provides another stunning example of the Court deriving important doctrine from no apparent source. In the course of invalidating a New York law as inconsistent with the concept of the substantive due process liberty of contract, the Court rejected the possibility that the law could be a legitimate regulation of the labor market as out of hand. Writing for the Court, Justice Peckham proclaimed the following:

> The question whether this act is valid as a labor law, pure and simple, may be dismissed in a few words. There is no reasonable ground for interfering with the liberty of person or the right of free contract, by determining the hours of labor, in the occupation of a baker.[307]

The Court provided no support beyond mere assertion for either the proposition that regulating the labor market was an invalid police power end or little more than citation to a few scattered precedents for the proposition that the right to contract was a specially protected aspect of due process liberty. In his classic dissent, Justice Holmes took issue with these claims, arguing that the Court had simply mistaken its own economic and social preferences for constitutional commands.[308] He noted that "a Constitution is not intended to embody a particular economic theory," and the law regularly "interfere[s] with the liberty of contract."[309] Consequently, he explained that "my agreement or disagreement has nothing to do with a majority [of the public] to embody their opinions in the law."[310] Clearly, Justice Holmes believed that the Court's disagreement was essentially all that served as a basis for its decision.

When the Court eventually rejected the doctrine of *Lochner* some thirty years later in *Nebbia v. New York*, it relied on the fact that there had been nothing behind the doctrine other than mere assertion.[311] The Court pointed out that "[t]he due process clause makes no mention of sales or of prices any more than it speaks of business or contracts or buildings."[312] And in *West Coast Hotel v. Parrish*,[313] which completed the rejection of *Lochner*, the Court asked "What is this freedom? The Constitution does not speak of freedom of contract."[314] This lead the Court to conclude that the state had a great measure of authority to regulate commercial activity, regardless of whether that included contracts or whether it consisted of regulation of the labor market as such.[315] With that recognition, *Lochner* was truly dead and gone.

In *Roe v. Wade*,[316] the Court determined that state laws severely limiting or prohibiting abortion violated the substantive component of due process liberty under the Fourteenth Amendment. In so deciding, Justice Blackmun formulated controversial doctrine governing abortion regulation, largely out of whole cloth. He adopted a trimester approach for regulation, under which there could be virtually no regulation in the first trimester on the grounds that, until that point, abortion was somewhat less risky to the woman than birth.[317] During the second trimester, the abortion procedure could not be prohibited but could be regulated to protect the woman's health.[318] Finally, since the fetus could, by definition, survive outside of the womb as of viability, the state could prohibit abortion entirely during the third trimester as long as it was not necessary to preserve the life or health of the woman.[319] Although Justice Blackmun did present a rationale for these rules, they were eventually discarded by the Court in *Planned Parenthood of Pennsylvania v. Casey*, which referred to them as an "elaborate but rigid construct."[320]

In defense of the trimester framework, Justice Blackmun argued that it was no different than the doctrinal constructs that the Court creates in all areas of constitutional law, such as the three levels of judicial scrutiny under the Equal Protection Clause.[321] In other words, it was simply another example of the need for the creation of intermediate principles. The trimester standards appeared to be different, however, because by their nature they drew distinctions that seemed within the competence of doctors as opposed to judges. Drawing a line based on "viability" is different from focusing on "compelling state interests" or less restrictive alternatives. As such, the Court seemed to have ventured beyond its domain of competence in *Roe* and needed to pull back in *Casey* in order to salvage those aspects of *Roe* that it considered to be at its core.

In the landmark cases of *Johnson v. Zerbst*,[322] the Court announced what was to become the prevailing standard for a waiver of constitutional rights, especially the right to counsel. The Court simply proclaimed that "[a] waiver is ordinarily an intentional relinquishment or abandonment of a known right or privilege."[323] The Court cited nothing in support of this statement, although it was almost certainly relying on common law principles. Nevertheless, this statement established the constitutional benchmark for decades to come. Moreover, it was not the only conceivable alternative, as the Court could well have devised either a more or less demanding standard for waiver. Rather it simply created language that it deemed to be appropriate under the circumstances.

In *United States v. O'Brien*,[324] the Court produced a significant doctrinal test for assessing the constitutional validity of governmental regulation of conduct where there is an incidental impact on freedom of speech. The question presented was whether an act of Congress requiring draft-age persons to be in possession of their draft cards violated freedom of speech where there was at least some evidence that a few members of Congress may have voted for the law as a means of punishing persons who had burned their draft cards in order to protest the Vietnam War.[325] The Court stated that such regulation would be upheld if

> [i]t is within the constitutional power of the Government; if it furthers an important or substantial governmental interest; if the governmental interest is unrelated to the suppression of free expression; and if the incidental restriction on alleged First Amendment freedoms is no greater than is essential to the furtherance of that interest.[326]

The Court cited a few prior cases for bits and pieces of this formula, but for the most part it simply produced this test on the spot as a rational approach for addressing the problem. The test proved to be a sensible method of analyzing the issues, involving non-content based regulation of speech and has become an important tool in the First Amendment area.

In *City of Boerne v. Flores*, the Court concluded that the enforcement section five of the Fourteenth Amendment gave Congress the power to provide remedies for violations of the amendment but no power to change its meaning.[327] The Court then explained that in order for action pursuant to the Fourteenth Amendment to qualify as remedial, there had to be congruence and proportionality between the injury to be prevented or remedied and the means chosen to accomplish this.[328] This is an example of doctrine created to resolve a particular problem on the spot, as the Court cited nothing what-soever as a source for the congruence and proportionality requirements. Rather, the Court simply must have concluded that this was as good of a way as any for distinguishing laws that provide a remedy from those that alter the substantive right.

Another example of doctrine being created from whole cloth occurred in *INS v. Chadha*, in which the Court, finding it necessary to decide whether the action by the House of Representatives in overruling the suspension of a deportation order constituted legislative action, concluded that it did because it "had the purpose and effect of altering the legal rights, duties and relations of persons."[329] The Court did not explain where this definition of legislative action came from or why it was appropriate. Indeed, it would seem that this is hardly a precise or well thought out definition of legislation, considering that judicial, executive, and administrative action are also easily capable of altering the rights of persons. In fact, Justice Powell, concurring, believed that the action in question was unconstitutional because it was judicial in nature as opposed to legislative.[330]

Massiah v. United States[331] provides yet another example of doctrine materializing almost out of thin air. There the Court held that a police officer could not testify to information that he overheard as part of a conversation between an indicted defendant and his codefendant who was wearing a radio transmitter, because the admission of such evidence would violate the Sixth Amendment right to counsel.[332] The Court discussed a case that was hardly on point but otherwise provided virtually no analysis or reasoning for its holding.[333] Justice White, dissenting, exposed the deficiencies of the Court's opinion but to no avail.[334]

In his dissenting opinion in *Cruzan v. Missouri Department of Health*, Justice Brennan asserted without authority (other than off-point dicta from a prior decision) that a "State's general interest in life must accede to Nancy Cruzan's particularized and intense interest in self-determination in her choice of medical treatment."[335] Justice Stevens agreed with this position.[336] Justice Scalia quite properly pointed out in dissent that Justices Brennan and Stevens could produce no authority for this proposition other than their own values and opinions.[337]

爨 VI. Conclusion

The derivation of constitutional principle and doctrine is one of the most important functions that the Supreme Court performs. Most constitutional questions that come before the Court now are resolved largely with reference to the Court's accumulated doctrine or through the creation of new doctrine. Sometimes doctrine springs out of whole cloth with little if any citation of authority. More often, however, it is created incrementally over a series of cases, working through issues and slowly deriving rules and analytical frameworks to resolve questions in the future. The doctrine is often supported by a variety of sources, including text, original understanding, structure, precedent, purpose, necessity, as well as prudential and institutional considerations.

NINE

Shaping, Clarifying, and Changing Doctrine

۩ I. Introduction

After deriving constitutional doctrine, the Court must then apply it. Initially, the Court will mold the doctrine based on a variety of considerations. Taking account of the context in which it will apply, the Court will determine whether the doctrine should be bright-line, rule-oriented, whether a balancing approach would be better, or whether it should be a more fact-specific totality of the circumstances approach. The Court will consider whether the doctrine can be applied in a principled and consistent manner and whether it can be understood by the primary actors who must govern their conduct accordingly.

Doctrine will often endure for decades beyond its initial creation and will be applied by the Court in dozens of cases and by lower courts in thousands of cases. When this happens, conflicts and inconsistencies are bound to occur. Doctrine will become frayed around the edges. From time to time the Court will find it necessary to clean up the doctrinal messes that occur and to clarify its analytical approaches. This chapter will also discuss how the Court chooses between competing lines of doctrine when it is unclear which is most applicable, as well as how the Court changes doctrine from time to time.

۩ II. Shaping Doctrine

A. Defining the Issue

A crucial aspect in the application of doctrine is the determination of what doctrine to apply. That may depend on how the issue before the Court is defined. One of the classic examples of identifying and defining the issue appears in Justice Harlan's opinion in *Cohen v. California*.[1] There the petitioner had been convicted under a California statute prohibiting "maliciously or willfully disturbing the peace and quiet of a neighborhood or person by offensive conduct"[2] for wearing a jacket that said "fuck the draft" in a courthouse. Before defining the issue, Justice Harlan briefly considered and rejected several First Amendment doctrines that might have been but in fact were not implicated by the facts of the case. First, he noted that the case involved speech and not conduct.[3] Moreover, the speech was not likely to incite imminent lawless action within the seditious speech exception.[4] Nor could the conviction be justified as protecting the decorum of the courthouse, as the statute at issue had state-wide application.[5] The speech did not fall under the obscenity doctrine because it did not appeal to the prurient interest in sex.[6] Likewise, it would not be considered fighting words because it was not specifically directed at anyone,[7] nor was it likely to cause a violent reaction by a hostile audience as there was nothing in the record to that effect.[8] The captive audience doctrine would not apply, given that the act took place in public.[9]

Having rejected all of these doctrines as inapplicable, Justice Harlan defined the issue as simply "whether California can excise, as 'offensive conduct,' one particular scurrilous epithet from the public discourse, either upon the theory of the court below that its use is inherently likely to cause violent reaction or upon a more general assertion that the States, acting as guardians of public morality, may properly remove this offensive word from the public vocabulary."[10] Noting that the first theory must be rejected because the hostile audience doctrine can only apply where there is specific evidence of a likely reaction, Justice Harlan analyzed the second theory as the true issue of the case.[11] Rarely does a justice spend as much time as Harlan did in *Cohen* detailing what was not involved in the case. As such, Cohen presents a textbook of a highly skilled justice engaging in careful and persuasive framing and definition of the issue, which led to clear and precise analysis and decision.

B. Empirical Support for Doctrine

Sometimes the Court devises doctrine that is based on assumptions as to how persons and institutions behave. More often than not, the Court does not provide any empirical support for these assumptions but rather seems to base them on intuition, common sense, or mere assertion.[12] To some extent, the Court takes judicial notice of at least some facts. As the Court put it in *Jacobson v. Massachusetts* in evaluating the utility of vaccination against small pox, "[w]hat everybody knows the court must know."[13] As such, the Court took "judicial notice of the fact that it is the common belief of the people of the state . . . that vaccination is a preventive of small pox."[14]

In *Chambers v. Maroney*,[15] the Court concluded that if the police have probable cause to search an automobile when it is stopped on the highway, and hence the right to search it without a warrant, then they should still be able to search it without a warrant after the suspects have been taken into custody and the car has been taken to the police station and is fully within the control of the police. Writing for the Court, Justice White explained that "which is the 'greater' and which the 'lesser' intrusion is itself a debatable question, and the answer may depend on a variety of circumstances."[16] Thus, he concluded "[f]or constitutional purposes, we see no difference between on the one hand, seizing and holding a car before presenting the probable cause issue to a magistrate and, on the other hand, carrying out an immediate search without a warrant."[17] Justice Harlan, dissenting, argued that "the lesser intrusion will almost always be the simple seizure of the car for the period . . . necessary to enable the officers to obtain a search warrant."[18] He pointed out that this was especially true, given that the owner could always consent to a search if he concluded that the wait for the warrant was too burdensome.[19] Intuitively, it would seem that Justice Harlan had the stronger argument; however, neither he nor the majority cited any empirical support for their conclusions, depending instead on what would appear to be their own hunches.

Even in the area of civil liberties, the state is not necessarily required to prove the validity of the interest that it is trying to promote with mathematical certainty. In *Paris Adult Theatre v. Slaton*,[20] the Court recognized that the state has several valid interests in stemming the distribution and display of obscene material in public, including in adult theaters, and that the state need not establish these interests with empirical proof. The Court noted that "[f]rom the beginning of civilized societies, legislators and judges have acted on various unprovable assumptions."[21] It further reasoned:

> If we accept the unprovable assumption that a complete education requires the reading of certain books . . . and the well nigh universal belief that good books, plays, and art lift the spirit, improve the mind, enrich the human personality, and develop character, can we then say that a state legislature may not act on the corollary assumption that commerce in obscene books, or public exhibitions focused on obscene conduct, have a

tendency to exert a corrupting and debasing impact leading to antisocial behavior?[22]

Gertz v. Welch[23] was a case in which the Court adopted major doctrinal changes largely based on speculation and intuition about how persons and institutions would behave. For instance, in rejecting the rule that a higher standard of proof should apply when the defamatory statement involved a matter of public concern and instead should apply only where the plaintiff was a public figure, Justice Powell reasoned that public figures generally will find it easier to defend themselves in the press because the press will be more likely to report their replies.[24] In dissent, Justice Brennan challenged this as an "unproved, and highly improbable, generalization."[25] Justice Powell's assumption is not necessarily improbable, but Justice Brennan was certainly correct in characterizing it as unproved, in that Justice Powell had cited nothing whatsoever in support of it. On the other hand, Justice Brennan's assertion that a reasonable care standard would exacerbate press self-censorship was as much based on intuition and speculation as Justice Powell's assumptions.[26]

Justice White, dissenting, challenged Justice Powell's opinion from the opposite extreme as Justice Brennan, arguing that it interfered significantly with the common law's traditional protection of reputation. He rejected Justice Powell's conclusion that private libel suits were likely to cause the press to engage in self-censorship and declared that "I know of no hard facts to support that proposition, and the Court furnishes none."[27] Likewise, with respect to the Court's assumption that presumed and punitive damage awards in the absence of a showing of actual malice might exert a chilling effect on the press, Justice White responded that "[t]he Court points to absolutely no empirical evidence to substantiate its premise."[28] As Justice White was defending the long-established approach, he was able to argue that the burden of proof should lie with the Court because it was imposing significant changes in the law. To the extent that judicial doctrine is based on assumptions as to how people and institutions will behave, the doctrine may be counterproductive if those assumptions prove to be false. Nevertheless, many of the predicates for the Court's doctrine seem to be based on little more that intuition and speculation.

In *Bates v. State Bar of Arizona*,[29] the Court invalidated long-standing prohibitions on attorney advertising, at least of routine services, as inconsistent with the First Amendment. In so holding, the Court rejected the six justifications for the prohibition set forth by the Arizona Bar, including the inherently misleading nature of attorney advertising, adverse effects on professionalism, the administration of justice, and the quality of services.[30] As was the case in *Gertz*, the Court rejected these rationales based on little more than speculation and citation to some secondary authority.[31] Whether the Court's assessment of the impact of attorney advertising was correct, its explanation for the rejection of such a long-standing prohibition seemed thin, if not wholly inadequate.

A series of cases under the Establishment Clause provides another example of the Court basing doctrine on speculation and later reversing course. In *Meek v. Pittenger*, the Court invalidated a program that provided state funding for remedial education in parochial schools out of fear that in the process religious indoctrination might occur.[32] In *Grand Rapids School District v. Ball*, the Court relied on the same presumption to strike down a program providing supplemental courses in parochial schools, out of the same fear, speculating that such conduct might occur and go undetected, despite the fact that there was no evidence in the record of any instance.[33] In her dissenting opinion in the companion case of *Aguilar v. Felton*, Justice O'Connor argued that

[g]iven that not a single incident of religious indoctrination has been identified as occurring in the thousands of classes offered in Grand Rapids and New York City over the past two decades, it is time to acknowledge that the risk identified in *Meek* was greatly exaggerated.[34]

Justice O'Connor attributed this lack of evidence to the professionalism and good faith of the teachers administering the program.[35] She further observed that carrying this speculative fear to its logical conclusion would require the closing of the public school system, given that it is always possible that a teacher will use the classroom to convey a religious message.[36] These cases provide an example of the degree to which doctrine is often based on little more than hunch, and an arguably biased hunch at that. A decade later in the case of *Agostini v. Felton*,[37] the Court concluded that, as Justice O'Connor had argued in dissent, there was in fact no basis for its factual predicates with respect to possible indoctrination and reversed the earlier cases. This is an unusual case in which the Court revisited and rejected its prior factual assumptions as incorrect.

Sometimes the status of "social facts" is a matter of great dispute. In *Lee v. Weisman*[38] Justice Kennedy argued that, given the nature of peer group pressure among adolescents, a prayer delivered by a rabbi at a middle school graduation would have at least a psychologically coercive effect by requiring students (including nonbelievers) to stand in silence in violation of the Establishment Clause. Justice Kennedy stated that "given our social conventions, a reasonable dissenter in this mileau could believe that the group exercise signified her own participation or approval of it."[39] Justice Scalia, dissenting, disagreed completely with Justice Kennedy's assessment of the impact of the graduation prayer, arguing that it was ludicrous to conclude that students who stand in respectful silence during a prayer have in any sense been coerced into assenting to its substance.[40]

Ultimately, this comes down to a matter of opinion (although Justice Kennedy cited various psychological studies in support of his position), and as it happened his opinion garnered one more vote than Justice Scalia's. Likewise, Justice Kennedy argued that Justice Scalia's argument that there was no coercion present because the students were not legally required to attend graduation was "formalistic in the extreme," given the social significance of the event.[41] Reasonable people could differ as to how these practices would generally be perceived. Given the doctrinal approach taken by the Court, such an assessment was crucial to the decision. That in and of itself suggests the weakness of the doctrine in that it turns on such ephemeral and debatable conclusions.

In the *Prize Cases* the Court held that President Lincoln possessed the legal authority to blockade Southern ports based on its conclusion that a state of civil war existed "in fact" regardless of whether it had been legally declared.[42] The Court wrote that "[t]he President was bound to meet [the insurrection] in the shape it presented itself, without waiting for Congress to baptize it with a name."[43] In other words, whether there was a war to which the president could respond was a factual matter of which the Court could take judicial notice as opposed to a legal question. Justice Nelson, dissenting, disagreed, arguing that "civil war . . . under our system of government, can exist only by an act of the Congress. . . ."[44] Thus for Justice Nelson, the fact of war was irrelevant to the decision.

In *Lochner v. New York* the Court concluded that regulating the baking trade as a "labor law, pure and simple" could not possibly serve a legitimate police power purpose.[45] In other words, the state had no right to regulate the labor market merely to affect the economics of that market. In reaching that conclusion, the Court proclaimed that there was no reason to believe that bakers were any less capable of protecting their rights in the workplace than anyone else.[46] The Court cited no evidence to support these conclusions. There is nothing in the opinion to suggest that these statements were based on anything more than the personal opinions of the justices. A mere seven years earlier in *Holden v. Hardy*, the Court had upheld a law of this nature with respect to miners and had proceeded on the assumption that it was perfectly proper for the state to regulate working conditions where it had reason to believe that there was an inequality of bargaining power.[47] *Lochner* is another example of the Court seemingly basing its underlying conclusions on speculation rather than on any evidence in the record.

C. The Impact of Doctrine

In developing a doctrinal test, the Court will often be heavily influenced by whether it will cause problems for those who must rely on the law in planning their conduct. The nature of the doctrine that the Court derives is often shaped by the needs of the persons and institutions that must rely on that doctrine in the future. Such was the case in *Gertz v. Welch*,[48] in which the Court was concerned with setting forth a set of rules resolving the conflict between freedom of the press and private plaintiff defamation actions. The Court recognized that simply relying on a case-by-case balancing of interests would afford the press insufficient predictability, perhaps resulting in the very kind of self-censorship that it was attempting to avoid.[49] Consequently, it decided that it was necessary to "lay down broad rules of general application."[50] The Court recognized that such rules are not perfect in that they "necessarily treat alike various cases involving differences as well as similarities."[51] Having decided that broad rules were in order, however, it proceeded to create several of them, including a requirement that the plaintiff prove that the press was at fault in publishing the defamatory material, the adoption of different standards of liability for public and private party plaintiffs, and the adoption of higher standards of proof for the recovery of punitive damages.[52]

This approach, which Professor Nimmer once referred to as "definitional balancing,"[53] attempts to balance the competing interests once and for all in the initial case in which the rules are set forth, rather than on a case-by-case basis. The Court relies on this approach with some frequency in the First Amendment area, given that there is a recognized need for clarity. Indeed, Justice Blackmun considered the need for clarity and predictability so great in *Gertz* that he concurred in the majority opinion simply to settle the matter, even though he disagreed with the Court's basic approach.[54] If there is a need for such broad-based, rule-oriented decision making, *Gertz* is an example of the Court executing it in a very detailed and thoughtful manner.

In shaping doctrine the Court will sometimes take account of the impact that the doctrine will have on the values protected by the provision in issue. For instance, in *City of Ladue v. Gilleo*, in the course of invalidating an ordinance that broadly prohibited persons from posting signs on their own lawns, the Court noted that such a prohibition cuts deeply into First Amendment interests in that it removes an inexpensive and easy form of communication, undermines a speaker's interest in being personally identified with the message, and makes it more difficult for a speaker to reach his neighbors.[55]

In *Kelo v. City of New London*, the majority declined to apply a heightened standard of review to the question of whether an economic development plan would actually lead to expected public benefits on the grounds that litigation over this fairly difficult issue would unduly delay the implementation of such plans.[56] In their dissenting opinions in *Kelo*, Justices O'Connor and Thomas pointed out that allowing governments to condemn private property for economic development by private entities would almost certainly benefit the wealthy and well connected at the expense of the poor and minorities.[57] Justice Thomas produced statistics indicating that racial minorities and the poor are usually the ones displaced by urban renewal, which has some-times been referred to as "Negro Removal."[58] The majority was unmoved by this argument, however. Both the majority and dissent took the potential impact of the rules and policies into account in justifying their respective approaches.

In evaluating doctrine to determine whether it should be modified, an obvious question that should be asked is whether the current doctrine has worked relatively well. In reply to Justice Scalia's argument in favor of rejecting the Court's neutrality doctrine under the Establishment Clause in his dissent in *McCreary County v. ACLU*, Justice O'Connor took the position in her concurring opinion that nations that have not adopted a policy of government neutrality toward religion have experienced far more societal turmoil over religion than has the United States.[59] This caused her to question why we would "trade a system that has served us so well for one that has served others so poorly?"[60] Presumably, there are factors other than legal doctrine that differentiate the United States from some of the countries that Justice O'Connor had in mind. Nevertheless, the question was certainly worth considering in determining whether doctrinal change might be warranted.

R.A.V. v. City of St. Paul[61] raised the issue of the extent to which First Amendment doctrine should be constructed to provide strategic protection for important free speech values. The majority had held that a city ordinance that punished fighting words that were based on a few discrete categories including race violated the First Amendment's prohibition against viewpoint discrimination, even though fighting words themselves were not protected speech.[62] In his concurring opinion in *R.A.V. v. St. Paul*,[63] Justice Blackmun criticized the majority's approach of extending the anti-content discrimination principle to all categories of speech on the grounds that it could result in the overall dilution of speech protection. He reasoned that "[t]he simple reality is that the Court will never provide child pornography or cigarette advertising the level of protection customarily granted political speech."[64] Thus, Justice Blackmun argued that the Court's doctrine should be constructed to ensure that the most significant speech would not receive less than adequate protection, even if that meant that less important speech would receive little if any protection at all. Justice Blackmun argued for the development of doctrine in a strategic manner designed to protect against backsliding in hard cases.

D. Line Drawing

Drawing lines, however arbitrary they might seem, is simply inherent in the development of judicial doctrine. Justice Holmes, in the case of *Irwin v. Gavit*, observed that:

> [n]either are we troubled by the question where to draw the line. That is the question in pretty much everything worth arguing in the law. . . . Day and night, youth and age, are only types.[65]

He expanded on this point in his dissent in *Louisville Gas & Electric Co. v. Coleman* in which he explained that

> [w]hen a legal distinction is determined, as no one doubts that it may be, between night and day, childhood and maturity, or any other extremes, a point has to be fixed or a line has to be drawn, or gradually picked out by successive decisions, to mark where the change takes place. Looked at by itself, without regard to the necessity behind it, the line or point seems arbitrary. It might as well or nearly as well be a little more to one side or the other. But, when it is seen that a line or point there must be, and that there is no mathematical or logical way of fixing it precisely, the decision

of the legislature must be accepted unless we can say that it is very wide of any reasonable mark.[66]

As such, Justice Holmes believed that there was indeed "a plain distinction" between large secured loans and small loans to individuals, and as such he would have upheld the law in question against an equal protection challenge.[67]

However, as Justice Frankfurter noted, "the fact that a line has to be drawn somewhere does not justify its being drawn anywhere."[68]

Doctrinal tests almost always produce hard cases near the margin where it is unclear whether or not an element of the test has been met. If law is to be applied at all, however, judgments must be made. As Justice Cardozo famously put it in his concurrence in *A.L.A. Schecter Poultry Corp. v. United States*, "the law is not indifferent to considerations of degree."[69] Lines must be drawn even when it cannot be done with complete clarity and precision. Indeed, in his concurrence in *Terry v. Adams*, Justice Frankfurter pointed out that the lines drawn by courts are essentially figure[s] of speech and as such cannot be expected to separate "the sheep from the goats" in the real world as opposed to in the mind of the judge.[70]

The Court has acknowledged that line drawing in constitutional law is not always neat and predictable. In the course of discussing the Establishment Clause in *Lynch v. Donnelly*, Chief Justice Burger observed that "[i]n each case, the inquiry calls for line drawing; no fixed, per se rule can be framed."[71] He acknowledged that "[t]he line between permissible relationships and those barred by the Clause can no more be straight and unwavering than due process can be defined in a single stroke or phrase or test."[72] Justice Scalia, dissenting in *Edwards v. Aguillard*, criticized this approach as highly unprincipled, arguing that it was time "that we sacrifice some 'flexibility' for 'clarity and predictability.'"[73]

Doctrine may be open to criticism if it is incapable of yielding principled boundaries, that is, if it is impossible to draw clear and predictable lines as to what is covered and what is not.[74] It is easy to overstate the "where will we draw the line" argument, however. Chief Justice Burger addressed this concern in *Walz v. Tax Commission* in which he noted that

> [t]he argument that making "fine distinctions" between what is and what is not absolute under the Constitution is to render us a government of men, not laws, gives too little weight to the fact that it is an essential part

of adjudication to draw distinctions, including fine ones, in the process of interpreting the Constitution.[75]

Justice Harlan, concurring, agreed, noting that "[t]he prospect of difficult questions of judgment should not be the basis for prohibiting legislative action that is constitutionally permissible."[76]

The Court's constitutional jurisprudence is filled with fine distinctions. In *Arizona v. Hicks*, for instance, the Court held that a police officer engaged in a search when he moved a turntable to obtain its serial number, and, because he did not have probable cause to believe that the stereo was stolen, the search was illegal.[77] Justice O'Connor, dissenting, would have characterized the officer's conduct as "a cursory inspection" rather than a search, and, as such, probable cause would not be required.[78] In the great majority of cases, whether police conduct constitutes a search will not be a matter of controversy. The *Hicks* case illustrates, however, that every category has its margins, and close and difficult cases will occur in these borderline situations.

The inability to make principled distinctions can be a good reason to reject doctrine that would require such distinctions to be made. In *Widmar v. Vincent*, for instance, in the course of rejecting a distinction between "worship" and other forms of religious speech, the Court noted that it would be a very difficult line to draw.[79]

E. Bright Lines

Frequently in developing doctrine, the Court chooses to employ relatively clear bright-line rules that tend to maximize predictability and at the same time inevitably minimize flexibility.[80] The Court may choose a bright-line approach for a variety of reasons. One of the most famous examples of the adoption of bright-line rules by the Court was the warnings promulgated in *Miranda v. Arizona*.[81] Prior to *Miranda*, whether a confession was given voluntarily was assessed by a fact-intensive totality of the circumstances approach.[82] The Court obviously found that inadequate, apparently because in practice it provided insufficient protection against the admission of coerced confessions, insufficient guidance to the police, and consumed an inordinate amount of judicial time. Consequently, the Court concluded that confessions obtained during the course of custodial interrogation would be inadmissible in evidence unless the suspect had been "warned that he had a right to remain silent, that any statement that he made may be used as evidence against him, and that he has a right to the presence of an attorney either retained or appointed."[83] Absent the warnings, the Court indicated that "[n]o amount of circumstantial evidence that the person may have been aware of [these] right[s] will suffice. . . ."[84] The adoption of this requirement obviously simplified the litigation process, although there would still be questions as to whether the warnings were properly given, whether there was an effective waiver, and whether there was in fact custodial interrogation.[85]

The *Miranda* approach could readily be criticized as inconsistent with the Court's traditional case-by-case approach to constitutional adjudication in that it reached out to decide a variety of issues not yet presented by the litigants. This opened the Court up to the charge that its action was more legislative than judicial. In dissent, Justice Harlan argued that the traditional totality of the circumstances approach was preferable to the Court's ironclad warnings in that through the judicial treatment "of one case at a time," it had "developed an elaborate, sophisticated, and sensitive approach to the admissibility of confessions."[86] However, the difficulty of reconstructing what had occurred during custodial interrogation, given that there would almost certainly be no one present other than the police and the suspect, provided some support for the Court's rule-oriented approach. Moreover, the Court's method is arguably quite useful to the police as well in that it allows them to engage in extensive interrogation with little risk of judicial second-guessing, as long as they begin with the administration of these relatively simple warnings. Thus, even conceding that Justice Harlan was correct in characterizing the imposition of the warnings as legislative in nature, it may still have been an easily defensible move by the Court, at least in the context in which it was decided.

The Fourth Amendment is another area in which the Court has emphasized the need for bright-line rules to ensure predictability.[87] As the Court put it in *Dunaway v. New York*, in the course of affirming the need for probable cause as a predicate for a lawful arrest, "[a] single, familiar standard is essential to guide police officers, who have only limited time and expertise to reflect on and balance the social and individual interests involved in the specific circumstances they confront."[88] The Court quoted this statement two years later in *New York v. Belton* in support of its decision to adopt a bright-line rule that "when a policeman has made a lawful custodial arrest of the occupant of an automobile, he may, as a contemporaneous incident of that arrest, search the passenger compartment of that automobile."[89]

In the companion case of *Robbins v. California*,[90] the Court announced a further bright-line rule to the effect that the police may not search closed containers in automobiles pursuant to the search incident to the arrest doctrine. Writing for a plurality, Justice Stewart declared that "as the disparate results in the decided cases indicate, no court, no constable, no citizen, can sensibly be asked to distinguish the relative 'privacy interests' in a closed suitcase, briefcase, portfolio, duffel bag, or box."[91] Justice Powell concurred in the judgment but contended that "[t]he plurality overestimates the difficulties involved in determining whether a party has a reasonable expectation of privacy in a particular container."[92] Thus, Justice Powell questioned whether there was a need for the rule under the circumstances. Justice Rehnquist, dissenting, questioned the utility of bright-line rules period, arguing that

> [o]ur entire profession is trained to attack "bright lines" the way hounds attack foxes. Acceptance by the courts of arguments that one thing is the "functional equivalent" of the other, for example, soon breaks down what might have been a bright line into a blurry impressionist pattern.[93]

There may be some truth to Justice Rehnquist's observation, but surely he overstated the difficulty with a bright-line approach. In *Michigan v. Jackson*, Chief Justice Burger, concurring, did caution against attempting to derive rules on a case–by–case basis from the cases that come before the Court, given that by definition they are the "hard cases" and as such may not give rise to useful rules for the more ordinary case.[94]

Sometimes, however, in an area in which it is important for non-lawyers to be able to make judgments as to the applicability of the law, such as the Fourth Amendment, too many lines, bright or otherwise, can be more of a hindrance than a help. In *Illinois v. Gates*,[95] for instance, the Court replaced the doctrinally complicated *Aguilar-Spinelli* test for evaluating whether an informant's tip provided sufficiently reliable information to meet the probable cause standard for issuance of a warrant. In rejecting the prior approach, the Court emphasized that "the evidence . . . collected must be seen and weighed not in terms of library analysis by scholars, but as understood by those versed in the field of law enforcement."[96] Thus, "probable cause is a fluid concept—turning on the assessment of probabilities in particular factual contexts—not readily, or even usefully, reduced to a neat set of legal rules."[97] The Court in *Gates* concluded that rules do not necessarily aid in understanding of constitutional principles.

Sometimes, as was the case with the unduly complicated approach that had developed in that particular area, they have made application of the law far more difficult and could indeed have the perverse effect of driving the police away from the warrant procedure instead of toward it.[98]

One reason why the Court may choose a bright-line approach is because of the importance of the constitutional right or interest in question. Such was the case in *New York v. United States*, in which the Court held that the structural principle prohibiting Congress from commandeering a state legislature to enact federal programs was so fundamental that it could not be overridden by a competing governmental interest, such as disposing of low-level radioactive waste, no matter how important that interest might be.[99] This led the Court to conclude that ultimately "the Constitution protects us from our own best intentions."[100] As a result, it rejected an interest-balancing approach in this context.

An obvious difficulty with a bright-line approach is that it does not allow for nuanced analysis or interest balancing. Chief Justice Burger, dissenting, in *In re Griffiths* from the Court's decision to apply strict scrutiny to invalidate a state law excluding aliens from the practice of law, noted that

> [i]n recent years the Court, in a rather casual way, has articulated the code phrase "suspect classification" as though it embraced a reasoned constitutional concept. Admittedly, it simplifies judicial work as do "per se" rules, but it tends to stop analysis while appearing to suggest an analytical process.[101]

This is almost certainly true, although such bright-line rules do offer the benefit of containing judicial discretion within previously defined boundaries once they have been adopted.

The Court recognizes that some areas demand so much flexibility that the development of bright-line rules would be counterproductive. For instance, in *Strickland v. Washington*,[102] the Court explicitly rejected a bright-line approach in developing standards for assessing whether assistance of counsel was inadequate under the Sixth Amendment. The Court concluded that effectiveness of counsel must be measured by whether it was reasonable in view of prevailing norms of professional conduct.[103] Consequently, "[n]o particular set of detailed rules for counsel's conduct can satisfactorily take account of the variety of circumstances faced by defense counsel or the range of legitimate decisions regarding how best to represent a criminal defendant."[104] As a result, "[a]ny such set of rules would interfere with the constitutionally protected independence of counsel and restrict the wide latitude counsel must have in making tactical decisions."[105] The Court concluded that, in assessing a claim of ineffective assistance of counsel, the fact finder must afford great deference to the decisions made by counsel, and relief may not be granted, absent a showing of prejudice.[106] It recognized that this was an area in which bright-line rules would not simply be unhelpful but would in fact undermine the constitutional values in question.

F. Interest Balancing to Create Doctrine

One prominent feature of the Court's constitutional doctrine is balancing. Usually the Court weighs a state interest against a constitutional right, but sometimes it weighs constitutional rights against each other.

Balancing has been a prominent mode of analysis in free speech cases. In *Schneider v. New Jersey*,[107] for instance, the Court balanced the right of persons to hand out leaflets on the public streets as a means of exercising their First Amendment rights against a city's interest in avoiding litter on the streets and concluded that the latter was insufficient to outweigh the former. This was an example of the Court placing weight or value on both the right and the state interest and concluding that the former was essentially heavier than the latter. The Court was also influenced by the fact that the state could rely on the less restrictive alternative of prohibiting littering as opposed to banning leafletting.[108]

The administrative search case of *Camara v. San Francisco*[109] is another example of the Court creating doctrine through interest balancing. Previously in *Frank v. Maryland*,[110] the Court had held that it was not necessary for the state to obtain a warrant to engage in an administrative search, for instance as part of a housing code compliance program. In *Camara*, the Court rejected the *Frank* Court's conclusion that no warrant was necessary but replaced it with the novel approach that an area-wide warrant, as opposed to a typical warrant specifying the particular property in issue, would suffice.[111] In reaching this conclusion, the Court relied on and balanced the competing interests.[112] It concluded that there is a sufficient privacy interest in a person's home, even where the point of the search is a random check for code compliance as opposed to a search for criminal evidence, to justify the issuance of a warrant by a judicial officer.[113] In determining that the area-wide warrant would satisfy Fourth Amendment concerns, the Court explained that "there can be no ready test for determining reasonableness other than by balancing the need to search against the invasion which the search entails."[114] In other words, the Court seemed to say that a balancing analysis was all but demanded by the constitutional text. Upon engaging in the balancing process, the Court took account of the fact that code-compliance programs had a lengthy history of public acceptance, the public interest in housing-code compliance was significant, and the invasion of privacy was limited because the inspection was not personal in nature and was not aimed at the discovery of criminal evidence.[115] Balancing these three factors led the Court to its conclusion that an area-wide administrative warrant would reconcile the competing interests. This is an excellent example of the Court confronting a somewhat different situation than the norm (under the Fourth Amendment) and adjusting existing legal doctrine to meet it through interest balancing. This was not an example of case-by-case balancing. Rather, the Court used the interest-balancing process to create doctrinal rules that would then apply in the future. Occasionally, the Court will proclaim as it did in *Dunaway v. New York*[116] that the Constitution, through the articulation of the "reasonableness" standard for searches and seizures, struck the balance, precluding the need for any further case-by-case interest balancing.

Another case where the Court relied on an explicit balancing of interests to develop a doctrinal rule is *United States v. Leon.*[117] There the Court held that evidence would not be excluded from a criminal trial where the police had relied in good faith on an apparently valid search warrant that was later overturned. Writing for the majority, Justice White engaged in an explicit cost benefit analysis. On the one hand, the Court noted that the purpose of deterring police misconduct would not be served where they were acting in good faith reliance on an apparently valid warrant.[118] The Court explained that it did not have reason to believe that magistrates or judges issuing warrants ignore the Fourth Amendment or that the exclusionary rule in this context would have any impact on their behavior in any event, given that, unlike the police, they have no vested interest in the conviction of the defendants.[119] In a lengthy footnote the Court expressed skepticism with respect to studies arguably minimizing the costs of the exclusionary rule, noting that the small percentages of defendants released under the rule "mask a large absolute number of felons who are released."[120] Ultimately, the Court concluded that "the marginal or nonexistent benefits produced by suppressing evidence obtained in objectively reasonable reliance on a subsequently invalidated search warrant cannot justify the substantial costs of exclusion."[121]

Justice Brennan, dissenting, took sharp issue with the Court's employment of its balancing analysis. He noted that the "cost/benefit analysis . . . creates an illusion of technical precision and ineluctability . . . [but in fact] the 'costs'. . . loom to exaggerated heights, and . . . the 'benefits' of such exclusion are made to disappear with a mere wave of the hand."[122] He criticized the Court for ignoring the benefit of removing the judicial system from the taint of reliance on illegally seized evidence.[123] Moreover, he argued that the Court's assessment of costs to law enforcement were based on "inherently unstable compounds of intuition, hunches, and occasional pieces of partial and often inconclusive data."[124] Essentially, Justice Brennan argued that there simply was not enough credible, empirical evidence to meaningfully balance the interests, and the balance set by the majority was rigged to undervalue the institutional interests in complying with the Fourth Amendment. Whether or not Justice Brennan's assessment was correct, he made a compelling case to the effect that cost benefit analysis in constitutional law should be undertaken with extreme care and can be readily misused.

The Court employed a naked balancing approach in *United States v. Nixon.*[125] Faced with the question of whether the president could assert a constitutionally implied privilege to resist a subpoena for tape recordings of conversations in the oval office that could provide evidence in criminal trials against some of his closest advisors, the Court recognized a qualified privilege but then balanced it against the public need for evidence in criminal cases.[126] It provided little guidance as to why the privilege should not be as absolute as other confidential communications privileges, why it should necessarily yield to the demand for evidence in criminal case, or why it would not always be overridden by such a demand. The case is probably best understood as an attempt to produce a unanimous opinion, which would require production of the tapes, given that there was good reason to suspect that they would incriminate the president (as in fact they did, leading to his resignation), without saying that the president was to be distrusted in this case. Consequently, it would seem to be an example of result-oriented balancing in that the Court calibrated the scales in advance to reach the result that it desired. If so, it reveals perhaps the most serious challenge to judicial interest balancing, that is, that there is generally little in the balancing process to provide any realistic check against manipulative decision making. Disagreement with how the balance is struck can simply be dismissed as a difference in evaluation of the competing interests.

Institutional concerns might limit the degree to which courts engage in the balancing of competing interests through the judicial process. In *Dennis v.*

United States, Justice Frankfurter, concurring, argued that the Court should engage in the explicit balancing of competing interests rather than simply employing doctrinal rules and exceptions.[127] At the same time, however, he argued that there were significant institutional limits on the Court's ability to do that, noting the following:

> Courts are not representative bodies. They are not designed to be a good reflex of a democratic society. Their judgment is best informed, and therefore most dependable, within narrow limits. Their essential quality is detachment, founded on independence. History teaches that the independence of the judiciary is jeopardized when courts become embroiled in the passions of the day and assume primary responsibility in choosing between competing political, economic and social pressures.[128]

Frankfurter was arguing for a combination of judicial candor and restraint.

G. Anti-Doctrine—Ad Hoc Judgment

The purpose of constitutional doctrine is to provide more specific and predictable guidance for the adjudication of constitutional cases. The development of doctrine usually leads to the development of tests for assessing constitutionality. Sometimes, however, the tests prove incapable of helping to decide cases in a sensible and consistent manner. When this happens, some justices may abandon the doctrine and simply decide specific cases based on their judgment as to what the constitutional provision seems to require. Justice Breyer took this approach in his concurring opinion in *Van Orden v. Perry*.[129] In deciding that a Ten Commandments monument on the Texas State Capitol grounds did not violate the Establishment Clause, he could "see no test-related substitute for the exercise of legal judgment"[130] in such a borderline case. Consequently, he fell back to the purposes of the clause, which he identified as protecting religious liberty, promoting religious tolerance, while avoiding religious divisiveness.[131] Considering all of the circumstances of the case, including the fact that there appeared to be a secular purpose, the context did not suggest that a religious message was being conveyed, and there had been virtually no objection to the monument during the forty years that it had stood on the capitol grounds, he concluded that it was not inconsistent with the purposes of the clause and indeed ordering its removal would foster the very type of religious divisiveness that the clause was intended to prevent.[132] Justice Breyer's approach can be faulted on the grounds that it provides little predictability and arguably results in decisions based on the personal preferences of judges.[133] His reply was that his decision was based on his understanding of the purposes of the clause and not on his own values.[134] As for predictability, the problem with the existing tests is that they did not seem to have been applied in a consistent manner either, especially to borderline cases.[135]

In *Burton v. Wilmington Parking Authority*,[136] the Court took a highly particularistic fact-oriented approach to determining whether seemingly private conduct constituted "state action" under the Fourteenth Amendment. There, a coffee shop located in a parking garage owned by a state authority discriminated based on race.[137] In determining that the state was sufficiently implicated, the Court concluded that it would be "an impossible task" to "fashion and apply a precise formula."[138] Instead, "[o]nly by sifting facts and weighing circumstance can the nonobvious involvement of the State in private conduct be attributed its true significance."[139] The Court then proceeded to consider all relevant facts identified in the record and concluded that they established a relationship of "interdependence" between the coffee shop and the state, bringing the Fourteenth Amendment into play.[140] The Court cautioned, however, that each subsequent case must be decided on its own peculiar facts.[141] Justice Harlan, dissenting, criticized this approach under which by "first indiscriminatingly throwing together various factual bits and pieces and then undermining the resulting structure by an equally vague disclaimer, seems to me to leave completely at sea just what it is in this record that satisfies the requirement of 'state action.'"[142] Though an example of extreme ad hoc decision making, *Burton* has remained a relatively isolated case in the state action area. Its approach has virtually never been followed since.

In the area of obscenity regulation, the Court had struggled to produce doctrine that could be applied in a consistent and predictable manner over a lengthy period.[143] In his dissenting opinion in *Paris Adult Theatre v. Slaton*,[144] Justice Brennan concluded that the quest for clarity was fruitless and that the inevitable vagueness of obscenity doctrine, despite the Court's best efforts to infuse it with some semblance of predictability, was reason enough to relinquish the task all together, permitting the state only to protect against exposure to minors and unconsenting adults. The majority disagreed, however, adopting a three-part test for obscenity that has brought stability to the area and has essentially provided sufficient guidance ever since.

In *Morrison v. Olson*, the Court applied an ad hoc approach in the course of upholding the Independent Counsel Act against a variety of constitutional challenges.[145] Taking account of a number of factors, the Court concluded that the insulation of the independent counsel against "at will" removal did not "impermissibly [burden] the President's power to control or supervise."[146] Justice Scalia objected strenuously to the Court's "totality of the circumstances" form of analysis, maintaining that such a decision was "ungoverned by rule, and hence ungoverned by Law."[147] He then noted that "[t]he ad hoc approach to constitutional adjudication has real attraction [since] . . . [i]t is guaranteed to produce a result, in every case, that will make a majority of the Court happy with the law [considering that] [t]he law is, by definition, precisely what the majority thinks, taking all things into account, it ought to be."[148] It would be difficult to set forth a more penetrating and concise critique of this form of analysis.

Writing for the Court in *Blakely v. Washington*,[149] Justice Scalia again criticized a relatively ad hoc approach to adjudication, in this instance permitting judges to invalidate sentencing guidelines that stray beyond acceptable limits. He maintained that "[w]ith *too far* as the yardstick, it is always possible to disagree with such judgments and never to refute them."[150] This is a point well taken, and yet there are areas of the law, such as the Takings Clause, where "not too far" seems close to the legal standard applied.

The question of whether regulation rises to the level of a taking has long caused the Court to engage in a relatively ad hoc balancing analysis. In the first significant regulatory takings case, *Pennsylvania Coal Co. v. Mahon*, Justice Holmes explained that "[g]overnment hardly could go on if to some extent values incident to property could not be diminished without paying for every such change in the general law."[151] Consequently, he concluded that "[t]he general rule at least is that while property may be regulated to a certain extent, if regulation goes too far it will be recognized as a taking."[152] Obviously, this approach provides little in the way of predictability or guidance. Several decades later in *Penn Central Transportation Co. v. New York*, Justice Brennan, writing for the majority in a major regulatory takings case, conceded that "this Court, quite simply, has been unable to develop any 'set formula' for determining when 'justice and fairness' require that economic injuries caused by public action be compensated by the government, rather than remain disproportionately concentrated on a few persons."[153] He described the approach as an "essentially ad hoc factual inquir[y]" but maintained that there were several factors to be considered in the balance, including "[t]he economic impact of the regulation on the claimant and, particularly, the extent to which [it] has interfered with distinct investment-backed expectations," "the character of the governmental action," as well as the importance of the governmental purpose.[154] The Court then gave several examples of laws that do not generally amount to a taking, including taxing and zoning.[155] This clarified the balancing process slightly but not much.

Voting rights cases involving the question of whether the shape of a district or the structure of the electoral process are racially discriminatory in violation of equal protection have been notoriously devoid of principled guidance. In *Rogers v. Lodge*,[156] for instance, the Court concluded that a multimember districting plan that was not initially adopted for discriminatory purposes was being maintained for such illicit purposes. In explaining this conclusion, the Court did little more than summarize the fact-findings of the district court without attempting to state any particular governing rule or principle. Justice Powell, dissenting, criticized the Court for placing reliance on the federal district court's "essentially free from any standards propounded by this Court."[157] In a lengthy dissent Justice Stevens argued that the Court's approach, "premised on a case-by-case appraisal of the subjective intent of local decision makers cannot possibly satisfy the requirement of impartial administration of the law that is embodied in the Equal Protection Clause of the Fourteenth Amendment."[158] In other words, Justice Stevens argued that the Court's ad hoc decision making process in the case actually amounted to a greater constitutional violation than the practices that it was reviewing. This is a strong statement; however, it is essentially true, given the lack of guidance or predictability inherent in the Court's approach.

H. Multifactor Tests

Especially in the latter half of the twentieth century, the Court has been highly inclined to create multifactor doctrinal tests for analyzing issues in all areas of constitutional law. These tests are far too numerous to set forth. In the area of freedom of speech alone, there may be more than a dozen different multifactor tests for evaluating different types of issues. An attempt to discuss these tests in any detail would require a lengthy chapter of its own. Because the development or refinement of many of these tests has been discussed in detail elsewhere in the book, this section will simply provide a flavor of the multifactor doctrinal approach in an effort to show how it fits together with some of the alternative analytical techniques.

Probably the most familiar and indeed the most frequently employed doctrinal approaches employed by the Court are the three standards of judicial scrutiny that it has developed over time to address equal protection issues. The baseline test for evaluating constitutionality in many contexts, and especially under the Equal Protection Clause, is the highly deferential rational basis test. In the equal protection context, the Court asks whether the legislative classification in issue is rationally related to a legitimate state purpose.[159] At the other end of the spectrum is the strict standard of review first articulated in *Korematsu v. United States*,[160] which the Court applies to legislative classifications that are suspect in nature, such as race, or to fundamental interests, such as voting in state elections, as recognized in *Kramer v. Union Free School District*,[161] or interstate travel, as in *Shapiro v. Thompson*.[162] This standard of review requires the state to establish that it has a compelling state interest, that the means chosen by the state to further that interest are narrowly tailored, and that there are no less discriminatory alternatives. This standard of review is quite demanding and difficult to satisfy. In *Craig v. Boren*[163] the Court also developed an intermediate standard of review for evaluating classifications based on gender. As the name suggests, it falls somewhat in between the deferential and strict standards requiring the state to set forth an important (though not compelling) state interest and a substantial (though not narrowly tailored) ends means relationship.[164] The development of this standard is discussed in some detail later in this chapter.[165]

These standards are rather generic and apply to all types of equal protection cases. The central focus of the tests involves an assessment of the weight of the government interest as well as a consideration of the appropriateness of the means chosen to effect that interest. However, in evaluating the significance of the state purpose, the Court has declared several possible state purposes to be off limits entirely, such as engaging in invidious racial discrimination,[166] perpetuating gender-based stereotypes,[167] giving one vote greater weight than another,[168] or penalizing interstate relocation on the basis of indigence or a need for social services.[169]

The Court has followed a similar pattern in the area of freedom of speech, where the tests tend to take account of the peculiarities of the specific context in which they arise. For instance, in the area of commercial speech the Court in *Central Hudson Gas & Electric v. Public Service Commission*[170] set forth a four-part intermediate-type standard in which it enquires (1) whether the speech in issue concerns lawful activity, (2) whether the regulation promotes a substantial governmental interest, (3) whether the regulation directly advances that interest, and (4) whether it is no more extensive than necessary. This is essentially a modified intermediate standard of review with some focus on the specific context. With respect to obscenity, the Court in *Miller v. California* settled on a three-part test that asks (1) whether the average person applying contemporary community standards would find the work taken as a whole to appeal to the prurient interest, (2) whether the work taken as a whole depicts specifically defined conduct in a patently offensive manner, and (3) whether the work taken as a whole lacks serious literary, artistic, scientific, or political value.[171] Unlike the test for commercial speech, which is a modified generic review standard, the obscenity test is entirely context specific. These are only two of the multifactor tests that the Court has developed. Dozens more could be cited.

Arguably, the most famous of the Court's modern doctrinal tests is the *Lemon* test for evaluating potential Establishment Clause violations, which the Court developed over a long line of cases, culminating in *Lemon v. Kurtzman*.[172] The development of the test is discussed in detail in the previous chapter.[173] Under *Lemon*, the Court asks whether the law in question (1) has a secular purpose, (2) has a primary effect of neither advancing or inhibiting religion, and (3) does not excessively entangle government and religion.[174] This test focuses on what the Court perceives to be the central issues raised under the Establishment Clause. Like many of the Court's doctrinal tests, the *Lemon* test looks both to purpose and effect.

The rather extreme proliferation of multifactor doctrinal tests by the Supreme Court over the past seventy years arguably evinces a desire by the Court to engage in relatively nuanced, but at the same time controlled, decision making. Presumably, the Court is attempting to achieve at least some of the predictability of bright-line rules, along with some of the flexibility of balancing, while hopefully avoiding the inflexibility of a bright-line approach and the unpredictability of balancing. Whether multifactor tests are capable of achieving this middle ground is subject to debate, but in any event this approach tends to dominate modern constitutional analysis by the Court.

I. Avoiding Evasion

Sometimes the Court takes notice of the fact that doctrinal rules could easily be evaded if it demands only formal as opposed to substantive compliance. For instance, in *Cummings v. Missouri*, in which the Court invalidated a post-Civil War Test Oath that had the equivalent impact of a bill of attainder, it noted that "[t]he Constitution deals with substance not shadows. Its inhibition was leveled at the thing, not the name."[175] Consequently, doctrine that has appeared to be too formalistic has often been criticized.[176]

The Court was concerned with preventing easy evasion of constitutional requirements when in *Smith v. Allwright*[177] it held that the state action limitation, and hence the duty not to exclude voters on account of race, could not be avoided simply by discriminating in the context of the purportedly "private" Democratic primary instead of the general election. The Court explained that "[c]onstitutional rights would be of little value if they could be thus indirectly denied."[178] The Court had previously faced attempts to avoid the constitutional prohibition against racial discrimination in voting through the use of privatized primaries or pre-primaries and was obviously attempting to convey the message that such evasion would not be tolerated.[179]

Likewise, in his dissenting opinion in *City Council of City of Los Angeles v. Taxpayers for Vincent*, Justice Brennan argued that the Court should apply a fairly demanding standard of review to attempts by governments to limit protected free speech activities in order to further aesthetic considerations, because such considerations are highly subjective and could therefore easily conceal an intent to discriminate on the basis of content.[180]

J. Implementing Doctrine Procedurally

An important aspect of constitutional doctrine is delineating how it will operate in the context of litigation. At some point the Court needs to be able to transform doctrinal rules into a form applicable in a trial court. In *Green County v. County School Board of New Kent County*,[181] the Court had held that a legally segregated or "dual" school system was under an obligation to eliminate all vestiges of segregation "root and branch." A few years later in *Keyes v. School District No. 1, Denver*,[182] the Court faced the question of whether a similar desegregation obligation applied to a district that was racially segregated in fact (de facto) but had never been legally segregated (de jure). The Court concluded that the plaintiff was required to prove that there had been an intent by the authorities to racially segregate at least a "meaningful portion" of the school district.[183] The question then became whether proof of such intent in a portion of the district (in the *Keyes* case encompassing about 10 percent of the students) was sufficient to warrant a district-wide desegregation order. At that point, the Court developed two legal presumptions to control litigation of this issue. The Court concluded that proof by the plaintiff that a meaningful portion of the district was intentionally segregated creates a presumption that the entire district was intentionally segregated, shifting to the defendant school district the burden of proving that it was not to avoid a district-wide desegregation order.[184] As the Court explained, proof of some significant intentional segregation creates two different presumptions.[185] First, if school officials had an illegal purpose in one portion of the district, there is reason to presume that they had such an illegal intent in other portions of the district as well.[186] Second, it will be presumed that intentional segregation in one portion of the district had a segregative impact in other portions of the district and that segregation existing today is the result of intentional segregative decisions made in the past.[187] The burden would then shift to the defendant to attempt to rebut these two presumptions. If it was unable to do so, then the entire school district would be considered a dual school system under *Green County* and a district-wide remedy to desegregate "root and branch" would follow.

This is an example of the Court developing doctrinal rules not simply in the abstract as it often does, but rather with an eye to their application in the course of litigation. Beyond that, however, it developed procedural rules that as a practical matter have a powerful substantive effect. It will generally be difficult to rebut either of the *Keyes* presumptions. That is, it would be hard to prove that segregative intent was not a factor in the decision making process within the district, given that there might need to be an inquiry into the reasoning behind thousands of decisions over several decades, there would probably not be adequate records, and many of the decision makers are likely to be unavailable. Separating causal factors in such a way so as to prove that intentional segregation in one part of the district had no impact in another would be difficult and often impossible, even where there was no impact. Because intention and causation in this area are difficult to prove one way or the other, a presumption in favor of one side will often be outcome determinative. Thus, in setting these presumptions as it did, the Court did not simply specify how the issues would be litigated. It also created an analytical framework that would—and almost certainly was intended to— heavily influence the outcomes in these cases. The *Keyes* rules provide an excellent example of the Court constructing legal doctrine in a form that will guide adjudication and at the same time almost certainly exercise a significant substantive impact.

% III. Clarifying Doctrine

Once the Court has developed a large body of constitutional doctrine through case-by-case adjudication, some inconsistency and confusion is bound to arise. Consequently, from time to time the Court will need to devote some effort to reconciliation and clarification if the doctrine is to remain manageable.

A. Principled Application

In developing constitutional doctrine, there is great value in adopting an approach that can be applied in a principled manner.[188] In criticizing the approach of selectively applying the Bill of Rights to the states in *Adamson v. California*, Justice Frankfurter argued that "[s]ome are in and some are out, but we are left in the dark as to which are in and which are out."[189] The obvious difficulty, however, was that the very same criticism could be raised against the fundamental fairness approach that he championed. As such, Justice Frankfurter conceded that the enterprise of determining which procedures are protected by due process requires "an exercise of judgement"; however, there remain objective benchmarks to ensure that "judges are [not] wholly at large."[190] This might answer concerns about subjectivity, although it would not necessarily allay the problem of lack of predictability.

The debate continued in *Rochin v. California*, in which the Court held that extracting evidence from a criminal defendant "shocks the conscience" and thus violates due process of law under the Fourteenth Amendment.[191] Writing for the majority, Justice Frankfurter insisted that "the vague contours of the Due Process Clause do not leave judges at large."[192] Rather, judges must rely on "considerations deeply rooted in reason and in the compelling traditions of the legal profession," including whether the practices in question "offend those canons of decency and fairness which express the notions of justice of English-speaking peoples."[193] He conceded that an interpretation so dependent on judicial judgment "is bound to fall differently at different times and differently at the same time through different judges."[194] This prospect proved too much for Justice Black, who concurred in the result but was highly critical of the "nebulous standards" and "accordion-like qualities" of the majority's analytical approach.[195] Beyond the issue of incorporation of the Bill of Rights, the Court has continued to struggle with the issue of defining substantive due process liberty in a principled manner.

Principled and consistent application of doctrine has been a major problem in the area of the Establishment Clause. In *McCollum v. Board of Education,* the Court's second modern Establishment Clause opinion, Justice Jackson, concurring, warned of this problem, stating that

> [t]he task of separating the secular from the religious in education is one of magnitude, intricacy and delicacy. . . . It is idle to pretend that this task is one for which we can find in the Constitution one word to help us as judges to decide where the secular ends and the sectarian begins in education. Nor can we find guidance in any other legal source. It is a matter on which we can find no law but our own prepossessions.[196]

Over a series of cases, the Court attempted to provide some doctrinal guidance with the adoption in *Lemon v. Kurtzman,*[197] of a three-part test for evaluating whether state conduct, especially state aid to sectarian schools, violated the Establishment Clause of the First Amendment. Essentially, the Court asked whether the state action had a primarily secular purpose, whether the effect was to advance or disadvantage religion, and whether there was a danger of excessive entanglement of the state in religious matters.[198] Although, the *Lemon* test was an improvement over the standard-less and subjective inquiry suggested above by Justice Jackson, in application it was not capable of delivering even minimally consistent results.

Dissenting in *Wallace v. Jaffree,* Justice Rehnquist summarized the state of the law as it then stood as follows:

> [A] State may lend to parochial school children geography textbooks that contain maps of the United States, but the State may not lend maps of the United States for use in a geography class. A State may lend textbooks on American history, but it may not lend a film on George Washington, or a film projector to show it in history class. A State may lend classroom workbooks, but may not lend workbooks in which the parochial school children write. . . . A State may pay for bus transportation to religious schools but may not pay for bus transportation from the parochial school to the public zoo or natural history museum for a field trip. A State may pay for diagnostic services conducted in the parochial school but therapeutic services must be given in a different building; speech and hearing "services" conducted by the State inside the sectarian school are forbidden. . . . but the State may conduct speech and hearing diagnostic testing inside the sectarian school. Exceptional parochial school students

may receive counseling, but it must take place outside of the parochial school. . . . A State may give cash to a parochial school to pay for the administration of state-written tests and state-ordered reporting services, but it may not provide funds for teacher-prepared tests on secular subjects. Religious instruction may not be given in public school, but the public school may release students during the day for religious classes elsewhere. . . .[199]

As absurd as these rules seem, they were the results of the Court's struggle to apply the *Lemon* test and its predecessors to various forms of financial aid to parochial schools. There are few if any examples of greater inconsistency of result in all of Supreme Court history. Not surprisingly, the *Lemon* test has been heavily criticized. In *Mitchell v. Helms*,[200] the Court concluded that the distinction between the provision of textbooks, which was constitutionally permissible, and instructional materials, which were not, was untenable and as a result overruled *Wolman v. Walter*[201] and *Meek v. Pittenger*,[202] which had prohibited the latter.

In *McCreary County v. ACLU*[203] the Court struck down display of the Ten Commandments in a courthouse, while in the companion case of *Van Orden v. Perry*[204] it upheld the constitutionality of a display of the Ten Commandments monument on the grounds of the Texas State Capitol. In his dissenting opinion in *McCreary*, Justice Scalia criticized the Court's doctrine in the Establishment Clause area for its utter lack of consistency and predictability. He wrote:

> What distinguishes the rule of law from the dictatorship of a shifting Supreme Court majority is the absolutely indispensable requirement that judicial opinions be grounded in consistently applied principle. That is what prevents judges from ruling now this way, now that—thumbs up or thumbs down—as their personal preferences dictate. Today's opinion . . . admits that it does not rest upon consistently applied principle.[205]

Justice Scalia then listed a series of cases in which the Court appeared to have ignored its neutrality principle and argued that this was proof that it should be rejected.[206]

Addressing these doctrinal inconsistencies in his concurring and dissenting opinion in *Wolman v. Walter*, Justice Powell noted that, if attempting to preserve a balance between Establishment Clause values and the positive values of sectarian schools "means a loss of some analytical tidiness, then that too is entirely tolerable."[207] Justice Powell recognized that there are values higher than doctrinal consistency. At some point, however, glaring doctrinal inconsistency becomes both an embarrassment as well as a negative influence on legal stability. Justice Powell's remarks and the results of the Court's Establishment Clause jurisprudence suggest that at least occasionally, unless the Court is prepared to adopt a bright-line rule that fails to capture the complexity of the constitutional provision in issue or abdicate adjudication in the area entirely, a degree, indeed even a high degree, of doctrinal inconsistency may be inevitable.

B. Doctrine in Flux

Sometimes, dissatisfaction with doctrine reaches a point at which several justices are prepared to reexamine it, and yet there is no majority to either clearly reaffirm it or reject and alter it. At that point, the doctrine appears unstable yet still controlling. This appeared to be the state of the law with respect to the public forum doctrine in *International Society for Krishna Consciousness, Inc. v. Lee*.[208] The public forum doctrine provided a three-category approach, dividing public property into traditional public forums, dedicated public forums, and non-public forums for purposes of determining the extent to which a person could exercise free speech rights on public property. The approach had been vigorously criticized by dissenting justices in prior cases.[209] Writing for a plurality in the *Lee* case, Justice Rehnquist not only continued to apply the "categorical" approach to questions of speech on public property but even added greater doctrinal complexity.[210] Applying this analysis, the plurality concluded that an airport was not a public forum.[211]

Justice Kennedy, writing for four justices, disagreed with the Court's analytical framework, arguing that "our public forum doctrine ought not be a jurisprudence of categories rather than ideas. . . ."[212] He argued that the strict categorical nature of the analysis had transformed it from a speech-protective to a speech-restrictive device by giving the government almost complete control over how the property is categorized.[213] He maintained that when doctrine grows inconsistent with its underlying purpose, in this case encouraging vigorous exercise of freedom of speech, then the doctrine must be reformulated. Instead of attempting to categorize the forums, Justice Kennedy believed that the Court should consider a number of relevant factors, the most significant being the compatibility of expressive activity with the legitimate governmental uses of the property.[214] Justice Souter also objected to the Court's categorical analysis and also would have focused on compatibility.[215] The *Lee* case illustrates an instance in which what appeared to be established doctrine is now under sufficient challenge on the Court itself to suggest that it has become unstable and could very well be rejected were one more of the justices to reconsider it. Nevertheless, the Court has not addressed the matter in the decade since *Lee*, despite the appearance of instability.

C. Resolving Doctrinal Conflicts

Occasionally the Court is faced with a case that must be decided at the intersection of seemingly conflicting lines of doctrine. In such a case, the Court must either reconcile the apparent conflict or choose between the alternatives.

In *Johnson v. California*,[216] the Court was faced with the question of whether a California prison policy that required that newly admitted prisoners be double-celled with prisoners of the same race should be subjected to the strict standard of judicial review. On the one hand, the Court had held that all racial classifications (of which this was clearly one) must be subjected to strict scrutiny.[217] On the other hand, the Court had also developed a doctrine that courts should be deferential to prison officials and should generally subject constitutional challenges to prison regulations to the rational basis standard of review. The *Johnson* Court had to choose between these two options and chose the former, holding that, unlike many other constitutional guarantees in which deference to prison officials is warranted, the strong constitutional policy against racial discrimination need not be sacrificed to the demands of incarceration, and the reasons for strict review of racial classifications apply equally to prisoners.[218] Consequently, the Court held that the two lines of authority were not really in conflict, but, to the extent that they were, one should obviously take precedence over the other.[219]

Justice Thomas read the cases quite differently, concluding that there was no special basis for according prison reliance on race any less deference than any other policy.[220] Rather, the reason for such deference was judicial lack of competence in evaluating the demands of the prison environment, which would hold equally true with respect to the need to occasionally employ racial classifications for purposes of prison security.[221] Thus, Justice Thomas resolved the purported conflict by concluding that the rationale behind the deferential standard demanded application in all circumstances.[222] *Johnson* is a good example of the choice that the justices sometimes have to make between conflicting lines of doctrine and the fact that different justices can quite reasonably reach different conclusions as to which line of doctrine should prevail.

D. Justifying Doctrine

Regardless of how doctrine is initially derived, the Court will often find it convenient to justify the doctrine, especially when it is under attack. The Court did this with the principle that the government must be neutral toward religion in *McCreary County v. ACLU*.[223] The Court acknowledged that the term *establishment* in the First Amendment "is certainly not self-defining."[224] It noted that the issues raised by the religion clauses are especially difficult, as there is an apparent tension between the Establishment and Free Exercise Clauses.[225] The Court then explained that, given these "interpretive problems," tension has best been accommodated by the neutrality principle, which the Court has long applied in this area.[226] It conceded that, given its generality, the neutrality principle was not capable of providing an answer to every hard question; however, "invoking neutrality is a prudent way of keeping sight of something the Framers of the First Amendment thought important."[227] The Court attempted to link the principle to original understanding but relied primarily on its contemporary utility to explain why the principle was worth keeping.

E. Choice of Doctrine

Sometimes the justices will agree on a result but differ significantly on the best constitutional approach to the issue. *Edwards v. California*[228] was such a case. The Court unanimously invalidated a California statute that made it a crime to bring an indigent person into the state. The majority found that this constituted discrimination against interstate commerce, in that the it had long held that personal migration was covered by the Commerce Clause.[229] In separate opinions joined by two other members of the Court, Justices Douglas[230] and Jackson[231] argued that the Commerce Clause provided an inadequate doctrinal foundation for a decision that essentially involved civil rights and that it should rest instead on the seldom-used Privileges or Immunities Clause of the Fourteenth Amendment.

As Justice Douglas put it, "the right of persons to move freely from State to State occupies a more protected position in out constitutional system than does the movement of cattle, steel, fruit and coal across state lines."[232] Although the Privileges or Immunities Clause may have seemed a more appropriate doctrinal choice, the Court's long-standing hesitancy to rely on it almost certainly steered it toward the more established Commerce Clause.

Likewise, in *Railway Express Agency v. New York*,[233] Justice Jackson, concurring, provided a theoretical explanation for why it was preferable to examine state regulation pursuant to the Equal Protection rather than the Due Process Clause of the Fourteenth Amendment. He pointed out that if the Court declared that a law violates due process, it "leaves ungoverned and ungovernable conduct which many people find objectionable."[234] However, such would not be the case with equal protection because it would merely mean "that the prohibition or regulation must have a broader impact."[235] Moreover, equal protection analysis is more desirable because

[t]here is no more effective practical guaranty against arbitrary and unreasonable government than to require that the principles of law which officials would impose upon a minority must be imposed generally. Conversely, nothing opens the door to arbitrary action so effectively as to allow those officials to pick and choose only a few to whom they will apply legislation and thus to escape the political retribution that might be visited upon them if larger numbers were affected.[236]

Thus, of the two alternatives, Justice Jackson maintained that equal protection offered advantages both from the perspective of the state and the individual. At least in cases in which the Court could choose between these theories, it has definitely preferred equal protection, as Justice Jackson maintained that it should.

F. Cleaning up a Doctrinal Mess

Often, constitutional doctrine develops in an incremental, haphazard manner with little internal coherence. Each case may make sense on its own facts, but the cases simply do not fit together well. When this occurs, the Court may attempt to use a single case to sort it out and provide some clarification.

1. Fundamental Rights and Suspect Classification

Such was the case with the Court's equal protection jurisprudence in the early 1970s. In 1973, in the course of ruling on the constitutionality of the Texas educational financing system, Justice Powell attempted to sort through the area of suspect classifications and fundamental interests, which the Court had developed as a part of its Equal Protection Clause analysis, and to create some order out of the chaos. The specific issue was whether classifications based on wealth (in that case, district property wealth) were constitutionally suspect, and whether education was a fundamental interest.[237] If so, the strict standard of review would apply, and the financing plan would probably be struck down as unconstitutional. There was a significant amount of precedent in the area, but it was far from consistent. Both Justice Powell in the majority and Justice Marshall in dissent worked over the cases and attempted to deduce controlling principles.

For Justice Powell, the Court's cases involving classifications based on wealth or ability to pay were best understood as holding that strict scrutiny was appropriate only where a person was totally deprived of a benefit on account or a complete inability to pay. [238] Moreover, the prior cases were limited to classifications based on personal wealth, not group wealth.[239] Justice Marshall read the cases differently, concluding that the precedents could not adequately be explained by these principles alone and that classifications based on group wealth were sufficiently problematic to warrant strict scrutiny.[240]

On the question of whether education should be recognized as a fundamental interest again leading to the application of strict scrutiny, Justice Powell explained the prior cases as establishing that an interest must explicitly or at least implicitly be protected by the Constitution before it may be considered fundamental; thus, mere social importance was insufficient.[241] As with wealth-based classifications, Justice Marshall disagreed with Justice Powell's analysis and read the prior cases recognizing fundamental interests in voting in state elections, interstate travel, and rights in the criminal appellate process as standing for the proposition that an interest was fundamental if there was a nexus to constitutional rights.[242] Justice Powell argued that the prior cases simply could not be read to support that proposition.[243]

At a doctrinal level, Justice Powell argued that the prior cases established that there were a relatively finite number of fundamental interests and suspect classifications, which led to the application of strict scrutiny;

otherwise, the deferential standard of review was applicable.[244] Justice Marshall again disagreed, arguing for a sliding scale approach that would increase the standard of review incrementally as the classification became more worrisome and the interest grew in constitutional significance.[245] This is merely a thumbnail sketch of the debate between Justices Powell and Marshall on fundamental interests, suspect classifications, and strict scrutiny. To fully capture the argument would require several pages of analysis. This summary does illustrate two points, however. First, at some point after significant doctrinal development has taken place, there will often come a point at which the Court must think seriously about tying up loose ends and bringing some clarity and order to somewhat incoherent precedent. Second, when the Court attempts to do that, the very disorder of the case law will provide the basis for alternative readings. Consequently, it will be possible to clarify the law in very different ways, and attempts will almost certainly be made to do just that. Usually, both readings will be defensible, as was the case in *Rodriguez*, although one may be preferable for independent reasons.

But even where the Court attempts to bring greater clarity to the law as it did in *Rodriguez*, that hardly means that it will stay clarified. Unless the newly developed doctrinal structure is reenforced in subsequent hard cases, it may well unravel. That seemed to happen, at least to an extent, following *Rodriguez* when the Court decided *Plyler v. Doe*.[246] In *Plyler*, the Court held that a Texas statute that required the children of undocumented immigrants to pay substantial tuition to attend public schools violated the Equal Protection Clause.[247] As with *Rodriguez*, there was a question as to whether there was anything in the case that would warrant the application of the strict standard of review. If not, then under the *Rodriguez* framework, the deferential rational basis standard would apply. The Court was unwilling to hold that a classification based on undocumented status, or a payment requirement, or the impact on education was sufficient to invoke strict scrutiny.[248] Rather than dropping the standard of review to the deferential rational basis standard as *Rodriguez* would presumably require, the Court instead cited a variety of significant factors presented by the case and then applied an intermediate standard of review, or at least a fairly rigorous version of the rational basis standard.[249] In reaching this conclusion, the Court relied on the fact that the children themselves had presumably not entered the country illegally on their own accord but rather had been brought in by their parents, that education, though not constitutionally fundamental, is very important to success, and that immigration policy is not generally the domain of the states.[250]

Taking account of these factors together and then adjusting the standard of review accordingly seemed quite similar to the sliding scale approach propounded by Justice Marshall in *Rodriguez* but rejected by the majority. Justice Marshall concurred in *Plyler* with the notation that the Court's opinion demonstrated why his sliding scale methodology was superior to Justice Powell's "rigidified approach" in *Rodriguez*.[251] Recognizing the tension between the analysis of *Rodriguez* and *Plyler*, Justice Blackmun joined in the opinion in *Plyler* but stated that, while he agreed with the *Rodriguez* approach in general, he did not believe that it was capable of resolving every case that might arise.[252] Justice Powell, the author of the *Rodriguez* opinion, distinguished it on the grounds that in *Plyler* a group of children were being totally deprived of education, whereas in *Rodriguez* the question was one of relative deprivation.[253] Consequently, he had no problem with the application of an intermediate standard of review in *Plyler*.[254] Justice Burger, in dissent, emphasized the inconsistency between the analytical framework in the two cases.[255]

The Court's subsequent opinion in *City of Cleburne v. Cleburne Living Center*,[256] however, seemed to indicate that *Plyler* should be read simply as an unusual and sympathetic factual situation and not as an abandonment of the *Rodriguez* analytical framework. The Court struck a local zoning law that prohibited the establishment of a home for the mentally retarded. In so doing, however, the Court refused to treat mental retardation as a "quasi suspect classification," thereby requiring the application of an intermediate standard of review but instead applied the more lenient rational basis standard.[257] It pointed to the facts that there are often legitimate reasons for treating the mentally retarded differently: they are frequently the subject of beneficial treatment in the legislative process, they wield a fair amount of political power, and taking this step would lead to a slippery slope with respect to other groups claiming similar treatment.[258] Even so, the Court ultimately invalidated the law under the rational basis standard for lack of a legitimate state purpose.[259]

In a lengthy concurrence, Justice Marshall argued that the law would not have been invalidated under a mere rational basis standard, and, consequently, the Court had applied something more akin to his sliding scale approach and should so admit.[260] The very fact that Justice Marshall made a relatively convincing case that the Court was applying something beyond a traditionally deferential rational basis standard reenforced the conclusion that the Court had decided to stick with the *Rodriguez* framework, at least nominally, even when the facts might call for somewhat more demanding scrutiny, as they did in *Plyler*. Apparently, the Court concluded that a certain degree of doctrinal distortion was a price worth paying to avoid the subjectivity and unpredictability of the far more nuanced approach propounded by Justice Marshall. In other words, sometimes the Court needs to bend or distort doctrine in order to save it.

2. The Right to Travel

In *Saenz v. Roe*,[261] the Court attempted to bring greater analytical clarity to its "right to travel" doctrine. It had long recognized constitutional protection for a right to travel and had declared it to be a fundamental right under equal protection doctrine in *Shapiro v. Thompson*.[262] Still, the right seemed to flow from several different constitutional sources[263] and protected a variety of different types of interests. Recognizing the confusion in the area, the majority in *Saenz* attempted to dissect the right to travel cases and explain them with greater clarity and particularity. In so doing, it concluded that there were actually three distinct interests protected by right to travel doctrine.

> It protects the right of a citizen of one State to enter and to leave another State, the right to be treated as a welcome visitor rather than an unfriendly alien when temporarily present in the second State, and, for those travelers who elect to become permanent residents, the right to be treated like other citizens of that State.[264]

Each of these interests was protected by different parts of the Constitution. The first was protected by a variety of constitutional sources, the second by the Article IV Privileges and Immunities Clause, and the third by the Fourteenth Amendment Privileges or Immunities Clause.[265] Without changing the substance of the doctrine but rather simply explaining it better, the Court was able to bring more coherence to an area that had become somewhat chaotic.

3. Obscenity

Arguably, there has never been a messier and more incoherent area of constitutional law than that of obscenity, especially between the Court's initial foray into the area in 1957 in *Roth v. United States*[266] and its relatively successful attempt to provide greater clarity and certainty in *Miller v. California*[267] in 1973. This doctrinal confusion was the direct result of the Court's inability to build a majority on the issue of how the concept of obscenity should be defined and analyzed under the First Amendment. In *Roth*, Justice Brennan did write for a majority of the Court in concluding that obscenity was not protected by the First Amendment.[268] The difficult question, however, was how should obscenity be defined. The Court in *Roth* rejected the English standard derived from the case of *Regina v. Hincklin*, which permitted a finding of obscenity to be based on the impact of isolated passages from the work.[269] Instead, the Court adopted a standard that had been applied by several lower courts and provided that material would be considered obscene if "to the average person, applying contemporary community standards, the dominant theme of the material taken as a whole appeals to purient interests."[270]

Justice Harlan wrote a concurring and dissenting opinion, arguing that a more speech protective standard should be applied in federal as opposed to state obscenity cases.[271] Justice Douglas, joined by Justice Black, wrote a dissenting opinion, arguing that obscenity should not be removed from the coverage of the First Amendment.[272] The Court ultimately concluded that obscenity was a constitutional fact, and, as such, each obscenity case required the appellate courts to engage in independent constitutional review of the allegedly obscene material.[273] It was in this context in *Jacobellis v. Ohio* that Justice Stewart made his famous and oft-quoted statement that, although he could not define obscenity, "I know it when I see it."[274]

In 1966 in *Memoirs of a Woman of Pleasure v. Massachusetts*,[275] Justice Brennan, writing for a three-justice plurality, interpreted *Roth* and subsequent cases as setting forth a three-part test for judging whether a work was obscene.[276] In addition to the dominant theme appealing to the prurient interest and patent offensiveness by contemporary community standards as recognized in *Roth*, Justice Brennan added a third requirement that the work had to be "utterly without redeeming social value."[277] Justices Clark and White, dissenting, objected strenuously to the addition of the "utterly without redeeming value" element to the existing *Roth* standard, arguing that it was clearly inconsistent with the holding of *Roth*.[278] Justice Clark noted that the "utterly" element had previously appeared only in an opinion written by Justice Brennan and joined by one other justice.[279] As such, it carried no precedential weight. A fair reading of the cases clearly confirms Justice Clark's view. By the time of *Redrup v. New York*[280] in 1967, the Court acknowledged that it was divided into several different camps on the issue of obscenity, with no position garnering more than two votes. Consequently, it decided cases by per curiam opinions, offering virtually no guidance as to the proper legal standards or analysis.[281]

Finally, in 1973 in *Miller v. California*,[282] probably due to changes in personnel, a majority of the Court was finally able to agree on a standard for defining obscenity for the first time since *Roth*. The Court agreed that there had been no basis whatsoever for the "utterly without redeeming social value" standard of *Memoirs*, so it rejected that at the outset.[283] It essentially retained the *Roth* test as originally stated and added a third element in place of the Memoirs "utterly" standard.[284] As a result, the Court settled on a three-part test that defined obscenity as material that is specifically defined by state law and that "taken as a whole, appeal[s] to the prurient interest in sex, which portray sexual conduct in a patently offensive way, and which, taken as a whole, do not have serious literary, artistic, political, or scientific value."[285]

This standard returned the Court much closer to where it had started in *Roth*, successfully ended the era of extreme doctrinal confusion, and stabilized the law under an approach that has commanded majority support ever since. Not only was the *Miller* Court able to clean up what was arguably the worst doctrinal mess that it had ever created, but it was also able to put to rest the notion that it was somehow impossible for the Court to create clear and workable legal standards in this particular area.[286] The journey from *Roth* to *Miller* may illustrate that it is dangerous to attempt to impose new doctrinal requirements as Justice Brennan did in *Memoirs*, where there is clearly no majority on the Court to back them up. The result is likely to be a badly splintered Court, as was the case for the better part of a decade in the obscenity area. *Miller* illustrated the importance of the Court, resolving internal doctrinal differences and building a majority around a set of doctrinal principles, however imperfect they may be. Once *Miller* achieved that, questions that had bedeviled the Court for over a decade essentially vanished.

G. Changing Doctrine

1. The Affirmative Commerce Clause

Sometimes the Court concludes that its doctrine is mistaken and needs to be revised or even changed dramatically. One of the most significant instances of such a doctrinal shift occurred in the area of the Commerce Clause in the mid-1930s. Up to 1937, the Court had construed the Commerce Clause somewhat narrowly, taking the position that Congress could not regulate local activities such as mining, agriculture, and manufacturing, and instead the Tenth Amendment reserved regulation of these areas to the states.[287] This type of analysis, treating the regulatory authority of the federal and state governments as largely mutually exclusive, was known as dual federalism. Even if local activity had a clear economic impact on interstate commerce, it would not be considered part of interstate commerce if the effects were "secondary and indirect."[288] This type of doctrinal analysis was open to criticism as being unduly formalistic. In defending Commerce Clause legislation before the Court, the government attempted to convince the Court to take a more realistic approach to the impact of occurrences at the local level on interstate commerce.

This effort finally succeeded in 1937 in *NLRB v. Jones & Laughlin Steel*,[289] in which the Court upheld the jurisdiction of the National Labor Relations Board to regulate labor stoppages at a steel mill. In rejecting the prior approach, which had emphasized the closeness of the connection with interstate commerce rather than the magnitude of the effect, the Court remarked that "[w]e are asked to shut our eyes to the plainest facts of our national life and to deal with the question of direct and indirect effects in an intellectual vacuum."[290] Rather, the Court concluded that effects on interstate "commerce must be appraised by a judgment that does not ignore actual experience."[291] The Court concluded that a local strike in the steel industry could have a "catastrophic" effect on interstate commerce.[292] The contrast between the analysis and results in *Carter Coal* and *Jones & Laughlin Steel* could not be clearer. The factual background in the two cases was remarkably similar. The Court reached a different result by rejecting its prior doctrinal framework and replacing it with a new and different approach.

The Court completed the doctrinal transformation five years later in *Wickard v. Filburn*,[293] in which it held that Congress could limit the amount of a crop grown to be consumed on a farm. At the outset Justice Jackson noted "that questions of the power of Congress are not to be decided by reference to any formula which would give controlling force to nomenclature such as 'production' and 'indirect' and foreclose consideration of the actual effects of the activity in question upon interstate commerce."[294] The Court then engaged in an economic analysis of the wheat market, noting that in the aggregate, home-grown wheat can affect prices in interstate commerce by satisfying demand or increasing supply.[295] The transformation of doctrine from formalistic to realistic was complete. This was one of the most significant doctrinal changes in Supreme Court history. The prior doctrine had been under attack for years. The Court did not simply replace one doctrinal formulation with another but instead changed its entire analytic perspective from one of formalism to economic realism, as well as moving from a relatively engaging to a far more deferential mode of analysis with respect to congressional exercise of the commerce power. That these changes occurred in challenges to legislation that clearly had a significant economic impact during the height of the Great Depression has cemented their place in constitutional history as landmark decisions.

2. Defining a Search—From Property to Privacy

Over several decades, Fourth Amendment search and seizure doctrine changed its focus from whether the search was of a "constitutionally protected area" and involved a physical trespass to whether it constituted an invasion of protected privacy.[296] As a result of this change, the Court shifted from the position that wiretapping did not constitute a search and seizure[297] to the position that it did. In *Katz v. United States*, the Court ultimately rejected the earlier approach, arguing that it had essentially been abandoned by intervening precedent.[298] The majority replaced the prior protected area approach with a somewhat ill-defined emphasis on privacy.[299] Justice Harlan, concurring, attempted to provide a more struc-tured analysis, concluding that, as he understood the precedents, for there to be Fourth Amendment protection, "a person [must] have exhibited an actual (subjective) expectation of privacy and, second, that the expectation be one that society is prepared to recognize as 'reasonable.'"[300] Perhaps because the Harlan approach was easier to grasp and apply, it seems to have had more influence in subsequent cases than the majority's analysis.[301] This was a major doctrinal change that had been called for ever since Justice Brandeis's classic dissent in the *Olmstead* case some thirty-five years earlier. As with the changes in Commerce Clause jurisprudence, it did not constitute a mere change in doctrinal formulation but rather a major shift in the Court's very conception of the Fourth Amendment and its purpose. This shift in perspective was sufficiently well thought out and backed by enough of a judicial consensus to easily stand the test of time.

3. Free Exercise and the Standard of Review

Eventually, doctrine will be replaced if it is no longer followed. In *Employment Division v. Smith*,[302] Justice Scalia, writing for the majority, replaced the compelling state interest standard with a rational basis standard in free exercise cases involving challenges to neutral and general laws restricting religiously motivated conduct on the grounds that as a practical matter the Court had either failed to apply the former standard unless the free exercise claim was combined with another constitutional claim that would also require application of the stricter standard of review or had virtually always found that the state had satisfied its burden. Consequently, Justice Scalia concluded that the compelling interest test served no useful purpose in this area.[303] Justice O'Connor, concurring, disputed Justice Scalia's characterization of the disposition of the prior cases and hence the need to change the doctrinal standard.[304] Still, a majority of the Court supported the change. Had the Court applied the strict standard in free exercise cases with its customary rigor, it is unlikely that a majority of the Court would have been persuaded to make the dramatic doctrinal change that it did in *Smith*.

4. Battling over the Standards of Review and Gender Discrimination

Sometimes, the Court alters doctrine without admitting what it is doing at the time, only to recognize the alteration in a subsequent decision. In *Reed v. Reed*,[305] the Court applied a seemingly more rigorous version of the rational basis standard in invalidating a state law that classified based on gender. A few years later in *Frontiero v. Richardson*,[306] a four-justice plurality would have extended the strict standard of review to gender-based classifications; however, there was no majority for that approach. Then, in 1976 in *Craig v. Boren*,[307] the Court simply announced that " [t]o withstand constitutional challenge, previous cases establish that classifications by gender must serve important governmental objectives and must be substantially related to achievement of those objectives." This marked the introduction of the "intermediate standard of review" into equal protection jurisprudence. Contrary to the Court's assertion, the previous cases established no such thing. Justice Brennan went on to describe how these cases seemed to apply more than a traditionally deferential rational basis standard, but he was scarcely able to contend that they had adopted a new and higher standard of review.

As Justice Rehnquist pointed out in dissent, the Court's adoption of the new standard of review "apparently comes out of thin air."[308] Indeed, Justices Powell[309] and Stevens[310] concurred in the decision but explicitly took the position that, despite the Court's language, they did not understand its opinion as recognizing a new standard of review. But that is in fact what it did, and, ever since, *Craig v. Boren* has been cited for the proposition that gender-based classifications must be subjected to an intermediate standard of review.[311] Justice Brennan might have used the prior cases to make the argument that the next logical step was to create an intermediate standard of review to address the cases employing gender-based classifications, but to simply assert that the prior cases stood for that proposition seemed disingenuous and manipulative.

The struggle over the standard of review with respect to gender-based classifications continued well after *Craig*. At least in cases in which the male was disadvantaged by the gender classification, Chief Justice Rehnquist was reluctant to concede that the intermediate standard of review applied. In *Michael M. v. Superior Court*, decided five years after *Craig v. Boren*, Chief Justice Rehnquist, writing for a plurality, noted that "the Court has had some difficulty in agreeing upon the proper approach and analysis in cases involving challenges to gender-based classifications."[312] He pointed out that *Reed v. Reed* had applied a more focused rational basis standard, while Craig "restated the test" in the language of intermediate scrutiny; however, he was hesitant to admit that the latter approach had apparently carried the day.[313]

Just as Justice Rehnquist resisted accepting the intermediate standard of review, others on the Court seemed equally intent on pushing the Court beyond the intermediate standard in cases involving gender classifications. In *Personnel Administrator of Massachusetts v. Feeney*,[314] the Court noted that a law designed to prefer men over women in public employment "would require an exceedingly persuasive justification to withstand a constitutional challenge." The Court indicated, however, that the appropriate standard of review was the intermediate standard adopted in *Craig*,[315] and it did not appear in context that the Court was attempting to modify or increase that standard. Still, on its face this language appeared somewhat more demanding than the "important state interest" language of *Craig*. Two years after *Feeney* in *Mississippi v. Hogan*, the Court quoted the "exceedingly persuasive justification" language and noted that the state must "at least" satisfy the *Craig* standard of an "important governmental objective" and a "substantial relationship" to its achievement.[316] Moreover, the Court observed that "we need not decide whether classifications based on gender are inherently suspect."[317]

Finally, in *United States v. Virginia*, in the course of striking down the ban on women at the Virginia Military Institute, the Court repeatedly referred to the need for an "exceeding persuasive justification," labeling the standard "skeptical scrutiny" with only a passing reference to the intermediate standard of *Craig v. Boren*.[318] Unlike, *Feeney*, in which the "exceedingly persuasive justification" language originated, the Court in *United States v. Virginia* almost certainly seemed to be using that language to raise the standard of review. Justice Rehnquist concurred in the decision but urged the Court to stick with the "firmly established" standard of *Craig v. Boren*,[319] and Justice Scalia argued in dissent that the Court's application of the "exceeding persuasive" test was far more demanding than intermediate scrutiny.[320] It is easy to make too much of the verbal formulations that the Court employs. Arguably, the Court decides most of these cases on the facts and equities and simply relies on these legal standards for after-the-fact explanation. The standards do seem to have some substance, however, and the gender discrimination cases present an interesting study in the origin of a legal standard and a subsequent judicial tug of war to modify it.

5. Discrimination against Aliens

The Court's doctrine with respect to the appropriate standard of review to apply in equal protection challenges to laws discriminating against aliens has also been subject to change. In *Graham v. Richardson* in 1971, citing a few earlier cases in which it had invalidated laws discriminating against aliens, the Court declared that its "decisions have established that classifications based on alienage, like those based on nationality or race, are inherently suspect and subject to close judicial scrutiny."[321] In fact, the Court had done no such thing. Indeed two of the three cases that the Court relied on had been decided decades before the Court had ever recognized the concept of strict scrutiny.[322] Rather, *Graham* recognized this principle for the first time in the course of invalidating state laws that precluded lawful resident aliens from receiving welfare benefits.

The Court employed strict scrutiny to invalidate several laws that discriminated against aliens over the next several years.[323] In *Sugarman v. Mcl. Dougall*, the Court invalidated a law that prohibited aliens from holding civil service jobs; however, it observed that the state may employ a citizenship requirement with respect to positions essential to the preservation of "a political community," including "persons holding state elective or important non elective executive, legislative, and judicial positions, for officers who participate directly in the formulation, execution or review of broad public policy."[324] A few years later in *Foley v. Connelie*,[325] the Court quoted this language for the proposition that, where such positions were involved, strict scrutiny did not apply, and an exclusion of aliens would be sustained if it was rationally related to a legitimate state interest. The Court concluded that the position of state trooper fell within this category, given the important role that law enforcement officers play in executing governmental powers.[326] This exception to strict scrutiny could arguably cut deeply into its overall application, depending on how broadly it is interpreted. The majority argued that it was simply building upon the law as it had developed.[327] The dissents charged that the Court had seized on some relatively insignificant dicta in *Sugarman* and used it to fundamentally rework the doctrine.[328] Justice Stewart agreed with the dissents that the majority was changing the doctrine significantly but concurred on the grounds that that should in fact be done.[329] In the twenty-five years since *Folie* was decided, there has not been any significant doctrinal development, so it is not clear to what extent the *Folie* exception may have swallowed the *Graham* rule. It is an excellent example, however, of how lingering dicta in earlier decisions can be readily employed to affect significant shifts in doctrine.

※ IV. Conclusion

Over its 200-plus year history, the Court has constructed a massive doctrinal framework that it employs as perhaps the most frequently utilized methodology to decide constitutional cases. In constructing this doctrinal superstructure, it chooses between a variety of possible approaches, including bright-line rules, definitional balancing, case-by-case balancing, and ad hoc decision making. The impact of the doctrine, as well as questions of ease of administration and avoidance of evasion are taken into account in the determination as to which approach makes the most sense in a particular context. The complicated doctrinal structure that the Court has created is often in need of fine-tuning. From time to time, the Court finds it necessary to justify doctrine, resolve doctrinal conflicts, clean up doctrinal messes, and often significantly change or even reject prior doctrine. The Court's doctrinal framework is sufficiently fluid to give rise to more than one plausible reading. As a result, the justices will often differ as to exactly what the doctrine is, as well as the direction in which it should be taken. When this happens the majority will forge the path for future doctrinal development, though often in the face of spirited dissent.

TEN

Consequential Reasoning

✇ I. Introduction

Throughout history, the Court or individual justices have often relied on the possibility of unacceptable consequences as a reason for rejecting a particular rule or result.[1] That is, they argue that if the Court takes a certain course of action, bad consequences will almost certainly follow. On its face, the argument should at least cause a justice to pause and think before proceeding as a rational person would ordinarily wish to avoid a decision that is likely to have an adverse impact. Thus, the bad-consequences argument tends to have logical and intuitive appeal. Moreover, it is an easy argument to make. Decisions, especially legal decisions, generally do have consequences, and it will usually be difficult to determine exactly what they will be with any certainty. The future, by definition, is uncertain. And yet, it only takes a modicum of imagination to speculate about what very well might happen. The argument of bad consequences can be a powerful tool in the hands of the advocate because it tends to place the opponent in the uncomfortable position of attempting to refute the speculative state of affairs that presently exists only in the advocate's imagination. As Justice Powell noted in his dissenting opinion in *Rummel v. Estelle*, "[s]uch a 'floodgates' argument can be easy to make and difficult to rebut."[2]

Given the appeal of this argument, it is hardly surprising that it has been employed with great frequency by the courts and continues to play a significant role in contemporary constitutional interpretation. It has been utilized by the Court in many of its most memorable decisions, including *Marbury v. Madison*,[3] *McCulloch v. Maryland*,[4] *Lochner v. New York*,[5] *Youngstown Steel & Tube Co. v. Sawyer*,[6] *New York Times Co. v. Sullivan*,[7] *Mapp v. Ohio*,[8] *Griswold v. Connecticut*,[9] *Miranda v. Arizona*,[10] *United States v. Nixon*,[11] and *Bakke v. Regents of the University of California*,[12] just to mention a few. Although bad consequences is an easy argument to make and a frequent argument made, it is not always a convincing one. Nor is it necessarily a bad argument. To a large extent, it depends on the advocate's ability to persuade the Court that bad things are, in fact, likely to occur if a particular course of action is followed. There are a number of obvious responses, including the arguments that there is no reason to believe that these bad consequences will actually happen; that the bad consequences might occur but can be prevented; that the consequences are really not that bad after all; or that if the bad consequences occur, we simply must suffer them in order to achieve other important ends. Each of these responses can be found in the case law. It should also be noted that there are two somewhat different types of bad consequences—those over which the courts will have some control and those over which they will not. Often the argument is made that a particular rule or result is undesirable because it will prove unworkable, confusing, or easily abused. Presumably, these consequences may be avoided or tempered somewhat through further judicial supervision. On the other hand, when the bad consequences will result from the independent conduct of third parties in response to the judicial ruling, the courts may have less ability to contain the damage.

This chapter will examine a variety of instances in which the Court or individual justices have put forth a bad-consequences argument and examine when the Court tends to consider such arguments persuasive and when it does not.

II. Classic Consequential Arguments

Bad-consequences arguments have been set forth by the Court and justices throughout its history in many leading cases. Indeed, Chief Justice Marshall made such an argument at a crucial point in the foundational cases of *Marbury v. Madison*. In the course of justifying judicial review of congressional legislation, he relied heavily on the fact that we have a written Constitution intended to define and limit governmental power.[13] Near the end of his opinion, he argued that the absence of judicial review "would subvert the very foundation of all written constitutions . . . [and would reduce] to nothing what we have deemed the greatest improvement on political institutions—a written constitution."[14] Marshall had a point, but, with his characteristic vigor, he arguably took the argument too far. Judicial review does provide a significant—probably the most significant—method of enforcing constitutional limitations. As such, bad consequences might very well follow, in that constitutional limitations might not as readily be honored.

However, judicial review is by no means the only method of ensuring that the Constitution is taken seriously, as Marshall would have us believe. Marshall was not challenged on this point because the decision was unanimous; however, scholars have since observed that constitutional limitations can indeed be enforced through the political process itself, as is done in many countries that have written constitutions but do not have judicial review of actions by coordinate branches of government.[15]

In *Lochner v. New York*,[16] the majority was obviously quite troubled by the consequences that might follow if the legislature were permitted to limit the hours that a baker could work. In concluding that the Fourteenth Amendment substantive due process liberty of contract prohibited the New York legislature from limiting the maximum hours that a baker could work, it opined that

> [a] printer, a tinsmith, a locksmith, a carpenter, a cabinetmaker, a dry goods clerk, a bank's, a lawyer's, or a physician's clerk, or a clerk in almost any kind of business, would all come under the power of the legislature, on this assumption. No trade, no occupation, no mode of earning one's living, could escape this all-pervading power, and the acts of the legislature in limiting the hours of labor in all employments would be valid, although such limitation might seriously cripple the ability of the laborer to support himself and his family.[17]

Thus the *Lochner* Court believed that if it did not hold firm in the case before it, the slide down the slippery slope toward pervasive regulation of all trades would be inevitable and irreversible. Although bad-consequence arguments are often exercises in rhetorical overkill, that was not the case in *Lochner*, given that all of the Court's fears were realized once the liberty of contract doctrine was laid to rest some thirty years later in *Nebbia v. New York*[18] and *West Coast Hotel v. Parrish*.[19] The question is whether the consequences were in fact as bad as the majority believed them to be.

The Court has been especially concerned that a failure to maintain a rigid boundary line in the area of Congressional power under the Commerce Clause would lead to serious adverse consequences. In the seminal case of *Gibbons v. Ogden*,[20] Chief Justice Marshall recognized that the very enumeration of the power to regulate interstate commerce presumed that there must be something beyond which Congress could not reach. For nearly two centuries, the Court has struggled to define that boundary. In these cases, the fear that the inability to draw the line will result in erasing the boundary entirely has been a constant concern of the Court. As the battle over the scope of the Commerce Clause came to a head in the mid-1930s in cases such as *Carter v. Carter Coal Co.*[21] and *A.L.A. Schechter Poultry Corp. v. United States*,[22] the Court invalidated congressional attempts to regulate wages, prices, and business practices for fear that, under the government's theories, "federal authority would embrace practically all the activities of the people, and the authority of the state over its domestic concerns would exist only by sufferance of the federal government."[23] Shortly thereafter, the Court gave up the fight and chose to defer to Congress and, as with *Lochner*, the consequences that the Court feared came to pass.

Within the past decade the Court has determined once again to play a role in defining the boundary of congressional authority under the Commerce Clause. In the course of concluding in *United States v. Lopez*[24] that a federal criminal law prohibiting the carrying of a firearm in or near a school exceeded the Commerce power, the Court appeared to be heavily moved by the need for some assurance that there is some real limitation on the scope of the Commerce Clause. It noted the following:

> Under the theories that the Government presents . . . it is difficult to perceive any limitation on federal power, even in areas such as criminal law enforcement or education where States historically have been sovereign. Thus, if we were to accept the Government's arguments, we are hard pressed to posit any activity by an individual that Congress is without power to regulate.[25]

In this context, the prospect of bad consequences has arguably become a significant structural principle. If the government is unable to offer at least some limiting principle to its Commerce Clause theory, then the theory is constitutionally inadequate. In this sense, the bad-consequences argument is used to reenforce the point that there are constitutional boundaries that must be maintained. An inability to explain how those boundaries will be enforced in a principled manner presents a risk that the Court may be unwilling to take.

The argument has been employed in the dormant Commerce Clause area as well. In his opinion for the Court in *H.P. Hood & Sons v. DuMond*, Justice Jackson set forth a classic "parade of horribles" as reason to prohibit states from controlling the export of goods produced within the state.[26] He opined as follows:

> We need only consider the consequences if each of the few states that produce copper, lead, high-grade iron ore, timber, cotton oil or gas should

decree that industries located in that state shall have priority. . . . May Michigan provide that automobiles cannot be taken out of that State until local dealers' demands are fully met?. . . . Could Ohio then pounce upon the rubber-tire industry, on which she has a substantial grip, to retaliate for Michigan's auto monopoly?[27]

Hopefully not, but there would almost certainly be economic as opposed to legal reasons why such extreme protectionism would be unlikely to occur. The argument is powerful rhetorically because it does illustrate that carried to its logical conclusion, the principle would lead to unfortunate results that were indeed the very type of results that the framers of the Constitution meant to avoid. The argument is persuasive more because of its ability to demonstrate what could happen as opposed to what probably would happen.

III. Will the Bad Consequences Occur?

A. Avoiding the Risk

One obvious response to a bad-consequences argument is to counter that it is highly unlikely that the bad consequences will actually come to pass. In *Cohens v. Virginia*, Chief Justice Marshall made a classic bad-consequences argument to the effect that if the Supreme Court cannot review the decisions of the highest courts of a state on questions of federal criminal law, then states could criminally harass federal officials executing federal law within the states without protection or recourse.[28] Marshall readily conceded that the examples put forth by counsel for the petitioner were "extreme cases" that may "never occur."[29] But his answer in turn to this concession was, even though the probability is slim, the lack of judicial protection "would contribute in no inconsiderable degree to their occurrence."[30] In other words, an absence of judicial supervision would increase the likelihood that the bad consequences would materialize. This is a nice example of a skilled justice raising a bad-consequences argument, considering the counterargument, and then dispatching the counterargument with his own counterargument.

B. The Danger of Small Risks

There are other instances as well where the Court has conceded that the likelihood that truly bad consequences will occur is small but, nevertheless, the risk itself is worth avoiding. For instance, in his influential concurring opinion in *Youngstown Steel & Tube Co. v. Sawyer*, Justice Jackson noted that permitting the president to seize and operate the steel mills during war time would not "plunge us straightway into dictatorship, but it is at least a step in that wrong direction."[31] Likewise, in *Boyd v. United States*, the Court recognized that, though a subpoena for private papers is "divested of many of the aggravating incidents of actual search and seizure . . ., illegitimate and unconstitutional practices get their first footing . . . by silent approaches and slight deviations from legal modes of procedure."[32] If anything, the modesty of these observations is far more persuasive than the more catastrophic predictions that the Court sometimes makes.

Another standard use to which the bad-consequences argument can be put is to emphasize that it is important not to be blinded by the seemingly insignificant impact of the facts before the Court, but to remain aware that the principle will apply to harms of a greater magnitude as well. For instance, in *Crandall v. Nevada*,[33] the Court invalidated a tax of one dollar on every person leaving the state by vehicle for hire. In the process, it pointed out, however, that the potential harm was hardly limited to one dollar per head because "if the State can tax a railroad passenger one dollar, it can tax him one thousand dollars . . . If one State can do this, so can every other State."[34]

C. Remote Possibilities

Sometimes, bad-consequences arguments carry little force simply because the likelihood that the consequences will occur seems quite remote. For instance, in *Griswold v. Connecticut*, the Court invalidated a Connecticut law that criminally prohibited the use of contraceptives by anyone, including married couples.[35] In the course of invalidating this law, Justice Douglas wondered whether we would "allow the police to search the sacred precincts of marital bedrooms for telltale signs of the use of contraceptives?"[36] The threat seemed frightening, but at the same time unlikely to ever occur. In dissent, Justice Stewart pointed out that there had not been any such search.[37] Moreover, any attempt by the police or prosecutors to actually embark on the bedroom search contemplated by Justice Douglas would almost certainly amount to political suicide. As a result, Justice Douglas's bad-consequence argument in *Griswold* must be taken as rhetorical flourish rather than concern as to realistic probabilities, and it was no doubt recognized as such. In his concurring opinion in *Griswold v. Connecticut*,[38] Justice Goldberg argued that if the Constitution did not prohibit the Connecticut law that banned the use of contraceptives by married people, then it would not prohibit the "far more shocking" prospect of governmental limitation of family size. This would appear to be a truly bad consequence. It might or might not follow logically from the upholding of the Connecticut contraceptive law, but as a matter of political reality, it seems far-fetched. As such, it was not a persuasive argument.

Likewise in *Field v. Clark*,[39] the petitioner argued that unless the passage of a law by Congress was required to be noted in the respective house journals before it became effective, congressional leaders could conspire to declare that a bill had become law even though it had never been passed by one or both houses. The Court rejected this argument, noting that the possibility of such a "deliberate conspiracy" was "too remote to be seriously considered," and it would be inconsistent with the proper respect that the Court owed the legislative branch to indulge in such speculation.[40] In other words, at some point, the bad consequences are simply too far-fetched to be taken seriously.

Justice Scalia made this point in *Harmelin v. Michigan*[41] in the course of rejecting Justice White's argument that if the Cruel and Unusual Punishment Clause does not prohibit sentences that are disproportional to the crime, then nothing would stop a state from punishing overtime parking with life imprisonment. Justice Scalia explained that the strength of a "parade of horribles" argument

> [i]s in direct proportion to 1) the certitude that the provision in question was meant to exclude the very evil represented by the parade, and 2) the probability that the parade will in fact materialize. Here . . . there is no cause to believe that the provision was meant to exclude the evil of a disproportionate punishment. . . . Nor is it likely that the horrible example imagined would ever in fact occur. . . .[42]

In other words, at some point, common sense and political realities are a more than adequate answer to bad consequence or parade of horribles arguments. As Justice Scalia further explained, we should not assume that "the Constitution prohibited everything that is intensely undesirable."[43]

In his concurring opinion in *McCollum v. Board of Education*,[44] Justice Jackson warned that a strict enforcement of the concept of a wall of separation between church and state in the area of public education would result in the removal from the curriculum of much of the present education in art, literature, music, and philosophy.[45] As he put it:

> [N]early everything in our culture worth transmitting, everything which gives meaning to life, is saturated with religious influences, derived from paganism, Judaism, Christianity—both Catholic and Protestant—and other faiths accepted by a large part of the world's peoples.[46]

To some extent, Justice Jackson's concerns have been borne out by litigation over religious influence in schools but hardly to the extent he feared. The courts have been able to draw lines short of the banishment of all religiously influenced work from public education, but those lines have been jagged and subject to much criticism. Consequently, this would appear to be another example of a bad-consequences argument with a solid kernel of truth, but which greatly overstated the threat.

Twenty years later in *Board of Education v. Allen*, Justice Black, the author of *Everson*, now dissenting, argued that permitting the state to lend secular textbooks to students in religious schools could lead to the state building religious schools, paying the salaries of the teachers, and finally paying all of the bills of the institutions.[47] As with Justice Jackson's argument in McCollum, this assumed that once one step was taken down the slippery slope, there would be no possibility of stopping the inevitable fall. Once again, lines were drawn, however inartfully. The very same all-or-nothing approach raised by Justice Black in *Allen* could just as easily have been employed to challenge the result reached by his opinion for the Court in *Everson* upholding government payment of the transportation costs to parochial schools.

D. Proving Bad Consequences

The bad-consequences argument is persuasive only to the extent that the likelihood of occurrence seems realistic. It is generally easy enough to argue that any course of action will lead to unfortunate results, but how does the Court know that these things will actually come to pass? To what extent should it be the obligation of the proponent of such an argument to provide some support for the dire predictions? It is not unusual for the Court to speculate about the impact of its decision and yet make no effort whatsoever to provide any empirical grounding for its predictions. In recognizing a qualified presidential communications privilege in *United States v. Nixon*, the unanimous Court opined that

> allowance of the privilege to withhold evidence that is demonstrably relevant in a criminal trial would cut deeply into the guarantee of due process of law and gravely impair the basic function of the courts. . . . The President's broad interest in confidentiality of communications will not be vitiated by disclosure of a limited number of conversations preliminarily shown to have some bearing on the pending criminal cases.[48]

The Court offered no factual basis for this conclusion. Intuitively, one might believe that the Court had it backwards—that there was likely to be a sizeable chill on communications and very little need for law enforcement. *Nixon* was a strange case, decided under political and deadline pressure, so perhaps the Court's bald assertions may be understood, if not excused. Still, it provides a sterling example of a tendency of the Court to offer up the bad-consequences argument on faith alone. Because *Nixon* was unanimous, there was no one to raise these questions in dissent.

Usually, bad-consequences arguments are speculative, based on predictions of what might happen in the future. That does not need to be the case, however. In his dissenting opinion in *Times Film Corp. v. Chicago*,[49] Chief Justice Warren illustrated the actual bad consequences that flowed from pre-exhibition licensing of motion pictures by citing literally pages of examples in which innocuous or valuable motion pictures were suppressed under licensing schemes, often for political reasons. This made for a particularly powerful argument. Although it did not carry the day in that case, the majority's approach was eventually rejected in favor of the dissent.

Likewise, the famous case of *Miranda v. Arizona*[50] provides an example of at least an attempt by the Court to reply to a bad-consequences argument with some empirical proof that the fear was groundless. The opponents of the Court's *Miranda* warnings, including the dissenters, charged that the rules would impair the ability of the police to obtain confessions necessary to solve crime[51] and would return murderers and rapists to the street.[52] These would indeed be bad consequences if they were to occur and very well might result in a reduction in the public's esteem for the Court. But the Court was not without a defense to this argument. It was able to point out that both the FBI and English police had delivered similar warnings for quite some time with little apparent trouble.[53] That is not to say that these examples might not be distinguishable from the state systems to which Miranda would apply;

however, as a practical matter, the burden of persuasion had been thrown back to the dissenters and critics.

In *United States v. Brewster*, the Court replied to the dissent's prediction that permitting a congressman to be sued for criminal conduct even tangentially related to his legislative responsibilities might lead to executive harassment of congressmen by noting that "we are not cited to any cases in which the bribery statutes, which have been applicable to Members of Congress for over 100 years, have been abused by the Executive Branch."[54] In other words, if the bad consequences were likely to occur, they would have already happened Moreover, if such abuse were to occur, Congress could amend or repeal the statutes to protect itself.[55]

IV. Can the Court Prevent Bad Consequences from Occurring?

When the Court is contemplating the prospect that a rule or decision will lead third parties to engage in conduct that may result in bad consequences, it may have to acknowledge that once it sets the process in motion, there will be little that it can do to stop the harm from occurring. However, where there is concern that a decision or legal rule will cause future courts to issue decisions or build on the rule in a manner that would be harmful, the Court must consider whether it will be able to tailor the rule to avoid this harm. Will the bad consequences necessarily occur, or can they be avoided? Can a sensible line be drawn, or will it be arbitrary? Will there be a slippery slope, or will there be footholds?

A. Can a Principled Line be Drawn?

Many of the bad-consequences arguments in the Supreme Court revolve around these questions. One common variant of the bad-consequences argument attempts to defeat a particular legal approach by asserting that it will result in a series of incorrect legal decisions in the future that the courts themselves will be incapable of avoiding. For instance, in *Proprietors of Charles River Bridge v. Proprietors of Warren Bridge*,[56] the Court declined to read a covenant not to issue a competing charter into the charter previously issued to the owner of a bridge on the grounds that it would undermine the development of roads and bridges in an expanding economy, and that the

Court would be hard-pressed to alleviate the problem as it would require the creation of an arbitrary set of rules as to what is and is not permissible.[57] In other words, although the Court's doctrine would have created the problem, it would be difficult to devise an adequate doctrinal solution.

Bad-consequences arguments assume that there is no way of distinguishing the present case from those future cases to be avoided if at all possible. Rather, those cases will necessarily follow if the Court decides the present case in a particular way. As Justice Cardozo, concurring in *A.L.A. Schecter Poultry v. United States*, put it, where the question was whether the regulation of the sale of poultry that had moved interstate but would now be resold in state affected interstate commerce, "[t]o find immediacy or indirectness here is to find it almost everywhere."[58] Under the Court's analytical framework, that was almost certainly correct. A few years later, the Court avoided the problem by rejecting its doctrine and embarking on a new approach. In other words, if the doctrine will not permit sensible lines to be drawn, then perhaps the doctrine should be rejected.

Chief Justice Marshall's famous thesis in *McCulloch v. Maryland* that the power to tax is the power to destroy, which led him to conclude that a state may not impose a specific tax on a federal instrumentality,[59] is based on the assumption of unavoidable bad consequences. To illustrate, Marshall noted that, if permitted, "they may tax the mail; they may tax the mint; they may tax patent-rights; they may tax the papers of the custom house; they may tax judicial process; they may tax all the means employed by the government, to an excess which would defeat all the ends of government."[60] This was a classic parade of horribles indeed! But it was hardly obvious that it would be unavoidable. A century later, however, in response to the argument that the power to tax is the power to destroy, Justice Holmes succinctly responded, not "while this Court sits."[61] In other words, the Court itself could minimize or alleviate the harm through case-by-case review. Moreover, if state taxation truly threatened federal interests, the Congress could create blanket or targeted immunity by statute. In either instance, the evil could be avoided without the constitutional rule that Marshall seemed to argue was essential.

B. Taking a Case-by-Case Approach

The Court does frequently take that position, that there will be time enough to worry about bad consequences that may flow from the present decision in future cases should they arise. In *Champion v. Ames*, for instance, it was argued that if Congress could exclude lottery tickets from interstate commerce, then it could exclude anything, including perfectly harmless items as well.[62] The Court's basic response to this argument was "[i]t will be time enough to consider the constitutionality of such legislation when we must do so."[63] It concluded that if the Congress were to pass legislation that abused its commerce power, then "upon the courts will rest the duty of adjudging that its action is neither legal [n]or binding upon the people."[64] Thus the back stop of judicial review on a case-by-case basis provided a fair amount of protection against this parade of horribles.[65]

Justice Goldberg, concurring in *Abington Township v. Schempp*, noted that

> [i]t is of course true that great consequences can grow from small beginnings, but the measure of constitutional adjudication is the ability and willingness to distinguish between real threat and mere shadow.[66]

This expressed a traditional confidence in the ability of the Court through common law type adjudication to draw meaningful distinctions and avert real harm. The difficulties encountered by the Court in attempting to draw principled lines in this area suggest, however, that the problem was more serious than Justice Goldberg had assumed.[67]

In *Kelo v. City of New London*,[68] Justice O'Connor, dissenting, argued that permitting a city to rely on economic redevelopment as a public purpose that could justify the taking of private property would permit a city to take property from A and transfer it to B simply because B would put it to a use that would generate more taxes. In dissent, Justice O'Connor argued that "[n]othing is to prevent the State from replacing any Motel 6 with a Ritz-Carleton, any home with a shopping mall, or any farm with a factory."[69] The majority replied that the case before it involved a comprehensive development plan, and it would address the hypothetical involving a transfer of property simply to obtain increased tax revenue if it were ever to arise.[70] The Court also noted that "parade of horribles" arguments are generally unpersuasive in takings cases because the person whose property is taken still receives just compensation.[71] Justice O'Connor responded that if that case should arise, the Court has not provided any principled basis for deciding it differently than the case before the Court.[72] The Court's response to Justice O'Connor's point does recognize that it would be inappropriate for the Court to attempt to decide a series of hypothetical cases not presented to the Court. That is beyond argument. However, Justice O'Connor's point that was well-taken is that at least the Court should be obliged to fashion a principle reasonably capable of preventing bad consequences in the future. The reply to this concern, however, is that under a case-by-case method of adjudication, future courts faced with actual factual situations would be more adept at molding limiting principles than the Court that launches the initial principles.

In answer to the argument that recognition of a particular rule or power might be abused, the Court or individual justices have often responded as Justice Story did in *Martin v. Hunter's Lessee*, that "[i]t is always a doubtful course, to argue against the use or existence of a power, from the possibility of its abuse."[73] The general point is valid, but Justice Story went too far. The argument for potential abuse is not "always" a bad argument. Sometimes it is a good argument. Some powers are more likely to be abused than others. Some rules are more likely to prove arbitrary, or create confusion, or to inevitably lead to undesirable results than others. The key is to determine when the bad-consequences or abuse argument is sensible and when it is not. To return again to Justice Holmes, "where to draw the line . . . [i]s the question in pretty much everything worth arguing in the law."[74]

In his dissent in *Walz v. Tax Commission*, Justice Douglas charged that permitting states to grant property tax exemptions to churches "may seem deminimis. . . . [b]ut it is, I fear, a long step down the Establishment path."[75] The majority dismissed concerns about a "foot in the door" or "the nose of the camel in the tent," concluding that "[a]ny move that realistically 'establishes' a church or tends to do so can be dealt with 'while this Court sits.'"[76] Justice Harlan agreed, noting that "I, for one, however, do not believe that a 'slippery slope' is necessarily without a constitutional toehold."[77] The very next year in *Lemon v. Kurtzman*, in the course of invalidating a state salary supplement for parochial school teachers (teaching secular subjects), Chief Justice Burger warned that

> [a] certain momentum develops in constitutional theory and it can be a 'downhill thrust' easily set in motion but difficult to retard or stop. Development by momentum is not invariably bad; indeed, it is the way the common law has grown, but it is a force to be recognized and reckoned with. The dangers are increased by the difficulty of perceiving in advance exactly where the 'verge' of the precipice lies.[78]

Chief Justice Burger recognized that he had not been moved by the slippery-slope argument the previous year in *Walz* but argued that in that case, unlike in *Lemon*, there had been significant historical support for the practice in issue, which in itself provided a basis for limiting the principle.[79] It is still rather remarkable that Chief Justice Burger should stake out such contrasting positions in such a short period of time in the course of construing the same constitutional provision. It simply illustrates, however, that in fact sometimes slippery slopes should be a matter of significant concern and sometimes they should not. It all depends on the circumstances.

Plessy v. Ferguson[80] should caution against automatically assuming that courts will necessarily come to the rescue and provide protection against bad doctrinal consequences should they materialize. In upholding a Louisiana law requiring separate railroad cars for blacks and whites, the Court went out of its way to reject the arguments set forth by "learned counsel for the plaintiff" to the effect that the decision would authorize the state to

> enact laws requiring colored people to walk upon one side of the street, and white people upon the other, or requiring white men's houses to be painted white, and colored men's black . . . [since] [t]he reply to all this is that every exercise of the police power must be reasonable, and extend only to such laws as are enacted in good faith for the promotion of the public good, and not for the annoyance or oppression of a particular class.[81]

Sixty years of hard-core segregation constructed on the edifice of *Plessy* demonstrated the insight of "learned counsel for the plaintiffs" and the woeful inadequacy of the Court's reliance on the reasonableness principle, an error which Justice Harlan clearly recognized in dissent.[82] Sometimes very bad consequences will indeed follow.

C. The Inability to Impose Limits as a Decisive Factor

Employment Division v. Smith,[83] a highly controversial case in the area of Free Exercise of Religion, is a contemporary example of judicial fear of an inability to draw defensible lines. Writing for the majority, Justice Scalia construed the Free Exercise Clause to stand for the principle that neutral and general laws that simply burdened the exercise of religion do not violate the Free Exercise Clause.[84] In settling on that principle, he relied on the bad-consequences argument raised in *Reynolds v. United States*,[85] the Court's first Free Exercise decision. The Court in Reynolds had decided that absent such a rule of neutrality, every person would become a law unto themselves, resulting in anarchy.[86] Justice Scalia believed that the Court could not alleviate the problem through future line drawing because it would be inappropriate, if not impossible, for the Court to attempt to determine whether a particular practice was central to a religious faith.[87] Concurring in the result but not the opinion, Justice O'Connor objected to Justice Scalia's neutrality approach with her own bad-consequences argument: that it was an undesirable rule because it would unduly restrict the Free Exercise Clause to providing protection against only the fairly unusual law that specifically targets religious practices.[88]

In dissent, Justice Blackmun argued that it was improper to adopt a rule simply because a preferable alternative might be subject to abuse, an argument which he noted could always be raised.[89] Frequently, the bad-consequences argument is window dressing. *Smith*, however, is an important case in which it appears that it played a significant role. Justice Scalia's fear that alternatives would either create chaos or force the Court into an institutionally inappropriate position would seem to be the primary rationale behind his decision. In rejecting Justice O'Connor's and Justice Blackmun's alternative approaches, Justice Scalia and the majority essentially decided that the bad consequences that he envisioned were indeed worse than those contemplated by Justice O'Connor.

Washington v. Davis[90] would seem to be another case in which the prospect of unavoidable bad consequences played a significant role in the decision. There, the Court concluded that, under the Equal Protection Clause, a plaintiff must show discriminatory intent rather than simply adverse impact in order to establish an Equal Protection violation based on race.[91] Although the Court relied on arguments of precedent, doctrine, and principle, looming over the decision was its conclusion that an impact standard

"would raise serious questions about, and perhaps invalidate, a whole range of tax, welfare, public service, regulatory, and licensing statutes that may be more burdensome to the poor and to the average black man than to the more affluent white. Given that rule such consequences would perhaps be likely to follow."[92]

That was obviously a risk that the Court was unwilling to take. It was simply not convinced that it might be avoided by drawing distinctions on a case-by-case basis or through the employment of procedural devices such as presumptions and the shifting burdens of proof. Consequently, it was better to stay away from the application of an impact standard entirely under the Equal Protection Clause.

In *Washington v. Glucksberg*, both the majority and Justice Souter, concurring, agreed that there would be a severe slippery slope problem if the Court were to recognize that a right to assisted suicide was protected by Fourteenth Amendment Due Process Clause.[93] Justice Souter worried that such a right "would not be readily containable by reference to facts about the mind that are matters of difficult judgment, or by gatekeepers who are subject to temptation, noble or not."[94] This would appear to be yet another case in which the possibility of unavoidable bad consequences played a crucial role in the decision.

D. Bad Consequences for the Court and its Doctrine

Bolling v. Sharpe,[95] a companion case to *Brown v. Board of Education*,[96] is another case in which the risk of bad consequences, to some extent to the Court itself, may have been quite important to the decision. In *Bolling*, the Court found for the first time in the Fifth Amendment Due Process Clause an equality principle allowing it to invalidate segregation in the District of Columbia schools. The doctrinal obstacles to this result were formidable; however, the Court candidly admitted that "[i]n view of our decision that the Constitution prohibits the states from maintaining racially segregated public schools, it would be unthinkable that the same Constitution would impose a lesser duty on the Federal Government."[97] The Court essentially admitted that it had no choice but to so construe due process in order to avoid the serious adverse consequences of being seen as hypocritical by allowing segregation to continue in its own backyard that would in turn severely undermine voluntary compliance with *Brown*. This was an instance where, as a prudential matter, the threat of adverse institutional consequences was so severe that it may have been a controlling factor.

V. Are the Consequences Really that Bad?

Another response to a bad-consequences argument is that however bad the consequences might seem, they were in fact anticipated and indeed intended. In the *Slaughter-House Cases*, the Court recognized that "[t]he argument . . . is not always the most conclusive which is drawn from the consequences urged against the adoption of a particular construction of an instrument."[98] Despite this admonition, however, it concluded that the Privileges or Immunities Clause of the Fourteenth Amendment could not have been intended to provide federal constitutional protection to the fundamental rights of citizens against state government, in that it would have

> "constitute[d] this court a perpetual censor upon all legislation of the States, on the civil rights of their own citizens . . . [been] so great a departure from the structure and spirit of our institutions . . . to fetter and degrade the State governments by subjecting them to the control of Congress . . . [and] radically [change] the whole theory of the relations of the State and Federal governments to each other."[99]

Given these dire consequences, the Court concluded that the argument against this interpretation "has a force that is irresistible."[100] But in view of the catastrophic changes wrought by the Civil War, which the Court itself had detailed earlier in its opinion, it is hardly unreasonable to assume that such fundamental structural changes were indeed intended by the framers of the Fourteenth Amendment. Justice Field so argued in his dissent.[101] Whether intended or not, they have largely been wrought through 100-plus years of interpretation of the Amendment. Thus, although the majority in the *Slaughter-House Cases* could not imagine that these consequences could have been intended, subsequent courts reached the opposite conclusion.

In his dissent in *Wesberry v. Sanders*, Justice Harlan argued that the logical consequence of the Court's decision was that the overwhelming number of congressional districts were unconstitutionally apportioned and would need to be redrawn.[102] His prediction was certainly correct, but they were redrawn and life and politics went on. From the majority's perspective, the consequences simply were not that bad; in fact, they were probably quite good, and the country readily adjusted to them.

VI. Should the Possibility of Bad Consequences Influence the Decision?

The question can be raised as to whether the possibility that bad consequences might flow from the decision is even a relevant consideration.

It certainly could be argued that the duty of the Court is simply to decide the case as best it can and let the chips fall where they may. The Court addressed this to some extent in *Cooley v. Board of Wardens*.[103] There the issue was whether state pilotage laws that had been in effect for over sixty years violated the dormant Commerce Clause of the Constitution. Presumably if these laws were unconstitutional, sixty years worth of fees might have to be repaid. The Court indicated that if the violation were clear, it would be duty bound to invalidate them "with deep regret."[104] The Court upheld the constitutionality of the laws, however, seemingly indicating that in a close case, the cost and dislocation of the decision was worthy of consideration.

In *Payton v. New York* where the Court held that the police could not arrest a suspect in his home without a warrant, the Court rejected the argument that law enforcement would suffer as a result of this rule for lack of supporting evidence, but it also noted that such a policy argument must yield in any event to a clear constitutional command.[105] In other words, if the law is clear, accepting adverse consequences is simply part of living with constitutional limitations that can sometimes impose significant harm in order to achieve the larger good.

In *New York v. United States*, Justice Frankfurter warned against over-reliance on bad-consequences arguments, noting that

> [t]he process of Constitutional adjudication does not thrive on conjuring up horrible possibilities that never happen in the real world and devising doctrines sufficiently comprehensive in detail to cover the remotest contingency."[106]

His concern was not with the bad-consequences argument per se but rather with carrying it to the absurd extremes of highly unlikely possibilities.

※ VII. Bad Consequences as Rhetorical Argument

Occasionally, the bad-consequences argument is presented almost as a matter of rhetorical overkill. If the Court reaches a particular result, all hell will break loose. The famous nineteenth-century political question doctrine case of *Luther v. Borden*[107] presents a well-known example of an assertion of "really" bad consequences. The issue there was whether the Court should determine which of two competing groups was, in fact, the legitimate government of Rhode Island. As Chief Justice Taney put it, if the existing charter government should be deemed to have been illegitimate,

> then the laws passed by its legislatures during that time were nullities; its taxes wrongfully collected; its salaries and compensation to its officers illegally paid; its public accounts improperly settled; and the judgements and sentences of its courts in civil and criminal cases null and void, and the officers who carried their decisions into operation answerable as trespassers, if not in some cases as criminals.[108]

This was essentially a prudential or institutional argument. The Court was saying that, even if it could decide between these two governments, it should not, because that would lead to extremely dire consequences. In the context of the entire case, the argument may well be something of a makeweight as there were several other considerations prompting the Court's decision that it seemed to consider more significant. The bad-consequences argument in *Luther* certainly gets the reader's attention, but it readily appears to be little more than rhetorical hyperbole.

Obviously, one could ask why an invalidation of the existing government, whether by the Court, the president, or Congress must inevitably throw Rhode Island into a retroactive state of anarchy. That would seem to be a state of affairs to be avoided if at all possible. Why could not the Court simply have declared that, as of the decision, the charter government was illegitimate, and that, to avoid chaos, its authorized actions up to that time would be accepted? In other words, the obvious response to catastrophic consequences can be that they simply do not have to happen, even if the Court takes the course of action in question.

Sometimes both the majority and dissent argue that truly bad consequences will occur if the other's conclusions prevail. In *Flagg Brothers v. Brooks*, for instance, the majority argued that if "state action" were found to exist when the state simply permitted a warehouseman to sell the property of a person who had failed to pay the storage fee, then state action would exist whenever the state failed to prevent private deprivations of property.[109] Justice Stevens, dissenting, however, contended that under the Court's approach, the state "could authorize 'any person with sufficient physical power,' . . . to acquire and sell the property of his weaker neighbor."[110] Both of these predictions are certainly rhetorical overstatements of the likely consequences of the competing rules. One must assume that future courts would develop limiting principles to prevent either of these extremes from occurring. Despite the Court's decision, Justice Stevens' prophecy has not come to pass.

⅏ VIII. Conclusion

The argument of bad consequences is a staple element of legal reasoning. It appears with great regularity in the Supreme Court's constitutional jurisprudence. More often than not, it is employed as an adjunct to some other form of argument. Frequently, it appears to be a minor consideration, if not a makeweight. It is easily raised but often easily answered as well. The validity of the argument is often dependent upon predictions about unknowable future events that sometimes lead to dueling parades of horribles with no obvious method of resolution. This is particularly true when it is asserted that a rule or decision will cause nonjudicial actors to engage in action that will result in bad consequences. On the other hand, when it is asserted, as it often is, that a rule will result in adverse consequences because it will be difficult to apply or limit in the future, at least it is arguable that the Court itself may be able to solve these problems through careful case-by-case adjudication. Whether that is in fact true, however, will depend on the circumstances.

ELEVEN

Ethical Argument

✹ **I. The Nature of Ethical Argument**

In his book *Constitutional Fate*, Professor Bobbitt identified the concept of ethical argument as a legitimate method of constitutional interpretation. He explained that an ethical argument "relies on a characterization of American institutions and the role within them of the American people."[1] An ethical argument is not a moral argument but rather is based on "the character or ethos, of the American polity."[2] Ethical argument is not established as a legitimate form of constitutional interpretation in the same sense as textualism, original understanding, or any of the other methodologies discussed so far in this book. That is almost certainly because both judges and commentators, to the extent that they think about ethical argument at all, are likely to fear that it may pose either an unacceptable danger of subjectivity or at the very least an unacceptable danger of the appearance of subjectivity. Consequently, the Court often only hints at ethical argument and never relies upon it as the sole source of interpretation in a case. Much of the work occurs beneath the surface. Still, Professor Bobbitt may be on to something. Ethical argument has played a role in the explanation of the Court's decision or reasoning in a sufficient number of cases to make it worthy of consideration. Although Professor Bobbitt first recognized and explicated the concept of ethical argument, I do not purport to apply it exactly as he might. Rather, I take the concept, which I consider to be a legitimate one, and attempt to identify it in a variety of Court opinions.

This chapter will examine several lines of cases in which ethical argument has arguably played a role. Perhaps the clearest examples of reliance on ethical argument are the Court's cruel and unusual punishment cases, especially those involving the death penalty. Arguably, the Court's interpretive approach in this area assumes that ethical argument will play a major role. As Professor Bobbitt recognized, the Court's modern substantive due process cases are also an area in which consideration of the American ethos has an impact, often explicitly. This chapter considers the Court's use of ethical argument in two different branches of substantive due process litigation— those considering whether punitive damages awards are unconstitutionally excessive and those addressing issues of personal privacy. Then the chapter considers *Reynolds v. Sims*, a landmark case in which ethical considerations played an implicit but significant role in the decision. Finally, it will address the degree to which the Court's conception of societal values may possibly influence its decisions.

𝕸 II. Ethical Argument and Cruel and Unusual Punishment

A. The Eighth Amendment and Evolving Standards

The Court could have limited the concept of cruel and unusual punishment to those punishments that were considered so at the time of the adoption of the Eighth Amendment. Having with good reason declined to do that, however, the Court has all but adopted an approach that is largely guided by ethical argument. The very concept of cruel and unusual requires comparison to some external benchmark. With respect to punishment, that benchmark or norm has tended to be that which is accepted within the American ethos.

The Court has recognized from the outset, starting with *Weems v. United States*,[3] its first major cruel and unusual punishment case that whether a punishment should be considered cruel and unusual will be based on American values as they have evolved as of the time of the decision in the case. In *Weems*, the Court invalidated a punishment called "cadena temporal," imposed in the Philippines for alteration of a public document. Under this punishment the prisoner would serve twelve years hard labor in chains and would be permanently disqualified from public service positions.[4] *Weems* is most notable in that it clearly rejected the position that the prohibition of cruel and unusual punishments was limited to either those punishments condemned by the predecessor of the Cruel and Unusual Punishment Clause in the English Bill of Rights or those considered to be cruel and unusual at the adoption of the Eighth Amendment in 1791.[5] In the process, the Court set forth the most vigorous, evolving constitutional approach to appear anywhere in the United States Reports.[6] This in turned led the Court's cruel and unusual punishment jurisprudence down a path that would inevitably require it to make judgments as to whether a particular type of punishment was in fact consistent with contemporary American standards. The Court in *Weems* did not engage in a detailed ethical analysis; however, it did declare that

> [s]uch penalties for such offenses amaze those who have formed their conception of the relation of a state to even its offending citizens from the practice of the American commonwealths, and believe that it is a precept of justice that punishment for crime should be graduated and proportioned to [the] offense.[7]

This in itself is a clear statement of the ethical approach. The imposition of such severe punishment for a relatively minor offense with no leeway for taking account of degrees of culpability was simply inconsistent with the Court's conception of the proper relation between the state and the individual.

The Court continued to build on the *Weems* approach some forty-five years later in *Trop v. Dulles*.[8] There, a four-justice plurality held that Congress did not have the constitutional power to authorize deprivation of citizenship upon court martial for military desertion in time of war and that such a penalty violated the Eighth Amendment's ban on cruel and unusual punishments.[9] Building on *Weems*, Chief Justice Warren proclaimed that:

> [T]he basic concept underlying the Eighth Amendment is nothing less than the dignity of man. While the State has the power to punish, the Amendment stands to assure that this power be exercised within the limits of civilized standards.[10]

As a result "[t]he Amendment must draw its meaning from the evolving standards of decency that mark the progress of a maturing society."[11] These statements, which have often been quoted in subsequent cruel and unusual punishment cases, solidified the Court's commitment to an ethical approach in this area. Chief Justice Warren argued that because denaturalization as punishment had not been authorized prior to 1940, it was unusual and out of line with traditional American values.[12] In the course of rejecting denaturalization as punishment for desertion, the plurality relied not simply on the American ethos but also on the world ethos, noting that of eighty-four nations surveyed by the United Nations, only the Philippines and Turkey permitted expatriation as a punishment for desertion.[13]

Robinson v. California, the Court's next cruel and unusual punishment case, invalidated a law that made it a crime to be a drug addict.[14] Presumably, the Court's decision was driven by the fact that criminal punishment for status as opposed to conduct was inconsistent with contemporary American values; however, the Court's opinion was so terse and conclusory that it is hard to determine the basis of the decision.[15]

B. The Death Penalty Cases

1. *Furman v. Georgia*

From the early seventies onward, the Court has subjected the procedures for the imposition of capital punishment to review under the Eighth Amendment, invalidating many of the death penalty statutes passed in the United States. In the course of so doing, the Court—or at least several of the justices—has relied heavily upon the foundation laid in cases such as *Weems* and *Trop*.

In perhaps the most significant of its death penalty cases, the Court effectively invalidated all existing death penalty statutes in the country with a 5-4 decision in *Furman v. Georgia.*[16] Five justices joined a brief per curiam opinion and filed separate concurrences. Justice Douglas published an opinion that can best be described as rambling and incoherent.[17] Justice Brennan wrote a lengthy concurrence in which he quoted heavily from *Weems* and *Trop* and attempted to deduce four principles for adjudicating cruel and unusual punishment claims.[18] He argued that in assessing such a claim the Court should consider whether the punishment 1) is so severe as to be degrading to human dignity, 2) is arbitrarily severe, 3) is unacceptable to contemporary society, and 4) is not excessive.[19] Arguably, each of these principles implicates an ethical approach, but certainly the third—acceptability to contemporary society—does so explicitly. Justice Brennan concluded that despite the enactment of death penalty statutes by over thirty states and continued approval of the death penalty in public opinion polls, the great infrequency with which the death penalty was imposed and administered suggested strongly that "contemporary society views this punishment with substantial doubt."[20]

Concurring, Justice Stewart also emphasized the infrequent administration of the death penalty as proof that it was cruel and unusual, but not because it demonstrated societal rejection but rather because it rendered its imposition "wanton" and "freakish."[21] Justice White also concurred, emphasizing the infrequent imposition of the death penalty; however, the significance of that fact to him was that it no longer served sufficient societal purposes of deterrence or retribution.[22] Dissenting, Justice Powell responded that the decline in the imposition and administration of the death penalty over the past several years was largely attributable to judicial decisions as opposed to any particular change in societal attitudes.[23] Also dissenting, Justice Burger characterized the decline in death penalty sentences as "a refinement on, rather than a repudiation of, capital punishment."[24]

Justice Marshall wrote a lengthy concurrence. Like Justice Brennan, he attempted to derive principles for determining whether a punishment was cruel and unusual. He argued that a punishment would violate the Eighth Amendment if "popular sentiment abhors it"; that is, if "citizens found it to be morally unacceptable."[25] He then spent several pages reviewing and rejecting the various justifications offered in support of capital punishment.[26] Justice Marshall conceded that "[t]here are no prior cases in this Court striking down a penalty on this ground, but the very notion of changing values requires that we recognize its existence."[27] He conceded that forty-one states authorized the death penalty. He discounted this, however, by arguing that the public was not sufficiently informed as to the true nature of the death penalty. He explained that the proper question

> [i]s not whether a substantial proportion of American citizens would today, if polled, opine that capital punishment is barbarously cruel, but whether they would find it to be so in the light of all information presently available.[28]

Applying this approach he argued that

> I believe that the great mass of citizens would conclude on the basis of the material already considered that the death penalty is immoral and therefore unconstitutional.[29]

Justice Marshall's approach would seem to be dangerously elitist. On the one hand, he maintained that the death penalty is cruel and unusual because it is inconsistent with public values and morality, but, on the other, he substituted his personal conceptions of what the public should think for what in fact it does think.

In his dissenting opinion, Justice Powell took aim at Justice Marshall's conclusions of societal opinion and values. He argued that the best source of evidence of public opinion on the death penalty was the legislative enactments authorizing it and the jury verdicts imposing it.[30] This approach would eventually carry the day in Eighth Amendment adjudication, at least for a time. Chief Justice Burger, in dissent, noted that the absence of judicial decisions invalidating penalties on the ground that societal values had changed "is powerful evidence that in this country legislatures have in fact been responsive—albeit belatedly at times—to changes in social attitudes and moral values."[31] Turning to Justice Marshall's conclusions concerning informed public opinion, Justice Powell maintained that it was quite inappropriate for the Court to invalidate capital punishment based on "a prediction regarding the subjective judgments of the mass of our people under hypothetical assumptions that may or may not be realistic."[32] Indeed, Justice Powell argued that it is not at all certain that the public would experience deep-felt revulsion if the States were to execute as many sentenced capital offenders this year as they executed in the mid-1930s.[33]

In response to Justice Marshall's argument that retribution was never a legitimate justification for capital punishment,[34] Justice Powell argued that "in order to maintain respect for law, it is essential that the punishment inflicted for grave crimes should adequately reflect the revulsion felt by the great majority of citizens. . . ."[35] Likewise, although he joined the majority invalidating the death penalty, Justice Stewart rejected Justice Marshall's claim that retribution was not a legitimate justification.[36] He explained that

> [t]he instinct for retribution is part of the nature of man, and channeling that instinct in the administration of criminal justice serves an important purpose in promoting the stability of a society governed by law. When people begin to believe that organized society is unwilling or unable to impose upon criminal offenders the punishment they deserve, then there are sown the seeds of anarchy—of self-help, vigilante justice, and lynch law.[37]

In a sense, Justice Powell and Justice Stewart turned the tables on Justice Marshall and argued that society needed at least the option to impose capital punishment as opposed to having rejected it. Their conception of the American ethos was quite the opposite of Justice Marshall's, which highlights the risk involved when the Court or a justice relies on ethical argument.

In *Furman*, only Justice Brennan and Justice Marshall concluded that capital punishment was unconstitutional under all circumstances. Although *Furman* effectively invalidated the death penalty in all forty-one states in which it had been authorized and despite Justice Marshall's conclusion that it was out of step with contemporary mores, many states reenacted capital punishment statutes, providing juries with far more guidance following *Furman.*

2. *Gregg v. Georgia*

In *Gregg v. Georgia*,[38] the Court upheld the death penalty procedures enacted by the Georgia legislature following *Furman*. There Justice Stewart, writing for a three-justice plurality, agreed that "an assessment of contemporary values concerning the infliction of a challenged sanction is relevant to the application of the Eighth Amendment."[39] However, in making such an assessment, the Court must "look to objective indicia that reflect the public attitude."[40] Considering such criteria in some detail, the plurality concluded that

> it is now evident that a large proportion of American society continues to regard it as an appropriate and necessary criminal sanction.
>
> The most marked indication of society's endorsement of the death penalty for murder is the legislative response to Furman. The legislatures of at least 35 States have enacted new statutes that provide for the death penalty for at least some crimes that result in the death of another person. And the Congress of the United States, in 1974, enacted a statute providing the death penalty for aircraft piracy that results in death.
>
> . . . .
>
> In the only statewide referendum occurring since Furman . . . the people of California adopted a constitutional amendment that authorized capital punishment.
>
> . . . .
>
> A December 1972 Gallup poll indicated that 57% of the people favored the death penalty, while a June 1973 Harris survey showed support of 59%.[41]

Thus, the plurality was willing to indulge the assumption that strong societal disapproval might undermine the constitutionality of a penalty. It simply did not find such strong disapproval after examining the relevant evidence of popular opinion.

Justice Marshall filed a dissent in *Gregg* in which he admitted that he "would be less than candid if [he] did not acknowledge that [the reenactment of the death penalty by 35 state legislatures following Furman] have a significant bearing on a realistic assessment of the moral acceptability of the death penalty to the American people."[42] He cited a survey that purported to confirm his view that the American people had little familiarity with the actual administration of the death penalty and would feel differently about it if they were better informed.[43] Even assuming that the current reenactment reflected the views of an informed citizenry, however, Justice Marshall would still have ruled it unconstitutional as an excessive penalty in that it did not serve a legitimate purpose.[44]

In the companion case of *Roberts v. Louisiana*, where the majority invalidated a death penalty provision reenacted after *Furman* that provided the jury with virtually no discretion, Justice White, dissenting, noted that the reenactment of the death penalty by thirty-five states foreclosed the argument that is was unacceptable to contemporary society.[45] He emphasized that:

> [i]t will not do to denigrate these legislative judgments as some form of vestigal savagery or as purely retributive in motivation; for they are solemn judgments, reasonably based, that imposition of the death penalty will save the lives of innocent persons.[46]

Combining the Stewart plurality in *Gregg* with the White dissent in *Roberts*, seven justices forcefully rejected Justice Marshall's conclusion that the death penalty was inconsistent with contemporary societal values.

In *Woodson v. North Carolina*,[47] another companion case to *Gregg*, the Court invalidated a mandatory death penalty adopted by North Carolina. In so holding, the Court relied on the historical pattern of rejection of a mandatory death penalty over the course of American history leading up to *Furman* as proof of societal disapproval of such laws.[48] The Court quite properly attributed the enactment of such laws subsequent to Furman to confusion over what the Court demanded.[49] Woodson established that even as of *Gregg*, a majority of the Court was willing to find a punishment invalid under the Eighth Amendment on the grounds that it was inconsistent with contemporary values, if objective record evidence supported that conclusion.

3. *Coker v. Georgia*

The following year in *Coker v. Georgia*,[50] the Court again looked to evidence of societal values to invalidate a Georgia law that imposed the death penalty for rape of an adult woman. The Court relied on the fact that as of *Furman*, only sixteen jurisdictions imposed the death penalty for rape; after *Furman* and *Gregg* Georgia was the only state to authorize capital punishment for rape of an adult woman, although two other states imposed the death penalty for rape of a child.[51] In addition, the Court relied on the fact that nine out of ten juries in Georgia declined to impose the death penalty in rape cases.[52] The Court explained that this evidence was not conclusive but lent strong support to its decision that the death penalty was sufficiently disproportionate to the offense of rape to constitute cruel and unusual punishment.[53] Dissenting Chief Justice Burger argued that the Court should have taken account of the fact that the defendant had raped three women within a three-year period, killing one and attempting to kill another.[54] In addition, he argued that the five-year period between *Furman* and the present, when the number of death penalty statutes for rape declined significantly, was far too short of a period during which to evaluate a shift in societal consensus, given that state legislatures were still attempting to comply with the demands of *Furman* and *Gregg*.[55]

4. Enmund and Felony Murder

Four years later in *Enmund v. Florida*,[56] the Court held that the Eighth Amendment prohibited imposing the death penalty on an accomplice—in that case a lookout—to a crime resulting in a murder. In reaching its decision, the Court engaged in a lengthy analysis of the practices of all states that administered the death penalty. Although it conceded that the evidence of rejection was not as compelling as in *Coker*,[57] the Court noted that eight states permitted imposition of the death penalty solely for participation in a robbery in which a murder occurred, whereas eleven others required some degree of a culpable state of mind.[58] The Court also emphasized that juries rarely impose the death penalty in cases where the defendant did not participate in the murder as such.[59]

Dissenting, Justice O'Connor argued that *Coker* and *Lockett* required not simply that the death penalty be largely rejected by both legislatures and juries but also that it be disproportionate to the offense in question.[60] She maintained that the Court's evidence with respect to both legislatures and juries simply did not show the degree of overwhelming rejection necessary for societal consensus.[61] She was able to show that twenty-three states, or neatly two-thirds that allowed the death penalty, permitted its imposition in cases in which the defendant neither killed the victim nor specifically intended that the victim die.[62] Justice O'Connor made a compelling case that this did not come close to the degree of consensus on which the Court had relied in prior cases. Consequently, the Court's decision was almost certainly based on its own independent conclusions as to the appropriateness of the death penalty for felony murder, regardless of societal beliefs. As Justice O'Connor recognized, the Court in *Enmund* seemed to be diluting the degree of proof that it had previously required to establish a societal consensus against a form of punishment. Several years later in *Tison v. Arizona*,[63] Justice O'Connor wrote an opinion for the Court in which she concluded that there was no societal consensus against imposing the death penalty on a person who had been a substantial participant in a murder and who acted with reckless indifference toward human life.

5. The Death Penalty and Mental Disability

The question of whether a state may execute a mentally retarded person caused the Court to take account of a perceived change in objectively expressed societal attitudes on the matter and ultimately reverse course. In *Ford v. Wainwright*,[64] the Court relied on the fact that executing a person who had become insane was prohibited at common law, was not permitted in any of the fifty states, and as such was clearly inconsistent with the Eighth Amendment. Given that the execution of the insane was prohibited in Florida, where Ford was on death row, the ultimate question in the case was whether he had an adequate opportunity to raise and litigate the issue. [65] In terms of societal values, however, this was a clear case for the Court.

In *Penry v. Lynaugh*,[66] the Court reversed the death sentence of a retarded man because the jury may not have been permitted to consider all of the potential mitigating evidence. However, the Court rejected the argument that a societal consensus had developed against execution of the mentally retarded, noting that only two of the states that permitted capital punishment prohibited it with respect to the mentally retarded.[67] The Court acknowledged three public opinion polls indicating that anywhere from 66 to 73 percent of the public opposed the imposition of the death penalty on the mentally retarded.[68] It declined to find a societal consensus, however, until such opinion "find[s] expression in legislation, which is an objective indicator of contemporary values upon which we can rely."[69] Writing only for herself in the final section of the opinion, Justice O'Connor concluded that given the wide variation in degrees of mental retardation, absent a societal consensus to the contrary, it should remain a mitigating factor rather than a bar to capital punishment.[70]

Thirteen years after the decision in *Penry*, the Court revisited the question of whether execution of the mentally retarded constituted cruel and unusual punishment in *Atkins v. Virginia*[71] and held that it did. The decisive factor for the Court was almost certainly the fact that in the decade since Penry eighteen states had passed legislation prohibiting the execution of the mentally retarded.[72] It explained that "[i]t is not so much the number of these States that is significant, but the consistency of the direction of change."[73] In a footnote, the Court also cited position papers by professional organizations, world opinion, and public opinion polls in support of its conclusion.[74] Writing for the majority, Justice Stevens concluded that "[t]he practice . . . has become truly unusual, and it is fair to say that a national consensus has developed against it."[75] The Court also concluded that execution of the mentally retarded was unlikely to serve the legitimate purposes of retribution and deterrence behind the death penalty and that the very fact of mental retardation was likely to hamper the defendant in presenting mitigating factors in his defense.[76]

Justice Scalia, dissenting, charged that "[s]eldom has an opinion of this Court rested so obviously upon nothing but the personal views of its Members."[77] He noted that although 18 states had recently banned the execution of the mentally retarded, 20 others had not.[78] This led him to ask how "agreement among 47% . . . amounts to a consensus[.]"[79] He explained that this figure would not have come close to representing a national consensus in prior cases.[80] In response to the Court's emphasis on the direction of change, Justice Scalia wondered, "in what *other* direction *could we possibly* see change," given that virtually all states permitted the execution of the mentally retarded as of the time of *Penry*?[81] Both Justices Scalia[82] and Rehnquist[83] were highly critical of the Court's reference to public opinion surveys and professional and world opinion, even though Justice Stevens only cited it in a footnote and did not seem to place heavy reliance on this material. Justice Scalia ultimately concluded that the Court's decision seemed to be based on its own views about the morality of executing the retarded as opposed to societal opinion on the matter.[84]

6. The Death Penalty for Juveniles

In 1988 in *Thompson v. Oklahoma*,[85] the Court held that the Cruel and Unusual Punishment Clause precluded the execution of a person who was under sixteen years of age at the time the murder was committed. Finding a societal consensus against such an execution, Justice Stevens, writing for a four-justice plurality, emphasized that no state permitted a person under sixteen to vote or serve on a jury, only one state allowed a person under sixteen to drive, and only four to marry without parental consent.[86] He emphasized that all eighteen of the states that had adopted a minimum age for the death penalty had set it at sixteen or above.[87] The plurality also relied on the opinions of professional organizations and the practices of other nations[88] and cited the fact that juries have rarely imposed the death penalty on persons under sixteen years of age.[89] The plurality also noted that due to immaturity, persons under the age of sixteen who commit murder are less culpable.[90]

Justice O'Connor was unwilling to conclude that a societal consensus had formed against the execution of persons under sixteen but concurred in the judgment on other grounds.[91] Justice Scalia dissented, arguing that states that permitted the death penalty but imposed no minimum age should be counted as opposed to a minimum age, in which case a bare majority of states permitting capital punishment would be viewed as so opposed.[92] Justice Stevens would have excluded consideration of these states as irrelevant on the ground that it was unclear whether they had even considered whether there should be a minimum age.[93] This type of argument over whether to count states that either permit or prohibit the death penalty in general but do not address the specific application reappears before the Court in case after case on the issue of whether a societal consensus exists.

In *Stanford v. Kentucky*,[94] the Court held that no societal consensus had developed against executing defendants who were older than sixteen but younger than eighteen at the time the murder was committed, because a majority of the states that permitted capital punishment allowed it in these circumstances.[95] As frequently occurs in these types of cases, the majority and dissent differed significantly as to how to tally the statistics.[96] In the final section of the opinion writing for a four-justice plurality, Justice Scalia maintained that in assessing whether there was a societal consensus, public opinion polls, and the views of interest groups and professional associations were irrelevant and only legislative acts would be considered.[97] The dissent would rely on this information as well as the practices of other nations.[98] Justice Brennan dissented, arguing that relying exclusively on legislative enactments made interpretation of the Eighth Amendment dependent on the vary institution that it was intended to limit.[99] Justice Scalia responded that the Bill of Rights was intended to bind the judiciary as well and restrain it from simply imposing its own value preferences on the public.[100] Writing for a plurality, he rejected reliance on age-based laws outside of the area of capital punishment—such as the age for driving, drinking, or voting—as irrelevant.[101] Justice O'Connor, concurring,[102] and Justice Brennan, dissenting,[103] disagreed with this conclusion.

Sixteen year later in *Roper v. Simmons*,[104] the Court overruled *Stanford v. Kentucky* and declared that executing a person who committed a murder while under 18 years of age constituted cruel and unusual punishment. It conceded that the pace of legislative change was considerably slower than that in *Atkins*, because during the fifteen-year period since *Stanford* only five jurisdictions had either legislatively or judicially rejected the execution of persons under eighteen at the time of the murder.[105] As with *Atkins*, however, the Court placed great emphasis on the direction of the change.[106] It suggested that the slower pace of change might be attributable to the fact that as of *Penry* only two states had prohibited the execution of the mentally retarded, while as of *Stanford* twelve death penalty states had already banned the execution of a person under eighteen and fifteen had prohibited the execution of a person under seventeen.[107] Thus, the movement toward banning the execution of juveniles was well under way prior to *Stanford*. The Court concluded that "a majority of States have rejected the imposition of the death penalty on juvenile offenders under 18, and we now hold this is required by the Eighth Amendment."[108]

In the course of its opinion, the Court noted various ways in which juveniles differ from adults, including a lack of maturity and underdeveloped sense of responsibility, greater susceptibility to negative influences, and a lesser development of character.[109] These differences translated into a lesser degree of culpability for juvenile offenders.[110] This led the Court to conclude that execution of persons under eighteen was less likely to promote the goal of deterrence or retribution.[111] The Court concluded that *Stanford* was incorrect in indicating that the Court should rely only upon objective indicators of societal disapproval and should not bring its own independent judgment to bear on whether a penalty is cruel and unusual under the Eighth Amendment.[112] Finally, the Court observed that the United States was the only nation that executed persons under eighteen.[113] Although it conceded that this did not control its interpretation of the Constitution, it "does provide respected and significant confirmation for our conclusions."[114]

Justice O'Connor dissented, noting that the Court "refrains from asserting that its holding is compelled by a genuine national consensus" and indeed it "rests ultimately, on its independent moral judgment that death is a disproportionately severe punishment for any 17-year old offender."[115] She pointed out that death penalty states were almost evenly split on the issue before the decision, and, unlike *Atkins*, two states had recently reaffirmed their decisions to permit execution of offenders under eighteen.[116] She then argued that *Atkins* ultimately rested on the Court's conclusions as to the immorality of executing the mentally retarded, which simply could not justify a complete ban on the execution of juveniles.[117] Rather "the differences between 'adults' and 'juveniles' appear to be a matter of degree, rather than kind."[118] Consequently, a blanket prohibition is not warranted.

Justice Scalia also dissented and argued that "[w]ords have no meaning if the views of less than 50% of death penalty States can constitute a national consensus."[119] Rather he maintained that "our previous cases have required overwhelming opposition to a challenged practice, generally over a long period of time."[120] He also criticized the Court for counting non-death penalty states as part of the opposition to imposition of the death penalty on offenders under eighteen.[121] He then attempted to turn the Court's methodology against it, arguing that

> [o]n the evolving-standards hypothesis, the only legitimate function of the Court is to identify a moral consensus of the American people. By what conceivable warrant can nine lawyers presume to be the authoritative conscience of the Nation?[122]

7. Death Penalty for Rape of a Child

In *Coker v. Georgia*, the Court held that the Eighth Amendment prohibited the imposition of the death penalty for the rape of an adult woman. Thirty-two years later in *Kennedy v. Louisiana*,[123] the Court extended that prohibition to the rape of a child as well. As it had done in its more recent death penalty decisions, the Court purported to rely on both the objectively verifiable national consensus as well as it own independent judgment. As to the former, it concluded that the fact that only six states authorized the death penalty for rape of a child and only two defendants had been sentenced to death for such an offense in the past thirty years indicated that the evolving consensus was opposed to the practice.[124] The fact that the six states in question had enacted the penalty relatively recently was insufficient to convince the Court that the trend was evolving in favor of the penalty.[125] Justice Alito, dissenting, made a persuasive case that no consensus could be discovered in this context, given that dicta in *Coker* had suggested to many state courts and legislatures that the death penalty for child rape was also prohibited by the decision.[126] However, the majority disagreed.[127]

As with *Atkins* and *Roper*, it would appear that the Court's own independent judgment played a more decisive role in its determination than the objective evidence of consensus. The majority argued that imposition of the death penalty for child rape could have adverse effects on the victim and that it would be difficult to create standards for adjudicating such cases.[128] However, as Justice Alito pointed out in dissent, these factors were at best of marginal relevance to the Eighth Amendment issue.[129] As such, the Court concluded that in a case involving an individual victim (i.e., as opposed to a case involving terrorism or treason) the death penalty is disproportionate to a crime that does not involve the taking of life.[130] The Court did concede "that there are moral grounds" for questioning the elimination of the death penalty in a child rape case.[131] However contrary to the Court's conclusion that a crime involving the taking of human life is qualitatively more serious from a moral standpoint, Justice Alito maintained the following:

> I have little doubt that, in the eyes of ordinary Americans, the very worst child rapists—predators who seek out and inflict serious physical and emotional injury on defenseless young children—are the epitome of moral depravity.[132]

This is almost certainly correct and highlights the fact that in evaluating the death penalty, the Court's jurisprudence is now driven by the subjective moral judgments of a majority of the justices on the Court with only the slightest concern for whether these judgments reflect those of the public at large.

As the dissents of Justices O'Connor, Scalia, and Alito illustrate, the Court's most recent decisions in cases addressing categorical bans on capital punishment—*Atkins v. Virginia, Roper v. Simmons,* and *Kennedy v. Louisiana*—indicate a significant shift in the methodology employed by the majority. Reliance on objective indications of societal consensus seems to play a significantly diminished role. An assessment of societal values, which at one point seemed to be the predominate factor now may be little more than window dressing. The Court's own moral assessment, bolstered by professional and international opinion, now seems to be determinative. It is at least possible that this shift portends a movement toward outlawing the death penalty at some point in the future under the Eighth Amendment, even in the absence of a solid societal consensus. Consequently, ethical argument based on objective evidence as opposed to the Court's own intuitions, which for a time seemed at the very center of the Court's death penalty analysis, has become increasingly marginalized.

C. The Length of Sentence Cases

Another line of cruel and unusual punishment cases that implicate judicial consideration of ethical argument or societal values are the cases addressing the length of punishment. In *Rummel v. Estelle*,[133] the Court rejected the argument that life imprisonment of a defendant who had been convicted of credit card fraud, passing a forged check and obtaining $120 by false pretenses under the Texas recidivist statute violated the Eighth Amendment. Thirteen years earlier in *Spencer v. Texas*, the Court had indicated in dicta that the same statute was not facially invalid under the Cruel and Unusual Punishment Clause.[134] Since the Court acknowledged that the death sentence is qualitatively different, it found the capital punishment line of cases, including *Furman, Gregg,* and *Coker,* to be of limited relevance.[135] Although *Rummel* was able to establish that the Texas recidivist statute was arguably the strictest in the country, the Court found the differences between states to be matters of degree and recognized that as long as states pass their own sentencing legislation, some state is bound to have the strictest approach.[136] It also rejected the argument that life imprisonment for three nonviolent felonies was sufficiently disproportionate to violate the Eighth Amendment, as it was for the states to determine which offenses created the most serious danger to society.[137]

Dissenting, Justice Powell engaged in the type of comparative analysis common in the Court's death penalty cases and concluded that three quarters of the states do not have habitual offender statutes that would impose life imprisonment for the commission of two or three nonviolent felonies and in no other state would Rummel have received a life sentence for his offenses.[138] He also cited recommendations of the American Bar Association and the American Law Institute favoring terms of years rather than life for recidivists.[139] Justice Powell also pointed out that the only first-time offenders subject to life imprisonment in Texas were persons convicted of capital murder.[140] Thus, Justice Powell concluded that an analysis of the objective factors ordinarily considered in cruel and unusual punishment cases showed that the punishment imposed on Rummel was constitutionally disproportionate to the offenses he committed.[141] Appealing to the ethical approach, Justice Powell concluded the following:

> We are construing a living Constitution. The sentence imposed upon the petitioner would be viewed as grossly unjust by virtually every layman and lawyer.[142]

Only three years later in *Solem v. Helm*,[143] Justice Powell wrote the majority opinion for the Court, invalidating a life sentence without possibility of parole for an individual with seven felony convictions, including three for burglary, one for obtaining a money order under false pretenses, one for grand larceny, one for driving while intoxicated, and the final one for uttering a no-account check.[144] The Court began its analysis by declaring that the proportionality principle first recognized in *Weems* applied to prison sentences.[145] In order to apply this approach to criminal sentences, the Court declared that it would consider (1) the gravity of the offense and the harshness of the penalty, (2) sentences imposed for other crimes by the same jurisdiction, and (3) sentences imposed for the same crime by other jurisdictions.[146] Applying these criteria Justice Powell noted that Helms's final crime was passive in nature, and, unlike Rummel, there was no possibility of parole.[147] Next, the Court noted that the jurisdiction in question, South Dakota, otherwise authorized a life sentence for murder, treason, first-degree manslaughter, arson, and kidnapping.[148] Finally, Justice Powell pointed out that Helms could have received a life sentence without parole for the type of offenses he had committed in only one other state.[149] He distinguished *Rummel* from *Helms* in that Rummel was eligible for parole and in fact was paroled shortly after the Court's decision in his case; whereas Helms would be eligible for commutation of his sentence only after having served at least twenty-one years.[150]

Chief Justice Burger dissented, arguing that under *Rummel*, the *Weems* proportionality analysis was only appropriate in cases involving barbaric punishment and not with respect to a typical prison sentence.[151] Otherwise, any sentence would be unconstitutional if "it is more severe than five justices think appropriate."[152] He concluded that *Rummel* had categorically rejected the method of analysis employed by the majority.[153]

Seven years later in *Harmelin v. Michigan*,[154] the Supreme Court changed course. There it rejected the claim that a mandatory life sentence without possibility of parole and without consideration of any mitigating circumstances for possession of 650 grams of cocaine constituted cruel and unusual punishment.[155] In a section of the opinion joined only by Chief Justice Rehnquist, Justice Scalia declared that *Solem v. Helm* had misread the precedent, including *Rummel*, and that outside of capital punishment or the type of barbaric punishment in *Weems*, the Eighth Amendment contained no disproportionality principle applicable to length of sentencing.[156] Justice Scalia reached this conclusion following an extensive review of the history of the clause and an analysis of why a disproportionality principle would inevitably lead to highly subjective judicial judgments.[157]

Justice Kennedy wrote an opinion concurring in the judgment, joined by Justices O'Connor and Souter, maintaining that the precedents—particularly *Rummel* and *Solem*—did support a narrow disproportionality principle applicable to criminal sentences, but that it would not apply to the sentence in issue in the case.[158] He concluded that the Eighth Amendment only banned "extreme sentences that are 'grossly disproportionate' to the crime."[159] Given the serious nature of the crime in issue, Justice Kennedy explained that there was no need for any comparison between the sentence and with sentences within the jurisdiction or in other jurisdictions.[160]

Justice White, dissenting, argued that the Cruel and Unusual Punishment Clause did indeed embody a disproportionality principle recognized by precedent and applicable to prison sentences.[161] Likewise, he rejected Justice Kennedy's conclusion that comparative analysis was unwarranted when the sentence was not grossly disproportionate to the severity of the crime.[162] Applying the three-part *Solem* analysis, Justice White would have found that the sentence violated the Eighth Amendment.[163]

Presently, the Court's approach to disproportionate sentences appears to be in a state of flux and has been for quite some time. From the outset, the Court has been concerned with the potential that this type of review could easily get out of hand. The *Solem* Court appeared willing to engage in a comparative analysis that would take at least some account of societal standards and values, at least as expressed through legislation. It is unclear whether a majority of the Court would follow that approach today, however. Arguably, testing the length or severity of criminal sentences by either an intra- or inter-jurisdictional comparative approach in any but the most extreme case (and perhaps not even then) would cut too deeply into the values of federalism in allowing states to set their own standards of punishment and would also embroil the Court in an analysis that would smack too strongly of the imposition of judicial value choices. As such, an explicitly ethical analysis under the Eighth Amendment may be confined to cases involving the death penalty.

III. Substantive Due Process Cases

A. The Punitive Damage Cases

Another area in which the Court brings ethical considerations to bear, at least implicitly, is the line of cases decided over the past two decades, considering the constitutionality of large, punitive damage awards. The Court first confronted the issues in *Browning-Ferris Industries of Vermont v. Kelco Disposal, Inc*,[164] where it held that the Eighth Amendment Excessive Fines Clause did not apply to punitive damage awards in civil cases. It held that the history and purpose of the Eighth Amendment showed that it was concerned with limiting governmental power and not private remedies.[165] Two years later in *Pacific Mutual Life Insurance Co. v. Haslip*,[166] the Court considered but rejected a due process challenge to an $800,000 punitive damage award against an insurance company whose agent had defrauded a customer. It concluded that the standards applied by the Alabama courts in the case ensured that the award was not so unreasonable as to violate due process of law.[167] Justice Scalia, concurring in the judgment, objected to the fact that the Court even considered the reasonableness of the punitive damage award, given that the awarding of punitive damages has been well established throughout American history.[168] Justice O'Connor dissented, arguing that the Court should employ the Due Process Clause to police punitive damage awards because vague jury instructions often:

> encourage inconsistent and unpredictable results by inviting juries to rely on private beliefs and personal predilections. Juries are permitted to target unpopular defendants, penalize unorthodox or controversial views, and redistribute wealth. Multimillion dollar losses are inflicted on a whim.[169]

According to Justice O'Connor, the Constitution imposes at least some limitation on the award of punitive damages because "the Due Process Clause does not permit a State to classify arbitrariness as a virtue."[170]

Two years later in *TXO v. Alliance Resources*,[171] a slander of title action involving valuable oil leases, the Court held that a punitive damage award of $10 million—where the actual damages awarded were nineteen thousand dollars—was not grossly excessive and that the procedures followed by the trial court did not violate due process. Writing for a plurality, Justice Stevens rejected the type of inter- or intra-jurisdictional comparative approach for assessing punitive damage awards that the Court had employed in the sentencing context because there were simply too many variable factors in individual punitive damage cases to permit meaningful comparison.[172] He was unwilling to find that the award was grossly excessive in view of the defendant's bad faith, the amount of money at stake, and the degree of harm that could have occurred.[173] Justice Kennedy concurred but objected to the Court's reasonableness analysis on the ground that it provided no realistic guidance.[174] Justice Scalia concurred, but on the grounds that the Due Process Clause placed no limit on punitive damage awards at all.[175] Justice O'Connor dissented, repeating the criticisms that she had previously raised in her *Haslip* dissent.[176] Thus as of *TXO*, the Court was deeply divided on the issue of punitive damages. A majority seemed to believe that there was room for some type of limited review of awards pursuant to substantive due process, but there was little agreement as to what that review should entail.

Finally, in *BMW v. Gore*,[177] the Court invalidated a punitive damage award as grossly excessive in violation of due process. An Alabama jury had awarded $2 million in punitive damages because the defendant had failed to notify purchasers of cars that they had been repainted, resulting in actual damages to the plaintiff of $4,000. The Court attempted to provide greater guidance for evaluating punitive damage awards by proposing a three-part inquiry that focused on the degree of reprehensibility of the plaintiff's conduct, the disparity between the harm or potential harm caused and the punitive damage award, and a comparison with civil penalties authorized for the same offense.[178] It concluded that each of these factors contradicted the reasonableness of the award.[179] Justice Breyer concurred and expanded on the need for clear standards for both imposing and reviewing awards of punitive damages.[180] Among other things, he noted that "I cannot find any community understanding or historic practice that this award might exemplify and which, therefore, would provide background standards constraining arbitrary behavior and excessive awards."[181] He pointed out that punitive damages awards this disproportionate to actual damages were a relatively recent occurrence.[182] Consequently, he claimed the lack of constraining legal or historical standards rendered the punitive damage award in issue unconstitutionally excessive based on disproportionality alone.[183] Justice Scalia, dissenting, again argued that the Constitution did not forbid punitive damage awards however unfair they might seem and that the Court's "decision, though dressed up as a legal opinion, is really no more than a disagreement with the community's sense of indignation or outrage. . . ."[184] Justice Ginsburg also dissented, arguing that the Court had no business assessing the constitutionality of punitive damage awards.[185]

Seven years later in *State Farm Mutual v. Campbell*,[186] the Court struck down an award of punitive damages of $145 million as inconsistent with due process in which the award of actual damages was a million dollars in a case involving an alleged bad faith refusal to settle an insurance claim. The Court applied and expanded on the *Gore* analysis. With respect to reprehensibility, it emphasized that it was improper for the jury to take account of other dissimilar acts by the defendant.[187] As for proportionality, the Court suggested that a punitive damage award that exceeded a single digit ratio (i.e., greater than 9 to 1) would generally not satisfy due process, and that a fairly large compensatory award, such as the million dollar award in this case, would in itself provide a certain degree of deterrence and punishment.[188] As for comparable civil or criminal penalties, the Court pointed out that the maximum criminal fine for the conduct in issue would have been $10,000.[189] As all three factors favored the defendant, the Court concluded that the $145 million punitive damage award "was neither reasonable nor proportionate to the wrong committed."[190]

The Court's recent line of due process punitive damage cases seem to involve some degree of ethical consideration, although certainly not as explicitly as in the death penalty cases. Both the majority and dissents rely on ethical considerations to some extent. Given that there were virtually no guiding constitutional principles limiting state punitive damage awards prior to the Court's involvement over the past two decades, it is difficult to attribute its intervention to anything other than a conclusion that massively disproportionate awards violate a conception of fundamental fairness. It is unlikely that the Court meant to judge these awards based on its own personal convictions but rather based on its understanding of societal mores. In other words, its fairly cautious approach in this area suggests that it leans heavily in favor of deferring to the results reached by juries but recognizes that occasionally an award can cross all boundaries of reasonableness. Justice Breyer's comment in *Gore* that there is no historical or even contemporary societal support for these massively disproportionate punitive damage awards is acknowledgment that these decisions are based on the conclusion that these juries are simply out of line with any accepted convention of fairness and justice. On the other hand, Justice Scalia argued that the decision of the juries in these cases are the best barometers of societal mores and that there was simply no objective basis by which the Court could claim that its judgment was a better gauge of fairness.

B. The Due Process Privacy Cases

One of the most obvious areas in which ethical considerations have a bearing on the Court's constitutional decision making is in the area of due process privacy. Even more than the Cruel and Unusual Punishment Clause, due process liberty is extraordinarily open-ended, especially when interpreted to impose substantive as opposed to procedural limitations. For the most part, the Court has not explained these decisions with explicit invocation of ethical argument. Rather, it has relied upon more traditional, interpretive methodologies as discussed in prior chapters. There are cases, however, in which it seems obvious that ethical argument played a role, and there are important instances in which ethical argument seems obvious.

1. *Skinner v. Oklahoma*

Skinner v. Oklahoma,[191] though decided under the Equal Protection Clause, is the first of the Court's modern privacy decisions. The Court set aside a law that required sterilization of a person convicted of at least two felonies of moral turpitude on the grounds that the state's classification of crimes of moral turpitude was arbitrary.[192] Doctrinally, Skinner was a ground-breaking case in that it was the first instance in which the Court recognized a fundamental right—procreation—and applied the strict standard of review in an equal protection case.[193] There can be little doubt, however, that by the time *Skinner* was decided in 1942 with the rise of Hitler in Germany, the Court simply concluded that despite judicial approval in an earlier era,[194] mandatory sterilization, certainly for the types of petty offenses involved in *Skinner*, was quite inconsistent with contemporary American values. Justice Stone would have invalidated the law on procedural due process grounds.[195] Justice Jackson agreed with both rationales and came closer than the other justices to an ethical approach in noting that "[t]here are limits to the extent to which a legislatively represented majority may conduct biological experiments at the expense of the dignity and personality and natural powers of a minority—even those who have been guilty of what the majority define as crimes."[196] Ultimately, he did not rely on this substantive due process–based approach, but in merely articulating it he probably came closer to the moving force behind the decision than did the explanations of the other justices.

2. *Poe* and *Griswold*

In what is arguably the most influential of the substantive due process privacy opinions, in his *Poe v. Ullman*[197] dissent, Justice Harlan provided a doctrinal framework within which ethical argument can be taken into account. In *Poe*, Justice Harlan was prepared to employ substantive due process in a manner that involved reliance on history and tradition but also incorporated a degree of explicit interest balancing. Justice Harlan was prepared to invalidate the Connecticut law banning the use of contraceptives by married people, which the Court did in fact strike down four years later in the landmark case of *Griswold v. Connecticut*. In an oft-quoted phase, Justice Harlan explained that due process represents "the balance which our Nation, built upon postulates of respect for the liberty of the individual, has struck between that liberty and the demands of organized society."[198] This approach would seem to permit explicit consideration of societal norms. Indeed, it seems to define substantive due process as the ultimate product of the American ethos. However, Justice Harlan was quite sensitive to the charge that the Court would simply define liberty with its own values and preferences. Consequently, he explained that history and tradition would provide an objective anchor for the elaboration of due process liberty.[199]

A focus on tradition and history most certainly considers the American ethos, but despite Justice Harlan's comment that "tradition is a living thing,"[200] it almost certainly does so in a backward-looking manner. The objective indicators of tradition that the Court is likely to rely upon, most especially state legislative and judicial action, will often reflect past rather than present values. Justice Harlan summed up this approach by noting that due process liberty "is a rational continuum which, broadly speaking, includes a freedom from all substantial arbitrary impositions and purposeless restraints."[201] By placing primary emphasis on the balancing approach proposed by Justice Harlan in *Poe*, the Court could focus on its conception of the current American ethos in defining due process liberty. Justice Souter seemed to argue for such an approach in his concurring opinion in *Washington v. Glucksberg*.[202] However, such an approach would seem to unduly denigrate the importance of history and tradition in Justice Harlan's analytical framework. In *Poe*, Justice Harlan readily rejected the Connecticut law as inconsistent with due process liberty, noting that there was no other similar law in the United States or among other nations.[203]

Four years after *Poe*, the Court did invalidate the law in *Griswold*. Justice Douglas relied on a novel, privacy-based theory, and most of the other concurring justices relied on Justice Harlan's substantive due process *Poe* analysis.[204] Although none of the justices relied on ethical considerations as such, it is hard to imagine that they did not influence the decision, given that the law in question was so clearly out of step with contemporary values. Indeed, as Professor Bobbitt recognized, *Griswold* would have been the ideal case in which to rely on ethical argument.[205]

3. *Roe* and *Casey*

The due process privacy cases reveal the limitations of ethical argument. To the extent that the Court is indeed looking to the American ethos—the mores and values recognized by society—the argument becomes difficult to make when society is bitterly divided over the practice in question. That would certainly have been the case with *Roe v. Wade* and abortion, where the Court effectively struck down abortion prohibitions nationwide and a significant segment of society, quite possibly a majority, disagreed vigorously with the decision. The only way in which the Court could even attempt to justify the decision based on ethical reasoning would be at a high level of generality, which essentially evades the specific issue before the Court. The joint opinion in *Planned Parenthood v. Casey* attempted to do just that in the portion of the opinion in which it explained that the case involved "the right to define one's own concept of existence, of meaning, of the universe, and of the mystery of human life."[206] Consequently, the state could not prohibit a previability abortion because the woman's "suffering is too intimate and personal for the State to insist . . . upon its own vision of the woman's role, however dominant that vision has been in the course of our history and our culture."[207] Perhaps the Joint Opinion was appealing to some societally recognized conception of liberty, at least at a high level of abstraction, in support of its conclusion, and yet it explicitly conceded that it was prepared to impose that conception in the very teeth of a cultural consensus to the contrary. Consequently, it remains difficult to understand the abortion decisions as legitimately explainable based on even an implicit ethical approach.

4. *Bowers* and *Lawrence*

Bowers v. Hardwick and *Lawrence v. Texas*, the former sustaining the constitutionality of a law criminalizing homosexual sodomy and the latter invalidating such laws, do arguably rely to some extent on ethical argument. In sustaining the Georgia law in 1986, the *Bowers* majority cited the historical and legislative support for such laws.[208] This in itself served to reject any claim that the law in question, like the law in *Griswold*, was out of step with contemporary mores. Two decades later, when the Court finally overruled *Bowers* in *Lawrence v. Texas*, it argued that the *Bowers* Court's conclusions as to an historical and cultural consensus were incorrect,[209] but perhaps more importantly it made the case that whatever support for such laws may have existed in 1986 had dwindled to almost nothing.[210] The Court quoted the "mystery of life" language from *Casey*[211] and maintained that there was no longer a societal consensus in support of criminalization of homosexual sodomy but did not explicitly argue that a clear consensus to the contrary had developed. Rather, it was enough that *Bowers* could no longer be supported by an appeal to widely shared beliefs or values. This is arguably an instance in which an appeal to the American ethos would not be sufficient to support the Court's decision, but it certainly would not support the opposite result either.

5. *Washington v. Glucksberg*

The Court's decision in *Washington v. Glucksberg*,[212] rejecting a due process right to assisted suicide, may also be an example of a case in which any appeal to the ethos or societal values undermined the claim for such a right. In rejecting the claim, the Court relied heavily on the overwhelmingly strong historical and societal consensus against such a right.[213] Against this showing there was simply no room to appeal to an ethical argument to the contrary.

The due process privacy cases would seem to be an area in which ethical argument could operate. For the most part, however, that is not the case. Unless there is a relatively clear societal consensus either against the legislation challenged as in *Griswold* or in support of it as in *Glucksberg*, ethical argument is likely to seem hollow or manipulative. As such, it will be little more than window dressing for a decision better explained on other grounds.

⅄ IV. One Person, One Vote

Arguably, one outstanding example of an implicit appeal to ethical argument can be found in *Reynolds v. Sims*,[214] the Court's landmark reapportionment decision in which it held that the Equal Protection Clause required that legislative bodies be apportioned based on population equality or one person, one vote as it became known. At first glance, *Reynolds* might appear to be a strange case in which to perceive an appeal to ethical argument, in that the Court essentially invalidated the legislative apportionment plans of most states, and, as it would turn out over time, most municipalities as well. In that sense, one might argue that the societal consensus was to the contrary. Yet for the most part, the gross malapportionment invalidated by the Court in *Reynolds* reflected political entrenchment rather than deliberate choice.[215]

The *Reynolds* dissents argued quite persuasively that population equality was simply one of several viable theories of political representation, and there was no basis for concluding that it was embodied in the Constitution. However, the Court's strong suit was that its alternative—one person, one vote or majority rule—did indeed seem to be the fairest and indeed most obvious method for constituting a political body. It was most likely the way in which many familiar organizations and clubs operated. As such, the Court was able to bring about a monumental change in the operation of the American political system in a manner in which the public response would almost certainly be quite favorable. The Court did not explicitly rely on ethical argument. Rather, it simply declared that "[l]egislators represent people, not trees or acres."[216] But, to a large extent, as the dissenters argued in vain, it appears that the Court pulled its standard out of a hat.[217] That the Court was able to do so with such confidence is almost certainly attributable to the fact that it understood that its approach reflected deeply held American values of fairness.

⅄ V. Ethical Argument Everywhere?

The Court rarely relies explicitly on ethical argument, and when it does, as in the instance of the death penalty cases, the results may be somewhat chaotic.

However, reliance on at least the Court's conception of American values lies beneath the surface of many of its decisions in the area of civil liberties. It could be argued that the justices' conception of what America stands for—at least in terms of procedural fairness, equality, individual privacy, and freedom of thought and expression—may have at least influenced decisions such as *Brown v. Board of Education*,[218] striking down racial segregation in public schools; *Reed v. Reed*,[219] promoting gender-based equality; *Gideon v. Wainwright*,[220] requiring counsel for indigent criminal defendants; *Miranda v. Arizona*,[221] providing protection against potentially coercive custodial interrogation; *New York Times v. Sullivan*,[222] increasing protection of free speech against liability for defamation; and *Mathews v. Eldridge*,[223] providing greater procedural protection against adverse governmental action, just to name a few.

To maintain that these cases were influenced by ethical considerations is pure speculation, even if it is possible. The Court explained these decisions in far more traditionally accepted terms. An explicit appeal to ethical argument will almost certainly be lambasted by critics as an admission that the justices are simply deciding cases based upon their own subjective values. That danger is always present, whether or not the case is explained in ethical terms, but certainly doing so brings it closer to the surface. Because many of the cases cited above were unpopular, controversial, or at least against the grain of existing law, it might well be questioned how they could be based on an appeal to widely shared societal values. And they probably could not, at least in the sense of reflecting values that at the time of the decisions had permeated the culture. Yet in most if not all of these instances, the Court's decisions have become deeply entrenched in American culture and at some point after the fact have become a part of the American ethos. This illustrates that the Court plays an important role in developing, as opposed to simply reflecting, American societal values.

However, the fact that the Court is sometimes successful in this endeavor hardly means that is always the case. The Court's initial approach to the death penalty in *Furman* provides an example of an area in which an attempt to influence societal values fell flat. Many of the Court's attempts to push in the direction of the separation of church and state have also met significant resistance and have not resulted in a broad-based societal consensus. The same can be said of the Court's abortion decisions. Thirty-five years after *Roe v. Wade*, society still remains bitterly divided. Reliance upon existing societal consensus, objectively manifested in positive law, may be a relatively safe but not particularly potent methodology, given that honestly applied, it simply allows the Court to strike down laws that are already outside of the societal mainstream. An attempt to influence or lead societal values is a more hazardous undertaking. That may explain to some extent why the Court is hesitant to attempt to do so explicitly.

TWELVE

Rhetoric in Constitutional Interpretation

❧ I. Introduction

Constitutional argument is often advanced by the use of rhetoric. Sometimes the Court's use of rhetoric does more to create or establish a constitutional principle than does its reliance on traditional sources of constitutional interpretation such as text, original understanding, or precedent. Not only is rhetoric an effective method of prevailing in a constitutional argument, but it can create principles that will be far more enduring than if stated in more mundane language. Some of the great stylists in the history of the Court, including Justices Holmes, Brandeis, and Jackson in classic opinions such as *Abrams, Whitney*, and *Barnette*, provide evidence of the power of rhetoric to create enduring principles. One form of rhetoric that can be effective but also misleading is the use of metaphor. This chapter will consider the checkered career of the Court's most famous metaphor—Thomas Jefferson's "wall of separation" between church and state as a foundational principle under the Establishment Clause. The chapter will also examine the role that rhetoric plays in dissenting opinions and will consider instances when rhetoric proves to be unpersuasive.

❧ II. Rhetoric to Bolster Principle

A. At the Outset—*Marbury v. Madison*

Some of the most famous and most influential statements in the history of the Supreme Court are examples of pure rhetoric. One such example is Chief Justice Marshall's statement in *Marbury v. Madison* that

> [t]he government of the United States has been emphatically termed a government of laws, and not of men. It will certainly cease to deserve this

high appellation, if the laws furnish no remedy for the violation of a vested legal right.[1]

Marshall purported to bolster the authority of this statement by proclaiming that someone, presumably someone important, has termed this government one of laws and not men, but he failed to tell us who that someone was. Doubtlessly, someone did so term it, and that someone probably was important. The persuasive power of the statement flows not from its unnamed source but rather from Marshall's clear and concise summary of an attractive and foundational principle. Marshall had delivered an effective early nineteenth century sound bite.

B. First Amendment Classics

1. Holmes in *Schenck, Abrams,* and *Gitlow*

Often the rhetoric of an opinion dominates all else. Justice Holmes's short opinion in *Schenck v. United States*[2] provides a classic example. The case is almost certainly best remembered for Holmes's statement that "[t]he most stringent protection of free speech would not protect a man in falsely shouting fire in a theatre and causing a panic."[3] This remark is of only tangential significance to the Court's analysis, yet it is branded in the memory of almost everyone even minimally familiar with constitutional law. Likewise, in *Schenck*, Holmes introduced the clear and present danger test into First Amendment jurisprudence. The test has been criticized by scholars, was largely limited to the fairly narrow area of seditious speech, and has since been replaced by an incitement approach; yet, due in part to the Holmes pedigree and the rhetorical power of the phrase itself, it still tends to symbolize the central tenet of free speech analysis for the uninitiated.

Justice Holmes wrote with even greater eloquence the following year in dissent in *Abrams v. United States*.[4] He explained the following:

Persecution for the expression of opinions seems to me perfectly logical. If you have no doubt of your premises or your power and want a certain result with all your heart you naturally express your wishes in law and sweep away all opposition. To allow opposition by speech seems to indicate that you think the speech impotent, as when a man says that he has squared the circle, or that you do not care whole heartedly for the result, or that you doubt either your power or your premises. But when men have realized that time has upset many fighting faiths, they may come to believe even more than they believe the very foundations of their own conduct that the ultimate good desired is better reached by free trade in ideas—that the best test of truth is the power of the thought to get itself accepted in the competition of the market, and that truth is the only ground upon which their wishes safely can be carried out. That at any rate is the theory of our Constitution.[5]

Holmes's introduction of the marketplace of ideas theory as an explanation of why freedom of speech should be highly protected remains one of the most eloquent and quotable passages in all of American constitutional law. It was written in Holmes's characteristic style, which is at once cryptic, conversational, and insightful. He employed several images that capture the imagination of the reader and led toward acceptance of the thesis. Early on, the image of the overconfident regulator "sweep[ing] away all opposition" possibly calls to mind the poor sport in a chess match, angrily sweeping the opponent's pieces off the board in order to avert certain defeat. The image is negative and turns one against the regulator of speech at the outset. Likewise, the image of impotent speech as "a man who says he can square the circle" evokes not simply unpersuasive speech but rather ridiculous speech. This understates the risk of tolerating false speech, as this example involves speech that is both demonstrably false and harmless. That will not necessarily be the case with the type of speech that the government has an interest in restricting. Thus Holmes used an image that stacked the deck in favor of his conclusion. The image of the overthrow of "fighting faiths" suggests historical movements of epic proportion. So much the better that Holmes provided no examples. The reader is free to imagine what he will.

The metaphor of the market also provides power to the argument, as it is so easily understood by the reader. Based on experience, the reader is likely to conclude that competition among goods in the marketplace does yield positive benefits and usually, or at least often, does result in the triumph of the superior product. Holmes called this to mind and then moved on. The obvious assumption is that the same process will work with ideas as well. Holmes does not pause to question whether there are important differences between the marketplaces of goods and ideas, which undermines the analogy, or for that matter whether there even is a marketplace of ideas in any meaningful sense. Holmes raised far more questions than he answered, but his argument works extraordinarily well by presenting the reader with identifiable images and then enlisting the reader to use his own imagination to carry it forward.

Holmes spoke again with rhetorical flourish in his dissent in *Gitlow v. New York*.[6] In response to the majority's conclusion that the petitioner's speech incited violent and illegal activity, Holmes responded:

> Every idea is an incitement. It offers itself for belief and if believed it is acted on unless some other belief outweighs it or some failure of energy stifles the movement at its birth. The only difference between the expression of an opinion and an incitement in the narrower sense is the speaker's enthusiasm for the result. Eloquence may set fire to reason.[7]

In this instance, Holmes's rhetoric outstripped his analysis. His statement that opinion and incitement are differentiated only by the enthusiasm of the speaker may sound good initially, but it simply is not so, either literally or legally. Incitement is generally understood as a call to immediate action, regardless of the enthusiasm with which it is offered. Consequently this is an instance in which Holmes's rhetoric is more misleading than illuminating.

2. Judicial Rhetoric at its Best—Brandeis in *Whitney*

Perhaps the most stirring rhetoric about the values of the freedom of speech ever to appear in a Supreme Court opinion came in Justice Brandeis's concurrence in *Whitney v. California*,[8] where the majority upheld a conviction under a statute similar to that in *Gitlow*. Brandeis wrote eloquently and passionately about how civic courage was a dominant value essential to democracy and promoted by freedom of expression.[9] He attempted to explain why freedom of speech that seemed dangerous and threatening should be permitted by attributing all of his conclusions to the framers, beginning sentence after sentence with "they believed" or "they recognized" or "they did not,"[10] and yet he supported his claims as to the views of the framers with nothing more than two quotes from Jefferson.[11] Whether or not all of Brandeis claims were in fact embraced by the framing generation, attributing these views to them gives force to the argument. Brandeis effectively argued that because the wise and respected men who lived in fearful times displayed and believed in courageous toleration of threatening speech and because the nation that they founded has in fact survived for over 113 years, should not we show such courage as well?

He masterfully used language to build his argument, moving from one point to the next. For example, he stated the following:

They valued liberty both as an end and as a means. They believed liberty to [be] the secret of happiness and courage to be the secret of liberty.[12]

With a deft turn of phrase, Brandeis moved from liberty to happiness to courage. Liberty and happiness are easy to accept. Courage is harder. By tying courage to liberty and happiness, Brandeis tried to make the embrace of courage natural and inevitable. He continuously built "one thing leads to another"-type arguments with finely turned phrases that march the reader toward his inevitable conclusion. For instance, he argued:

that it is hazardous to discourage thought, hope, and imagination; that fear breeds repression; that repression breeds hate; that hate menaces stable government; that the path of safety lies in the opportunity to discuss freely supposed grievances and proposed remedies; and that the fitting remedy for evil counsels is good ones.[13]

Brandeis constructed a thesis that led logically from the premise that suppression of speech is a problem to the conclusion that free debate is the solution. His rhetoric is strong and his reasoning is tight, leaving little room for disagreement. Moreover, the points he made seem intuitively correct; it seems like common sense.

Focusing again on the dangers of giving way to fear, Brandeis wrote the following:

Fear of serious injury cannot alone justify suppression of free speech and assembly. Men feared witches and burnt women. It is the function of speech to free men from the bondage of irrational fears.[14]

There may be no more powerful piece of rhetoric in all of the United States Reports. The sentence "men feared witches and burnt women," harkening back to a dark and frightening incident in colonial history, carries extraordinary emotional power because it is concise yet true. Turning to doctrine, Brandeis cautioned that

[t]he wide difference between advocacy and incitement, between preparation and attempt, between assembling and conspiracy, must be borne in mind.[15]

The differences that Brandeis mentions are important legal distinctions in the area. Brandeis drew the distinctions with unparalleled precision. Returning to the framers, he noted:

> Those who won our independence by revolution were not cowards. They did not fear political change. They did not exalt order at the cost of liberty.[16]

Through his short declarative sentences, Brandeis issued a challenge. He invoked the founders as men of great moral courage and urged us to be more like them. Many more examples of Brandeis stirring rhetoric in the *Whitney* concurrence could be cited. His position on free speech doctrine was sound and ultimately carried the day.[17] But there are many instances of justices who were ahead of their times and were vindicated by later courts. Brandeis's *Whitney* concurrence is special because of the singular combination of precision, logic, and devastatingly effective, emotionally charged rhetoric. It is a true classic.[18]

C. The Rhetoric of Justice Jackson

Justice Jackson, one of the Court's most elegant writers, added to the canon of stirring rhetoric in support of the free speech principle in his famous opinion in *West Virginia Board of Education v. Barnette*,[19] invalidating a state statute that required public school children to salute the flag and repeat the pledge of allegiance. The opinion relied more heavily on ringing rhetoric than on traditional legal analysis. Memorable phrases are sprinkled throughout the opinion, including "[c]ompulsory unification of opinion achieves only the unanimity of the graveyard."[20] However, *Barnette* is best remembered for Justice Jackson's stirring statement of principle near the very end of the opinion, where he observed the following:

> If there is any fixed star in our constitutional constellation, it is that no official, high or petty, can prescribe what shall be orthodox in politics, nationalism, religion, or other matters of opinion or force citizens to confess by word or act their faith therein.[21]

This stated a key First Amendment principle, and as such it would have been significant however blandly set forth. Justice Jackson's stellar metaphor and stirring rhetoric magnified it well beyond its doctrinal importance, causing it to be quoted in dozens of subsequent opinions. This is an excellent example of the degree to which the rhetorical force of an opinion can substantially increase its impact on the law.

Few justices have used the pithy phrase more effectively than Justice Jackson. In explaining why the Smith Act's prohibition of communist party organizational activity did not violate the First Amendment, he proclaimed "[t]he Constitution does not make conspiracy a civil right"[22] and "[t]here is no constitutional right to 'gang up' on the Government."[23] He displayed his rhetorical skills again in *Edwards v. California*, where he wrote that

> [u]nless this Court is willing to say that citizenship of the United States means at least this much to the citizen, then our heritage of constitutional privileges and immunities is only a promise to the ear to be broken to the hope, a teasing illusion like a munificent bequest in a pauper's will.[24]

In *H. P. Hood & Sons v. DuMond*[25] Justice Jackson relied on stirring rhetoric to bolster a near absolute prohibition of state discrimination against interstate commerce. He wrote that "[o]ur system, fostered by the Commerce Clause, is that every farmer and every craftsman shall be encouraged to produce by the certainty that he will have free access to every market in the Nation, that no home embargoes will withhold his export, and no foreign state will by customs duties or regulations exclude them."[26] Justice Black dissented, unimpressed with Justice Jackson's rhetoric and with the absolutist approach that he believed it was designed to support.[27] He argued that Justice Jackson's "eulogy to the framers" and concerns about guarding against "commercial and even shooting wars among the states . . . have strong emotional appeals and when skillfully utilized . . . obscure the vision" that they are attempting to install.[28] Justice Black perceived this to be an example of rhetoric employed to deceive rather than to clarify.

III. Rhetoric to Emphasize Strength of Conviction

Sometimes the Court uses bold rhetoric to highlight the strength of its conviction to a particular principle. Such was the case in *Chambers v. Florida*,[29] where a unanimous Court condemned the dragnet incommunicado coercive interrogation of a large group of African Americans in a homicide investigation. In denouncing such practices, Justice Black wrote the following:

> The testimony of centuries, in governments of varying kinds over populations of different races and beliefs, stood as proof that physical and mental torture and coercion had brought about the tragically unjust sacrifices of some who were the noblest and most useful of their generations. The rack, the thumbscrew, the wheel, solitary confinement, protracted questioning and cross questioning, and other ingenious forms of entrapment of the helpless or unpopular had left their wake of mutilated bodies and shattered minds along the way to the cross, the guillotine, the stake and the hangman's noose. And they who have suffered most from secret and dictatorial proceedings have almost always been the poor, the ignorant, the numerically weak, the friendless, and the powerless.[30]

The Court almost certainly used this strong and soaring rhetoric to attempt to bring home to renegade law enforcement agencies, especially in the Deep South, that brutal and coercive methods of interrogation would no longer be tolerated by the Court. It is one of the strongest statements of this nature in the history of the Court.

Another example of this would be Justice Robert's dissent in *Korematsu v. United States*, where he referred to the internment camps to which persons of Japanese ancestry on the Pacific Coast were sent during World War II as "concentration camps."[31] Likewise, Justice Murphy, dissenting, argued that the thinking behind the order in issue "has been used in support of the abhorrent and despicable treatment of minority groups by the dictatorial tyrannies which this nation is now pledged to destroy."[32] Comparison of U.S. military policies upheld by the Court to the tactics of Nazi Germany was quite obviously a means by which the dissenters attempted to convey their extreme distress at those practices as well as the Court's deference to them. Not surprisingly, the majority was offended by the comparison. Justice Black responded that "we deem it unjustifiable to call them concentration camps with all the ugly connotations that term implies."[33] For a justice who took the protection of civil rights and liberties as seriously as did Black, his response to the dissents rhetorical barbs was quite restrained.

🖎 IV. Enduring Rhetoric

One of the key advantages of stirring rhetoric in judicial opinions is that it is likely to live on and exert influence long after more pedestrian analysis is forgotten. An example of this is Justice Brandeis's famous rhetorical flourish near the conclusion of his opinion in *New State Ice Co. v. Liebmann.*[34] The majority had struck down an Oklahoma law regulating the ice business as a violation of substantive due process. Justice Brandeis offered a lengthy dissent filled with careful analysis of precedent, as well as his characteristic reliance on empirical sources. With the rejection of the *Lochner* doctrine a few years later, the case would be forgotten were it not for Justice Brandeis's closing comments. In the course of explaining why the Court should be hesitant to invalidate state social and economic regulation, Brandeis wrote that

> [t]o stay experimentation in things social and economic is a grave responsibility. Denial of the right to experiment may be fraught with serious consequences to the nation. It is one of the happy incidents of the federal system that a single courageous state may, if its citizens choose, serve as a laboratory; and try novel social and economic experiments without risk to the rest of the country.[35]

Justice Brandeis's rhetoric has resonated over the years, has been quoted in dozens of cases and hundreds of books and articles, and serves as a summarization of one of the key arguments in favor of taking federalism seriously. This almost certainly would not have been the case had he made the same point in a less elegant prose.

The rhetoric of Justice Brandeis in his famous dissent in *Olmstead v. United States*[36] provides another example of judicial rhetoric that has assumed a life of its own and is quoted both by the Court and by commentators with great frequency. In *Olmstead,* the majority held that a wiretap of a telephone conversation did not constitute a search or seizure under the Fourth Amendment, given that there was no physical trespass and given that a conversation was an intangible thing incapable of being seized.[37] Objecting to what he perceived to be an unduly narrow conception of the purpose and scope of the Fourth Amendment by the majority, Justice Brandeis wrote the following:

> The makers of our Constitution undertook to secure conditions favorable to the pursuit of happiness. They recognized the significance of man's spiritual nature, of his feelings and of his intellect. They knew that only a part of the pain, pleasure and satisfactions of life are to be found in material things. They sought to protect Americans in their beliefs, their thoughts, their emotions and their sensations. They conferred, as against

the government, the right to be let alone—the most comprehensive of rights and the right most valued by civilized men.[38]

As with his classic concurrence in *Whitney*, Brandeis focused on the general right to pursue happiness, and then through powerful rhetoric he attempted to explain what that entails as a matter of constitutional law. Also as in *Olmstead*, he attributed the views that he propounds to the framers with no particular citation to support this claim. As was the case with his earlier classic law review article,[39] Brandeis summed up his conclusion by recognizing a right to privacy embodied in the Fourth Amendment that he characterizes as "a right to be let alone." With this rhetoric in dissent, Brandeis effectively launched privacy as the value underlying the Fourth Amendment's protection against unreasonable searches and seizures, although it would be four decades before a majority of the Supreme Court agreed. It is probable that the concept of privacy would have carried the day in any event, even absent the Brandeis rhetoric of *Olmstead*; however, there can be no doubt that the power of Brandeis's language added to its momentum.

But Brandeis was not finished. He concluded his opinion with grand rhetorical flourish, explaining why it is worthwhile to exclude evidence unlawfully obtained that could otherwise be used to convict a guilty defendant. He wrote:

> In a government of laws, existence of government will be imperiled if it fails to observe the laws scrupulously. Our government is the potent, the omnipresent teacher. For good or for ill, it teaches the whole people by example. Crime is contagious. If the government becomes a law breaker, it breeds contempt for law; it invites every man to become a law unto himself; it invites anarchy. To declare that in the administration of the criminal law the end justifies the means—to declare that the government may commit crimes in order to secure the conviction of a private criminal—would bring terrible retribution. Against that pernicious doctrine this court should resolutely set its face.[40]

With short declarative sentences and memorable phrases such as "[o]ur government is the . . . omnipresent teacher" and "[c]rime is contagious," Brandeis produced a memorable paragraph that is quoted at least in part whenever the Court attempts to remind the readers of its opinions that the costs of enforcing constitutional limitations on police conduct are worthwhile.

V. Metaphor

A metaphor can prove to be a very effective rhetorical device in constitutional argument. However, it is capable of misuse as well. The most famous and controversial metaphor in American constitutional law is Jefferson's statement in his letter to the Danbury Baptist Association that the First Amendment was intended to create "a wall of separation between church and state." This figure of speech was first introduced into Supreme Court jurisprudence in the late nineteenth century in *Reynolds v. United States*.[41] The metaphor was thrust into a state of prominence, however, in *Everson v. Board of Education*, the Court's first modern Establishment Clause case, when Justice Black declared that it summarized the historical purpose of the Establishment Clause.[42] This figure of speech has had tremendous staying power in constitutional law because of the clear picture that it paints, because it does capture the principle that many believe to be the correct approach to issues of church and state, and because of the respect paid to its author, Jefferson, especially on matters of freedom of religion.

Ever since the wall of separation was introduced into constitutional jurisprudence, justices have built upon the wall to tweak it to their liking. In the course of concluding that the state program at issue in Everson did not violate the Establishment Clause, Justice Black declared that the "wall must be kept high and impregnable [but it] has not been breached here."[43] Justice Rutledge, dissenting, argued that "[n]either so high nor so impregnable today as yesterday is the wall raised between church and state."[44] In his concurring opinion in the next significant Establishment Clause case, *McCollum v. Board of Education*, Justice Frankfurter accepted the wall metaphor and the principle behind it but cautioned that "[a]ccommodation of legislative freedom and Constitutional limitations upon that freedom cannot be achieved by a mere phrase."[45] He concluded his opinion by noting that "Jefferson's metaphor in describing the relation between Church and State speaks of a 'wall of separation,' not of a fine line easily overstepped."[46] Concurring in *McCollum* but with grave reservations as to the Court's approach, Justice Jackson concluded that "we are likely to make the legal 'wall of separation between church and state' as winding as the famous serpentine wall designed by Mr. Jefferson for the University he founded."[47] Dissenting in *Zorach v. Clauson*, the next major Establishment Clause case to come before the Court, Justice Jackson proclaimed that "[t]he wall which the Court was professing to erect between Church and State has become even more warped and twisted than I expected."[48]

Justice Stewart also objected in his dissent in *Engel v. Vitale*:

[t]he Court's task, in this as in all areas of constitutional adjudication, is not responsibly aided by the uncritical invocation of metaphors like the 'wall of separation,' a phrase nowhere to be found in the Constitution.[49]

In *Committee for Public Education v. Nyquist*, Justice Powell rejected Justice Jackson's earlier charge that "the wall . . . has become as winding as the famous serpentine wall."[50]

Justice Rehnquist challenged the wall of separation metaphor vigorously in his dissent in *Wallace v. Jaffree*.[51] He wrote:

[w]hether due to its lack of historical support or its practical unworkability, the Everson "wall" has proved all but useless as a guide to sound constitutional adjudication. It illuminates only too well the wisdom of Benjamin Cardozo's observation that "[m]etaphors in law are to be narrowly watched, for starting as devices to liberate thought, they end often by enslaving it." . . . The "wall of separation between church and State" is a metaphor based on bad history, a metaphor which has proved useless as a guide to judging. It should be frankly and explicitly abandoned.[52]

After calling for its abandonment, however, Justice Rehnquist could not resist continuing to tweak the metaphor himself, noting that "[t]he Court has more recently attempted to add some mortar to Everson's wall through the three part test of *Lemon v. Kurtzman*," which he also rejected as not "based on either the language or intent of the drafters."[53] In his dissent in *Zelman v. Harris*, Justice Stevens warned that "[w]henever we remove a brick from the wall that was designed to separate religion and government, we increase the risk of religious strife and weaken the foundation of our democracy."[54]

One response to the argument that the wall of separation metaphor is an inaccurate picture of the original understanding of the Establishment Clause is simply to claim, as Justice Stevens did in his dissent in *Van Orden v. Perry*, that whether the metaphor is historically accurate or not the Court has entrenched the separation principle into its Establishment Clause jurisprudence, and it is a good principle even if it does not capture the original understanding.[55]

As of *Larkin v. Grendel's Den* in 1982, the 'wall' of separation had become "a useful signpost"[56] as opposed to a clear doctrinal dividing line. Regardless of whether the wall metaphor captures the correct principle of the relationship between government and religion, the lengthy rhetorical battle in case after case as to the current health of the wall seems to illustrate the Cardozo wisdom quoted by Chief Justice Rehnquist that metaphors can easily get out of hand and prove more misleading than helpful. There will inevitably be some danger when the Court substitutes other language for that of the text. The phrase "Congress shall make no law respecting an establishment of religion" might well translate into the principle of "a wall of separation between church and state." However, the difficulty that the Court has encountered in employing that metaphor as a workable principle, starting with *Everson*, suggests that it simply fails to capture the complexity of the relationship between church and state. It promises far more than the Court has been willing or able to deliver. Thus, an attempt to stick with the metaphor, despite persistent controversy, has led to confusion and frustration rather than enlightenment.

VI. Rhetoric in Dissent

Some of the most stirring examples of rhetoric in Supreme Court opinions are found in dissenting opinion, including many of the examples cited in this chapter. By definition, dissenting justices are unhappy with the result or the reasoning of the majority opinion. Because these justices have lost the argument on the Court itself, the dissent will attempt to alert other constituencies, including future courts, political institutions, the bar, the academy, and the public, to the deficiencies of the majority opinion in the hopes that it will be reconsidered, modified, or rejected in the future. Because the dissent attempts to attract attention and challenge the decision of the majority and because the dissenting justices are unconstrained by the need to hold on to a majority, a dissent generally has more leeway to employ overblown rhetoric in the course of condemning the majority's decision. Even so, the dissent can overplay its hand by employing so much rhetorical bombast that it loses all credibility.

Justice Brennan's dissent in *National League of Cities v. Usery*[57] seemed to cross this line. The Court had held that the application of the Federal Labor Standards Act to state governments could in certain instances violate the state's constitutionally protected domain of sovereignty and autonomy. In the course of his dissent, Justice Brennan referred to the majority opinion and decision as a "patent usurpation," a "manufactured abstraction without

substance," which "must astound scholars of the Constitution," a "repudiation of a line of unbroken precedent," an "ill conceived abstraction," with a
"paucity of legal reasoning," in "patent derogation," with "no principle giving
meaningful content," "ominous," "leaves one incredulous," "alarming" "is the
startling restructuring of our federal system," "a thinly veiled rationalization,"
"disregard of precedents" delivering a "catastrophic judicial body blow to the
powers of Congress."[58] Justice Brennan's near hysterical rhetoric was out
of proportion to anything that the majority opinion said or did. Although
it would seem too shrill to be persuasive, *National League of Cities* was
overruled nine years later, and Justice Brennan's position, without the
bombast, essentially prevailed in Justice Blackmun's majority opinion for
the Court in *Garcia.*

VII. Ineffective Rhetoric

Sometimes judicial rhetoric does not ring true and actually weakens the
opinion. Such was the case in *Texas v. Johnson*, in which the Court invalidated
a Texas statute that made it a crime to desecrate, among other things, an
American flag.[59] The Court's holding was controversial and flew in the face
of strong public opinion. Writing for the majority, Justice Brennan made a
sound legal argument as to why the Texas statute constituted impermissible
content-based discrimination.[60] He concluded the opinion with a rhetorical
flourish, however, writing that

> [t]he way to preserve the flag's special role is not to punish those who
> feel differently about these matters. It is to persuade them that they are
> wrong. . . . We can imagine no more appropriate response to burning
> a flag than waving one's own, no better way to counter a flag burner's
> message than by saluting the flag that burns, no surer means of preserving
> the dignity even of the flag that burned than by—as one witness here
> did—according its remains a respectful burial.[61]

Seldom has a justice so thoroughly missed the mark with rhetoric. Given
the deep emotions stirred by flag burning, Justice Brennan's conclusion that
those offended should be content to wave their own flags and gather and
dispose of the ashes of desecrated flags was hollow, condescending, and
insulting. Dissenting, Chief Justice Rehnquist was surely correct in characterizing Justice Brennan's rhetoric as "a regrettably patronizing civics lecture"

and in noting that it is quite inappropriate for the Court "[to admonish] those responsible to public opinion as if they were truant school-children."[62]

Justice Blackmun's concurring and dissenting opinions in *Webster v. Reproductive Health Services* and *Planned Parenthood v. Casey* provide examples of very ineffective rhetoric. Justice Blackmun, the author of *Roe v. Wade*, seemed to take a proprietary interest in the preservation of *Roe* against the consistent challenges to it. Once it appeared that *Roe* might be overruled in the not too distant future, Justice Blackmun attempted through overwrought rhetoric to rally its supporters to the cause. In *Webster*, where the Court construed the statutes in question to avoid a direct constitutional challenge to *Roe* but indicated that it might be prepared to reconsider *Roe* in a future case, Justice Blackmun wrote the following:

> I fear for the future. I fear for the liberty and equality of the millions of women who have lived and come of age in 16 years since *Roe* was decided. I fear for the integrity of, and public esteem for, this Court.[63]

Near the end of his lengthy dissent, he stated the following:

> "[N]ot with a bang, but a whimper," the plurality discards a landmark case of the last generation and casts into darkness the hopes and visions of every woman in this country who had come to believe that the Constitution guaranteed her the right the right to exercise some control over her unique ability to bear children.[64]

He closed with the warning that "the signs are evident and very ominous [that] a chill wind blows."[65] Rarely if ever has a justice written with such anxiety or apprehensiveness. From its outset, *Roe* was an extremely controversial decision. Reasonable people could readily disagree as to its legitimacy and whether it should be overruled. Justice Blackmun's hand wringing over its possible demise suggested a defensiveness and emotional attachment to the decision on his part, arguably inappropriate for a supposedly impartial justice to maintain. Unfortunately, Justice Blackmun continued in the same vein in his concurring and dissenting opinion in *Planned Parenthood v. Casey*, in which the Court declined to overrule *Roe* but did modify it substantially. He wrote that

> [a]ll that remained between the promise of Roe and the darkness of the plurality was a single flickering flame. Decisions since Webster gave

little reason to hope that this flame would cast much light. . . . But now, just when so many expected the darkness to fall, the flame has grown bright. . . . And I fear for the darkness as four Justices anxiously await the single vote necessary to extinguish the light.[66]

This overblown and stilted rhetoric confirmed that Justice Blackmun possessed no poetic attributes. He closed his opinion by noting the following:

I am 83 years old. I cannot remain on this Court forever, and when I do step down, the confirmation process for my successor well may focus on the issue before us today. That, I regret, may be exactly where the choice between the two worlds will be made.[67]

This final comment confirmed the degree to which Justice Blackmun viewed the battle over *Roe* as a personal crusade on his part to preserve a decision in which he had invested so much emotional energy. In these dissents Justice Blackmun engaged in lengthy and careful legal analysis of the opinions he criticized, making a strong case that the changes the plurality in each favored were legally unsound. He should have left it at that. His personalized, emotionally charged rhetoric in these dissents fell flat and is embarrassing rather than inspiring.

VIII. Rhetoric Wars

Occasionally, the majority and the dissent will become engaged in a rhetorical battle. In *Zorach v. Clausen*, after paying homage to the principle of separation between church and state, Justice Douglas proclaimed that "[w]e are a religious people whose institutions presuppose a Supreme Being."[68] In the course of upholding the released time program at issue, he concluded that "[w]e cannot read into the Bill of Rights . . . a philosophy of hostility to religion."[69] The dissenters objected to this rhetoric as unfair. Justice Black, dissenting, criticized "the Court's legal exaltation of the orthodox and its derogation of unbelievers."[70] Justice Jackson seemed to take particular offense to the majority's rhetoric, declaring that

[a]s one whose children, as a matter of free choice, have been sent to privately supported Church schools, I may challenge the Court's

suggestion that opposition to this plan can only be antireligious, atheistic, or agnostic. My evangelistic brethren confuse an objection to compulsion with an objection to religion.[71]

He went on to condemn the "epithetical jurisprudence used by the Court . . . to beat down those who oppose pressuring children into some religion. . . ."[72] It seems obvious that Justice Douglas had managed to get under Justice Jackson's skin in *Zorach*. Justice Douglas's "we are a religious people" statement has assumed a life of its own and is often repeated, both in judicial opinions and in political debate over the church and state issue. It may well be that Justice Jackson was particularly irritated, recognizing that that would almost certainly be the case.

※ IX. Colorful Rhetoric

Occasionally, a justice will use rhetoric to add color or personality to an opinion, sometimes with a humorous twist. In *Browning-Ferris Industries v. Kelco Disposal, Inc.*, where the Court held that the word *fine* in the Excessive Fines Clause was not intended to include civil damages, Justice O'Connor dissented, quoting William Shakespeare in *Romeo and Juliet*, where Prince Escalus states the following:

> But I'll amerce you with so strong a fine, That you shall all repent the loss of mine.[73]

Justice O'Connor noted that Shakespeare used the word *amerce*, signifying civil damages and fine interchangeably, implying that at least in the late sixteenth century there was no perceived difference between the two.[74] This caused Justice Rehnquist, writing for the majority, to take up the poet's pen and write:

> Though Shakespeare, of course, Knew the Law of his time,
> He was foremost a poet, In search of a rhyme.[75]

Justice Scalia has established a reputation for colorful and memorable rhetoric especially in dissent. For instance in *Lambs Chapel v. Moriches Union*

Free School District,[76] he criticized the Court's sporadic reliance on the *Lemon* test for analyzing establishment clause issues as follows:

> Like some ghoul in a late-night horror movie that repeatedly sits up in its grave and shuffles abroad, after being repeatedly killed and buried, *Lemon* stalks our Establishment Clause jurisprudence once again, frightening the little children and school attorneys. . . .

Likewise in his dissent in *Lee v. Weisman*[77] Justice Scalia was critical of the majority's conclusion that a student attending a public school graduation ceremony at which a prayer had been delivered had been subtly coerced into endorsing or participating in the religious ceremony. Justice Scalia replied that:

> We indeed live in a vulgar age. But surely "our social conventions,". . . have not coarsened to the point that anyone who does not stand on his chair and shout obscenities can reasonably be deemed to have assented to everything said in his presence."[78]

Rhetoric such as this by Justice Scalia certainly catches and holds the attention of and is remembered by the reader. Many other examples could be cited as well.

X. Conclusion

Rhetoric is not a means of interpreting the Constitution. Stirring rhetoric does not itself provide a reliable source of constitutional meaning. However, it can play a significant role in cementing a particular interpretation into the fabric of constitutional law. A well-turned description of a constitutional principle or an evocative explanation of its rationale will be inspiring and will be cited and quoted for decades if not centuries to come. Consequently, justices who were capable of explaining their approaches with effective rhetoric, such as Holmes, Brandeis, and Jackson, have had a greater impact upon the development of constitutional law than almost certainly would otherwise have been the case.

Yet rhetoric does have its dangers. Just as it can be persuasive, it can also be misleading, sometimes obscuring rather than clarifying analysis. Figures of speech such as metaphors can sometimes be enlightening but can often complicate rather than simplify analysis. Moreover, evocative and memorable rhetoric is not easy to produce. Few Supreme Court justices have had the gift of truly elegant expression. Clumsy or hollow attempts at creating enduring rhetoric can be both embarrassing and counterproductive. Supreme Court justices are not chosen for their ability to write unforgettable opinions. Indeed, most of the Supreme Court's work, even in the area of constitutional interpretation, does not lend itself to nor is aided by evocative exposition. Occasionally it does, and we have been fortunate to have had several justices who were indeed capable of expounding constitutional principles in language that captures their essence and continues to inspire readers decades later.

THIRTEEN

Synthesis

MOST OF THIS BOOK has been devoted to pulling specific interpretive methods out of the cases and examining them discretely in isolation from the remainder of the case. This is useful, indeed necessary, to create understanding of the details of these methods and the ways in which they are employed by the Court. It is rare, however, for the Court to rely on only one methodology in deciding a major case. All of these methods of interpretation have long been and continue to be influential because they can be quite persuasive. In explaining why a case has been decided in a particular manner, in criticizing a decision in a dissenting opinion, or in defending an opinion against such criticism, a justice will almost certainly use every weapon available. Thus, it is not uncommon for an opinion to rely on a variety of different interpretive methods, to the point where it is difficult—if not impossible—to attribute the result to any particular approach. Thus, a study of how the Court interprets the Constitution and explains its decisions would not be complete without some consideration of how the Court weaves these different methods together, as well as how concurring and dissenting opinions rely on alternative methods to reach different results than the majority. This chapter will work through five important cases, each from a different period in the Court's history in order to illustrate how the Court synthesizes the different interpretive methods into a coherent justification for its decision.

I. *Cohens v. Virginia*

Cohens v. Virginia is one of Justice Marshall's classic opinions on judicial review. He had previously established that the Court could invalidate an act of Congress as inconsistent with the Constitution in *Marbury v. Madison.* The Court also established its power to strike down an act of a state legislature as unconstitutional in *Fletcher v. Peck.* And in *Martin v. Hunter's Lessee,*

Justice Story, writing for the majority, established that the Court had the constitutional authority to reverse a state court's interpretation of the Constitution. *Cohens* was the final piece in the puzzle. The Court held that it had the authority to reverse a state court's decision in a criminal case on constitutional grounds. As with *Martin, Cohens* involved a battle between the Supreme Court of the United States and the courts of Virginia over the relationship of the federal and state governments under the Constitution. For the most part, Marshall could have written a relatively brief opinion, relying heavily on Justice Story's opinion in *Martin*. Instead, he wrote a full-blown and lengthy opinion, working the case over in detail and using virtually every legal argument available to him. Perhaps he wanted to have his own say on the matter, but more likely he understood that while the precise question raised by the facts was minor, the larger issue raised by Virginia's challenge to the Supreme Court's authority under the Constitution went to the very heart of constitutional structure and indeed could threaten to tear the country apart, as it ultimately did several decades later.

Cohens was convicted of selling a lottery ticket in violation of a prohibition passed by the state legislature.[1] In state court he relied unsuccessfully on the fact that a federal law permitted the sale of lottery tickets.[2] Because the trial court was the highest state court that could hear his case, he brought his appeal directly to the Supreme Court of the United States.[3]

Justice Marshall began his opinion proclaiming that if the contentions of the state were accepted dire consequences would follow for the Union, because it would be unable to enforce its laws and there would be an extreme lack of uniformity.[4] Thus at the very outset, Marshall blended arguments of rhetoric, structure, and consequences to impress upon the reader that, as he put it, the issue before the Court was of "great magnitude."[5] Had he cited *Martin v. Hunter's Lessee* on this point, he could have relied on precedent as well.

Marshall then turned directly to the text of Article III, noting that it gave the Court jurisdiction both over types of cases based on subject matter, those "arising under," and others based on the nature of the parties, such as the state and a citizen of another state.[6] Marshall relied on the explicit text to refute the state's structural argument that, under a Constitution maintaining a federal system, it would be unwarranted for a federal court to assert jurisdiction over a decision from a state court.[7] Here again, Marshall was simply repeating an argument made previously by Justice Story in *Martin*; however, it was equally applicable here.

At that point Marshall blended textual and structural arguments with even a nod to original understanding. He pointed out that the people had been taught by experience that "a close and firm Union [was] essential to their liberty and to their happiness" and thus adopted the present Constitution "in the conventions in their respective States."[8] This was an obvious though implicit reference to the experience under the Articles of Confederation and an explicit reference to the framing generation's response. Having bestowed upon his interpretation the aura of original understanding, he immediately bolstered it with the text of the Supremacy Clause, proclaiming it "the authoritative language of the American people; and . . . of the American States."[9] Rhetorically Marshall explained that this text is binding on the states, even under their own state sovereignty–based compact theory.

Justice Marshall then made a textual/structural argument explaining that the Constitution grants great powers to the Congress, which obviously cut deeply into the sovereignty of the states, and so it is with the judicial power as well.[10] This led Marshall to conclude that his structural vision of a powerful federal government, at least within areas of constitutionally enumerated power, overrides Virginia's competing structural vision of semiautonomous states.[11] Marshall used text skillfully to reenforce his structural argument.

At that point, Marshall turned back to the text, echoing but not citing *Martin* again with the argument that the structure or spirit of the Constitution could hardly exclude states from the jurisdiction of federal courts when in several instances Article III makes such jurisdiction dependent upon the fact that the state is a party to the litigation. Next, Marshall raised the consequentialist argument that a denial of federal jurisdiction over state courts could lead to a pattern of defiance of federal law within the states, and, even if such was an unlikely occurrence, recognizing federal impotence might well encourage it.[12]

Turning again without citing it to perhaps the strongest argument set forth by Story in *Martin*, the need for uniformity with respect to the interpretation and application of federal law, Marshall built a structural/textual argument by contrasting the importance of judicial independence under the federal Constitution with the lack thereof in many states.[13] This provided a solid argument in favor of federal jurisdiction over state cases raising federal issues. As was the case in *Martin*, there was simply no adequate counterargument to this point.

Marshall followed with another originalist reference to the failures of the Articles of Confederation, noting the inability of the federal government during that period to enforce legal obligations against the states.[14] As against the state's argument that in time of massive state defiance, "parchment stipulations" would not save the Union, Marshall essentially replied pragmatically that something is better than nothing.[15]

He then turned back to the textualist canon that no word or phrase in the Constitution should be viewed as mere surplus. He used this conclusion to reject the state's structural argument that there is no need for federal jurisdiction over a suit between a state and its own citizens because there is no reason to believe that a state would be prejudiced against its own citizens.[16] Marshall replied that such an argument ignores the fact that Article III also provides jurisdiction for cases "arising under" the Constitution, and it is certainly possible that a citizen can be involved in a case with its own state, such as the one before the Court in which a federal question has been raised.[17]

Having established that the Constitution can and does provide the Supreme Court with jurisdiction over cases involving states, a point that had already been resolved by *Martin*, Chief Justice Marshall then addressed the state's argument that such jurisdiction could only be exercised as an original rather than as an appellate matter because the Constitution provided for original jurisdiction when the state is a party.[18] Marshall pointed out, however, that the Constitution also provided for appellate jurisdiction for cases "arising under" federal law, and certainly the state could be a party to such a case.[19] Marshall then set for himself the task of construing the document "as to give effect to both provisions, as far as it is possible to reconcile them, and not to permit their seeming repugnancy to destroy each other."[20] He attempted this reconciliation by reading these provisions to mean that "the framers designed to include in the first class those cases in which jurisdiction is given, because a State is a party; and to include in the second, those in which jurisdiction is given, because the case arises under the constitution or a law."[21] This construction was supported by the canon that the Constitution should be construed to ensure that all of its provisions carried meaning.

Marshall supported his reading by combining an argument based upon the apparent purpose of the text with a consequentialist argument. Textually, he conceded that sometimes affirmative text implies a negative, but not where such a reading would defeat the purpose of the provisions in question.[22] In this instance, Marshall argued that this would be true because important cases involving federal law could arise after the cases had been commenced or states or foreign nations could be sued in state courts.[23]

In either case, reading a grant of jurisdiction on one basis to prohibit the exercise on the other would preclude the Court from hearing cases that Article III almost certainly intended it to hear.[24] This was an example of Marshall illustrating, based on potential consequences, that it was highly unlikely that Virginia's reading could be correct.

Given that Marshall was so often writing on a blank slate, he did not need to address precedent to the extent that a later Court would. However, in *Cohens*, his reading of Article III was arguably in conflict with language in his own landmark opinion in *Marbury v. Madison*. Consequently, he found it necessary to distinguish *Marbury*.[25] He began by cautioning that dicta in prior cases should be considered but not given controlling effect.[26] In *Marbury*, Justice Marshall had relied upon the canon that an affirmative in the text implies a negative in support of his conclusion that the Article III division between original and appellate jurisdiction precluded Congress from creating original where the Constitution only authorized appellate.[27] To the extent that the language in *Marbury* suggested that a case that could be heard in original could never be taken to the Court in its appellate jurisdiction, Marshall cautioned that the principle was laid down "in terms much broader than the decision."[28] Thus, Marshall maintained that the application of the canon made sense on the facts of *Marbury* but not with respect to those of *Cohens*.[29] Consequently, Marshall concluded that under Article III, the Court may be authorized to exercise appellate jurisdiction in all cases arising under the Constitution or laws of the United States, even if the state is a party.[30]

Marshall then turned to the state's argument that the Eleventh Amendment, which barred a suit against a state by a citizen of another state, prohibited the appeal. Marshall began consideration of this argument with an appeal to the original understanding of the amendment supported by textual analysis. Citing nothing but relying on the common understanding of the relatively recent events that had led to the adoption of the Eleventh Amendment, Marshall explained that it was indeed the product of the filing of lawsuits in states by out-of-state creditors.[31] Turning to the text, he explained that the purpose of the amendment could not have been to protect the dignity of states against having to appear in court because Article III clearly provided jurisdiction over suits against states by other states or by foreign states.[32] Because the amendment was passed in response to suits by creditors, Marshall concluded that it was concerned with lawsuits prosecuted by individuals and not lawsuits in general.[33] Then, in a close and lawyerly reading of the text of the amendment, Marshall argued that the "commencement" or "prosecution" of a "suit" meant the initiation of a legal proceeding in a court and did not contemplate the continuation of such a proceeding through an appeal.[34] Thus, a criminal proceeding brought by the state against an individual is not converted into a suit by the individual against the state within the Eleventh Amendment simply because the individual appeals his conviction to the Supreme Court.[35]

Marshall then addressed Virginia's claim, which the Court had previously rejected in *Martin*, that the Supreme Court could not constitutionally exercise jurisdiction "over the judgment of a State Court."[36] This was once again essentially, as Marshall well understood, a fundamental argument over the very nature of the United States of America. As such, he turned to structural argument to make the case for a close-knit federal Union and government created by the people.[37] As he put it "the American people are one; and the government which is alone capable of controlling and managing their interests . . . is the government of the Union."[38] As such, the federal government must be able to "control all individuals or governments within the American territory."[39]

Continuing with his structural argument, Marshall explained that it was appropriate that the federal judiciary be entrusted with the construction of federal law, and a principle that prohibited the Supreme Court from reviewing an interpretation of federal law by a state court would undermine this ability, as well as the need for uniform construction of federal law.[40] Having established a structural vision of a strong Union with a judiciary capable of interpreting federal law, Marshall cited the text, noting that it gave the federal courts jurisdiction of all cases arising under such laws.[41] He then turned to the original understanding for further support. First, he noted that the very point of the framing of the Constitution was to produce a more powerful and effective central government.[42] Even under the far weaker and more state-oriented Articles of Confederation, federal courts had jurisdiction to hear appeals from state courts in prize cases.[43]

At that point, Marshall invoked the *Federalist Papers*, which he characterized as a "great authority" and "a complete commentary on our constitution."[44] He quoted at length from a passage in the Federalist that stated quite explicitly that the Supreme Court's appellate jurisdiction "ought to be construed to extend to the State tribunals."[45] He also pointed out that an authority equal in stature to the Federalist, the First Congress, composed of many "eminent members of the Convention," passed the act providing the Supreme Court with appellate jurisdiction over state tribunals.[46] In an era in which arguments of original understanding were not well developed,

Marshall made a strong originalist case based on a combination of well-understood purpose, pre-Constitutional practice, the *Federalist Papers*, and the action of the First Congress. A modern Court would have certainly employed more citations to authority; however, the basic line of reasoning would have been the same.

Turning to tradition and practice, Marshall noted that with a single exception (presumably Virginia) state courts had readily accepted the Supreme Court's appellate jurisdiction over their decisions construing federal law.[47] Finally, he dismissed the argument of Virginia that Supreme Court appellate jurisdiction over state courts would convert the state courts into federal courts as exaggerated rhetoric, ultimately based on an incorrectly narrow conception of the nature of the federal Union.[48] Marshall then finished the opinion with consideration of the state's statutory argument that the Judiciary Act did not cover the cases in issue.

Cohens is not Marshall's or the Marshall Court's best opinion. It is neither as magisterial nor as important as *McCulloch*, and on the basic issue before the Court it is not as tight and lawyerly as Justice Storey's opinion in *Martin v. Hunter's Lessee*. However, it is an excellent example of Chief Justice Marshall, our greatest expounder of the Constitution, easily blending textual, structural, originalist, and precedential arguments into a powerful defense of the Court's decision and of foundational constitutional principle.

🎞 II. The *Slaughter-House Cases*

The *Slaughter-House Cases*[49] constituted the first opportunity for the Court to construe the recently enacted Fourteenth Amendment. The majority and the three dissents produced opinions that have had a significant impact on the direction of constitutional law ever since. Following the Civil War and as part of Reconstruction, the Fourteenth Amendment was ratified in 1868. Four years later in the *Slaughter-House Cases*, the Court rejected a challenge to a Louisiana law that had created a monopoly for one group of butchers in the city of New Orleans. In the process, the Court worked over the recently passed Thirteenth and Fourteenth Amendments in detail.

Justice Miller delivered the opinion of the Court. He began his analysis by citing Chancellor Kent and Justice Shaw of the Massachusetts Supreme Court for the proposition that the state has broad authority to regulate private property and activities for the public good pursuant to "the police power."[50] He then cited several leading Supreme Court cases, including

Gibbons v. Ogden, City of New York v. Miln, and the *License Cases* to establish that as a matter of constitutional precedent, the states did indeed have extensive regulatory powers over local affairs that were beyond the scope of congressional regulation.[51]

Focusing on to the Reconstruction Amendments, Justice Miller acknowledged that the decision in this case was of the most importance.[52] He immediately turned his attention to the purpose and original understanding of the Reconstruction Amendments, which, as he acknowledged, "is fresh within the memory of us all."[53] In this respect, the cases presented the highly unusual situation in which the relevant and important original understanding upon which the Court would rely was for the most part not a matter of distant history but rather of nearly current events. At that point, Justice Miller provided a short history of the events leading up to the adoption of the Thirteenth Amendment, including the Civil War and the abolition of slavery.[54]

Addressing the text of the Thirteenth Amendment, Justice Miller explained that its "two short sections seem hardly to admit of construction, so vigorous is their expression and so appropriate to the purpose...."[55] Thus for Justice Miller and the majority, this was an instance in which the plain meaning of the text should easily prevail. This led the Court to conclude that the obvious meaning of the term *servitude* in the amendment was something akin to slavery and not a common law servitude on property.[56]

Turning then to the Fourteenth Amendment, Justice Miller again relied upon the history leading to its passage, especially the enactment in Southern states of Black Codes designed to deny recently freed slaves any significant legal rights or protection.[57] Despite the fact that the Thirteenth and Fourteenth Amendments were written in general terms, the Court concluded that both their text as well as "events, almost too recent to be called history" establish that "the one pervading purpose" was to provide freedom and legal protection to recently freed slaves.[58] Thus, by combining text with original understanding, the majority determined that though the language was not limited to the protection of recently freed slaves, it should at least be read in light of that purpose.[59]

Focusing specifically on the phrase "citizens of the United States" as set forth in the first sentence of the Fourteenth Amendment, Justice Miller explained that the point of recognizing and defining this concept was to overrule the *Dred Scott* decision and thereby establish that the recently freed slave were citizens.[60] Sticking with the text of the first sentence, the Court noted that it clearly distinguished U.S. and state citizenship.[61] This caused the Court to conclude that the reference in the next sentence to "privileges or immunities of citizens of the United States" must have been intended to exclude those of state citizens because "the change in phraseology was adopted understandingly and with a purpose."[62]

Because the plaintiffs were relying on the Privileges or Immunities Clause of the second sentence, it was crucial that the Court come to grips with those privileges or immunities that were dependent upon U.S. citizenship.[63] That led Justice Miller to construe this language in terms of original understanding, related textual provisions, and its purpose and precedent. He noted that the phrase "privileges and immunities" of state citizens first appeared in the Articles of Confederation.[64] Similar language was then placed in Article IV of the Constitution in an effort to achieve the same type of protection.[65] To define the meaning of this language, Justice Miller turned to precedent, most particularly Justice Washington's circuit court opinion in *Corfield v. Coryell*, in which he defined privileges and immunities of state citizenship as the "fundamental rights" of citizens of free governments.[66] The Court concluded that this was intended to encompass "nearly every civil right for the establishment and protection of which organized government is instituted."[67] The Court quoted its decision in *Paul v. Virginia* for a similar understanding.[68] Thus, at least prior to the passage of the Fourteenth Amendment, these rights were created and protected by the states. The only role of the federal government under Article IV was to secure the same degree of protection against a state government for out-of-state citizens that in-state citizens received.[69]

Consequently, the question that Justice Miller then posed was whether the passage of the Fourteenth Amendment was intended to change that understanding and vest in the federal government the authority to protect the basic civil rights of citizens against infringement by their own state governments.[70] Relying on its conception of the structural relationship between the federal and state governments and the extent to which construing the clause would empower Congress and the federal courts to intrude upon the preexisting domain of the state governments, the Court concluded that "no such results were intended by the Congress which proposed these amendments, nor by the legislatures of the States which ratified them."[71] Thus, through a combined structural/consequential argument the majority concluded that the Privileges or Immunities Clause of the Fourteenth Amendment was incapable of protecting the type of basic rights to pursue a profession implicated in the case.

Then in dicta, Justice Miller suggested some of the rights that might be protected by the privileges and immunities of U.S. citizenship, such as the right to come to the seat of government, the right to receive protection by the federal government on the high seas, the right to peaceably assemble, and the right to avail oneself to habeas corpus, in order to show that his interpretation had not robbed the clause of all meaning.[72]

Having rejected the petitioners' privileges and immunities argument, the Court focused briefly on the other two substantive clauses of sentence two of the Fourteenth Amendment—Due Process of Law and Equal Protection. The Court quickly dismissed the due process argument, noting that the Fifth Amendment and many state constitutions contained similar if not identical clauses and none had ever been construed to reach the type of regulation in issue.[73] As for equal protection, the Court, relying on its conception of the purpose of the clause as deduced from its history, concluded that it was unlikely that it would ever be held to provide protection against anything other than racial discrimination.[74]

Finally, Justice Miller addressed what is probably the strongest argument against the result that the Court reached; that is, that its conception of the federal structure reflected a pre-Civil War understanding that the Reconstruction Amendments were most definitely intended to change. He acknowledged the force of this argument but concluded that, while the Reconstruction Amendments were certainly designed to place new limitations upon the states, they were not intended "to destroy the main features of the general system" then in existence.[75]

Whether right or wrong, Justice Miller, writing for the majority in the *Slaughter-House Cases*, produced a careful and lawyerly opinion that wove together text, original (though very recent) understanding, structure, precedent, and consequential reading to defend what is admittedly a narrow reading of the Thirteenth and Fourteenth Amendments.

Justice Field filed a lengthy dissent. He acknowledged that the police power was quite broad but argued that it did not extend to depriving a person of his right to pursue his calling.[76] He did not ultimately rely on the Thirteenth Amendment; however, he did observe that the term *involuntary servitude* was intended to cover more than slavery.[77] Moreover, the Civil Rights Act of 1866, passed pursuant to the enforcement provisions of the Thirteenth Amendment, arguably covered the conduct in issue, suggesting that it fell within the broad scope of the amendment.[78] Thus, in a relatively brief treatment of the Thirteenth Amendment, Justice Field relied both on text and original understanding to suggest a broader interpretation than had the majority.

He then turned to the Fourteenth Amendment, which he explained was at the heart of the case.[79] He began by stating that the purpose of the amendment was to provide a secure constitutional basis for the Civil Rights Act previously passed pursuant to the Thirteenth Amendment and "to place the common rights of American citizens under the protection of the National government."[80] Thus, at the outset, Justice Field understood the Fourteenth Amendment as doing precisely what the majority had concluded that it did not do.

Justice Field explained that prior to the Civil War there was a debate both in Congress and in the Supreme Court—as exemplified in the *Dred Scott* decision—over whether a person could be a citizen of the United States without first being a citizen of a state.[81] He pointed out that the first sentence of the text of the Fourteenth Amendment effectively ended that debate, recognizing that those born in the United States are citizens of the United States and of the state wherein they reside.[82]

Focusing on the text, Justice Field contended that it did not create privileges or immunities but merely recognized those that already existed.[83] Relying on the canon that the text should be read to avoid surplus, Justice Field argued that the majority's reading would reduce the Privileges or Immunities Clause to nothing because all of the rights it deemed to be covered were already independently protected by the Constitution in any event.[84] This led Justice Field to inquire, "[w]hat, then, are the privileges and immunities which are secured against abridgment by State legislation?"[85] To answer that question, Justice Field turned to the original understanding of the amendment, most particularly the need to provide a firm constitutional basis for the Civil Rights Act of 1866.[86]

He then worked through the same historical sources as the majority.[87] He quoted Justice Washington's opinion in *Corfield v. Coryell* at even greater length than did the Court.[88] Although Justice Washington in Coryell was construing Article IV, which by its terms only applied to the privileges and immunities of state citizenship, Justice Field pointed out that in the debate over the passage of the Civil Rights Act of 1866, Senator Trumbull quoted the passage from *Coryell* as indicative of the scope of privileges and immunities of U.S. citizenship as well.[89] This convinced Justice Field that the purpose of the Privileges or Immunities Clause of the Fourteenth Amendment was to provide the same type of protection against "hostile and discriminating legislation" by state governments against in-staters that Article IV provided against out-of-staters.[90] Justice Field then provided a lengthy history from Common Law England, through colonial America as well as post-constitutional state law to illustrate the degree to which monopolies over trades were considered inconsistent with the basic rights of citizens.[91]

Relying on essentially the same text and to a large degree the same original understanding sources as the majority, Justice Field made a forceful argument that the text and well-understood purpose of the Privileges or Immunities Clause was quite the opposite of the majority's interpretation.

Justice Bradley also filed a dissenting opinion. Like Justice Field, he reasoned that the Fourteenth Amendment confirmed the primacy of U.S. citizenship.[92] As with Justice Field then, the central interpretive issue was to determine what are the privileges or immunities of U.S. citizenship.[93] Declaring that "citizenship means something,"[94] Justice Bradley turned to history in an attempt to determine exactly what that might be. He maintained that "[t]he people of this country brought with them to its shores the rights of Englishmen."[95] He then traced the development and nature of these rights from the Magna Carta through Blackstone to the colonial governments and the Declaration of Independence.[96] Like Justice Field, Justice Bradley found that the right to pursue a common calling was easily included within the privileges or immunities of citizenship, but in addition he indicated that it was an aspect of liberty or property protected by due process of law as well.[97]

As with the majority and Justice Field, Justice Bradley quoted extensively from Justice Washington's opinion in *Corfield v. Coryell* but he did acknowledge like the majority that Justice Washington was only speaking of the privileges and immunities of state citizenship. Whether or not *Coryell* was pertinent, Justice Bradley maintained that an expansive catalog of the privileges or immunities of U.S. citizenship could be gleaned from the Bill of Rights as well as from common understanding, and the right to pursue a common calling would certainly be included among them.[98]

Turning then to both common understanding and English history, Justice Bradley argued that restricting the right of persons to pursue a common calling could not possibly qualify as a legitimate police power regulation.[99] Returning to the text of the amendment, Justice Bradley argued that the monopoly in question clearly violated the Privileges or Immunities Clause and moreover constituted a violation of both liberty and property protected by the Fourteenth Amendment's Due Process Clause.[100] The latter conclusion would serve as one of the foundation stones for the substantive due process approach that the majority of the Court would adopt within a decade and that would play a dominant role in its jurisprudence for the next fifty years.

In response to the majority's claim that the purpose of the Fourteenth Amendment was to guarantee the rights of recently freed slaves, Justice Bradley pointed out that "the language is general, embracing all citizens, and I think it was purposely so expressed."[101] In other words, the plain meaning of the text overrides speculation as to its purpose. Finally, again in response to one of the majority's primary concerns, Justice Bradley argued that there was no reason to believe that a generous construction of Privileges or Immunities would lead to significant congressional intrusion into the state domain because the clause only protected fundamental rights that are already well defined.[102]

Justice Swayne also added a dissenting opinion. He began by arguing that indeed the Reconstruction Amendments did radically change the relationship of the federal government and the states. As he put it, they "rise to the dignity of a new Magna Charta."[103] For Justice Swayne, the language of the first section of the Fourteenth Amendment was so clear that " [t]here is no room for construction."[104] As such, there was no basis for the majority's conclusion that the amendment would protect only against racial discrimination.[105] Therefore, the decision turned "what was meant for bread into a stone."[106] He closed by noting that "I earnestly hope that the consequences to follow may prove less serious and far reaching than the minority fear they will be."[107] His fears were indeed justified, however, in that the impact of the decision was to minimize the significance of the Privileges or Immunities Clause, which had arguably been intended as the centerpiece of post-Civil War protection of civil rights and liberties against the states.

The *Slaughter-House Cases* presented a constitutional controversy of the greatest significance, as all of the justices recognized. It was the Court's first opportunity to construe the recently enacted Fourteenth Amendment, and it would have a lasting impact on constitutional law. By a narrow margin the Court construed all of the provisions of the amendment, virtually eliminating the Privileges or Immunities Clause as a significant provision. In so doing, the majority and all three of the dissenting opinions relied upon the text and essentially the same background sources but read them quite differently. Relying on its conception of the purpose of the text, its understanding of federal structure and the consequences that might follow from a contrary decision, the Court concluded that none of the provisions of either the Thirteenth or Fourteenth Amendments should be read to invalidate the monopolies granted by the Louisiana legislature to the butchers. The dissenters reached the opposite conclusion, relying on the plain meaning of the text and a very different conception of the purpose of the

Reconstruction Amendments and the degree to which they had significantly altered constitutional structure with respect to federalism. Over the course of the next 150 years, the dissents' conception of the significance of the Reconstruction Amendments would eventual prevail, although the Privileges or Immunities Clause itself would never recover. The case illustrates the degree to which differences in interpretive approach can have a profound and lasting impact on constitutional law.

▓ III. *Powell v. Alabama*

Decided in 1932, *Powell v. Alabama*[108] is one of the Court's great civil liberties decisions. It involved the infamous "Scottsboro boys" trial, in which several young black men, who the Court described as "ignorant and illiterate" and "residents of other states," were tried and convicted of raping two white women and sentenced to death in court proceedings amid extreme hostility and prejudice.[109] The question before the Court in *Powell* was whether the right to counsel was a fundamental right at least in a capital case and there-fore applicable against the states as an aspect of Fourteenth Amendment due process liberty. Although the trial judge had made a gesture of appointing "all members of the bar" to help the defendants and permitted a lawyer to intervene on their behalf immediately before the trials began, as a practical matter they did not have the assistance of counsel in their trials.[110]

After Justice Sutherland, writing for the majority, stated the facts in a fair amount of detail, he turned his attention to whether due process required appointment of counsel in the cases. To determine whether the right to assistance of counsel was a fundamental aspect of due process liberty, the Court turned to history, as its precedents had determined that historical practice was indeed crucial. It conceded that the right to counsel was not protected in England at the time of the framing of the Constitution.[111] What was crucial to Justice Sutherland, however, was that the English approach had been soundly rejected in colonial America.[112] Citing its own doctrine, the Court explained that due process was defined by prior English practice only to the extent that it was consistent with "the civil and political conditions of our ancestors."[113]

At that point the Court found it necessary to turn to precedent. It acknowl-edged that *Hurtado v. California* had held that Fourteenth Amendment due process did not encompass the right to indictment by a grand jury because the Fifth Amendment contained both the right to indictment and a Due Process Clause, and holding that the latter encompassed the former would seem to render the former redundant.[114] Presumably, the same argument could be made with respect to the Sixth Amendment right to counsel and due process.[115] The Court acknowledged the basic validity of this argument but pointed out that it had also made important exceptions.[116] Justice Sutherland noted that the Court had recognized that the that due process prevented a state from taking private property without just compensation, despite the fact that the Fifth Amendment included the Takings Clause, and it also prevented the state from abridging freedom of speech, despite the fact that the First Amendment includes the Freedom of Speech Clause.[117] Reconciling these precedents, the Court concluded that *Hurtado* simply recognized a presumption rather than a per se rule, and the presumption would be overcome if the Court concluded that the right in question, though explicitly set forth in the Bill of Rights, was nevertheless fundamental in nature.[118] Thus, the Court both cleared a troublesome precedent out of its way and provided some clarity to the law at the same time.

The Court then turned its attention to the question of whether the right to counsel in a capital case was indeed a fundamental aspect of due process. It started its analysis by looking at precedent to define the essence of due process and concluded that at the very least it demanded notice, hearing, and a legally competent tribunal.[119] The Court then looked at American history and practice to conclude that due process "has always included the right to counsel when desired and provided by the party."[120] Then, in a paragraph eloquently describing the role and purpose of the right counsel, the Court detailed how an innocent person unfamiliar with the rules of law might readily be convicted, absent "the guiding hand of counsel at every step of the proceedings against him."[121] This would be especially true with respect to illiterate defendants like those in the case.[122] The Court supported this conclusion with citations and quotations from several of its precedents, lower court precedents, and from Cooley on *Constitutional Limitations* and Cooley's revision of Story's *Commentaries*.[123]

Rather than stating a per se rule that all criminal defendants or criminal defendants in capital cases were entitled to the right to counsel as a matter of due process, the Court instead engaged in a "totality of the circumstances"-type of analysis, emphasizing "the ignorance and illiteracy of the defendants, their youth, the circumstances of public hostility, the imprisonment and the close surveillance of the defendants by the military forces, the fact that their friends and families were all in other states and communication with them necessarily difficult, and above all that they stood in deadly peril of their lives. . . ."[124]

Finally, turning to practice and tradition, the Court pointed out that the federal government and all states had legislation or court rules that required appointment of counsel at the very least in capital cases.[125] The Court concluded its opinion by noting that this provided "convincing support" for its conclusion.[126]

Powell was a cutting-edge case in which the Court not only addressed a previously unresolved issue but created doctrine to address future cases. The Court's flexible and ad hoc totality of the circumstances approach held sway for the next thirty years until it was replaced with a per se rule requiring the appointment of counsel in all felony cases in *Gideon v. Wainwright*.[127]

Powell is one of the Court's great civil liberties decisions. It justified its result and transformed the law with a carefully reasoned opinion, mixing original understanding, purpose, precedent, rhetoric, tradition, and doctrinal creation. It did not take the law to the place where it eventually ended up; however, it started the Court in the right direction with an opinion that provided a solid foundation for further advancement.

🎜 IV. *New York Times v. Sullivan*

New York Times v. Sullivan [128] is one of the Court's landmark cases in the field of freedom of speech. Justice Brennan wrote a truly masterful opinion for the Court in which the law of libel was subjected to First Amendment scrutiny for the first time. In the process he made important pronouncements on freedom of speech principles and devised a doctrinal framework that continues to prevail. The case involved an appeal from a one-half million dollar judgment against the *Times* in a libel suit brought by the Birmingham, Alabama, public affairs commissioner, stemming from a slightly inaccurate advertisement submitted to the paper by a civil rights coalition.[129]

Speaking for the majority Justice Brennan was faced with the task of explaining how the First Amendment could limit the common law of libel, given that it had been taken for granted for over 150 years that libelous speech was not protected by the First Amendment. Borrowing from the brief submitted by Herbert Wechsler on behalf of the *Times*,[130] Justice Brennan set forth a brilliant explanation of why the First Amendment was necessarily implicated, at least when a public official sued for libel based upon statements concerning the performance of his public duties. He quickly disposed of the arguments that there was no state action present and that the advertisement constituted commercial speech unprotected by the First Amendment.[131]

Justice Brennan explained that libel per se, as involved in this case, was a strict liability tort with truth as the sole defense.[132] Initially, he dismissed dicta in two prior cases, suggesting that libel was beyond the scope of the First Amendment, noting that none of the prior cases "sustained the use of libel laws to impose sanctions upon expression critical of the official conduct of public officials."[133] Indeed, in analogous areas, the Court had rejected exclusions from First Amendment coverage with respect to "insurrection, contempt, advocacy of unlawful acts, breach of the peace, obscenity [and] solicitation of legal business."[134] Consequently, precedent did not require rejection of the challenge.[135]

Justice Brennan quoted from several prior decisions for the proposition that speech on public issues was at the heart of the First Amendment. Following a lengthy quote from Justice Brandeis's classic dissent in *Whitney v. California*, Justice Brennan wrote that "we consider this case against the background of a profound national commitment to the principle that debate on public issues should be uninhibited, robust, and wide open. . . ."[136] This statement of First Amendment principle has been quoted repeatedly in subsequent opinions. It emphasizes the democratic or Meiklejohn theory of freedom of speech under which speech on public or governmental issues is at the very core of the First Amendment. Justice Brennan did not create this principle, but, by relying upon it heavily in such an important case, he helped to cement it firmly into First Amendment jurisprudence.

Given that the advertisement in question was a criticism of a public official, the question became whether it forfeited First Amendment protection on account of the falsity of some of the allegations.[137] Again quoting from several precedents, Justice Brennan proclaimed that First Amendment protection was not dependent upon "any test of truth."[138] He explained that in the course of public debate, "erroneous statement is inevitable."[139] As such, freedom of speech needs "breathing space" in order to flourish.[140] Relying on precedent prohibiting criminal contempt citations for criticism of judges, Justice Brennan maintained that the same principle must apply to civil liability with respect to the injury to the reputation of other public officials as well.[141] The precedents in question were not directly on point, to be sure; however, Justice Brennan was able to make use of them by way of analogy.

Faced with explaining why the law of libel was now subject to the First Amendment after having been deemed outside of its coverage for over

170 years, Justice Brennan turned to the historical controversy surrounding the Alien and Sedition Act in the early days of the republic.[142] He noted that the act made it a crime punishable by fine and imprisonment to "publish . . . any false, scandalous and malicious writing or writings against the government."[143] He then pointed out that, although there were several convictions under the act, Madison and Hamilton denounced it vigorously in the Virginia Resolutions, and the persons convicted under the act were pardoned by Jefferson and the fines were repaid by Congress.[144] Though never judicially invalidated, Justice Brennan declared that the verdict of history is that the act was unconstitutional.[145] He then explained that the significance of the Alien and Sedition controversy was that "[w]hat a State may not constitutionally bring about by means of a criminal statute is likewise beyond the reach of its civil law of libel."[146] He noted that in adjusted dollars the libel judgment in issue was 100 times greater than the maximum fine under the Alien and Sedition Act, and, moreover, a civil libel judgment did not carry the protections available in the criminal process.[147] Thus, with a very clever argument, Justice Brennan made the case that a large libel verdict in favor of a public official was inconsistent with the original understanding of the First Amendment.

Justice Brennan then noted that the defense of truth could not save such a libel action from invalidation; an attempt to ensure that statements were true would inevitably result in a chilling effect on speech as it is often difficult to verify the truth of every factual assertion.[148] Thus, there was a need for strategic protection to ensure that speech pertaining to the conduct of public officials was truly unrestrained.[149]

At that point it was necessary to determine to what extent if at all the law of libel and the First Amendment might coexist in a case involving a public official plaintiff. Relying on state law accommodations, especially as expressed in the 1908 Kansas case of *Coleman v. MacLennan*, Justice Brennan settled upon what he termed an "actual malice" standard, that is, in order to recover, the public official must prove that the statement was made with knowledge of falsity or reckless disregard for the truth.[150] He noted that because public officials receive an absolute privilege against libel judgments for criticism of private citizens, at the very least citizen critics should receive a qualified privilege as a matter of fairness.[151]

Applying the newly announced standard, the Court reversed the verdict in question.[152] In addition, Justice Brennan concluded that in a case such as this, the proof would need to meet a clear and convincing evidence standard.[153]

He also concluded that a public official could not recover a judgment for libel when the statements in question were critical of the government but did not name the official.[154] To allow such a recovery would come dangerously close to a forbidden seditious libel law. Justices Black and Goldberg each wrote concurring opinions, arguing that a libel defendant sued by a public official should receive an absolute rather than a qualified privilege under the First Amendment.[155]

Justice Brennan's opinion for the Court in *New York Times v. Sullivan* is without question one of the great civil liberties opinions in the history of the Court. Relying primarily on precedent, which was never really on point, as well as dicta in prior cases along with free speech principle and history, Justice Brennan brought the law of libel, at least with respect to public officials, within the coverage of the First Amendment for the first time and constructed a doctrinal framework for evaluating such cases. Ultimately, a degree of First Amendment protection was extended to virtually all libel defendants in *Gertz v. Welch*,[156] although not in the manner that Justice Brennan himself would have chosen. The majority opinion in *New York Times v. Sullivan* is an example of constitutional exposition at its finest.

▓ V. *Lee v. Weisman*

The Establishment Clause has consistently provided a particularly rich domain for the study of constitutional interpretation because so many of the methods of interpretation can be applied effectively in this area and because the Court has had so much difficulty reaching any consensus on the proper approach. Consequently, Establishment Clause cases often provide especially strong examples of contrasting interpretive approaches. The relatively recent case of *Lee v. Weisman*,[157] in which the Court invalidated the delivery of a school-sponsored invocation and benediction as part of a middle school graduation ceremony provides such a contrast in approach.

Justice Kennedy wrote the opinion for the 5-4 majority, striking down the prayers. At the outset, Justice Kennedy announced that the case would be governed by the anticoercion principle developed in the Court's school prayer cases from the 1960s, and as such there was no need to consider the significance of the far more recent religious display cases in which the Court's doctrinal approach seemed to be in a state of flux.[158] Thus, Justice Kennedy established that the case would be decided based on precedent, doctrine, and principle but even then on one line of authority rather than another.

Turning to the facts, Justice Kennedy focused immediately on the school's provision of guidelines to the rabbi who wrote and delivered the prayer and explained that pursuant to *Engel v. Vitale*, the Court's New York regent's prayer decision from 1962, the Establishment Clause prohibits state participation in the composition of a prayer, even if the purpose of such participation was to create a relatively nonsectarian prayer.[159] Turning briefly to original understanding, Justice Kennedy quoted Madison's influential "Memorial and Remonstrance" for the proposition that religious liberty was intended to protect the church against corruption by the state as well as the rights of the nonbeliever.[160] This suggested that any attempt by the state to produce acceptable civic religious exercises was inconsistent with this historically grounded, nonparticipation principle. Thus, Justice Kennedy molded an argument based on precedent, doctrine, and original understanding.

He attempted to distinguish freedom of speech principles that clearly permitted the state to sponsor messages the audience might find disagreeable or offensive from freedom of religion principles that banished state participation in the promulgation of religious messages.[161] He attributed this distinction to "the lesson of history" that in the area of religion, the state is likely to indoctrinate and coerce; however, he did not cite any specific examples. Thus, the appeal to originalism at this point was quite superficial.

Justice Kennedy then turned his attention away from the state's participation in the creation and delivery of the prayer to the impact on the student audience. He cited several cases, expressing a special concern with the presence of coercive pressure in elementary and secondary schools.[162] In view of the absence of any legal coercion in this instance, Justice Kennedy declared that the inherent pressure to stand in respectful silence during the invocation and benediction amounted to legally cognizable subtle coercion of the nonbeliever or dissenter.[163] He supported this with citations to academic works discussing the impact of peer group pressure on the young.[164]

This was the crux of the case. Justice Kennedy essentially relied on analogy to attempt to establish that respectful silence at a voluntary graduation exercise was constitutionally equivalent to being forced to participate in or at least witness a prayer in the context of a classroom where attendance was legally mandated. Given the social importance of graduation, Justice Kennedy rejected the stipulation in the record that it was wholly voluntary.[165] He concluded that the very reason why the school supported the prayer—the importance of the event—explained why it should not be considered voluntary in nature.[166] Justice Kennedy then distinguished

Marsh v. Chambers, in which the Court had permitted opening prayers at legislative sessions on the grounds that the case had involved adults who were free to come and go as they pleased.[167] Thus, Justice Kennedy's majority opinion relied almost exclusively on factual analogies to the anticoercion principle derived from the school prayer cases.

Justice Blackmun, writing for Justices Stevens and O'Connor, concurred in the Kennedy opinion but nevertheless wrote a relatively lengthy separate concurrence. Unlike Justice Kennedy, Justice Blackmun considered it important to walk through several of the Court's prior Establishment Clause decisions, including *Everson, Engel, Schempp, Epperson*, and *Lemon*. The point of Blackmun's concurrence seemed to be to emphasize that, although proof of coercion could prove an Establishment Clause violation, it certainly was not essential.[168] Rather that the government was sponsoring or participating in religious activity was enough to render it unconstitutional.[169] As with Justice Kennedy, Justice Blackmun's approach was based on precedent and doctrine; however, Blackmun clearly believed that Kennedy's emphasis on anticoercion doctrine threatened to minimize an equally if not more important doctrinal theme—anti-endorsement or sponsorship. Justice Blackmun continued by arguing that government endorsement of religious belief undermined democratic values.[170]

The Blackmun concurrence, joined by Justice O'Connor, is perhaps best viewed as a continuation in the doctrinal battle that had developed between Justice Kennedy, who favored a coercion-based approach, and Justice O'Connor, who would focus on endorsement as the key concept. The contrast between the Kennedy opinion for the Court and the Blackmun concurrence for three of the five justices in the majority illustrates that even when the Court agrees on a particular interpretive approach, in this case prior doctrine, the justices will often still disagree as to which aspects of doctrine should control.

In addition to the Blackmun concurrence, Justice Souter, who had joined the Kennedy opinion for the majority, also added a concurrence joined by Justices Stevens and O'Connor. Like Justice Blackmun, Justice Souter wrote to emphasize that proof of coercion was not essential to an Establishment Clause claim; however, he also wrote to dispute Justice Scalia's contention in dissent that the Establishment Clause was concerned only with government preference for one religion over another. Like Justice Blackmun, Justice Souter emphasized the Court's decision followed almost automatically from the Court's Establishment Clause precedent beginning with *Everson*.[171]

Justice Souter then turned his attention to the originalist challenge to the precedent set forth judicially by Chief Justice Rehnquist in his dissenting opinion in *Wallace v. Jaffree*.[172] Based on historical scholarship, Chief Justice Rehnquist had argued that the purpose of the Establishment Clause had been to prohibit the government from preferring one religious denomination over another.[173] Justice Souter engaged in a lengthy review of the original understanding in an attempt to discredit that approach. He worked through the drafting of the Religion Clauses of the First Amendment, starting with Madison's initial proposal, which was changed by the House Select Committee, which was in turn changed by Committee of the Whole, which was then changed again by the House.[174] The Senate then went through several drafts, and the Conference agreed to language closer to the House version.[175] Justice Souter showed that although both the House and Senate had at one point adopted language focusing on nonpreferentialism, both ultimately rejected it in favor of language prohibiting "state support for 'religion' in general."[176] Citing the Virginia Bill for Religious Freedom and Madison's "Memorial and Remonstrance" as proof that the framers appreciated the difference between preferential and nonpreferential establishments, Justice Souter concluded that, given the drafting history and the ultimate language of the Establishment Clause, there was no reason to substitute an antipreferentialist approach for the broader approach to which the Court had long adhered.[177] Thus, in response to an originalist argument, Justice Souter presented a solid originalist reply.

Before turning away from the issue, however, Justice Souter added a consequentialist argument to the effect that a nonpreferentialist approach would require the Court to engage in the troublesome task of determining whether a particular belief system was indeed religious and consequently barred from government support by the First Amendment.[178]

In the second part of his opinion, Justice Souter relied on precedent and doctrine to make the argument that there need not be coercion for there to be an Establishment Clause violation.[179] Citing several precedents, Justice Souter pointed out that in the past the Court had invalidated several noncoercive laws under the Establishment Clause.[180] He supported this argument by turning to the text and noting that the language prohibiting laws "respecting" religion would seem to cover more than coercive, state-established churches.[181] Moreover, again focusing on the text, Justice Souter argued that because the Free Exercise Clause would almost certainly prohibit coercion of religious belief, requiring coercion would render the Establishment Clause redundant.[182]

Justice Souter then considered the argument pressed by Justice Scalia in dissent that the context and practices of the framing generation indicated that the Establishment Clause was only intended to apply to coercive practices.[183] He cited Madison's "Memorial and Remonstrance" for a broader principle.[184] With respect to the issuance of religiously oriented Thanksgiving Proclamations, Justice Souter noted that both Jefferson and Madison indicated subsequently that they believed their actions to have been inconsistent with the Establishment Clause.[185] Justice Souter conceded that some of the practices in the early republic, such as paid chaplains for Congress and religiously oriented Thanksgiving Proclamations, are inconsistent with the strong separationist approach of Madison and Jefferson but simply indicate that there was some division of opinion within the framing generation on the issue.[186] He conceded that it was impossible to know how the framing generation understood the Establishment Clause; however, there was enough support for the separationist approach that the Court had taken to warrant its continuance.[187]

Finally, Justice Souter turned to principle and doctrine and attempted to define neutrality as a key concept in Establishment Clause jurisprudence. Applying this principle, he maintained that to be neutral, permissible accommodation of religious belief must lift a burden imposed by government, which was simply not the case with respect to state-sponsored graduation prayer.[188]

Thus, while joining the majority opinion, Justice Souter wrote a lengthy concurrence employing textual analysis, original understanding, precedent, and doctrine designed to reject some of the potential implications of Justice Kennedy's opinion for the Court as well as the arguments raised by the petitioners and by Justice Scalia's dissent, although he did not reference it directly. The fact that four of the five justices who joined the Kennedy opinion for the Court either wrote or joined opinions cautioning against its approach suggests that these justices perceived Justice Kennedy's analysis, which was essential to a majority holding, to be doctrinally troubling for the future of the Establishment Clause jurisprudence.

Justice Scalia wrote a dissent joined by Chief Justice Rehnquist, Justice White, and Justice Thomas. He relied heavily on history and tradition to support his conclusion that graduation prayers were perfectly consistent with the Establishment Clause.[189] Justice Scalia walked through the historical tradition in detail, quoting from the Declaration of Independence, Washington's, Jefferson's, and Madison's inaugural addresses, as well as Washington's first Thanksgiving Proclamation.[190] He then cited the history of Thanksgiving Proclamations by presidents, prayer at the opening of congressional sessions and the opening of the Court's sessions with the invocation "God save the United States and this Honorable Court."[191] More specifically, Justice Scalia noted that history indicated that a prayer was delivered at the first public high school graduation in 1868, during the very same month the Fourteenth Amendment was ratified.[192] Thus, for Justice Scalia and the dissenters, solid history and tradition were more than sufficient to validate the practice.

Justice Scalia then turned to Justice Kennedy's doctrinal approach and attacked the conclusion that there was legally cognizable coercion in the delivery of the graduation prayers with vigor. As a factual matter he objected to the majority's conclusions that attendance at graduation was not voluntary and that standing in silence effectively constituted endorsement or participation.[193] Justice Scalia also challenged the Court's conclusion that school officials had meaningfully participated in the drafting of the prayers.[194] He then argued that, as both a historical and doctrinal matter, the only type of coercion that could lead to an Establishment Clause violation was actual legal coercion.[195] The school prayer cases such as *Engel* and *Schempp* were readily distinguishable on the ground that mandatory attendance laws did constitute actual legal coercion.[196] Finally, Justice Scalia criticized the Court for allowing Establishment Clause jurisprudence to turn on "formulaic abstractions" instead of "long-accepted constitutional traditions."[197]

From the perspective of interpretive methodology, *Lee v. Weisman* is a fascinating case. As is so often true in the area of the Establishment Clause, the justices were deeply divided, not simply in terms of the correct result but also in terms of the appropriate method of analysis. Moreover, the division was not simply between the majority and the dissent but among the justices in the majority as well. Over the course of sixty pages in the United States Reports, the four opinions, each joined by at least three justices, relied upon text, original understanding, tradition, precedent, doctrine, and rhetoric. The justices in the majority agreed that precedent and doctrine were controlling but did not agree on which lines of precedent and which doctrines were of the greatest importance to the resolution of the case. Justices Souter and Scalia both relied on original understanding, the former on the drafting history of the Establishment Clause, the latter on the historical practices around the time of the framing, to reach diametrically opposite conclusions. Justice Kennedy and Justice Souter both found coercion relevant but in radically different ways, with the former relying on psychological coercion while the latter relied on actual legal coercion. *Lee v. Weisman* readily illustrates the flexibility in constitutional interpretation, at least in cutting-edge cases, and how easy it is for the justices to reach well-supported though contrary results through the application of different methodologies.

Notes

Introduction

1 Akhil Amar, *Intratextualism*, 112 Harv. L. Rev. 742 (1999).

Chapter 1 Textualism and Its Canons

1 25 U.S. 419, 437 (1827).

2 5 U.S. 137 (1803).

3 Id. at 176.

4 Id. at 177.

5 Id.

6 See Chapter 6, section II, part A.

7 See, e.g., *Chisholm v. Georgia*, 2 U.S. 419, 431–32 (1793) (Iredell, J.), at 451 (Blair, J.), at 466 (Wilson, J.), 467–69 (Cushing, J.), 477 (Jay, J.).

8 505 U.S. 833, 1000–01 (1992).

9 22 U.S. 1, 188 (1824).

10 Id.

11 Id.

12 See Chapter 2, section II for a detailed discussion of reading constitutional text in light of its purpose.

13 17 U.S. 316, 407 (1819).

14 Id. at 415.

15 Id.

16 Id. at 407. Justice Story had made much the same argument a few years earlier in *Martin v. Hunter's Lessee*, 14 U.S. 304, 326 (1816), noting that "[t]he constitution unavoidably deals in general language."

17 343 U.S. 579, 596 (1952).

18 Id.

19 367 U.S. 497, 540 (1961).

20 Id.

21 Id. at 542–43.

22 See Chapter 5, section V.

23 116 U.S. 616, 635 (1886). See also *Home Building & Loan Assn v. Blaisdell*, 290 U.S. 398, 428 (1934) (the contract clause "is not absolute and is not to be read with literal exactness like a mathematical formula").

24 See *Fisher v. United States*, 425 U.S. 391, 399–401 (1976).

25 277 U.S. 438, 464 (1928).

26 Id.

27 Id. at 472–74.

28 389 U.S. 347 (1967).

29 See, e.g., *Smith v. Maryland*, 442 U.S. 735, 742–46 (1979) (pen register recording numbers called from a telephone is not a search).

30 111 U.S. 53, 57 (1884).

31 Id. at 58 (quoting Worcester).

32 Id. at 58.

33 314 U.S.160, 183 (1941).

34 Id.

35 83 U.S. 36, 78–80 (1872). The Court has read the clause somewhat more broadly in the recent case of *Saenz v. Roe*, 526 U.S. 489 (1999); however, it is too soon to tell whether *Saenz* is simply a unique counterexample to the narrower reading of the clause or whether it portends a more expansive reading in the future. *Saenz* will be discussed in more detail in subsequent chapters.

36 Id. at 90, 93, 106 (Field, J., dissenting), 114–16, 123 (Bradley, J., dissenting), 124–26 (Swayne, J., dissenting).

37 See Chapter I, section V, Chapter 13, section II.

38 *Saenz v. Roe*, 526 U.S. 489, 527–28 (1999) (Thomas, J., dissenting) (suggesting that any effort to read the Privileges or Immunities Clause more broadly should be accompanied by a narrowing of Due Process and Equal Protection).

39 22 U.S. 1, 188 (1824). See also *Heller v. District of Columbia*, 128 S. Ct. 2788 (2008); *United States v. Sprague*, 282 U.S. 716, 731 (1931) ("The Constitution was written to be understood by the voters; its words and phrases were used in their normal and ordinary as distinguished from technical meaning . . .").

40 22 U.S. 1, 189 (1824).

41 Id. at 189–90.

42 Id. at 194.

43 Id. at 196.

44 5 U.S. 137, 175 (1803).

45 In *McCulloch v. Maryland*, Marshall maintained that the word *necessary* in the Necessary and Proper Clause could easily be understood to mean convenient rather than absolutely essential. He made reference to its use "in the common affairs of the world, or in approved authors," although he failed to cite any specific examples. 17 U.S. 316, 413 (1819). See also *Cherokee Nations v. Georgia*, 30 U.S. 1, 16–18 (1831) (Chief Justice Marshall noted the differences between Indian tribes and foreign nations in support of the argument that the ordinary meaning of the former is different from the latter) id. at 21–29 (Justice Johnson made similar arguments). But see Id. at 56–57 (for the argument by Justice Thompson that Indian tribes should be equated with foreign nations). And in *Cohens v. Virginia*, Chief Justice Marshall explained that where the letter of the Constitution would seem to extend jurisdiction to "all cases arising under" it, it must be so understood unless an exemption claimed on the "spirit and true

meaning must be so apparent as to overrule the words which its framers have employed." 19 U.S. 264, 380 (1821). In other words, he seemed to concede that a reading based on spirit or purpose could prevail over relatively plain text, but only if the case for that reading was extremely compelling. Justice Marshall went on to note that the state of Virginia attempted to trump the text in this instance with a structural argument, but he rejected that argument as incorrect. Id. at 380–81.

46 17 U.S. 122 (1819).

47 Id. at 202.

48 14 U.S. 304, 326 (1816). Justice Story relied on this canon on a couple of occasions in the course of his analysis. Id. at 338, 347.

49 Id. at 338. A few years later in *Cohens v. Virginia*, 19 U.S. 264, 383–84 (1821), Chief Justice Marshall made similar arguments in justifying the Supreme Court's hearing of an appeal from a Virginia state court in a criminal case.

50 14 U.S. at 343.

51 Id.

52 Id. at 346.

53 Id. at 347.

54 279 U.S. 655, 679 (1929).

55 Id.

56 Id. at 680.

57 Id. at 681.

58 253 U.S. 221, 227 (1920).

59 521 U.S. 507, 519–20 (1997).

60 457 U.S. 202, 211–15 (1982).

61 494 U.S. 872, 893 (1990).

62 83 U.S. 36 (1872).

63 Id. at 126.

64 See Chapter 13, section II.

65 109 U.S. 3, 11 (1883).

66 Id. at 46–47 (Harlan, J., dissenting).

67 Id.

68 332 U.S. 46, 63 (1947) (Frankfurter, J., concurring).

69 Id. at 74–75.

70 See *District of Columbia v. Heller*, 128 S. Ct. 2783, 2800 (2008) ("the phrase 'Security of a Free State' and close variations seems to have been terms of art in the eighteenth-century political discourse"); *United States v. Verdugo-Urquidez*, 494 U.S. 259, 265 (1990) ("'the people' seems to have been a term of art employed in select parts of the Constitution"); *Williamson v. United States*, 207 U.S. 425, 435–46 (1908) (at the time of the drafting of the Constitution, "breach of peace," as used in the clause prohibiting arrest of legislators, did not mean a misdemeanor as it does today but rather a wide range of crimes constituting a breach of the King's peace).

71 3 U.S. 386, 390 (1798).

72 Id.

73 Id. at 391. See also *Cooley v. Board of Wardens*, 53 U.S. 299, 314 (1851) ("Imposts and duties on imports, exports, and tonnage were then known to the commerce of a civilized world to be as distinct from fees and charges for pilotage"; thus the latter was not covered by the imposts and duties clause).

74 See *Stogner v. California*, 539 U.S. 607, 611–15 (2003).

75 71 U.S. 277 (1866).

76 71 U.S. 333 (1866).

77 Id. at 387 (Miller, J., dissenting).

78 Id. at 388–90.

79 71 U.S. at 325.

80 328 U.S. 303 (1946).

81 Id. at 321.

82 Id.

83 Id. at 323.

84 381 U.S. 437 (1965).

85 Id. at 442.

86 Id. at 462.

87 433 U.S. 425, 471–72 (1977).

88 Id. at 475–76.

89 19 U.S. 264, 405 (1821).

90 Id. at 407.

91 Id. at 407–08.

92 Id. at 408–09.

93 59 U.S. 272, 276 (1855).

94 211 U.S. 78, 100 (1908).

95 Id. at 101.

96 Id. at 105.

97 *Malloy v. Hogan*, 378 U.S. 1 (1964).

98 See Chapter 5, part V.

99 342 U.S. 165, 170 (1952).

100 Id. at n.3.

101 See *Williams v. Florida*, 399 U.S. 78 (1970) (Due Process does not require a twelve-person jury in state criminal case); *Apodaca v. Oregon*, 406 U.S. 404 (1972) (Due Process does not require a unanimous jury in state criminal cases).

102 399 U.S. 78, 99–103 (1970).

103 406 U.S. 404, 410–13 (1972).

104 17 U.S. 316, 414 (1819).

105 See Chapter 2, section I, part A.

106 14 U.S. 304, 374 (1816).

107 Id. at 334.

108 Id. at 334–35.

109 74 U.S. 700 (1868).

110 Id. at 721.

111 Id.

112 Id.

113 Id. at 732–34.

114 506 U.S. 224, 230–31 (1993).

115 Id. at 240.

116 Id. at 241–42.

117 487 U.S. 654, 671 (1988).

118 Id. at 671.

119 Id. at 718–19.

120 Id. at 719–23.

121 *Cohens v. Virginia*, 19 U.S. 264, 391 (1821) (part of the "arising under" jurisdiction would be surplus if jurisdiction was entirely dependent on the character of the parties); *TXO Products Corp v. Alliance Resource Corp.*, 509 U.S. 443, 471 (1993) (Scalia, J., concurring) (reading due process to prohibit excessive awards of punitive damages would render the excessive fines clause meaningless).

122 83 U.S. 36, 96 (1872).

123 110 U.S. 516, 534–35 (1884).

124 Id. See *Adamson v. California*, 332 U.S. 46, 66 (1947) (Frankfurter, J., concurring) (arguing that construing the Due Process Clause as merely summarizing the other provisions of the Bill of Rights would charge "Madison and his contemporaries . . . with writing a meaningless clause").

125 332 U.S. 46, 66 (1947). Likewise in *Poe v. Ullman*, Justice Harlan, dissenting, argued that the very fact that there was a Due Process Clause in the Fifth Amendment counseled against construing the Fourteenth Amendment Due Process Clause as simply incorporating the Bill of Rights against the states as it would render the Fifth Amendment Due Process Clause rather meaningless. 367 U.S. 497, 542 (1961).

126 287 U.S. 45, 67 (1932).

127 381 U.S. 479, 490–91 (1965). But see *Trop v. Dulles*, 356 U.S. 86, 101 n.32 (1958) where the Court suggested that it was unclear "[w]hether the word 'unusual' has any qualitative meaning different from 'cruel'" in the Eighth Amendment; however, it continued by noting that if it does, then it would be "something different from that which is generally done." Id.

128 381 U.S. at 491.

129 Constitution of the United States, Ninth Amendment.

130 514 U.S. 549, 587–89 (1995).

131 Id. See also *Kelo v. City of New London*, 545 U.S. 469, 511 (2005) (Thomas, J., dissenting) (Necessary and Proper Clause would allow government to take property for a "public purpose," so the public use clause must require something different from a mere public purpose or it would be surplus).

132 435 U.S. 765, 799 (1978).

133 Id. at 800–01.

134 356 U.S. 86, 101 n.32 (1958).

135 Id.

136 Id.

137 5 U.S. 137, 174 (1803). See *Strauder v. West Virginia*, 100 U.S. 303, 308 (1879) (the prohibitory language of the Fourteenth Amendment "implies the existence of rights and immunities").

138 5 U.S. at 174.

139 Id.

140 22 U.S. 1, 194–95 (1824).

141 Id. at 195.

142 See *United States v. Lopez*, 514 U.S. 549, 553 (1995) (quoting the above language from *Gibbons* in the course of holding that a law prohibiting a person from bringing a gun into a school zone exceeded congressional power under the Commerce Clause).

143 19 U.S. 264, 395 (1821).

144 Id. at 395.

145 Id. at 394–96.

146 Id. at 397–98.

147 Id. at 400–42.

148 79 U.S. 457, 544–45 (1870).

149 Id. at 545.

150 79 U.S. at 649.

151 Id.

152 381 U.S. 479, 489–90 (1965).

153 317 U.S. 1 (1942).

154 Id. at 40–42.

155 Id.

156 462 U.S. 919, 955 (1983).

157 Id.

158 506 U.S. 224, 230 (1993).

159 22 U.S. 1, 191 (1824).

160 Id.

161 U.S. Constitution, Article I, section 9.

162 22 U.S. 1, 216–17 (1824).

163 25 U.S. 419, 438 (1827).

164 Id.

165 Id.

166 Id.

167 381 U.S. 479, 509 (1965).

168 Id. at 510.

169 389 U.S. 347 (1967).

170 Id. at 351.

171 Id. at 373.

172 Id. at 365.

173 Id. at 350.

174 345 U.S. 461, 473 (1953).

175 545 U.S. 469, 501–02 (2005) (O'Connor, J., dissenting). She cited the cases of *Berman v. Parker*, 348 U.S. 25, 32 (1954) and *Hawaii Housing Authority v. Midkiff*, 467 U.S. 229, 240 (1984) as examples of where the Court had misconstrued the phrases.

176 545 U.S. at 505–06.

177 545 U.S. 1, 69 (2005) (Thomas, J., dissenting).

178 Id.

179 548 U.S. 140, 146 (2006).

180 Id. at 153.

Chapter 2 Intratextualism and Textual Purpose

1 Akhil Amar, *Intratextualism*, 112 Harv. L. Rev. 747 (1999).

2 17 U.S. 316, 412–15 (1819).

3 See *Okanogan v. United States*, 279 U.S. 655, 683 (1929) (the word *house* is used several times in the Constitution and always refers to the chambers assembled and prepared to conduct business rather than in adjournment); *Hawke v. Smith*, 253 U.S. 221, 227–28 (1920) (Framers used the term *legislature* at several points in the Constitution to mean a "representative body which made the laws of the people"); *Morrison v. Olson*, 487 U.S. 654, 719 (1988) (Scalia, J., dissenting) (*inferior* means "subordinate to" in Article III, with respect to inferior courts; so it should carry the same meaning in Article II, with respect to "inferior" officers).

4 17 U.S. at 414–15.

5 Id. at 415.

6 Id. In *Kelo v. City of New London*, 546 U.S. 469, 508–10 (2005), Justice Thomas, dissenting, made a similar argument with respect to the Public Use Clause of the Fifth Amendment. He conceded that contemporary dictionaries recognized that it carried a narrower meaning of "employed by" and a broader meaning of "convenient." He argued that the narrower meaning was correct in that it was the only meaning that made sense in the two other instances in which "use" appeared in the original constitution—the clause stating that duties and imposts shall be for the "use" of the treasury, and the clause giving Congress the right to raise and support Armies but no money should be put to that "use" for more than two years. The canon provides that it should be assumed that words carry the same meaning unless there is some reason to believe that a different meaning is intended. It is certainly quite possible that the framers meant to call forth different meanings of the word *use* in these three instances.

7 14 U.S. 304, 329–30 (1816).

8 410 U.S. 113, 157–58 (1973).

9 Id.

10 Id.

11 494 U.S. 259, 265 (1990).

12 Id.

13 Id.

14 Id.

15 Id. at 276.

16 Id. at 287.

17 128 S. Ct. 2783, 2790 (2008).

18 Id. at 2791.

19 Id. at 2827 (Stevens, J., dissenting).

20 Id. at 2800.

21 Id.

22 Id.

23 Id.

24 330 U.S. 1, 32 (1947).

25 17 U.S. 316, 418–19 (1819).

26 2 U.S. 419, 477 (1793).

27 422 U.S. 806, 820 (1975).

28 Id.

29 Id. at 838–39, 845 (Burger, C. J., dissenting).

30 128 S. Ct. 2783, 2801 (2008).

31 Id.

32 Id. at 2826 (Stevens, J., dissenting).

33 Id. at 2824 (Stevens, J., dissenting).

34 Id. at 2847–48 (Breyer, J., dissenting).

35 See, e.g., *United States v. Brewster*, 408 U.S. 501, 521 (1972) ("the privilege against arrest is not identical with the Speech or Debate privilege, but it is closely related in purpose and origin [thus] [i]t can hardly be thought that [it] totally protects what the sentence preceding it has plainly left open to prosecution, i.e., all criminal acts."); *Escobedo v. Illinois*, 378 U.S. 478, 497 (1964) (White, J., dissenting) (incongruous to read the Sixth Amendment right to counsel as limiting custodial interrogation when the Fifth Amendment privilege against self-incrimination was meant to deal with the admissibility of confessions).

36 14 U.S. 304, 329–31 (1816).

37 Id. at 339–40.

38 Id. at 340 quoting Article VI, U.S. CONST.

39 Id. at 341–42. He gave the examples of the Contract Clause raised in defense in a state civil case or the Ex Poste Facto Clause raised in defense in a state criminal case.

40 *Eldred v. Ashcroft*, 537 U.S. 186, 218–19 (2003), the Court relied on the fact that the Copyright Clause and the First Amendment were added to the Constitution nearly contemporaneously as some proof that the framers believed that copyright could readily coexist with freedom of speech. Moreover, the Court argued that the aims of these provisions were compatible in that the very purpose of copyright was to encourage the production of the type of expressive material protected by the First Amendment. Id.

41 19 U.S. 264 (1821).

42 Id. at 393.

43 Id. at 393–94.

44 Id. at 383.

45 Id. at 426.

46 Id.

47 Id.

48 32 U.S. 243, 248–49 (1833).

49 Id.

50 Id. at 250.

51 30 U.S. 1 (1831).

52 Id. at 18.

53 Id.

54 Id. at 19.

55 Id. Marshall was obviously responding to Justice Thompson's argument in dissent that words sometimes do carry different meanings in different clauses.

56 Id. See *United States v. Lopez*, 514 U.S. 549, 587 (1995) (Thomas, J., concurring) (arguing that the reference in the Commerce Clause to commerce with Indian tribes and foreign nations makes more sense if commerce is limited to trade as opposed to manufacturing, and that the Port of Preference Clause also supports the narrower reading of the word *commerce*).

57 30 U.S. at 42–43.

58 83 U.S. 36, 74 (1872).

59 Id.

60 501 U.S. 957, 978 n.9 (1991).

61 347 U.S. 497 (1954).

62 Id. at 499.

63 Id.

64 Id. at 500.

65 428 U.S. 153, 177 (1976).

66 376 U.S. 1, 22 (1964).

67 Id. at 25–26.

68 Id. at 26.

69 Id. at 26–33.

70 Id. at 29–30.

71 See also *Reynolds v. Sims*, 377 U.S. 533, 611–12 (1964) (Harlan, J., dissenting) (for an argument that if the framers of the Fourteenth Amendment had intended to cover discrimination with respect to voting rights, there would have been no need for the Fifteenth Amendment prohibiting exclusion from the franchise based on race, and the Nineteenth Amendment prohibiting exclusion from the franchise based on gender); *Lee v. Weisman*, 505 U.S. 577, 621 (1992) (Souter, J., concurring) (rejecting Justice Kennedy's argument that coercion is the key to the Establishment Clause, on the ground that it would render the Free Exercise Clause redundant).

72 343 U.S. 579, 641–44 (1952).

73 Id. at 643.

74 Id. at 644.

75 Id. at 643–44.

76 Id. at 631.

77 Id.

78 116 U.S. 616, 633 (1886).

79 *United States v. Fisher*, 425 U.S. 391, 399–401 (1972).

80 *Cantwell v. Connecticut*, 310 U.S. 296, 303 (1940).

81 374 U.S. 203, 309–10 (1963).

82 Id.
83 Id. at 254–56.
84 Id. at 255.
85 17 U.S. 316, 419–20 (1819).
86 Id.
87 5 U.S. 137 (1803).
88 Id. at 156.
89 19 U.S. 264 (1821).
90 Id. at 384.
91 Id. at 384–85.
92 22 U.S. 1, 188–89 (1824). See also *Youngstown Sheet and Tube v. Sawyer*, 343 U.S. 579, 646 (1952) (Jackson, J., concurring)("[t]he purpose of lodging [the] titles[of President and Commander-in-Chief] in one man was to insure that the civilian would control the military, not to enable the military to subordinate the presidential office"); *New York v. United States*, 505 U.S. 144, 156–57 (1992) (the Tenth Amendment does not set up an explicit barrier against federal intrusion into state autonomy, but its purpose was to serve as a reminder of its importance).
93 See, e.g., *Prigg v. Pennsylvania*, 41 U.S. 539, 611 (1842) (the Fugitive Slave Clause should be read in light of its well-understood purpose to secure the rights of slaveholders in their slaves); *Home Building & Loan Association v. Blaisdell*, 290 U.S. 398, 427–28 (1934) (the Contract Clause should be read in light of purpose of preventing legislatures from undermining contractual obligations through debtor relief legislation, which the Court then proceeded to ignore).
94 22 U.S. at 190. See also *Trustees of Dartmouth College v. Woodward*, 17 U.S. 518, 628 (1819) (the Contract Clause should be read as prohibiting the preconstitutional practices, which gave it rise, and not every internal agreement of the state).
95 22 U.S. at 190.
96 See Chapter 1, Section III, part B.
97 17 U.S. 316 (1819).
98 Id. at 413.
99 Id. at 415.
100 65 U.S. 66, 98–99 (1860).
101 Id. at 99.
102 Id. at 99–101.
103 Id. at 99.
104 Id. at 100.
105 279 U.S. 655 (1929).
106 Id. at 683–85.
107 Id. at 684–85.
108 Id. at 685.
109 408 U.S. 606, 617–18 (1972).
110 Id. at 616, 617–18.
111 Id. at 625.
112 277 U.S. 438 (1928).

113 Id. at 464. In *Hester v. United States*, 265 U.S. 57, 59 (1924), decided a few years prior to *Olmstead*, the Court excluded activity taking place in "open fields" from the protection of the Fourth Amendment on the ground that such a place did not constitute "persons, houses, papers or effects" within the meaning of the Fourth Amendment. Despite the shift toward a privacy-basis analysis in *Katz v. United States*, 389 U.S. 347 (1967), the Court stuck with this textual analysis in *Oliver v. United States*, 466 U.S. 170, 176–77 (1984).

114 277 U.S. at 487. Justice Butler made the same point in his dissent, arguing that

> This court has always construed the Constitution in light of the principles upon which it was founded. The direct operation or literal meaning of the words used do not measure the purpose or scope of its provisions. Under the principles established and applied by this court, the Fourth Amendment safeguards against all evils that are like and equivalent to those embraced within the ordinary meaning of its words. Id. at 487–88.

115 392 U.S. 93, 95–96 (1968).

116 Id. at 96–97, (citing *Joint Anti-Facist Refugee Committee v. McGrath*, 341 U.S. 123, 150 (1951) (Frankfurter, J., concurring)); *Coleman v. Miller*, 307 U.S. 433, 460 (1939) (Frankfurter, J., separate opinion).

117 Id. at 95.

118 Id. at 102–04.

119 403 U.S. 602, 612 (1971).

120 See Chapter 13, Section V.

121 489 U.S. 257, 266 (1989).

122 528 U.S. 495 (2000).

123 Id. at 517.

124 Id. at 513–17.

125 378 U.S. 478, 485 (1964).

126 Id. at 494–95 (Stewart, J., dissenting).

127 Id. at 485.

128 Id.

129 Id. at 486.

130 83 U.S. 36, 71–72 (1872).

131 Id. at 81.

132 Id. at 89–90 (Field, J., dissenting).

133 Id. at 123 (Bradley, J., dissenting).

134 343 U.S. 214 (1952).

135 Id. at 225, 229.

136 343 U.S. 579, 650 (1952).

137 Id.

138 457 U.S. 731, 750 n.31 (1982).

139 Id.

140 Id.

141 17 U.S. 316 (1819).

142 Id. at 406–07.

143 Id. at 407.

144 134 U.S. 1 (1890).

145 Id. at 13–14.

146 2 U.S. 419 (1793).

147 134 U.S. at 12–16.

148 517 U.S. 44 (1996).

149 527 U.S. 706 (1999).

150 517 U.S. at 110, 115, 119.

151 Id. at 110.

152 Id. at 110–11.

153 Id. at 54.

154 Id. at 110.

155 Id. at 68.

156 Id. at 68.

157 Id. at 69.

158 Id. at 69–70.

159 527 U.S. at 723.

160 Id.

Chapter 3 Original Understanding: Preconstitutional Sources and the Drafting and Ratification Process

1 176 U.S. 581, 602 (1900).

2 332 U.S. 46, 64 (1947).

3 128 S. Ct. 2783, 2805 (2008).

4 See *Hamdi v. Rumsfeld*, 542 U.S. 507, 555, 557–59 (2004) (Scalia, J., dissenting, detailing the history of the evolution of Habeas Corpus in England to illustrate the importance of reliance on legal process as a predicate to confinement).

5 165 U.S. 275, 281 (1897).

6 94 U.S. 113, 123 (1876).

7 Id.

8 Id. at 126.

9 59 U.S. 272, 276–77 (1855).

10 For a much more recent example, see *Pacific Mutual Life Insurance Co. v. Haslip*, 499 U.S. 1, 28 (1991), where Justice Scalia, concurring, relied heavily on the conclusion that the inclusion of the Due Process Clause in the Bill of Rights was intended to encapsulate the concept of the "law of the land" as set forth in the Magna Carta.

11 110 U.S. 516, 522 (1884).

12 Id. at 529.

13 Id. at 530.

14 Id. at 532.

15 Id. at 530–31.

16 386 U.S. 213, 223 (1967).

17 499 U.S. 1, 31–32 (1991) (italics in original).

18 Id. at 34–35.

19 *BMW of North America v. Gore*, 517 U.S. 559 (1996).

20 103 U.S. 168, 183–89 (1880).

21 Id. at 202.

22 408 U.S. 501 (1972).

23 Id. at 508.

24 See, e.g., *Browning-Ferris Industries v. Kelco Disposal Inc.*, 492 U.S. 257, 267 (1989) (in the course of construing the Excessive Fines Clause of the Eighth Amendment, the Court noted that "[t]he Framers of our Bill of Rights were aware and took account of the abuses that led to the 1689 Bill of Rights," on which the Eighth Amendment was based).

25 395 U.S. 486, 521–22 (1969).

26 Id. at 523–31.

27 116 U.S. 616 (1886).

28 Id. at 626–30 (1886). In *Miranda v. Arizona*, 384 U.S. 436, 459 (1966), the Court relied on events surrounding the trial of John Lilburn in 1637 before the Star Chamber as crucial to the development of the privilege against self-Incrimination.

29 116 U.S. at 626–30.

30 Id. at 626–27. In *Faretta v. California*, 422 U.S. 806, 822–26 (1975), the fact that in England, prior to the Constitution, the only instance in which the right of self-representation was denied an accused was in the infamous Court of the Star Chamber provided strong evidence for the Court that such a right had been highly valued.

31 See Chapter 7, Section II.

32 *United States v. Fisher*, 425 U.S. 391, 399–401 (1976).

33 362 U.S. 60, 64 (1960).

34 Id. at 65.

35 Id. at 64.

36 Id. at 70.

37 See also *Grosjean v. American Press Co.*, 297 U.S. 233, 245–49 (1936) (English history showed that the First Amendment was concerned with prohibiting government licensing of the press); *Richmond Newspapers v. Virginia*, 448 U.S. 555, 564–66 (1980) (Burger, C.J., plurality opinion), id. at 589 (Brennan, J., concurring) (the fact that trials in England had been conducted in public as far back as historical records could trace provided evidence of both its importance and of the fact that it was probably accepted as a given by framers of the Constitution).

38 330 U.S. 1, 8–9 (1947).

39 Id. at 9–11.

40 370 U.S. 421, 425–34 (1962).

41 Id.

42 Id. at 428–30.

43 Id. at 445.

44 370 U.S. at 446.

45 368 U.S. 420, 470 (1961).

46 Id.

47 103 U.S. 168 (1880).

48 9 Ad and E 1, 112 Eng. Rep. 1112 (K.B. 1839).

49 103 U.S. at 202.

50 408 U.S. 606, 624 n.14 (1972).

51 Id. at 656.

52 Id. at 657.

53 128 S. Ct. 2783, 2797 (2008) (italics in original).

54 Id.

55 Id.

56 Id. at 2798–99.

57 Id. at 2838 (Stevens, J., dissenting).

58 501 U.S. 957, 967–75 (1991).

59 420 U.S. 103, 114 (1975).

60 Id.

61 Id. at 115.

62 See the *Slaughter-House Cases*, 83 U.S. 36, 105 (1872) (Field, J., dissenting) (noting that following the American Revolution, the common law of England "was completely incorporated into the fundamental law of this country" and that law forbids the establishment of monopolies in trades and occupations).

63 423 U.S. 411, 420–23 (1976).

64 Id. at 420–21.

65 Id. at 438–41.

66 445 U.S. 573, 591 (1980).

67 Id. The Court detailed some of those differences in a lengthy footnote. Id. at n.33.

68 Id. at 593–96.

69 Id. at 596.

70 Id. at 597–98. See also *Tumey v. Ohio*, 273 U.S. 510, 526–31 (1927) (complete absence of practice at common law of allowing judges to be compensated from fines of convicted criminal defendants indicates that such a practice was not consistent with due process of law). Cf. Virginia v. Moore, 128 S. Ct. 1598, 1603 (2008) (no evidence that framers of the Fourth Amendment "intended to incorporate subsequently enacted statutes into the Amendment's coverage").

71 445 U.S. at 598.

72 Id. at 604–07.

73 Id. at 606.

74 Id. at 611.

75 297 U.S. 233, 249 (1936).

76 Id. at 248–49.

77 Id. at 249.

78 Id.

79 314 U.S. 252, 264 (1941), quoting Schofield, *Freedom of the Press in the United States*, 9 Pub Amer. Socil Soc. 67, 76.

80 Id. at 265.

81 Id. at 285.

82 77 U.S. 557, 563 (1870).

83 Id.

84 Id.

85 Id.

86 53 U.S. 443, 454–57 (1851).

87 *Washington v. Glucksberg*, 521 U.S. 702, 712 (1997).

88 5 U.S. 137, 162, 165 (1803). See also, *Slaughter-House Cases*, 83 U.S. 36, 115 (1872) (citing Blackstone's classification of fundamental rights).

89 418 U.S. 323, 381 n.14 (1974), quoting J. Hurst, The Growth of American Law: The Law Makers 257 (1950).

90 Id., citing 4 W. Blackstone, Commentaries*150–53.

91 *Schenck v. United States*, 249 U.S. 47, 51–52 (1919).

92 527 U.S. 706, 715 (1999).

93 395 U.S. 784, 795 (1969).

94 *U.S. Term Limits, Inc. v. Thornton*, 514 U.S. 779, 799 (1995).

95 *Near v. Minnesota*, 283 U.S. 697, 713–14 (1931).

96 *Strauder v. West Virginia*, 100 U.S. 303, 308 (1879).

97 *Linkletter v. Walker*, 381 U.S. 618, 622–23 (1965).

98 *Ex Parte, Garland*, 71 U.S. 333, 380–81 (1866).

99 *McGowan v. Maryland*, 366 U.S. 420, 434 (1961), id. at 475 (Frankfurter, J., concurring).

100 *Washington v. Glucksberg*, 521, U.S. 702, 712 (1997).

101 542 U.S. 507, 555 (2004).

102 Id.

103 545 U.S. 469, 510 (2005) (citing 1 Blackstone's Commentaries 135).

104 Id.

105 128 S. Ct. 2783, 2799 (2008).

106 386 U.S. 213, 225 (1967).

107 Id., quoting Warren, *History of the American Bar* 174 (1911).

108 Id., quoting Bowen, *The Lion and the Throne* 514 (1956).

109 *Richmond Newspapers v. Virginia*, 448 U.S. 555, 567–68 (1980) (Burger, C. J., plurality) (relying on colonial history of open criminal trials as evidence that the framers of the First Amendment assumed that criminal trials would be open to the public); *Saenz v. Roe*, 526 U.S. 489, 523–24 (1999) (Thomas, J., dissenting) (relying on usage of the term "privileges and immunities" in colonial charters to establish that as used in the Constitution, it was intended to refer to fundamental rights); *Faretta v. California*, 422 U.S. 806, 826–31 (1975) (emphasizing the importance of the right of self-representation in colonial America); *Boyd v. United States*, 116 U.S. 616, 624–25 (1886) (relying on the controversy over the writs of assistance in 1761 to shed light on the meaning of the Fourth Amendment's prohibition against unreasonable searches and seizures).

110 See *Richmond Newspapers v. Virginia*, 448 U.S. 555, 568 (1980) (Burger, C.J., plurality) (quoting from the letter's reference to the preservation of open criminal trials in support of the proposition that there is a constitutional right to a public trial).

111 283 U.S. 697, 717 (1931). The Court has relied on this letter as evidence of the importance of freedom of speech and press in other cases. See, e.g., *Roth v. United States*, 354 U.S. 476, 484 (1957).

112 303 U.S. 444, 452 (1938).

113 362 U.S. 60, 65 (1960).

114 Id.

115 Id.

116 Id. at 64–65.

117 530 U.S. 57, 91 (2000).

118 391 U.S. 145, 152 (1968). *Slaughter-House Cases*, 83 U.S. 36, 115–16 (1872) (Bradley, J., dissenting) (citing the Declaration's language that "life, liberty, and the pursuit of happiness" are inalienable rights as evidence of the fundamental nature of the right to pursue a common calling).

119 343 U.S. 579, 641 (1952).

120 17 U.S. 316, 406–07 (1819).

121 Id. at 407.

122 14 U.S. 304, 345 (1816). Marshall made the same point five years later in *Cohens v. Virginia*, 19 U.S. 264, 417 (1821).

123 83 U.S. 36, 75 (1872).

124 Id.

125 526 U.S. 489, 524–28 (1999).

126 Id.

127 Id.

128 65 U.S. 66, 101–02 (1860).

129 Id. 103.

130 19 U.S. 264, 380 (1821).

131 Id.

132 Id. at 388.

133 98 U.S. 145 (1878).

134 Id. at 165–67.

135 Id. at 162–63.

136 Id. at 163.

137 Id. The language of the Eight Amendment's Cruel and Unusual Punishment Clause first appeared in the Virginia Declaration of Rights of 1776. As such, the legislative debate over that provision has been cited as shedding light on the meaning of the constitutional provision. See *Furman v. Georgia*, 408 U.S. 238, 319–22 (1972) (Marshall, J., concurring).

138 98 U.S. at 163.

139 Id.

140 Id. at 163–64.

141 Id. at 164.

142 Id.

143 Id.

144 Id. at 165.

145 330 U.S. 1, 9–10 (1947).

146 Id. at 11.

147 Id. at 12.

148 Id.

149 Id. at 13.

150 Id.

151 Id. at 34–39.

152 Id. at 39.

153 366 U.S. 420, 437–40 (1961).

154 Id.

155 Id. at 438.

156 Id. at 430.

157 397 U.S. 664, 683 (1970).

158 Id. at 683.

159 392 U.S. 83, 125 (1968).

160 Id. at 125–26, quoting C. Antieau, A. Downey & E. Roberts, *Freedom from Federal Establishment* (1964).

161 Id. at 126.

162 462 U.S. 919, 947–50 (1983).

163 Id. at 947, citing M. Farrand, The Records of the Federal Constitution of 1787, 301–02 and 304–06.

164 Id. at 948–49, quoting M. Farrand; id. at 254, quoting James Wilson.

165 Id. at 951.

166 377 U.S. 533, 595–602 (1964). Section two does explicitly require the reduction of a state's representation in Congress in proportion to the number of its citizens disenfranchised.

167 332 U.S. 46, 92–123 (1947).

168 Id. at 64.

169 79 U.S. 457, 655–56 (1870).

170 Id. at 656.

171 176 U.S. 581, 601 (1900).

172 Id. at 601. See also *Afroyim v. Rusk,* 387 U.S. 253, 262–64 (1967), where the Court relied on statements made by three members of Congress during the debates on the Fourteenth Amendment to the effect that Congress did not have the power to deprive a citizen of his citizenship. The Court conceded, however, that statements made during the debate might lead to conflicting inferences. Id. at 267. Justice Harlan, dissenting, argued that these three isolated statements said nothing as to what the majority of Congress believed with respect to the question. Id. at 273–74.

173 366 U.S. 420, 440–42 (1961).

174 Id. at 440.

175 Id. at 441.

176 Id.

177 Id.

178 Id.

179 Id. at 442.

180 Id.

181 505 U.S. 577, 613–16 (1992) (Souter, J., concurring).

182 472 U.S. 38, 93–99 (1985).

183 Id. at 98–99.

184 Id. at 99.

185 *Powell v. McCormack*, 395 U.S. 486, 538–39 (1969).

186 *Nixon v. United States*, 506 U.S. 224, 231 (1993).

187 445 U.S. 573, 607–11 (1980).

188 Id. at 585.

189 Id. at 611.

190 Id., quoting N. Lasson, The History and Development of the Fourth Amendment to the United States Constitution 101 (1937).

191 Id. at 611.

192 See, e.g., *West Virginia Bd. of Educ. v. Barnette*, 319 U.S. 624, 649–50 (1943) (Frankfurter, J., dissenting) (pointing out that the state of New York had a Council of Revision for fifty years before the adoption of the Constitution but that the framers had deliberately rejected this notion).

193 381 U.S. 479, 513 n.6 (1965) (summarizing the Council of Revision Provisions and their rejection).

194 Id.

195 478 U.S. 714, 729 (1986).

196 298 U.S. 238, 292 (1936).

197 See *NLRB v. Jones & Laughlin Steel Corp.*, 501 U.S. 1 (1937).

198 505 U.S. 144, 164–65 (1992).

199 521 U.S. 507, 519–23 (1997).

200 Id. at 520–21.

201 Id.

202 Id. at 522.

203 Id.

204 *Abington Township v. Schempp*, 374 U.S. 203, 256 n.21 (1963) (Brennan, J., concurring) (citing authorities for the debate).

205 Id. at 256–57.

206 Id.

207 Id. at 257.

208 128 S. Ct. 2783, 2796 (2008).

209 Id. at 2835 (Stevens, J., dissenting).

210 Id. at 2796.

211 Id. at 2836 (Stevens, J., dissenting).

212 *Powell v. McCormack*, 395 U.S. 486, 540–41 (1968) (statements made during state ratification conventions confirm that delegates believed Congress could only exclude a member for failing to meet the standing qualifications); *Hans v. Louisiana*, 134 U.S. 1, 14 (1890) (quoting statements by Madison and Marshall during the Virginia Ratifying Convention, declaring that persons could not sue a state in federal court); *Home Building & Loan v. Blaisdell*, 290 U.S. 398, 461–63 (1934) (Sutherland, J., dissenting) (citing statements made during the ratification debates to confirm that the Contract Clause was intended to prohibit debtor forgiveness acts); *Gregg v. Georgia*, 428 U.S. 153, 170 n.17 (1976)

(Stewart, J., plurality) (debates on the ratification of the Constitution suggest that delegates did not intend to adopt the English conception of cruel and unusual punishment); *District of Columbia v. Heller*, 128 S. Ct. 2783, 2833–36 (2008) (Stevens, J., dissenting) (relying on debates and amendments set forth during the state ratifying conventions to maintain that the Second Amendment was intended to quiet fears that Congress would disarm or abolish state militias).

213 17 U.S. 316, 404–04 (1819).

214 17 U.S. at 402.

215 Id. at 402–03.

216 Id. at 403.

217 Id. at 404.

218 Id. at 404–05.

219 14 U.S. 304, 351 (1816).

220 32 U.S. 243, 250 (1833).

221 514 U.S. 779, 812–15 (1996).

222 Id. at 812–13.

223 Id. at 813–14.

224 Id. at 812.

225 Id. at 814–15. In his dissent in *Reynolds v. Sims*, challenging the Court's conclusion that the Equal Protection Clause required that state legislatures be apportioned on a one person, one vote basis, Justice Harlan pointed out that two-thirds of both the loyal states and reconstructed states supporting ratification explicitly required malapportioned state legislatures and that Congress was aware of this (at least with respect to the reconstructed states) and ignored it. 377 U.S. 533, 602–08 (1947).

226 514 U.S. at 900 (Thomas, J., dissenting).

227 505 U.S. 144, 164–66 (1992).

228 366 U.S. 420, 486 (1961).

229 Id.

230 Id. at 580 n.11.

231 See *United States v. Verdugo-Urquidez*, 494 U.S. 259, 289 (1990) (Brennan, J., dissenting) ("throughout the entire process [of drafting the Bill of Rights] no speaker or commentator, pro or con, referred to the term 'the people' as a limitation").

232 391 U.S. 145, 174–75 (1968).

233 Id.

234 Id. at 175 n.9.

235 Id. at 165.

236 422 U.S. 806, 832 (1975). In *United States v. Nixon*, 506 U.S. 224, 233 (1993), the Court addressed the question of whether Senate procedures in an impeachment trial were subject to judicial review. In concluding that they were not, the majority suggested that the absence of any discussion of the possibility of judicial review of impeachment convictions was significant, considering that there was discussion of judicial review of other actions.

237 397 U.S. 664, 682 (1970). Justice Brennan quoted a historical work for the proposition that "'[a]s far as anyone has been able to discover, the topic was never mentioned in the debates which took place prior to the adoption of the First Amendment.'" Id. at n.1 citing C. Antieau, P. Carroll, T. Burke, Religion Under the State Constitutions 122 (1965).

238 383 U.S. 169, 177 (1966).

239 Id. at 177–78.

240 492 U.S. 257, 264 (1989).

241 Id. at 264–65.

242 Id. at 265.

243 See, e.g., *INS v. Chadha*, 462 U.S. 919, 947 (1983) (relying on Federalist 73 to illuminate the significance of the Presentment Clause), id. at 949 (relying on Federalist 22 & 51 to illuminate the purpose of bicameralism); *Bowshers v. Synar*, 478 U.S. 714, 722 (1986) (quoting Federalist 47 on the importance of the separation of powers); *Nixon v. GSA*, 433 U.S. 425, 443 n.5 (1977) (quoting Federalist 47 for the proposition that the branches of the federal government are interdependent and not completely separated), Id. at 512 n.6 (Burger, J., dissenting) (quoting Madison in Federalist 48 as to the dangers of legislative encroachment on the other branches); *Powell v. McCormack*, 395 U.S. 486, 540 (1968) (relying on Federalist 52 to support the argument that Congress could only exclude members for failing to meet standing qualifications); *U.S. Term Limits v. Thornton*, 514 U.S. 779, 806 (1995) (quoting Federalist 52 for the proposition that there needed to be uniform qualification standards for members of Congress); *Hans v. Louisiana*, 134 U.S. 1, 12 (1890) (relying on Federalist 84 for the proposition that states were not subject to suit without their consent); *Home Building & Loan v. Blaisdell*, 290 U.S. 398,427 (1934) (quoting Federalist 44 on the background of the Contract Clause);*United States v. Brown*, 381 U.S. 437, 443–44 (1965) (quoting and citing Federalist 47, 48, 49, 51 on the importance of avoiding the accumulation of too much power in one branch of government).

244 19 U.S. 264, 418–19 (1821).

245 Id. at 419–20.

246 17 U.S. 316 (1819).

247 Id. at 433.

248 Id. at 434.

249 Id.

250 Id.

251 505 U.S. 144, 163 (1992) (quoting Alexander Hamilton, Federalist 15).

252 488 U.S. 361, 380–81 (1989) (quoting Federalist 47 and 51.)

253 521 U.S. 898, 971 (1997), quoting Federalist 27.

254 Id. at 910–15.

255 Id. at 915 n.9.

256 381 U.S. 479, 489 (1965).

257 Id. at 489 n.3, n.4.

258 Id.

259 Id.

Chapter 4 Original Understanding: Contemporaneous Understanding and Interpretive Issues

1 79 U.S. 457, 607 (1870).

2 See, e.g., *Browning-Ferris Industries of Vermont v. Kelco Disposal, Inc.*, 492 U.S. 257, 265 n.6 (1989) (relying on Coke's Institutes and two eighteenth-century dictionaries to establish that the word *fine* as used in the Excessive Fines Clause referred to a payment to the state); *Allegheny v. ACLU*, 492 U.S. 573, 649 n.5 (1989) (relying on Thomas Sheridan's dictionary of 1796 and Samuel Johnson's dictionary of 1785 for definitions of "respect" as used in the Establishment Clause); *Nixon v. United States*, 506 U.S. 224, 230 (1993) (the Court relied on Sheridan's 1796 dictionary and Johnson's 1785 dictionary to establish that the word *try* in the Impeachment Clause had different meanings at the time of the framing); *Wallace v. Jaffree*, 472 U.S. 38, 106 (1985) (Rehnquist, C.J., dissenting, quoting Webster's dictionary of 1826 for the proposition that "'establishment [was defined] as 'the act of founding, ratifying or ordaining' such as, in '[t]he episcopal form of religion, so called in England.'")

3 357 U.S. 186, 199 (2003).

4 Id. at 199.

5 128 S. Ct. 2783, 2791 (2008).

6 Id.

7 Id. at 2792.

8 Id. at 2793.

9 Id. at 2828.

10 514 U.S. 549, 585–86 (1995) (quoting from contemporary dictionaries of Johnson (1793), Bailey (1789), and Sheridan (1796)).

11 Id. at 586 citing Federalist 4, 7, and 40, Federal Farmer 5, and Smith, and address to the People of the State of New York.

12 Id. at 586–87 quoting Federalist 12, 21, and 36 as well as State Ratification Debates. See also *Saenz v. Roe*, 526 U.S. 489, 523–24 (1999) (Thomas, J., dissenting) (citing preconstitutional materials to establish that the phrase "privileges and immunities" was understood to signify "fundamental rights"). In his concurring opinion in *First National Bank of Boston v. Bellotti*, 435 U.S. 765, 798–99 (1978) quoting Andrew Bradford and Leonard Levy, Justice Burger relying on a 1734 letter as well as assessments by a noted colonial historian concluded that prior to the drafting of the First Amendment, the term "freedom of press" was used interchangeably with "freedom of speech" as opposed to carrying a distinct meaning.

13 545 U.S. 469, 508 (2005) citing 2 S. Johnson, A Dictionary of the English Language 2194 (4th ed., 1773) as well as J. Lewis, Law of Eminent Domain S 165, p 224 n.4 (1888) (citing dictionaries contemporaneous with the drafting of the amendment).

14 Id.

15 Id. at 509.

16 Id.

17 See, e.g., *City of Boerne v. Flores*, 521 U.S. 507, 551–57 (1997) (O'Connor, J., dissenting) (relying on Free Exercise provisions of state constitutions and state

legislation as evidence of the meaning of the Free Exercise Clause of the First Amendment).

18 3 U.S. 386, 391–92, 397 (1798).

19 287 U.S. 45, 59–62 (1932). See also *Duncan v. Louisiana*, 391 U.S. 145, 152 (1968) (the fact that all of the state constitutions provide for a right to jury trial at the time of ratification indicates that it should be considered a fundamental right as a matter of due process of law).

20 Id.

21 128 S. Ct. 2783, 2793 (2008), id. at 2802–03.

22 Id. at 2795–96.

23 Id. at 2825–26 (Stevens, J., dissenting).

24 341 U.S. 494, 521 (1951).

25 418 U.S. 323, 380 (1974).

26 Id. at 381.

27 354 U.S. 476, 482–83 (1957).

28 Id. at 483.

29 540 U.S. 712, 723 (2004).

30 Id.

31 Id. at 727–28.

32 501 U.S. 957, 977–78 (1991).

33 See *Washington v. Glucksberg*, 521 U.S. 702, 715 (1997) (the Court noted that "[b]y the time the Fourteenth Amendment was ratified, it was a crime in most States to assist a suicide"); *44 Liquormart v. Rhode Island*, 517 U.S. 484, 517 (1996) (Scalia, J., concurring) ("I consider more relevant the state legislative practices prevalent at the time the First Amendment was adopted, since almost all of the States had free speech constitutional guarantees of their own . . .").

34 410 U.S. 113, 175–76 n.1 (1973) (Rehnquist, J., dissenting) (listing the thirty-six states).

35 514 U.S. 779, 823–27 (1995).

36 Id.

37 Id.

38 Id.

39 Id. at 866 (Thomas, J., dissenting). In his concurring opinion in *United States v. Nixon*, 506 U.S. 224, 250 (1993), Justice Stevens argued that the fact that some state and colonial governments held impeachment hearings before legislative committees was evidence that the current similar Senate practice was not unconstitutional.

40 94 U.S.113, 124–26 (1876).

41 Id.

42 435 U.S. 618, 622–25 (1978).

43 Id.

44 Id. at 637.

45 521 U.S. 507, 539–40 (1997).

46 See *Boyd v. United States*, 116 U.S. 616, 630–31 (1886) (modifications to procedures for the production of documentary evidence passed by the First Congress shed

light on the proper understanding of the Fourth Amendment drafted at about the same time).

47 36 U.S. 420, 583 (1837).

48 Id. quoting the Northwest Ordinance of 1787.

49 Id.

50 472 U.S. 38, 100 (1985) (Rehnquist, J., dissenting).

51 377 U.S. 533, 573 (1964).

52 521 U.S. 898, 905–09 (1997).

53 Id. Justice Stevens, dissenting, argued that in the early days of the republic, it was not uncommon for judges to perform executive functions and consequently congressional assignment of enforcement tasks to state judges should be viewed as akin to the assignment of such tasks to state executive officials. Id. at 950–52.

54 Id. at 949.

55 463 U.S. 783, 788 (1983).

56 Id. at 816.

57 Id. at 815 n.32, quoting Bernard Schwartz, The Bill of Rights: A Documentary History 1171 (1971).

58 83 U.S. 36, 90 (1872).

59 *Faretta v. California*, 422 U.S. 806, 812–13 (1975) (the fact that right of self representation was recognized by the First Congress in the Judiciary Act of 1789 shows that the framers considered it quite important); *Harmelin v. Michigan*, 501 U.S. 957, 980–81 (1991) (Scalia, J.) (the fact that the First Congress imposed the death penalty for forgery of government securities or running away with goods valued over $50 indicates that it did not believe that the Cruel and Unusual Punishment Clause contained a proportionality principle).

60 14 U.S. 304, 351 (1816).

61 Id.

62 19 U.S. 264, 420 (1821). See also *Ableman v. Booth*, 62 U.S. 506, 522 (1858) ("many of the members of the Convention were also members of this Congress, and it cannot be supposed that they did not understand the meaning and intention of the great instrument"); *Myers v. United States*, 272 U.S. 52, 174–75 (1926) (the First Congress "[w]as a Congress whose constitutional decisions have always been regarded, as they should be regarded, as of the greatest weight in the interpretation of that instrument"); *Kentucky v. Dennison*, 65 U.S. 66, 104 (1860) (placing heavy reliance on a construction of the Extradition Clause embodied in an act of 1793, noting that it was "[t]he construction put upon it almost contemporaneously with the commencement of the Government itself, and when Washington was still at its head, and many of those who had assisted in framing it were members of the Congress which enacted the law"); *Pollock v. Farmers Loan and Trust Co.*, 157 U.S. 429, 615–16 (1895) (White, J., dissenting) (an Act of Congress from 1794 should provide dispositive evidence as to the meaning of the phrase "direct" tax as "each member of the congress, even although he had not been in the convention, had, in some way, either directly or indirectly, been an influential actor in the events which led up to the birth of that instrument").

63 465 U.S. 668, 674 (1984).

64 478 U.S. 714, 724 n.3 (1986). The Court concluded that the rejection by the First Congress in the Decision of 1789 of a congressional role in the removal of executive officials "provides 'contemporaneous and weighty evidence' of the Constitution's meaning[,]" quoting *Marsh v. Chambers*, 463 U.S. 783, 790 (1983).

65 17 U.S. 316 (1819).

66 Id. at 401. *Cooley v. Board of Wardens*, 53 U.S. 299, 315 (1851) (relying on pilotage law passed by the first Congress in 1789).

67 17 U.S. at 402.

68 Id. at 417.

69 395 U.S. 486, 547 (1969).

70 Id. In *Afroyim v. Rusk*, the Court placed some reliance on the fact that the Congress has declined to pass laws permitting voluntary expatriation under certain circumstance in 1794, 1797, and 1818 to bolster its conclusion that Congress did not have such authority. 387 U.S. 253, 258 (1967).

71 545 U.S. 844, 886 (2005) (Scalia, J., dissenting).

72 Id.

73 Id. See also *Wallace v. Jaffree*, 472 U.S. 38, 101–02 (1985) (Rehnquist, J., dissenting).

74 545 U.S. at 886.

75 Id. at 887. See also 472 U.S. at 100.

76 *Wallace v. Jaffree*, 472 U.S. at 103 (Rehnquist, J., dissenting).

77 545 U.S. at 887.

78 Id. at 887–88.

79 472 U.S. at 103–04.

80 Id. at 99–106 (Rehnquist, J., dissenting); 545 U.S. at 885–88.

81 545 U.S. at 878–81.

82 *McCreary County v. ACLU*, 545 U.S. 844, 877–78 (2005). *Van Orden v. Perry*, 545 U.S. 677, 722–26 (2005) (Stevens, J., dissenting).

83 545 U.S. 844, 895 (2005).

84 Id. at 877–78; *Van Orden v. Perry*, 545 U.S. at 722–26 (2005) (Stevens, J., dissenting).

85 545 U.S. 844, 896–97 (2005).

86 505 U.S. 577, 626 (1992) (Souter, J., concurring). Justice Souter cited Madison's subsequent disavowal of his earlier wartime proclamations calling for public prayer. Id. at 625–26.

87 Id.

88 376 U.S. 254, 273–77 (1964).

89 In *Bridges v. California*, 314 U.S. 252, 266–67 (1941), the Court looked to post-ratification incidents as strong evidence that the First Amendment had rejected the English practice of a permissive use of the contempt power with respect to press criticism of judicial proceedings. In particular, it emphasized that Judge Peck was in fact impeached by Congress for using the contempt power against a lawyer who had criticized one of his decisions.

90 See chapter 13, Section IV for additional discussion of the argument.

91 See *District of Columbia v. Heller*, 128 S. Ct. 2783, 2807–09 (2008) (citing pre-Civil War state cases construing state constitutional analogs of the Second Amendment as evidence of the original understanding of the latter).

92 83 U.S. 36, 71 (1872).

93 Id. at 96–97 (Field, J., dissenting).

94 332 U.S. 46, 51–52 (1947).

95 Id. at 53.

96 6 Fed. Case 546 No 3, 230 (CCED Pa. 1825).

97 526 U.S. 489, 522–23 (1999).

98 Id. at 524–27.

99 19 U.S. 264, 420–21 (1821).

100 103 U.S. 168, 204 (1880).

101 521 U. S. 507, 542–43 (1997).

102 Id.

103 463 U.S. 783, 817 (1983).

104 Id.

105 544 U.S. 709, 729–30 (Thomas, J., concurring).

106 Id.

107 See, e.g., *Valley Forge Christian Academy v. Americans United*, 454 U.S. 464, 494 (1982) (Brennan, J., dissenting) (quoting Madison for the proposition that constitutional rights were to be enforced by the judiciary); *United States v. Verdugo-Urquidez*, 494 U.S. 259, 266 (1990) (quoting Madison for the proposition that absent a Bill of Rights, Congress had the power to engage in unreasonable searches and seizures).

108 283 U.S. 697, 718 (1931).

109 See, e.g., *Lee v. Weisman*, 505 U.S. 577, 590 (1992), id. at 608 (Blackmun, J., concurring), Id. at 622 (Souter, J., concurring).

110 515 U.S. 819, 854–58 (1995).

111 Id. at 868–73.

112 Id. at 854–55 (Thomas, J., concurring).

113 Id. at 869–70 (Souter, J., dissenting).

114 397 U.S. 664, 685 (1970).

115 Id. at 685. He continued, "[a]nd if they had not either approved the exemptions, or been mild in their opposition, it is probable that their views would be known to us today. Both Jefferson and Madison wrote prolifically about issues they felt important, and their opinions were well known to contemporary chroniclers." Id.

116 Id. at 685 n.5.

117 Id.

118 297 U.S. 1, 65–66 (1936).

119 Id. at 66.

120 Id. at 67.

121 Id. at 76–77.

122 521 U.S. 898, 915 n.9 (1997).

123 Id.

124 See *Johanns v. Livestock Marketing*, 544 U.S. 550, 572 (2005) (Souter, J., dissenting) (quoting Jefferson's objection to public funding of opinions with which the individual disagrees, rendered in the context of the funding of a state church, as evidence of objection to any sort of compelled funding of belief or opinion);

Hamdi v. Rumsfeld, 542 U.S. 507, 564, 565 (2004) (Scalia, J., dissenting) (relying on a letter from Jefferson to Madison in 1788 questioning the wisdom of the Suspension of Habeas Corpus Clause); *Dennis v. United States,* 341 U.S. 494, 522 n.4 (1951) (Frankfurter, J., concurring) (quoting a statement in a letter to Abigail Adams to the effect that the First Amendment does not apply to the states for the proposition that the First Amendment is not absolute, a conclusion that was not necessarily advanced by the quote); *United States v. Brown,* 381 U.S. 437, 446 n.20 (1965) (quoting Jefferson's notes on the state of Virginia for the proposition that the legislature should not be allowed to exercise executive or judicial powers).

125 See Chapter 12, Section III.

126 457 U.S. 731, 750 (1982) quoting from 10 The Works of Thomas Jefferson 404 n. (P. Ford ed., 1905) (emphasis in the original).

127 Id. at 778 n.23.

128 Id.

129 408 U.S. 606, 615 (1972), citing T. Jefferson, Manual of Parliamentary Practice, S. Doc No 92-1, p. 437 (1971).

130 Id. at 652–55 (1972), quoting 8 The Works of Thomas Jefferson 322–27 (Ford ed., 1904).

131 Id. at 655.

132 *Kilbourn v. Thompson,* 103 U.S. 168, 204 (1880) (quoting Justice Story on the scope of the Speech and Debate Clause); *Gitlow v. New York,* 268 U.S. 652, 666–68 (1925) (quoting Story's Commentaries for the proposition that freedom of speech is not absolute); *Hamdi v. Rumsfeld,* 542 U.S. 507, 556 (2004) (Scalia, J., dissenting) (quoting Story for the proposition that due process of law is equivalent to presentment or indictment); *Powell v. Alabama,* 287 U.S. 45, 70 (1932) (relying on Story's Commentaries as updated by Cooley for the proposition that the right to assistance of counsel was encompassed in the concept of due process of law); *United State v. Verdugo-Urquidez,* 494 U.S. 259, 276 (1990) (Kennedy, J., concurring) (quoting Story for the proposition that the Constitution was not a compact between the states or the people of the states); *Cummings v. Missouri,* 71 U.S. 277, 323 (1866) (quoting Story's Commentaries on the meaning of a Bill of Attainder); *District of Columbia v. Heller,* 128 S. Ct. 2783, 2839–41 (2008) (Stevens, J., dissenting) (arguing that "there is not as much as a whisper" in Story supporting an individual rights approach to the Second Amendment).

133 492 U.S. 257, 268 (1989) (quoting 2 J. Story, Commentaries on the Constitution of the United States 624 (T. Cooley, 4th ed., 1873)).

134 457 U.S. 731, 749 (1982) (quoting 3 J. Story, Commentaries on the Constitution of the United States § 1563, pp. 418–19 (lst ed. 1833)).

135 Id.

136 381 U.S. 479, 490 (1965), quoting J. Story, Commentaries on the Constitution of the United States 626–27 (6th ed., 1891).

137 Id. at 490.

138 505 U.S. 144, 156 (1992), quoting 3 J. Story Commentaries on the Constitution of the United States 752 (1833).

139 Id.

140 462 U.S. 919, 949 (1983).

141 143 U.S. 649, 669–71 (1892).

142 Id.

143 *Wallace v. Jaffree*, 472 U.S. 38, 52–53 n.36 (1985) (citing and quoting Joseph Story's Commentaries on the Constitution).

144 Id.

145 Id. at 104–05.

146 217 U.S. 349, 371–72 (1910).

147 Id. at 372.

148 514 U.S. 779, 799, 802 (1995) (citing Story for the proposition that powers which states never possessed are not reserved under the Tenth Amendment).

149 Id. at 856 (Thomas, J., dissenting).

150 Id.

151 *Hurtado v. California*, 110 U.S. 516, 527–28 (1884) (1884) (quoting Cooley for the correct understanding of the concept of due process of law).

152 *Wallace v. Jaffree*, 472 U.S. 38, 105 (1985).

153 See, e.g., *Maxwell v. Dow*, 176 U.S. 581, 593–94 (1900) (quoting Cooley on the meaning of the Fourteenth Amendment Privileges or Immunities Clause); *Hamdi v. Rumsfeld*, 542 U.S. 507, 555 (2004) (Scalia, J., dissenting) (quoting Cooley for the proposition that due process affirms the right to trial by legal process).

154 *Wallace v. Jaffree*, 472 U.S. 38 at 105–06 (1985)(quoting Cooley's Constitutional Limitations at 470–71 for the proposition that practices such as legislative prayer, appointment of military chaplains, proclamations of Thanksgiving, and tax exemptions for churches did not violate the Establishment Clause);*United States v. Brown*, 381 U.S. 437, 445 (1965) (quoting Cooley on the purpose of the prohibition against Bills of Attainder).

155 128 S. Ct. 2783, 2811–12 (2008).

156 274 U.S. 357, 372, 375–77 (1927).

157 Id. at 375–77.

158 310 U.S. 586, 594 (1940).

159 See, e.g., *Home Building & Loan v. Blaisdell*, 290 U.S. 398, 454–67 (1934) (Sutherland, J., dissenting) (providing a lengthy history of the circumstance leading to the adoption of the Contract Clause to show that its purpose was to prohibit debtor forgiveness laws that interfered with existing contractual obligations).

160 176 U.S. 581, 602 (1900).

161 294 U.S. 511, 522 (1935).

162 Id. at 523.

163 Id.

164 83 U.S. 36 (1872).

165 Id. at 71.

166 Id.

167 100 U.S. 303, 307 (1879).

168 330 U.S. 1, 8–15 (1947). In dissent, Justice Rutledge emphasized the importance of history to the creation and understanding of the religion clauses. Id. at 33.

169 Id. at 15.

170 Id. at 16.

171 98 U.S. 145, 164 (1878).

172 330 U.S. at 18. The dissenters found Justice Black's conclusion to be "utterly discordant" with his wall of separation. Id. at 19 (Jackson, J., dissenting). Justice Rutledge wrote "[n]either so high nor so impregnable today as yesterday is the wall raised between church and state . . ." Id. at 29.

173 333 U.S. 203, 244–50 (1948).

174 462 U.S. 919, 947 (1983).

175 381 U.S. 479, 488 (1965).

176 Id. at 489.

177 Id. at 489–90.

178 *Abington Township v. Schempp*, 374 U.S. 203, 237 (1963) (Brennan, J., concurring) (noting that with respect to public prayer, "the historical record is at best ambiguous, and statements can readily be found to support either side of the proposition"). Compare *United States v. Verdugo-Urquidez*, 494 U.S. 259, 266–68 (1990) (framing generation did not believe that the Fourth Amendment applied to noncitizens outside of the territory of the United States), with id. at 287–90 (original understanding does not support such a limitation) (Brennan, J., dissenting).

179 376 U.S. 1 (1964).

180 Compare id. at 10–16 with id. at 31–42.

181 Id. at 30–31. Justice Harlan noted that there "were . . . many statements favoring limited monarchy and property qualifications for suffrage and expressions of approval or disapproval for unrestricted democracy. Such expressions prove as little on one side of this case as they do on the other." Id. at 30.

182 Id. at 34.

183 392 U.S. 83, 95–96 (1968).

184 Id. at 94.

185 Id. at 96, citing Justice Frankfurter's concurrence in *Joint Anti-Fascist Refugee Committee v. McGrath*, 341 U.S. 123, 150 (1951) and his separate opinion in *Coleman v. Miller*, 307 U.S. 433, 460 (1939).

186 392 U.S. at 83, 96.

187 Id. at 96 citing the letter from Chief Justice Jay to Secretary of State of Jefferson.

188 521 U.S. 507, 538–40 (1997) (Scalia, J., concurring); Id. at 551–56 (O'Connor, J., dissenting).

189 Id.

190 Id. at 554.

191 494 U.S. 872 (1990).

192 521 U.S. at 540–41.

193 539 U.S. 607 (2003).

194 Id. at 622–25.

195 Id. at 643–49.

196 Id. at 626.

197 *Seminole*, id. at 131–59; *Alden*, id. at 764–81.

198 527 U.S. at 724.

199 *Alden*, id. at 778–79, 789, 794; *Seminole*, id. at 139, 149.

200 457 U.S. 731, 750 n.31 (1982).

201 Id.

202 Id. at 772–78

203 Id. at 750 n.31.

204 157 U.S. 429 (1895).

205 Id. at 568–74.

206 Id. at 573–74.

207 Id. at 641.

208 Id. at 616.

209 3 Dall 171.

210 157 U.S. at 617–18.

211 Id. at 620.

212 Id. at 570–72.

213 472 U.S. 38, 99 (1985).

214 Id. at 98.

215 Id.

216 Id. at 99.

217 *Alden v. Maine*, 527 U.S. 706, 715–27 (1999). See also *Seminole Tribe of Florida v. Florida*, 517 U.S. 44 (1996).

218 517 U.S. at 54; 527 U.S. at 745–48.

219 517 U.S. at 107 n.5; 527 U.S. at 770 n.8.

220 See *Burnett v. Coronado Oil and Gas Co.*, 285 U.S. 393, 406 (1932) (Brandeis, J., dissenting) ("Stare decisis is usually the wise policy, because in most matters it is more important that the applicable rule of law be settled than it be settled right.")

221 399 U.S. 78 (1970).

222 Id. at 96–97.

223 Id. at 98–99.

224 347 U.S. 483, 489 (1954).

225 Id.

226 Id.

227 Id. at 489–90.

228 Id. at 489.

229 Justice Brennan made the same argument with respect to prayer in public schools in his concurring opinion in *Abington Township v. Schempp*, 374 U.S. 203, 230–39 (1963), noting that "the structure of American education has greatly changed since the First Amendment was adopted," given that it "was . . . main[ly] confined to private schools more often than not under strictly sectarian supervision." He then provided a history of the development of public education in the United States in a lengthy textual footnote. Id. at 239 n.7. He also pointed out that the growth in religious diversity, especially with respect to non-Christian religions in modern America undermines the utility of the framing generation's views on the matter. Id. at 240.

230 343 U.S. 579, 634–35 (1952).

231 545 U.S. 844, 879 (2005).

232 Id.

233 408 U.S. 238, 258 (1972).

234 Id. at 263.

235 Id. at 265–66.

236 217 U.S. 349, 373 (1910).

237 17 U.S. 316, 407 (1819).

238 17 U.S. 518, 644 (1819).

239 277 U.S. 438, 473 (1928).

240 389 U.S. 347, 366 (1967).

241 374 U.S. 203, 234–35 (1963).

242 Id. at 236–37, quoting Justice Jackson in *West Virginia State Board of Education v. Barnette*, 319 U.S. (624, 639 (1943). In *Allegheny v. ACLU*, 492 U.S. 573, 590 (1989), Justice Blackmun, writing for a plurality, cited Professor Laycock for the proposition that the intolerance of eighteenth-century Americans toward Catholics, Jews, Moslems, and atheists should not be a basis for interpreting the Establishment Clause.

243 374 U.S. at 234.

244 Id., quoting *West Virginia State Bd. of Education v. Barnette*, 319 U.S. 624 (1943).

245 Id. at 241.

246 472 U.S. 38, 52–55 (1985).

247 Id.

248 Id. at 52 n.36.

249 Id. at 52–56.

250 Id.

251 Id. at 53 n.38.

252 528 U.S. 495, 512 (2000).

253 319 U.S. 624, 639–40 (1943).

254 391 U.S. 145, 188 (1968).

255 Id.

256 347 U.S. 483, 489–90 (1954).

257 Id. at 490.

258 Id.

259 Id. at 492–93.

260 Id. at 493.

261 545 U.S. 677, 728–30 (2005).

262 Id. at 691–92.

263 545 U.S. 844, 886–89 (2005) (Scalia, J., dissenting).

264 545 U.S. 677, 728–31 (2005). Justice Stevens relied on several sources from early American history, including Justice Story's Constitutional Commentaries. Id. The *McCreary* majority made this same point but not in as much detail as the Stevens dissent in the companion case of *Van Orden*. 545 U.S. 844, 876–81 (2005).

265 545 U.S. 677, 728–31 (2005).

266 Id. at 730.

267 545 U.S. 844, 898 (2005) quoting 6 The Papers of George Washington, Presidential
     Series 285 (D. Twohig ed. 1996).
268 545 U.S. 677, 728 (2005) (Stevens, J., dissenting).

Chapter 5 Tradition and Practice

  1 See, e.g., *Boyd v. United States*, 116 U.S. 616, 622 (1886) ("No doubt long usage,
     acquiesced in by the courts, goes a long way to prove that there is some plausible
     ground or reason for it in the law, or in the historical facts which have imposed
     a particular construction of the law favorable to such usage" but finding no
     such usage with respect to the practice in issue); *Vieth v. Jubelirer*, 541 U.S. 267,
     274–76 (2004) (plurality) (existence of political gerrymandering from well before
     the ratification of the constitution to the present presumably provides some
     reason why it should be considered a nonjusticiable political question); *Field v.
     Clark*, 143 U.S. 649, 683–90 (1892) (relying on a series of similar legislative actions
     extending back to the time of the Washington presidency); *Nixon v. GSA*, 433
     U.S. 425, 510 (1977) (Burger, C.J., dissenting) (majority should not have ignored
     practice of presidential control over his papers extending back to Washington in
     upholding an Act of Congress depriving President Nixon of custody of his papers).
  2 299 U.S. 304, 327–28 (1936). The Court drew this conclusion following a lengthy
     review of the legislative and executive practices. Id. at 322–28.
  3 17 U.S. 316, 401 (1819).
  4 Id. at 401.
  5 Id. at 402.
  6 22 U.S. 1, 190 (1824).
  7 5 U.S. 299 (1803).
  8 Id. at 309.
  9 22 U.S. 1, 192 (1824).
 10 Id.
 11 Id.
 12 Id. at 193.
 13 53 U.S. 299, 315 (1851). In dissent, Justice McLean reached a contrary conclusion,
     reasoning that the Congressional Act of 1789 incorporating by reference existing
     state pilotage acts should be understood as indicating that absent such legislation,
     the state acts would violate the Commerce Clause. Id. at 322.
 14 Id. at 321. See also *Myers v. United States*, 272 U.S. 52, 175 (1926) where the Court
     noted that

> [t]his Court has repeatedly laid down the principle that a contemporaneous
> legislative exposition of the Constitution, when the founders of our
> government and framers of our Constitution were actively participating in
> public affairs, acquiesced in for a long term of years, fixes the construction to
> be given its provisions.

 15 53 U.S. at 321.
 16 Id.
 17 267 U.S. 132, 151 (1925).

18 537 U.S. 186, 200–01 (2003).

19 Id.

20 Id. at 213–14. *Rutan v. Republican Party of Illinois*, 497 U.S. 62, 95 (1990) (Scalia, J., dissenting) (arguing that "when a practice not expressly prohibited by the text of the Bill of Rights bears the endorsement of a long tradition of open, widespread, and unchallenged use that dates back to the beginning of the Republic, we have no proper basis for striking it down"); *United States v. Virginia*, 518 U.S. 515, 568 (1996) (Scalia, J,. dissenting) (arguing that this principle protected the male-only policy of the Virginia Military Institute from invalidation under the Equal Protection Clause as the tradition of government-funded single-sex military institutes predates the passage of the Fourteenth Amendment).

21 343 U.S. 579, 610 (1952).

22 Id. at 610–11. Likewise, speaking particularly of the Due Process Clause, Justice Frankfurter in *Rochin v. California*, 342 U.S. 165, 169–70 (1952) wrote the following:

> [W]ords being symbols do not speak without a gloss. On the one hand the gloss may be the deposit of history, whereby a term gains technical content . . . . On the other hand, the gloss of some of the verbal symbols of the Constitution does not give them a fixed technical content. It exacts a continuing process of application.

23 343 U.S. at 612–20.

24 Id. at 683–700.

25 Id. at 701.

26 279 U.S. 655 (1929).

27 Id. at 690–91.

28 488 U.S. 361, 399–401 (1989).

29 Id. at 401.

30 17 U.S. 316, 402 (1819).

31 Id.

32 453 U.S. 57, 72 (1981).

33 370 U.S. 421, 446 (1962).

34 Id. at 446.

35 Id.

36 Id.

37 Id. at 449.

38 Id.

39 Id.

40 Id.

41 Id. at 450.

42 465 U.S. 668, 674–78 (1984). Justice Scalia emphasized the same historical practices with respect to governmental prayer in his dissenting opinion in *Lee v. Weisman*, 505 U.S. 577, 633–36 (1992) in support of his position that a prayer delivered by a rabbi at a public school graduation did not violate the Establishment Clause.

43 465 U.S. at 719.

44 Id. at 720.

45 Id. at 723–24.

46 Id. at 724.

47 Id.

48 545 U.S. 677, 686–87 (2005).

49 Id. at 688–89.

50 Id. at 690.

51 Id.

52 Id. at 740–42.

53 Id. at 724. Justice Souter raised similar arguments in his concurrence in *Lee v. Weisman*, 505 U.S. 577, 623–26 (1992), responding to Justice Scalia's reliance in his dissent on historical examples of public prayer in the founding era.

54 Id. at 82 n.27.

55 See *Burson v. Freeman*, 504 U.S. 191, 206 (1992) (the fact that all fifty states prohibit electioneering in close proximity to polling places is evidence that this restriction serves a compelling state interest).

56 366 U.S. 420, 495–96 (1961).

57 Id. at 509–11 (1961).

58 Id. at 510–11.

59 397 U.S. 664, 677–78 (1969).

60 Id. at 678.

61 Id.

62 Id. at 676. Justice Brennan made the same point in his concurring opinion. Id. at 687. See also *Reynolds v. United States*, 98 U.S. 145, 165 (1878) (the fact that all states had prohibited polygamy from the very outset to the present showed that the practice was not protected by the Free Exercise Clause of the First Amendment).

63 397 U.S. at 681.

64 Id.

65 Id.

66 Id. at 681–87.

67 403 U.S. 602, 624 (1971).

68 463 U.S. 783 (1983).

69 Id. at 787–90.

70 Id. at 792.

71 545 U.S. 844, 894 (2005).

72 Id. at 877.

73 Id. at 884.

74 307 U.S. 496, 515 (1939).

75 See, e.g., *Schneider v. State*, 308 U.S. 147, 161 (1939) (interest in avoiding littering was insufficient to justify a ban on leaf letting on public property).

76 460 U.S. 37 (1983).

77 Id. at 45–47.

78 Id. at 45.

79 Id. at 46–47.

80 505 U.S. 672 (1992).

81 Id. at 680. Justice O'Connor, concurring and dissenting separately, agreed with this analysis, id. at 685, but would invalidate the ban on leaf letting even in a nonpublic forum.

82 Id.

83 Id.

84 Id. at 681–82.

85 Id. at 697.

86 Id. at 697–98.

87 Id. at 698.

88 Id. at 700. He voted to invalidate the ban on leaf letting but to uphold the ban on solicitation of funds either as reasonable time, place, and manner regulation, or as regulation of conduct rather than speech. Id. at 703.

89 Id. at 710.

90 In his dissenting opinion in *Ray v. Blair*, 343 U.S. 214, 233 (1952), Justice Jackson drew a distinction between using tradition to explicate open-ended constitutional provisions such as due process as opposed to other more specific provisions. There the Court had relied to some extent on the long-standing state custom of expecting presidential electors to remain loyal to the national party's candidate in support of the constitutionality of a state law imposing an obligation of loyalty. Id. at 229. Justice Jackson disagreed arguing that

> [i]f custom were sufficient authority for amendment of the Constitution by Court decree, the decision in this matter would be warranted. Usage may sometimes impart changed content to constitutional generalities, such as "due process" of law, "equal protection," or "commerce among the states." But I do not think powers or discretions granted to federal officials by the Federal Constitution can be forfeited by the Court for disuse.

Id. at 233. With respect to structural provisions, he concluded that "[a] political practice which has its origin in custom must rely on custom for its sanctions."

91 260 U.S. 22, 31 (1922).

92 211 U.S. 78, 107–08 (1908).

93 Id. at 108–09.

94 316 U.S. 455 (1942).

95 Id. at 467–71, 477–80 (Appendix summarizing state practices).

96 338 U.S. 25, 28–38 (1949) (pointing out that twenty-six of twenty-seven states that had considered the issue had rejected the exclusionary rule).

97 Id. at 46. *Adkins v. Children's Hospital*, 261 U.S. 525, 560 (1923) (rejecting proof that social welfare type legislation was constitutional because it had been widely adopted by the states with the observation that proof of constitutionality "cannot be aided by counting heads").

98 367 U.S. 643, 651 (1961).

99 391 U.S. 145 (1968).

100 Id. at 151–54.

101 Id. at 156.

102 Id. at 183.

103 381 U.S. 479 (1965).

104 367 U.S. 497, 543–45 (1961).

105 Id. at 542. See *Ingraham v. Wright*, 430 U.S. 651, 676 (1977) (The "balance struck" by history indicates that corporeal punishment in schools does not violate substantive liberty protected by Fourteenth Amendment Due Process as long as it is carried out within the bounds of the common law privilege of justification).

106 Id. at 542–43.

107 381 U.S. 479, 500 (1965).

108 Id. at 511–12.

109 367 U.S. at 552.

110 Id. at 553.

111 See, e.g., *Moore v. City of East Cleveland*, 431 U.S. 494, 503–04 (1977) (due process liberty protects family life because it is so deeply embedded in our history and tradition).

112 410 U.S. 113, 130–47 (1973).

113 See id. at 174 (Rehnquist, J., dissenting) (noting that most states have prohibited abortion for over a century).

114 521 U.S. 702 (1997).

115 Id. at 710.

116 Id. at 710–11. *Cruzan v. Missouri Department of Health*, 497 U.S. 261, 271–84 (1990) (cataloguing how state law had long protected the interest in the preservation of life in the course of approving of Missouri's imposition of higher burden of proof before life support systems could be terminated). See also *Roth v. United States*, 354 U.S. 476, 484–85 (1957) (contending that the conclusion that "obscenity as utterly without redeeming social importance . . . is mirrored in the universal judgment that obscenity should be restrained reflected in the international agreement of over 50 nations, in the obscenity laws of all of the 48 States, and in the 20 obscenity laws enacted by Congress from 1842 to1956").

117 521 U.S. 702, 722 (1997). The Court concluded that in order to recognize assisted suicide as a fundamental right, "we would have to reverse centuries of legal doctrine and practice, and strike down the considered policy choice of almost every State." Id. at 723.

118 Id. at 756 n.4.

119 Id. at 722 n.7.

120 478 U.S. at 186, 190 (1986) (quoting *Griswold v. Connecticut*, 381 U.S. 479, 505 (1965)).

121 Id. at 193.

122 Id. at 196–97.

123 Id. at 199, 206.

124 Id. at 217.

125 Id. at 210.

126 Id. at 216.

127 539 U.S. 558, 568–70 (2003).

128 Id. at 570.

129 Id. at 571. The Court cited decisions by five state courts that had rejected the *Bowers* approach under their own constitutions. Obviously these state court

decisions have no controlling effect on interpretation of the United States Constitution; however, the Court deemed them to be some evidence of the direction that the law was taking.

130 Id. at 597–98.

131 478 U.S. 186, 192–93 (1986).

132 Id. at 568–70.

133 Id. at 595–96.

134 356 U.S. 86, 102 (1958).

135 Id.

136 521 U.S. 702, 718 n.16 (1997).

137 Id. at 734.

138 Id. at 785–87.

139 478 U.S. 186, 196 (1986).

140 539 U.S. 558, 567–73 (2003).

141 Id. at 573.

142 Id.

143 Id. at 577.

144 Id.

145 Id. at 598, quoting *Foster v. Florida*, 537 U.S. 990 n.* (2002) (Thomas, J., concurring in denial of cert.).

146 491 U.S. 110 (1989).

147 Id. at 114–15. The child through her guardian was also attempting to obtain visitation rights for her natural father.

148 Id. at 127 n.6.

149 Id. at 127.

150 Id. at 125–27.

151 Id. at 139.

152 Id. at 127 n.6.

153 Id.

154 Id.

155 Id.

156 Id. at 137.

157 Id. at 127 n.6.

158 Compare id. at n.6 with id. at 139.

159 Id. at 139–40.

160 Id. at 127 n 6.

161 Id. at 132.

162 505 U.S. 833, 847–48 (1992).

163 Id. at 847.

164 388 U.S. 1, 12 (1967).

165 505 U.S. at 848.

166 Id.

167 521 U.S. 702, 771 n.11 (1997).

168 478 U.S. 186 (1986).

169 539 U.S. 558 (2003).

170 478 U.S. at 188.

171 Id. at 190.

172 Id. at 199, 202.

173 Id. at 199 (quoting Oliver Wendell Homes, *The Path of Law*, 10 Harv. L. Rev. 457, 469 (1897)).

174 Id. at 199.

175 Id. at 217–18.

176 539 U.S. 558, 566–67 (2003).

177 Id. at 567.

178 *Planned Parenthood of Southeastern Pennsylvania v. Casey*, 505 U.S. 833, 848–50 (1992).

179 252 U.S. 416, 433 (1920). See also *Rummel v. Estelle*, 445 U.S. 263, 307 (1980) (Powell, J., dissenting) ("we are construing a living Constitution.")

180 343 U.S. 495, 518 (1952).

181 341 U.S. 494, 517, 521 (1951). He repeated this observation again a few pages later. Id. at 523.

182 319 U.S. 141, 152 (1943).

183 Id. at 152–53.

184 398 U.S. 398, 442 (1932).

185 110 U.S. 516, 529 (1884). The Court elaborated, noting that

> [i]t is more consonant to the true philosophy of our historical legal institutions to say that the spirit of personal liberty and individual right . . . was preserved and developed by a progressive growth and wise adaption to new circumstances and situations of the forms and processes found fit to give, from time to time, new expression and greater effect to modern ideas of self-government.

Id. at 530. 110 U.S. at 538. In *Williams v. Illinois*, for instance, the Court indicated that there would be a "need to be open to reassessment of ancient practices other than those explicitly mandated by the Constitution" where circumstances had changed. 399 U.S. 235, 240 (1970). This led the Court to conclude that despite historical tradition, imprisoning a criminal defendant for a period of time exceeding the amount of the maximum permitted by the statute due to inability to pay a fine violated Equal Protection of the Law in view of the increase in reliance on fines as criminal punishment. Id.

186 351 U.S. 12, 20–21 (1956).

187 Id. at 21.

188 383 U.S. 663 (1966).

189 Id. at 669.

190 Id. at 678. Justice Harlan also objected to the Court's approach arguing that "it is all wrong, in my view, for the Court to adopt the political doctrines popularly accepted at a particular moment of our history and to declare all others to be irrational and invidious. . . ." Id. at 686. See also *West Coast Hotel v. Parrish*, 300 U.S. 379, 402–03 (1937) (Sutherland, J., dissenting) (arguing that the Constitution is "made up of living words that apply to every new condition"; however, the words must still apply to a situation today as they would have when written).

191 356 U.S. 86, 101 (1958).

192 536 U.S. 765, 785 (2002).

193 Id. at 785–86.

194 Id. at 786.

195 Id.

196 Id. The Court cited the tradition relied upon in *Burson v. Freeman*, 504 U.S. 191 (1992).

197 376 U.S. 1, 42–43 (1964).

198 Id. at 43–44.

199 Id. at 45.

200 Id.

201 435 U.S. 618, 622–25 (1978).

202 Id. at 625.

203 478 U.S. 186, 192–94 (1986), id. at 196–97 (Burger, C.J., concurring).

204 539 U.S. 558, 572–74 (2003). The Court noted that as *Bowers* had pointed out, all fifty states had outlawed sodomy as of 1961; however, by the time *Bowers* was decided, the figure had dropped to twenty-five, and by the time of *Lawrence* seventeen years later, the number had dropped to thirteen, with only four exclusively targeting homosexuals. Id. at 572.

205 445 U.S. 573, 598 (1980).

206 Id.

207 Id. at 599.

208 Id.

209 Id.

210 Id.

211 536 U.S. 304, 314–16 (2002).

212 Id. at 315.

213 Id. at 316.

214 Id.

215 Id.

216 Id. at 342.

217 Id. at 343.

218 Id. at 344–45.

219 283 U.S. 697, 718 (1931).

220 273 U.S. 510, 531 (1927).

221 521 U.S. 898, 906–08 (1997). Justice Stevens, dissenting, argued that the opposite inference should be drawn, given that in the early days judges routinely carried out many executive duties, and as such, the imposition of such duties on state courts was equivalent to the imposition of these duties on executive officials. Id. at 951–52.

222 369 U.S. 186, 300–25 (1962).

223 369 U.S. 186, 301 (1962).

224 Id.

225 377 U.S. 533 (1964).

226 504 U.S. 191, 200–06 (1992).

227 Id. at 206.

228 Id. at 220–22.

229 Id. at 220.

230 Id. at 221–22.

231 Id. at 222.

232 536 U.S. 304, 316 n.21 (2002).

233 Id. at 322 (Rehnquist, J., dissenting), id. at 346–48 (Scalia, J., dissenting).

234 Id. at 322 (Rehnquist, J., dissenting).

235 Id. at 322–24.

236 Id. at 344–46.

Chapter 6   Structural Reasoning

1 Charles L. Black, Jr., Structure and Relationship in Constitutional Law (1969).

2 Id. at 13.

3 5 U.S. 137 (1803).

4 14 U.S. 304 (1816).

5 17 U.S. 316 (1819).

6 See C. Black, id. at 7.

7 After making his structural case, Marshall then noted "the peculiar expressions of the constitution of the United States furnish additional arguments. . . ." 5 U.S. at 178.

8 Id. at 176.

9 Id. at 177.

10 Id. at 178.

11 Id.

12 14 U.S. 304 (1816).

13 Id. at 339–40, 343.

14 Id. at 351–52.

15 Id. at 352.

16 Id. at 348. Chief Justice Marshall made much the same argument a few year later in *Cohens v. Virginia*, 19 U.S. 264, 386 (1821) where the question was whether the United States Supreme Court had jurisdiction over the final judgment of the highest court of a state when a federal issue was presented in a state criminal case. See also *Ableman v. Booth*, 62 U.S. 506 (1858) for a similar argument.

There are areas, however, where as a structural matter, the Court has recognized that there is a valid constitutional interest in diversity among states. For instance, in the area of obscenity, the Court has recognized that Maine or Mississippi need not have the same community standards of acceptability as Las Vegas or New York. *Miller v. California*, 413 U.S.15, 32 (1972).

17 See 17 U.S. 316 (1819). C. Black, supra note at 13–14.

18 17 U.S. at 411.

19 Id. at 407.

20 Id. at 409–10.

21 Id. at 407, 411.

22 Id. at 426.

23 Id.

24 Id.

25 Id. at 434–35.

26 Id. at 435–36.

27 Id. at 436.

28 Id. at 428.

29 See Chapter 6, section IV, part D.

30 Id. at 428–29.

31 19 U.S. 264 (1821).

32 Id. at 413.

33 Id. at 414. See also *Ableman v. Booth*, 62 U.S. 506, 517–21 (1858) (making a structural argument to justify federal judicial supremacy over state action implicating federal concerns).

34 221 U.S. 559, 566, 575 (1911).

35 74 U.S. 700 (1868).

36 Id. at 725.

37 Id. at 726.

38 17 U.S. 316, 404–05 (1819).

39 149 U.S. 698, 711 (1893). Despite the breadth of this power over immigration, the modern Court would not sustain a Congressional Act as tinged with racism and as devoid of due process as the Act in question.

40 Id. at 737.

41 Id. at 757.

42 103 U.S. 168, 191 (1880).

43 Id. at 192.

44 312 U.S. 569, 574 (1941).

45 Id. at 576. In his dissenting opinion in *Saia v. New York*, 334 U.S. 558, 565 (1948) where the Court had invalidated a law prohibiting the use of loud speakers without a permit, Justice Frankfurter wrote that "[o]ur democracy presupposes the deliberative process as a condition of thought and of responsible choice by the electorate." This lead Justice Frankfurter to conclude that preserving the conditions for such thought and deliberation by prohibiting the noise that might interfere with it should not be unconstitutional. Id. Indeed, in the previous sentence, he had pointed out that the framers of the Constitution "had the street outside Independence Hall covered with earth so that their deliberations might not be disturbed by passing traffic." This, of course, is a structural argument.

46 268 U.S. 510, 535 (1925). In 1923, in the case of *Meyer v. Nebraska*, 262 U.S. 390, 399 (1923), the Court summarized this endeavor to that date as follows:

> [Liberty] denotes not merely freedom from bodily restraint but also the right of the individual to contract, to engage in any of the common occupations of life, to acquire useful knowledge, to marry, establish a home and bring up children, to worship God according to the dictates of his own conscience, and generally to enjoy those privileges long recognized at common law as essential to the orderly pursuit of happiness by free men.

The Court would later rely on much of this catalogue of protected aspects of liberty as providing the foundation for its constitutional right of privacy.

47 197 U.S. 11 (1905).

48 197 U.S. 11, 26 (1905).

49 367 U.S. 497, 542 (1961).

50 299 U.S. 304 (1936).

51 Id. at 312.

52 Id. at 315.

53 Id. at 316–17.

54 Id.

55 Id. at 318.

56 See, e.g., Charles Lofgren. United States v. Curtiss-Wright Export Corporation: An Historical Reassessment, 83 Yale L.J. 1 (1973).

57 Id. at 317.

58 Id. at 319–20.

59 542 U.S. 507 (2004).

60 Id. at 579–85.

61 Id. at 580–82.

62 Id. at 581, quoting Federalist 70.

63 Id. at 581–84.

64 Id. at 589–90.

65 Id. at 535–37.

66 517 U.S. 44 (1996).

67 527 U.S. 706 (1999).

68 517 U.S. at 47.

69 Id. at 72–73.

70 Id. at 77.

71 Id. at 100.

72 527 U.S. at 712.

73 Id. at 713.

74 Id.

75 Id. at 759, 762–94, 796–802.

76 517 U.S. at 67, 68.

77 527 U.S. at 713.

78 Id. at 728.

79 Id. at 729.

80 Id. at 748–53.

81 Id. at 763.

82 Id. at 734.

83 505 U.S. 144 (1992).

84 Id. at 168–69. Justice Scalia, writing for the Court, emphasized the same considerations in *Printz v. United States*, 521 U.S. 898, 919–22 (1997) in the course of holding that Congress could not commandeer state executive officials to carry out federal regulatory programs either.

85 Id.

86 Id. at 181.

87 Id. at 206.

88 19 U.S. 264, 386–87 (1821).

89 Id. at 387.

90 17 U.S. 316, 427–31 (1819).

91 Id. at 436.

92 Wechsler, The Political Safeguards of Federalism, in *Principles and Politics and Fundamental Law* (1961).

93 22 U.S. 1 (1824).

94 Id. at 197.

95 303 U.S. 177 (1938).

96 Id. at 185 n.2.

97 See J. Ely, Democracy and Distrust (1980) for a detailed explication of this theory of judicial review.

98 325 U.S. 761, 768 n.2 (1945). The Court relied on this reasoning again in the dormant Commerce Clause context in *West Lynn Creamery v. Healy*, 512 U.S. 186, 200–01 (1994). In the course of invalidating a Massachusetts program that imposed a nondiscriminatory tax on all milk dealers but distributed the funds raised only to in-state dairy farmers, the Court noted that the program had the effect of essentially buying off the dairy farmers—the in-state group otherwise most likely to object to the tax. Justice Scalia, concurring, and Justice Rehnquist, dissenting, both expressed skepticism as to whether such interest group process oriented analysis should play any role whatsoever in the Court's decision. Id. at 207 (Scalia, J., concurring), id. at 212 (Rehnquist, C.J., dissenting).

99 394 U.S. 144, 153 n.4 (1938).

100 Id.

101 Id.

102 Id.

103 See Chapter 8, section IV, part C.

104 426 U.S. 833 (1976).

105 Id. at 842–52, 855.

106 Id. at 843–44, n.12.

107 Id. at 858–76.

108 Id. at 876–77.

109 See Chapter 6, section II, part C.

110 Id. at 876–77.

111 469 U.S. 528 (1985).

112 Id. at 538–47, 556. He elaborated, noting that

> [o]f course, we continue to recognize that the States occupy a special and specific position in our constitutional system and that the scope of Congress' authority under the Commerce Clause must reflect that position. But the principal and basic limit on the federal commerce power is that inherent in all congressional action—the built-in restraints that our system provides through state participation in federal governmental action.

113 Id. at 551.

114 Id. at 552–53.

115 Id. at 552–53.

116 Id. at 565–67.

117 Id. at 564 n.8.

118 Id. at 565–67.

119 Id. at 565 n.8. Justice O'Connor wrote a separate dissenting opinion emphasizing the threat to state autonomy posed by the growth in the national economy followed by an increase in federal regulation. She faulted the Court for failing to take account of this trend in its analysis of federal encroachment on the states. Id. at 580–89.

120 Id. at 568–69, quoting or citing Samuel Adams, George Mason, James Madison, and debates in the state ratifying conventions.

121 469 U.S. at 551.

122 Id. at 567. The Court has often reaffirmed the central role of judicial review in the context of separation of powers. See, e.g., *Powell v. McCormick*, 395 U.S. 486 (1969); *Flast v. Cohen*, 392 U.S. 83 (1968).

123 514 U.S. 549, 577–79 (1995).

124 Id. at 577.

125 Id. at 576.

126 Id. at 578.

127 506 U.S. 224, 233–35 (1993).

128 Id.

129 Id. at 235.

130 Id. at 244–45.

131 Id. at 235.

132 521 U.S. 507 (1997).

133 Id. at 523–24.

134 Id. at 529.

135 73 U.S. 35 (1867).

136 Id. at 39.

137 Id. at 45.

138 Id. at 43.

139 See, e.g., *Shapiro v. Thompson*, 394 U.S. 618 (1969); *Saenz v. Roe*, 521 U.S. 507 (1999).

140 521 U.S. 507 at 510–11, quoting U.S. Const., Amd. 14 S 1.

141 448 U.S. 555 (1980).

142 Id. at 565–77.

143 Id. at 587–88. For these propositions, Justice Brennan cited commentators, including Alexander Meiklejohn, Judge Robert Bork, and John Hart Ely as well as his own opinion for the Court in *New York Times v. Sullivan*, 376 U.S. 254 (1964). Id.

144 448 U.S. at 589.

145 Id. at 593–97. Justice Souter, dissenting in *Johanns v. Livestock Marketing Association*, 544 U.S. 550, 571–72 (2005) raised a structural argument as a check against abuse. He maintained that a program permitting governmental use of

taxes to propagate a commercial message is not constitutionally troublesome as long as the fact of government sponsorship is clear to the audience as the political check of the democratic process will guard against abuse; however, it does raise a First Amendment problem when the government sponsorship of the message is omitted or concealed.

146 272 U.S. 52 (1925).

147 Id. at 126.

148 Id. at 130–35.

149 Id. at 245 (Brandeis, J., dissenting).

150 Id.

151 Id. at 247.

152 Id.

153 Id. at 248.

154 Id. at 293.

155 Id. at 295.

156 Id.

157 295 U.S. 602 (1934).

158 Although Congress can provide protection to federal officers against arbitrary removal by the president, it may not participate in the removal process itself other than through impeachment. *Bowsher v. Syner*, 478 U.S. 714, 734 (1986).

159 295 U.S. at 626–30.

160 343 U.S. 579 (1952).

161 Id. at 588.

162 Id. at 635.

163 Id.

164 Id. at 636–38.

165 Id. at 638–55.

166 457 U.S. 731, 748 (1982).

167 Id.

168 Id.

169 Id. at 749.

170 Id. at 750.

171 Id. at 753.

172 Id.at 750.

173 Id. at 758.

174 Id. at 779.

175 418 U.S. 683 (1974).

176 Id. at 704.

177 Id. at 705.

178 Id. at 707.

179 Id.

180 19 U.S. 264 (1821).

181 Id. at 377.

182 Id. at 379–83.

183 Id. at 384.

184 514 U.S. 779 (1995).

185 Technically, the Arkansas law at issue did not completely bar the election of a congressman who had already served three consecutive terms, but it simply prohibited his name from being listed on the ballot. Id. at 783. Though he could still run and win election as a write-in candidate, the Court quite properly viewed this limitation as effectively imposing a term limit. Id. at 828–31.

186 The most relevant textual provision was the Qualifications Clause of Article I, s 5, cl 1.

187 The leading precedent was the Court's decision in *Powell v. McCormick*, 395 U.S. 486 (1969).

188 514 U.S. at 800–02.

189 Id. at 804–05.

190 Id.

191 Id. at 822.

192 Id. at 837–38.

193 Article I, section 5, cl 1.

194 Article I, section 6.

195 Article I, section 4, cl 1.

196 514 U.S. at 803–04.

197 Id. at 820–21.

198 Id. at 793.

199 Id. at 838.

200 Id. at 840.

201 Id. at 841–42.

202 Id. at 846.

203 Id. at 847.

204 Id. at 848.

205 Id. at 848, 853.

206 Id. at 857–58.

207 Id. at 858.

208 Id. at 864–73.

209 Id. at 877.

210 527 U.S. 706, 728 (1999).

211 Id. at 748–53.

212 Id. at 758.

213 Id. at 801–03.

214 Id. at 798–99.

215 See, e.g., *United States v. Lopez*, 514 U.S. 549 (1995); *United States v. Printz*, 521 U.S. 898 (1996); *New York v. United States*, 505 U.S. 144 (1992).

216 462 U.S. 919, 960 (1983).

217 Id. at 952–54.

218 Id. at 964–65.

219 478 U.S. 714 (1986).

220 Id. at 727–33.

221 Id. at 737.

Chapter 7 Precedent

1 116 U.S. 616 (1886).

2 Id. at 617–18.

3 Id. at 618.

4 19 How St Tr 1029.

5 116 U.S. at 622.

6 Id. at 638.

7 232 U.S. 383 (1914).

8 Id. at 390.

9 Id. at 393.

10 Id. at 392.

11 251 U.S. 385, 391–92 (1920).

12 338 U.S. 25 (1949).

13 Id. at 26.

14 Id. at 27–28.

15 Id. at 28.

16 Id. at 29.

17 Id. at 31–32. Justice Black concurred on the grounds that the exclusionary rule was a judicially created remedy rather than an element of the Fourth Amendment itself. Id. at 39–40.

18 Id. at 42–45.

19 367 U.S. 643 (1961).

20 Id. at 646–48.

21 Id. at 649.

22 Id. at 651–53. The Court pointed out that in a series of cases decided since *Wolf*, it had eliminated methods by which federal officials could avoid the exclusionary rule of *Weeks*. Id. at 654.

23 Id. at 655–56.

24 Id. at 661–62.

25 Id. at 678–81.

26 381 U.S. 618 (1965).

27 Id. at 636–37.

28 Id. at 637–38.

29 Id. at 649.

30 414 U.S. 338 (1974).

31 Id. at 347.

32 Id. at 348.

33 Id. at 351–52. In *United States v. Janis*, 428 U.S. 433 (1976), the Court reached the same result with respect to the introduction of illegally seized material in civil proceedings.

34 Id. at 352.

35 Id. at 356.

36 Id. at 357, quoting *Weeks v. United States*, 232 U.S. 383, 391–92, 394 (1914). Justice Brennan also quoted from the classic dissents of Justices Brandeis and Holmes in *Olmstead v. United States*, 277 U.S. 438, 485, 575 (1928).

37 Id. at 359, quoting *Mapp v. Ohio*, 367 U.S. at 651.

38 Id. at 362–63. In response to the majority's argument that the petitioner in *Silverthorne* had already been indicted, Justice Brennan pointed out that the prosecutor could quite possible have been seeking further charges. Id.

39 428 U.S. 465, 482 (1976).

40 Id. at 486.

41 Id. at 487–95. Justice Burger, concurring, noted that the exclusionary rule had initially been created in *Weeks* out of a concern to protect private papers; however, it has since been transformed into a means of excluding evidence of the bodies in murder cases. Id. at 502.

42 468 U.S. 897, 922 (1984).

43 Id. at 906.

44 Id.

45 Id. at 916–17.

46 Id. at 928.

47 Id. at 932–33.

48 Id. at 935–41.

49 Id. at 943. He continued: "A doctrine that is explained as if it were an empirical proposition but for which there is only limited empirical support is both inherently unstable and an easy mark for critics." Id.

50 Id. at 952–56.

51 See *Pennsylvania Bd. of Probation v. Scott*, 524 U.S. 357, 364 (1998) (exclusionary rule does not apply to parole revocation hearings); *Arizona v. Evans*, 514 U.S. 1, 14 (1995) (evidence should not be excluded on account of a clerical error); *INS v. Lopez-Mendoza*, 468 U.S. 1032, 1050 (1984) (exclusionary rule does not apply to deportation hearings).

52 126 S. Ct. 2159, 2165 (2006).

53 Id. at 2168.

54 Id. at 2175.

55 411 U.S. 1 (1973).

56 Id. at 20.

57 351 U.S. 12 (1956).

58 372 U.S. 353 (1963).

59 411 U.S. 1, 20 (1973).

60 Id. at 21.

61 Id. at 22–23.

62 Id. at 118–19.

63 Id.

64 Id.

65 323 U.S. 214, 246 (1944).

66 320 U.S. 81 (1943).

67 323 U.S. at 246.

68 Id. at 247.

69 Id.

70 381 U.S. 479 (1965).

71 Justice Douglas began his analysis by denying the charge leveled by Justice Black in dissent that the decision was based on the substantive due process reasoning of *Lochner v. New York*. Id. at 482.

72 Id. at 483.

73 268 U.S. 510 (1925).

74 262 U.S. 390 (1923).

75 381 U.S. at 482–83.

76 291 U.S. 502 (1934).

77 300 U.S. 379 (1937).

78 357 U.S. 449 (1958).

79 381 U.S. 481–83 (1965).

80 357 U.S. at 463–66.

81 381 U.S. at 482–83.

82 Id. at 484. The concept of penumbral rights was first mentioned by Justice Holmes in his dissenting opinion in *Olmstead v. United States*, 277 U.S. 438, 469 (1928).

83 Id.

84 Id. at 485.

85 Id. at 485–86.

86 Id. at 499–500.

87 Id. at 509–10.

88 405 U.S. 438 (1971).

89 381 U.S. at 485–86 (Douglas, J., opinion of the Court) (focusing on "privacy surrounding the marital relationship"); id. at 495, 498 (Goldberg, J., concurring, describing the right as privacy in "the martial relationship and the martial home" and noting that laws prohibiting adultery and fornication are unquestionably constitutional); id. at 505 (White, J., concurring, recognizing that it would be permissible for the state to outlaw premarital and extramarital sexual activity).

90 367 U.S. 497, 546 (1961).

91 405 U.S. 438 (1972).

92 Id. at 453.

93 Id.

94 319 U.S. 624, 633–36 (1943).

95 430 U.S. 705, 714 (1977).

96 Id. at 715.

97 Id. at 715.

98 Id. at 720–22.

99 370 U.S. 660 (1962).

100 392 U.S. 514 (1968).

101 370 U.S. at 666.

102 Id.

103 392 U.S. at 532.

104 Id. at 567.

105 Id. at 533.

106 Id. at 534.

107 Id. at 538–45.

108 53 U.S. 299, 324 (1851).

109 27 U.S. 245 (1829).

110 341 U.S. 494, 504–05 (1951).

111 Id. at 504.

112 Id. at 504–05.

113 Id. at 528.

114 Id. at 534–39.

115 436 U.S. 149 (1978).

116 Id. at 160 n.10. The three cases were *North Georgia Finishing, Inc. v. Di-Chem, Inc.*, 419 U.S. 601 (1975); *Fuentes v. Shevin*, 407 U.S. 67 (1972); *Sniadach v. Family Finance Corp.*, 395 U.S. 337 (1969).

117 Id. at 174.

118 193 U.S. 197, 400–01 (1904).

119 403 U.S. 713 (1971).

120 Id. at 753 (Harlan, J., dissenting).

121 Id. at 714.

122 Id. at 753.

123 418 U.S. 683 (1974).

124 Id. at 687–89.

125 Id. at 704–12.

126 Id. at 706, 712 n.19.

127 531 U.S. 98 (2000).

128 Id. at 104–11.

129 Id. at 112–22.

130 505 U.S. 833, 872–73 (1992).

131 410 U.S. 113 (1973).

132 505 U.S. at 871.

133 Id. at 873–75.

134 Id. The Court partially overruled *Ohio v. Akron Center for Reproductive Health*, 497 U.S. 502 (1990) and *Thornburgh v. American College of Obstetricians and Gynecologists*, 476 U.S. 747 (1986).

135 Id. at 944 (1992). He argued that *Roe* was wrongly decided and should be overruled. Id. later in the opinion the Chief Justice remarked that "Roe continues to exist, but only in the way a storefront on a western movie set exists: a mere facade to give the illusion of reality." Id. at 954.

136 Id. at 993.

137 326 U.S. 501 (1946).

138 Id. at 503.

139 Id. at 505–08.

140 Id. at 506.

141 Id. at 512.

142 391 U.S. 308, 325 (1968). At the time the picketing occurred, the mall had only two tenants.

143 Id. at 323–24.

144 Id. at 318–19.

145 Id. at 324.

146 Id. at 318.

147 Id. at 318–22.

148 Id. 320 n.9.

149 Id. at 331.

150 Id. at 330.

151 Id. at 331.

152 Id. at 338–39.

153 407 U.S. 551 (1972).

154 Id. at 562.

155 Id.

156 Id. at 564.

157 Id. at 584.

158 424 U.S. 507, 518 (1976).

159 Id. at 519–520.

160 Id. at 520.

161 332 U.S. 46 (1947).

162 Id. at 59.

163 Id. at 62.

164 Id.

165 Id. at 72–74 (Black, J., dissenting).

166 211 U.S. 78 (1908).

167 336 U.S. 77, 89 (1949).

168 See, e.g., *Slaughter-House Cases*, 83 U.S. 36 (1872) (6-3); *Mapp v. Ohio*, 367 U.S. 643 (1961) (5-4); *Furman v. Georgia*, 408 U.S. 238 (1972) (5-4); *Regents of the University of California v. Bakke*, 438 U.S. 265 (1978) (5-4); *U.S. Term Limits, Inc., v. Thornton*, 514 U.S. 779 (1995) (5-4); *District of Columbia v. Heller*, 128 S. Ct. 2783 (2008) (5-4).

169 494 U.S. 872, 879 (1990).

170 310 U.S. 586 (1940). Justice Scalia failed to acknowledge that *Gobitis* had been overruled, although that would be common knowledge among constitutional experts.

171 19 U.S. 264, 399–400 (1821).

172 Id. See, e.g., *United States v. Gonzalez-Lopez*, 548 U.S. 140, 156 (2006) (Alito, J., dissenting) (It is unreasonable to read statements in earlier denial of the choice of counsel cases as addressing the issue of prejudice as that issue was not presented in those cases.) It is well accepted that the Court should rarely discuss or purport to decide issues not yet presented. It is a rule that is not always followed, however. One of the most stunning examples of disregard for this general rule is Justice Brennan's concurring opinion in *Abington Township v. Schempp*, in which he went out of his way for several pages to address and attempt to resolve virtually every conceivable freedom of religion issue that might arise in the future. 374 U.S. 203, 290–304 (1963).

173 19 U.S. at 400.

174 Id.

175 Id. at 401.

176 426 U.S. 229 (1976).

177 403 U.S. 217 (1971).

178 Id. at 219.

179 Id. at 259–60 (White, J., dissenting).

180 Id. at 224–25.

181 Id. at 224–26.

182 426 U.S. at 244–45.

183 Id. at 242–43.

184 Id. at 243.

185 Id. at 244–45.

186 391 U.S. 145 (1968).

187 176 U.S. 581 (1900).

188 391 U.S. at 155.

189 Id. at 184 n.24.

190 517 U.S. 44, 67 (1996) (citing 292 U.S. 313, 321–23 (1934)).

191 Id.

192 Id. at 123–27.

193 Id. at 67.

194 The Court in *Seminole* did quote language from concurring opinions of Justices Kennedy and O'Connor that seemed to support this approach. Id. at 67, quoting from *County of Allegheny v. ACLU, Greater Pittsburg Chapter*, 492 U.S. 573, 668 (1989) (Kennedy, J., concurring); *Sheet Metal Workers v. EEOC*, 478 U.S. 421, 490 (1986) (O'Connor, J., concurring). Justice Souter's primary argument in favor of the Common Law basis for sovereign immunity was that the holdings of several other lines of cases established that the Court itself had not taken the language that the majority relied on seriously in the past. Thus, he argued that the Court would not have held that states could consent to federal jurisdiction in citizen suits if there was a complete constitutional bar against such jurisdiction. 517 U.S. at 126–128.

195 387 U.S. 253, 261 (1967), citing 22 U.S. 738 (1824).

196 Id. at 276.

197 Id.

198 542 U.S. 507 (2004).

199 4 Wall. 2 (1866).

200 542 U.S. at 567–68 (Scalia, J., dissenting).

201 Id. at 522 (O'Connor, J., writing for a plurality).

202 Id. at 522–23.

203 Id. at 571–72 (Scalia, J., dissenting).

204 402 U.S. 183 (1971).

205 408 U.S. 238, 311–14 (1972) (White, J., concurring). Justice White emphasized the absence of standards guiding the jury, and his opinion was necessary to support the holding.

206 Id. at 400–01 (Burger, C.J., dissenting).

207 428 U.S. 153, 195 n.47 (1976) (Stewart, J., plurality).

208 Id.

209 Id.

210 See, e.g., *Southern Pacific v. Arizona*, 325 U.S. 761, 783 (1945) (States have a greater interest in regulating highways, as recognized in *South Carolina v. Barnwell*, than in regulating railroads because states are generally responsible for the maintenance of highways within their states.)

211 391 U.S. 367, 382 (1968).

212 Id. at 384 n.30.

213 Id. at 384–85.

214 448 U.S. 555, 564, 580–81 (1980) (Burger, C.J., plurality), Id. at 584 (Stevens, J., concurring), Id. at 584–86 (Brennan, J., concurring).

215 443 U.S. 368 (1979).

216 394 U.S. 557 (1969).

217 Id. at 564.

218 Id. at 565.

219 Id. at 565–66.

220 Id. at 566, 567, 568.

221 402 U.S. 351, 354 (1971).

222 413 U.S. 49, 65–67 (1973).

223 188 U.S. 321, 358–59 (1903).

224 247 U.S. 251 (1918).

225 Id. at 272.

226 Id. at 278–80.

227 312 U.S. 100, 115–17 (1941).

228 494 U.S. 872, 881–82 (1990).

229 Id. at 895–97.

230 Id.

231 262 U.S. 447 (1923).

232 392 U.S. 83 (1968).

233 Id. at 102–104.

234 Id. at 117–30.

235 Id. at 121–22.

236 Id. at 127. Even Justice Fortas, who concurred in the Court's opinion, stated that "[t]his thesis [that the Establishment Clause specifically limits the spending power], slender as its basis is, provides a direct 'nexus' . . . between the use and collection of taxes and the Congressional action here. . . ." This was hardly a glowing endorsement of the Court's reasoning. Id. at 115.

237 454 U.S. 464 (1982).

238 Id. at 479–80.

239 Id. at 510. Justice Stevens, dissenting, argued that the majority's distinctions would "trivialize the standing doctrine." Id. at 514.

240 Id. at 511–12.

241 127 S. Ct. 2553 (2007).

242 Id. at 2559–60.

243 Id. at 2566.

244 487 U.S. 589 (1988).

245 127 S. Ct. at 2567–68.

246 Id. at 2571–72.

247 Id. at 2580.

248 Id. at 2582.

249 Id. at 2584.

250 413 U.S. 717, 718 n.1 (1973).

251 432 U.S. 1 (1977).

252 Id. at 9 n.11.

253 Id. at 15 n.*.

254 501 U.S. 808, 827 (1991).

255 339 U.S. 56 (1950).

256 Id. at 86.

257 157 U.S. 429, 651 (1895).

258 530 U.S. 428, 443 (2000).

259 321 U.S. 649, 665 (1944). See *Payne v. Tennessee*, 501 U.S. 808, 828 n.1 (1991) (citing thirty constitutional decisions partially or completely overruled in the prior twenty years).

260 298 U.S. 38, 94 (1936).

261 321 U.S. at 665–66.

262 Id. at 669.

263 505 U.S. 833, 854 (1992).

264 Id. at 844. The Court noted that this was the fifth case in which the United States had asked the Court to overrule *Roe*.

265 410 U.S. 113 (1972).

266 505 U.S. at 854.

267 Id. at 855.

268 Id. at 844–55.

269 Id. at 865.

270 Id. at 866.

271 Id. at 867.

272 Id.

273 Id. at 868.

274 Id. at 869.

275 Id. at 963.

276 Id. at 995–96. He stated that "the notion that we would decide a case differently from the way we otherwise would have in order to show that we can stand firm against public disapproval is frightening." Id. at 998.

277 *Dred Scott v. Sandford*, 60 U.S. 393 (1856).

278 505 U.S. at 1001–02.

279 *Seminole Tribe of Florida v. Florida*, 517 U.S. 44, 63 (1996) (overruling *Union Gas v. Pennsylvania*, in part because it "deviated sharply" from prior precedent by holding that Congress could enlarge the Court's Article III jurisdiction, since the Court had maintained that the state sovereign immunity recognized by the Eleventh Amendment was a limitation of Article III jurisdiction);

Gideon v. Wainwright, 372 U.S. 335, 342–44 (1963) (overruling *Betts v. Brady's*, 316 U.S. 455 [1942] and its holding that an indigent state felony defendant was entitled to appointment of counsel only where "special circumstances" were present, on the ground that *Betts* itself had made "an abrupt break with its own well-considered precedents").

280 247 U.S. 251 (1918).

281 312 U.S. 100 (1941).

282 247 U.S. at 270–71.

283 Id.

284 312 U.S. at 117.

285 Id. at 116–17.

286 515 U.S. 200, 226–27 (1995).

287 Id.

288 Id. at 231.

289 Id. at 233.

290 501 U.S. 808, 822 (1991).

291 482 U.S. 496 (1987).

292 490 U.S. 805 (1989).

293 501 at 828–30 (1991). The Court cited 33 cases that it had overruled in the past 20 terms. Id. at n.1.

294 See *Katz v. United States*, 389 U.S. 347, 353 (1967) (overruling *Olmstead v. United States* and *Goldman v. United States* on the ground that the trespass doctrine on which they relied had been abandoned); *Seminole Tribe of Florida v. Florida*, 517 U.S. 44, 63 (1996) (overruling *Union Gas v. Pennsylvania*, in part because it was a solitary departure from precedent in that the Court had not relied on it in the five years since it was decided).

295 505 U.S. 833, 855 (1992).

296 Id. at 857.

297 Id. at 993–98.

298 127 S. Ct. 2553, 2584 (2007).

299 Id. at 2583–84 (2007) (*Flast v. Cohen* should be overruled because it failed to appreciate the separation of powers component of the standing doctrine).

300 *Munn v. Illinois*, 94 U.S. 113, 134 (1876) (regulation of grain storage elevators does not violate due process because the business is affected with the public interest).

301 291 U.S. 502 (1934).

302 Id. at 531.

303 Id. at 536.

304 Id.

305 Id. at 555.

306 300 U.S. 379 (1937).

307 261 U.S. 525 (1923).

308 300 U.S. at 400.

309 Id.

310 521 U.S. 203 (1997).

311 473 U.S. 402 (1985).

312 521 U.S. at 234–35. Justice Souter, dissenting, disagreed with the majority's conclusions that intervening decisions had altered the governing legal principles. Id. at 246–47.

313 Id. at 208–09.

314 277 U.S. 438 (1928).

315 316 U.S. 129 (1942).

316 389 U.S. 347 (1967).

317 277 U.S. at 457.

318 365 U.S. 505, 511 (1961).

319 389 U.S. at 353.

320 Id.

321 53 U.S. 443, 456–57 (1851).

322 23 U.S. 42 (1825).

323 53 U.S. 443, 456 (1851).

324 338 U.S. 25, 31 (1949).

325 367 U.S. 643, 652, 656 (1961).

326 347 U.S. 483, 492–93 (1954).

327 163 U.S. 537, 544 (1896).

328 347 U.S. at 490.

329 Id. at n.5.

330 163 U.S. at 544.

331 347 U.S. at 491–92.

332 Id. at 489–90, 492–93.

333 Id. at 489–90.

334 Id. at 493.

335 163 U.S. 537, 551 (1896).

336 347 U.S. at 495.

337 Id. at 494.

338 Id. at 494 n.11.

339 Id. at 495.

340 *Seminole Tribe of Florida v. Florida*, 517 U.S. 44, 116–159 (1996) (Souter, J., dissenting) (arguing that the Court's opinion in *Hans v. Louisiana* was clearly incorrect for several reasons but that it should not be overruled because it had been relied upon for over 100 years).

341 53 U.S. 443, 458 (1851).

342 515 U.S. 200, 234 (1995).

343 514 U.S. 549, 574 (1995).

344 Id.

345 505 U.S. 833, 855–56 (1992).

346 Id. at 856.

347 Cf. Laurence Tribe, *The Curvature of Constitutional Space: What Lawyers Can Learn from Modern Physics*, 103 Harv. L Rev. 1, 23 (1989).

348 505 U.S. at 956. He argued that "[s]urely it is dubious to suggest that women have reached their 'places in society' in reliance upon Roe, rather than as a result of

their determination to obtain higher education and compete with men in the job market. . . ."

349 Id. at 957.

350 539 U.S. 558, 577 (1992).

351 Id. at 589–90.

352 127 U.S. 2553, 2584 (2007).

353 See *Payne v. Tennessee*, 501 U.S. 808, 829–30 (1991) (overruling two prior decisions in part on the grounds that the lower courts could not consistently apply them), id. (relying almost exclusively on unworkability) (Souter, J., concurring).

354 469 U.S. 528 (1985).

355 426 U.S. 833 (1976).

356 Id. at 852.

357 Id.

358 469 U.S. at 538–39.

359 Id.

360 Id. at 539.

361 Id. at 540, (quoting *Fry v. United States*, 421 U.S. 542, 558 (1975) (Rehnquist, J., dissenting)).

362 Id. at 540.

363 Id. at 540–41.

364 Id. at 543–44.

365 Id. at 549.

366 478 U.S. 109 (1986).

367 Id. at 127 (White, J., plurality opinion), 161 (Powell, J., concurring).

368 541 U.S. 267, 281–84 (2004).

369 Id. at 279–292.

370 Id. at 312 (Kennedy, J., concurring), 334–40 (Stevens, J., dissenting), 346–51 (Souter, J., dissenting), 360–66 (Breyer, J., dissenting).

371 517 U.S. 44, 45 (1996).

372 491 U.S. 1 (1989).

373 Id. at 19–20.

374 517 U.S. at 62–63.

375 Id.

376 Id. at 63–64.

377 Id. at 64.

378 505 U.S. 833, 862–64 (1992).

379 Id.

380 Id. at 961–62.

381 See, e.g., *Gayle v. Browder*, 352 U.S. 903 (1956) (racially segregated buses violate equal protection); *Holmes v. City of Atlanta*, 350 U.S. 879 (1955) (racially segregated golf courses violate equal protection); *Mayor of Baltimore v. Dawson*, 359 U.S. 877 (1955) (racially segregated public beaches violate equal protection).

382 300 U.S. 379, 390–91 (1937).

383 See *Payne v. Tennessee*, 501 U.S. 808, 830 (1991) (overruling *Booth v. Maryland* and *South Carolina v. Gathers*, in large part simply because they were "wrongly

decided"); *Seminole Tribe of Florida v. Florida*, 517 U.S. 44, 63 (1996) (overruling *Union Gas v. Pennsylvania*, in part because it was "poorly reasoned").

384 505 U.S. 833, 864 (1992).

385 In dissent, Chief Justice Rehnquist questioned why a decision that was wrong when it was handed down needed to be even more wrong at a later date in order to be overruled. Id. at 955–56.

386 310 U.S. 586 (1940).

387 319 U.S. 624 (1943).

388 Id. at 635–42.

389 Id. at 643–44.

390 Id. at 636–40.

391 Id. at 638.

392 75 U.S. 603 (1869).

393 79 U.S. 457, 487 (1870).

394 395 U.S. 752, 767–68 (1969) (overruling *Harris v. United States*, 331 U.S. 145 (1947) and *United States v. Rabinowitz*, 339 U.S. 56 [1950]).

395 526 U.S. 489, 527 (1999).

396 Id.

397 Id. at 528.

398 *Propeller Genesee Chief v. Fitzhugh*, 53 U.S. 433, 456 (1851) (prior case the *Thomas Jefferson*, which set forth the ebb and flow of the tide rule did not adequately focus on the issue now before the Court and thus is not entitled to great respect as a precedent).

399 164 U.S. 112 (1896).

400 545 U.S. 469, 515–16 (2005).

401 Id.

402 Id. at 523.

403 367 U.S. 643, 667–68 (1961) (Harlan, J., dissenting).

404 Id. See also *Gravel v. United States*, 408 U.S. 606, 630 (1972) (Stewart, J., dissenting) (noting that the critical question of whether a congressman could be forced to testify before a grand jury about sources of information used in preparation for the performance of legislative acts was not encompassed in the petition for certiorari or discussed in the briefs and was mentioned only tangentially in the oral argument).

405 508 U.S. 520, 571 (1993).

406 494 U.S. 872 (1990).

407 128 S.Ct. 2783, 2814–15 (2008).

408 Id. at 2845.

409 545 U.S. 844, 889 (2005).

410 Id. (citing opinions by a majority of sitting justices "repudiating" the Court's Lemon test).

411 508 U.S. 520, 574–75 (1993).

412 Justice Souter also argued that *Smith* should be subject to reconsideration, given that Justice Scalia, writing for the majority in *Smith*, had conceded that the Court's result was a permissible reading of the Free Exercise Clause but

was certainly not compelled by the text. Id. at 574. In other words, the more discretionary the Court's holding, the greater chance that it might be erroneous and therefore worthy of reconsideration.

413 517 U.S. 44, 120–21 (1996).

414 Id.

415 Id. at 68–69.

416 Id. at 122 n.17.

417 483 U.S. 219 (1987).

418 65 U.S. 66 (1860).

419 517 U.S. 44, 122 n.17 (1996).

Chapter 8 Deriving Doctrine

1 261 U.S. 525, 568 (1923).

2 Id.

3 250 U.S. 616, 624, 630 (1919) (Holmes, J., dissenting).

4 Id. 630.

5 Id.

6 Id.

7 It was prominently set forth by John Milton in Areopagitica—A Speech for the Liberty of Unlicensed Printing (1664) and by John Stuart Mill in On Liberty (1859).

8 274 U.S. 357, 372 (1927).

9 Id. at 374–75.

10 Id. at 375.

11 Id. at 375.

12 Id. at 377.

13 Id. at 375–76.

14 See, e.g., *Frohwerk v. United States*, 249 U.S. 204 (1919); *Debs v. United States*, 249 U.S. 211 (1919).

15 315 U.S. 568 (1942).

16 Id. at 571–72.

17 403 U.S. 15 (1971).

18 Id. at 25–26.

19 Id. at 25.

20 Id.

21 Id.

22 Id. at 26.

23 Id.

24 Id. at 15.

25 The *Slaughter-House Cases*, 83 U.S. 36, 68–69, 71 (1872) (primary purpose of the Fourteenth Amendment was to ensure civil rights and equal treatment to recently freed slaves); *Strauder v. West Virginia*, 100 U.S. 303, 304 (1879) (purpose of Fourteenth Amendment was to protect the rights of recently emancipated slaves).

26 163 U.S. 537 (1896).

27 Id. at 544–49.

28 Id. at 549–550.

29 Id. at 551.

30 Id.

31 100 U.S. 303, 308 (1879).

32 118 U.S. 356, 373–74 (1886).

33 Id.

34 163 U.S. at 559.

35 Id. 559.

36 323 U.S. 214, 216 (1944).

37 Id. at 216–18.

38 347 U.S. 483 (1954).

39 438 U.S. 265 (1978).

40 Id. at 289, quoting *Shelley v. Kramer*, 334 U.S. 1, 22 (1948).

41 Id. at 295–99.

42 Id. at 298–99.

43 Id. at 299.

44 Id. at 327.

45 Id. at 357–58.

46 Id. at 360–62.

47 Id. at 412.

48 488 U.S. 469 (1989).

49 Id. at 492.

50 Id.

51 Id. at 498–508.

52 Id. at 505.

53 515 U.S. 200 (1995).

54 Id. at 223–24.

55 Id. at 227.

56 539 U.S. 306, 326–27 (2003). Justice Kennedy, dissenting, argued that Justice O'Connor may have remained true to the Powell *Bakke* approach at a level of general principle but deviated from it in application. Id. at 387.

57 377 U.S. 533 (1964).

58 376 U.S. 1, 13–14 (1964). The Court relied heavily on historical analysis to reach this conclusion. Id. at 8–17. Justice Harlan, dissenting, disputed the Court's historical analysis. Id. at 26–42.

59 377 U.S. at 560.

60 Id. at 560–65.

61 Id. at 560–61.

62 Id. at 562.

63 In adopting the "one person, one vote" principle, the Court rejected another analogy: the federal analogy; that is, the fact that the Constitution creates a Senate in which states receive equal representation regardless of population. Id. at 572. The Court disposed of this, largely on the grounds that this was a product

of political necessity, part of the Great Compromise essential to agreement on the Constitution in the first instance. Id. at 572–74.

64 Id. at 564–65.

65 Id. at 562.

66 Id. at 623–24.

67 Id. at 565.

68 Id. at 590.

69 410 U.S. 113, 152–56 (1973).

70 Id. at 152–53.

71 Id. at 153.

72 Id.

73 505 U.S. 833, 845 (1992).

74 505 U.S. 833, 851 (1992).

75 Id. at 849.

76 Id. at 852.

77 367 U.S. 497, 522 (1961) (Harlan, J., dissenting).

78 505 U.S. at 849–50.

79 418 U.S. 241 (1974).

80 Id. at 248–54.

81 Id. at 252, quoting 376 U.S. 254, 270 (1964).

82 418 U.S. at 258.

83 Id. at 255–56.

84 Id. at 257, quoting *New York Times v. Sullivan*, 376 U.S. at 279.

85 Letter of Thomas Jefferson to the Danbury Baptist Assn (Jan. 1, 1802), The Papers of Thomas Jefferson (Manuscript Division, Library of Congress).

86 98 U.S. 145, 164 (1878).

87 330 U.S. 1, 16 (1946).

88 Id.

89 Id. at 29 (Rutledge, J., dissenting).

90 333 U.S. 203, 210, 212 (1948).

91 Id. at 213.

92 Id. at 213–220.

93 Id. at 238.

94 472 U.S. 38, 92 (1985).

95 343 U.S. 306 (1952).

96 Id. at 308–09. The majority found that the released time program involved permissible cooperation but no coercion. Id. at 311–313. The dissent disagreed. Justice Jackson, dissenting, argued that under the program, the school "serves as a temporary jail for the pupil who will not go to church." Id. at 324.

97 Id. at 312.

98 Id.

99 Id. at 313.

100 Id. at 314.

101 Id.

102 Id. at 319.

103 Id.

104 Id. at 325.

105 374 U.S. 203, 222 (1963).

106 Id. at 222.

107 Id. at 306.

108 Id. Justice Stewart, dissenting, commented that:

> a compulsory state educational system so structures a child's life that, if religious exercises are held to be an impermissible activity in schools, religion is placed at an artificial and state-created disadvantage. Viewed in this light, permission of such exercises for those who want them is necessary if the schools are truly to be neutral in the matter of religion. And a refusal to permit religious exercises thus is seen not as the realization of state neutrality, but rather as the establishment of a religion of secularism, or, at the least, as government support of the beliefs of those who think that religious exercises should be conducted in private.

Id. at 313.

109 392 U.S. 236, 243 (1968).

110 Id.

111 Id. at 244–48. Justices Black, Douglas, and Fortas objected that the textbooks had been selected initially by the religious schools and only then been approved by the state, giving the schools a significant opportunity to choose books that would further their religious mission. Id. at 252–53 (Black, J., dissenting); id. at 257 (Douglas, J., dissenting) ("There's nothing ideological about a bus"); id. at 270–71 (Fortas, J., dissenting).

112 397 U.S. 664, 668–69 (1970).

113 Id. at 668. Justice Burger noted that "[t]he course of constitutional neutrality in this area cannot be an absolutely straight line," and "short of . . . expressly proscribed governmental acts there is room for play in the joints." Id. at 669. Justice Harlan agreed with these points in his concurrence, noting that "it is far easier to agree on the purpose that underlies the First Amendment's Establishment and Free Exercise Clauses than to obtain agreement on the standards that should govern their application." Id. at 694.

114 Id. at 674.

115 Id. at 674–76.

116 403 U.S. 602, 613–14 (1971).

117 Id. at 612–13.

118 Id. at 616–21.

119 *Wallace v. Jaffree*, 472 U.S. 38, 68–69 (1985) (the Lemon test should be reexamined and refined but not completely abandoned) (O'Connor, J., dissenting); id. at 91 (calling for a reconsideration of the Court's Establishment Clause precedents) (White, J., dissenting), (Lemon test has no grounding in text or history and has proven to be unworkable) (Rehnquist, J., dissenting).

120 403 U.S. 672, 678 (1971).

121 Id.

122 Id. at 680–82.

123 Id.

124 426 U.S. 736, 762–67 (1976).

125 473 U.S. 373, 385–97 (1985).

126 465 U.S. 668, 688 (1984).

127 Id. at 689–90.

128 Id. at 688.

129 Id.

130 Id. at 692.

131 473 U.S. 373, 389–92 (1985).

132 492 U.S. 573, 590–93 (1989) (opinion of Blackmun, J., with O'Connor, J. & Stevens, J., concurring).

133 Id. at 668–69.

134 509 U.S. 1, 12–13 (1993).

135 521 U.S. 203, 223–25 (1997).

136 Id. at 232–34.

137 530 U.S. 793, 810–13 (2000).

138 Id. at 837–39.

139 391 U.S. 145, 174 (1968), citing Jaffe, *Was Brandeis an Activist?: The Search for Intermediate Premises*, 80 Harv. L. Rev. 986 (1967).

140 Id.

141 Id. at 176.

142 298 U.S. 238, 327 (1934).

143 205 U.S. 454, 462 (1907).

144 249 U.S. 47, 52 (1919).

145 Id.

146 250 U.S. 616, 624 (1919).

147 Id. at 630.

148 268 U.S. 652 (1925).

149 Id. at 673.

150 274 U.S. 357, 372, 376–77 (1927).

151 Id.

152 Id. at 378–79.

153 341 U.S. 494, 507 (1951).

154 Id. at 510–11.

155 Id. at 509.

156 Id. at 580 (Black, J., dissenting).

157 395 U.S. 444, 447 (1969).

158 341 U.S. 494, 543 (1951).

159 Id. In his opinion for the plurality in *Dennis* Justice Vinson noted the following:

> Nothing is more certain in modern society than the principle that there are no absolutes, that a name, a phrase, a standard has meaning only when associated with the considerations which gave birth to the nomenclature.

Id. at 508.

160 Id., quoting *Hyde v. United States*, 225 U.S. 347, 384 (1912).

161 341 U.S. at 542–43, quoting Freund, On Understanding the Supreme Court 27–28.

162 Id. at 544. In his concurring opinion in *Kovac v. Cooper*, 336 U.S. 77, 90 (1949), Justice Frankfurter expressed similar distress at the notion that freedom of speech held a "preferred position" under the First Amendment, meaning that any state regulation in the area of freedom of speech was presumptively unconstitutional. He argued that the phrase is "mischievous" because "it radiates a constitutional doctrine without avowing it." Id. He then set forth a lengthy history of the evolution of this phrase in the case law in an attempt to demonstrate that this concept had never commanded a majority of the Court. Id. at 90–95, however Justice Rutledge, dissenting, argued that Justice Frankfurter had in fact demonstrated just the opposite. Id. at 106. Justice Frankfurter's primary concern, however, was with the Court's tendency to rely on verbal formulas rather than engage in detailed factual analysis. After discussing Justice Holmes's criticism of this trend, Justice Frankfurter explained that it is a mistake "to fall into the ways of mechanical jurisprudence through the use of oversimplified formulas" in that it "treats society as though it consisted of bloodless categories." Id. at 96.

163 *United States v. Carolene Products Co.*, 304 U.S. 144, 152 (1938).

164 Id. at 152 n.4.

165 *Skinner v. Oklahoma*, 316 U.S. 535, 541 (1942).

166 304 U.S.144, 152 n.4 (1938).

167 Id. at 152–54.

168 Id. at n.4.

169 Id.

170 Id.

171 Id.

172 301 U.S. 1 (1937).

173 291 U.S. 502 (1934).

174 300 U.S. 379 (1937).

175 336 U.S. 77, 90–91 (1949).

176 316 U.S. 535 (1942).

177 Id. at 541.

178 Id.

179 323 U.S. 214, 216 (1944).

180 395 U.S. 621, 626 (1969).

181 Id.

182 377 U.S. 533 (1964).

183 394 U.S. 618 (1969).

184 Id. at 630 n.8. The Court mentioned the Article IV Privileges and Immunities Clause, the Fourteenth Amendment Privileges or Immunities Clause, the Commerce Clause, and the Due Process Clause.

185 Id. at 662.

186 Id. at 662–63.

187 Id. at 658–62.

188 *Buck v. Bell*, 274 U.S. 200, 208 (1927).

189 376 U.S. 254 (1964).

190 Id. at 279–80.

191 Id. at 299.

192 Id. at 293 (Black, J., concurring) & 297 (Goldberg, J., concurring).

193 See, e.g., *Curtis Publishing Co. v. Butts*, 388 U.S. 130 (1967).

194 403 U.S. 29, 43 (1971).

195 418 U.S. 323 (1974).

196 Id. at 340–42.

197 Id. at 343–44.

198 Id. at 344–46.

199 Id. at 344–45.

200 Id. at 348–49.

201 Id. at 349.

202 Id. at 353.

203 Id. at 361–69.

204 Id. at 369–400.

205 Id. at 382–400.

206 *Brown v. Board of Education*, 349 U.S. 294 (1955).

207 *Brown v. Board of Education*, 347 U.S. 483 (1954).

208 349 U.S. at 301.

209 Bernard Schwartz, Decision 102–03 (1996).

210 377 U.S. 218, 234 (1964). The Court was forced to declare the end of all deliberate speed four years later in *Green v. County School Board*, 391 U.S. 430, 438 (1968).

211 391 U.S. at 438–39.

212 402 U.S. 1 (1971).

213 Id. at 15–31.

214 369 U.S. 186 (1962).

215 Id. at 210.

216 Id. at 211–18.

217 48 U.S. 1 (1849).

218 328 U.S. 549 (1946).

219 369 U.S. at 222.

220 Id. at 223.

221 Id. at 210.

222 Id. at 216.

223 Id. at 226–27.

224 Id. at 228.

225 369 U.S. at 280.

226 Id. at 289–90.

227 Id. at 295–96.

228 Id. at 295.

229 Id. at 297–99. He argued that it was in fact "a Guarantee Clause claim masquerading under a different label." Id. He continued: "where judicial competence is wanting, it cannot be created by invoking one clause of the Constitution rather than another." Id.

230 Id. at 277.

231 Id. at 301. Justice Harlan, dissenting in *Baker*, argued that "there is nothing in the Federal Constitution to prevent a State, acting not irrationally, from choosing any electoral legislative structure it thinks best suited to the interests, temper and customs of its people." Id. at 334.

232 See, e.g., *Powell v. McCormack*, 395 U.S. 486, 518–19 (1969); *Nixon v. United States*, 506 U.S. 224, 228–29 (1993).

233 514 U.S. 549 (1995).

234 317 U.S. 111 (1942).

235 514 U.S. at 560.

236 Id. at 561.

237 404 U.S. 336 (1971).

238 514 U.S. at 562.

239 494 U.S. 1, 17 (1990).

240 514 U.S. at 562–63.

241 Id. at 566.

242 Id. at 565–67.

243 Id. at 567–68.

244 Id. at 574.

245 Id. at 584.

246 Id. at 603 (Souter, J., dissenting), id. at 615 (Breyer, J., dissenting).

247 529 U.S. 598 (2000).

248 Id. at 610–13.

249 Id. at 613–18.

250 See, e.g., *Goldberg v. Kelly*, 397 U.S. 254, 263–64 (1970) (degree of the due process protection to which a person is entitled is a function of importance of the liberty or property interest at stake as well as the nature of the governmental interest). In *Powell v. Alabama*, 287 U.S. 45, 69 (1932), for instance, the Court concluded that at least in some cases a fair hearing as an aspect of due process of law entails the right to assistance of counsel. As the Court explained:

> [t]he right to be heard would be, in many cases, of little avail if it did not comprehend the right to be heard by counsel. Even the intelligent and educated layman has small and sometimes no skill in the science of law. . . . He requires the guiding hand of counsel at every step in the proceedings against him. Without it, though he be not guilty, he faces the danger of conviction . . . Id.

Thus, the purpose of due process in ensuring a fair hearing could not be achieved without the participation of counsel in many instances.

251 357 U.S. 449 (1958).

252 Id. at 451–52.

253 Id. at 459–60.

254 Id. at 460.

255 Id. at 461.

256 Id. at 462.

257 468 U.S. 609, 617–18 (1984).

258 Id. at 618–19.

259 Id. at 620.

260 509 U.S. 630, 647–48 (1993).

261 Id.

262 448 U.S. 555, 570–76 (1980) (Burger, C.J., plurality), id. at 592–97 (Brennan, J., concurring).

263 426 U.S. 794 (1976).

264 Id. at 810.

265 Id. at 828–29.

266 343 U.S. 579, 635–38 (1952).

267 Id. at 635.

268 Id. at 635–38.

269 See, e.g., *United States v. Nixon*, 418 U.S. 683, 703 (1974); *Nixon v. GSA*, 433 U.S. 425, 443 (1977) (Justice Jackson's approach has carried the day).

270 343 U.S. at 634.

271 Id. at 640.

272 380 U.S. 51 (1965).

273 Id. at 52.

274 Id. at 56–59.

275 Id. at 58.

276 Id.

277 Id.

278 343 U.S. 579 (1952).

279 Id. at 653.

280 Id. at 653–54. Justice Douglas made much the same point in his separate concurrence. Id. at 633.

281 53 U.S. 299, 320 (1851).

282 Id. at 319–21.

283 303 U.S. 177, 189–92 (1938).

284 325 U.S. 761 (1945).

285 Id. at 770.

286 Id. at 770–71.

287 Id. at 771.

288 Id. at 766–70.

289 Id. at 789–91.

290 397 U.S. 137, 142 (1970).

291 Id.

292 Compare *Kassel v. Consolidated Freightways*, 450 U.S. 662, 672–77 (1981) (Powell, J., plurality applying a fairly rigorous balancing test similar to *Pike*) with id. at 679–80 (Brennan, J., concurring), id. at 687, 696–702 (Rehnquist, C.J., dissenting) (arguing for a more deferential approach to safety justifications in burden cases).

293 156 U.S. 1, 15–17 (1895).

294 Id. at 13–15.

295 Id. at 43–44.

296 17 U.S. 316, 421 (1819).

297 Id.

298 392 U.S. 1 (1967).

299 Id. at 30–31 (1967).

300 340 U.S. 349, 354 (1951).

301 Id. at 358.

302 Id. at 354.

303 Id. at 300.

304 3 U.S. 386, 390 (1798).

305 See *Stogner v. California*, 539 U.S. 607, 611 (2003).

306 198 U.S. 45, 57 (1905).

307 Id. at 57.

308 Id. at 75.

309 Id.

310 Id.

311 291 U.S. 502, 532 (1934).

312 Id.

313 300 U.S. 379 (1937).

314 Id. at 391.

315 Id.

316 410 U.S. 113 (1973).

317 Id. at 163.

318 Id.

319 Id. at 163–64.

320 505 U.S. 833, 872–73 (1992).

321 Id. at 930–31, quoting his dissenting opinion in *Webster v. Reproductive Services*, 492 U.S. 490, 548 (1989).

322 304 U.S. 458, 464 (1938).

323 Id. at 464.

324 391 U.S. 367, 377 (1968).

325 Id. at 382–84.

326 Id. at 388.

327 521 U.S. 507, 519–20 (1997).

328 Id. at 520.

329 462 U.S. 919, 952 (1983).

330 Id. at 960.

331 377 U.S. 201 (1964).

332 Id. at 206.

333 Id.

334 Id. at 208–13.

335 497 U.S. 261, 314 (1990) (Brennan, J., dissenting).

336 Id. at 350 (Stevens, J., concurring).

337 Id. at 299–300 (Scalia, J., concurring).

Chapter 9 Shaping, Clarifying, and Changing Doctrine

1 403 U.S. 15 (1971).

2 Id. at 16, quoting Cal. Penal Code section 415.

3 Id. at 18.

4 Id.

5 Id. at 19.

6 Id. at 20.

7 Id.

8 Id.

9 Id. at 21.

10 Id. at 22–23.

11 Id. at 23–24.

12 See Justice Brennen's argument in dissent in *United States v. Leon*, 468 U.S. 897, 942 (1984) that the Court's conclusion to limit the scope of the exclusionary rule was based on "intuition, hunches, and occasional pieces of partial and often inconclusive data."

13 197 U.S. 11, 30 (1905).

14 Id. at 35.

15 399 U.S. 442 (1970).

16 Id. at 51–52.

17 Id. at 52.

18 Id. at 63.

19 Id. at 64.

20 413 U.S. 49, 59–64 (1973).

21 Id. at 61.

22 Id. at 63.

23 418 U.S. 323 (1974).

24 Id. at 343–45.

25 Id. at 363.

26 Id. at 366.

27 Id. at 390.

28 Id. at 397.

29 433 U.S. 350 (1977).

30 Id. at 368–78.

31 Id.

32 421 U.S. 349, 370–72 (1975).

33 473 U.S. 373, 388 (1984).

34 473 U.S. 402, 428 (1985) (O'Connor, J., dissenting).

35 Id. at 427.

36 Id. at 429.

37 521 U.S. 203 (1997).

38 505 U.S. 577, 593–96 (1992).

39 Id. at 593.

40 Id. at 637 (Scalia, J., dissenting).

41 Id. at 595.

42 67 U.S. 635, 669 (1862).

43 Id.

44 Id. at 690.

45 198 U.S. 45, 57 (1905).

46 Id.

47 169 U.S. 366, 397 (1898).

48 418 U.S. 323 (1974).

49 Id. at 343.

50 Id. at 343–44.

51 Id. at 344.

52 Id. at 346–51.

53 M. Nimmer, *The Right to Speak from Times to Time: First Amendment Theory Applied to Libel and Misapplied to Privacy*, 56 Cal. L Rev. 935, 942–43 (1965).

54 418 U.S. at 353.

55 512 U.S. 43, 55–57 (1994).

56 545 U.S. 469, 488 (2005). Justice Thomas, dissenting, argued that as a result the Court will closely review a state's decision to authorize a search of a home but will not "'second-guess the City's considered judgments' . . . when, the issue is, instead, whether the government may take the infinitely more intrusive step of tearing down petitioners' homes." Id. at 518.

57 Id. at 505 (O'Connor, J., dissenting), id. at 522 (Thomas, J., dissenting).

58 Id. at 522 (Thomas, J., dissenting).

59 545 U.S. 844, 882 (2005).

60 Id.

61 505 U.S. 377 (1992).

62 Id. at 391–92.

63 Id. at 415.

64 Id.

65 268 U.S. 161, 168 (1925).

66 277 U.S. 32, 41 (1928).

67 Id.

68 *Pearce v. Commissioner*, 315 U.S. 543, 558 (1942) (Frankfurter, J., dissenting). Quoting this statement in his dissenting opinion in *Rummel v. Estelle*, Justice Powell criticized the Court for choosing "the easiest line rather than the best." 445 U.S. 263, 306 (1980).

69 295 U.S. 495, 554 (1935).

70 345 U.S. 461, 471 (1953).

71 465 U.S. 668, 678 (1984).

72 Id. at 678–79.

73 482 U.S. 578, 640 (1987).

74 See, e.g., *Printz v. United States*, 521 U.S. 898, 927–28 (1997) (rejecting an attempt to draw a line between "policymaking" and "implementation" by state executive officials as impossible to draw in a principled manner).

75 397 U.S. 664, 679 (1970).

76 Id. at 700. See, e.g., *Brown v. Maryland*, 25 U.S. 419, 441 (1827) (hard distinctions will be made as the cases arise).

77 480 U.S. 321, 324–25 (1987).

78 Id. at 335.

79 454 U.S. 263, 269 n.6 (1981). In his dissenting opinion in *Mistretta v. United States*, Justice Scalia rejected reviving the non-delegation doctrine on the ground that it would be impossible to draw principled lines. 488 U.S. 361, 415–16 (1989).

80 See *Federal Election Committee v. Wisconsin Right to Life*, 127 S. Ct. 2652, 2665–66 (2007) (rejecting an intent-based approach that would prove too uncertain to protect freedom of speech) (Roberts, C.J., plurality), id. at 2680–81 (arguing that the plurality's approach did not provide sufficiently clear protection for speech either) (Scalia, J., concurring in the judgment).

81 384 U.S. 436 (1966).

82 Id. at 508–09 (Harlan, J., dissenting).

83 Id. at 444.

84 Id. at 471–72.

85 See also *United States v. Gonzalez-Lopez*, 548 U.S. 140, 150 (2006) (attempting to analyze cases in which a defendant was denied his choice of counsel under a harmless error standard would require the Court to consider what might have happened in a "parallel universe").

86 384 U.S. at 508.

87 *United States v. Robinson*, 414 U.S. 218, 235 (1973) (concluding that the police need clear rules when conducting searches and seizures and hence when the police arrest a suspect they may conduct a full search of his person for weapons or evidence without a warrant), but see id. at 238 (Marshall, J., dissenting) arguing that case-by-case contextual adjudication was essential in this area.

88 442 U.S. 200, 213–14 (1979). See also *Oliver v. United States*, 466 U.S. 170, 181 (1984), citing the need for bright-line rules in the search and seizure area as a reason for the conclusion that a search of an open field is not covered by the Fourth Amendment.

89 453 U.S. 454, 460 (1981). The Court noted that "[w]hen a person cannot know how a court will apply a settled principle to a recurring factual situation, that person cannot know the scope of his constitutional protection, nor can a policeman know the scope of his authority." Id.

90 453 U.S. 420, 428–29 (1981).

91 Id. at 427.

92 Id. at 434 n.3.

93 Id. at 443.

94 475 U.S. 625, 637 (1986).

95 462 U.S. 213, 231–41 (1983).

96 Id. at 232.

97 Id.

98 Id. at 236.

99 505 U.S. 144, 178 (1992). The Court drew the same conclusion with respect to the commandeering of state executive officials. *Printz v. United States*, 521 U.S. 898, 932 (1997) (balancing analysis is inappropriate in these circumstances).

100 Id. at 187.

101 413 U.S. 717, 730 (1973).

102 466 U.S. 668, 688–89 (1984).

103 Id.

104 Id.

105 Id. at 689.

106 Id. at 689–93.

107 308 U.S. 147, 162 (1939).

108 Id.

109 387 U.S. 523 (1967).

110 359 U.S. 360 (1959).

111 387 U.S. at 530–36.

112 Id. See also *Delaware v. Prouse*, 440 U.S. 648, 661 (1979) ("The marginal contribution to roadway safety possibly resulting from a system of spot checks cannot justify subjecting every occupant of every vehicle on the roads to a seizure").

113 387 U.S. at 532–33.

114 Id. at 536–37.

115 Id.

116 442 U.S. 200, 214 (1979).

117 468 U.S. 897 (1984).

118 Id. at 916.

119 Id. at 917.

120 Id. at 907 n.6.

121 Id. at 922.

122 Id. at 929.

123 Id. at 933.

124 Id. at 942.

125 418 U.S. 683 (1974).

126 Id. at 706–09.

127 341 U.S. 494, 524–25 (1951).

128 Id. at 525. Justice Frankfurter made much the same point in his dissent in *Baker v. Carr*, 369 U.S. 186, 267 (1962). In his dissenting opinion in *Troxel v. Granville*, Justice Scalia argued that if errors are to be made, legislative errors will do less harm than errors made by the Court in the course of constitutional interpretation, as "state legislatures have the great advantages of doing harm in a more circumscribed area, of being able to correct their mistakes in a flash, and of being removable by the people." 530 U.S. 57, 93 (2000).

129 545 U.S. 677, 698 (2005).

130 Id. at 700. Justice Breyer relied on a concurring opinion by Justice Goldberg in *Abington Township v. Schempp*, 374 U.S. 203 (1962), which had rejected doctrinal tests in favor of purpose-based analysis to resolve difficult Establishment Clause questions. He concluded that "as Justices Goldberg and Harlan pointed out, the Court has found no single mechanical formula that can accurately draw the constitutional line in every case." Id. at 699.

131 Id.

132 Id. at 701–03.

133 Id. at 697 (Thomas, J., concurring).

134 Id. at 700.

135 Id. at 698–99.

136 365 U.S. 715 (1961).

137 Id.

138 Id. at 722.

139 Id.

140 Id. at 725. See also *Escobedo v. Illinois*, 378 U.S. 478, 490–91 (1964) (where the Court took a very factually particularistic approach to when the right to counsel would prohibit police interrogation of a suspect who has retained counsel).

141 365 U.S. at 726–27. In his dissenting opinion in *Jackson v. Metropolitan Edison Co.*, Justice Douglas criticized the majority for engaging in a "seriatim "rather than an "aggregate" examination of the relevant factors, thereby making it more difficult to find state action in a particular case. 419 U.S. 345, 359 (1974).

142 365 U.S. at 728.

143 See Chapter 9, Section III, Part F, Subpart 3.

144 Id. at 78–104.

145 487 U.S. 654 (1988).

146 Id. at 692.

147 Id. at 733.

148 Id. 734. Justice Scalia raised a similar criticism of the Court's decision, upholding the constitutionality of the federal sentencing commission in *Mistretta v. United States*, 488 U.S. 361, 426 (1989). He argued that under the Court's approach "the functions of the Branches should not be commingled too much—how much is too much to be determined, case-by-case, by this Court." Id. See also *Harmelin v. Michigan*, 501 U.S. 957, 985–86 (1991) (Justice Scalia objected to any attempt by the Court to determine whether a criminal sentence is cruel and unusual as disproportionate to the crime, on the grounds that it inevitably leads to judges imposing their own value judgments).

149 542 U.S. 296, 306–08 (2004).

150 Id. at 308.

151 260 U.S. 393, 413 (1922).

152 Id. at 415.

153 438 U.S. 104, 124 (1978).

154 Id. at 124.

155 Id.

156 458 U.S. 613 (1982).

157 Id. at 629.

158 Id. at 643.

159 See, e.g., *Massachusetts Bd. of Retirement v. Murgia*, 427 U.S. 307, 314 (1976).

160 323 U.S. 214 (1944).

161 395 U.S. 621 (1969).

162 394 U.S. 618 (1969).

163 429 U.S. 190 (1976).

164 Id. at 197.

165 See Chapter 9, Section III, Part G, Subpart 4.

166 *Strauder v. West Virginia*, 100 U.S. 303, 307 (1879).

167 *Mississippi Univ. for Women v. Hogan*, 458 U.S. 718, 726 (1982).

168 *Reynolds v. Sims*, 377 U.S. 533, 567–68 (1964).

169 *Shapiro v. Thompson*, 394 U.S. 618, 631 (1969).

170 447 U.S. 557, 566 (1980).

171 413 U.S. 15, 24 (1973).

172 403 U.S. 602 (1971).

173 See Chapter 8, Section III, Part B.

174 Id. at 615.

175 71 U.S. 277, 325 (1866).

176 See, e.g., *McMann v. Richardson*, 397 U.S. 759, 784 (1970) (Brennan, J., dissenting) (arguing that the Court's conclusion that a plea of guilty was voluntary if entered into voluntarily in open court formalistically ignores the fact that it may have been heavily influenced by prior unconstitutional conduct).

177 321 U.S. 649, 664 (1944).

178 Id.

179 See, e.g., *Nixon v. Herndon*, 273 U.S. 536 (1927) (equal protection was violated by exclusion based on race from state democratic primary); *Nixon v. Condon*, 286 U.S. 73 (1932) (equal protection was violated by racial exclusion by state democratic executive committee).

180 466 U.S. 789, 822–26 (1984).

181 391 U.S. 430 (1968).

182 413 U.S. 189 (1973).

183 Id. at 208.

184 Id.

185 Id.

186 Id.

187 Id.

188 See, e.g., *Lee v. Weisman*, 505 U.S. 577, 616–17 (1992) (nonpreferentialist approach to the Establishment Clause would require judges to engage in exercises of comparative theology quite beyond their competence).

189 332 U.S. 46, 65 (1947).

190 Id. at 67–68.

191 342 U.S. 165, 172 (1952).

192 Id. at 170.

193 Id. at 169, 171.

194 Id. at 170.

195 Id. at 175, 177.

196 333 U.S. 203, 237–38 (1948). He added:

> . . . To lay down a sweeping constitutional doctrine as demanded by complainant and apparently approved by the Court, applicable alike to all school boards of the nation, "to immediately adopt and enforce rules and regulations prohibiting all instruction in and teaching to religious education in all public schools," is to decree a uniform, rigid and, if we are consistent, an unchanging standard for countless school boards representing and serving highly localized

groups which not only differ from each other but which themselves from time to time change attitudes. It seems to me that to do so is to allow zeal for our own ideas of what is good in public instruction to induce us to accept the role of a super board of education for every school district in the nation.

Id. at 237.

197 403 U.S. 602 (1971).

198 Id. at. 612–13.

199 474 U.S. 38, 110–11 (1985).

200 530 U.S. 793 (2000).

201 433 U.S. 229 (1977).

202 421 U.S. 349 (1975).

203 545 U.S. 844 (2005).

204 545 U.S. 677 (2005).

205 545 U.S. at 890–91. Justice Scalia cited a footnote in which the majority stated that its Establishment Clause doctrine "lacks the comfort of categorical absolutes." Id. at 891, quoting id. at 859 n.10.

206 Id. at 891–92. In the companion case of *Van Orden v. Perry*, Justice Thomas, concurring, argued that by attempting to create a compromise on when religious displays on governmental property are constitutionally permissible, the Court provided no principled way to choose between "displays which are constitutional and those which aren't" "the incoherence of the Court's decisions in this area renders the Establishment Clause impenetrable and incapable of consistent application." 545 U.S. 677, 694. This lack of predictability gives rise to the appearance that the decisions "turn on judicial predilections." He argued that the compromise that suggests that certain religious displays have little or no religious meaning "is not fully satisfying to either non-adherents or adherents." Id. at 696.

207 433 U.S. 229, 263 (1977). Three years later a majority of the Court made the same point in *Committee for Public Education and Religious Liberty v. Regan*, where it noted that "our decisions have tended to avoid categorical imperatives and absolutist approaches at either end of the range of possible outcomes." 444 U.S. 646, 662 (1980). It conceded that "[t]his course sacrifices clarity and predictability . . . ." Id.

208 505 U.S. 672 (1992).

209 See, e.g., *Perry Education Assn v. Perry Local Educators Assn.*, 460 U.S. 37, 56 (1983) (Brennan, J., dissenting).

210 505 U.S. at 678–85.

211 Id. at 681–85. Justice O'Connor agreed with the plurality's categorical analytical framework, its conclusion that an airport was not a public forum, and its conclusion that the airport authority's ban against solicitation was reasonable, hence constitutional; however, she disagreed that the ban on leaf letting was reasonable, hence her vote along with four other justices resulted in the invalidation of that regulation. Id. at 685–87.

212 Id. at 693–94.

213 Id. at 695.

214 Id. at 698–99. Justice Kennedy ultimately concluded, however, that although the leafletting ban was unconstitutional, solicitation was subject to abuse and could be prohibited in the terminal even though it was a public forum. Id. at 706–07.

215 Id. at 709–11.

216 543 U.S. 499 (2005).

217 See, e.g., *Adarand Constructors Inc. v. Pena*, 515 U.S. 200, 227 (1995).

218 543 U.S. at 507.

219 Id. at 510–13.

220 Id. at 524.

221 Id. at 529–32.

222 Id.

223 545 U.S. 844, 860 (2005).

224 Id. at 874–75.

225 Id. at 875.

226 Id. at 875–76.

227 Id. at 876.

228 314 U.S. 160 (1941).

229 Id. at 175–76.

230 Id. at 178–81.

231 Id. at 182–85.

232 Id. at 178.

233 336 U.S. 106, 112 (1949).

234 Id.

235 Id.

236 Id. at 112–113.

237 *San Antonio Independent School Dist. V. Rodriguez*, 411 U.S. 1 (1973).

238 Id. at 22–23.

239 Id. at 28.

240 Id. at 122.

241 Id. at 33–38.

242 Id. at 111–17.

243 Id. at 35–36.

244 Id. at 54–55.

245 Id. at 98.

246 457 U.S. 202 (1982).

247 Id. at 230.

248 Id. at 220–23.

249 Id. at 223–24.

250 Id. at 220–25.

251 Id. at 230–31.

252 Id. at 232–33.

253 Id. at 239 n.3.

254 Id. at 239.

255 Id. at 243–47.

256 473 U.S. 432 (1985).

257 Id. at 442.

258 Id. at 443–46.

259 Id. at 449–50.

260 Id. at 456–57.

261 526 U.S. 489 (1999).

262 394 U.S. 618 (1969).

263 Id.

264 526 U.S. at 500.

265 Id.

266 354 U.S. 476 (1957).

267 413 U.S. 15 (1973).

268 354 U. S. at 485–86.

269 Id. at 489.

270 Id.

271 Id. at 496.

272 Id. at 508, 514.

273 *Jacobellis v. Ohio*, 378 U.S. 184, 190 (1964).

274 Id. at 197.

275 383 U.S. 413, 418 (1966).

276 Id.

277 Id.

278 Id. at 442 (Clark, J., dissenting), id. at 461 (White, J., dissenting).

279 Id. at 442 (Clark, J., dissenting).

280 386 U.S. 767, 770 (1967).

281 Id. According to Justice Brennan's dissent in *Paris Adult Theatre v. Slaton*, 413 U.S. 49, 82 n.8 (1973), thirty-one cases were decided by such per curiam opinions.

282 413 U.S. 15, 21–24 (1973).

283 Id. at 21.

284 Id. at 24.

285 Id.

286 Justice Brennan, the author of both *Roth* and the two-justice *Memoirs* plurality, continued to make that argument vigorously in the companion case to *Miller*, *Paris Adult Theatre v. Slaton*, 413 U.S. 49, 85–93 (1973).

287 See, e.g., *Carter v. Carter Coal Co.*, 298 U.S. 238, 299 (1936) (manufacturing is not commerce); *United States v. E.C. Knight Co.*, 156 U.S. 1, 12 (1895) (manufacturing is not commerce).

288 298 U.S. at 301 .

289 301 U.S. 1 (1937).

290 Id. at 41.

291 Id.

292 Id.

293 317 U.S. 111 (1942).

294 Id. at 120.

295 Id. at 125–29.

296 *Katz v. United States*, 389 U.S. 347, 350 (1967).

297 *Olmstead v. United States*, 277 U.S. 438 (1928).

298 389 U.S. at 353.

299 Id. at 350.

300 Id. at 361 (Harlan, J., concurring).

301 See, e.g., *Smith v. Maryland*, 442 U.S. 735, 740 (1979) (applying Justice Harlan's Katz analysis to hold that placing a pen register on a telephone does not constitute a search); *Kyllo v. United States*, 533 U.S. 27, 34 (2001) (using thermal imaging to measure heat emanating from a home was a search using the Harlan objective/subjective approach of *Katz*).

302 494 U.S. 872, 883–84 (1990).

303 Id.

304 Id. at 894–901.

305 404 U.S. 71 (1971).

306 411 U.S. 677 (1973).

307 429 U.S. 190, 197 (1976).

308 Id. at 220.

309 Id. at 210 n.*.

310 Id. at 211.

311 See, e.g., *Califano v. Webster*, 430 U.S. 313, 316–17 (1977).

312 450 U.S. 464, 468 (1981).

313 Id. at 468–69, 476. Justice Brennan in dissent scolded the Rehnquist plurality as well as the Stewart and Blackmun concurrences for resisting the *Craig v. Boren* standard. Id. at 489 n.2.

314 442 U.S. 256, 273 (1979).

315 Id.

316 458 U.S. 718, 724 (1982).

317 Id. at n.9 (1982).

318 518 U.S. 515, 531, 533, 534, 546, 556 (1996).

319 Id. at 559. Justice Scalia also contended that the majority opinion "drastically revises our established standards for reviewing sex-based classifications." Id. at 566.

320 Id. at 572–74.

321 403 U.S. 365, 371–72 (1971).

322 The Court cited its prior cases of *Yick Wo v. Hopkins*, 118 U.S. 356, 369 (1886); *Truax v. Raich*, 239 U.S. 33, 39 (1915); and *Takahashi v. Fish & Game Comm'n.*, 334 U.S. 410 (1948).

323 *In re Griffiths*, 413 U.S. 717 (1973) (invalidating ban on aliens becoming attorneys); *Matthews v. Diaz*, 426 U.S. 67 (1976) (invalidating denial of Medicare to nonpermanent resident aliens who have lived in the country for less than five years); *Nyquist v. Mauclet*, 432 U.S. 1 (1997) (invalidating denial of tuition benefits to aliens who did not intend to apply for citizenship); *Sugarman v. Mcl. Dougall*, 413 U.S. 634 (1973) (invalidating denial of aliens to hold civil service jobs); *Examining Board v. Flores de Otero*, 426 U.S. 572 (1976) (invalidating ban on aliens becoming licensed professionals).

324 413 U.S. 634, 647 (1973).

325   435 U.S. 291, 295–96 (1978).

326   Id. at 297–98.

327   Id. at 295–97.

328   Id. at 303–04 (Marshall, J., dissenting).

329   Id. at 300.

Chapter 10 Consequential Reasoning

1 See, e.g., *Simon & Schuster v. N.Y. State Crime Victims Bd.*, 502 U.S. 105, 121–22 (1991) (law seizing the proceeds from a book describing the authors' crimes and redistributing them to victims could have inhibited works by many important authors, including Martin Luther King, Jr., Henry David Thoreau, and Malcolm X); *Town of Castle Rock v. Gonzalez*, 545 U.S. 748, 772 (2005) (Souter, J., concurring) (permitting a person to assert a property interest in a state procedural provision would turn every state failure to comply with statutory provision into a potential substantive deprivation of due process); *Reynolds v. United States*, 98 U.S. 145, 166–67 (1878) (protecting religiously motivated conduct rather that simply religious belief might permit human sacrifice); *Allen v. Wright*, 468 U.S. 737, 755–56 (1984) (if an allegation of abstract stigmatic injury was sufficient to establish standing, any black person in the country could bring a discrimination claim against the IRS for failing to deny a tax exemption to a discriminatory institution); *Gonzales v. Raich*, 545 U.S. 1, 69 (2005) (Thomas, J., dissenting) (under the Court's definition of economic activity the Congress "may now regulate quilting bees, clothes drives, and potluck suppers throughout the 50 States" under the Commerce Clause); *Nixon v. United States*, 506 U.S. 224, 236 (1993) (permitting judicial review of a presidential impeachment could result in years of uncertainty and questions as to legitimacy); Civil Rights Cases, 109 U.S. 3, 13 (1883) (construing the Fourteenth Amendment to permit Congress to prohibit private discrimination could lead to congressional regulation of all local activity); *Prigg v. Pennsylvania*, 41 U.S. 539, 619 (1842) (construction of the Constitution that would prohibit Congress from enforcing the Fugitive Slave Clause would also prevent Congress from enacting several other well-accepted laws pursuant to the Necessary and Proper Clause).

2 445 U.S. 263, 304 (1980) (Powell, J., dissenting).

3 5 U.S. 137, 178 (1803).

4 17 U.S. 316, 426 (1819).

5 198 U.S. 45, 59–64 (1905).

6 343 U.S. 579, 635–56, 651–53 (1952) (Jackson, J., concurring).

7 376 U.S. 254, 267, 279, 292 (1964).

8 367 U.S. 643, 654, 660 (1961).

9 381 U.S. 479, 484–85 (1965).

10 384 U.S. 436, 483 (1966), id. at 516 (Harlan, J., dissenting), id. at 542 (White, J., dissenting).

11 418 U.S. 683, 713 (1974).

12 438 U.S. 265, 309 (1978).

13 5 U.S. 137, 175 (1803).

14 Id. at 178.

15 See William Van Alstyne, *A Critical Guide to Marbury v. Madison*, Duke L. J.1, 17 (1969).

16 198 U.S. 45 (1905).

17 Id. at 59. The Court continued in this vein for the better part of three pages. See also The Civil Rights Cases, 109 U.S. 3, 12 (1983) (permitting Congress to reach private conduct under section 5 of the Fourteenth Amendment would allow Congress to effectively write a complete municipal code).

18 291 U.S. 502 (1934).

19 300 U.S. 379 (1937).

20 22 U.S. 1, 194–95 (1824).

21 298 U.S. 238 (1936).

22 295 U.S. 495 (1935).

23 Id. 546. The Court made a similar argument with respect to the Spending Power in *United States v. Butler*, 297 U.S. 1, 75 (1936) where it concluded that permitting the government to regulate agricultural production through conditional contracts would result in a "total subversion of the governmental powers reserved to the individual states." Id.

24 514 U.S. 549 (1995).

25 Id. at 564. The Court made similar arguments in the course of invalidating a portion of the Violence Against Women Act that created a civil damage remedy for gender-based assaults in *United States v. Morrison*, 529 U.S. 598 (2000). The Court reasoned that the theory underlying the Act would allow Congress to regulate any violent crime as well as any area of family law. Id. at 615.

26 336 U.S. 525 (1949).

27 Id. at 538–39.

28 19 U.S. 264, 385 (1821).

29 Id. at 386.

30 Id.

31 343 U.S. 579, 653 (1952) (Jackson, J., concurring).

32 116 U.S. 616, 635 (1886).

33 73 U.S. 35 (1867).

34 Id. at 46.

35 381 U.S. 479 (1965).

36 Id. at 485.

37 Id. at 537, 529. Justice Frankfurter had made the same point in the earlier case of *Poe v. Ullman* where the Court had dismissed a challenge to the law. 367 U.S. at 501.

38 Id. at 497. See also *United States v. Butler*, 297 U.S. 1, 84 (1936) (Stone, C.J., dissenting) (if Congress cannot attach conditions to ensure that federal appropriations are spent for the intended purpose, federal funds would be misused and wasted).

39 143 U.S. 649, 672–73 (1892).

40 Id.

41 501 U.S. 957, 986 n.11 (1991).

42 Id.

43 Id.

44 333 U.S. 203 (1948).

45 Id. at 235–36.

46 Id. at 236. Likewise in *Zorach v. Clausen*, 343 U.S. 306, 312–13 (1964). Justice Douglas made a classic bad-consequences argument in support of the doctrinal position that separation of church and state cannot possibly mean complete separation because

> [m]unicipalities would not be permitted to render police or fire protection to religious groups. Policemen who helped parishioners into their places of worship would violate the Constitution. Prayers in our legislative halls; the appeals to the Almighty in the messages of the Chief Executive; the proclamations making Thanksgiving Day a holiday; 'so help me God' in our courtroom oaths—these and all other references to the Almighty that run through our laws, our public rituals, our ceremonies would be flouting the First Amendment.

47 392 U.S. 236, 253 (1968).

48 418 U.S. 683, 712–13 (1974).

49 365 U.S. 43, 50, 68–74 (1961).

50 384 U.S. 436 (1966).

51 Id. at 516 (Harlan, J., dissenting).

52 Id. at 542 (White, J., dissenting).

53 Id. at 483–90.

54 408 U.S. 501, 523–24 (1972).

55 Id. at 524.

56 36 U.S. 420 (1837).

57 Id. at 552. *Hein v. Freedom from Rel-igion Foundation*, 127 S. Ct. 2553, 2569 (2007) (Alito, J., plurality) (permitting standing here would allow standing to challenge any executive action), id. at 2572–73 (Kennedy, J., concurring) (permitting standing here would allow challenges to executive branch speeches), id. at 2584 (Scalia, J., concurring and dissenting) (Court should overrule *Flast v. Cohen* because it has shown that it is incapable of drawing principled lines in this area).

58 295 U.S. 495, 554 (1935). Likewise in *United States v. Butler*, 297 U.S. 1, 75 (1936), the Court held that allowing Congress to tax and spend in order to regulate agricultural production would allow Congress to regulate "all industry throughout the United States" by similar measures that could result in the central government exercising uncontrolled police power in every state of the Union." Id. As with *Schechter*, significant doctrinal shifts disposed of the problem. In other words, if a particular interpretation will result in bad consequences, the Court does have the power to change the interpretation.

59 17 U.S. 316, 426 (1819).

60 Id. at 432. Marshall employed bad consequences to aid his textual argument of defining the word *necessary* broadly in the Necessary and Proper Clause to mean

"appropriate," rather than narrowly to mean "essential," by contending that the narrower reading would lead to the undesirable result of precluding Congress from addressing unforeseen exigencies, although it is not altogether clear why such consequences would follow. Id. at 413–15.

61 *Panhandle Oil Co. v. Mississippi ex Rel Knox*, 277 U.S. 218, 223 (1928) (Holmes, J., dissenting).

62 188 U.S. 321, 362–63 (1903).

63 Id. at 362.

64 Id. at 363.

65 See, e.g., *Wood v. Miller*, 333 U.S. 138, 144 (1948) (judicial review will provide protection against potential abuses of the war power in the future); *Employment Division v. Smith*, 494 U.S. 872, 902 (1989) (O'Connor, J., concurring) (courts have been able to strike a reasonable balance between compelling government interests and Free Exercise claims, thereby avoiding Justice Scalia's concern that every claimant could become a law unto himself).

66 374 U.S. 203, 308 (1963).

67 See Chapter 9, Section III, Part A.

68 545 U.S. 469, 500–01 (2005).

69 Id. at 503.

70 Id. at 486–87.

71 Id. at 487 n.19.

72 Id. at 502–03.

73 14 U.S. 304, 344 (1816). See also *Worcester v. Georgia*, 31 U.S. 515, 561, 572 (1832) (McClean, J., dissenting).

74 *Irwin v. Gavit*, 268 U.S. 161, 168 (1925).

75 397 U.S. 664, 716 (1970).

76 Id. 678.

77 Id. at 699–700.

78 403 U.S. 602, 624 (1971).

79 Id. at 624.

80 163 U.S. 537 (1896).

81 Id. at 549.

82 Id. at 552, 557–58. (Harlan, J., dissenting).

83 494 U.S. 872 (1989).

84 Id. at 877–79.

85 98 U.S. 145 (1878). There the Court opined that if the Free Exercise Clause protected polygamy, the state would be unable to prohibit human sacrifice as part of religious worship or a wife from throwing herself onto her husband's funeral pyre. Id. at 166. This is certainly one of the Court's more memorable parades of horribles, and yet both of these examples refer to actual religious practices.

86 98 U.S. at 166–67.

87 494 U.S. at 887. Justice Scalia believed that Justice Blackmun essentially favored such an approach through his focus on the impact of the practice. Id. at n.4.

88 Id. at 893–94, 902–03.

89 Id. at 916–17. In *Lee v. Weisman*, 505 U.S. 577 (1992), a recent Establishment Clause Case, Justices Souter, concurring, and Scalia, dissenting, engaged in dueling battles of bad doctrinal consequences. Justice Souter charged that Justice Scalia's nonpreferentialist approach would require the Court to engage in comparative theology to evaluate prayers, id. at 616, while Justice Scalia responded that Justice Souter's separationist approach would outlaw many well-accepted practices such as placing the phrase "In God We Trust" on coins. Id. at 639.

90 426 U.S. 229 (1976).

91 Id. at 239–41.

92 Id. at 248. The Court expressed similar concerns in *McCleskey v. Kemp*, 481 U.S. 279, 315–17 (1987), where it concluded that a challenge to the imposition of the death penalty on the grounds that racial discrimination played an improper role must establish intent to discriminate by the particular jury rather than through statistical evidence of system-wide bias. The Court worried that reliance on statistical evidence alone might call into question a host of other decisions throughout the criminal process where disparities might exist. Id. Justice Brennan, in dissent, argued that the death penalty was readily distinguishable from other sentences and punishments. Id. at 340 (Brennan, J., dissenting).

93 512 U.S. 702, 733 n.23 (1997), id. at 785 (Souter, J., concurring). The Court and Justice Souter found that practice in the Netherlands, where assisted suicide was legal, bolstered this concern. Id. at 734; Id. at 785–86 (Souter, J., concurring).

94 Id. at 785 (Souter, J., concurring).

95 347 U.S. 497 (1954).

96 347 U.S. 483 (1954).

97 347 U.S. 497, 500 (1954).

98 83 U.S. 36, 78 (1872).

99 Id. The Court made a similar argument a few years later in the Civil Rights Cases, 109 U.S. 3, 13 (1883), maintaining that if Congress was not limited to state action by the Fourteenth Amendment, it could readily enact a full municipal code reaching all forms of private activity within the states.

100 83 U.S. at 78.

101 Id. at 92.

102 376 U.S. 1, 21 (1964).

103 53 U.S. 299, 321 (1851).

104 Id.

105 445 U.S. 573, 602 (1980).

106 326 U.S. 572, 583 (1946).

107 48 U.S. 1 (1849).

108 Id. at 38–39. The Court made a similar argument in *Cooley v. Board of Wardens*, 53 U.S. 299, 321 (1851), when it observed that if the local pilotage law in question violated the Commerce Clause, then sixty years of illegally collected fees would need to be repaid.

109 436 U.S. 149, 165 (1978).

110 Id. at 170.

Chapter 11   Ethical Argument

1 Philip Bobbitt, *Constitutional Fate* 94 (1982).

2 Id.

3 217 U.S. 349 (1910).

4 Id. at 364.

5 Id. at 373–74.

6 Id. See Chapter 4, section II, part G.

7 Id. at 366–67.

8 356 U.S. 86 (1958).

9 Justice Brennan concurred on the ground that the statutes was beyond congressional power. Id. at 105.

10 Id. at 100.

11 Id. at 101.

12 Id.

13 Id. at 102–03.

14 370 U.S. 660 (1962).

15 Several years later in *Powell v. Texas*, 392 U.S. 514 (1968), the Court declined to extend *Robinson* to cover a criminal conviction for public drunkenness because the offense punished conduct rather than status. Id. at 532–33.

16 408 U.S. 238 (1972).

17 Id. at 239.

18 Id. at 265–282.

19 Id. at 271–79.

20 Id. at 300.

21 Id. at 310.

22 Id. at 311–13.

23 Id. at 436 n.18.

24 Id. at 388.

25 Id. at 332.

26 Id. at 341–61.

27 Id. at 332.

28 Id. at 362.

29 Id. at 363.

30 Id. at 437–40.

31 Id. at 384.

32 Id. at 444.

33 Id. at 444.

34 Id. at 362.

35 Id. at 453.

36 Id. at 308.

37 Id.

38 428 U.S. 153 (1976).

39 Id. at 173.

40 Id.

41 Id. at 179–81.

42 428 U.S. 227, 232 (1976).

43 Id.

44 Id. at 233–34.

45 428 U.S. 325, 352–53 (1976).

46 Id. at 355.

47 428 U.S. 280 (1976).

48 Id. at 294.

49 Id. at 298–99.

50 433 U.S. 584, 593–97 (1977).

51 Id. at 595–96.

52 Id. at 597.

53 Id.

54 Id. at 606.

55 Id. at 614–16. A year later in *Lockett v. Ohio*, 438 U.S. 586 (1978), the Court invalidated a death penalty statute that did not allow for the consideration of all possibly relevant mitigating factors. The Court did not attribute this to any explicit conception of recognized public values. It did rest its conclusion on "[t]he need for treating each defendant in a capital case with that degree of respect due the uniqueness of the individual." Id. at 605. It is likely that the Court's conclusion reflected its understanding of widely shared public values, embracing both the uniqueness of the individual as well as concern that the death penalty, though appropriate, only be imposed in cases where it was most justified.

56 458 U.S. 782 (1982).

57 Id. at 793.

58 Id. at 789–90.

59 Id. at 794.

60 Id. at 815–16.

61 Id. at 818–19.

62 Id. at 823.

63 481 U.S. 137, 158 (1987).

64 477 U.S. 399, 408–09 (1986).

65 Id. at 410.

66 492 U.S. 302 (1989).

67 Id. at 334.

68 Id. at 334–35.

69 Id. at 335.

70 Id. at 340.

71 536 U.S. 304 (2002).

72 Id. at 314–15.

73 Id. at 315.

74 Id. at 316 n.21.

75 Id. at 316.

76 Id. at 318–21.

77 Id. at 338.

78 Id. at 343.
79 Id.
80 Id. at 343–44.
81 Id. at 344.
82 Id. at 347–48.
83 Id. at 324–28.
84 Id. at 349–50.
85 487 U.S. 815 (1988).
86 Id. at 823–24.
87 Id. at 829.
88 Id. at 830–31.
89 Id. at 832.
90 Id. at 835.
91 Id. at 849.
92 Id. at 867.
93 Id. at 826–29.
94 492 U.S. 361 (1989).
95 Id. at 372–73.
96 Compare Id. at 372–73 (states that prohibit capital punishment period should not be counted) with Id. at 384–85 (all states should be counted) (Brennan, J., dissenting).
97 Id. at 377.
98 Id. at 388–92.
99 Id. at 391–92.
100 Id. at 378–80.
101 Id. at 374–76.
102 Id. at 382.
103 Id. at 394–96.
104 543 U.S. 551 (2005).
105 Id. at 565.
106 Id. at 566.
107 Id.
108 Id. at 568.
109 Id. at 569.
110 Id. at 571.
111 Id. at 571–72.
112 Id. at 574–75.
113 Id. at 577.
114 Id. at 578.
115 Id. at 588.
116 Id. at 595–97.
117 Id. at 597–601.
118 Id. at 600.
119 Id. at 609.
120 Id.

121 Id. at 610.

122 Id. at 616.

123 128 S. Ct. 2641 (2008).

124 Id. at 2657.

125 Id. at 2656–57.

126 Id. at 2668 (Alito, J., dissenting).

127 Id. at 2656.

128 Id. at 2662–64.

129 Id. at 2673 (Alito, J., dissenting).

130 Id. at 2659–61.

131 Id. at 2658.

132 Id. at 2676 (Alito, J., dissenting).

133 445 U.S. 263 (1980).

134 385 U.S. 554, 560 (1967).

135 445 U.S. at 272.

136 Id. at 282.

137 Id. at 282–83.

138 Id. at 296–98.

139 Id. at 300 n.21.

140 Id. at 301.

141 Id. at 302.

142 Id. at 307.

143 463 U.S. 277 (1983).

144 Id. at 280–81.

145 Id. at 290.

146 Id. at 292.

147 Id. at 297.

148 Id. at 298.

149 Id. at 299–300.

150 Id. at 303.

151 Id. at 308.

152 Id. at 305.

153 Id. at 308.

154 501 U.S. 957 (1991).

155 Id.

156 Id. at 965.

157 Id. at 966–94.

158 Id. at 997–98.

159 Id. at 1001.

160 Id. at 1004.

161 Id. at 1013–14.

162 Id. at 1020–21.

163 Id. at 1027.

164 492 U.S. 257 (1989).

165 Id. at 266.

166 499 U.S. 1 (1991).

167 Id. at 22.

168 Id. at 25. Justice Kennedy largely agreed with Justice Scalia. Id. at 40.

169 Id. at 43.

170 Id. at 59.

171 509 U.S. 443 (1993).

172 Id. at 457–58.

173 Id. at 462.

174 Id. at 466–67.

175 Id. at 470–71.

176 Id. at 473.

177 517 U.S. 559 (1996).

178 Id. at 574.

179 Id. at 575–86.

180 Id. at 586–88.

181 Id. at 594.

182 Id.

183 Id. at 596.

184 Id. at 600.

185 Id. at 607.

186 538 U.S. 408 (2003).

187 Id. at 420–23.

188 Id. at 425–26.

189 Id. at 428.

190 Id. at 429. Recently in *Exxon Shipping Co. v. Baker*, 128 S. Ct. 2605 (2008), the Court vacated a $5 billion punitive damage award against Exxon with respect to the Exxon Valdez oil spill. Under the circumstances, the Court indicated that an award of $500 million in punitive damages, equivalent to the size of the compensatory damage award, would have been appropriate. Id. at 2634. However, the Court's decision was based entirely on its power as a common law admiralty court and as such sheds little if any light on its due process jurisprudence.

191 316 U.S. 535 (1942).

192 Id. at 541.

193 Id.

194 Writing for the Court, Justice Holmes had approved of sterilization of a mentally retarded person in the infamous case of *Buck v. Bell*, 274 U.S. 200 (1927).

195 Id. at 543–44.

196 Id. at 546.

197 367 U.S. 497, 522 (1961).

198 Id. at 542.

199 Id.

200 Id.

201 Id. at 543.

202 521 U.S. 702, 763–64 (1997).

203 367 U.S. at 554–55.

204 See Chapter 5, section V, part B.

205 P. Bobbitt at 168–175.

206 505 U.S. 833, 851 (1992).

207 Id. at 852.

208 478 U.S. 186, 193–95 (1986).

209 539 U.S. 558, 568–71 (2003).

210 Id. at 572–574.

211 Id. at 574.

212 521 U.S. 702 (1997).

213 Id. at 710–719.

214 377 U.S. 533 (1964).

215 The companion case of *Lucas v. Forty-Fourth General Assembly of Colorado*, 377 U.S. 713 (1964) was an obvious exception, given that a recent state referendum had consciously approved deviations from population equality for the express purpose of providing greater representation to important but sparsely populated regions of the state.

216 Id. at 562.

217 Id. at 590 (Harlan, J., dissenting).

218 349 U.S. 294 (1955).

219 404 U.S. 71 (1971).

220 372 U.S. 335 (1963).

221 384 U.S. 436 (1966).

222 376 U.S. 254 (1964).

223 424 U.S. 319 (1976).

Chapter 12 Rhetoric in Constitutional Interpretation

1 5 U.S. 137, 163 (1803).

2 249 U.S. 47 (1919).

3 Id. at 51.

4 250 U.S. 616, 230 (1919).

5 Id.

6 268 U.S. 652, 672–73 (1925).

7 Id. at 673.

8 274 U.S. 357, 372 (1927).

9 Id. at 375–77.

10 Id. 375–77

11 Id. at 375 n 3.

12 Id. at 375.

13 Id. at 375.

14 Id. at 376.

15 Id.

16 Id. at 377.

17 See *Brandenburg v. Ohio*, 395 U.S. 444, 447–48 (1969) (requiring incitement and an imminent threat of harm before seditious speech could be suppressed).

18 Another excellent example of rhetoric used to bolster principle is Justice Brandeis's classic dissent in *Olmstead v. United States*, 277 U.S. 438, 471 (1928).

19 319 U.S. 624 (1943).

20 Id. at 641.

21 Id. at 642. Justice Frankfurter, whose opinion in *Minersville School District v. Gobitis*, 310 U.S. 586 (1940) was overruled by *Barnette*, began his dissent rhetorically by noting that "[o]ne who belongs to the most vilified and persecuted minority in history is not likely to be insensible to the freedoms guaranteed by our Constitution." 319 U.S. at 646 (Frankfurter, J., dissenting).

22 *Dennis v. United States*, 341 U.S. 494, 572 (1951).

23 Id. at 577.

24 314 U.S. 160, 186 (1941).

25 336 U.S. 525, 539 (1949).

26 Id.

27 Id. at 558–59.

28 Id. at 558, 563.

29 309 U.S. 227 (1940).

30 Id. at 237–38.

31 323 U.S. 214, 226 (1944).

32 Id. at 240.

33 Id. at 223.

34 285 U.S. 262 (1932).

35 Id. at 311.

36 277 U.S. 438, 469 (1928).

37 Id. at 464–65.

38 Id. at 478.

39 Warren and Brandeis, *The Right of Privacy*, 4 Harv. L. Rev. 193 (1890).

40 277 U.S. at 485.

41 98 U.S. 145 (1878).

42 330 U.S. 1, 16 (1947).

43 Id. at 18.

44 Id. at 29.

45 333 U.S. 203, 213 (1948).

46 Id. at 231.

47 Id. at 238.

48 343 U.S. 306, 325 (1952).

49 370 U.S. 421, 445–46 (1962).

50 413 U.S. 756, 761 (1973).

51 472 U.S. 38, 107 (1985).

52 Id.

53 Id. at 108.

54 536 U.S. 639, 686 (2002).

55 545 U.S. 677, 709 n.4 (2005).

56 459 U.S. 116, 123 (1982).

57 426 U.S. 833, 857 (1976).

58 Id. at 857–80.

59 491 U.S. 397 (1989).

60 Id. at 414–18.

61 Id. at 419–20.

62 Id. at 434–35. Chief Justice Rehnquist, dissenting, quoted extensively from a variety of literary sources that honored the flag, including Emerson's "Concord Hymn," Key's lyrics to the "Star Spangled Banner," and Whittier's "Barbara Frietchie." 491 U.S. 397, 422–24 (1989).

63 492 U.S. 490, 538 (1989).

64 Id. at 557.

65 Id. at 560.

66 505 U.S. 833, 922–23 (1992).

67 Id. at 943.

68 343 U.S. 306, 313 (1952).

69 Id. at 315.

70 Id. at 319.

71 Id. at 324.

72 Id.

73 492 U.S. 257, 290 (1989) (quoting *Romeo and Juliet*, Act III, scene 1, lines 188–89).

74 Id.

75 Id. at 265 n.7.

76 508 U.S. 384, 398 (1993).

77 505 U.S. 577, 636 (1992).

78 Id.

Chapter 13 Synthesis

1 19 U.S. 264, 375 (1821).

2 Id.

3 Id. at 376.

4 Id. at 377.

5 Id.

6 Id. at 378–79.

7 Id.

8 Id. at 381.

9 Id. at 381.

10 Id. at 382.

11 Id. at 383.

12 Id. at 385–86.

13 Id. at 386–87.

14 Id. at 388.

15 Id. at 389.

16 Id. at 391.
17 Id.
18 Id. at 393.
19 Id.
20 Id.
21 Id. at 393–94.
22 Id. at 394–95.
23 Id. at 395–98.
24 Id.
25 Id. at 399–400.
26 Id. at 400.
27 Id. at 400.
28 Id. at 401.
29 Id.
30 Id. at 405.
31 Id. at 406.
32 Id.
33 Id. at 406–07.
34 Id. at 408–09.
35 Id. at 410–12.
36 Id. at 413.
37 Id. at 413–14.
38 Id. at 414.
39 Id.
40 Id. at 415–16.
41 Id. at 416.
42 Id. at 416–17.
43 Id. at 417.
44 Id. at 418.
45 Id. at 419.
46 Id. at 420.
47 Id. at 421.
48 Id. at 421–23.
49 83 U.S. 36 (1872).
50 Id. at 62.
51 Id. at 63–64.
52 Id. at 67.
53 Id. at 68.
54 Id. 68.
55 Id. at 69.
56 Id.
57 Id. at 70.
58 Id. at 71.
59 Id. at 72.
60 Id. at 73–74.

61 Id.

62 Id. at 74.

63 Id.

64 Id. at 75.

65 Id.

66 Id. at 75–76.

67 Id.

68 Id.

69 Id. at 77.

70 Id.

71 Id. at 78.

72 Id. at 79.

73 Id. at 80–81.

74 Id. at 81.

75 Id. at 82.

76 Id. at 88–89.

77 Id. at 90.

78 Id. at 91–92.

79 Id. at 93.

80 Id.

81 Id. at 94–95.

82 Id. at 95.

83 Id. at 96.

84 Id.

85 Id.

86 Id. at 96–97.

87 Id. at 97–98.

88 Id. at 97.

89 Id. at 98.

90 Id. at 100–01.

91 Id. at 104–10.

92 Id. at 112–13.

93 Id. at 113.

94 Id. at 114.

95 Id.

96 Id. at 114–16.

97 Id. at 116.

98 Id. at 118–19.

99 Id. at 119–21.

100 Id. at 122.

101 Id. at 123.

102 Id. at 123–24.

103 Id. at 125.

104 Id. at 126.

105 Id. at 129.

106 Id.
107 Id. at 130.
108 287 U.S. 45 (1932).
109 Id. at 51–52.
110 Id. at 53, 55–56, 58.
111 Id. at 60.
112 Id. at 60–65.
113 Id. at 65.
114 Id. at 65–66.
115 Id.
116 Id. at 66–67.
117 Id. at 66–67.
118 Id. at 67–68.
119 Id. at 68.
120 Id.
121 Id. at 69.
122 Id.
123 Id. at 69–70.
124 Id. at 71.
125 Id. at 73.
126 Id.
127 372 U.S. 335 (1963).
128 376 U.S. 254 (1964).
129 Id. at 258–61.
130 Anthony Lewis, *Make No Law*, 117–19 (1991).
131 376 U.S. at 265–66 (1964).
132 Id. at 267.
133 Id. at 268.
134 Id. at 269.
135 Id.
136 Id. at 270.
137 Id. at 271.
138 Id.
139 Id.
140 Id. at 272.
141 Id. at 272–73.
142 Id. at 273.
143 Id. at 273–74.
144 Id. at 274–76.
145 Id. at 276.
146 Id. at 277.
147 Id. at 277–78.
148 Id. at 278–79.
149 Id.
150 Id. at 279–80.

151 Id. at 282.
152 Id. at 284.
153 Id. at 285–86.
154 Id. at 288–92.
155 Id. at 293–305.
156 418 U.S. 323 (1974).
157 505 U.S. 577 (1992).
158 Id. at 587.
159 Id. at 588–89.
160 Id. at 590, *quoting* Memorial and Remonstrance Against Religious Assessments (1785) in 8 Papers of James Madison 301 (W. Rachal, R. Rutland, B. Ripel & F. Teute eds. (1973).
161 Id. at 591–92.
162 Id.
163 Id. at 593.
164 Id. at 593–94.
165 Id. at 595–96.
166 Id. at 595.
167 Id. at 597.
168 Id. at 604.
169 Id.
170 Id. at 607.
171 Id. at 610–11, discussing *Everson v. Bd. Educ.*, 330 U.S. 1 (1947).
172 Id. at 612, discussing *Wallace v. Jaffree*, 472 U.S. 38, 106 (1985) (Rehnquist, J., dissenting).
173 472 U.S. 38, 92–106 (1985).
174 505 U.S. at 612–13.
175 Id. at 613–15.
176 Id. at 615.
177 Id. at 616.
178 Id. at 616–17.
179 Id. at 618.
180 Id. at 619.
181 Id. at 620–21.
182 Id. at 621.
183 Id. at 622.
184 Id.
185 Id. at 623–25.
186 Id. at 626.
187 Id.
188 Id. at 629.
189 Id. at 632–35.
190 Id. at 633–35.
191 Id. at 635.
192 Id.

193 Id. at 638.
194 Id. at 640.
195 Id. at 640–41.
196 Id. at 643.
197 Id. at 644.

Table of Cases

Index